JURA: ISLAND OF DEER

To Margaret

JURA

Island of Deer

PETER YOUNGSON

Birlinn

First published in Great Britain in 2001 by
Birlinn Ltd, 8 Canongate Venture,
5 New Street, Edinburgh EH8 8BH

www.birlinn.co.uk

The publisher gratefully acknowledges
financial assistance from The Russell Trust

ISBN 1 84158 136 4

British Library Cataloguing-in-Publication Data
A catalogue record for this book is available
from the British Library

Typeset in Sabon by Carnegie Publishing, Lancaster
Printed and bound by Creative Print and Design, Ebbw Vale, Wales

Contents

List of illustrations, maps and figures

Colour plates

Sources: Nos 3; 4; 6; 7; 8; 9; 15; 16; 17; 19; the author. Nos 1; 10; 11; 12; 13; 14; Norman Tait. No.2; Willie Macdonald. No.5; Gordon Wright.

Black and white illustrations

Sources: Nos 3; 4; 5; 6; 7; 9; 10; 13; 14; 16; 17; 19; 21; 22; 23; 24; 25; 26; 27; 28; 30; 31; 32; 33; 34; 35; 36. All of these were given to the author by members of the Jura community, with permission for him to reprint them. Nos 8 and 15; Norman Tait's collection. No. 2; 'Jura, an Island in Argyll', D. Budge. No.1 by permission of John Dewar. No.12 by permission of Glasgow Musueums: Art Gallery & Museum, Kelvingrove.

Maps

Sources: Nos 1; 2; 3; 4; 7; 8; 9; 10; 11; 12; 13; 17; drawn by the author. Nos 5 and 6; 'Geology of Knapdale, Jura and North Kintyre' (1911). No.14 by permission of the National Library of Scotland (Map Department). No.15; Thomson's Atlas of Scotland (1832). No.16 from 'The Highland Scots of North Carolina' by Duane Meyer, copyright © 1961 by the University of North Carolina Press, renewed 1989 by Duane Meyer, used by the permission of the publisher.

Figures

Sources: Figs 1 and 2. I am grateful to the Society of Antiquaries of Scotland and the artist Susan Mercer for permission to reproduce these. Fig. 3 from Effie Lindsay's Scrapbook with her permission to reprint. Fig.4 with the permission of the National Archives of Scotland (NAS ref; GD64/3/81). Fig.5 from Calum MacArthur's 'Placenames of Ardfernal', with permission.

Preface

I first spent a holiday in the Island of Jura in 1970, and returned in each of the next four summers with my wife and children. There was much to delight us in these visits, and they may have prepared me to accept the Call to be Jura's Parish Minister in 1975. We stayed for twelve years, and would no doubt be there still if my parents' frailty had not made it necessary for us to return to the mainland. I had formed a strong affection for the island during my summer months, but nothing had prepared me for the experience of living and working in Jura all the year round. As the weeks and months went by I gradually became aware that I was appreciating the island in many new and different ways.

The physical nature of the island took some time to come to terms with. There was its sheer size, for one thing. A visitation by the Presbytery of Kintyre in 1724 had reported, 'The Isle of Jura is from south-west to north-east in length twenty-four miles, and those so long that in just measure they would make upwards of thirty.' Indeed, anyone who spends his or her life travelling up and down the island's one road comes to know the truth of that heartfelt statement. On Jura the miles are exceedingly long. Indeed, when I came to feel the need for a simple guide for visiting drivers, and wrote a small pamphlet, I could find only one suitable title: 'The Long Road'.

But there was much more to Jura than sheer scale. For one thing there was its great natural beauty. I had never lived on an island before, and was unprepared for the way the views display an ever-changing interface between sea and land. Each turn in the road reveals another bay, and a new seascape to delight the eye. The hills, the moors and the lochs change with the weather and the seasons.

The residents of the island were also full of surprises. Many of them were descendants of native Jura stock, with their own particular dialect of Gaelic, and their own special store of local tales. They were wise and cultured and many of them willingly shared their experience of island life with me.

As the years passed I found myself becoming the guardian of more and more information about the island. If a specialist in some branch of natural history visited the island he would often be directed to the Manse, and shortly the Minister would be out in the wilds, dogging the footsteps of some expert in sedges and rushes, or setting light traps for moths.

If descendants of the emigrants to North Carolina had an urgent desire to trace their ancestry they, too, would arrive on the doorstep of the Manse, wearing stetsons and be-slung with cameras, to ask the local Minister to 'tell us who we are!'

Gradually a mountain of data began to accumulate. Population records of every kind, photos of people and places of earlier days, scientific facts of the most abstruse nature. If a bird or a bat was found dying or dead, it would be brought to the Minister; if a turtle or a dolphin was stranded in some remote cove, the Minister would be expected to set off and examine it.

If sheer exposure to information creates expertise, then, after twelve years of incessant such exposure I must surely qualify as an expert. And yet, no matter how long you stay on Jura, there are many things which to understand fully, or even partly, you have to have been born on the island.

Gradually a feeling grew in me of being responsible for doing something with all this material. Many kindnesses and courtesies helped me accumulate it. Family photographs were lent and presented; stories were told; lessons were given in cutting peat and in working the glebe. Perhaps the way to pay back some of the debts I had incurred was to write it all down.

But surely there was no need of 'yet another book about Jura?' Or so I thought until I began to review the situation. Study quickly revealed that there was no book about Jura in print. True, there had recently been two books. *Jura: An Island in Argyll* had been written and published by the Rev. Donald Budge. Donald Budge, a native of Skye and a Gaelic speaker, had been Minister in Jura from 1949 until his retirement in 1970, and published his own account of the island in 1960. It is an extraordinary story, revealing great insights into the island. The book soon sold out, and second-hand copies are now eagerly sought.

In 1974 Blackie & Son published a volume in their Island Series entitled *Hebridean Islands: Colonsay, Gigha and Jura*, which they commissioned John Mercer to write. It was of course never intended to deal solely with the Island of Jura, and for those with a special interest in that isle it always suffered from its need to be fair-handed with Colonsay, Oronsay and Gigha in the same volume. For this reason I have always considered it to be 'disqualified' from filling the concept of 'a book about Jura.'

No other volume dealing with the island exists, nor has one ever been written. Jura must be the largest and most significant island in the British Isles to have been so neglected.

Thirteen years have passed since I left Jura to follow my Ministry elsewhere. During these years my enthusiasm for the island has not diminished, and the accumulated information I acquired has not gone away. Now I have retired from the Ministry of the Church of Scotland, and having, by the grace of God, been given time to apply myself to this old obsession, I have undertaken my long-postponed project to write 'a book about Jura.'

Here it is. I hope it will prove to be both informative and enjoyable.

Acknowledgements

This book about Jura probably began to germinate thirty years ago when I and my family first made the acquaintance of the island. The parish church was between Ministers in 1970 and we came to the unfurnished Manse for a summer month while I occupied the pulpit. The island quickly involved us and we returned each year on holiday, at first to the Harrisons' cottage at Ardfernal, and later to Corran House, which we bought as a holiday home. In 1975 a 'Call' was extended to me to become the next Minister of Jura. We accepted and settled into the Manse, where we remained for twelve very happy years. Had my aged parents not required the kind of attention and support which could not be provided from the remoteness of a Hebridean island, we would probably be living there still. However, we left at the end of 1987, and our lives took a different direction.

From my arrival as the Minister in 1975 my interest in Jura slowly grew to become a passion, and by degrees an obsession, out of which this book was ultimately born. Those who fed the obsession were many, and I think with profound gratitude of the native people in those early years who spoke freely of their island and its life and stories. To me they seemed a collection of giants, and they remain so in my mind and memory. I am happy to mention by name many of the full-time residents of my first years in Jura. They are set down here in the order I became most accustomed to, going round the island anti-clockwise, starting at Inver. I can still see each one clearly in my mind's eye, and hear their voices inside my head. Many of their stories and much of their knowledge of Jura have found their way into these pages.

I acknowledge my debt for friendship and information to Donald and Isa Darroch of Inver; Angus and Nancy McDonald of Ardfin, and Norman McDonald of Ardfin; Charlotte Darroch of Woodside; Betsy McKechnie of Bealach Dearg; Jeannie McIsaac of the shop house; Alec McIsaac of Braeside. There were many from the long shoreline between the Village Hall and Burnside Jack and Rhona Paton; Morag Head; Katie McLean of Faskadh; Janet McKechnie of the Post Office; Mrs Nellie Prosser; Dan and Effie McDougall of Frisco; Betty Bateman of An Gala; Katie Keith; John Shaw; Peggy McLeod and Jean Handley; Mary Marshall; the folk of Keils; Alick and Mary Keith; Archie Black; May Keith; the people of Burnside; Katie Darroch; Jeannie Shaw of Crackaig; Calum and Mary McArthur and their daughters together with Ian Cameron; Charlie and Nancy McLean; Sarah Robertson; Aggie McDonald; Mary Shaw and Effie Kerr; Dougie and Tottie Buie of Carraig; the people of Knockrome Sandy and Nan Buie; Sandy Darroch and his sisters Katie and Annie; Bella Leonard; the Rozgas and the Boyles; Neil Shaw, Morag Shaw and John Shaw of Ardmenish; Neil and Lily McInnes of Gatehouse; Robert and Flora Shaw of Lagg; Chrissie

Kingsberry of Lussagiven; the folk of Inverlussa: – Angus McKechnie; Mrs Welsh; Mary Shaw; Alistair Ruadh; Peter and Annette Campbell of Ardlussa.

To these must be added the people whose main home was elsewhere, but whose hearts were always in Jura, either from ancestral ties or from long, long involvement. Among such were the Nicholsons of the Excise House; the Paterson sisters, Elsie and Catriona; Alec Darroch of Holly House; Calum McArthur of Ardfernal; and Margaret Darroch of Tarbert;

The owners of the island's Estates floated in and out of my relationship with my Parish, often contributing unexpected anecdotes or accounts of Jura residents. Such were Tony and June Riley Smith; Sir William Lithgow; the Rickman family and Viscount Lord Astor. Margaret and Ronan Nelson of Ardlussa were in a special category of their own, with ready friendship on offer and an intimate relationship with the north part of the island from which I benefited in many ways.

Within this considerable list I want to note that a few were truly great storytellers. Between them, the following five individuals seemed to know most of the tales of Jura: Katie Darroch, Sandy Buie, Archie Black, Dan McDougall and Angus McKechnie. It was to these that I went again and again to have confirmation of the many stories all the people in the earlier long list shared with me. All these great people are now dead, but I am comforted to think that many of their recollections live on in the pages of this book.

I arrived as the Minister of Jura determined to become a proficient speaker of the Gaelic tongue. Unfortunately I turned out to have no aptitude or talent for the language and was always a poor student. What little Gaelic I know is the result of the patient instruction of Katie Darroch, Dan McDougall and Archie Black, but I fear they were ill rewarded by my achievements. However, although local folk used to say my attempts to speak Gaelic were ruined by the fact that everything I said had the 'blas Sasunnach' (the flavour of the English); without such progress as I did make I would have been unable to comprehend the remarkable work on Gaelic place-names of Jura undertaken by Calum McArthur, much of which is reproduced in the book.

Calum McArthur brings to the place-names of Jura a combination of native ancestry and local instincts, together with a scholarly understanding of the Gaelic tongue. His work on the Gaelic names enshrined in the Ordnance Survey maps of Jura, together with his detailed study of the local names of the crofting townships of Ardfernal and Knockrome, and his identification of some of the early place names of Dean Munro, is vital to an understanding of Jura.

My shortcomings as a Gaelic student were often a stumbling block to ambition. Some years ago I published the stories collected on Jura between 1908 and 1914 by the Rev. Charles Robertson. I was quickly in trouble with the Gaelic content, and was rescued by my friend and colleague the Rev. Dr Roderick MacLeod, the Minister of Cumlodden, Lochfyneside and Lochgair, and a notable Gaelic scholar. Roddie has come to my help again in connection with this larger venture, and for his patience and his unerring scholarship I am most grateful.

Gaelic isn't the only language I have trouble with, and Richard Spencer of Cluny has helped me considerably with some difficult Latin as well.

To return to my own life on Jura. My early attempts to learn its ways were ably fostered by Sandy Buie, who taught me to cut peat; and by Alec McIsaac, who taught me to net sea trout, and my early attempts to farm the glebe were built on instructions from every quarter, but mainly from Alick Keith and Angus McDonald, who between them taught me all they could about cattle and hay and potatoes, and from Big Alan McDonald, who taught me to plough. All of these new disciplines gave me more impetus to identify with the island, and that determination lies behind my desire to write about it.

As I began to learn about the island's wildlife the gamekeepers all seemed willing to initiate me. Neil McInnes was a mine of information, and Willie McDonald, shared his enthusiasm for Jura's animals and birds, about which he was most knowledgeable. Peter Campbell taught me to skin and butcher my first stag. Without these experts I would have remained forever on 'the outside' in Jura.

As far as the natural history of Jura is concerned, I brought my own lifetime enthusiasms with me, especially an interest in shells and the seashore. Early in the 1970s came Barry Pendlebury, highly placed in the Nature Conservancy Council, who introduced his enthusiasm for entolomology and taught me the dragonflies and damselflies of Jura, and in due course persuaded me to take on the indefinite loan of a light trap, and all its accompanying impedimenta from the NCC; to begin to trap and identify the moths of the island. Others such as Tony Church of Arran joined the insect quest, and a profile began to emerge. Into this came Norman and Pearl Tait from Renfrew, bringing a range of expertise, and in particular Norman's insect and other nature photographs. Various experts have always been ready to identify and check material, of which Peter Wormell of the NCC and Iain Christie of Helensburgh were early in the field along with Dr R. P. Knill-Jones. In recent years Keith Bland of Edinburgh has been a continual support.

Other experts began to arrive. The Woodland Survey brought Nick Stewart, a brilliant field botanist, who tried unsuccessfully to teach me sedges and rushes, but whom I followed around the island, encountering exciting rarities at almost every turn. Nick had a disconcerting habit of crouching suddenly to identify some tiny scrap of green, and if you were following too closely you could easily tumble over him. I also received help and support from Michael Jarvis, Dr K. D. Bennett, Alan Stirling and Vince Giavarini.

Other closed doors also began to open. Norman and Pearl Tait were able to build on Pearl's profession as a mycologist, and a start was made on identifying the fungi of Jura.

Dr Shelagh Smith arrived on a shore study, and put my amateur interest in shells and the shoreline on a sound professional footing.

Gordon Booth, the 'bird man of Islay', came many times to Jura, and a succession of holidaying ornithologists sent back their summer notes.

On the archaeological and paleontological front Jack Stevenson and Dr Graham Ritchie came for a number of years for the Royal Commission on the Ancient and Historical Monuments of Scotland, and it was an excitement and a privilege to be able to see at first-hand the emergence of the Round House at Cul a' Bhaile. The *Argyll Inventory* which in due course emerged is the source for much of my information on Jura's prehistory, and descriptions of sites are reproduced here with permission and grateful thanks.

Marion Campbell of Kilberry and her companion Mary Sandeman were also a continual inspiration in my attempts to come to terms with Jura's early history.

In this area my relationship with John Mercer, then living for much of the year at Lealt, was vital. John and Susan were happy to share their discoveries, and from their work and their sites I gained a first-hand insight into the remote life of the Mesolithic people of Jura. John's monographs on the sites he discovered and excavated, together with Susan's illustrations were all printed in the *Proceedings* of the Society of Antiquaries of Scotland. Some of the material in these reprints illuminates this study, and is reproduced here with permission.

John was a notable polymath, whose interests, enthusiasms and abilities knew no bounds. His natural history insights could be startling. Who could forget being shown completely unexpected and unpredictable freshwater mussels in the Lealt Burn?

Another expert who spent time on Jura, and who was friendly and accessible was Professor A. G. Dawson, who studied the raised beaches and other geological features of the island, and again much of the outcome of his work, in a simplified form, appears here.

Dr Dawson stayed with our GP, Dr Joan Johnson, who was also gaining a rapid insight into the Island of Jura, and who, with her family, stimulated many discussions and ideas.

Here I must thank her successor, Dr Stewart Garrett, who not only offered his friendship and a close working partnership between our two professions, but taught me to sail his racing dinghy and his Dart catamaran. This introduced to me to a brand new world, full of strange terminology and extraordinary excitement, and it also qualified me in due course to be entrusted with *The Morag*. This small Wetherby 'Nimrod' belonged to Joe Darroch, another Jura descendant, living in Kent. In *The Morag* I was able to set off on voyages of exploration. One, with the owner, from the west coast of Jura to the headwaters of Loch Tarbert, was an extraordinary journey made entirely 'under sail'. Another, with my deep-water skipper, Roland Worthington-Ayre, enabled me to visit all the scattered islands to the north of Jura, and in a religious fancy, to land on each of them and re-claim them as part of the Parish of Jura. Time spent wandering on the ghostly island of Belnahua, and exploration of the myterious Garvellachs allowed me later to write from first-hand experience about these remote places. Fortunately Joe Darroch never had reason to regret his generosity, and this note may help me to express my huge debt of gratitude to him and to his wife Val and their family.

Contemporary written accounts of Jura are few and far between, and not all lend themselves to inclusion in a book like this. Mary Sandeman's *When the Years Were Young* is a collection of charming tales of her childhood as the Doctor's daughter on Jura, but I have always considered them essentially very personal, and have not quoted from them. Mr Nicholson's recollections of the Jura Regatta seem to me to fall into the same category. I have, however, leaned heavily on the remarkable scrapbook of Neil Lindsay of San Francisco.

My colleague in the Ministry, the Rev. John Wright, of Kildalton Parish in Islay, found in his family records the unpublished letters of a distant ancestress, Mary Edgar. These letters contained the fascinating account of her Missionary visit to Lagg in Jura, which find a place in this book. Without John Wright's goodwill these letters would have remained in obscurity.

I am indebted to many many professional scholars for encouragement and information, for example, to Ian Fisher of the Royal Commission on the Ancient and Historical Monuments of Scotland; and for access to the extensive work done under the auspices of the School of Scottish Studies, University of Edinburgh, by John McLean of Lewis, on farming customs and traditions of Jura. Margaret Storrie's work on Islay has also been a frequent inspiration, and her support and friendship over many years a continual encouragement. I also acknowledge help and guidance from Murdo MacDonald, the Archivist in Lochgilphead, with important records of the Poor Board, and of the Commissioners of Supply, and recently with valuable twentieth-century records.

I have been a continual user of the National Archives of Scotland, where in my studies of Census Records and Statutary Registers I have always been made most welcome; the 'Campbell of Jura Papers' are a resource without which a book on Jura could not possibly be written. Peter Morrison of Rothesay has brought me up to date with recent versions of some important records, and in particular the newly available version of the 1881 National Census on computer.

The National Library of Scotland has also been of great assistance through the years, and in particular its Map Department.

Emigration from Jura to North Carolina became my interest in the 1970s when eager Americans began to arrive at the Manse to ask for help in tracing their ancestry. Handicapped by a complete absence of knowledge or information, I felt embarrassed to be able to offer so little assistance. Individual inquirers soon became close personal friends, and following their invitation, my wife and I went to North Carolina on three occasions to pursue the relationship between Jura and its emigrant cousins.

Tom Shaw of Fayetteville was instrumental in arranging all of this, and from this beginning many friendships developed which informed the entire topic. Judge Sandy McKinnon of Lumberton was anxious to write his own contributions on the subject, and he and others visited Scotland. Lt-Col. Victor Clark was an indefatigable researcher, writer and organiser, editing the important book *A Colourful Heritage*, and publishing *The Argyle Colony Plus*, a magazine which became an essential resource for all studies of emigration from Jura, and which is extensively quoted from in this work. Vic Clark also pointed me towards many important American books whose titles will be found in the Bibliography.

Dr Scott Buie of Fort Worth began to study the early baptismal records of Jura, and was the first to employ computer technology to analyse and understand them. This work gave a huge impetus to my own, and underlies much of my later efforts. More recently Scott took over the production of the *Argyle Colony Plus* for some years, and now issues a regular *Newsletter* which acts as a clearing ground for genealogical and other Jura-related inquiries. This continues to be a goldmine of information. The list of other active supporters in the United States is a long one, perhaps too long for inclusion here. They will all know of my obligation to them, without their having to be mentioned individually. Most recently I have been encouraged by the work of Dr Douglas F. Kelly of North Carolina, whose *Carolina Scots* (1998), has been of enormous help.

When one is engaged in an ambitious attempt to write an account like this, the most common experience is one of feeling that you have got out of your depth. It is at such times that 'experts' seem to emerge, almost by accident, with experience and information about exactly the subject about which you are most at a loss. Prominent among such is Ross Noble, the Director of the Highland Museums of Kingussie and Newtonmore. His knowledge of the 'vernacular' culture of Scotland in the seventeenth, eighteenth and nineteenth centuries has proved invaluable.

My own personal friend and local GP, Dr John Gilmour, of Kirriemuir, has been of immense help in looking at matters of 'sicknesses' and 'causes of death', in the nineteenth century, and has also helped me to avoid many foolish mistakes in the field of medicine.

I return to Norman Tait. Apart from our mutual interest in natural history, Norman early became associated with my efforts to create a collection of photographs based on the personal 'snaps' in the possesion of elderly residents. This project had been given its initial impetus by a gift of some early photos of her husband, by Sarah Robertson, the aged widow of the Rev. Donald John Robertson of Jura. Norman Tait was enthusiastic about these, and undertook the increasingly laborious task of re-photographing every picture that I acquired, thus creating a stock of safely conserved negatives, and a supply of copies which could be put on public display. This display has continued to be maintained in Jura Parish Church, and after I left the island, Norman's interest in Jura's past continued in a fruitful collaboration with Gordon Wright of Jura Hotel, and resulted in the publication of fascinating collections of pictures and stories.

Since the mantle of local historian and knowledgeable consultant about Jura, tended to fall on Gordon after I left the island, along with a great deal of responsibility for the Parish Church, it would have been understandable if he had seen my continued interest in Jura as increasingly inappropriate as the years went by. It is to his lasting credit that he always conveyed quite the opposite impression, and that until his recent sad death he was an enthusiastic supporter of this project, which relationship continues with his wife Carol.

Gordon and Carol's family also produced their nephew David Horne, a young geologist who produced a most helpful book about Jura's rocks, from which I have borrowed freely.

In a similar way my relationship with the Taits survived my departure, and in due course has blossomed into the co-operation which has resulted in Norman being solely responsible for the photographic illustrations in the book and for the final form of the maps and figures. Their quality is I think exceptional, and speaks volumes for his expertise and dedication. My debt to him is quite beyond price.

Although I am in no way 'computer literate', this book has been written on a word processor. As a computer 'layman' I am grateful to Ian Martin of

Kirriemuir, who has been responsive to my panic-stricken calls day and night; has never at any time been baffled, and even makes 'house calls'.

I turn now to the question of my literary sources. In writing a book about an island like Jura it seems reasonable to include the accounts of the visitors who came and wrote of their visits. The book inevitably includes the writings of Dean Munro; Martin Martin; Thomas Pennant; John Walker; Daniel, Lord Teignmouth; and the accounts of the Rev. Francis Stewart; the Rev. Alexander Kennedy and the Rev. Donald Budge, who wrote the first, second & third Statistical returns on the Island. The volume entitled *Origines Parochiales* gives the result of much research into the history of the Parish and Church. Extracts from many other accounts have been incorporated into my text. I am pleased to acknowledge my debt to all of these, and the value of the many quotations I have included. All such works are listed in the Bibliography.

Other important sources have been the Minutes of the Presbytery of Kintyre; the Minutes of the Commissioners of Supply, 1744–74; Records of the Parochial Poor Board, 1845–90; and Records of the Crofters Commission sitting on Jura, 1894.

Other volumes on which I have relied for researched information are quoted in the Bibliography, and I hope that in general those concerned with their copyright, or with the significance of the research contained within these works will be pleased that I have quoted from them. I have tried at all times to make it clear where these invaluable sources have come from.

Some of these written works have been peculiarly significant in my attempt to understand what was happening in Jura during the past few centuries.

I have been greatly indebted to W. H. Murray, author of *The Islands of Western Scotland*, 1973, and I have relied on Mr Murray for many general ideas and detailed investigation.

I was privileged to know Donald McKechnie of Keils in Islay during my time on Jura. His book *The Lands of the Lordship* has been a powerful resource through my years of study. I hope that my enthusiasm for continuing to propagate Donald's lively, accurate and fertile ideas through this book will be acceptable to all concerned with his interests and research.

There remain two completely pivotal and vital works about Jura, my relationship with which requires some explicit explanation.

In my Preface I referred to Donald Budge's and John Mercer's books on Jura. I feel that I need to be more explicit about my relationship with these books and their authors.

Donald Budge's book was the first thing that opened my eyes to Jura's history. I read it again and again, and quoted from it continually in my discussions with local inhabitants. I was not privileged to meet either Mr Budge or Mrs Eleanor Budge, as plans to do so were overtaken first by his death and then by hers. I understood from his widow, that Donald Budge had known of my hopes to write about Jura, and to rely heavily on his own research and writing. Donald Budge died in 1978. I then had some correspondence with his widow, who was generous in support of my hopes of reprinting a good deal of her late husband's book in a future book about Jura. She was clear that in this matter I had a 'free hand' (her own words) in any matter concerning the reproduction of part or all of her late husband's book. It has been entirely within the spirit of this relationship, that I have reprinted verbatim many passages from his book. I have been always conscious that as a Gaelic speaker, and as the ministerial incumbent some twenty years before my own time, Donald Budge was able to tap into a priceless store of information about the island that I could never hope to access. I do hope, that in producing this book about Jura, I am being essentially true to Donald Budge's distinctive insights into the history and life of his Parish.

I recall my relationship with John Mercer up until his sad and premature death, as a rich and fruitful one at many levels. We had lively discussions and arguments about many issues including the inevitable relationship between politics and the Church. However, our essential relationship survived such doctrinal tensions, and we often discussed Jura, and our mutual but individual interests in it. John was clear that his early enthusiasm had been to write a book about Jura, but that in his negotiations with his publisher he had been obliged to research and write about Colonsay and Gigha as well as Jura. I recall a number of discussions in which I mooted with him the possibility that I might at some future date embark on an attempt to write a further book about 'Jura and Jura alone'. John's reaction was to encourage the enterprise, and to say again and again that it would be wasteful for me to re-engage in original research on topics which he had worked through exhaustively for his own book. It is in the spirit of these, to me vitally important, recollected discussions, that I reproduce here many of John Mercer's important discoveries about Jura, and many of his distinctive insights into its life and history.

There only remain to be mentioned the influences upon this work of members of my own family. My daughter Lyn illustrated an earlier publication of 'Tales of Jura', and has been happy to decorate the dust cover and title page of this book and produce new illustrations to some of the stories. My son-in-law, Richard Ovenden, a professional librarian, has kindly given me quick and easy access to vital texts relating to my study of the Island of Jura. Richard's help, skill, understanding and sympathy for the problems I have faced are also beyond my adequate thanks.

I cannot complete this account of those to whom I am profoundly indebted for the fact that the book has arrived at this point, without reference to the fact that my wife Margaret has not only been unvaryingly patient and supportive as I have worked on it over many months, but has spent many hours patiently reading and re-reading successive drafts for misspellings; misprints and general 'nonsense'. Thank you, Margaret, for getting the text right.

Margaret has stuck with me through forty-four years of marriage in which there have been many things to try her patience. In the last few years a 'book on Jura' must have often figured high on the list of such trials. As can be seen, this book is dedicated to her. After all she has gone through with it, it could be dedicated to no one else.

I

The Island and its Wild-Life

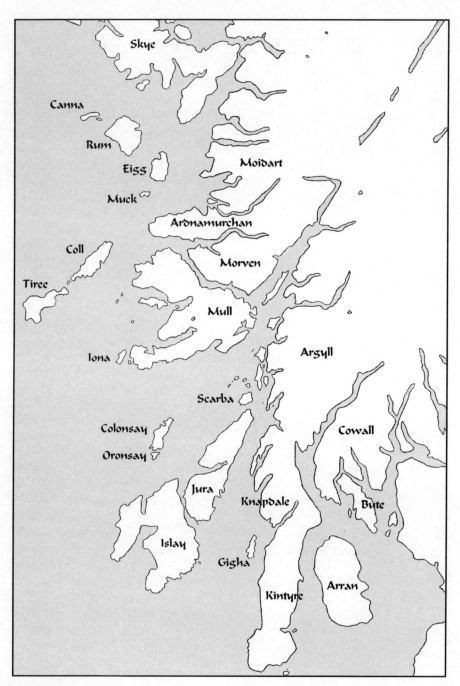

Map 1. Jura in relation to the mainland and its surrounding islands.

I

A Physical Description

The Hebrides are a large number of islands of various sizes which lie off the west coast of Scotland. They are conventionally divided into two groups: the Outer Hebrides and the Inner Hebrides. The Outer Hebrides, 35–50 miles from the mainland, form a compact line 130 miles long. The Inner Hebrides are scattered in a double rank 142 miles long, and lie close in to the coast. The main islands of the Inner Hebrides fall naturally into three groups around Skye, Mull and Islay. It is to the third of these groups that the Island of Jura belongs. Scholars seem generally agreed that Jura got its present name from the Viking period through association with the Norse word for 'deer' (see a fuller note in Chapter 13).

The Islay group is composed of Islay, Gigha and Cara, Colonsay and Oronsay, with Jura and Scarba. Jura is the second largest island in the group, and the fourth largest in the Inner Hebrides taken as a whole, coming in size after Skye, Mull and Islay.

Immediately to the north of Jura lies a considerable group of smaller islands, which, for historical reasons, have long been associated with it. These islands are Scarba; Lunga; Rubha Fiola, Eilean Dubh Mòr and Eilean Dubh Beag; Ormsa, Fladda and Belnahua; and the Garvellachs, or Isles of the Sea, consisting of Dun Chonnell, Garbh Eileach, A'Chuli, and Eileach an Naoimh. Further north than any of these, and marking the limit of the ancient Parish of Jura is Dubh-fheidh, two small rocks, submerged at low tide.

Jura is in area about 140 square miles (89,600 acres) or 36,261 hectares, while the islands to the north together amount to about 6½ square miles (4160 acres) or 1683 hectares.

Jura is a little over 27¼ miles long (44 km). It is nearly bisected by the sea loch, Loch Tarbert, which runs nearly 6½ miles (10.25 km) from its headlands on the west coast to three-quarters of a mile (1.25 km) from the east coast.

The island's broadest crossing lies to the south of the loch from Brein Phort to Ardfernal, and is nearly 7½ miles (12 km). The widest point north of the loch, from a little north of Shian Bay on the west coast is just over 6½ miles (10.6 km), and from there the island gradually tapers to the north, until at Barnhill, before it begins to curve sharply towards its northern point, the crossing is only a little under three miles (4.7 km)

Jura's orientation lies along its almost straight east coast, and is about 30 degrees east of north. This brings the island naturally in line with the north-west coasts and promontories of Knapdale and Craignish to the west.

Jura is separated from its nearest neighbour, the Island of Islay, by the Sound of Islay. The Sound runs roughly north to south and is some 11 miles (18 km) long. At its narrowest point at Feolin Ferry it is less than half a mile

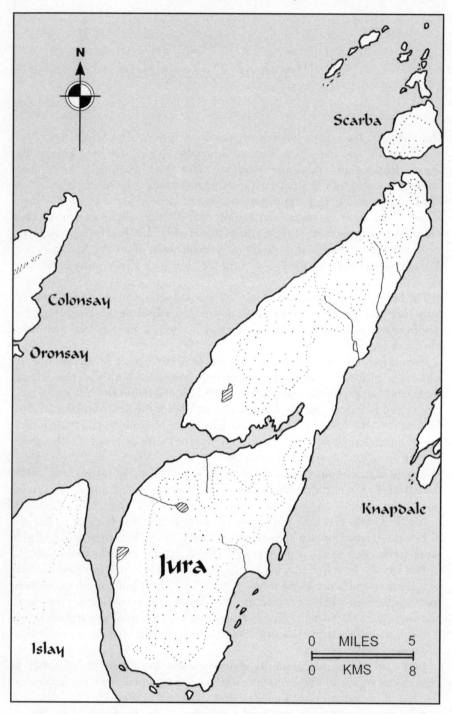

Map 2. Jura in relation to its nearest neighbours.

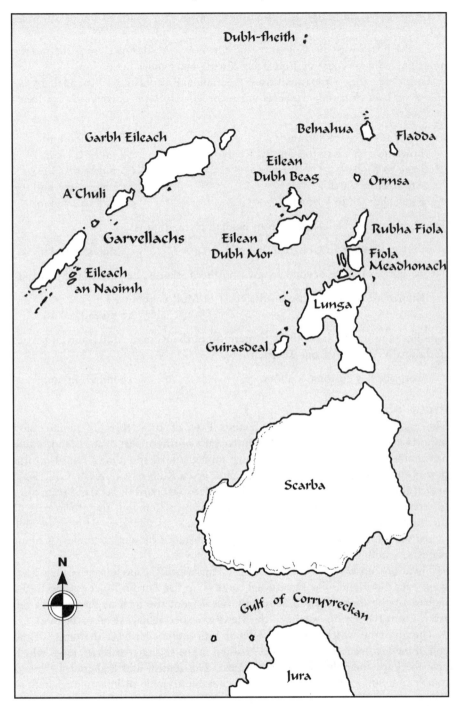

Map 3. The islands to the north of Jura.

(.75 km) across, although it opens out to north and south to about 2½ miles (4 km).

To the north-west lie Colonsay and Oronsay, the distance from the nearest point on the west coast of Jura being almost eight miles (12.75 km).

To the east Jura is separated from the mainland peninsula of Knapdale by the Sound of Jura. Various crossings are recorded, working northwards up Jura's east coast:

Small Isles Bay to Ormsary	12½ miles (20 km)
Lowlandman's Bay to Point of Knap	8 miles (13 km)
Lagg to Keills	5¾ miles (9.25 km)
Ardlussa to Carsaig	5 miles (8.25 km)
Kinuachdrach to Crinan	5½ miles (8.75 km)

The shortest possible crossing from landfall to landfall is

Port a' Tiobart to Craignish Point	3 miles (4.75 km)

To the north of Jura, beyond its own northern islands, lies the Island of Mull.

Kinuachdrach to Carsaig on the coast of Mull is about	
	20 miles (32 km)

Iona lies significantly just off the western tip of the Ross of Mull. Funeral parties traditionally left Jura from Corpach Bay.

Corpach Bay to Iona is about	25 miles (40 km)

HILLS

The major hills of Jura are the famous Paps of Jura, three in number and important features on the skyline even from the northern part of the island. These mountains dominate not only their own immediate surroundings, but also form part of the seascape for many miles around. From Kintyre, Colonsay, Coll, Tiree and Mull, and from the high tops of the western seaboard of Scotland from Skye to Arran, and even from the Isle of Man and Ben Lomond, they form part of the distant horizon. Residents of the tower blocks of Glasgow claim to be able to see the Paps of Jura on a clear day, at a distance of some 60 miles. (Colour plates 1, 2 and 3)

There are no easy ways to climb the Paps since the prelude is a long hard walk over moorland. The most usual route is up the Corran River and on to the highest of the three. Plate 6 shows the view from the loch at the head of the river. From the various summits the views are spectacular. (Colour plate 4)

The quartzite which forms the hills of Jura underwent frost shattering at the end of the last Ice Age, and this has resulted in the spectacular scree slopes which give the Paps their distinctive appearance. The central and highest trio have a fourth companion, and this group has a notable triangle of hills immediately to their south, and a further group of three encircling them to the north.

Dean Munro, writing in 1549, lists the three Paps and their companion: 'Foiranent uther is the greatest hills thairin are chieflie Ben quheillis, Ben senta, corben, Ben noir.' From the names given below it should be possible to disentangle Munro's names.

The names and heights are as follows:

The Paps

Beinn an Oir (Peak of the Edge ('Gold'?))	2572 ft (784 m)
Beinn Shiantaidh (Peak of Storms)	2477 ft (755 m)
Beinn a'Chaolais (Peak of the Narrows or Sound)	2408 ft (734 m)

The Companion

Corra Bheinn (Steep Peak)	1867 ft (569 m)

The Southern Triangle

Glas Bheinn (Grey Peak)	1840 ft (561 m)
Dubh Bheinn (Black Peak)	1739 ft (530 m)
Aonach-bheinn (Moor Peak)	1637 ft (499 m)

The Northern Ring

Scrinadle (Scree Dale)	1571 ft (479 m)
Beinn Bhreac (Speckled Peak)	1440 ft (439 m)
Beinn Tarsuinn (Crossways Peak)	1305 ft (398 m)

North of Loch Tarbert the hills string out to the north-west and towards the northern tip of the island.

RIVERS

The Presbytery's delegation on their visit in 1724 said of Jura: 'In it are eight waters of so rapid a current that at some times they cannot be passed, there being no bridges. And many have perished in them.' Jura has two substantial rivers: the Corran and the Lussa.

Fortunately there are now bridges along the main road, although there are still many obstacles to progress if one is walking in the interior of the island, for Jura is a wet place at all seasons and there is plenty of standing water, frequently surrounded by boggy ground.

The stream which runs into Whitefarland Bay on the Sound of Islay is nowadays called the River Inver from the name of the nearby Estate Lodge.

Together with the three rivers there are many conspicuous streams of which these are the most important: (a) Abhainn an Daimh-Sgeir; (b) Allt a'Mhoirt (Burn of the Murder); (c) Allt a'Mhuilinn (The Mill Burn); (d) Abhainn Mhic-ill-Libhri (McLever's (or McIvor's) River) and Abhainn na Coite (River of the Boat, or of the Share); (e) Glenbatrick River (River of the Pasture Harbour); (f) Abhainn Liundale (River of the Spring or Well Dale); (g) Abhainn Gleann Aoistall (River of Horse Glen); (h) Lealt Burn. This takes its name from the settlement, Lealt, which means 'all to one side of the burn'.

LOCHS

The part of the island south of Loch Tarbert has about seventy patches of open fresh water on the Landranger Map. Only nine are considered here. Five of these

Map 4. The major hills of Jura.

produce streams of the same name, and they have been covered in our Rivers section. They are The Market Loch; Glen Astaile Loch; Cnocbreac Loch; Loch an t'Siob and Loch na Fudarlaich. The remaining three lie farther north, near Loch Tarbert: Loch Lesgamaill; (Loch of the Chestnut Mare); Loch Losguinn; (Frog Loch), and Loch Sgitheig; (Hawthorn Loch).

The north part of Jura is covered by countless lochs and lochans, whose names can be found on the Pathfinder Map.

Two more need mention. Loch na Pearaich lies a little west of the head waters of Loch Tarbert, possibly Loch of the Vetch, but known locally as 'Parrot Loch'. A little inland from the road above Lussagiven is Loch Cathar nan Eun (Loch of the Mossy Place of the Birds). In Blaeu's sixteenth-century map this loch is shown and called Loch Cardinan, which is a reasonable attempt at Loch Cathar nan Eun.

The total coastline of Jura is about 98 miles (158 km). The coast is extremely variable with examples of many different features. There are cliffs, and beaches, and two large bays, and one fiord-type sea-loch.

In the neighbouring Island of Colonsay, a 'machair-type' Hebridean island, there are numbers of wide sandy beaches with inland dune systems and fine grassland. By contrast, Jura has few of these features, and sandy beaches are scarce.

RAISED BEACHES
Between the bays and beaches listed the east coast is rocky, with little foreshore, and a number of areas where the bedrock plunges sheer into the Sound. The Sound of Islay and the west coast are similar, but on the north-west stretches there are many impressive cliffs, in connection with which the Ordnance Survey Maps show more than forty caves, and a number of natural arches. Several of the caves, in particular in the region of Ruantallain, have a long history of human use.

Much of the extensive shoreline of Loch Tarbert is rocky and often has a rather bleak and forbidding appearance which enhances its sense of remoteness.

The shoreline of Jura is perhaps most famous as a result of its 'raised beaches', which are featured in geology textbooks, and visited by students of the subject.

Raised beaches are a widespread feature of the west coast of Scotland where the land, long burdened by the weight of ice-sheets during the glaciated periods, moved upwards once the ice had melted, carrying the previous shoreline clear of the present sea level. Once the eye is accustomed to looking for such former shores they can be readily spotted, often terminated by later cliff faces, which may themselves have been lifted above the present shore.

Many of these beaches are heavily vegetated, being covered with turf, peat, or even forests. Indeed, once a reasonable amount of sandy soil has accumulated on them, the raised beaches provide fertile ground for crops, and the underlying shingle gives good drainage. On Jura, some of the productive fields of the east coast settlements are situated on raised beaches.

The extraordinary aspect of Jura's most famous raised beaches is that they are not covered by any kind of vegetation. The stretches of shingle, high above sea-level, extend for great distances and cover large areas, and appear to be largely sterile. They provide a foothold for some small lichens, and a number of primitive insects, such as springtails. In some places colonies of gulls nest on the shingle, but that is all. Presumably the reason is that the depth of the deposits, the size of the individual cobbles, and the petrological composition of the shingle all create a situation where fierce western winds blow, and heavy rainfall continually washes off any potential colonists in the form of seeds, or even organic debris. The most spectacular examples of Jura's raised beaches are a long way from anywhere on the outer shore of Loch Tarbert, and on the far west coast. More accessible are those on the Sound of Islay, a few miles north of Inver. (Colour plate 5)

The largest part of Jura's 140 square miles is moorland and blanket bog. It is on these great acreages of moorland that Jura's varied population of wildlife exists, discussed in Chapter 4.

Prehistoric evidence makes it clear that Jura was extensively wooded, but those days are long gone, and the trees disappeared by a combination of climatic change and human activity.

There is some learned disagreement about whether there are any remnants of the primitive woods of Jura still surviving. R. N. Campbell of the Nature Conservancy Council gave it as his opinion in 1968 that there are remnants of the natural primitive woodland of Jura at Doire Dhonn, above Tramaig Bay, north of Ardlussa, and at the ravine along the Lealt burn. Further north, the woodlands of Con Tom and Glen Trosdale may be undisturbed relics of earlier tree cover.

The other trees on Jura have all been planted by man and can be found in association with human activity. A number of large forestry plantations can be seen from the main road.

A physical description of the island of Jura would not be complete without reference to the number of small islands which lie just offshore. There are three groups: the islands in Small Isles Bay on the east coast, the islands in the Sound of Islay and the islands in Loch Tarbert.

SMALL ISLES BAY
There are five islands in the bay: Eilean nan Gabhar (Goat Island); Eilean nan Coinen (Rabbit Island); Eilean Diomhain (The Idle or Useless Island); between Rabbit Island and the shore lies Pladda. This name is usually translated simply as 'Flat Island', although the connection with 'pladar' (a circular dish, or plate) is attractive. Indeed, Pladda is very flat, with a maximum height of about one metre. Pladda and Rabbit Island used to be grazed from the Manse. Eilean Bhride (Bridget's Island) completes the group.

SOUND OF ISLAY
There are three significant islands comprising from north to south:

Glas Eilean (Grey Island) This small island lies just off the south-west shore of Jura, and, contrary to its name, is really a very green island. It is not often visited, but is worth the effort as Glas Eilean has a most interesting geological significance, featuring 'pillow lavas' not otherwise found in this part of the Western Isles.

Am Fraoch Eilean (Heather Island) This island had a high historical profile because of the presence of Claig Castle (Castle of the Trench), which features in our consideration of historical sites. 'Fraoch Eilean' was the ancient battle cry of Clan Macdonald. Separated from Jura by Caolas a' Phlota (Narrow Sound of the Flood Tide), Heather Island has wonderful views to the south.

Brosdale Island This beautiful island seems to have had various different names during its history. Dean Monro, in 1549, called it Ellan na cravich (Wooded Island). The island lies offshore from Poll a' Cheo (Misty Pool), and Rubha na h-Acarsaid (Point of the Anchorage). Seen from the shore at this point Brosdale Island is an impressive feature.

THE ISLANDS OF LOCH TARBERT
The complex form of Loch Tarbert, with its spectacular outer and inner 'narrows' is further complicated by the presence of a number of small islands. Malcolm McArthur's research, which is referred to in detail later, has revealed that Dean Monro actually listed all the islands of Jura which we have already considered, and even some of the islands of Loch Tarbert. His island lists normally seem to deal with a central island, and its surrounding islets. However, islands 37–52 defeat all attempts to identify with Lorn, and turn out to be near Jura. The islands off Small Isles Bay and to the south of Jura are all easily identified. The others on the list turn out to be more difficult. Monro gives Ellan Righ (King's Isle) (39); Ellan Duff (Black Isle) (40); Ellan Naheglis (Kirk Isle) (41); Ellan Chriarache (42); Ellan Ard (High Isle) (43); Ellan Iisal (Laich Isle) (44).
Some of these still show on the modern Ordnance Survey Map, which gives:

Eileann Gleann Righ (Island of the King's Glen)   (Monro's 39)
Eilean Dubh a' Chumhainn Mhóir Black (Island of the Big Narrows)
                                                       (Monro's 40)
Eilean Iosal (Low Island)   (Monro's 44)
Eilean Ard (High Island)   (Monro's 43)
Eilean Chraoibhe chaorinn (Hazel Wood Island)   (Monro's 42)
Eilean na h-eaglais (Kirk Isle)   (Munro's 41)
Eilean an Easbuig (Island of the Bishop)

Monro gives two more islands: Ellan Anthian (37) and Ellan Uderga (38).
MacArthur proves that the first is Shian Island off Shian Bay, and the second is probably the unnamed island offshore from Glenbatrick.

THE NORTHERN ISLANDS
The ancient Parish of Jura has always included the islands to the north, and a physical description of the study area of this book would not be complete without some brief reference to them. They will of course appear again under various headings: human population, natural history, etc.

Scarba. The name is from the Norse, 'skarf' + 'ey', Cormorant Island. This is by far the largest of the northern islands. Very roughly a square, it is 3 miles (5 km) from east to west at its widest point, and about 2¾ miles (4.5 km) at its greatest measurement from north to south. In area it is about 5½ square miles (14.5 square km) Being composed largely of Jura quartzite, Scarba is rugged and inhospitable. It rises in the centre to the summit of Cruach Scarba Hill of Scarba at 1473 ft (449 m). (Colour plate 6)

Lunga. From the Norse for 'Heather Island'. This is the name loosely attached to a group of closely related islands lying just a short distance to the north of Scarba. The passage which separates the islands, 'Bealach a' Choin Ghlais' (Strait of the Grey Dog), is only 200 yards (183 m) wide. The group comprises Lunga itself, with a small island offshore to the south-west called Guirasdeal. To the north are the islands called Fiola, perhaps a Norse name. There are Fiola Meadhonach (Middle Fiola), with the little islets of Eilean Iosal (Low Isle) and Fiola an Droma (Fiola with the Ridge), hugging its western shore, and connected to it at low water, creating a small, almost land-locked inlet. Immediately north of Fiola Meadhhonach lies Rubha Fiola (Fiola Rock).

Ormsa. Probably, Island of Snakes, this small bare quartzite rock lies a third of a mile (0.6 km) north of Rubha Fiola, and is at the apex of an inverted triangle formed by the next two islands.

Fladda. From the Norse 'flat' r + 'ey', Flat Island. Another bare outcrop, this was the site of an important lighthouse in the past, and is now a holiday home. Some slate was extracted from Fladda in the eighteenth and nineteenth century. Fladda is conspicuous in any passage of the Sound of Luing.

Belnahua/Beul na h-uamha (Mouth of the Cave). This is the northern apex of the triangle. The quartzite has veered somewhat to the west, and Belnahua is in the commercially important bands of slate. Already quarried on a small scale in the sixteenth century, Belnahua, Fladda and the rest of the Easdale Dalradian Slates were exploited commercially from about 1750. The Belnahua slate was 'medium fine' and of quite high grade. (Colour plate 7)

Dubh-fheith (Black Bog). 2¾ miles (4.5 km) north of Belnahua lie the two almost submerged rocks of Dubh-fheith, which have have no special significance except that they mark the northernmost point of the geographical Parish of Jura.

Eilean Dubh Mór and *Eilean Dubh Beag (Big* and *Small Black Islands).* We return south to the region of the Fiolas, where six-tenths of a mile (1km) to the west lie these two small islands.

The Garvellachs. Known from ancient times as 'The Isles of the Sea', the name of the group is the plural of the name of the largest island, Garbh Eileach. This probably is derived from Gaelic words meaning a Rough Rocky Island. This group comprises four large islands and an assortment of small outlying rocks. From north to south, they are: (a) Dùn Chonnuill (Fort of Conal), a personal name – this small rocky island stands at the north-east of the group; (b) Garbh

Eileach, the largest of the group, measures 1 mile (1.6 km) in length, by about six-tenths of a mile (1 km) in breadth; (c) A' Chuli, the old name for this small island was Cul Brandon, or the Back Place of Brendan − less than half a mile long and a quarter of a mile across, A' Chuli is a beautiful little island, mirroring the general shape of Garbh Eileach, and with its own version of the same superb cliffs.

Eileach an Naoimh (Sacred, or Holy, or Consecrated Rocky Place). (Colour plate 8)

THE SEA
The sea has had an enormous effect on Jura's historic development; on its wildlife and on its human population. The seascape around the island is almost every-where bounded by a land horizon. Only certain very specific views to the west avoid the sight of land.

Apart from when it is close inshore, the sea gives little away about its depth, or the shape and structure of the sea bed around the island. The tide range varies considerably around the island from as little as about one metre in Craighouse Bay, to over three metres on the north-west coast.

Weather conditions farther offshore can have a great effect on the local tides, and strange and memorable phenomena occur from time to time. Extreme low spring tides are recorded in Small Isles Bay which seemed to remain low for a very long period, and these occurrences are supported by local recollections of the day when 'you could walk out to the islands through the sea-wrack'.

The depth of water around Jura is also very variable. If you stand at Small Isles Bay and look across the dozen or so miles to the Point of Knap on the mainland, you are looking across the Sound of Jura, and the depth increases steadily as you move towards the mid-point of the Sound, by which time it is more than 200 metres deep.

There is a shallower passage between Lagg and Keills, but a similar deep trench becomes established before the latitude of Tarbert, and veering towards the mainland coast, continues north to Crinan.

By contrast, if you stand anywhere on the western shore of Jura about the latitude of Colonsay and Oronsay and look across the eight miles of sea, you are surveying an expanse of much shallower water; often less than 20 metres and never as much as 100 metres, except for a narrow trench off the south-east coast of Colonsay.

The Sound of Islay is all shallow; nowhere more than 50 metres, although conditions of wind and tide can make it run like a torrent. The notably difficult water immediately to the south of Jura is also less than 50 metres in depth.

It is at the northern end of Jura that the nature of the sea becomes both interesting and also notorious. A narrow trench runs close to the east shore of the island from Lealt to Kinuachdrach, and goes as deep as 125 metres. Immed-iately north of the limit of this trench the water is much shallower, and it is possible to cross from Port an Tiobart, to Reis an t'Ruith (Rock in the Midst of the Stream), and thence to Craignish Point, without being over more than 50

metres of water at any point in the crossing. There is somewhat deeper water a
little to the north, but at this point one can envisage a land bridge between Jura
and the mainland at any time when the sea level was 175 feet or so below its
present depth. Geologists suggest that the sea level about 12,000 BC, was likely
to have been some 180 feet lower than today, so this seems a possible route for
Jura's post-glacial fauna to colonise the island.

Only a mile or so farther north still and matters change dramatically, as the
eastern end of the trench which runs between Jura and Scarba juts out into the
Sound.

Off the north-west coast of the island, there is water more than 100 metres
deep close inshore from a little north of Corpach to the northern end of the
island. This deep water continues north-west into the south-west approaches to
the Firth of Lorn in a confusing pattern of deep inlets and trenches, with an
especially deep one running from south-west to north-east to the south and
south-east of the Garvellachs. Here depths of 250 metres are attained, unusual
for anywhere on the Continental Shelf. Presumably it is the presence and
distribution of this deep water which influences the structure of perhaps the most
famous feature associated with Jura: the Gulf of Corryvreckan.

THE GULF OF CORRYVRECKAN

Between the northern tip of Jura and south coast of Scarba lies 'The Corryvreckan'. It has attracted the attention of the earliest historical writers, whose
impressions will be quoted later on, but first there is the dispassionate account
of *Sailing Directions* of Clyde Cruising Club:

> Between the island of Jura and Scarba is the Gulf of Corryvreckan, 1½ miles
> long and a little more than ½ mile wide at its narrowest point. The warnings
> which invariably accompany descriptions of this notorious gulf should be
> carefully heeded, but definite distinctions can be drawn between the flood and
> the ebb, whether these are Spring or Neap, and the prevailing weather condi-
> tions. In calm weather at slack water the whole gulf becomes placid and gives
> no hint of its ferocious nature under certain conditions of wind and tide. It is
> at its most dangerous when an Atlantic swell, having built up after several
> days of strong West winds, meets a flood tide. A passage at this time would
> be unthinkable.
>
> The Flood surges over the deep, uneven bottom, and is impeded by a high
> shelf which stretches out from Scarba, ending abruptly at the 29 metre sounding
> 600 yards south-west of Camas nam Bairneach. Above the comparatively shal-
> low shelf the flood gains in velocity, but meets resistance in the water ahead
> where a backward-rearing overfall is formed. The remaining dangerous over-
> falls extend five miles west.
>
> The overfalls close to the 29 metre sounding are invariably the most awesome,
> on occasion with breaking crests and spume at their tops. In calm weather at
> Spring Tides the first can rise to a height of four metres, and may be accom-
> panied by a loud roaring noise as it plunges from the Scarba shelf. A heavy
> western swell can double its height to eight metres (26 feet), when it and the

remaining overfalls drop to the bottom of deep and possibly angled troughs. In extreme conditions the roar can continue for several hours, audible even at Crinan, six miles distant.

This turbulence is coupled, on ebb as well as flood, with spasmodic upthrusts of bottom water. The latter have non-rotating, foam-flecked circumferences, which, if viewed from above, look remarkably like whirlpools, although their effect is precisely the opposite. Indeed, the only whirlpools in the Corryvreckan are of small size.

Beware of the flood in a sudden calm preceded by several days of strong west winds. On the last of the remaining swell an overfall can occur north of the north tip of Jura. Prolonged strong west winds can make an overfall, perhaps better described as a solid wall of water, stretch from here, and also from the shelf, right across the gulf.

The famous Norwegian whirlpool is called The Maelstrom, but *Chambers Dictionary* also defines maelstrom as 'a confused, disordered state of affairs; any resistless overpowering influence for destruction', and that sums up the Corryvreckan very well. (Plate 1)

A little farther north lies the Bealach a Choin Ghlais (Gap of the Grey Dog), the narrow channel between Scarba and its northern neighbour, Lunga. The Clyde Cruising Club's account of this is only a little less alarming than that of The Corryvreckan:

> Better known as the Little Corryvreckan, it is divided into two channels by islets in the middle. The broader channel is a mere 100 yards wide. The tide runs like a mill race, reaching on flood and ebbs 8½ knots. When the tide is running there is a constant danger of being swept on to the islets.

> The unnavigable part is just south of the islets. The water forms two distinct levels here, creating a short, but spectacular downhill torrent. On the flood an overfall forms north of the point, and in heavy weather this can be seen from a distance of 1 mile to the south-east.

> Due to the velocity of the tide, the narrowness of the channel, and the restriction caused by the islets in the middle, manoeuvrability is all but impossible. It should be treated at all times with the same caution as the Gulf of Corryvreckan.

It is worth noting that the waters around the most northerly of the islands – Fladda, Belnahua and the Garvellachs – also produce interesting and odd effects for the yachtsman, and should all be treated with considerable caution.

No study of the seas surrounding Jura is complete without mentioning its own sea-loch, Loch Tarbert. This is a very long inlet indeed, and has two notable 'narrows' before reaching the muddy headwaters. It has a considerable commercial history, having been the home of a herring fishery in the nineteenth century, and its remote bothy at Cruib has often been the centre for 'outward bound'-style youth activities. Little used these days, except by the owners of the estate, it must have been an important sea route, and its local names testify to a fascinating past.

2

Climate and Weather

The climate in the Inner Hebrides has changed often and dramatically since the ice-sheets melted, and since the later period of the Lomond Re-advance about 8000 BC. In the section on the flora and fauna of Jura, these changes will be traced briefly, but at this point the present climate of Jura is discussed, as it has been during the last decades of the twentieth century. In the Hebrides in general the present mean summer temperatures range from 55°F (12.78°C) to 57°F (13.89°C). These temperatures are about 1°F lower than those for the east coast of Scotland. The winter temperatures are more significant. The average temperature during the winter months is 41°F (5°C) to 42°F (5.56°C) for the whole length of the Hebrides. These temperatures are 3°F (1.66°C) higher than those for the east coast.

The large difference in winter temperatures is caused by the North Atlantic Drift of the Gulf Stream, by prevailing westerlies, and by the fact that the islands are small in size. The coastal strips of the Hebrides and the low inner islands are milder than anywhere in Britain except the south-west of England and the western fringes of Wales and Ireland.

Thus the Hebrides are virtually free of snow, except on the mountains, where it never lies as long or as heavily as on mainland hills. North-westerly blizzards are brief. Scotland's principal snowfalls come on east or south-east winds which discharge over the Highlands before reaching the Hebrides. Snow comes on low ground lightly and infrequently. Frost is neither prolonged nor extreme.

Temperature records for Jura come from Craighouse, Small Isles Bay, from 1966 to 1970.

Month	Average daytime temperature °F	°C	Days of sleet or snowfall	Days of ground frost
January	45	7.2	1	8
February	44	6.5	1	13
March	48	8.6	1	10
April	51	10.5		8
May	57	13.6		2
June	64	17.6		
July	63	17.1		
August	64	18.0		
September	60	15.7		
October	56	13.3		1
November	48	9.1		7
December	46	7.9	1	8

The above figures show an average temperature for June, July and August of 63.6°F (17.58°C) and for December, January and February of 45°F (7.2°C)

The average number of days when snow or sleet fell during the years in question was fewer. The number of days when ground frost was recorded was 57.

Rainfall in the Inner Hebrides is considerably heavier than on the east coast. Indeed the West Highlands is the wettest region of Europe. The highest rainfall of 120 inches or more comes, not on the coast, but several miles inland along the high mountain spine on which the ice-cap was once centred. Rainfall is almost as closely related to land-height as temperature; a few miles from the base of a mountain the rainfall may be only half that of the summit. The Hebrides lie well beyond the heavy rain belt. In general, they have a fall of 40–60 inches, except on the mountains of Harris, Skye, Rum and Jura, where it rises to 60–80 inches, and 120 inches on central Mull.

The records for Craighouse during the five years in question fall directly within the parameters given here by W. H. Murray:

Month	Rainfall (inches) Monthly total
January	4.9
February	4.4
March	5.0
April	2.9
May	3.4
June	3.2
July	3.7
August	3.2
September	6.3
October	8.3
November	7.7
December	6.5
Annual Totals	59.5

The statistics make interesting reading to anyone with experience of long-term residence on Jura, and also to those who spend holiday breaks there in the summer. It is easy to remember the many occasions in the 1970s and 1980s when summer visitors retreated from the island in some disgust, having experienced rainfall on every one of the 14 days of their stay in July or August, although the statistics do tend to confirm an experience of fine weather in the months of April and May.

An important climatic feature of the Hebrides, indeed, often its outstanding feature, is wind; strong and persistent. It comes off the Atlantic, laden with moisture, and, although the rain clouds continually renew themselves out of the west, the wind drives them across the low islands to precipitate mainly on the Highlands. Thus the Outer Hebrides, and the Inner too, where low-lying, have long hours of sunshine, especially in April, May and June. There are no good records for sunshine on Jura, but the long-term average for May sunshine is 234 hours on Tiree some 24 miles north of Craighouse.

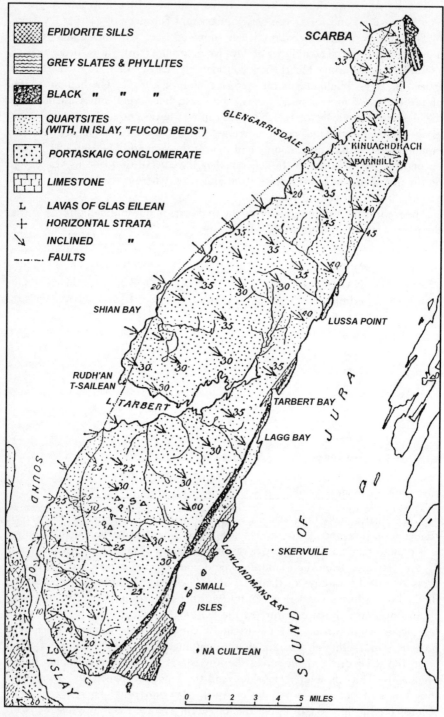

Map 5. Geological map of the rocks of Jura.

3

Geology

Jura is composed largely of a metamorphic rock called quartzite which had its origin in the Dalradian age (late Pre-Cambrian). This rock is interpreted as having been deposited as sandy layers on a shallow marine shelf dominated by tidal currents. Scotland and the Hebrides lay under this Cambrian Sea for 150 million years. Presumably as the sediments accumulated their weight depressed the sea bed, and ultimately the resultant layers were over three miles thick.

During the later part of the deposition of these layers, a rapid subsidence flexed the sea floor downwards to the north of Jura. From the resulting slope detritus poured into a deep basin to form what would become the Scarba Conglomerate. The rocky and pebbly material which formed this gradually became finer, turning into the Easdale Slates, a mainly muddy sequence deposited from dilute turbidity currents.

All these sediments form part of the Dalradian Series which are estimated at about 570 million years old. Present theory describes how these buried sediments were compressed, folded and metamorphosed, to be raised up later in a mountain chain we call the Caledonian. This mountain building period gave the Highlands and Islands their prevailing north-east to south-west grain. In the region of Jura the entire sequence became folded downwards as part of a great U-shaped formation called the Loch Awe Syncline which results in all the rocks of Jura being inclined downwards some 30–40 degrees in a south-east direction. If you go east across the Sound of Jura into Knapdale, you find the same strata in reverse order, and now inclining downwards to the north-west. The centre of this enormous valley lies beneath the Sound of Jura.

During the long ages of the Ordovician and Mesozoic eras, the Caledonian Highlands in the region of Jura were much reduced by erosion. Cracks in these rocks were filled by molten magma, and much later in the Lower Tertiary period, some 56 million years ago, there was a period of volcanic activity, the most prolonged and intense in Britain's history.

There were at least seven centres of eruption in the north-west, and doubtless many others now hidden under the sea. The centres in Arran and Mull would seem to be the most significant in their effect on Jura. The volcanic action developed in two main phases. First came the outpouring of plateau lavas. From vents and fissures they rolled out in flows spreading far and wide across the land, and reaching, over millions of years, an enormous thickness. Skye and Mull still show signs of these lava flows. Some of these lavas have left a remnant on the east coast of Jura from Ardfernal south towards Brosdale Island. These flows are termed epidiorite sills. Secondly, upwelling magma exploded through the crust in volcanoes of large vent. These explosion vents were accompanied by a

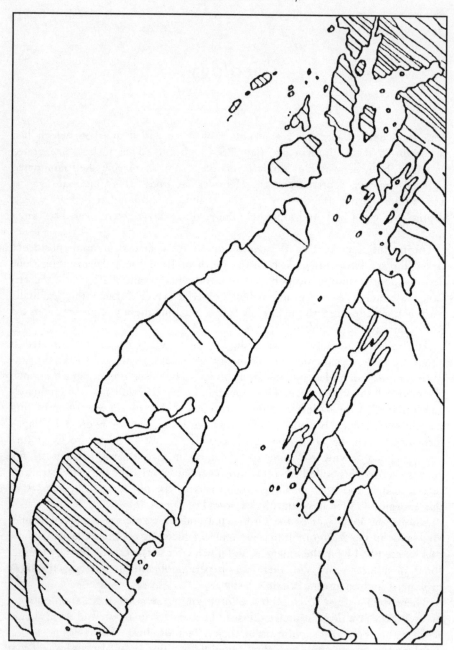

Map 6. The Tertiary volcanic dykes of Jura.

shattering of the earth's crust. From each centre, linear dykes swarmed out exactly as in glass shattered by a bullet hole.

These volcanic dykes were evidently of interest to Jura's eighteenth-century visitors, for J. Clevely recorded a 'Whyn-dyke' in the Sound of Islay, close to the cottages of Daimhsgeir.

During the Tertiary the whole area reached the stage of a peneplain, including the planing down of the basalt-dolerite dykes. A further uplift movement then took place. This produced in the south-west the present landscape of rugged pinnacles and ridges where the weak strata have become valleys and the faults have become lochs with a SW/NE orientation. The 2500 foot Paps of Jura, made of highly resistant quartzite, owe their conical erosion to their lack of weaknesses and faults. Far from the main 2500 foot zone, the Paps are simply assumed to have suffered some 1000 feet less erosion than the rest of the area.

ICE AGE

During the Pleistocene period, which began some two million years ago, Scotland was covered with ice four times, with milder interglacial phases intervening. At its maximum the continuous ice sheet was several thousand feet thick. Only the peaks of a few mountains would have protruded from it. The summit of the Paps of Jura may well have been amongst those peaks which remained above the ice at the period of 'maximum glaciation', although some authorities suggest a thickness of ice twice the height of the Paps.

In the early 1900s Jura was visited by S. B. Wilkinson, whose work for the Geological Survey showed that the direction of the ice flow was from east to west across Jura, as revealed by the scratches or striae left on the rock surfaces.

Other signs of the passage of the ice include deposits of 'till', mainly on low ground, and one very striking medial moraine on the north-west-facing slope of the highest of the Paps of Jura, Beinn an Oir. Another notable feature of this period is a fossilised rock glacier on the eastern side of Beinn Shiantaidh. A note on these follows:

Sgriob na Caillich (The Old Woman's Slide) (OS 473766). This is interpreted as a medial moraine deposited between two streams of the ice-sheet as they converged after sweeping around and through the Paps from the east. It is 3.5 km long and drops from 450 m OD to 30 m OD at which point the boulder belts are cut off by a low cliff and raised coastal platform. The complex is composed in places of up to four parallel lines of angular blocks made up almost entirely of quartzite, and having no evidence of striation or ice moulding. A. G. Dawson (1979) suggests that the moraine was produced during the waning of the Late Devensian ice-sheet. He considers that the peaks of the Paps protruded above the ice as 'nunataks' and that the boulders of the moraine were deposited from them on to a relatively thin, yet very active, ice-mass. No other medial moraine in Scotland can compare with Sgriob na Caillich in either size or complexity.

Fossil Lobate Rock Glacier (OS 522748). This feature was identified and described by A. G. Dawson in 1976. It consists of an accumulation of angular quartz boulders at the base of Beinn Shiantaidh. Backed by a scree slope, and facing ENE, the boulder field comprises a series of roughly concentric ridges and depressions occupying an area of 45,000 sq. metres. The mass has a sharply defined frontal margin. This fascinating feature, which is best viewed from the slopes of Corra Bheinn (OS 526755), has strong similarities with structures described in Colorado, Canada and Alaska. Such rock glaciers are composed of coarse debris that is moved downslope by interstitial ice or buried ice. (Colour plate 9)

RAISED BEACHES

The coastal area of western Jura contains a remarkable assembly of raised shoreline landforms. These include shore platforms and the best-developed spreads of late glacial shingle ridges in Britain. Although these features occur on both east and west coasts of the island, they are best seen on the west coast, as they are somewhat concealed by vegetation on the east coast. The raised shingle spreads of the west coast of Jura were first described by Wilkinson and Peach at the Geological Survey of 1900. The first major study was by McCann (1961) who sought to describe and explain the origin of the shingle spreads and relate them to patterns of sea-level change connected with late glacial activity. More recently A. G. Dawson (1979) has investigated the area in detail.

The following is a brief digest of glacial and sea-level chronology in Jura, Scarba and north-east Islay provided by Dawson.

Three million years ago.   Start of the Quaternary ice ages. Repeated ice sheets covered Jura; each one eroding rock, and depositing glacial debris until *c.* 45,000 years BC.

Second last inter-glaciation (Hoxnian).   High rock platform formed along the entire coast, height 33–36 metres, followed by its erosion. Only fragments remain in sheltered west facing areas.

Last inter-glaciation.   Formation of low rock platform, height 1–2 metres.

Last glaciation. Maximum at 15,000 BC. Westward-moving mainland ice overwhelmed Jura leaving evidence of glacial erratics, striae and glacial till accumulations.

14,000 BC.   Rapid melting of ice. Medial moraine formed at Sgriob na Caillich. North-east Islay and west Jura the first ice-free areas. Ice still covered the rest. A high shore terrace formed between Ruantallain and Corpach Bay at 40 metres sloping down to 26.5 metres in north-east Islay. South-west Jura remained ice covered.

13,500 BC.   South-west Jura now ice-free and a high shoreline formed along south-west Jura coast (30 metres at Glenbatrick, 24 metres north of Inver). At this time the highest beaches between Ruantallain and Shian Bay were formed under stormy conditions. The longshore current was from north-east to south-west at this time. There was pack-ice offshore. Land uplift continued as a result of the release of the ice-load. Relative marine regression occurred and resulted in the formation of the west Jura shingle spreads. The relative sea level fell from 35 metres to 19 metres. The shingle source was from the marine erosion of glacial deposits.

13,500–11,000 BC.   Continuing land uplift. Ice had now retreated north up the Firth of Lorne and Sound of Jura The whole area was now ice-free. By 10,000 BC the climate might have been slightly warmer than at present.

9300 BC.   The beginning of the final cold period. The Lomond Re-advance. Due to the relatively low altitude of Jura hills no glaciers developed as the climate became colder. The period of most intense cold was from 8800 to 8300 BC. Sea level continued to fall, and reached its lowest levels during the cold period of the Loch Lomond Stadial. There was much marine erosion of rock during this time, and this resulted in the formation of a wide raised rock platform along all of the west Jura coast and parts also of the east coast. This was the time of the rock glacier and of the accumulation of scree slopes as a result of frost action. The raised caves of Jura also date from this time.

8000 BC.   The climate began to warm up. Temperatures rose rapidly with a change from tundra vegetation to the development of forest. By 5550 BC the climate was warmer than at present, and sea level was also higher. Sea level rose to between 8.5 and 10 metres, and submerged the previously formed coastal rock platform. Water washed into caves and resulted in the deposition of water rounded cobbles on cave floors. The relative retreat of the sea to the present day is recorded in the shingle spreads north of Inver.

Apart from the low-lying lands along the east coast everything else that can be seen on Jura is composed of Jura quartzite. The best exposures are on high ground, or on the western shores of the island. On the Paps and their companion, Corra Bheinn, the thick, tilted beds of hard white, pink or grey quartzite dominate the landscape. The long, even, south-easterly slopes often follow the bedding planes in the rock.

There are good exposures around the head of Loch Tarbert, which is more easily reached than the Paps.

The west coast was evidently of interest to visitors, and the geologist Robert Jamieson visited it in 1774.

While considering the quartzite itself, it should be noted that it is quite easy to inspect the frost shattering effects of the Lomond Re-advance by walking to the Paps, and climbing up them. The walking on the higher slopes is most uncomfortable, and the screes can be experienced at first hand. The fossil glacier should probably be visited more often, but is really quite inaccessible. It can best be seen from the south-west slopes of Corra Bheinn.

The outcrops of Scarba Conglomerate and Port Ellen Phyllite which form much of the eastern coast of Jura, are clearly visible. Craighouse, for example, rests on both of them, although there is actually little conglomerate at the southern end of the island. A good exposure of Port Ellen Phyllites can be seen on the right of the road which gives access to the main pier, just before the pier itself. The rocks are green or grey with silver foliated surfaces due to the parallel alignment of flakes of mica.

If you walk out along the shore south of the pier until you get to the islands in Small Isles Bay in a north-east-facing line, you are looking along the line of the Epidiorite lava sills already mentioned. A visit to Ardfernal, and a climb to the top of Ardfernal Hill will show the line of these resistant sills very clearly.

A good place to see the Scarba Conglomerate is at Lussa Bay. The bay itself is eroded out of slate (formerly quarried nearby at Inverlussa) and coarser sandstones and conglomerates form the coastal ridges to the east.

There are interesting signs of volcanic activity on the small island in the Sound of Islay, known as Glas Eilean (Grey Island). This little island is almost connected with Jura, and it is possible to wade across at spring tide low water. Some reddish-brown basalt lava flows can be seen here – very different from the quartzites only a few hundred yards away on Jura. The lavas are vesicular (having gas bubbles) and amygdaloidal (the vesicles have been filled in with minerals such as quartz) Some flows show slaggy tops, covered with thin layers of sandstone. This red sandstone may link this small outcrop with the Lower Old Red Sandstone of Central Scotland, and the volcanic series of Lorne.

4

Natural History

In area, Jura is the fourth largest of the Inner Hebrides, after Skye, Mull, and Islay. In terms of its natural history it is a fascinating product of its geology and its geographic location.

The island's extremely hard metamorphic quartzite has resulted in little development of arable land, and consequently a comparatively small human population during its post-glacial lifespan. This underlying geology has meant that it has been hard for people to scrape a living from Jura, but the consequence has been that the island has not had to endure the impact of human endeavour which has so changed the face of other parts of the United Kingdom.

The human population of the island has been restricted to the comparatively fertile strips of land along the eastern seaboard, where the glacial till has provided some fertile soil. In consequence of this physical situation, which everyone in their own way has had to come to terms with, the hinterland of Jura is largely devoid of human activity. In this considerable area of Scotland you are unlikely to encounter people at all. Those you may see will be involved in the business of shooting red deer, during the stalking season. This activity is overseen and controlled by the Red Deer Commission, and is in operation from 1 July to 20 October for stags, and 21 October to 15 February for hinds. During this time there is heightened anxiety amongst landowners regarding the possibility that unaware and thoughtless citizens may inadvertently disturb the concentration of the stalkers, whose fees keep the estates solvent.

Other people who may be encountered in the remote vastnesses of Jura are the fell runners, who for a few days each year are involved in a Paps of Jura race. There are also a few hardy souls prepared to try to walk on the remote west coast and ready to make a bivouac if time does not allow them to reach the east coast.

There is a single remote lodge, built for the Astors at Glenabedrig, or nowadays, Glenbatrick, where one may occasionally find the landowner or his guests. At the extreme north end, Glengarrisdale still stands as a bothy.

Those who visit Jura with an interest in its natural history and wildlife find it very different from the neighbouring island of Islay, which has a much more varied landscape, with big areas of farmed land. The keen bird-watcher can spend a summer week in Islay and see a great variety of British birds. His one-day trip to Jura gives time only for a drive up the main road and back, and he leaves with the impression that there is very little on the island, and nothing of interest. Nothing could be further from the truth, but Jura's wildlife doesn't come up and say, 'Look, here I am!' – at least not in the summer months.

In the course of the last few centuries various notable travellers have visited Jura, and many have commented on its natural history. During the twentieth century a considerable number of specialist naturalists came to study various aspects of Jura's wildlife, many of them under the auspices of the Nature Conservancy Council.

In 1983 the Royal Society of Edinburgh published the results of a Symposium, organised by the Nature Conservancy Council and entitled *The Natural Environment of the Inner Hebrides*. The topics covered are far-ranging and provide a good background to anyone who wishes to study the natural history of any of the islands in the Inner Hebrides in depth. Serious students of the question are recommended to read this report, although many of the topics will be touched on in this chapter. The report will be referred to as *NEIH*.

VEGETATION

After the Ice Age, the newly cleared landscape was colonised by plants. Dr S. E. Durno of the Macaulay Institute for Soil Research in Aberdeen, did an analysis of ancient peat cores from Jura between 1967 and 1970. This showed that in the earliest times there were few pine trees, but oak and elm were common. During the Boreal period, up to about 5500 BC, the dominant trees were birch and hazel, but with the coming of the wetter Atlantic period alder took over from hazel, with birch and alder continuing into the present.

The island was probably largely covered with trees in the Boreal period, but these have gradually given way to grasses, sedges and heather, leading ultimately to Jura's present state of almost treeless moorland.

In recent times the island has seen a policy of moor-burning, together with heavy grazing by domestic animals and by large numbers of red deer. Regeneration of trees is impossible as long as young trees are eaten as fast as they spring up. Of course, human interference is nothing new. The pollen analysis shows that people began to clear the best ground for cultivation in Neolithic times.

The main influence on the vegetation is the underlying geology. Jura's rocks are all, to a greater or lesser degree, acid. Between the rock and the vegetation comes the soil, in Jura very often a layer of peat. This is encouraged to form by water-logged conditions, generally low temperatures, high acidity and lack of plant nutrients, and once it has begun this cycle simply continues.

The vegetative landscape falls largely into three main zones. The first and most low-lying consists of arable ground, now in many places reverting to pasture or even to a wild natural state. These lands rest on silts, sands, gravels and beaches of glacial, river and marine origin. The second zone lies on the margins of the first, and usually rises inland. Here are patches and belts of comparatively dry, hilly grassland, with varying amounts of mat grass and purple moor grass. The third and uppermost zone consists of subalpine peat moors. These are characterised by heather on dry slopes, by patches of bracken on dry good soil, and by sedges such as cotton and deer grass in the wetter areas, with much bent and sphagnum. In these areas grow Jura's mosses, grasses, sedges, rushes, and flowering plants, together with its native trees and shrubs.

Jura's natural history attracted the attention of some of its early visitors, and the Rev. Dr John Walker, author of *Experiments on the Paps*, made a considerable collection of botanical specimens on the island. The Rev. John Lightfoot published his *Flora Scotica* in 1777, and accompanied Thomas Pennant on his second tour of Scotland, which brought him also to Jura, and resulted in a number of observations on its plants.

If someone comes to visit the island with no previous experience of Scotland's Highlands and Islands, the vegetative cover can come as something of a shock. Even as far south as Jura, there is no general tree cover, only fragments of ancient scrub and modern plantations.

The walk from the road to climb one of the Paps of Jura, for example, will take one across seemingly endless miles of moorland. Off any beaten track, the going is difficult, with deep uneven tussocks of purple moor grass, interspersed with easier springy cover of calluna, or ling. The flowering plants are sparsely scattered, small, and close to the ground. In their season can be seen the yellow tormentil, milkwort, lousewort, sundew and boga sphodel, with areas of the other two native heathers, bell heather and cross-leaved heath. The day may be spent on ground which bears less than a couple of dozen species of plants. This means that one can quickly become quite knowledgeable about the flowers of Jura's moors.

The story is different in the small lush meadows close to the sea, as for example below Knockrome or Ardfernal. Here can be found a much larger variety of flowers and shrubs, with heavy and sometimes impenetrable thickets above the shoreline. Here in season can be found a number of species of orchid, including the fragrant and the lesser butterfly, also machair-type flowers such as centaury and grass of Parnassus. (Machair is the name for the close-cropped turf found above the beaches of many Hebridean islands; there is almost no true machair on Jura.)

Walks by Jura's roadsides, especially in the north, reveal more flowers and many species of ferns. Amongst the trees there are rich growths of lichens in the unpolluted atmosphere, and in the north the uncommon lungwort hangs from the branches.

The island is large and takes a very long time to be explored properly. Nothing can be taken for granted, as the valley just beyond the last one visited may contain something quite unexpected. Thus on the west coast there are a few scattered examples of the aspen tree. In scrub woods at Ardfernal a broad-leaved helleborine orchid turned up one year, the first for the Inner Hebrides, but was never repeated.

A well-known botanist from the Nature Conservancy Council visited the north of Jura in 1967, and left behind with the proprietor of the Ardlussa estate a short list of plant species which he believed had not been previously recorded on Jura. The list consisted of nine species, but gave no information as to where they had been found. Determined searching has probably rediscovered seven, but at the time of writing dwarf cornel (*Chamaepericlymenun suecicum*), little bog orchid (*Hammarbya paludosa*) and parsley fern (*Cryptogramma crispa*) all seem still to have eluded even the most experienced botanists.

A. Currie and C. W. Murray in *NEIH* provide a considerable study of the flora and vegetation of the whole region. They note a few special records.

Four flowers are listed which occur only on Jura in the area covered: pale willowherb (*Epilobium roseum*); rockrose (*Helianthemum chamaecistus*); cross-wort (*Galium cruciata*); and bog blaeberry (*Vaccinium uliginosum*).

Three species are listed only from Islay and Jura: tubular water dropwort (*Oenanthe fistulosa*); reflexed salt-marsh grass (*Puccinellia distans*); and great water dock (*Rumex hydrolapathum*).

Two species, both orchids, have been recorded only from Skye, Mull and Jura: sword-leaved helleborine (*Cephalanthera longifolia*); and broad-leaved helleborine (*Epipactis helleborine*).

In considering the plants of Jura, the student not only has to deal with a very large island, some of which is quite inaccessible, but must bear in mind the great variety of habitats that are present.

This summary mentions only a few of the flowers of the island, but a comprehensive list, compiled by Nick Stewart is available among papers published on Jura itself.

WOODLANDS

The author is indebted to M. E. Ball of the Nature Conservancy Council for the following brief account which appears in *NEIH*:

There is almost no native woodland remaining on the infertile soils of the Dalradian quartzite rocks which dominate the whole of this hilly and rocky island, the only exceptions being the degraded birchwoods of Coille na h'Uanair on the coast facing the sound of Islay, and in Glentrosdale in the extreme north. On the richer Dalradian schists outcropping in a narrow band parallel to the east coast, where soil and shelter factors are more favourable, woodland has survived. Although the majority of this natural woodland is grazed and browsed by sheep and deer it still survives in a relatively natural state except for small areas at Sannaig in the south-east and near Tarbert on the east coast where there is some underplanting of conifers.

All stand-type examples occurring in the Hebrides are represented in Jura at least once, such is the variety of site types present. Elm-ash has a single representation at Craighouse ravine in the south-east, which is also one of the finest sites in the Hebrides for its oceanic cryptogam flora. The related ash-hazel group on the other hand is found only on the north-east coast, where stand-type variety is greatest and includes small alder-grey sallow stands in addition to both facies of oak-birch and associated birch-hazel stands. Some stands, for example at Doire Dhonn, Ardlussa, are difficult to classify and seem to represent intermediates between the ash-hazel and oak-birch on mull soils.

Together with this brief, but authoritative assessment can be added the two woods designated as Sites of Special Scientific Interest. The designations and descriptions are brief:

Kinuachdrach. 'The best native woodland relic habitat in Jura with a flora characteristic of highly oceanic conditions.'

Doire Dhonn. On the steep slope above Tramaig Bay, north of Ardlussa, 'an unspoiled fragment of oakwood grading into the brackish saltmarshes of Tramaig Bay'.

There are also similar fragments at Ardmenish, and on the steep slopes at Ardfernal and near Inver, and the above-mentioned Ravine at Craighouse. These woods consist of birches with quantities of oak, alder, rowan and hazel, and some ash, as well as holly and sallow. There are black poplars at Lagg, and a very few aspens on the north-west coast.

It seems likely that tree planting around the two main estate houses, Jura House and Ardlussa, took place in the late 1800s, and mixed deciduous woodland occurs there with a variety of non-native species. Mr Evans undertook planting around Jura Forest Lodge, and the author found a considerable number of post-mature sycamores growing around the Manse. These were sown about 1880. There were beeches of a similar age. Some tree-planting also took place around Lagg.

Beginning in 1951, the Forestry Commission acquired some 2000 acres in Jura. Their plantations are on the Sannaig coast, east of Jura House; inland and west of Craighouse, and above the coast between Lagg and Tarbert. Landowners also did some planting with the aid of 'Small Woods' grants and under the 'Dedication' scheme.

The Commission planted some 900 acres of Sitka spruce; 200 acres of Sitka spruce mixed with 100 acres of Lodgepole Pine; 64 acres of Japanese larch, and some acres of Scots and Corsican pines; Norway spruce; Douglas fir and other conifers. In recent years the future of these plantations has often been in doubt. Ancient and important features in the island's history are submerged in these areas, such as the settlements of Sannaig and Dunans, and the standing stones of Carraig a'Ghlinne. The great views across the Sound around Corrynahera have also disappeared. Perhaps as the harvesting cycle continues and areas are clear-felled, these locations and views will re-emerge.

THE REMAINING PLANT GROUPS
Before leaving the general area of plant life on Jura, it should be noted that the island is rich in grasses, sedges, rushes, mosses, ferns, lichens and fungi. A full list of all of these is available on Jura.

BRYOPHYTES
The division Bryophyta contains the classes Musci, or mosses, and Hepaticae, or liverworts. M. F. V. Corley produced a full report on their occurrence in the Inner Hebrides, which can be studied in full in *NEIH*. Jura features prominently in this report, and the species list with which it concludes records 321 different species on the island. Since identification presents such problems for the amateur, and since few species have English names, this list has not been made widely available.

However this study of bryophytes deserves mention in this chapter. 'Of just under 1000 species of bryophytes known in the British Isles, 597 are recorded in the Inner Hebrides. Naturally the Inner Hebrides are rich in species with an oceanic distribution in the British Isles. A number of species are thought to be

Tertiary relicts in the British Flora.' The author, M. V. F. Corley, lists a number of Atlantic or Oceanic groups of species:

> The Northern Atlantic group is well represented in the Inner Hebrides, especially on Mull, Rum, Skye and Jura, and includes species whose worldwide distribution covers one or more of the following – Atlantic Norway, Faeroes, Himalayas, Yunnan, Alaska, British Columbia, Appalachian Mountains.
>
> The Southern Atlantic group species are absent from the most northerly parts of the west coast of Scotland, but tend to occur along the western coast of Europe south to Portugal. In Britain their occurrence is predominantly south-western with most species being most abundant in south-west Ireland. These species mainly grow in sheltered sites at low altitudes, particularly in deep-shaded ravines on Islay, Jura, Mull, Rum and Skye. They are presumably intolerant of desiccation and frost. It is hard to imagine these species occurring close to glaciated areas during the Ice Age, so one is led to the conclusion that they have colonised Britain from further south since the Ice Age. Notable species in the group include the endemic *Fissidens celticus, Cyclodictyon laetevirens* on Islay and Jura, and *Lejeunea holtii* on Jura. *Dumortiera hirsuta* is a widespread tropical species, also found on Jura.

It seems clear that Jura should be a 'Mecca' for the bryophyte specialist, with Craighouse Ravine as the 'holy of holies' in the matter of exotic mosses.

LICHENS

The renowned lichen expert Francis Rose visited Jura in 1974 and produced a report for the then Nature Conservancy Council. The *NEIH* Report of 1983 publishes the results of his work in the neighbouring island of Colonsay, but declares that the work on Jura was not yet ready for publication. Enthusiasts should request sight of Dr Rose's more recent reports.

FUNGI

The *NEIH* contains an assessment of fungi in the Inner Hebrides by R. W. G. Dennis and Roy Watling, but Jura is specifically exluded. A preliminary report of fungi on Jura was prepared by the mycologists Norman and Pearl Tait in 1982, and this is available on Jura.

THE ANIMAL KINGDOM

Consideration of the animal kingdom starts with the many phyla of invertebrates. Apart from the various classes of insects, which will be examined separately, the terrestrial examples of the phyla of invertebrates do not seem to have attracted the attention of specialists as far as Jura is concerned.

There seems to have been no study of flukes, flatworms, earthworms, roundworms and leeches, nor of land crustacea, inhabiting lochs and streams, such as water fleas and woodlice.

A notable omission is that land snails and freshwater snails seem to have attracted no interest, although one freshwater bivalve is well recorded. Although predominantly an island of acid soils, Jura has a number of quite conspicuous land snails, and it is perhaps surprising that no one has yet had a serious look at them. A noted bivalve is the pearl mussel (*Margaritifera margaritifera*), which, despite the acidity of the surrounding moors, lives happily in the Lealt Burn.

Although there are certainly a good number of spider experts in Scotland, there seems to be no list of spiders for Jura, nor anything about myriapods, centipedes and millipedes.

THE SEASHORE
The author has long had a keen amateur interest in the seashore, and has been a shell-collector all his life. Becoming the Parish Minister of Jura presented him with a wonderful opportunity to continue this enthusiasm. However, during his tenure the island was visited by several professional zoologists. In October 1979 the shores of Islay were studied by a party from the Royal Scottish Museum and, in June 1982, a team from the Nature Conservancy Council, headed by Shelagh M. Smith returned to Islay, but broadened their field of study to include Jura. Part of the survey was based on MV *Ocean Bounty* so a number of remote stations on Jura were visited from the sea. This resulted in a limited coverage of the shores of Jura, and the visit was restricted to the northern half of the island. Five sites were studied in Loch Tarbert, three in the inner loch and one on each shore of the outer. Three sites were listed for Lagg Bay.

Despite the fact that this expedition was not able to visit the, presumably, significant south-eastern bays like Lowlandman's and Small Isles, nor the entire Sound of Islay, the lists that were produced of marine life were detailed and expert, and remain the only professional account of the shorelife of Jura. Lists of species are available on Jura.

SEAWEEDS
As land animals live on a landscape covered with plants, so our shoreline animals live in an environment where plants also play an important part.

There are no surprises in the seaweeds which inhabit the predominantly rocky coastline of Jura, and they can be found on any similar shore in the Western Isles.

The five fucoid species (wracks) colonise the rocks in horizontal bands according to the amount of tidal exposure. From the high-water mark they go: channelled wrack (*Fucus caniculata*); flat wrack (*Fucus spiralis*); knotted wrack (*Ascophyllum nodosum*); bladder wrack (*Fucus vesiculosus*); and at the lowest level, serrated wrack (*Fucus serratus*). In the highest tidal pools lives the green weed (*Enteromorpha intestinalis*), which looks, as its name suggests, like green intestines.

Below the wracks, and growing abundantly on the flat bottom of shallow bays such as Small Isles Bay, live the oarweeds or tangleweeds, hugely significant in the times of the kelp industry and later as much-needed fertiliser on poor farmland. There are three main species: furbelows (*Saccorhiza polyschides*); oarweed (*Laminaria digitata*); and *Laminaria saccharina*, which leaves a sweet white deposit on drying. Another brown weed occurs with these: sea lace (*Chorda filum*).

In the rock pools live carrageen (*Chondrus crispus*); sea lettuce (*Ulva lactuca*); and thong weed (*Himanthalia lorea*); with thick encrustations of pinkish-red

Lithothamnion, a calcium carbonate fixing weed; the tiny spiky bushes of *Corallina officinalis*, and the delicate green fronds of *Cladophora rupestris*. In sheltered places at low water the beautiful green *Codium tomentosum* occurs in a few places. Many red weeds live offshore and are thrown up after storms, among which dulse (*Rhodymenia palmata*) is perhaps the commonest.

A list of some of Jura's seaweeds, taken from Shelagh Smith's report, is available on Jura.

SHORE INVERTEBRATES

Porifera (sponges). There are many species of sponges in the offshore waters, but the easiest to identify on rocks at extreme low water is breadcrumb sponge (*Halichrondia panicea*).

Hydrozoa (sea-firs). Many sea-firs live on the seaweed fronds at the low tide marks. They are very much a specialist study.

Siphonophora. The Portuguese man-of-war did not appear on the Jura coasts during the author's time there, but its relative, by-the-wind-sailor (*Velella aurigans*), did occasionally arrive. There was a major stranding of this curious creature at Shian Bay on the west coast of Jura in the summer of 1979 when countless specimens lay in a deep layer along the shore.

Scyphozoa (jellyfish). At least three species of jellyfish occur on Jura's coasts. *Aurelia aurita* is extremely common on all shores, the large globular *Rhizostoma octopus* occurs occasionally, as does the unpleasant lion's mane (*Cyanea capillata*).

Anthozoa (sea anemones). The Beadlet anemone (*Actinia equina*) is everywhere on the low shore, while the dahlia anemone (*Tealia felina*), is widespread on the lowest shore, and the snakelocks anemone (*Anemonia sulcata*) is common on oarweed fronds at low spring tides. Various members of the *Sagartia* family also occur but are hard to identify.

Worms (Nemertini, ribbon worms, Polychaeta, marine bristle worms). Many species of these inhabit the low shores of Jura Most are hard to identify, but a few are worthy of mention. Occasionally a blackish-brown worm may be encountered coiled up under a stone at the lowest tide mark. This worm is extremely long – 15 feet is commonplace. This is the bootlace worm (*Lineus longissimus*). Several flat bristle worms with overlapping scales are common but need to be identified from a suitable key. On sand at low tide the small volcanic hollows in the sand conceal the lugworm (*Arenicola marina*), universally used for bait. Many stones and shells on the low shore are encrusted with the tubes of *Pomatoceros triqueter*, which are triangular in section and have a keel running along the top. There are a number of other similar tube worms, also a variety of fan or peacock worms such as *Lanice conchilega*, whose tubes are composed of sand grains, and which may be washed up in huge numbers on the shore. The tiny clockwise coil of *Spirorbis borealis* may be seen in immense numbers on the fronds of the wracks and oarweeds.

ARTHROPODS AND CRUSTACEA

Cirripedia (barnacles). Most of the rock-encrusting barnacles in Jura are *Balanus balanoides*, but the large (1 cm across) *Balanus crenatus* can be thrown up from deep water on shells and stones, and the stalked goose barnacle (*Lepas anatifera*) may sometimes be found attached to timber that has been a long time in the water.

Isopoda are things resembling woodlice. Many species are encountered and can be identified from a key. The sea slater (*Ligia oceanica*) is a large, common and fast-moving animal, living under stones and seaweed. The many Amphipoda or sandhoppers are similarly difficult to identify. Members of the *Gammarus* family, compressed sideways, and jumping for cover when disturbed, occur in immense numbers under seaweed and stones on the upper shore.

DECAPODA: SHRIMPS, PRAWNS, CRABS AND LOBSTERS

Many of these live on Jura's rocky shores and bays. The common prawn and the common shrimp occur frequently, especially cut off in tide pools, for example at Lagg Bay.

Lobster (*Homarus vulgaris*) and crawfish or spiny lobster (*Palinurus vulgaris*) are both quite abundant around Jura's shore. Both are, of course, eagerly pursued as a commercial product and seldom encountered on the shore. Small squat lobsters of the Galathea family are occasionally found in low tide rock pools; most likely to be found is *Galathea squamifera.*

Several crabs are very common: the shore crab (*Carcinas meanas*); the velvet swimming crab (*Portunus puber*); the edible crab (*Cancer pagarus*); the broad-clawed porcelain crab (*Porcellana platycheles*); and the hermit crab (*Eupagarus bernhardus*). All of these may be encountered under rocks on the low shore and in rock pools.

Cast up on sandy beaches may be the carapaces of the masked crab (*Corystes cassivelaunus*), also various parts of the shells of the Norway lobster or Dublin Bay prawn (*Nephrops norvegicus*), are often found on the shore. These animals are fished for offshore. At extreme low spring tides a few species of spider crab are common on laminaria tangles in the bays.

A specimen of the uncommon angular or box crab (*Goneplax angulata*), was brought to the author. It lives in mud at some depth, and occurs in Loch Tarbert.

Pycnogonida. The Sea Spider (*Pycnogonum littorale*) lives under stones, on sea anemones and among jetsam on the lower shore.

Echinodermata. Common starfish, purple sunstar and common sunstar all occur at extreme low water as do various members of the brittle starfish group. The common sea-urchin is abundant and other smaller species such as *Psammechinus miliaris* also occur. Sea-cucumbers are present offshore, but are seldom encountered.

Tunicata, tunicates or sea-squirts. These are technically vertebrates, although you would not know it to look at them. They pass through an early stage not unlike that of a tadpole.

The colonial, star sea-squirt (*Botryllus schlosseri*) encrusts rocks with a typical star-shaped pattern, and is widespread. Small upstanding bag-shaped objects which squirt liquid when compressed are in this family. Individuals should be identified from a suitable key.

Many species of the above groups are listed in a report available on Jura.

MOLLUSCS

The phylum Mollusca contains a number of distinct classes: chitons or coat-of-mail shells, marine snails and sea-slugs, or gastropods; bivalves, or lammeli-branchs; elephant's tusk shells, or scaphopods; and cuttlefish, squids and octopuses, or cephalopods.

Dr Shelagh Smith is a renowned expert on marine molluscs, and her comprehensive checklist of the molluscs of the sites visited can be obtain on Jura. Dr Smith's interests show clearly in her work. She has done a great deal of original research on the Littorina family, known to most people as 'winkles', and has shown that the species of this group are much more complex than was earlier thought. Her list reveals the up-to-date situation, and the reader must not expect to find some of these species in older books. As noted earlier, Jura's very long shoreline has certainly not all been examined for the molluscs which may be present, so unexpected discoveries are always liable to be made. For the unskilled shell collector, Lagg Bay at low spring tide is likely to prove an exciting locality, and test powers of identification to the full.

INSECTS

There are a very considerable number of classes of insects, and it should be made clear at the outset that, although all these are studied by eminent experts, there has been a shortage of suitable specialists on Jura, so some of these classes have not been investigated. Those known to have received some attention follow, and lists of species recorded can be obtained on Jura.

Dragonflies and damselflies have been studied in detail, and Jura is fortunate in having a good variety of these attractive creatures. These families were looked at in Jura by Barry Pendlebury in the 1970s, and by Norman Tait, whose photographs of this order provide a vivid record. (Colour plate 10)

Butterflies and moths have received some attention. The author collected butterflies on Jura over a span of twelve years, and attempted to collate any other information which came his way. Collecting butterflies failed to produce a specimen of the small white. It must surely be present on Jura, but every small white examined turned out to be a green-veined white, over many years, so it is not yet included. The marsh fritillary colonies were historically involved in the reasons and description for SSSI listings in the far north. A number of other species are living successfully very near to Jura, for example the chequered skipper over on Knapdale, but there has been no sign yet of colonies on the west of the Sound. (Colour plate 11)

The author had the interesting experience of light trapping for moths on Jura at the behest of the Nature Conservancy Council, and with the use of its equipment. The entire undertaking was a revelation, since most of the species recorded in the trap were unsuspected previously of being on the island. Indeed, aged crofters, all their lives on Jura, stoutly denied that the mounted specimens shown to them could have come from the island. 'They could not have been here,' they would say, 'or we would have known of it.'

The island has a number of quite large and flamboyant species which were already well known; the emperor, and the fast-flying northern eggar and fox moths. Others such as large yellow underwings were long known from houses and farm buildings. The cinnabar moth is common on ragwort. The elephant hawk moth is quite common, its spectacular caterpillars living on fuschia bushes. The island has small colonies of six-spot burnet, a day flying moth, and, in the far north at Kinuachdrach, a colony of the vivid green forester moth, which also flies by day. The humming bird hawk moth gets as far as Jura, and turns up occasionally in gardens.

The island list must be far from complete, as trapping was only carried out in a few locations near Craighouse; and the woodlands at the north, for example, would have been a prime location. As far as beetles are concerned, the island was visited by E. J. Pearce in 1923, and subseqently R. Colin Welch published a study of Coleoptera in the Inner Hebrides in 1981, which updates all records of Jura. There appear to be 204 different species of beetle recorded from Jura.

The Diptera, or true flies, of Jura appear in Grimshaw's 'Diptera Scotica; Western Isles', which is printed in the *Scottish Naturalist* of 1914-16. All the references to Jura come from a visit made by entomologist, James Waterston, in September 1907. He compiled a list of 166 species of fly on the island at that time. The species names are of course given solely in Latin, and would be unintelligible to all but a specialist. This list can be consulted only in the *Scottish Naturalist*.

THINGS THAT BITE!

There are four creatures living on Jura which are mainly responsible for inflicting pain and irritation on humans: the cleg, the tick, the ked and of course the midge.

Cleg is the Scottish name given to the yellow horse-fly (*Haematopota crassicornis* Wahlberg). This is common in high summer, and often abundant on a hot day in bright sunshine. It was always a pest in the hay field, and can sometimes descend in large numbers on folk walking in the hills on a sunny summer day. It is possible sometimes to see one's companion, a few steps ahead on the path, with many clegs, having alighted, and covering their back. The cleg inflicts a painful bite, which swells, producing a white 'bump' which itches. It settles quietly and often the sudden pain is the only warning that it is there. Clegs are slow to react once they have bitten, and the victim often has the satisfaction of successfully swatting the fly. The flattened body often leaves a smear of one's own blood.

The deer ked (*Lipoptena cervi*) belongs to the family of biting flies (Hippoboscidae). It is not very common on low ground, but can be present in bracken and heather. It can infest red deer in great numbers. The animal flies and alights. It has a flat scale-like appearance, and clings closely to clothing or skin, making it hard to remove. It inflicts a painful bite, and on removal may sometimes leave the proboscis in the wound. To many people deer keds are repulsive in appearance, and are cordially disliked. The effects of the bite may be long lasting, producing a small hard callous which lasts a long time.

The tick or hard tick (*Ixodes ricinus*), an arachnid, or spider relative, waits on the tops of grasses for its mammal host to pass by. It is active in daylight, with peaks in March–May and September–October. Hairiness attracts ticks, so that dogs can come in from the hill covered in the things. It is the female which bites, pushing a proboscis under the skin. The beast starts out very small, and does not attract attention as the initial puncture is not painful. If not noticed, however, the tick can grow to nearly a centimetre long, and swells with blood to the size and shape of a very small grape. The discovery of such a hitchhiker, when getting undressed, comes as a shock, whether it is on oneself or one's companion. Again the proboscis tends to remain when the beast is removed, and causes a long-lasting small itchy and painful swelling.

It should be noted that ticks can spread infectious organisms from animals to human. In Scotland the only disease known to be transmitted by ticks is Lyme disease. This is caused by the bacterium *Borrelia burgdorferi*, which usually lives on deer, but can also infect dogs. The symptoms of Lyme disease are a red dot which may appear at the site of the tick bite and gradually expand into a reddened area up to 5 mm across. Sometimes, however, the bite passes unnoticed. Fever, headache, lethargy and muscle pains may develop, followed by a characteristic joint inflammation, with redness and swelling, typically affecting the knees and other large joints. Anyone developing symptoms after a tick bite should consult a doctor. The diagnosis of Lyme disease can be confirmed by a blood test. The disease can usually be cleared up by anitbiotic drugs, especially if diagnosed quickly.

The Highland midge (*Culicoides impunctatus*) is a major menace throughout the Western Isles, and is certainly most prolific in Jura. The female midge needs blood for fertility and attacks mammals. It is very small, 1.6 mm long, but breeds in vast numbers in damp places, and occurs all over the island, except on the very highest ground. There are various 'hatchings' during the summer months, and at their worst, midges make life outside intolerable. They are not usually a problem during the main hours of daylight, and in bright weather, being at their worst in early morning and in the evenings. On a late afternoon or early evening, on a damp warm and sultry day, especially after a shower of rain they can materialise around unsuspecting visitors in almost tangible dark clouds. A high-piched whine in the outer ear is often the first warning. In most people the actual bite produces a small red circle, which itches for a time and then fades. People extensively bitten can look quite bizarre. Some few individuals react badly to midge bites, and for them the matter is more than just a nuisance. People who can tolerate the various proprietary brands of anti-midge creams can gain a good measure of protection, but some find these, applied liberally, as they need to be, to be as bad as the insects. It seems an over-reaction to go about the island wearing some kind of protective hood, although they are available. The best remedy for midges is simply to remain indoors when they are most active.

FISH

As far as the freshwater fish of Jura are concerned, the number of species is limited to four, no doubt because of the acid nature of the island's rocks.

Sea-trout and salmon run up several rivers to spawn. The Inver, the Corran, and the Lussa certainly are streams to which they return regularly.

The burns of Jura have many brown trout, and a good number of its lochs have them as well.

Other species of freshwater fish one might expect are all absent from Jura. Only the three-spined stickleback inhabits the streams, although eels are quite plentiful in the island.

The two most important inshore fish for the people of Jura were the lythe and the saithe. The lythe is known in the south as the pollack, and the saithe is called the coalfish. The two species are very alike. Both fish are an olive colour with three dorsal fins and two ventral fins, indeed it is not always easy to tell small individuals apart, but the saithe gets much larger than the lythe. Both fish come close enough to land to be caught with a rod and line from the shore, and it was quite usual for them to be caught this way in the past with a reasonably long pole. They were also taken from small boats in the bays, or from the rocks on the islands. Saithe and lythe were then gutted and split open and hung out on long lines to dry in the sun, and stored for later use.

Mackerel, cod, dogfish and grey mullet also come into inshore waters, and in the sandy bays flatfish lie concealed as the tide goes out. Dabs, plaice and flounder are common.

Sea-trout and salmon also come close inshore. They travel laterally along the coast following the distinctive flavour of the fresh water coming into the bay.

Other inshore fish are pipefish, lumpsucker and the Cornish sucker fish. Pipefish regularly end up in tidal pools, as do very small lumpsuckers. However, large lumpsuckers are also present as evidenced when the Manse otter left one of about 5 lb weight on the shore. The otter had eaten only the eggs of this female fish, before discarding the rest.

The Cornish sucker fish should revel in the distinction that it was discovered in Jura by the famous visitor, Thomas Pennant, who named it the Jura sucker fish. Pennant knew that it was found in Cornwall, and since it turned out to have been previously described there, by the law of priority it is now officially called the Cornish sucker fish. The same fate befell the attempt of John Mac-Culloch, author of *A Description of the Western Isles of Scotland*, to register a lamprey he found at Jura, and it ends up without a 'Jura' label either. This seems a pity for *Petromyzon Jurae* would have been a fine title.

Skin diving among the oarweed forests in Jura's bays reveals a number of fish of the wrasse family, mostly ballan wrasse, but evidence of these is seldom seen on shore. Gobies also live in the sandy shallows.

Although one would have thought it well placed, Jura does not provide evidence of the passing of the great monsters, the basking sharks, seen from other islands. Perhaps if the cliffs of the west coast were regularly frequented, and sightings from there were reported, these great fish would turn out also to be neighbours.

AMPHIBIANS
Although there are many places in Britain where frogs and toads are becoming

scarce, this problem does not affect Jura, where both are abundant. No one seems to have been much concerned about newts on Jura, but the author found that the palmate newt is present on the island in considerable numbers. In Jura the habitat of this small newt is brackish pools above the high tide mark. There is, for example, a considerable colony to the south-east of the jetty at Lagg Bay.

REPTILES

There are three reptiles living on Jura: the adder, the slow worm and the common lizard. All are abundant, although not always easy to see. Slow worms hide under sheltered surfaces, and can often be found by gently lifting old abandoned sheets of corrugated iron.

Lizards sun themselves on dry stone dykes, and can be surprised doing so on many places on the island. Adders are very common indeed all over the island. They presumably do very well on the above-mentioned population of frogs and toads. They also like to sun themselves, and will often be seen on bare patches on moorland paths. They can often be found under the tabular gravestones in Kilearnadill Cemetery.

Tales and stories record beliefs and superstitions about the adder, and elderly residents were quite ready to recall the occasions on which they were bitten in their childhood. The English word they used to describe this experience was always 'stung'. The bite would come invariably at the hay-making, when an adder would be stood on in the long grass at the margins of a field. Three or four old ladies told of this experience, which resulted in a painful, swollen leg or foot, and, if it wasn't during the school holidays, a couple of days off school until the swelling went down. Local folk were quite dismissive of the suggestion that an adder bite might be more serious than this, or that it might lead to death.

Late in the 1970s, the local doctor shared with me the experience she had of treating an English walker who had been camping overnight near Glenbatrick. This young man had seen a large adder near his tent, but since adders were unknown in his home town, he believed this to be a grass snake and harmless. (Grass snakes are not found as far north as the Hebrides.) He tried to take a photograph, but the animal unobligingly went into a thick tussock of grass. It left its tail sticking out, and our hero, believing it was a grass snake and therefore not venomous, pulled it out by its tail into a more favourable photographic posture. He was not a little aggrieved when the snake bit him on the hand, near the base of the thumb. Thinking the snake was not poisonous, he was quite annoyed when the bite became painful, and his hand and lower arm began to swell. He then he took a couple of Disprin and went to sleep. The next day the arm was still swollen and throbbing, so, having packed up his tent and walked out to the east coast, he presented himself at surgery. He was a tall, well-built and powerful young man. When seen, his arm was swollen, with a much-enlarged elbow joint and a swelling under the armpit. There were four clear punctures in the hand. The GP gave him an anti-tetanus and sent him on his way with some anti-histamines. The toxin seems to have been reasonably hostile to his system, however, for some months later he wrote, thanking the good doctor for her care, and evidencing that his arm had later produced large discoloured swellings, and even later some skin eruptions, which lasted for some time.

This episode was the only occasion the author had indirect contact with an adder bite. The judgement seems to be that adders are best avoided, although serious consequences are not at all likely. It should be pointed out that this victim of adder bite pulled the snake out of the place where it was attempting to hide by its tail. Adders will leave you alone if you give them half a chance.

Local people of old seem to have killed adders on sight. This may have something to do with old Presbyterian superstitions that go back to the story of the serpent in Genesis, or more likely because they undoubtedly were responsible for the death of sheepdogs. There were two dogs who died in this way during the author's stay on Jura. There was also the questionable death of a young calf. The animal had a swollen muzzle, and may have been bitten there while feeding. It may have become unable to breathe properly and then died. This was certainly the opinion the vet gave as to cause of death.

The author's own attempts to befriend adders encountered on a path were always unsuccessful. Although the literature suggests that they make good pets, and are actually most reluctant to bite, any individuals the author approached with a friendly hand tended to put their heads up and back in what seemed a most threatening pose, and uttered alarming hissing sounds. Perhaps someone with a more pro-reptilian attitude would have been more successful.

TURTLES

The western isles of Scotland are sometimes visited by exotic marine animals which, having arrived in these inhospitable waters, end their lives on our shores.

Into this category comes the leatherback or leathery turtle, a giant creature about six feet long. News that such an animal had been stranded on the west coast of Jura came to the Manse in September 1979. The journey was undertaken, but by the time the Minister arrived on the scene there was no sign of the animal or its carcass. It seems that a visiting inshore fisherman, confusing turtles with 'tortoiseshell' and scenting a profit, had tried to cut off the deceased animal's carapace. Leatherback turtles don't have a true carapace. Since the operation was unsuccessful, this unknown individual seems to have towed the animal out to sea. However, before the Minister arrived, holiday-makers had walked along the shore, and seen the animal. In due course a letter arrived, and accompanying photographs. It appears that the turtle was first seen still alive just off shore, and had died only a short time before having its photograph taken. Strandings of leathery turtles are rare in Scotland, with only three recorded between 1971 and 1984.

BIRDS

The Island of Jura is a large land mass in the southern Inner Hebrides and, as such, might well be expected to have a large and varied population of birds, and this turns out indeed to be so. The list of species recorded from the island and its surrounding seas comes to about 145.

In an island where the various landowners are hugely interested in the business of hunting and shooting for sport, it may be found surprising that so many raptors are to be seen. The island has strong populations of merlins, kestrels, sparrowhawks, hen harriers, peregrines, buzzards, golden eagles, tawny owls, short-eared owls and barn owls. This situation must of course go back to the practices and attitudes of the keepers. Jura does not support a commercial population of red grouse, and such pheasant as are stocked remain on small areas of the east coast. Traditional shoots of woodcock and snipe are less important than they were in the past. The author has often been told by gamekeepers that the presence of a 'goldie' in the sky over a successful 'kill' of a good stag, could be worth an additional gratuity to the keeper concerned. Reed, Currie and Love in *NEIH* record, 'By 1887 the golden eagle had been exterminated on Jura. Reduced levels of keepering during the First World War led to many sites there and elsewhere in the Hebrides being reoccupied by the 1920s. Around this time golden eagles took vacant coastal sea eagle territories.'

This probably gives an accurate account of what was happening 100 years ago, but it seems that attitudes have changed in more recent times. Landowners in Islay were still paying a disgraceful cash bounty for 'hooked beaks' as recently as the 1960s, but it seems that in Jura keepers were under no pressure to kill raptors, and the presence of a variety of hawks, endangered elsewhere, is the happy result.

Pennant recorded the 'Arctic gull' in Jura in 1776, 'which breeds here on the ground'. It still breeds on Jura, and the *Atlas of Breeding birds* shows this to be its most southerly breeding territory. (Colour plate 12)

A comprehensive list of the birds of Jura prepared by the author is one of the publications available on Jura. A few further comments are attached here. Divers, shags, gannets and various auks are seen as would be expected. Geese and ducks are less frquent than on Islay, but many can be seen. Ptarmigan are often reported. Black grouse are still present. Waders and gulls are not as plentiful as on Islay, but many species can be seen. Occasional visitors – snowy owl, red-backed shrike, great grey shrike – are of interest; choughs are present and ravens abundant. Ring ouzels are common. Parties of snow buntings visit in winter.

MAMMALS

As an offshore island, Jura is populated by many forms of life which have been able to fly or swim to it. It seems, however, that the land bridge was submerged before a number of mainland animals could establish themselves on the island.

There is an interesting list of Scottish mammals, present on the mainland, but absent from Jura: fallow deer, sika deer, roe deer, wild cat, weasel, pine marten, mink, badger, fox, grey and red squirrel, water vole and bank vole, black rat, brown hare, water shrew, hedgehog, mole.

Only a small number of mammals now live on Jura, and only a handful of reasonably large ones. These are: red deer, feral goat, grey seal, common seal, otter, mountain hare and rabbit. The smaller ones are: stoat, brown rat, house mouse, field mouse, short-tailed vole, pipistrelle bat, long-eared bat, pigmy shrew and common shrew. Feral cats are recorded from time to time, and counting these, the total number of wild mammals present is seventeen.

The absent mammals need comment. Some of them have not made it yet, and may turn up. Sika deer could be expected to swim over at some point, they have swum from Kintyre to Gigha, and it is probably only a matter of time before mink arrive. Grey squirrels are also increasing their range nearby.

A number of now absent species seem to have been present in the past on Jura.

One mammal now extinct in the British Isles was certainly on Jura. The wild boar was hunted in the Middle Ages, and Budge says that in 1960 'there are still traces to be seen of the moats into which the wild boar were driven'. Fallow deer, common on Jura in the nineteenth century, were deliberately cleared by estate managers. There was recently a notable herd of fallow deer on Scarba. The fox, present in Skye to the north, is witnessed to by a bone recently excavated in north Jura. The brown hare was plentiful in the last century. The Campbell game books record hares being shot and, for example, in 1880, the year's bag was 80 hares. The last mention of the brown hare may have been in the 1919 sales prospectus for the Jura estate. Weasels were recorded in Jura between 1892 and 1900, although the status of the special Jura stoat, a small island version, means that there may always have been confusion in identification, and stoats may have been meant.

The hedgehog deserves some comment. Here is the relevant passage from the author's wildlife diary for 29 May 1983:

> It's happened at last; the Hedgehog Folly has finally reached Jura. It seems that there is some lunatic about from the far south with a private crusade to introduce hedgehogs to the Hebrides. No one appears to know who he is, or what his technique is, but he visited Islay a year or two back, and flattened hedgehogs are now commonplace on Islay roads. Today produced a very fine specimen from the road at Corran Beach, Jura. It was squashed of course, and rather high, but recently dead. I suppose if you're going to make some introduction or another, the hedgehog is about as inoffensive animal as you could find, but I still feel furious at the sheer arrogance of the Hedgehog Fancier. All right, so we have a deficient mammal fauna because some things didn't make it across the land bridge – but we're quite proud of what we have, and would like to keep it that way.

The author was on Jura for a further four years, and is pleased to report that no further evidence of hedgehogs was reported. It may be that the experiment failed.

Of those mammals which do live on Jura, the dominant species is the red deer. Miss Campbell told the Crofters' Commission that the deer had been on Jura since time immemorial, and that is probably true. The most likely derivation for the name 'Jura' is that it stems from the Norse for 'Deer Island'.

In 1549 Dean Monro called it 'ane uther fine firrest for deiris', and recorded, 'infinite deir slain there'. In 1695 Martin Martin reported 300 deer on Jura. Pennant gave 100 stags in 1772; Scrope, 500 in 1839. During the second half of the nineteenth century, protection and the elimination of much farming in the interests of the 'deer forest' resulted in a population of about 2800 in 1892. The numbers fluctuated in the early part of the twentieth century, but the figure had risen to 5435 in 1969 when the Jura herds comprised about 3 per cent of Scottish red deer.

The true habitat of the red deer is forest, a name quaintly perpetuated in the term 'deer forest', which in Jura applies to empty moorland. Under these conditions they do not attain the weight of forest living animals. The deer move freely throughout the island. They graze on the lower ground in the winter, and invade pasture land and abandoned arable. Sometimes they maraud into gardens. In the summer the hinds move to the high moors as the upper grazing improves, and to avoid biting flies and sportsmen. Mating, 'the rut' is in late September and October, when the barking roars of the stags echo around the hills. The young are born in June. Deer can reach thirty years old, but sixteen to nineteen years is a good average, with their prime from twelve to seventeen years. A big stag stands 44 inches at the shoulder, the heaviest recorded on Jura was twenty-six stone nine pounds, but sixteen stone is probably an average weight. Antlers are shed in March to May, with the new ones grown and out of 'velvet' about a month before the next mating. A fine pair of antlers with twelve points is called a 'royal', and there are usually a good number of such stags. Larger numbers of points are not very common on Jura, although there are always stories circulating, and the 'big stag of Knockrome' reputedly had eighteen. A good pair of antlers will span about 38 inches. Stags without antlers occur. These are called 'hummels', and can be very dominant. Not putting all their strength into the production of antlers, they are strong, and can often bundle antlered males off their feet. Jura has long been known for 'cromies', deer with malformed antlers which rise straight from the pedicles and, unless stunted, curve backwards.

The deer's coat is dark brown to grey in winter, becoming rich reddish-brown in summer. More nervous of humans than of vehicles, deer nevertheless are curious, and will stand and stare back at the visitor, and even when frightened will often stop during flight, and, ultimately from the skyline, look back. (Colour plate 13)

WILD GOATS

Jura has several hundred feral goats, possibly as many as 500. They are mostly dark brown in colour, although some are two-coloured with white patches. Generally the island's goats are shaggy creatures, at home on the steep cliffs, running just fast enough and far enough to get out of danger. The billies have scimitar horns, curving backwards and outwards and averaging two feet in length. The nannies have short round-sectioned prongs. Kids are born from late January. There have been occasional outbursts of 'trophy' shooting, by continental hunters, and one or two controversial 'exports' to introduce the goats to other parts of Scotland.

Goats were important domestic animals in the past, but the social changes of the mid-nineteenth century led to them being lost from the crofts. The overnight nature of emigration abroad and to the cities sometimes even left them behind on their pastures. This may be how they became feral.

OTHER MAMMALS

Grey and common seals. These are plentiful around Jura and can be seen both in the sea, and basking out on the rocks. R. W. Vaughan, of the Sea Mammal Research Unit, who produced an excellent report in *NEIH*, reports, 'Grey seals are likely to be seen over most of the area of the Inner Hebrides, particularly during the earlier part of the year. The main breeding sites in the area appear to be at Nave Island on the northern side of Islay, and at rocks south of Oronsay, but there are successful small colonies on the north side of Loch Tarbert, Jura.'

Loch Tarbert is also recorded as a breeding site for common seals, as are the islands fringing Small Isles Bay on the east coast of Jura.

Otters. They are well established in Jura, and apparently now safe from human persecution. There was a widespread practice of killing otters for their valuable pelts in Jura in the past, and elderly crofters of the author's acquaintance remembered such events as a 'windfall'. In Jura the otter appears to be largely a sea animal, not being seen very often inland. The author conducted some assessments in the 1970s by questioning local keepers, and found that there appear to be about twenty coastal territories, each most probably supporting a family of otters. The author felt privileged to have an otter's holt on the Minister's Burn for many years, only about 50 yards from the Manse, and this meant many opportunities to watch the animal. The chances of seeing an otter during a few days on Jura spent actively looking for it are quite good.

Hares and rabbits. Hewson suggests that the mountain hare was introduced to Jura about 1900, perhaps to promote eagles, as a food source. If so, it has certainly done very well for the mountain hare is now extremely abundant on Jura. A count conducted by keepers in the 1970s suggested something in excess of a thousand animals on the island. The mountain hare turns white in winter, but in Jura it does so on an island where there is very little snow. In the winter months it is possible to sit in the hills and pick out white hares over considerable distances.

The presence of Rabbit Island in Small Isles Bay suggests that the rabbit has been on Jura for a very long time. It is abundant, but the population swings in response to myxomatosis.

Stoats. Jura and Islay have their own sub-species of stoat (*Mustela erminea ricinae*). It has a smaller body than the mainland race, averaging 225 mm for males and 210 mm for females. The skull is also different from the mainland animal. The Jura stoat, like those on the mainland, turns white in winter. Stoats are considered vermin on Jura, and are taken by keepers whenever possible, nevertheless they still seem to be doing well, and are frequently seen. In the summer of 1982 a local keeper encountered a 'pack of stoats', which he estimated at thirty to forty!

Bats. The pipistrelle is very common on Jura. The long-eared bat is also recorded, and the author was pleased to have a specimen brought to him in 1982. This was found dead on the road at Ardlussa. Endless watching of pipistrelles around Jura Manse revealed the undoubted presence of a small number of individuals which were very much heavier and bigger, with a slower wing beat. The author was never able to confirm a species for these bats. No doubt someone will make up for this omission in the future.

Six small mammals are present on Jura: brown rat, field vole, wood mouse, house mouse, common shrew and pigmy shrew. Three of these animals are accorded special island sub-species status by some authorities. The Jura/Gigha common shrew, small and dark, is claimed as a close relative of the Islay shrew (*Sorex araneus granti*). The Jura wood mouse (*Apodemus sylvaticus larus*) has the darkest back among Hebridean forms, a silvery belly and a light yellow chest-spot. It has a small body and tail. Jura's field vole (*Microtus agrestis exsul*), is close to Gigha's and has long coarse black dorsal hairs and a peculiarly shaped skull. As with the stoat, there is much learned discussion as to how these distinct races may have evolved or arrived – and indeed whether they are distinct races at all. It seems the jury is still out.

All the above animals seem to do well on Jura and all are frequently encountered – the brown rat perhaps too frequently. The author had difficulty, however, with the house mouse and encountered similar problems to those of the small white butterfly. Although he begged for specimens and was shown many from all over the island, they all turned out to be wood mice and he never actually saw a house mouse during the twelve years he spent on Jura.

Whales and dolphins. As in the matter of the basking shark, Jura seems to be off the track for regular sightings of whales and dolphins. The common dolphin does come into bays from time to time, and is seen in Lowlandman's Bay quite often. Other cetaceans are seldom seen, although very occasionally an individual may be stranded.

During the author's time a Risso's dolphin (*Grampus griseus*) was found on the beach at Feolin Ferry in March 1979. Major organs were removed and sent to the Department of Anatomy in the University of Cambridge. In September 1986 a much rarer animal was stranded in Lagg Bay. This 15 foot whale was seen and photographed by local residents, but was washed out to sea on the next tide. Some weeks later the much decomposed carcass was found wedged in rocks north of Tarbert, and it was possible to salvage the head, and prepare the skull. The animal proved to be a Sowerby's whale (*Mesoploden bidens*), which rarely becomes stranded in Scotland.

THE NORTHERN ISLES
There seems to have been almost no systematic study of the natural history of the northern group of islands, with the possible exception of W. R. Hunter's study of the Garvellachs in 1954.

5

Prehistory

MESOLITHIC AGE

Jura has recently come into prominence in any consideration of British prehistory. That this has happened is due to the work of the late John Mercer, a palaeontologist who lived on the island in the 1960s, 1970s and 1980s. During the Palaeolithic Period there was a considerable amount of human settlement in the southern part of the British Isles, no doubt ebbing and flowing to fit with warm interglacial periods. In Scotland all traces of such inhabitants have been obliterated by the ice, and we must look for our most distant forbears in the period following the last ice age.

The received wisdom of the post-war years seems to have been to suggest that there may have been a considerable period after the departure of the ice-sheet during which there may have been little or no human colonisation. Mercer's view of the enterprising nature of our human ancestors made him feel that this was most unlikely to be the case. He was convinced that human hunter-gatherers would be found on the very edge of the retreating ice-sheets, probably living a seasonal life, not unlike that of the present-day Inuit or Eskimo peoples. The absence of evidence of the camp sites of such people, he believed, was due to the fact that the changes in sea-level which followed the disappearance of the ice would have tended to submerge coastal sites and obliterate evidence of the Mesolithic or Middle Stone Age, people who would undoubtedly have been living in Scotland at the time.

The isostatic uplift of the continental sheet is at its maximum on the extreme western seaboard of Scotland, and so it was to Jura that Mercer came in the belief that such camps would have stood a better chance or survival here than elsewhere. To look for such evidence, he extrapolated the level of the former shoreline, and from evidence and an uncanny ability to identify with the hunter's choice of ideal camp sites, he began excavation on some of his most likely chosen sites. His reward was an enormous amount of evidence, mostly in the nature of microlith stone tools, at Inverlussa, Lealt, An Carn, and other locations. This painstaking work was written up and published in the *Proceedings* of the Society of Antiquaries of Scotland, and this resulted in world-wide, if posthumous, recognition of his work and consequently of the Mesolithic Culture of the island of Jura.

Mercer suggested that Jura could have been occupied by man between 10,500 and 8800 BC, at least in the summers, and perhaps with Eskimo-style adaptation, possibly in the winters too.

The main archaeological sites all lie on the east shore of north Jura, the nearest landing place to the mainland. This suggests that they may have been the camping places of migrating hunters. Mercer is confident that Jura was occupied again from about 7000 BC. The final camps of the Jura Mesolithic hunters were made

45

on the rising beaches. The lowest site located is now about 20 feet above present sea level and probably dates from around 3000 BC.

Lussa Wood I (of the two sites) is Jura's most valuable single site. It is now 650 yards from the sea at a height of 53 feet. The washing limit of the early post-glacial transgression, marked by a narrow cross-going bog, runs across the terrace just behind the site. The oldest occupation left three continuous stone rings. These have carbon-14 ages of about 6000 BC, and are amongst the earliest stone structures in the British Isles. This site also produced over 3000 microliths – very small flint tools, pressure worked to give a sharp edge. Some would have served as barbs and tips of arrows, but most would be set on edge in grooved hafts of bone, wood or antler. Since camps like the ones on Jura reveal that their inhabitants did not have access to flint of the quality which could produce large blades or tools, and their largest tools seem to have been made from worked quartzite pebbles, the microlithic technique seems to have been the best way to make use of the raw material available. Microliths are characteristic of the Mesolithic period. However Jura's Mesolithic cultures also used flint tools such as scrapers and gravers. Throughout John Mercer's excavations, Susan Mercer produced a great number of superb drawings of these tools.

The main Lussa River camp below the wood has given radiocarbon dates of between 3450 and 2940 BC. It contained hammer stones, wood charcoal, about a thousand burnt hazel shells and great numbers of microliths.

Farther north lies the region of An Carn, a deserted village. Here there are several sites of importance. The two south Carn sites are on an extinct headland 65 feet above present sea level. South Carn I has produced 3000 microliths. The other site is Carn Cave, cut into the base of an ancient cliff immediately south of the headland. Mercer was unable to complete his proposed excavation of this site, which he hoped would produce tools related to Scotland's 'Obanian' culture.

The main site at Carn stands at 46 feet above sea level in the northern shadow of the extinct headland. This produced a small stone setting, sunk in the main area. With its back to the prevailing wind, and holding charcoal, it was clearly a small hearth. It produced a carbon-14 date of around 6000 BC. This site produced a large number of flints.

Between the Lussa Valley and Carn, John Mercer excavated another site near his Jura home of Lealt, above Lealt Bay. Pollen analysis from the site suggests that occupation began soon after 5500 BC. This Lealt site produced a huge number of quartzite and flint tools. Mercer said that one deposit held at least 50,000 pieces of humanly struck stone over its main area.

There is one other Mesolithic site to be mentioned. This is at Glenbatrick, and is the only one to be excavated on the west coast of the island. The site is on an extinct cliff 59 feet above sea level. The hunters appear to have camped on the shore of a sunken lagoon or waterhole, and their tools were found in a sticky clayey silt. Radiocarbon gave dates between 4000 and 3000 BC, and the site produced large numbers of tools.

The detailed analysis of microliths is a specialised subject. Mercer can trace relationships between the Jura material and tools from Teviec off the coast of north-west France, where sunken stone rings similar to the Lussa Wood structure

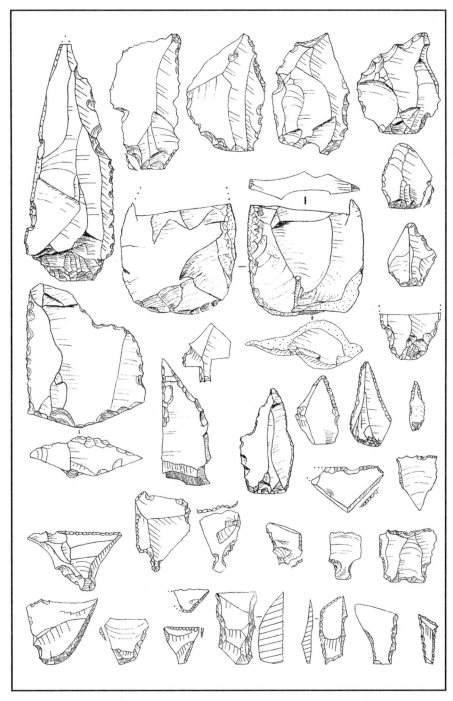

Figure 1. Flint tools from Lealt Bay. Tanged points and arrowheads.

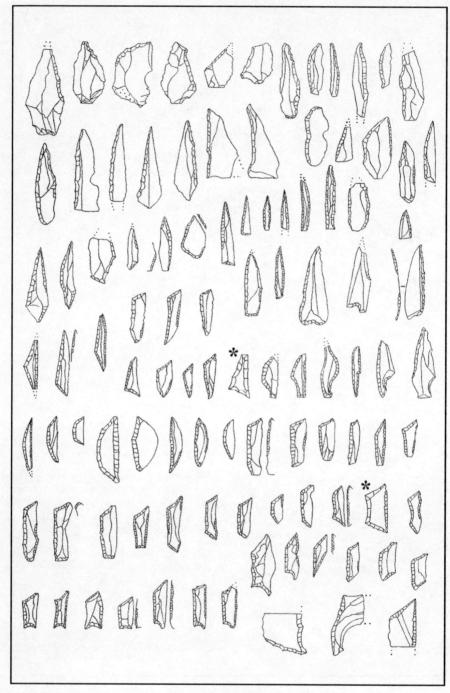

Figure 2. Microlith tools from Lealt Bay.

have also been excavated. The huge number of microliths yields readily to statistical analysis and provides the opportunity to compare the tools from Jura with those known from northern Ireland, north England and the Continent. The types are given various titles, for example trapezoid, micro-triangle, narrow-blade and broad-blade. John Mercer believed that the Jura Mesolithic was likely to have ended about 3000 BC, and may have overlapped with Neolithic settlers.

It is perhaps sad that such early camp sites as have been excavated by John Mercer are not suitable for any kind of preservation as later tombs or megaliths are. Even the methods of excavation do not reveal flint tools lying casually scattered around, but involve the slow and laborious washing and seiving of deposits from which the evidence gradually accumulates. Nevertheless, the sites themselves remain, and they can be visited and stood upon. The ground beneath our feet in these locations once felt the tread of ancestors who camped there over long periods many thousands of years ago.

NEOLITHIC AGE

The arrival date on Jura of Neolithic folk (*c.* 4000–2000 BC) is not known, since no charcoal found on Mesolithic sites can be definitely ascribed to Neolithic life. A period of Neolithic activity is shown by leaf-shaped and transverse arrowheads, and by chips from a polished axe of Antrim porcellanite from earlier Mesolithic sites. A single Neolithic axe-head has been found at Ardfernal.

However, in the absence of known settlement sites of Neolithic date, the best archaeological evidence comes from chambered cairns, of which the style known as 'Clyde Cairns' are known from six on Islay and one on Jura. These cairns are monumental structures designed to receive interments over a long period. There is a principal burial chamber, normally entered from the broader end of the cairn. It is parallel sided and constructed of upright side-slabs and end-slabs, with transverse slabs running across the chamber to divide the interior into a series of compartments. The roof slabs, which seldom survive in place, rested on top of the uprights, or on dry stone work on top of the uprights, designed to increase the height of the chamber.

The sole chambered cairn known in Jura is at Poll a Cheo (NR 504631) and is known locally as 'Cladh Chlainn Iain', MacDonald Graves. The cairn is greatly ruined and little remains to be seen. However, if one has visited a number of better examples, it is easier to interpret what is left here. The two portal stones still stand and, behind them, the upper edge of the only remaining side slab of the chamber. Kerb stones behind may indicate the rear of the chamber at a length of four metres, but Henshall suggests that the turf-covered stony ridge extending for a further six metres behind indicates the original outline. There is a suggestion of a crescentic facade, and much of the rough material that is spread around evidently comes from the original tomb. What the monument lacks in detailed structure is more than made up for by the beauty and peace of its setting. Jura's only Neolithic chambered cairn richly repays a visit.

BRONZE AGE

Although Jura was very much on the outer limit of settlement in southern

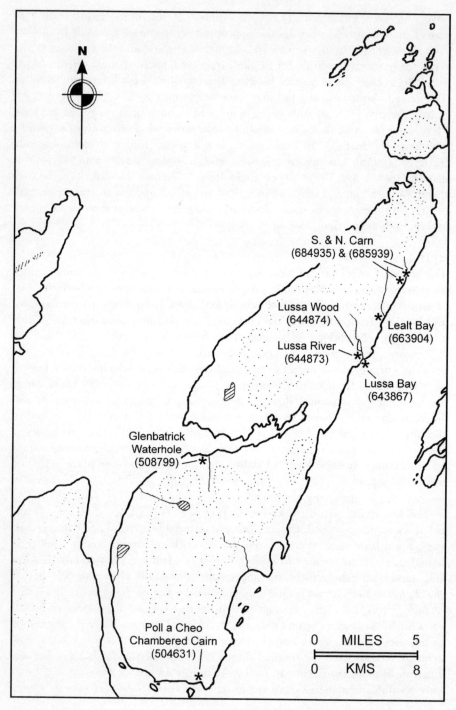

Map 7. The Mesolithic camp sites of Jura.

Scotland, it was not insulated from the movements of populations which brought new customs and habits with them. In due course the people who have often been called Bronze Age (2500–600 BC) arrived and took up residence.

These people abandoned the practice of burial in chambered tombs in favour of round cairns and cists to receive individual burials. They used pottery of a style which is now known as Beaker ware. They made ornaments of jet beads. These objects are occasionally associated with their burials, as for example, at Ardfin in Jura. These people also had developed the habit of making cup-shaped depressions in rock exposures. On the nearby mainland of Kintyre such depressions are often associated with encircling ring marks as well. These 'cup marks' tend to occur on natural rock outcrops.

Perhaps the most obvious sign of the presence of Bronze Age settlers is in the form of stone circles or standing stones. Jura has no actual stone circles, but standing stones are everywhere throughout the island, and will be noted and described.

The identification and investigation of Bronze Age settlements and field systems is a comparatively recent study, and it is interesting that a round structure, discovered near Knockrome by Mr Sandy Buie during peat-cutting and brought to the attention of the authorities by Miss Marion Campbell of Kilberry, turned out to be a hut circle which has now been thoroughly excavated by the Royal Commission on the Ancient and Historical Monuments of Scotland between 1976 and 1980. This hut circle at Cul a' Bhaile has an associated field enclosure and was occupied between the late second and early first millennium BC.

A comparative map would show the abundance of sites in neighbouring islands, but there is a respectable number of Bronze Age locations in Jura.

Full details of all the above Bronze Age monuments can be found in Volume 5 of the *Inventory of the Monuments of Argyll*, published by the Royal Commission on the Ancient and Historical Monuments of Scotland in 1984.

There follows a list of the titles and Map references of the sites:

Cairns (a) Abhainn na Sroine (NR 506632); (b) Barnhill (NR 705970); (c) Cnoc a Chuirn Mhoir (NR 682942); (d) Goirtean Fada (NR 525676); (e) Goirtean Uamh nan Giall (Clearing of the Field of the Foreigner) (NR 666983); (f) Keils (NR 529685 & NR 526686); (g) Kinuachdrach (NR 705988).

Cists (a) Ardfin Forest (NR 508633); (b) Craighouse (NR 530684); (c) Doir' a'Chlaiginn (NR 575757); (d) Kinuachdrach (NR 706990); (e) Lagg (NR 594782).

Cup Markings (a) An Carn (NR 680935); (b) Keils (NR 520679); (c) Knockrome (NR 557718); (d) Ardfernal (NR 561716). (Colour plate 14)

Standing stones (a) Ardfernal (NR 560717); (b) Camas an Staca (The Bay of the Pillar) (NR 464647); (c) Carragh a' Ghlinne (The Stones of the Glen) (NR 512664); (d) Knockrome (i) (NR 550714); (ii) (NR 548714); (iii) (NR 550719). Budge writes: 'There is an interesting relic of tradition with regard to the Knockrome stones, in that the local people, when passing between the two stones which are some distance apart, speak of passing between "the Two Juras". They are also said to mark the scene of a battle of early days. Going between the two stones was still

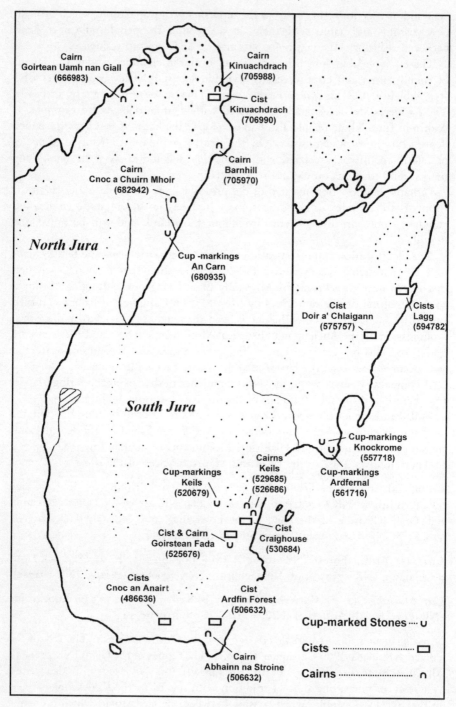

Map 8. Cup-marked stones, cists and cairns of Jura.

a current saying recently on the island, and to do so was supposed to bring good luck'. Presumably it was thought desirable to return by some other path; (e) Leargybreck (NR 538713); (f) Sannaig (NR 518648); (g) Strone (NR 507637); (h) Tarbert (NR 606822). (Colour plate 15)

In their various different settings Jura's standing stones are all worthy of a visit. It should be noted that a number feature in the work of Professor A. Thom, and are mentioned in his book, *Megalithic Sites in Britain*. Professor Thom visited Jura and believes that several of its stones have significance as prehistoric observatory sites.

Hut circles (a) Cul a' Bhaile (NR 549726) A hut circle and its surrounding enclosure are in open moorland 1km north-west of Knockrome on the south-east flank of a rocky knoll. Between 1976 and 1980 the hut circle and sections of the enclosure were excavated by Royal Commission members. The complete results of this investigation are published in the *Proceedings of the Society of Antiquaries of Scotland*, Vol. 114 (1984) and this should be consulted for details of the site. (b) Druim a' Chreagain (NR 512656); (c) Ardmenish (NR 565734).　·

The generally accepted picture nowadays appears to be that farmers and hunters probably coexisted for many generations after 4000 BC, while by 3000 BC a distinctive new culture seems to have become widely established with different burial customs, standing stones and cup-marked stones. It is hard to get much insight into the changing communities which inhabited Jura during the next 2500 years, although by the time of the Cul a' Bhaile house there is evidence of a good deal of sophistication both in house building and in farming practice. Once more the population is restricted by the underlying geology of the island to the raised beaches and fertile pockets strung out along the east coast, for it is there that all the evidence of their presence is concentrated. The population was no doubt quite small, but sufficient in numbers and organisational ability to raise such considerable monoliths as Camus an Staca, and several stone groups which may have had significant alignments.

IRON AGE

We know as little about the identity of the people living in Jura during the Iron Age (*c.* 600 BC–*c.* AD 400) as we do of those in the preceding period. No doubt Jura was part of the group of islands known to Ptolemy as the Ebudae or Ebudes. Once more we are dependent on what these folk have left behind. In Jura this consists of two types of fortified structures: forts and duns. Jura has no single example of an Iron Age broch, and even Islay has only one, being at the extreme southern edge of the distribution of these defensive towers.

Forts and duns, however, are found on Jura, although here again the listed monuments of Jura amount to only a fraction of those on neighbouring Islay. Jura has five listed forts and six duns as compared with the twenty-eight forts and forty-two duns of Islay. Even nearby Colonsay, only one-fifth the land mass of Jura but with its low lying and fertile ground, sports six forts and thirteen duns. Life on the quartzite and on the bogs of Jura was always very difficult. Only on the eastern shores could any of the successive waves of settlers become established.

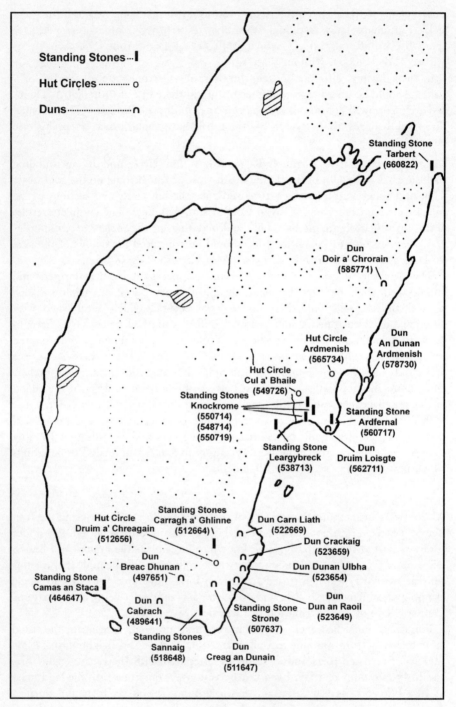

Map 9. Standing stones and duns of Jura.

As far as can be seen, the system of classification which separates forts from duns is primarily based on size and superficial appearance. A fort is a hilltop site defended by extensive drystone walls, often incorporating natural outcrops, and frequently protected by further outworks. A fort is usually a large and substantial structure.

A dun is generally a smaller enclosure perched on the top of a steep-sided natural outcrop and defended by a single enclosing wall. It should be noted that 'forts' in these islands are frequently named 'duns' on the map.

There follows a list of the Jura sites:

Forts (a) An Dunan, Ardmenish (NR 578730); (b) Breac Dhunan (NR 497651); (c) Creag an Dunain (NR 51164); (d) Druim Loisgte (NR 562711); (e) Dun an Raoil (NR 523649).

Duns (a) Cabrach (NR 489641); (b) Carn Liath (NR 522669); (c) Crackaig (NR 523659); (d) Dun Doir a' Chrorain (NR 585771); (e) Rubha Mor, Garbh Eilach, Garvellachs (NM 667117); (f) Dunan Ulbha (NR 523654).

With the above list of forts and duns, the evidence for the human occupation of Jura during the Iron Age appears to be exhausted. It seems little to show for a period of some 800 years, but again the difficulty of making a living on Jura and the comparatively small population rob us of much possible evidence.

II

Far-Off Times

6

The First Centuries of the Christian Era

We associate the Vikings with the eighth century AD, but Scandinavia was prosperous much earlier, certainly in the last two centuries BC. By then Norway had established slave-markets with the Mediterranean countries where Picts and Scots were bought and sold.

Boece (*Scotorum Historia*) states that Scandinavians were in Scotland at the time of Agricola, and Irish historians record the raising of an expeditionary force in the third century AD under Fionn MacCoul to drive the men of Lochlann, Scandinavian pirates, off the Hebrides and the mainland seaboard. Such an expedition was raised as a matter of self-interest in aid of Picts then fully committed to resisting Roman power. The Hebridean base for this expedition may have been in south-east Islay.

The probability that Viking longships were present in Hebridean waters gains support from the circumnavigation of Britain by a small Roman fleet in the period AD 80–85. The Romans brought back a name for the Hebrides, which Pliny (first century) spelt Hebudes, and Ptolemy (second century) rendered in Greek as Epoudai. The name appears to be a phonetic rendering of the Norse Havbredey, pronounced Haubredey. Haw means sea; bred means edge; and ey means island. In the plural it translates as Isles on the Edge of the Sea. No doubt the Romans picked up the name on their travels.

In the third and fourth centuries the Picts were increasingly helped by the Irish tribes that the Romans called Scotti. Before the Romans finally abandoned their walls in AD 388, Irish settlers were occupying Britain's west seaboard from Devon to Argyll.

The Irish tribe that began to colonise Argyll's peninsula of Kintyre and the isle of Islay from around AD 220 were Scots of Dalriada, a province of Antrim in Ulster. They came in peace as Celts to a Celtic land; Kintyre was held by the Epidii, where their Gaelic would be understood, and where mutual understanding had been established by trade. The main settlement, on the flat isthmus of Crinan, between Loch Fyne and the Sound of Jura, was, 300 years later, to become the capital of an independent kingdom of Scots. For the present, the Picts saw no threat.

Irish tradition tells how Cairbre Riata moved, with his people, from Munster to the extreme north of Ulster, and then across to Kintyre and the Inner Hebrides. This took place around AD 220. Cairbre Riata was the son of Conari II, the reigning High King of Erin (212–220). His descendants, the sons of Erc, continued the work of colonisation and conquest. The main invasion of Argyll, however, took place late in the fifth century. While the dates and, indeed, the facts seem somewhat confused the prime movers are supposed to have been Fergus, Loarn (later to give his name to Lorn) and Angus, said to have been sons of Erc.

According to mid-Argyll tradition, the invaders landed at Crinan, overran the Moine Mhor and seized the hill-fort of Dun Add, which they made their capital. Fergus, the eldest took Knapdale and Kintyre with Cowal. Later it would appear that Domingart, son of Fergus, reigned as a true king in what is now Argyll. His sons Gabhran and Comgall divided their father's kingdom. Gabhran took Mid-Argyll, Knapdale and Kintyre, while Comgall took the peninsula which still bears his name, Cowall. Lorn, obtained the northern part of Argyll that still bears his name.

Angus took Islay and Jura. One account says that he and his family did not conquer Islay, but inherited it from a Pictish ancestress. From this Angus came the clan whose descendants 600 years later were to produce Somerled, the kings of the Hebrides, and the Clan Donald, Lords of the Isles. All three petty kingdoms were later united. It seems clear that by the middle of the sixth century the Scottish Dalriada stretched from the Firth of Clyde to Ardnamurchan. If we accept the housing enumeration of the 'Chronicles of the Picts and Scots', we can make an estimate of the population of the Scots in Argyll:

	Houses	Armed muster
Clan Angus, holding Islay and Jura	430	500
Clan Lord, holding Lorn and Morvern	420	600
Clan Gabhran (from Fergus) holding Kintyre, Knapdale, Cowal, Arran and Bute	560	300
	1410	1400

The houses were apparently grouped in settlements of twenty, for they had a sea muster, assigning to each twenty houses fourteen benches for oarsmen. The armed musters give an average of one man to a house, suggesting a family unit, whose size, if taken at five or six, would give a population for Dalriada of 7000–8000 excluding the native Picts. This information gives us a curious opportunity to draw a tentative conclusion about the population of Jura. We have seen that the ratio of prehistoric monuments between Islay and Jura runs at about ten to one, so if Islay and Jura between them had 430 households, we might expect some forty or so households in Jura, with a total population of 240.

The National Census of 1841 has 210 households in Jura. This may represent something of a peak in population, and various studies have suggested that this was more than the island could support. Since that time the population has declined steadily, a decline which continues today.

The present population of just over 200 inhabitants, living in about fifty dwelling places seems to have brought the picture full circle after 1500 years.

Gabhran of Argyll was succeeded by his nephew, Conall, Comgall's son. Adomnán, Columba's chronicler implies that Columba visited with Conall for a time, and this may very well have been at Dunadd. When Columba conceived his mission to convert the northern Picts, Dalriada was ruled by Conall, who was his kinsman. Certainly Dunadd was besieged in 683 by yet another Angus who laid waste lands in Dalriada in 736.

While all of these distant events mention Jura only by implication, it should be remembered that it lay in a strategic position on the main routes from the south. While Columban monks may well have reached Iona by sailing up the west coast of Islay and cutting between Colonsay and Jura, thus avoiding the dangerous Sound of Jura, traffic bound for the capital at Dunadd was in a different situation. From Ireland it was possible to land at Southend in Kintyre and make the entire journey up the Mull of Kintyre by land, but from Islay it was a different story. As in the journeys to the cattle marts of the mainland in later centuries it was common practice to 'island hop', from Islay to Jura; to trek overland up Jura, and finish with the short sea crossing to Crinan.

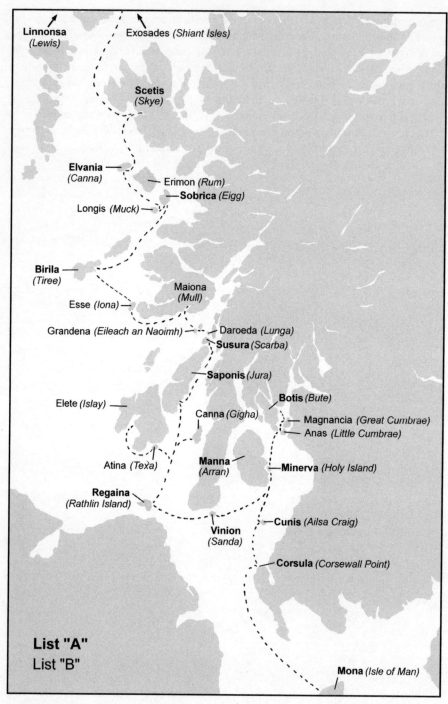

Map 10. The island names of the monk of Ravenna.

7

The Celtic Mission
and the Isle of Hinba

Our earliest written source of information about the area in which Jura and its surrounding islands lies comes from Adomnán's *Life of Columba*. Adomnán was elected abbot of Iona in 679, ninth in succession to Columba, its founder. Columba was ordained a priest about 551, and founded churches and monasteries in Derry and Durrow. He arrived in Iona, with twelve disciples in 563, and erected a church and monastery there. This became a springboard for the evangelisation of Pictish Scotland. Columba died in 597.

Although Adomnán's *Life* is concerned largely with prophecies, miracles and visions, and matters which are of little interest today, Adomnán mentions many places, and incidents concerned with them, and it is often possible to make an informed guess as to the modern locations his Latin labels refer to.

We will study this aspect of Adomnán, and also the work of Donald McEachern, a Gaelic scholar from Islay, writing in *The Lands of the Lordship* in 1976. McEachern researched not only Adomnán's list of island names, but compared them with lists developed from the writings of certain Roman authors. He considered that the Alexandrian geographer Ptolemy was vague and inaccurate about the Scottish west coast. To be fair, Ptolemy mentions that there are five islands which are called the Eboudai. Only one of Ptolemy's island names appeals to McEachern, for he is satisfied that 'Malios' is Mull.

He is far more interested in the work of an unknown monk from Ravenna, writing about 670, who appears to have found some old Roman itineraries, and who painstakingly prepared a sort of 'Gazeteer' of the Empire. He had quite a lot of material on Britain, but of course it was all out of date. His names reflect the Britain of the occupation some 300–400 years before he was writing.

We are here most concerned with his island names which seem to have come from the log of a naval commander on a reconnaissance expedition, He gives us a list of about fourteen or fifteen names of Scottish islands. He then goes on to say 'in another place are said to lie' and then gives a list of a further twelve Scottish island names. McEachern tries to match these with the modern places. Here are the names given by the Ravenna monk. The two lists appear to run parallel. It is possible that the first list were places visited by the fleet, and the second were places merely seen and named.

The first list: Corsula, Mona, Regaina, Minerve, Cunis, Manna, Botis, Vinion, Saponis, Susura, Birila, Elviana, Sobrica, Scetis, Linnonsa.

The second list: Magnancia, Anas, Atina, Elete, Daroeda, Esse, Gra (n)dena,
                    Maiona, Longis, Erimon/Eirimon, Exosades, where precious
                    stones grow.

The voyage starts from 'Corsula', Corsewall Point, above Stranraer in Galloway. It then proceeds to the Isle of Man, 'Mona', and on to Rathlin Island,
'Regaina'. From there it heads into the Firth of Clyde, to visit Minerve, Cunis,
Manna and Botis. Minerve is difficult. Possibly the 'M' can be ignored, which
would leave 'Iner(v)' which could be 'Inis' and island, so possibly Inchmarnock
or Holy Isle off Lamlash. Cunis, suggests Cone and so might be Ailsa Craig.
Botis and Manna must be Bute and Arran. The Gaelic for Bute is Bod. Arainn,
is the place of the God Aru. At this point the expedition leaves the Clyde and
heads south around Kintyre. Vinion occurs elsewhere as Avoyn, and now bears
the Norse name Sanda Sand isle, off Kintyre.

If we assume the names are more or less in order, we find the fleet moving
up the Sound of Jura, avoiding Islay and Gigha, but stopping at Saponis. Here
in the middle of the Ravenna monk's list we find what must surely be the Roman
name for the Isle of Jura. To a Roman fleet Jura was Saponis.

At the north end of Jura the fleet bears WNW to call at Tiree (Tir Idhe) which
beyond reasonable doubt is Birila. Susura, visited on the way is hard. It is just
possible that Scarba is not a Norse name, but a Norse rendering of S(usu)r(a).

The next name 'Elviana' is good Gaelic as 'Eilean' for 'the Island'. Faced with
a choice for 'the Island', and steering a course for Skye, McEachern plumps for
Canna. Sobrica puzzles him. On the itinerary it should be Eigg, but there is no
way to connect the name. 'Scetis' is Skye, An t-Eilean Sgitheanach. The first list
ends with Linnonsa, which is probably a corrupt form of the name the Norse
were to turn into Leous, Lewis. The letters 'n' and 'v' are easily confused, and
this name may have originally been Livvous, or the like.

Having completed the voyage, McEachern turns to the second list of places,
either places seen, but not visited, or visited on a different journey. He starts
again in the Firth of Clyde and round Kintyre as before.

First are Magnancia and Annas, presumably Great Annas and Little Annas,
and the two Cumbraes lie close at hand. Next come Cana, Atina and Elete. Atina
must be the name which occurs in Adomnán as Aithche, and in a survey of
Dalriada as Oideach, long ago identified with Texa. Ele(te) is of course Ile, or
Islay. Cana then would have to be Gigha, Norse 'Guo ey'. This may be for Cara
the islet off Gigha. The next recognisable name is Maiona, which is beyond
doubt meant for Malios, or Mull. If so, then Daroeda, Esse and Gra(n)dena must
lie between Jura and Mull. If the fleet sailed up the east coast of Jura, the
commander may have known enough to avoid the Corrievreckan and proceed
up past Scarba between Lunga and Luing. Daroeda is a puzzle, but by its position
in the order would have to be Lunga. E(ss)e suggests 'I' which is Iona, but
Gradena, the Cliff Place suggests Eileach an Naoimh, in the Garvellachs, which
St Brendan called Aileach, Cliff Place. Longos and Erimon can be taken together.
Remove the 'E' from Erimon and you get Rimon which is the older form of
Rum. It appears elsewehere as Ruimean, Rumind, and Dean Munro who visited
it in 1549 said the older folk called it Ronin. Longos is harder, but McEachern

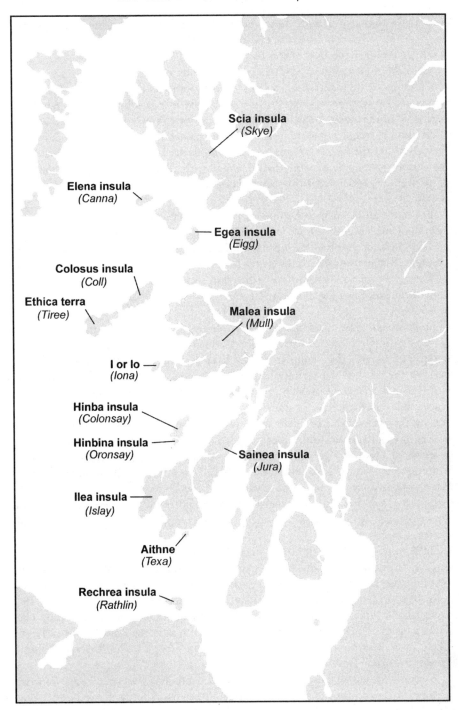

Map 11. The names used by Adomnán.

suggests a connection with pigs, and settles on Muck. The remaining name, Exosades has been identified by Lethbridge with the Shiant Isles.

This completes the lists of the Ravenna monk.

McEachern also made a study of all the islands Adomnán refers to in his Life of Columba. Adomnán wrote in Latin, and this masks the underlying Gaelic of the names he uses. Fortunately for us, he usually just tags on the Latin feminine ending 'a' to the existing name and follows it up with the 'cover all' term, 'insula' or 'island'. Adomnán mentions many fewer names than the Ravenna monk. It is evident that the names he employs are simply the labels he is familiar with for the various islands he has long had dealings with. They occur simply in the text of his account, and he probably never thought of them as having any geographical significance at all.

These are all the names Adomnán uses in the course of his Life of Columba: Airtraig, Colosus insula, Egea insula, Elena insula, Ethica Terra (?)Geona, Hinba insula, Hinbina insula, Ilea insula, I, Longa, Malea insula, Oidech/Aithche, Ommon, Rechrea insula, Saine insula (or Sainea), Scia insula.

With Adomnán's names there is no ship's captain's log to follow as in the time of the unknown Roman admiral. Here McEachern works out each reference individually.

Innis Aittraig, Isle by the Shore was shown by Watson to be the modern Shona, between Moidart and Ardnamurchan. Colosus insula may represent Old Irish masculine 'Colos'. The context makes it clear that the island meant is Coll. Perhaps the name was originally masculine, but became feminine by association with other island names which are almost all feminine. The name means 'hazel place'. Egea is Eigg, said to be from Old Irish 'eag', a notch, from the deep cutting through its centre. Elena was dealt with in the Latin list and shown to be the modern Canna. Ethica Terra, 'Tir Idhe' 'Corn land' hence Tiree. Geona is mentioned as the place from which a respectable old pagan gentleman came. Columba met him in Skye, but could only talk to him through an interpreter. If Geon was an island it may have been one of the Outer Isles.

Hinba insula and Hinbina insula have a special significance for this study, so we will leave McEachern's treatment of them until we consider the special question of 'Hinba'

Ile(a) has not changed its form since Adomnán wrote. It is still Islay. I, Io is Iona. It is an ancient name and appears to be connected with the yew-tree. It was probably a pagan sanctuary in prehistoric times. The island which Adomnán calls 'long' in Latin is impossible to identify with certainty. It may simply be 'the Long Island'. Like Ile, Male(a) remains virtually unaltered and is still Mull. The name appears to mean pre-eminent. Aithne/Oidech as in the Ravenna list is Texa. There is no clue to Ommon, which may be an error for the Ravenna Vinion Sanda. Rechre is Rathlin.

Next on Adomnán's list is Saine or Sainea. Saine is a 'lost' name. As we saw, it appears on the Ravenna list as Sapona. It seems likely that the Latin name had an introsive 'p' which would have disappeared. The meaning is unknown. From the Ravenna list we deduced that it was one of the southern isles. It belonged according to Adomnán, to the 'Cinel Loarn'. A south wind carried Columba and his men from Saine to Iona. Leaving Saine at dawn on a summer morning they were in Iona by nine in the morning. They were in fact returning from Ireland and had stopped at Saine to rest. Position as well as ownership narrows our choice down to Jura, for there is no other island of any size between Ireland and Iona of which we are in any real doubt as to the name, and, as if to clinch the matter, we have, on the west of the island, a cave called 'Uamh Mhuinntir Idhe', Cave of the Iona Party. The distance involved in travelling from that point to Jura would be about 30 miles. That would involve an unlikely speed of about six miles an hour. But perhaps Adomnán was making the point that the speed was miraculous. Just another miracle for Columba!

The author is quite convinced by McEachern's reasoning about Saine or Sainea, and accepts that this is the early name for Jura.

Scia is of course Skye, An t-Eilean Sgitheanach. The name may be connected with sgiath; a wing, but the derivation is doubtful.

HINBA

Donald McEachern deals with Adomnán's references to 'Hinba insula' and 'Hinbina insula' in a quite matter-of-fact way. This is what he says on the subject:

> According to a fairly reliable tradition, Hinb(a) is the old name of the island called Kolumbs ey, Columba's Isle by the Norse, now Colonsay. The 'b' between the 'm' and the 's' vanishes and the 'm' becomes 'n' by assimilation. The Columban monastery stood on Kiloran Bay. The meaning of Hinb is uncertain. There is one reference to an island called Hinbina insula, apparently Little Hinb, where there was a small priory to which penitents were sent. This would appear to be the adjacent islet of Oronsay, 'Oran's Isle'.

McEachern seems to have taken 'Hinba' in his stride, but in recent years controversy has arisen about the location of the island called Hinba by Adomnán The name cannot immediately be identified with any modern island, and yet Adomnán clearly thought it was significant in the life of Columba, and of his uncle Earnan and his foster son Baithene.

Heated academic debates have taken place on the question, and the two most favoured islands for the title of Hinba have been Eilach an Naoimh on the Garvellachs, and the island of Jura itself.

Both of these places lie within the remit of this present study, so it will be necessary to examine the question of "Hinba" once again, in the hope of arriving at some balance of probability as to its true identity.

Perhaps we should put Donald McEachern's assumptions about Hinba aside for a time while we look at the various other well-qualified people who have tackled the problem.

First we have Donald Budge. Mr Budge was the serving Church of Scotland minister in Jura at the time he wrote in 1960. He was a good Gaelic scholar, and devoted some thought to the matter in his book about Jura.

> The work of the Columban Church in Jura is largely associated with St Ernan, after whom the parish was, until recently, called Kilearnadil. Ernan is believed

to have been the brother of Eithne, the mother of St Columba, whose name is preserved in Kilmeny in Islay – Cill M'Eithne as it was in the Gaelic tongue.

Jura has also been identified by some authorities as the island 'Hinba' mentioned in Adomnán's *Life of Columba*. Professor Watson, in his Celtic place-names, strongly favours Jura as being the island with the lost name 'Hinba'. He reasons that we must look for the island among those which now have Norse names. It cannot be far from Iona for Columba often visited it. It lay in the track of vessels coming from Ireland; and it must have a wide bag-like bay or 'muir-bolg-mor'. Watson claims that either Jura or Colonsay must be the island referred to, and declares after examining the evidence 'that the claims of Jura to be the Hinba of Adomnán are strong claims'. Had he known Jura better, his conviction might have been even stronger, for he identifies Loch Tarbert in Jura as the possible bag-shaped bay. He was evidently unfamiliar with Lowlandman's Bay on the east side of the island. This bay exactly fits the description which is embodied in the name 'muir bolg-mor', for it is circular in shape, is almost land-locked, and is capacious enough and deep enough to shelter several vessels of considerable size. It might be argued that there are no ecclesiastical ruins in Jura, like those of Iona and Colonsay, but these buildings were raised several centuries later than the time of St Columba. There is a beautiful local tradition concerning Jura's St Ernan. The aged saint died somewhere outside of Jura, and when dying gave instruction concerning his burial. His body was to be conveyed to Jura and carried onward till they should come to a small glen over which a patch of mist would be hanging. They were to stop and bury his body in that spot. The burial party landed in the south of Jura at a rock known as Leac Ernan, and continued across the island until they came to the place which is now the churchyard of Kilearnadil.

It has been surprisingly difficult to establish clearly at what date the custom of identifying the Parish of Jura as 'Kilearnadil' fell out of use. It may be of interest to record that an account for chloride batteries for Mr Budge's Manse power plant, dated 23 July 1958, is addressed to 'The Manse of Kilearnadil'.

The earliest written reference to the name of the Parish of Jura comes in Dean Munro's *Western Isles of Scotland* of 1549, in which he refers to 'Ane chapell sumtyme the paroche kirk Kilernadill'. The Reformation Parish was of vast size, and included Gigha and Colonsay. Presumably the early centre of the pre-Reformation parish would have been at the Priory of Oronsay, and hence Jura might early have had a subordinate 'chapelle, sumtyme the paroche kirk'. Munro is the first to write the name as it remained for 400 years; apparently a mixture of Gaelic and Norse: Cill Earnan's Dale (The Church of Earnan's Dale).

The Rev. Charles Robertson, collecting Jura stories in about 1913, interviewed Dugald Buie and his brother Neil about this tradition. Robertson was an outstanding Gaelic scholar, and can be relied on in such matters. Here is his record of Dugald Buie's account.

Cill Earradail received its name from Earradail, who lived in Islay, and expressed his wish that when he died his remains should be taken to Jura, and carried onwards until a patch of mist, in the Gaelic 'bad ceo', should be seen, and that he should be interrred at the spot over which the mist was seen. His remains accordingly were landed in Jura at Leac Earradail at Daimhsgeir, and were committed to the earth where the first cloud of mist was seen at 'Cill Earradail'.

Neil Buie's story was identical except that he called Leac Earradail, 'Leac Airneadail'. 'Leac' is the Gaelic word for a slab. As can be seen, these accounts are substantially the same as the tradition recorded by Budge.

In the *First Statistical Account of Jura*, by the Rev. Francis Stewart, in 1794, the relevant passage reads as follows: 'The tutelary saint of the island was Fernadal; from him the burying ground is denominated Kil-fhearnadail. or the Cell of Fernadal; also a large oblong stone on the shore, three miles south west from the Cell, Leac-fhearnadail, or the stone of Fernadal.'

The graveyard is still in use. The slab can be found on the shore of the Sound of Islay at NR 444666.

John Mercer, in his *Hebridean Islands* in a discussion on 'Hinba', says:

Many have claimed that Hinba was Eilach an Naoimh, but there is good reason for doubt. The name 'inbe' meaning 'incision' tying up with Adamnan's placing of a 'muirbolc' or 'big sea-bag'; sea loch that is; in Hinba. The Garvellachs have no inlet worthy to name an island. Jura has the best claimant, the bag-ended Loch Tarbert; also there is the association on Jura of the ancient settlement of Keils, according to Muir, the island's first, and the burial ground of Kilearnadil, named after Ernan. The Hinba monastery should perhaps be sought at Keils on Jura, then.

The quote, 'many have claimed that Hinba was Eilach an Naoimh' seems to have originated with Dr W. Reeves in his *Life of St Columba* (1857).

Dr W. D. Lamont wrote a detailed account on the question in 1978, and for various reasons locates Hinba in the Coll and Tiree group, identifying it with the small island of Gunna.

William R. McKay entered the fray shortly after and, having disposed of Gunna to his satisfaction, concluded that there was no possibility of identifying Hinba from what Adomnán tells us:

The authors of the Royal Commission's Inventory on Argyll , writing in 1984, make their own contribution. Eilach an Naoimh has sometimes been identified with Hinba, where a monastery with an associated hermitage was founded in the sixth century by St Columba, and frequently visited by him. If Hinba indeed lay within the area covered by this volume a more probable identification is Jura, where the sheltered church-site at Cill Earnadail in the most fertile part of the island, may preserve the name of Ernan, an uncle of Columba who was briefly Prior of Hinba. There is, however, some reason to suppose the Hinba lay north of Mull, and the evidence is too slight for conclusive identification.

At this point we should remember that we must include Donald McEachern's opinions on Hinba from our earlier pages.

We have now assembled a list of authorities, including Donald McEachern, and we will now look at what Adomnán actually said about Hinba in his Life of Columba. Here follows a complete collection of his seven references to the island:

Book III At another time, when the illustrious man was staying in Hinba Island, one night in an ecstasy of mind he saw an Angel of the Lord sent to him.

XVII At another time, four holy founders of monasteries, coming over from Ireland to visit St Columba, found him in Hinba Island.

XVIII At another time, when the holy man was dwelling in the Isle of Hinba, the grace of holy inspiration was marvellously poured forth. He complained that his foster son Baithene was not present, for if he had chanced to be there he might have written down many things. Baithene however could not be present, detained as he was by a contrary wind in the island of Egea, until those three days and as many nights came to an end.

XXI At another time the Saint comes to the Hinbinan Isle, and on the same day orders that some indulgence in food should be allowed even to the penitents. But there was among the penitents a certain Neman, son of Cathir, who bidden by the saint, refused to accept the little indulgence offered.

XXIII Virgno who rowed over in those days from Ireland and remained for the rest of the days of his life in the Isle of Hinba, used often to narrate to the monks of St Columba that angelic vision, which, as aforesaid, he had undoubtedly heard from the lips of that aged Saint to whom it had been revealed. And this same Virgno, after many years passed blameless and in obedience among the Brethren, completed twelve more years in a place of anchorites in Muir-bulc-mor, leading the life of an anchorite as a victorious soldier of Christ.

XXIV At another time the blessed man, when staying in the Island Hinba, began to excommunicate other persecutors of the churches, namely the sons of Conall, son of Domnaill, of whom one was Ioan, of whom we have made mention of above.

XLV Again, at another time, the venerable man sent over Ernan, a priest, an old man, his uncle, to the presidency of that monastery which he had founded in Hinba Island many years before. And so when the Saint kissed and blessed him on his departure, he uttered this prophecy concerning him, saying; 'I do not expect to see again alive in this world this my friend now departing.' Accordingly the same Ernan, not many days afterwards, afflicted by some ailment, was at his own desire carried back to the Saint, who, greatly rejoiced at his coming, started to meet him at the haven. Ernan himself, although with faltering steps, was attempting with joyous activity to walk from the landing place to meet the Saint. But when there was between the two a space of about twenty-four paces, he was overtaken by sudden death before the Saint could look upon his face in life, and fell to earth, breathing his last. Wherefore in the same place before the door of the kiln a cross has been fixed; and another cross stands today fixed in like manner where the Saint stood when Ernan died.

This then is the full extent of our information about Hinba.

St Columba is recorded as having been staying in Hinba or Hinbina on five occasions, and the implication is that on some of these he was apparently 'in residence'. At least he was sufficiently settled to be carrying out a variety of different duties. This suggests that Hinba was easily accessible from Iona. Important visitors coming from Ireland found Columba in Hinba. This is ambiguous to the extent that they may have found him on their way to Iona, or may have visited Iona, and, not finding him in residence, gone on to Hinba.

Hinba has a monastery founded many years before the death of Columba's uncle Ernan. It also has a place for a religious recluse, or hermit, near a feature, 'Muir-bolc-mor', which has been variously translated but must at least be some kind of Bay.

Hinba had a very tenuous connection with Ernan, who was appointed as Abbot of its Monastery, when an old man, and only a few days before his death.

As we have already seen, most of the nearby islands have identifiable pre-Norse names, used by Adomnán, so they can all be ruled out as 'Hinba and Hinbina'.

Hinba must have been easily accessible from Iona because of the many visits made by Columba, and the amount of time he spent there.

The idea that Hinba was north of Iona is not an attractive one, since all the major islands to the north are accounted for, and Gunna, between Coll and Tiree, can definitely be discounted, because although a case may be made for a connection between Baithene and Tiree, and possibly for Coll as the residence of some of the miscreants dealt with by Columba, Gunna itself is only about 1.5 km in length and 400 m across. It has no bay of any size, and simply no room for religious settlements such as Adomnán writes of.

It is surely to the south that we must look, and to the south that we must dismiss the Garvellach Isles as the location for Hinba. Although plainly coming into prominence as a Columban settlement, and still containing one of the most important collections of Early Christian monuments in Scotland, it is surely unlikely that Eilach an Naoimh was as important to Columba as Hinba seems to have been. The author has sailed a good deal round the Garvellachs. There is only one rather doubtful anchorage off the south shore of Eilach an Naoimh. The waters are treacherously near to the fierce tide races of the Sound of Lorn and the mighty Corrievreckan whirlpool. The islands all have fierce cliffs to the north, and there is not a sign of any possible Muir-bolc-mor. Eilach an Naoimh is not an easy place to reach, and it is difficult to imagine Columba conducting the kind of business from it as described by Adomnán. It is 31 miles (50 km) from Iona to Eilach an Naoimh, and across treacherous coastal waters at that.

This seems to leaves us with the two possibilities of Colonsay and Jura.

Naturally, the author as the former Minister of Jura would be delighted to be able to settle on the definite opinion that Jura is Adomnán's island of Hinba. Present-day residents may also have an interest in the matter. But it isn't quite as simple as that.

There is no doubt that Jura can produce the most perfect 'muir-bolc-mor' anywhere in the Hebrides, in the form of Lowlandman's Bay, on its east coast. It is true also that this bag-shaped bay lies only three and a half miles from the ancient graveyard of Kilearnadail. Indeed the author wrote a children's song about 'Ships and Boats' in the 1970s, which contained this verse:

> Long ago from Isle of Iona, Columba and Earnan made their way,
> Old-time Diurachs saw them landing. Coracles in Lowlandman's Bay.

It was a hugely attractive picture, but Gaelic scholarship suggests that the strangers who gave the Bay its name were more likely to have been the Norseman, than Columban monks.

In the 'Hinba' discussion Jura has little else going for it, and many huge problems.

It is, as we have already seen, a difficult island to travel on. It is mountainous and boggy, and the inlet which cuts through almost to the east coast at Loch Tarbert is subject to fierce tides. There is some evidence that funeral parties from the mainland, bound for Iona, did sometimes portage the bodies of their deceased loved ones across Jura, and rest with them in the caves of the rocky west coast before sailing across to Iona. The author's opinion is that this route will have been taken only very reluctantly, and only by those folk living directly opposite on Knapdale, who would find it profitable to do so. We cannot imagine that it is a crossing which anyone in his right mind would undertake willingly, unless there was no possible alternative. With a dangerous crossing of the Sound of Jura, and a long sail from its west coast we can be sure that most parties would have preferred an easier route to the north or to the south of the island.

A visitor from Iona would face a 40 km sail merely to land on the west coast at Corpach. It is possible to sail through the island up Loch Tarbert, but at many times of tide not even a powerful modern launch can make this passage. The east coast of Jura, when reached, is very long and its earliest Christian settlements, three in number, are widely scattered.

It is hard to imagine where the communities of which Adomnán speaks, would be located, or how Columba would have reached them. As we have already seen in our study of the prehistoric settlements of the island, the human population of Jura has always been only a fraction of nearby Islay, or even of the much smaller Colonsay. And where would visitors from Ireland on their way to Iona find the saint in Jura? The island is vast and there were famously uncrossable streams even in the eighteenth century. Jura is not an island where you can land, and hope to spot the person you are coming to visit, and attract his attention with a cheerful wave. Indeed anyone who is well acquainted with Iona itself, and has landed on islands such as Tiree and Colonsay can begin to imagine that he knows when an island is likely to be 'Columban', and Jura has none of the features that make it feel right for such an early settlement.

It has been maintained that all of this argument pales into insignificance when it is pointed out that the parish from ancient times has been dedicated to and named after Columba's Uncle Ernan, who St Columba himself appointed abbot to its monastery, the community of Hinba.

It is this assumed connection which causes the author most concern. It seems quite possible that the consecration of the island has nothing whatever to do with St Ernan, who according to Adomnán was only abbot on Hinba for a matter of days.

Monro was no doubt correct in saying that the island has 'ane chapelle sumtyme the paroche kirk Kilernadil', and no doubt it had carried that title for many years before Monro's time. But does the title indicate a connection with Columba's Uncle Ernan? The author thinks not and, more importantly, the Rev. Francis Stewart in 1794 plainly did not think so either. He believed the island was dedicated to one St 'Fernadal', from which the burying ground takes its name of Kil-fhearnadail, or the Cell of Fernadal. He also knows about Leac fhearnadail, or the stone of Fernadal. Here we have to come to terms with the problems for non-Gaelic speakers of dealing with translations from the Gaelic. In the Gaelic the initial consonant 'f' takes an 'h' after it when qualified by another word. The 'fh' so formed is silent in Gaelic and so the initial 'f' simply disappears. A possible person called 'Fernadal' would therefore become 'Ernadal' the minute his name was qualified by another term which aspirates the initial 'f'.

Stewart has no interest in separating the suffix 'dil' or 'dail' or 'dal' from the saint's name, and thus needs no Norse 'Dale' to be added to the name.

The Buies of the Rev. Robertson's time equally attached the 'dail' on to the end of the man's name, although one of his sources has 'Earradail', which omits the 'n'.

If Kilearnadil, the present name of the graveyard, and the similar name 'Kilaridil' on our earliest map, of Blaeu and Pont (1789) means what it has always been supposed to mean – The Church of Earnan's Dale – then why should an isolated rock miles away on the south-western shore, and known as the spot where the patron saint's body was landed, have the suffix 'dail' as well?

Furthermore, if the oral tradition about St Earnan dying off the island of Jura, which Columba's uncle certainly did, – for we know that he died on Iona – is based on a far distant happening, then how could a party of monastic mourners fulfilling Earnan's wish to be buried on Jura land his body where Leac Earnadail is situated? Surely the man whose body was landed at Leac Earnadail on the Sound of Islay must have been someone who died on the Island of Islay, and wanted to have his wish satisfied to be buried on Jura?

On balance the author is now convinced that the religious sites on Jura, although undoubtedly derived from the Celtic Mission of Iona, are by no means as primitive as the years of Columba's own ministry, but arrived at a much later date, and only when there was a need to settle amongst, and work with, the small population of Jura on its large and inhospitable island.

This entire presentation leaves us face to face with Donald McEachern's original opinion that Hinba is Colonsay and Hinbina is Oronsay. McEachern is the only scholar to write on the subject who pays any attention at all to the fact that in extract XXI Adomnán refers to an island called 'Hinbina' – presumably 'Little Hinba'. Only Colonsay and Oronsay provide a large and little island.

It is a straightforward voyage of about 25 km, or 15 miles, from Iona to Colonsay, through open water, with no dangerous currents. Colonsay is on the direct route from Ireland, and travellers to Iona may well have routinely landed there for supplies and found Columba in residence. Colonsay has several reasonable bag-shaped bays; several with Columban chapels nearby; and if indeed the derivation of Hinba is to do with a division or separation, there is such a conspicuous division between Colonsay and Oronsay. Colonsay has a number of early Celtic Church foundations, and later supported the major development of the Priory of Oronsay.

Colonsay is a lush and fertile island, with a central hill which rises to less than 450 ft. It is easy to get about in, and has the same Hebridean quality of machair and sandy beaches shared by Iona and other so-called 'Columban' islands. When the Norsemen arrived they called Colonsay, Columba's Isle – 'Kolumbs-ey'– and it has remained so to this day.

In view of all these factors, the author has decided reluctantly to give up his vision of Columba and Earnan in Lowlandman's Bay, and will settle instead for identifying Hinba as Colonsay, with its little brother Hinbina as Oronsay. Sadly this also means giving up the fine bag-shaped bay, and the long-treasured dedication of the Parish of Jura to St Ernan.

It will be immediately evident to all readers that this is not an authoritative decree on the matter, but a personal opinion. The author believes that most of the available evidence has been presented here, and hopes that interested readers will make up their own minds on this question which has fascinated scholars for so long.

8

Early Ecclesiastical Sites

This seems a reasonable place to review the sites which have survived in some form from the early period of the Christian Church in the Western Isles. The monuments themselves can be described fairly simply. What is much harder is to be sure of their actual dates, and that field seems to remain open to considerable speculation.

We will look first at the island of Jura itself, and then at the notable sites on the Garvellachs. Once more the comparative abundance of religious foundations reflects the difference in the quality of life between Jura and its more fertile neighbours of Islay and Colonsay. In the *Argyll Inventory* there are some thirty-one monuments listed under the general heading of 'Chapel'. Only three of these sites are on Jura.

Frequently our studies reveal the presence of two different worlds on either side of the Sound of Islay, and here in the matter of Early Christian foundations can be found another striking piece of evidence.

Here are the Jura sites:

CHAPEL AND BURIAL GROUND, CILL CHALUIM CHILLE, TARBERT, JURA (NR 609822).
The remains of this early chapel lie within the graveyard on flat ground above Tarbert Bay. Donald Budge, in his book, records a tradition of the discovery of 'stone coffins and tombs' in the vicinity of the chapel, but the precise nature and location of these burials is not known.

The cross-marked stone within the graveyard has been mentioned under 'standing stones' and there is some disagreement about whether it is a prehistoric stone or not. It is a fine stone, 1.9 m high. Both its faces bear sunken Latin crosses.

In the 1980s there were twenty-three gravestones in the Tarbert Cemetery with some form of inscription on them. To the east of the graveyard, rising ground is bounded by a line of low cliffs. At the foot of these the Ordnance Survey map records the local traditional name of St Columba's Well, Tobar Chalum Chille. The authors of the *Argyll Inventory* found this difficult to identify, but local folk and this author know it well. Further round the headland there is a small cave with the local name Uamh an't Sar Tobar ('Cave of the Hero of the Well'). The word 'sar' has a variety of meanings with the general force of 'a worthy', and 'excellent or famous person', so these names may incorporate a tradition of an early monastic hermit who lived in the cave.

The Rev. Alexander Kennedy, writing in *The Second Statistical Account* in 1845, says: 'The ruins of many chapels are still extant in this island; their names, Kilmorie, Kilchianaig, Kilchattan, and Kilearnadale, furnish indications of their having been built at a period when the saints in the Romish calendar were held in higher repute than they are at the present time in the parish of Jura and Colonsay.'

Mr Kennedy does not identify these four sites, but there is evidence relating to them. Kilearnadale will be dealt with shortly, and is definitely identified with the present graveyard at Keils. Kilchianaig has an honourable history, and appears still on the current Ordnance Survey map at the cemetery at Inverlussa. Kilmorie is on Scarba, where it seems to be the Kilmore of Blaeu. This is the Kilmorie of John of Fordun who records in 1400 that many miracles were believed to have been performed there. This would leave the chapel at Tarbert to be associated with Kennedy's name, Kilchattan, the Church of St Catan. Dedications to St Catan are to be found in the Parish Church of Gigha and Cara, called Kilchattan, and in the Parish Church of Colonsay, still situated in the township of Kilchattan, so a dedication on nearby Jura seems quite likely. The connection with traditions linking it with the name of Columba himself would thus be broken, but perhaps oral tradition simply transferred the name of a Columban follower back to the saint himself. Where Mr Kennedy got his knowledge from in 1845 no one knows. Perhaps at that time he was dealing with a still lively tradition, no longer extant.

It should be noted that the Rev. Donald Budge, in his book of Jura, written in 1959, names the graveyard in Tarbert as Kilmhoire, which raises a question about the earlier evidence. Perhaps Kennedy should be taken literally when he says there are four ruins 'in this island', and consider that this rules out Scarba from the discussion. In that case, where is Kilchattan? There is no known other early foundation. The matter remains somewhat unclear.

CHAPEL SITE AND BURIAL GROUND, KILCHIANAIG,
INVERLUSSA, JURA (NR 644870)
There are no visible remains of a chapel in this graveyard, although foundations were seen by T. S. Muir in 1861 – 'very similar in size and shape to that at Tarbert'. The wall is nineteenth-century.

There is a small cross-shaped stone of local slate in use as a headstone. This may be medieval. An earlier note indicates, 'The earliest stone commemorates Malkum Buie, who died in 1746', but this was not legible in the 1980s. This cemetery is also the burial place of Mary McCraine, of famously disputed great age, and of whom stories occur in the chapter on longevity. There were over forty stones in the cemetery in the 1980s. In the case of this site, the name Kilchianaig does make its appearance on the Ordnance Survey map, tying it together with Mr Kennedy's fourth 'ruined chapel', and being confirmed in local tradition. The dedication may be to a saint with the Irish name 'Cianag'.

CHURCH SITE AND BURIAL GROUND, CILL EARNADAIL, KEILS,
JURA (NR 524687)
The main graveyard is situated some way up a small glen above Small Isles Bay, and to the north of the village of Keils. Nothing now remains of the church that once stood here. Local traditions vary. Some locate it at the north-east corner of

the existing cemetery, where it is suggested that the footings of the cemetery wall follow the line of two of the old chapel walls. Others place it in the heart of the graveyard, centred on the highest and most central area. The footings of a number of buildings are closely associated with this place. Some are visible immediately in front on the present main entrance, on the left. Others lie between the graveyard and the rising ground to the west, and yet more are lost within the gorse bushes to the east, on the other side of the burn. These presumably belonged to the former township of Killearnadale. Names with religious connotations lie nearby. On the flat ground in the bend of Abhainn a' Mhinisteir, the Minister's Burn, lies Acair a' Cleirich, the Clerk's or Curate's Acre, while some distance downstream is the Bishop's Well. On the abandonment of this site as the location for the main church in Jura, it is presumed to have moved to its present location about 1777, but there is good reason to suppose that there was a church in an unknown intermediate location in the previous centuries. (Plate 2) (Colour plate 16)

The monuments in this cemetery are of various dates and are recorded in detail in the *Argyll Inventory*, Volume Five; the Campbell Mausoleum is also described there.

The author mapped and recorded Kilearnadil in the late 1970s. However Argyll & Bute District Council embarked on a 'rationalisation' of the cemetery about 1980, as a result of which many of the uninscribed marker stones, traditional in the Western Isles, were moved, or even cast out of the cemetery. Many headstones were realigned to create straight rows to facilitate mowing. This activity caused great unhappiness in the community, and some elderly residents entirely lost confidence in the exact location of their family lair. In due course a modern extension was created to the old cemetery and, in 1985, the old entrance was demolished and a new and wider entrance provided.

When Budge wrote in 1959, he could mention only three recumbent slabs in the open area of the Kilearnadil graveyard. These he associated with the early Buies of Lergiebreac, and he mentioned these graves still being used by their descendants to this day. Indeed this was the situation when the author took up his appointment on Jura in 1975. However, Mary Campbell, a renowned lady of the community of Keils, long dead by that time, and an expert on the location of every grave in the cemetery, was remembered as prophesying that 'the day of the shears and the scissors' would come again to Jura. This saying was obscure, and not capable of any interpretation by the residents of her time. However, in the 1970s, the local authority supported a 'job-creation programme', and several men were employed to clean and tidy the cemeteries on the island. They probed down through the turf in many likely places, and revealed several more slabs, and there at last were the 'shears and the scissors'. They cannot have been hidden for so very long, for the 'scissors' is figured in *Carved Stones of Scotland* (1966), by Bannerman and Steers. The sketch which was the source for the figure in that book may, of course, have been made very much earlier than the date of publication.

Before we leave the mainland of Jura, and while considering burial places, we should note that the *Argyll Inventory* gives five further locations as burial grounds:

Ardmenish (NR 568737); Cladh Mhic Iain (NR 551713); Cladh nan Eireannach (NR 443705); Cnocbreac (NR 446732); and Kinuachdrach (NR 706985);

The author has recorded the inscriptions in the graveyards of Jura, and these lists can be obtained on the island.

We now consider the islands to the north. We deal first with Scarba, and then with the Garvellach Islands, all traditionally within the Parish of Jura. As above, these sites are listed and described in detail in the *Argyll Inventory*. Their titles and locations are given here.

CHAPEL, KILMORY, SCARBA (NM 718056)

The Garvellachs. It is on Eileach an Naoimh (the Holy, or Consecrated Mound) that we find the most celebrated Celtic remains in the area. They are of unique importance, but the Garvellachs are very difficult to get to, and the the monuments there are not visited as often as they deserve. Despite its remoteness, the site is protected from vandalism by a massive and unsightly metal enclosure, whose erection is an example of official insensitivity on an extraordinary scale.

EILEACH AN NAOIMH (NM 640097)

Here is a famous beehive cell and Eithne's grave. A small circular enclosure is identified in nineteenth-century local tradition as the burial place of St Columba's mother. (Colour plate 17)

9

The Viking Period

It was in 794 that the Vikings arrived. The Annals of Ulster record briefly, 'All coasts of Britain ravaged by the Gals.'. Iona Abbey was destroyed in 795, rebuilt and burned in 802, and levelled again in 806, when the Vikings murdered sixty-eight monks at Martyrs Bay; yet again in 825, when they killed the abbot and monks; and finally in 986, when they murdered the abbot and fifteen monks on the sands.

The monasteries on the islands closed down, but the Celtic Church survived. The monks went to earth, taking refuge in remote places. This persecution may have hastened the coming together of the Scots and the Picts who began to gather in communities known as Ceile De (or Culdees), the Companions of God. This Order founded churches widely in the Isles and kept the light alive for 200 years.

The Vikings made light of the sea voyages to the Isles; 200 miles to Shetland and 400 to Lewis, seemed little to them. They first seized the islands and used them as summer bases for mainland raids. Kenneth MacAlpin, King of Scots, was able to overthrow the Picts and unite the two kingdoms in 843 to defend in strength against a common enemy.

The Hebrides were completely conquered by the Vikings who by 850 had even driven Clan Angus out of Islay. The islands became known to the Scots as Innisgal, or Islands of the Foreigners. They were heavily involved in Norse politics. When, in 872, Harald Haarfager made himself first king of all Norway, and introduced a feudal system, many landowners went into exile rather than accept vassalage. From their settlements in the Isles they harassed the Norwegian coast, until in 891 Harald put together a fleet and conquered the Isles, which were ruled for the next 370 years by jarls who were nominal viceroys, but had a great deal of independence. The greatest of these jarls was Godred Crovan, who ruled the Isle of Man and the Hebrides.

Godred Crovan died on Islay in 1095, and his successor took the title of King of Man and of the Isles. This independent line and the growing power of the King of Scots alarmed King Magnus III of Norway and in 1098 he assembled a great fleet and sailed to the Hebrides to punish his rebellious compatriots. Bjorn Cripplehand wrote an eyewitness account of the campaign:

> Fire played in the fig trees of Lewis ... it mounted up to heaven. Far and wide the people were driven to flight. The king went with the fire over Uist. The glad wolf reddened tooth and claw in many a mortal wound within Tiree. The people of Mull ran to exhaustion.

Magnus devastated Lewis, Uist, Skye, Kintyre and all the Argyll islands. He forced Edgar, King of Scots, to acknowledge his claim to the Hebrides. Magnus was twenty-five at the time, and became fond of the Scots' kilt, which he introduced to Norway. This innovation earned him the name Barfod or bareleg.

But the rule of the Norse Kings of Man was coming to an end. The rightful King of Argyll, Gillebride of Clan Angus, had married a daughter of the King of Man, but was forced into exile in Ireland. His Norse wife had a son who was christened Sumarlidi (Summer Traveller), a name commonly given by the Norse to Vikings who voyaged in summer. The usual form is now Somerled. Around 1130, when Somerled had grown to manhood, he and his father returned to Scotland, raised the people of Morvern, and drove the Norsemen out of mainland Argyll. Established now as King of Argyll, Somerled made peace with Olav the Red, King of Man, whose sea-power seemed invincible, and married his daughter Ragnild. But, when Olav was succeeded by his tyrannical son Godred in 1152, the island people turned to Somerled. Somerled's sympathies inclined naturally to his Scots heritage, but he knew that the way to the Hebrides lay by sea-power. The Viking longships had always proved superior to the Scots galleys or birlinn. Somerled knew that he had to develop a better warship. He began secretly to build a new fleet. The ships would be shorter than the Norse longships, but they would have two new features. There would be a hinged rudder in place of the Norse steering oar, and a fighting top at the masthead. The design is clear on the Seal of Somerled. The new ships were called naibheag (nyvaig), meaning little ship, and he built fifty-eight.

When news of the threat reached Godred he sailed from Man for the Hebrides. On 6 January 1156 the two fleets met off the west coast of Islay. The battle raged all day, and at daybreak the next morning the Norse battle fleet was broken. Somerled's crews were too exhausted to follow up their victory. Somerled and Godred agreed to divide the Hebrides. Somerled took Bute and Arran, and the nominal title of the Scottish Crown, and all the islands south of Ardnamurchan point – Mull, Coll, Tiree, Jura, Islay, Colonsay, Gigha and lesser isles – under the suzerainty of the Norwegian Crown, to whom he and his successors paid tribute. Godred retained Man, the Skye group and the Outer Hebrides.

Somerled took up his seat in Islay. He berthed his fleet of nyvaigs at Lagavulin Bay on the south coast, where Dunyvaig Castle was later built for their protection by his grandson.

The twelfth century saw great upheavals in the political life of mainland Scotland. The growing Norman and Flemish influence came to a height when King David came to the throne in 1124, bringing with him many Anglo-Norman land-seekers to his court. Estates were given to a thousand of these men, Celtic owners presumably being dispossessed. The Gaelic tongue, which was by then the predominent language of Scotland fell into disuse in the Lowlands. Somerled, half Norse, half Scots, might acknowledge the suzerainty of Scottish and Norwegian kings, but like his ancestors on both sides he was not prepared to sacrifice his power, or give up land. When Malcolm IV succeeded his father David in 1153, Somerled and other Celtic chiefs made approaches to try to break the Anglo-Norman grip on the Crown. When they failed, they tried to force a treaty. In 1164 Somerled raised a fleet of 160 ships and sailed up the Firth of Clyde with 10,000 men from Argyll and the Isles. He marched to Renfrew with half his force and there received the king's Breton steward, Walter Fitz Alan, the Baron of Renfrew. Early in the morning, Somerled was found assassinated in his tent. This was a turning point in Hebridean history. Until then the Gaels had hope of halting the Anglo-Norman encroachment and of re-establishing a united Celtic kingdom. The hope and the opportunity were now gone. The split between the Lowland and the Island and Highland Scots became wide and permanent.

Somerled's three sons divided the islands between them. Ragnall held Islay and Kintyre, and the fleet of nyvaigs. Dughall, the founder of Clan Dougall, held all the other isles of Argyll, including Jura, and the mainland of Lorn. Angus held Arran and Bute. They felt no ties to the Scots Crown, whose court at Scone, beyond forested and well-nigh roadless mountains, was less accessible than Norway was by sea. In this island triumvirate the House of Islay was dominant, and all of Somerled's first five successors there held rank as Kings of the Isles.

Somerled's victory in 1156 had brought the Hebrides a hundred years of peace. His son Ragnall, or Reginald, was a strong supporter of the Christian Church, founding monasteries and rebuilding pillaged abbeys and chapels.

Donald I, who succeeded in 1207, gave his name to his clan, known thereafter as Clan Donald. He wished to consolidate his hold on the Hebrides, and made the journey to Norway to have his right to the Isles recognised by the Norse king. Alexander of Scotland sent messengers to Donald requiring him to hold his lands from the Crown of Scotland. Donald rashly killed the king's messenger, for which killing he later did penance in Rome. He ended his career by becoming a monk at Paisley, and died in 1237. Donald was succeeded by his son Angus Mòr

Meanwhile the power of Scotland was growing, and succeeding kings were exerting pressure on the Norse occupation of the mainland. In 1196, William the Lion reclaimed the north of Scotland from the Orkney jarls, and his grandson Alexander II instigated systematic attacks by the Earl of Ross and other mainland chiefs on Skye and the neighbouring islands.

Haakon of Norway was forced to reply and set sail with a great fleet, perhaps as many as 200 ships, in 1263. He anchored off Arran in the Firth of Clyde in late summer. He ravaged Bute and sent forty ships up Loch Long to be portaged across to Loch Lomond to plunder the surrounding countryside.

King Alexander had prepared well. He held the son of Angus Mòr of Islay as hostage against the King of the Isles supporting his sovereign Lord Haakon. He negotiated for a month, waiting for autumn gales. On the night of 1 October a great gale came out of the west, driving many of the longships on to the lee shore at Largs. Haakon landed men to try to salvage the ships, but the Scots attacked. The battle lasted all of the following day, while the storm at sea continued. Haakon was unable to reinforce his army with men or supplies from his wrecked and scattered fleet and was lucky to escape at nightfall, and be granted a truce to bury his dead and withdraw to sea. His broken fleet sailed for Orkney where he let all but twenty of the ships go home. He himself died of a fever in Kirkwall.

Alexander seized Skye and the Outer Hebrides and three years later in 1266 Norway formally ceded the Hebrides to Scotland at the Treaty of Perth.

10

The Viking Legacy

As far as Jura is concerned there is nothing to be seen on the ground that commemorates the lengthy period of Norse domination of its life. In one area, however, we are rich in Norse relics, for the invaders left their mark through their language, and the names they gave the natural features of the island. In our study of these names we are dependent on the work of Malcolm McArthur, a Gaelic scholar of Jura extraction, and on Donald McEachern of Islay.

Before proceeding it should be made clear again here that the name 'Jura' is itself Norse, replacing the older name which it has been suggested was Saine. Thus, Jura – 'Dýr ey' – Deer Island. (the Old Norse term for island is 'ey'); thence perhaps, to 'Diura' and so to 'Jura'.

David Dorward suggests that there was a personal Norse name which meant 'deer', and that Jura takes it name from that, thus 'Diorad's isle'. If, as this implies, the island was named after an early Viking chieftain who was called 'Deer', then all the ancient associations with red deer on the island would turn out to be mere coincidence, and the Norsemen didn't name Jura after the deer they found there at all!

It would be unwise to assume that the connection with deer is the only derivation for the name Jura. The Rev. Francis Stewart, writing in 1794 says: 'Some think it was so denominated from the great quantity of yew trees which grew in the island. The name of the yew, in Gaelic, is Juar; hence, they say Juarey and, in a contracted form, Jurey, 'the island of yew trees'.

Several contemporary scholars, such as McArthur, give credence to this argument. The present-day Gaelic for 'yew' is 'iubhar'. The fact that the yew has not grown on Jura in recent times may not be an argument against the derivation. The McSwein family of Jura have a tradition that Jura was notable in the past as a source of yew for the mainland.

In the matter of Norse names we can see the distinction between the fertile and well-populated Islay, and the rugged and inhospitable Jura. In Islay there are many traces of Norse terms to describe farms and homesteads, but these are quite absent from Jura.

A later generation who did not understand Norse often added a term like 'Gleann' or 'Port' to the early name, so that the result is tautological, e.g. Askaig; Ask vik; Ashtree harbour; so Port Askaig; The Harbour of Ashtree Harbour; or Grundale; graen dalr; the green glen; so Glen Grundale; The Glen of the Green Glen.

Most of the thirty-four names in Jura with a clear Norse provenance describe bold natural features, most of which can be seen from the sea. None describes settlements, although several became attached to farmhouses.

Here is the list, moving round the island anti-clockwise from the northern entry to the Sound of Islay, 'Ilar Sund'.

Gleann Asgeamail	ask – ash + muli – crag
Beinn Mhearsamail	fyrre – fir + muli – crag
Gleann Asdail	ass – ridge + dalr – glen
Gleann Iubharnadeal	ior-n – horse + dalr – glen
Feolin Ferry	feorlinn – eyr – shingle
Allt Gleann Bhisdeal	mid-dalr – mid-glen – burn of the glen
Daimhsgeir	dauf – blunt + sker – rock
Gleann Ullibh	possibly – wolf
Camas an Staca	Gael – camus – bay + N stac – column
Caolas a' Phlota	Gael. narrow sound + Nfloti – flood tide
Brosdale Island	broad glen
Rubha na Traille	praella nes – slave promontory
Sannaig	sand + vik – harbour
Crackaig	krak – crow + vik – harbour
Killearnadale	the dalr or glen of the cell of Earnan
Loch na Mile	fjall – fell – so loch of the fell
Gleann Grundale	green + dalr – the green glen
Ardfernal	aird – gravel isthmus + Gael. fearnal – alder
Ardmenish	aird + mjo – narrow + nes – nose
Loch Lesgamail	ljosg – chestnut mare + muli – crag
Lussa River	ljoss – bright + a – river
Tramaig Bay	tromr – edge + vik – harbour
Bog a' Chuirn	bodi – sunk rock or breaker of An Carn
Gleann Trosdale	tross – seaweed + dalr – glen
Ben Garrisdale	gardr – enclosure
Gleann Debadel	djup-r – deep + dalr – glen
Mi-mheall Dubh	mid-fell + Gael. – black
Mi-mheall Breac	mid-fell + Gael. – speckled
Rainberg Mor	rain mountain + Gael. – big
Rainberg Beag	rain mountain + Gael. – little
Cruib	krjupa – crouch
Liundale	lind – well or spring + dalr – glen
Glen Batrick	beit-ar – pasture + vik – harbour
Scrinadle	skrin – scree

It is a matter of interest that Norse names do not survive for the most prominent features of the island of Jura. Surely the Vikings had their own names for the Paps of Jura, which were a significant sailors' mark over long distances? Perhaps the pre-Norse names simply surfaced again once the Norsemen were gone?

At this point we had better consider two significant fortified sites: Claig Castle and Dùn Chonaill Castle.

CLAIG CASTLE (NR 471626)

Claig Castle (Castel Claidh, Castle of the Trench) is situated at the southern approaches to the Sound of Islay, occupying the flat-topped summit of the small island called Am Fraoch Eilean, or Heather Island. Commanding as it does the two main sea-lanes between the Mull of Kintyre and the southern Hebrides, namely the Sounds of Islay and Jura, the site is one of considerable strategic importance. The Mull itself is plainly visible from the castle on a clear day, while the eastward prospect includes the island of Gigha and much of the Kintyre coast.

There is an excellent description in the *Argyll Inventory*, in which the authors suggest that this building is of late medieval, fifteenth-century construction. The castle is not included in John of Fordun's late fourteenth-century list of island strongholds and has little recorded history. W. H. Murray, on the other hand, says that it was Somerled's chief castle, which he built around 1154 to command the Sound of Islay, and that it was the first castle in the Hebrides built to square Norman design. The *Inventory* states it was used on one occasion as a prison by Angus, son of John II, Lord of the Isles, and also featured briefly in Donald Dubh's unsuccessful rebellion of 1545.

Thomas Pennant visited Jura in 1772, and gives us an account of the castle:

> After dinner walk down to the sound of Ilay, and visit the little island of Fruchlan, near to the shore, and a mile or two from the Eastern entrance. On the top is a ruined tower of square form, with walls nine feet thick; on the West side the rock on which it stands is cut through to a vast depth, forming a foss over which had been the drawbridge. This fortress seemed as if intended to guard the mouth of the sound; and was also the prison where the Macdonalds kept their captives, and in old times was called the castle of Claig.

DÙN CHONAILL CASTLE, GARVELLACHS (NM 6712, 6812)

The island of Dùn Chonaill lies at the north-east end of the Garvellachs group, about midway between Jura and Mull. The site is one of great strategic import- ance, commanding as it does the two main sea routes giving access from the southern Hebrides to Lorn and the Sound of Mull. On a clear day the view from Dùn Chonaill embraces almost the entire southern approaches to the Firth of Lorn, extending from the Ross of Mull to the Gulf of Corryvreckan. Again there is an excellent account in the *Argyll Inventory*.

Dùn Chonaill was probably one of the four castles known to have been held by Ewen (MacDougall) of Lorn from King Hakon of Norway in the middle of the thirteenth century. It is first named in 1343, when David II granted custody of the royal castles of Cairnburgh, Iselborgh and Dùn Chonaill, together with the lands and small islands pertaining to them, to John I, Lord of the Isles. Eleven years later John of Lorn relinquished his own claims to the same castles, and in 1390, Donald, Lord of the Isles, granted to Lachlan MacLean of Duart various lands and castles, including half of the constabulary of the castles of Dùn Chonaill and Dunkerd, together with lands in and near the Garvellachs. Nothing further is heard of Dunkerd, but 'the great castle of Dunqhhonle' is included in a list of castles in the Western Isles compiled at about this time by the chronicler John of Fordun.

Dùn Chonaill continued in the possession of the MacLeans until, about the second quarter of the seventeenth century, when it passed to the Campbell Earls of Argyll, but, although this period is comparatively well documented, the castle has no record of military activity.

AN AROS, GLENGARRISDALE (NR 644969)

There are no identifiable remains of the supposed castle of the MacLeans of Lochbuie that is said to have stood here. Nearby is Clach nan Arm (rock of the weapons), the reputed burial place of those who fell in a battle fought between the MacLeans and the Campbells in 1647.

11

The Lords of the Isles

Alexander III now confirmed Angus Mòr in his kingship, thus suggesting a feudal overlordship without the need to prove it. In 1300 Angus Mòr died, leaving two sons, Alexander, and Angus Òg. Alexander made the mistake of taking the side of Balliol in the wars of the Scottish succession, with the result that his lands became forfeit, and he was himself imprisoned in Dundonald Castle, where he died in 1303. His brother Angus Òg, who succeeded him, was a personal friend of Robert Bruce, and supported him in every way. He sheltered Bruce in his island and mainland castles. He harried English warships with his fleet of nyvaigs, and fought with 1800 men of Islay on the right wing of Bruce's battle array.

A grateful king granted Angus Òg the islands of Mull, Jura, Coll and Tiree, which MacDougall of Lorn had forfeited by supporting the king's enemies.

At the same time Bruce caused consternation by asking the Island and Highland chiefs to show their charters. These charters did not exist. However, after the death of Robert Bruce in 1329, his son, David II, granted charters to Angus Òg's son and successor John MacDonald, Good John of Islay. Angus Òg had died in Islay in 1329 and was buried in Iona.

These charters gave John MacDonald title to Gigha, Scarba, Colonsay, Skye, and Lewis with Harris. John married Amie Macruari of Garmoran, who brought as dowry the islands of Eigg, Rum, the Uists, Eriskay and Barra, together with the mainland territories of Moidart, Knoydart and Morvern. With these titles inherited from his father, John MacDonald now ruled the entire Hebrides.

Further confirmation of various titles includes one of special interest to us. In 1335 Edward Balliol who served as puppet king under Edward III from 1332 to 1356 'granted in heritage to John of Ile for his allegiance the Island of Dure and others for the usual services by land and sea'. Presumably knowing that Balliol's signature was of little value, Edward II confirmed this grant the following year in 1336.

In 1343 King David II granted to Angus, son of John of the Isles – of the Ardnamurchan family – 'the island of Dewre and others, for the usual services', but in the same year the king granted the title again to John, Lord of the Isles.

In 1354 John of Larin, lord of Argyle 'quitclaimed' to John of Yle, Lord of the Isles, certain lands of which the latter had charters from King David II, or from King Robert Bruce, including the castle of Dunconill and the upper part of Duray.

This grant to The Lord of the Isles records for the first time the existence of an 'upper part of Duray', thus establishing the separation of north and south Jura which runs right through the next 500 years.

John of Islay had by this time relinquished the title of King, and assumed that of Lord of the Isles. In 1357 he divorced Amie and made a second marriage to

Margaret, daughter of Robert the Steward, who became King Robert II, the first Stewart King of Scotland.

In 1390, Donald of Ile, Lord of the Isles, granted to Lachlan Makgilleone a number of lands and castles, including half of the constabulary of the castles of Dunconail and Dunkerd, with the island of Garbealeach, the two islands of Garbealan and Scealda, the pennyland of Moylbuyg in Scarba, and the upper part of the lands of Dura. This list adequately describes Dùn Chonaill, with Garbh Eileac and Eileach an Naoimh. Scealda is probably the 'Little Island', from 'sgealb', a splinter, and thus A' Chuli. Mulbuie is in Scarba.

The Hebrides remained a separate kingdom, whose MacDonald princes negotiated treaties with the kings of England, Ireland, France and Scotland. Their vast territories were still further extended when John's grandson, Donald II, acquired the earldom of Ross, including not only Ross but much of Invernessshire. The Lords of the Isles now ruled the entire Atlantic seaboard from Assynt to the Mull of Kintyre, and from Lochaber to Rockall. Regional administration was based on the four centres of Islay, Mull, Skye and Lewis.

The Lords granted land to vassal clans of direct Donald descent and of other name. The principal clans of direct descent were:

Clan Ranald: of Moidart, Arisaig, Morar, Knoydart, the Small Isles, the Uists, Benbecula, Eriskay, Barra.
Clan Donald: of Sleat in Skye and of North Uist
Clan Iain: of Ardnamurchan with lands in Islay, Jura and Mull
Clan Iain: Mhor of Islay.

The principal island clans not having direct male descent from Donald were:

Clan Gillean: of Mull, Coll, Tiree, Luing, Scarba, North Jura, the Isles of the Sea, Morvern and Ardgour.
Clan Leod: of Lewis, Harris, west Skye, Raasay, Glenelg, Gairloch and Assynt.
Clan Neil: of Barra
Clan Neil: of Gigha
Clan MacPhee: of Colonsay
Clan MacKinnon: of central Skye and north Mull
Clan MacQuarie: of Ulva and Gometra

Here again the division is made clear, for Clan Iain has the south and Clan Gillean the north of Jura.

Donald II, Lord of the Isles, died about 1420 and is buried on Iona. His successor was his son Alexander, third Lord of the Isles and second Earl of Ross. The MacDonalds had now acquired so much power that King James I of Scotland felt compelled to try to restrain them. He called all the western chiefs to meet him at Inverness, and as they were entering the hall where they were to meet they were arrested and imprisoned, including not only the Lord of the Isles, but his mother, the Countess of Ross. Alexander was compelled to submit and was imprisoned in Tantallon Castle. The infuriated islesmen took the field under Donald Balloch of Dunnyveg, Islay, and won a victory at Inverlochy in 1431. Alexander was released and confirmed in his titles including the Lordship to

which James added the lordship of Lochaber. Alexander died in his castle at
Dingwall in 1448 and was succeeded by his eldest son John, fourth and last Lord
of the Isles and Earl of Ross. John was involved in several armed insurrections
against the Crown, but ultimately surrendered in the face of an army and a fleet
sent against him by James II. The Earldom of Ross passed to the Crown, and
the influence of the MacDonalds began to diminish.

About 1400 'Dura' was described by John of Fordun as 24 miles long, with
few inhabitants. In 1475 it was forfeited with the other islands by John, the last
Lord of the Isles, but in 1476 it was restored to him by King James III, who in
1478 confirmed the new grant.

John's son was Angus of Islay. He resented the surrender of his lands by his
father and rebelled against his father and against the king. For the first time the
house was divided. Angus attacked his father's fleet and destroyed it at the battle
in the Sound of Mull known as the battle of Bloody Bay. In retaliation, Angus's
young son, a child of three years of age, and later known as Donald Dubh, was
kidnapped from Islay and handed over to the custody of Argyll, who kept the
child, the son of his own daughter, a prisoner for many years. Angus was
assassinated by an Irish harper in 1485. His father lived on until 1498.

Donald Dubh, the legal heir of John, last Lord of the Isles, passed most of
his life as a prisoner.

In 1493, the youthful King of Scots, James IV, now eighteen, gained enough
energy and resources to bring John to trial and to break him. The Lordship was
abolished

In 1494 King James IV made a specific grant of parts of north Jura to John
McGilleon of Lochboye, and this is the first of a number of such records which
appear from the end of the fifteenth century, throughout the sixteenth and into
the early part of the seventeenth centuries.

These various land grants are mostly recorded in The Register of the Great
Seal of Scotland (*Registri Magni Sigilorum*), and they provide the first mention
of individual place-names in Jura and the northern isles. The forms of the names
are variable and often corrupt. Some of these charters will appear in the next
chapter.

Had James IV been more experienced, he might have let the Lordship stand,
shorn of its mainland strength, but strong enough to govern the Hebrides. He
visited the Hebrides in person and granted charters to the chief land-holders,
including members of the Council of the Isles. The king had strength of personality, and displayed a generosity of mind that won allegiance. He was the last
Scots king to speak Gaelic, and he might well have won the islesmen's hearts if
he had not, in a fit of impatience in 1499, thrown away all his gains by granting
the lieutenancy of the Isles to Campbell of Argyll – the one man whom the
Hebridean and Highland chiefs could not accept. James's termination of the
Donald Lordship, followed by his death at Flodden in 1514, left the island chiefs
and their clans without any common head, common policy, or any object of
loyalty. Thereafter it was every chief for himself and for his own clan.

In 1543 Donald Dubh escaped from Edinburgh Castle, and was acclaimed with
enthusiasm in the Isles. The youthful Mary, Queen of Scots had just come to the

throne, and owing to many problems and intrigues was not able to deal with the threat, so that for two years, supported by the English king, Donald was able to defy the government. This situation might have continued had not Donald Dubh died in 1545.

The headship of the Macdonald clans now fell to the House of Islay, Clan Ian Mhoir, of whom James Macdonald of Dunnyveg and the Glens was the chief. James had not taken part in Donald Dubh's rebellion. For one reason, he was married to a daughter of Colin, third Earl of Argyll.

James was elected Lord of the Isles by his clansmen on the death of Donald Dubh, but he made no attempt to back up his title, although he used the designation in a letter to the Privy Council. Although urged by his clansmen to rebel, he remained loyal to the crown. Some years later he went to help his brother Sorley Buy, who was fighting to hold on to estates in Ireland, and was taken prisoner and died there in 1565.

Angus of Islay succeeded his father in the chieftainship of Clan Ian Mhoir, his succession producing one of the longest and fiercest feuds in the history of the Hebrides. This resulted from a dispute over the Rhinns of Islay, but which we must deal with as it involves Jura as well.

At the time of the forfeiture of the Lordship of the Isles, the Crown granted the Rhinns of Islay to Maclean of Duart. Later, while the chief of Duart held that he had these lands direct from the Crown, Macdonald of Dunnyveg claimed that the lands were held under him. For a time Duart did not press his claim, but, when young Lachlan Maclean came of age, he revived it. An agreement was arrived at, and Angus Macdonald of Islay married Lachlan Maclean of Duart's sister.

In 1585, however, the feud broke out with great ferocity. Donald Gorm Macdonald, chief of Sleat, was travelling by sea to visit his cousin Angus of Islay. He ran into head winds and was forced to land on Jura and find shelter. The part of the island they landed on belonged to the Macleans of Duart. While they were there, two of Donald Macdonald's kinsmen landed a little distance away. These two were outlaws and were also his enemies. Their names were Hugh MacGilliespic-chleirich and Alexander Mac-Dhomnuill Herraich, and they had a party of men with them. These men wanted to stir up trouble between Donald Macdonald and the Macleans, so they rounded up some Maclean cattle during the night, and set sail with them when the weather improved. The plan worked out well, for the Macleans immediately blamed Donald Gorm and his men for the theft. Next night, as the men of Sleat were resting at Knockbreck, near Inver on Jura, they were attacked without warning by a large body of Macleans led by their chief Lachlan Mòr. Sixty of the unsuspecting men of Skye were killed. Donald Gorm and a few others escaped because they happened to be asleep aboard their vessel, which was anchored just offshore.

Donald Gorm was enraged by what he considered was a treacherous and unprovoked attack, and returning to Skye he raised his clan and all his other allies. Burnings and killings followed to such an extent that King James IV wrote to Roderick Macleod, chief of Dunvegan, asking him to do everything in his power to help Maclean against Clan Donald. Angus of Islay, as head of the leading clan did his best to make peace between Maclean of Duart, who was his brother-in-law, and Donald Macdonald of Sleat, who was his cousin. He went on a peace mission to Skye, where he stayed some days and then went on to visit Maclean in his castle of Duart. His advisers suggested it would be prudent to send negotiators to Maclean, but Angus was determined to go in person, and on his arrival at the castle with a small party of men, he found himself seized and thrown into the castle dungeon. To save his life and the lives of his men, Angus agreed to renounce his rights to the disputed Rhinns of Islay. He was then set free, but had to leave several hostages, including his brother and his son.

Angus returned to Dunnyveg, and planned revenge. Lachlan Maclean followed shortly after to have a deal about the Rhinns put into effect, and found the tables turned. At a banquet given for him and his men at Mullindry in Islay, he was captured together with eighty-six followers. His men were put to death, and he was only spared as a result of pleading on his behalf by young James of Islay.

Argyll was appointed mediator by the king, and managed to enforce a settlement, but the feud soon broke out again. Macdonald ravished Mull and Tiree, while Maclean plundered Rum, Eigg, Muck and Canna, enlisting a hundred Spanish soldiers from the Armada ship, *Florida*, which had been anchored in Tobermory Bay for some weeks. This ship was later blown up and sunk.

Soon after this, the king promised safe conduct to the chiefs if they would come to Edinburgh for a conference. They were all arrested immediately on their arrival, and released only on their promise to pay arrears of Crown dues. Angus Macdonald had to leave behind his son James as a hostage. He was going to have a long stay in Edinburgh, where he became a favourite at Court, and was knighted by the king.

The freed chieftains, once at liberty again, went back on their promises, were accused of treason and sentenced to forfeit their lands in 1594.

In an attempt to save his lost lands, Angus Macdonald made them over to his son, Sir James. The plan didn't work. The Privy Council, among other things, ordered Angus to keep good order in Jura, Islay and Colonsay. In November 1596, Angus made submission to the King and later went to Edinburgh to receive his pardon and learn the terms on which it was to be granted. These were the evacuation of Kintyre and the Rhinns of Islay, payment of the due arrears to the Crown, and the handing over of Dunnyveg Castle to the king's nominee. Sir James was to remain in Edinburgh as a hostage.

The following year, the king sent Sir James to Islay as an ambassador to his father. He immediately claimed the estates and assumed authority as successor to his father. The trouble between father and son seemed like a good opportunity to Lachlan Maclean of Duart, to raise again the issue of his own claim to the Rhinns of Islay. Sir James was willing for a compromise, but nothing less than complete title would satisfy Maclean.

Uncle and nephew prepared for war, and it came in the fierce and bloody battle of Gruinart Bay on Islay, Traigh Gruinart, in 1598. Lachlan Mòr of Duart arrived in Islay with 600 men. He landed on the tiny Nave Island at the mouth of Gruinart Bay, and leaving 340 on the island, he took the rest of his men to the Bay itself, accompanied by his son, Lachlan Òg. He found Sir James

Macdonald in a strong position behind the hill, and positioned his own men on the hill itself, after driving some Macdonald men off it.

Sir James Macdonald attacked with his men, but was driven back. Lachlan Òg Maclean was wounded, and his father sent him off to Nave Island with a small party of men. In Sir James's second attack, he came face to face with Lachlan Mòr, who came down the hill to meet his nephew.

Lachlan Mòr shouted 'James, son of my sister, get out of my way.' (The Gaelic is recorded: '*A Sheumais, a mhic mo pheathar, fag mo rathad.*')

He had scarcely called out these words when he was struck by an arrow shot by one of Macdonald's men, and fell to the ground. The Macleans were enraged by the fall of their chief and fought on with great fury. Sir James called out his own reserves, and the Macleans were overwhelmed. All but about seven or eight men were killed. According to tradition, the man who killed Lachlan Mòr was known as Dubhsith and was a native of Jura. Some say his name was Buie, but it is likely that the name Dubhsith is a variation of the name McDuffie, now called Macfie. He was short in stature, but a good marksman. William Livingstone, the Islay poet, described him as 'A dwarf hatched by the devil in Lagg in Jura' ('*Troich a ghuir an diabhul anns an Lag an Diura*'.)

On the morning of the fight, Dubhsith had offered his services to Lachlan Mòr of Duart. Maclean told him sharply that he would not disgrace his followers by having such a contemptible creature among his men. Dubhsith immediately went to Sir James Macdonald, who spoke kindly to him, and told him he would be very glad to have his services. Dubhsith was on the look-out all day for Lachlan Maclean, so that he could kill him, and during the fighting as Lachlan bent over, he saw an opening in his armour. Dubhsith took aim at once and loosed an arrow which entered just beneath Maclean's armpit so that he died.

Sir James Macdonald was himself badly wounded at Gruinart, and he was later arrested and taken back to Edinburgh. He was charged with treason and imprisoned in the Castle, from which he made repeated attempts to escape. In this he was spurred on by the knowledge that Argyll was pressing the king constantly to grant him a charter to Macdonald's lands in Islay.

In fact, in 1607 some of Sir James's lands were granted to Argyll. Kintyre and part of Jura were handed over, and from these places the Macdonalds were expelled and replaced by Campbell dependants.

Argyll had already offered to be responsible for the administration of these lands, but it was not until years later that he obtained full possession of the Macdonald lands in Jura. Old Angus Macdonald sold his possessions in Islay to Sir John Campbell of Calder in 1612, shortly before his own death in 1613. In April 1614, Sir James Macdonald in his prison in Edinburgh received word from his younger brother Angus Òg, that a certain Ranald Òg, who claimed to be a natural son of Old Angus of Islay, had surprised and captured the castle of Dunnyveg. When this news reached Angus Òg he sent out the fiery cross calling out his kinsmen to deal with the invaders. It was at this time that Coll MacGillespie Macdonald, best known as Colkitto (from 'ciotach', meaning left-handed), made his appearance in the great epic of the last days of the Macdonalds of Islay. Coll Macdonald was the son of Gillespie Macdonald, of the family of Dunnyveg, and was born in Ireland. After Coll's birth, the mother and child were sent to Colonsay, where Coll was brought up. Nothing was heard of him until 1614. At the time of the capture of Dunnyveg by Ranald Òg, Colkitto happened to be in Islay, and went with a dozen or more men, with the idea of re-taking the castle. In the meantime the Privy Council had ordered Andrew Knox, the Bishop of the Isles, who had been appointed Constable of the castle of Dunnyveg, to obtain its surrender, for which purpose he proceeded to Islay with seventy men. He was accompanied by his son, and by his nephew, the laird of Ranfurlie, as well as by Donald Gorm Macdonald of Sleat. On landing in Islay they found they were attacked by Colkitto, who had got together a force of a hundred men. He seized and destroyed the bishop's boats, and threatened to wipe out the whole of the bishop's party. The bishop was compelled to hand over the laird of Ranfurlie, and his own son Thomas Knox, to Colkitto as hostages, and to guarantee a settlement on Colkitto's own terms, which included the surrender of all Crown rights in Islay.

To prevent the Campbells from having a hand in the affair, Sir James Macdonald, from his prison in Edinburgh, offered to go to Islay, to obtain the surrender of Dunnyveg, and if necessary to hand Coll Macdonald over to the king. His offer was refused.

After the failure of the bishop's expedition, Sir John Campbell of Calder was put under pressure to try to recover the castle. As first he was reluctant to take this on, but eventually he accepted the commission from the Privy Council, and prepared to set sail for Islay. Several hundred soldiers were sent from Ireland to assist him under the command of Sir Oliver Lambert. They arrived in the Sound of Islay, and anchored off Ardfin in Jura. Donald Gigach Macian was the chief of the Macdonalds in Jura, and he kept Angus and Colkitto informed of the movements of the enemy.

Calder immediately laid seige to Dunnyveg, whose defenders soon realised that they would be unable to hold out against such a strong force. Angus asked for a parley, but no agreement was reached. Colkitto urged Angus to hold out for favourable terms, but by evening Angus was forced to surrender unconditionally. Both Angus and Colkitto's wives and families were taken prisoner, but Colkitto managed to escape to sea with a boatload of followers, and sailed north to Skye. There he embarked on a free-booting campaign throughout the Western Isles. With Macdonald kinsmen he raided the Macleod-owned island of St Kilda, killing all the cattle, and only sparing the lives of the inhabitants. He returned south as far as the Firth of Clyde, capturing Irish – as well as Glasgow-owned vessels, so that the name of 'Colkitto's Galley' was one that came to be widely feared.

In the meantime, Sir James Macdonald had learned that Campbell of Calder was plotting to have the death sentence which hung over him, finally carried out. With the help of Macdonald of Keppoch and some others, he managed to escape from his prison in Edinburgh. He crossed the Forth, narrowly escaping recapture, and headed west. Within a month he had joined Colkitto in the island of Eigg. They got together a force of 300 men, and, landing in Islay, they re-captured Dunnyveg. Meanwhile support for Sir James poured in from every quarter. Donald Gigach Macian crossed over from Jura with twenty men, Malcolm Macfie

came from Colonsay with forty men, and many others responded to Sir James'
call.

Sir James was now writing letters to people of influence in the government,
seeking to expose the plottings of the Campbells, and effect a reconciliation with
himself. His letters fell on deaf ears. His plan was to occupy loyal Kintyre, to
which he sent an advance party under the leadership of Donald Gorm Macdonald,
one of his illegitimate sons. He himself crossed over to Jura, and later joined
forces in Kintyre. His army had by now increased to between 700 and 800 men.

Although the Privy Council had pressed the Campbell lairds to call out more
men, the rally to the Argyll forces was poor until the Earl of Argyll returned
from England and took command. Sir James, now in Kintyre, split his army, and
took his half north to meet the Earl of Argyll's force, while Colkitto took the
other half south to meet Calder's army opposite Cara, just north of the island
of Gigha. After some fighting, Colkitto had lost most of his boats, but was still
able to retreat where he took refuge in the fortress on Loch Gorm. Sir James
also found himself unable to cope with Argyll's army, and, retreating south, he
also crossed over to Islay. When the Argyll battle fleet arrived Sir James realised
that further resistance was useless, and he fled to Ireland with Sir James
Macdonald of Keppoch, leaving the rest of his followers to their fate. When
Colkitto saw that the situation was hopeless, he tried to make terms with Argyll,
who was prepared to reach an agreement on condition that Dunnyveg and the
stronghold on Loch Gorm be surrendered, and the remaining rebels be rounded
up. Colkitto accepted the terms and handed over Malcolm Macfie of Colonsay
and nineteen others. The rebellion was over. Malcolm Macfie was pardoned and
released. Coll was given safe conduct to Edinburgh for the purpose of making a
formal submission. He was later pardoned and allowed to return to Colonsay,
where he displaced the Macfies and took over the island.

Sir James Macdonald left Ireland for Spain. He was later pardoned and
returned to London, where he died in 1626. Colkitto himself should have become
chieftain on Sir James' death, as he left no heir, but the clan was so disorganised
that it had almost ceased to exist. Eventually the chieftainship of Clan Macdonald
fell to the Macdonalds of Sleat in Skye.

Stories evidently accumulated around Colkitto, and one famous one was
collected by John Dewar in the middle of the nineteenth century, and deserves
its place here.

COLKITTO AND THE MEN OF CRAIGNISH
Colkitto on one occasion was in Jura with a number of his followers, and was
passing from the south-west of Jura to the west. The son of Fear Chraignish
(Laird of Craignish) and the two sons of Fear Searbhuain (another local chieftain)
were also in Jura at the time with some of their men. At nightfall Colkitto
intended to encamp at Inverneil and he and his men erected huts for shelter; they
also lit a fire and began to prepare a meal. Colkitto while walking near the camp
saw that another party had also built huts, and on approaching the sentry he
asked whose the huts were.

The sentry replied that they belonged to the son of Fear Chraignish and the two sons of Searbhuain, and some of their men. Colkitto replied, 'I had myself intended passing the night here, but since they are here, we shall move on to another place.' and he left the watchman. Colkitto's dog, however, went near to the tent of young Craignish and Craignish's dog rushed out and fought with Colkitto's dog. Coll turned back, and striking the Craignish dog, stopped the fight, and walked away with his own dog.

Young Craignish asked, 'Who was that man who passed?'

'That,' said the watchman, 'was Colkitto who has a party of men along with him.' Young Craignish was angry and nothing would satisfy him but to pursue Coll. The two sons of Searbhuain tried to persuade him to allow Coll to pass, but he would not listen to them. He set off after Coll, and the two sons of Searbhuain followed him with some of their men. They overtook Colkitto at a place called Knockrome, which is near to the sea. Young Craignish made an attack on Coll who at that time was somewhat advanced in years and past the fullness of his strength. Craignish, however, was at the peak of his strength and an able swordsman, and it looked as if Colkitto would be slain. The Jura dwarf, Dubhsith Macillesheanach, was near to Coll, and he was armed with a weapon called the 'stapull crom'.

Colkitto called out to him, 'Dubhsith, have you ever haughed a cow?' (To haugh is to hamstring, or cut the great tendon at the back of the knee.)

Dubhsith swung his weapon out past Coll and aiming a blow at young Craignish, haughed him, whereupon Colkitto killed him outright. Dubhsith followed Coll, keeping close to him, and whenever any foe came near to them Dubhsith killed him, haughing him with his 'stapull crom'.

Mac Fhear Chraignish, and the two sons of Fear Searbhuain, and forty men, were killed in the fight which took place at Knockrome, but Colkitto escaped without injury.

'Stapull crom' is obscure. 'Stapull' is usually a bar or bolt or staple. 'Crom' is curved or bent or crooked. It sounds like a long handled hook or sickle, like the old 'halberd'.

Colkitto was certainly not a man to simply fade away, and he appears one last time before passing out of the Highland story.

The tale centres on his son. Colkitto and his son are easily confused. Colkitto was Coll MacGillespic. His son was Alasdair Colkitto, lieutenant to Montrose in his unsuccessful attempt to win the throne back for the House of Stuart. Alasdair Colkitto was a man of great strength, great stature and great ferocity, who could well have become a great general. He went to join Montrose with a force of 2000 men. He landed in Ardnamurchan, took Mingary and Lochaline castles and advanced through Badenoch to Atholl, where he joined Montrose. The outcome of that meeting was the epic campaign which included the dash to the west through the snows of Lochaber, the destruction of the homelands of the Campbell lairds, including Inverary, the seat of the Earl of Argyll, and finally the near annihilation of the Campbells at the battle of Inverlochy.

In addition to his love of battle, Alasdair Colkitto was driven on by his bitter memories of humiliations suffered by the Macdonalds at the hands of Argyll. His need for revenge was a factor in the downfall of Montrose. After the victory at Kilsyth, Alasdair, with his Irish and his island men withdrew to the west to harry the Campbells still further, and was absent from the field of Philiphaugh, where Montrose met defeat. With Montrose's army broken up, there was little Alasdair Colkitto could do but continue to pillage the already devastated Campbell country, but eventually General Leslie bore down upon him with the Covenanting army, and drove him down into Kintyre. With 300 men he retreated into Dunaverty Castle, but after a siege he was forced to surrender, and the whole garrison, chiefly Macdougalls of Lorn, were put to the sword. Alasdair Colkitto escaped to Ireland where he ended his career a few months later at the battle of Cnocnanos in Cork.

A handful of his followers continued to hold out in Islay, where his father Colkitto, now seventy-seven years of age, defended the castle of Dunnyveg, where he was Constable. It was Colkitto's last fight. Before long Leslie arrived to lay siege to the castle. The defenders were forced to capitulate after a short but stubborn resistance. Terms of surrender were asked, and while the parley was going on Colkitto was imprudent enough to venture out to talk to his old friend Campbell of Dunstaffnage. Argyll, who was present insisted that he be taken prisoner, and the old warrior met his death by hanging. A contemporary account says: 'The final part of the ceremony was performed in the cleft of a rock in the neighbourhood of Dunstaffnage Castle. Across this cleft the murderers placed the mast of Colkitto's own galley, from which he was suspended, and perished, amid their fiendish yells.'

Sir James Turner was adjutant to General David Leslie. He was present, first at the surrender of Dunaverty in Kintyre and the massacre which followed, and second at the surrender of Dunnyveg. In his memoirs he gives a vivid account of Colitto's end, and incidentally a unique and early comment about Jura:

Dunnyveg after a stout resistence, for want of water, came to a parley. I am appointed to treat with one Captain O'Neal and Donald Gorm who came out of the house on the Lieutenant General's word. Life was promised them: all the officers to go where they pleased, the sogers to be transported to France. The articles I saw couched in writing and signed both by Argyll and Leslie. A little scurvy isle in the end of Isla was keeped by a bastard son of Coll Kittock, which we left to its fortune. Before we were masters of Dunnyveg, the old man Coll, coming foolishly out of the house to speak to his old friend the Captain of Dunstaffnage, was surprised and made prisoner, not without some stain to the Lieutenant General's honour. He was afterwards hanged by a jury of Argyll's sheriff deputy, one George Campbell, from whose sentence few are said to have escaped that kind of death. From Isla we boated over to Jura, a horrid ile and a habitation fit for deere and wild beasts, and so from ile to ile till we came to Mull.

Here Maclaine saved his lands, with the loss of his reputation, if he was ever capable of having any. He gave up his strong castle to Lesley, gave his eldest son for a hostage of his fidelity, and which was unchristian baseness in the lowest degree he delivered up fourteen very prettie Irishmen who had been all along faithful to him, to the Lieutenant General who immediately caused hang them all. It was not well done to demand them of Maclaine, but inexcusable ill done of him to betray them. Here I cannot forget one Sir Donald Campbell, a very old man shethed in blood from his very infancy who pressed that the whole clan of Maclaine be put to the sword. For my part I said nothing, for I did not care though he had prevailed in his sute, for the delivery of the Irish had so much irritated me against the whole name.

On reading this account it is easy to see that Sir James Turner was so depressed by all of this that he could see no beauty anywhere, not even in Jura.

Donald Gigach Macian has already been mentioned in connection with Calder's expedition to Dunnyveg. He was at the time the leading Macdonald in Jura. This branch of the Macdonalds, the Macians of Ardnamurchan, held lands in Jura for 150 years. Previous to this, there was no leading representative of the Macdonalds of Islay living in Jura. The prominent local families of that time were the Shaws and the Buies, both of whom were of Macdonald stock. Jura was little more than a hunting ground where the Lords of the Isles and the Macdonalds of Islay could come to hunt deer and wild boar. They had their stewards and foresters, and there were also native people living by crofting and fishing.

The Macians came to live in Jura about 1506. The story goes like this:

King James IV had taken strong measures to try to control the chieftains of the west, granting them new charters for their lands, but reserving to the Crown some of the best fortified castles. One of these was Dunaverty in Kintyre, which was part of the ancient patrimony of the Macdonalds. Sir John Macdonald of Dunnyveg, who was known as Iain Cathanach, was angered by the claim on Dunaverty, and took an expedition to attack it. He stormed the castle, and hanged the king's governor over the wall as the king's ships were sailing by.

The king was not immediately in a position to punish this insult, but soon found someone to take on the job. Macian of Ardnamurchan had a dispute with Iain Cathanach at this time over some land in Sunart. Macian, a man of great ambition with a considerable army at his disposal, was able to trick Iain Cathanach, and took him and his two sons prisoner. He brought them all to Edinburgh where they were condemned for treason and all three were executed. As a reward for his services Macian received from the king a renewal of all charters made in his favour with regards to the lands of Ardnamurchan and Sunart, and with them Dunnyveg in Islay, and in 1506 the king at Edinburgh confirmed to 'John macian, as heir to his grandfather, John vic Allister vic Ian, two merk lands and 6s 8d worth of land in Jura, viz. a large eighth part of Aridscarnula and an eighth part of Knock na seolaman, which he held of the late Donald de Insulas, on account of Sir John's treason.'

Two other sons of Sir John Cathanach, named Alexander and Angus, survived him and fled to Ireland. Macian was given orders to pursue and capture or slay. He returned after a long search and reported failure to the king. He concealed from His Majesty the fact that he had not only succeeded in finding the young men, but had given Alexander his daughter Catherine in marriage.

On the death of James IV at Flodden, and the accession of James V, this

Alexander Cathanach was received back into favour and re-settled his lands. There was much transference of lands and charters at this time, and at the same time the Campbells were exerting every possible pressure to get possession of Macdonald lands. In 1522 it is recorded that Alexander Cathanach entered into a bond of gossipry (a bond of friendship) with Sir John Campbell of Calder, in which he agrees that he and all the branch of Clan Donald that he is descended from are to serve Calder, and to do no harm to the Macians who hold land under Calder. Campbell of Calder also agrees to give Alexander certain lands in Jura for the space of five years.

We have seen that Donald Gighach Macian kept Colkitto informed about the enemy fleet in 1615, but he also took an active part in the fighting. In a letter to Lord Binning on 20 June 1615, Archibald Campbell, son of the Prior of Ardchattan wrote: 'I am certanlie informit be my spie that McFie of Collinsay, Donald Gigache in Jouray, hes gone with the rebels and are earnest transporting their gudis to Ilay.'

On that same day Hector McNeill wrote to Lord Binning:

Two speciall men that held of Argyll befoir ar newlie rebellit with thame, Mcduphe of Collinsay and his haill name, and Donald Gigaich Makean who held Jura of Argyll, those two chiftanes ar gaine with the rebels thriescore and foure and remaines in Kintyre in pairtis neirest Argyll as zit making thair boast and wowing to be at the Tarbert quhilk is nyne myls within Argyll's boundis this night or the morne.

It is not surprising to find these two 'chieftains' joining with Colkitto and Sir James Macdonald. In the first place, Mariota, the daughter of Macian, chief of Ardnamurchan, was married to Macfie of Colonsay, and Macfie had formerly held Colonsay from the Macdonalds of Islay. In the second place, although the Macians for a time held Jura from the Crown, they later held it from the Macdonalds of Islay. Although at the time of the rebellion they 'held' their lands 'of Argyll', they did so under compulsion, and took the first opportunity to assist Sir James.

There is another document which sheds light on this distant period. This is a bond of fostering – an agreement by which a son of a chieftain or person of superior rank was adopted till manhood by a minor family of the same clan or another. This was considered a very high honour and the agreement was upheld as a solemn obligation. The bond in question was entered into by Sir John Campbell of Calder and Neill McNeill of Gigha, it is dated the penultimate day of September 1520, and was drawn up at Camistack, Jura.

One of the witnesses is Angus Alexander Macian:

This indenture made at Camistack in Jura the penult day of September in the year of God, one thousand five hundred and twenty years, the which day and place it is fully appointed accorded and finally ended betwixt honourable men, viz. John Campbell of Calder, Knight on the one part and Neill McNeill of Gigha on the other part in manner form and effect as follows. That is to say that the aforesaid John Calder, Knight, binds and obliges him for to give to

Neill McNeill of Gigha in fostering his second son John, and if that son dies the next son or daughter that the foresaid John has to give to the aforesaid Neill when he desires any of them etc., etc. And for the more security and keeping of all the points above written etc. I the aforesaid Neill McNeill have affixed my proper seal to be set here together with my subscription and my hand upon the pen, year, day and place before written before these witnesses, Duncan Campbell of Inverliver, Angus Alexander Macian, McNachtan Mullerane McNeill and Donald of Lennox with others divers.

Neill McNeill of Geaye with my hand upon the pen

On the fall of Dunnyveg and the rebellion ending, Macfie of Colonsay was among those taken prisoner, conveyed to Edinburgh and afterwards released. Of Donald Gigach Macian of Jura we hear no more, nor of his men of Jura, most if not all of whom would lose their lives either in the fighting or in the executions which took place after the fall of the castles of Dunaverty and Dunnyveg.

III

People and Places

12

Settlements and Communities

The earliest records of places identified with people who were living in Jura's crofting townships come in the Land Charters of the fifteenth and sixteenth centuries. The various places mentioned are not immediately recognisable, but will be interpreted in the 'List of Settlements' which follows.

THE LAND CHARTERS

1 In 1494 King James IV granted anew to John McGilleon of Lochboye 2½ marks of Arlisay and Knockinsawyll in Dowray, and the pennyland of Kilmore in Scarba, together of the extent of 2 marks, one pennyland in Lunga, and other lands, all which were John McGilleon's in heritage, and were held by him of John of Ile, through whose forfeiture they were in the King's hands.

2 In 1496 King James IV granted in heritage to Lachlan Makgilleon, the natural son of Hector Makgilleon of Doward, with remainder to Hector and his heirs, to Hector's brother Donald and his heirs, and to Hector's heirs whomsoever bearing the surname and arms of Makgilleon, certain lands which Hector had resigned, and which were then erected into the barony of Doward, and included Dunconnill with the isles belonging to it, le Mulboy (or Mulroy) in Scarba, and Troeg, Owenegeill, Glennamuk, Ardskalanis, Cammys, Ernystill, and Ardmenys, in Jura.

3 In 1505 James confirmed to John Makkane of Ardnamurchan all grants he had formerly made to him of lands in the island of Durey and elsewhere.

4 In 1506 he granted to the same John 2½ marks in Dievra, namely a great eighth part *(magnam octuam partem)* of Aridscarnula, and an eighth of Knoknaseolaman, which had been held by his grandfather Alexander of the deceased Donald of the Isles lord of Doniewag and Glynis, and were in the King's hands by forfeiture of the deceased John, Lord of the Isles, the son of the deceased Alexander Earl of Ross.

5 In 1510 James IV granted in heritage to Duncan Stewart of Appin the lands of Dowart and others, including five marklands called Ardbanich, Cammis, Terbert, Troagh, Glennamuk, Hvanagell, and Myliroy, of the old extent of ten marks, lying in the island of Dura and sheriffdom of Perth, all which Duncan had acquired from the deceased Lauchlan MakGilleon of Dowart in lieu of a debt of 4500 marks, and redeemable on payment of that sum.

6 In 1536 Royal property in the isles apparently included Jura.

7 In 1534 John Makgilleoune of Lochboy granted to his son Murdoch various

lands, including the 2½ marks of Ardlisay and Knockinsawill in Dorray, and the pennyland of Kylmoyre in Scarba, together extending to two marklands, and one pennyland in the island of Lunga.

8 In 1538 King James V confirmed the above grant.

9 In 1540 the lands of the 1510 grant above, with the castle of Dunchonnaill and its isles, were resigned by Hector Makclane of Dowart, and granted by King James V to his son and heir, Hector Makclane and his male heirs, with the remainder to the heirs of Hector the elder, to his brother Alan and his heirs, to his brother John and his heirs, and to his own heirs whomsoever of the surname and arms of Makclane.

10 In 1542 the same lands were resigned by Murdoc Makgilleoun, and granted anew by King James V to him and his heirs male, in free barony, with remainder to his brother Charles Makgilleoun and his heirs male.

11 In 1615 Hector McCleane of Lochbowie was served heir to his great-grand-father Murdoch in the same lands, then included in the barony of Moy.

12 In 1545 the barony of Bar in North Kintyre, granted to James Makconnyl of Dunnyveyig by Queen Mary, granted anew or confirmed to the same James by Francis and Mary, king and Queen of Scots, in 1558, and granted by the same queen to Archibald the son and apparent heir of James Makconnyll in 1564, included 16s 8d of Ardornell and Knokprovin, 16s 8d of Heryne and Largebrek, 16s 8d of Kilharnadull and Auchichtoyvs, 16s 8d of Knokfelomane, 16s 8d of Crakage, 16s 8d of Sannok, 16s 8d of Achilleik, 16s 8d if Strowne, 16s 8d of Broasdulle, 16s 8d of Ardfin, and 16s 8d of Knokbrak, all in the isle of Jura and sheriffdom of Terbert.

13 About this time, in 1549, Archdeacon Monro was conducting his own visit to Jura, and together with his physical description, assigns to the lands to their landlords, as; part be Clandonald of Kyntyre, pairt be Macgillayne of Douard, pairt be Macgillane of Kinlochbuy, pairt be McDuffithe of Colonsay.

14 In 1616 the lands of Skenan in Jura, formerly belonging to the priory of Oransay as a part of its patrimony, were granted by King James VI to Andrew bishop of the Isles, and with other lands united into the tenandry of Oransay.

15 In 1630 Andrew, Bishop of Rapho and prior of Oransay, granted to Colin Campbell, rector of Craigness, the isles of Ilachinive and Kilbrandan, with the parsonage and vicarage teinds of the same, which belonged to the priory of Oransay. In 1635 Neill, bishop of the Isles to whose bishopric the priory of Oransay was annexed, with the consent of the dean and chapter, confirmed the grant of the bishop of Rapho, and granted also the same lands anew to the same Colin Campbell.

A number of the references in these above documents refer to islands to the north of Jura, and will be covered in a separate chapter. We restrict this study to Jura itself.

There is a considerable degree of unanimity within a good number of documents which mention established settlements, and a core of about twenty of these feature consistently from the late sixteenth century, and throughout the seventeenth and eighteenth centuries. Even the great variety in spellings begins to stabilise, and the names become more recognisable as time passes.

Within this period we encounter the Old Parish Registers – the records kept by Ministers of Baptisms, and Marriage Banns, and occasionally deaths, before the establishment of Statutory Registers of Births, Marriages and Deaths in 1855. Many of these documents have not survived, but in the case of Jura there is a curious 'survival' in the shape of a Record of Baptisms dating from 1704 to 1734. This thirty-year slot records the names of those who were living on the island, and who were having children, and also tells us where they were living.

We pick up various other early clues in the mention of places of residence for people who feature, e.g. in the Trial of the Rev. John McSwine, in 1691, and in the Discipline proceedings of the Presbytery of Kintyre in 1702 and 1707.

The work of the Commissioners of Supply in maintaining roads and ferries also mentions places in Jura in the 1740s.

In due course various mapmakers will mark the names of settlements with ever-increasing accuracy, and in later chapters we will see Pont's map and also Langland's map of 1801 and Thomson's Atlas of 1832.

In the nineteenth century we have an Old Parish Baptismal Record from 1810 to the start of the Statutory Register of 1855. Perhaps most important of all are the Census Records of 1841, 1851, 1861, 1871, 1881 and 1991.

The complete list of settlements is not long, comprising less than sixty different communities, and these will now be set down, with suitable comments. To avoid the need to produce a new set of names for successive centuries, the following list is reasonably comprehensive, and stretches forward to cover to the end of the nineteenth century.

PLACES WHERE PEOPLE HAVE LIVED

Knocbreac (also Cnocbreac) Speckled Hill. Recorded in the 1545 Charter as Knokbrak, this community was the only one of any size on the west coast of Jura. There were six baptisms here in the 1700s, and five houses on the 1841 census, but no entries on the 1851. Local tradition has always said it was 'Cleared', and certainly the ruins are still plain to be seen, but three of the five families were housed elsewhere in Jura by 1851. A fuller comment will be made later. Several North Carolina descendants record Knocbreac as their ancestral home.

Inver, Mouth of the River. By 1830 there was a dwelling here, presumably on the site of the present Inver House. The baptisms of the early nineteenth century showed four families in sequence, three with the surname Buie. Inver, oddly, is not mentioned in the 1841 census, although it appears on the 1851 census, and on each successive one to 1891. The modern house was built initially for an estate owner and survives as such to the present.

Feolin Ferry. The name probably contains the Norse root, 'eyr', shingle, and so gives a meaning the same as that for Feolin Farm. Since Change Houses were

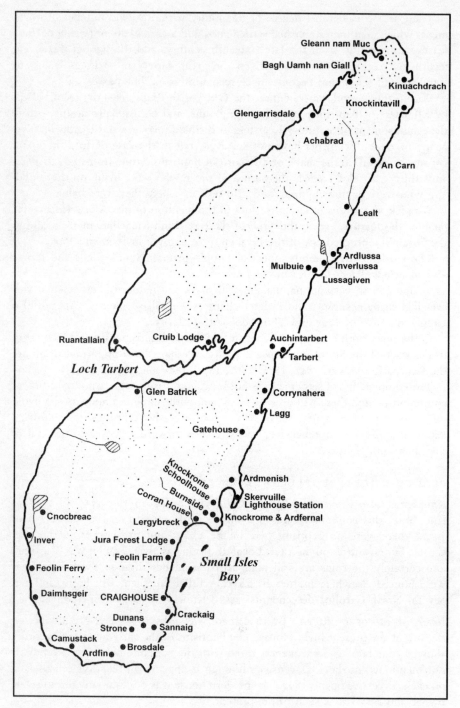

Map 12. The settlements of Jura.

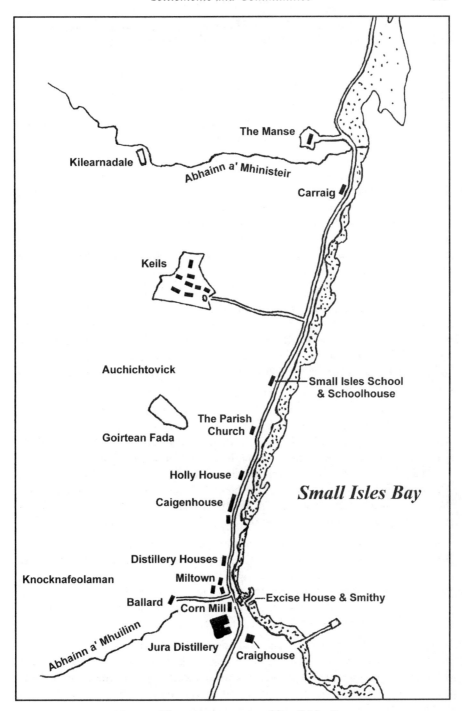

The Manse

Kilearnadale

Abhainn a' Mhinisteir

Carraig

Keils

Auchichtovick

The Parish
Church

Goirtean Fada

Small Isles School
& Schoolhouse

Holly House

Caigenhouse

Small Isles Bay

Distillery Houses

Knocknafeolaman

Miltown

Ballard

Excise House & Smithy

Corn Mill

Abhainn a' Mhuilinn

Jura Distillery

Craighouse

Map 13. The settlements around Small Isles Bay.

established at Craighouse, at Corran House and at Lagg, with the possibility of a final one up at Kinuachdrach, it seems certain that Feolin Ferry was already operating as the first of the string of inns by the time of the early eighteenth-century baptisms. Since no baptisms were recorded at the Ferry, we may consider that the innkeeper and his wife were a settled couple past child-bearing age. The house appears first in 1770, at which time it is spelt as 'Faorinn'. There are three houses in 1840; a farmer and a ferryman live there. There is a dwelling in all the nineteenth-century censuses. One house survives.

Daimhsgeir. Also spelt 'Dainskeir'; 'blunt skerry' or 'rock', often taken to mean Stag Skerry, referring to the fact that deer swim the Sound from Islay and land there, but the Gaelic for this would be Sgeir nan Damh. Daimhsgeir, if Gaelic, would have to mean Skerry of a single stag, which hardly makes sense. It is more likely to come from the Norse, dauf – sker, blunt rock. Appears on a Sasine Roll of 1757. No eighteenth-century baptisms were recorded. There were two cottages on all the censuses of the nineteenth century. A death was recorded from here in 1923. The cottages are now ruined.

Camustack, Bay of the Stone Pillar. There is no mention of this place in the eighteenth-century baptismal roll, but in 1812, Donald McColl and Peggy McPhee had a daughter called Ann at Camustack. It then appears on the 1841 census, when a single house is recorded, and remains on each of the subsequent censuses. The house remains standing today. The lack of earlier comment is very strange since 'Camistack' is the site of a Bond of Fostering in 1520, one of Jura's earliest documents. There are signs of lazy-bed cultivation close to the house.

Ardfin, White Promontory. Ardfin is on the 1545 Charter. When the Campbells of Sannaig built Jura House overlooking the Sound of Islay, the dwellings at Ardfin no doubt found themselves part of the home farm, as they are today. It is not clear whether any of the eighteenth-century foundations survive, but there are many signs nearby of ancient cultivation. Ardfin was a 16s 8d land in 1545. The baptismal register shows sixteen families here during the early 1700s and there were twenty-four baptisms between 1704 and 1734. The 1841 census shows six dwellings in addition to Jura House. Four houses are still inhabitable. (Plate 3)

Brosdale, The Broad Dale. Appears in the 1545 Charter as Broasdulle, and later Broastill, when it was a 16s 8d land. With a striking location overlooking the Sound, Brosdale was typical of so many of Jura's ancient townships. There were twenty-one baptisms in the early 1700s and ten dwellings in the 1841 census , but they were replaced by 'New Brosdale' by 1851. A substantial community, the ruins of both communities can still be seen.

New Brosdale. Between 1841 and 1851 the residents in Brosdale were compulsorily re-housed by the Laird in a newly built township. The transported community continued with ten to twelve dwellings throughout the century. Only the schoolhouse of Cabrach, which served its children, survives today. The last death recorded from New Brosdale was in 1913.

Strone, Nose. Appears in the 1545 Charter as Strowne, when it was a 16s. 8d. land. The baptismal record suggests a small community of several houses in the early eighteenth century but by 1841 Strone was a single house. It remained so throughout the nineteenth century, and still stands today.

Auchivelick (Achaleck, Achadh na lice), Field of the Slabs. Lies just behind Strone. It comes right after 'Strowne' on the 1545 charter as Achilleik, and is a 16s 8d land. This name is often difficult to read in the record, and is easily confusable with another quite similar one. The difficulty arises from the fact that the 1545 land grant confirms lands of Kilharnadull and Auchichtovys. The awkward name in the record would seem to be Auchichtovick. If Kilearnadil and Auchichtovick are close to one another then this may be land on the hillside above Small Isles Bay. There were seven baptisms at Auchivelick in the early 1700s, but there is no evidence of it in the records after 1718, although ruins can still be found today.

Dunans, Fortified Hill. The community of Dunans lies between Strone and Sannaig, close by a small Iron Age fort, or dun, and now within a forest. It appears first as Dunans House in 1815, and then as Dunans in 1822. There are six houses in the nineteenth-century censuses, but the community declined and became deserted by the 1920s. The last death was recorded in 1922. The settlement is now ruined. It produced US emigrants in the nineteenth century, but seems unlikely to have come into existence much before then.

Sannaig, Sand Harbour. An early name, and a 16s 8d land in the 1545 register. In the folklore of the island this was where the McDonald Chieftain of the Island lived, and from where he was dispossessed by Duncan Campbell. The first baillies of Jura called themselves Campbells of Sannaig, and indeed the baptismal register of the early 1700s records the baptism of Duncan, the eldest son of Archibald Campbell and his wife Barbara Campbell, the third of Sannaig, and grandson of Dunacha Maol. There was also a daughter, Janet, at this time. Several baptisms of the time indicate residence. There must have been a least one other dwelling at this time, but by the time of the1841 census there is only a single house. A marriage took place there in 1865. The house is now deserted and the site swallowed up by forestry, but the ruin can still be found.

Crackaig, Crow Harbour. This crofting township appears on the 1545 Charter as a 16s 8d land. Crackaig was a large township in 1841 with fourteen households. There were twenty-four baptisms between 1704 and 1734. The community declined steadily through the nineteenth century to two dwellings in 1891, and only one habitable house survives to the present day.

Trianintorran. This dwelling place is known only from a single reference in the eighteenth-century baptismal register. It was the residence of Donald McPhail and Mor McInnes, who had two daughters there; More in 1706 and Margrat in 1708. The name of the house would mean 'The Three Small Hillocks'. Just north of Crackaig stands a row of small hills called Cnoc Tigh nan Torran ('Hill of the House of the Little Hillocks'). There are possible ruins nearby, and in the absence of any other evidence, this is suggested as the probable site of Trianintorran.

Craighouse (taigh na creag), 'House of the Rock'. This was originally the name of the second change house or inn of Jura, and as such appears on the valuation of 1770. The name has now by custom become used for the entire village around Small Isles Bay. The baptismal record shows two successive innkeepers in the early eighteenth century. Craighouse continued through the nineteenth century as the residence of the publican, and is on every census. It remains the old centre of the modern hotel. (Plate 4)

Knocknafeolaman. This township name is almost forgotten, and to the oldest inhabitants has an air of mystery. It occupied the high ground above the present distillery, and there are many traces of ruins. It appears in the Charter of 1506; on Blaeu's map, and in wadsets leases, contracts and valuations of 1666, 1694, 1751, 1757, 1770. There were twenty-eight baptisms from seventeen families recorded there to residents between 1704 and 1733, which indicates a thriving community. It appears on Langland's map of 1801, and Thomson's Atlas of 1832, where the location approximates to the present Ballard. The last record is of an infant baptism there in 1810. A little later the name of Miltown makes its appearance nearby on the shore below. Even as early as 1716 the miller, John McArthur, is living in Knocknafeolaman, above the mill.

Ballard. There were five houses here on the 1841 census, dwindling to one by 1881. The single house still stands. Presumably Ballard took on the mantle of the declining Knocknafeolaman.

Milltown. Appears first in family records from 1810, and is on the 1841 census with six homes, which persist through the century. This was where the miller, the blacksmith and the exciseman all lived, and some dwellings still survive. Here stands the fine mill, now very dilapidated, and one the shore side of the road the famous 'excise house', portrayed on the well-known Daniell print of 1817. The smithy stood under a lean-to at one end, with a dwelling beneath the excise house, and in due course part of this building became the village store.

Distillery Houses. Jura Distillery was registered in 1810, and workers lived nearby from then on. In 1880 there was an expansion and a manager's house, and two houses for a maltman and cooper appear on the 1881 and 1891 censuses. These are some distance along the shore on the 1897 map, and are still there. In 1901 distilling ceased. A modern distillery now exists nearby.

Caigenhouse (house by the narrow passage up the cliff). This row of cottages appears for the first time in the 1841 census which lists nine dwellings. This number increased to seventeen by 1891. Various 'service occupation folk' lived here along with hand loom weavers, and nearby, the Inspector of Poor. The row is virtually still intact. At one time a number of retired sea captains lived here and Caigenhouse was known as 'Mariners' Row'. (Plate 5)

Holly House. By 1871 a solid stone house was built for the Inspector of Poor. It stands between Caigenhouse and the Parish Church, and seems to have been called Holly House from the start. It still bears the name. Later it housed the Free Kirk Missionary, and then the Doctor. Its last use before becoming a holiday home was as the Local District Council Office.

Church. Beyond Holly House stands the Parish Church, and a little way further north is Small Isles School, with its schoolhouse. The schoolteachers and their family lives are well documented in censuses and baptismal registers.

Auchichtovick. In the 1545 Charter as Auchichtoyvs, and a residence in 1714 and 1720, this is probably also Achachobhais, and possibly 'the field of the oath' in a story which links it with Kilearnadil. Local tradition places it near Keils. There is no record after 1720, and no ruins are known.

Keils (cill, a monk's cell), so kirk or graveyard. The crofting township of Keils appears for the first time as the residence for several families in the early 1700s. By the 1841 census it has twenty dwellings. Although Keils and Kilearnadale overlap in time in the Old Parish Records, and are linked in folk tales of the destruction of Kilearnadil by 'an carrasan', or plague, it seems likely that as Kilearnadil declined, Keils grew. Keils does not appear in any documentation before the baptismal register. One family is there from 1709 to 1717, but the first baptisms of the other five families recorded range from 1716 to 1726, which implies a settlement only just becoming established about that time. There were still seventeen houses in the 1891 census, although only four at the present time. The croft lands are still farmed. Keils was frequently photographed. (Plates 6 and 7)

Kilearnadale (kirk of Earnan's or Fearnan's glen). The community of houses around the graveyard appears in 1545. It is shown as a township on Blaeu's map of 1595 and in Wadsets, Valuations and Contracts on 1666, 1694, 1751, 1757 and 1770. The small community of seven families in the eighteenth-century baptismal register seems to have been dominated by the family McNamoile. They all disappeared before the 1841 census. Indeed, Kilearnadil is not mentioned as a dwelling place after the 1730s. Local tradition recalls that the community was wiped out by plague. There are no family records after 1810. A number of ruins can still be seen around the graveyard.

Carraig. The United Free Church had a short period of vigorous growth in Jura in the early twentieth century. A modest church with a somewhat 'prefabricated' appearance was built at Carraig, behind a substantial stone-built Manse. The venture was short-lived, being overtaken by the Church Union of 1929. The manse became a dwelling house which still survives.

Manse. In the mid eighteenth century a Manse was provided for the Parish Minister, and stood in its own glebe land beside the Minister's Burn. The building did not last long and a new Manse was built in 1840. A succession of Manse families were recorded in censuses and other documents.

Feolin Farm. A confusing name. It seems to be the 'Ernystill' of 1494, the 'Heryne' of 1545, the 'Erine' of 1704, and the 'Feorine' of Langland's map of 1801, while being also 'Feoline' in 1666; 1694 and 1751; 'Fouline' in 1770, and 'Feolin' from 1841 to the present day. The name probably contains the Norse root, 'eyr', 'shingle'. Feolin occurs in every document from 1494. There were eighteen baptisms between 1704 and 1734. It acquired the title 'Farm' in the 1841 census when there were six houses. There were still four in 1891. The main farmhouse survives, and there is one cottage.

Jura Forest Lodge. In 1881 Jura Forest Lodge appeared between Feolin and Lergybreck. The lodge was built by Henry Evans, a noted sportsman of his day, who took a long lease of Jura Forest in 1874.

Lergybreck or *Lergiebreac*. The name comes from 'learg', 'sloping place' + 'breac', 'speckled', so, 'Speckled Pasture Slope.' In a beautiful location overlooking Loch na Mile and Corran Beach this community is mentioned in the 1545 Charter as sharing a 6s 8d land with Heryne. Seven families appear in the eighteenth-century baptismal register. There are nine dwellings in 1841; mostly tenants, but a strong tradition suggests forcible clearance by a rascally estate factor, and by 1891 the old cottages have been pulled down, and new houses occupied by gamekeepers, a gardener and a caretaker for the 'deer forest', were built as part of Henry Evans' estate. Several of these still stand, but only one cottage now remains among the ruins of old Lergybreck.

Corran House (corran, sickle), hook of shingle curving into the sea. Corran House was built as the third Change House or local inn, and appears as a place of residence in 1706. A number of baptisms are recorded from the early eighteenth century. It was valued as a change house in 1770 and appears in all the nineteenth-century censuses. There was evidently a second dwelling nearby known as East Corran House, which probably sheltered only a single family. Latterly Corran became a croft house. It still stands today.

Small Isles Bay. By the early 1700s the baptismal register shows this encircled by communities. At the southern end stands the inn, close to the shore, and ready to serve not only travellers from the ferry, but ships coming into the bay. Nearby is the mill and above it Knocknafeolaman. A little to the north would be Auchichtovick on the hillside, perhaps near to Goirtean Fada, the Long Enclosure. Further along is Keils, and beyond that Kilearnadil, with its burial ground and parish church, although later in the century this would move down to the shore. Still further north are the lands of Erine with Lergiebreac, leading round Loch na Mile to the Corran Strand and Corran House, and to the north, and looking down over the whole scene would stand Knockrome and Ardfernal.

By the early years of the eighteenth century this ring would have housed nearly 200 young adults of child-bearing age, and about the same number of children, not to mention all those who were too young or too mature to appear in the baptismal register. The smithy was at Lergybreac at this time, and one might speculate that its population would support a shop, although there is no mention of a merchant here. Other buildings will appear later, such as distillery, school, excise house, Inspector of Poor, Manse, and the later community of Caigenhouse.

Burnside. The ruin of the SPCK School, called Burnside, can still be see on the left of the road to Knockrome.

Knockrome (cnoc, hill + crom, bent). In the 1545 Charter as a 16s 8d land with Ardfernal, and from then on is then mentioned continuously. There were many baptisms in the eighteenth century. Nineteen families are recorded as having children there in the register. Knockrome was likely the most overpopulated settlement in the island at that time, and remained the largest crofting township in Jura in the nineteenth century, with twenty-three dwellings in 1841. Although only a few houses are still habitable, elderly residents can remember many more within their lifetime. The croft land is still worked by residents. Many former dwellings are now farm sheds. There are many ruins to be seen.

Ardfernal. This is another place with a much debated name: 'aird', in this context, probably means a gravel isthmus, taken together with either, 'fearna', alder tree, or 'stearnal', Arctic tern. Local tradition records a pronunciation which may favour the second, as in 'Arst chyarnal'. Appears first in the 1506 Charter as Aridscarnula, then continously. There were many baptisms in the eighteenth century, and twenty-three houses in 1841 made it one of the largest crofting townships in Jura, although the number of dwellings fell to fourteen by 1851, and was down to eleven by the turn of the century. The land is still farmed, although not by anyone residing in the township There are five houses remaining. Many ruins are still visible. (Plate 8)

Knockrome Schoolhouse.   A school was established for Knockrome as early as 1796, but the schoolhouse does not merit a mention in the census until 1861.

Ardmenish (ard + mjo, narrow + nes, nose). Appears continuously from 1496. A crofting township on good land. There were nineteen baptisms between 1704 and 1734, and six houses in the censuses of the nineteenth century. There is still a habitable house.

Skervuile Lighthouse Station. A light was placed on the dangerous rock in the midst of the Sound of Jura (NR 604713) in 1839. Skervuile, 'Iron Rock', had its present lighthouse built in 1865, and at the same time the massive thick-walled houses were built to be the homes of the three lighthouse keepers and their families.

The lighthouse staff became well integrated into the life of the community, one Galbraith was renowned as an Elder of the Kirk in the 1870s. These families appear in the later censuses. When the Commissioners of Northern Lighthouses closed the buildings after the Second World War, they became holiday homes. Although the lighthouse has long been automatic, the lighthouse station still stands.

Gatehouse. A house appears here first in the 1861 census, and from then on. A long boundary fence stretched from here up to Loch Sgitheig, and doubtless there was an early gate on the road at this point, through which the cattle on their way to Lagg were forced to pass. The single fine house still stands here.

Lagg (hollow). The former name of Lagg was Camus or bay. It appears first in 1496 as Cammys, and continues to the present day. The community contained the next change house, and was also the end of the famous ferry crossing. Hew McCleisich and Doroty McPhetrus had children both in Lagg and in Corran House in the early 1700s, and he may well have been the innkeeper in both places.

There were fourteen families with children in the baptismal register. There were thirteen dwellings in 1841; eleven in 1881 and six in 1891. Lagg was a considerable crofting township, supporting, as well as the ferry, a post office, a school and a local catechist. Nine deaths were recorded from 1945, the last in 1963. Several early houses still survive, including the change house and the post office, and four or five are still habitable. (Plate 9)

Corrynahera (corrie of the boundary). This community makes its appearance in the register with twenty-two baptisms from 1704 onwards, and its nine families imply several dwellings. By 1841 it has just the one house, now dilapidated and deserted, but still standing by the road.

Tarbert (tar, across + bert, carry). Place of portage of vessels from sea to sea. Another ancient name, centred on a Celtic graveyard, and early traditions of Celtic activity. In the 1496 Charter Ardskalanis is given as the old name. By 1510 it is Terbert. From 1534 Tarbert is on every record. The eighteenth-century baptismal register has twenty-nine family entries, and fifty-six baptisms, which makes it the largest population on the island, judged by the numbers in the register. The seven houses on the 1841 census drop to two by 1891. In its greatest days there was a merchant, one Donald Shaw. Several old houses survive. The land is still farmed.

Auchintarbert (field of Tarbert). The ruins of three houses, recorded in the 1751 valuation and occupied throughout the census period of 1841–91 lie on the west of the road at Tarbert. Farther notes appear later.

Ruantallain (rubh an t' Sailean), rock of salt. Recorded as having two houses between 1841–91, but baptisms appear earlier, at least from 1810. This settlement is also noted in more detail later.

Glen Batrick. A holiday home on the west coast, south of Loch Tarbert. The name derives from the name of the glen. There are no baptism or census records.

Cruib Lodge. A bothy on the north shore of Loch Tarbert, near to a former hunting lodge of the Astors. There are no residence records.

Lussagiven (Lussa + dhio-mhaoin, idle). On the sasine roll in 1757 and on to the present. Eight houses made a crofting township between 1841–91 There were baptisms between 1814–34, and deaths are recorded until 1949. Several houses survive.

Upper Lussagiven. Mentioned in the sasine roll in 1757 and on Langland's map 1801. An alternative name, Mulbuie (maol, round hill + buie, yellow), appears on the 1871, 1881 and 1891 censuses with two cottages. A death was recorded here as late as 1908. The ruins lie on the landward side of the road above Lussagiven.

Inverlussa (mouth of Lussa River). In the 1871 census two houses appear at Inverlussa, By 1881 there were five homes here. These were reputedly built to house the workers at the slate quarry, which stands nearby, now in ruins. Oddly, none of the censuses records a single quarrier living here. The slate industry seems to have been of short duration. It had been promoted by Walter McFarlane, who owned Ardlussa for the last quarter of the nineteenth century, but the slate proved to be too brittle, and the quarry failed. The community was durable though, and lasted to modern times.

Ardlussa (ljoss, bright + 'a' river). On every record from the 1494 charter, where it is Ardlisay. There were forty-two baptisms between 1704 and 1734, in twenty-six families. There were three to five houses in the censuses of the nineteenth century. There are several dwellings in use. The fertile land is still farmed Ardlussa House stands in the midst.

Lealt (leth, half + allt, burn), on one side of the Burn. It appears in the sasine record of 1757, and in the baptismal register of 1811 as Lethalt. There are three dwellings in the in 1841 census, going down to one by 1881. It may have been in existence in the 1700s. A death is on record from 1939. One house survives.

An Carn (the cairn). This ruined settlement lies in a commanding situation north of Lealt. Carn is described in detail in a later chapter under 'clearances'.

Knockintavill (cnoc an t-sabhail), barnhill. A possible alternative derivation was from 'samhail', thus 'sorrel hil'l, Barnhill was known as 'Knockintavil' from the 1494 charter till after the 1891 census. The English name has been in use only since the twentieth century. There were eleven families listed in the 1700s baptismal register. By 1841 there were three households, going down to one by 1891. The fine single house is still habitable, and enjoyed fame as George Orwell's residence between 1947 and 1948 when he wrote *Nineteen Eighty–Four*.

Glengarrisdale (gardr, enclosure + dalr, glen). On the remote north-west coast. Two cottages with families appear in the 1891 census, and there is an earlier death record from 1872. There are no baptismal records. Occupied till after the Second World War. There is still a bothy.

Achabrad (achad braghad), field of the neck. On the map of 1801. There were two homes in the census of 1841. The last family record was in 1840, and the community was deserted by 1851. There are no baptismal records. There are some ruins in the valley above Glengarrisdale. The name survives on the 1898 Ordnance Survey map.

Bagh Uamh nan Giall (bay of the cave of hostages). Noted in the Charters of 1494/6 and 1506/10 as Owenegill and Hvanagell. This bay has no known record of human habitation.

Gleann nam Muc (glen of pigs). The same charter records as the last site. As a named human residence this location has also disappeared without trace, although the area is often visited.

Kinuachdrach (ceann, head + uachd, above + troach, ebb), headland above the ebb tide. First mentioned in the 1494 Charter as Troeg, then Troach, and thereafter continuously. In the 1707 Presbytery visit the name is given as 'Cean uachtarach'. There were twenty baptisms and twelve families between 1704 and 1734. It was probably always associated with the ferry crossing to the mainland. There were seven houses in 1841 and five in 1891. Ferrymen were present in the census. Late deaths were recorded from 1943 and 1944. A single house remains today.

13

People to the End of the Seventeenth Century

Who were the people of Jura at the end of the seventeenth century?

Thomas Pennant, writing about his visit in 1776, says: 'the very old clans are the Mac-il-vuys and the Mac-raines.'

Donald Budge wrote of the earliest names and from him we read of Buies, Darrochs, Blacks, Shaws, McCraines, Clarks, MacDougalls, and many others. These names occur in the earliest records, and they also appear in stories from the earliest traditions of the folklore of the island.

SHAW

The first mention of an identifiable individual who came from Jura comes from the battle of Gruinart in Islay, described in detail in a previous chapter. According to tradition, the man who slew Lachlan Mor was known as Dubhsith, and was a native of Jura. It was said that his name was Buie, but it is probably that Dubhsith is a variation of the name McDuffie, now called Macfie.

A man called Duffy Shaw lived in Lagg, and died there in 1858. His proper name was Dubh Seatha, and the 'Dubh' was presumably an abbreviation of Dubhsith. He seems to have claimed kinship with the ancient archer, and in a dispute with a neighbour from Gatehouse, called Lachunn Mor Maclean, brought up the story of the battle, which he himself had missed by about 200 years.

The Jura Shaws appear with a vengeance in the Manuscript of Craignish, where they feature in a clan blood feud with the Campbells of Barrichbeyan. They entered into a Bond of Good Behaviour in 1604. A number of men of Jura are listed in this document as having been 'art and part' in the slaughter of John Dou Campbell: Donald Shaw; Duncan Og; Gillechrist Gillecallum; John Odhar and John Og; also; John Shaw, Gilliecallum his son; Duncan Og his brother's son. A number of others appear by name as having been involved in the killings; John Macdonald Shaw; Neil Macdonald Shaw; Angus Macdunnachie (Vicgillie-chaynich) Shaw, father of Donald Macangus; Neil Macdunnachie Shaw; (these Shaws are called collectively 'Clan Macillehaynich').

From the appearance of the name 'Macdonald' in some of the Shaw names it is tempting to see this clan battle as part of the larger struggle between the Campbells and the Macdonalds, and the Shaws as supporters of the Macdonald side. The probable derivation of this name has been looked at already. Neil Shaw, for many years secretary to An Comunn Gaighealach, always wrote his name as Niall Macillesheathanaich. Inspection will show that only three letters from that fine name survive into English, 's', 'h' and 'a'!

We have already looked at the folk tale of a fight at Knockrome in which

Colkitto was involved, which would also be in the early years of the seventeenth century. The story features another Jura dwarf, now called Dubhsith Macille-sheanach, who crippled Colkitto's opponent. Perhaps the one tradition links to the earlier one at Gruinart.

BUIE

Along with Shaws, in the early stories, are encountered Buies and Darrochs An ancestral member of each family features in a number of old tales. The Darroch is dated as a contemporary of Duncan Campbell, the first of Sannaig, who was living in the middle of the seventeenth century, and by association his opponent Buie comes from the same period.

The name Buie is from the Gaelic 'buidhe' meaning yellow. The name appears in early records as Mac-ille-bhuidhe, the son of the yellow-haired lad. Mac is the Gaelic form of son, while 'ille' is what is left of 'gille', the lad, or servant. This appears still in a number of religious surnames, as, for example, Gilchrist, servant of Christ, and Gillies, 'gill-Iosa', servant of Jesus. We encounter individuals called Buie about the end of the seventeenth century. On their first appearance they are called McIlbhuy, but by 1704 we find they are being written conventionally as Bui, although by the middle of the eighteenth century the final 'e' has made its appearance and the name has taken on its modern form of Buie.

DARROCH

The name Darroch is more puzzling. The ancestral Darroch seems to have been called 'MacIain Riabhach', brindled or grizzled MacIain. The Jura Macdonalds were traditionally believed to be a branch of the family called 'Clann Vic Ian'. Other traditions name the ancestral and villainous Darroch, 'Mac Ille Riabhach', son of the grey-haired lad. By the early years of the eighteenth century Darrochs were numerous, although there seems little agreement about how the name should be spelled.

We find: McIlliroch; McIllirioch; McIliroch; McIliriach; McIlliriach; McIllirach; McIllereich; although by the 1720s the name seems most usually to be written 'McIllirioch'.

In 1733 the name Darroch appeared in the baptismal record as that of a woman called Mary Darroch, and over the next twenty-five years, the form Darroch began to replace McIliriach. Emigrants still went to the United States bearing the name McIliriach in 1754, but not in 1767, when there was one called Jenny Darach (*sic*). A list of tenants in the Inventory of Debts of 1764 shows fourteen families called McIlriach, and only two called Darroch. The process by which the one name changed into the other is very hard to understand, and has produced a great deal of discussion, which will no doubt go on and on.

The problem of a simple shift from the old name to the new centres on the intrusion of the 'd' sound at the beginning of the name Darroch, for 'McIlriach' contains no 'd' sound at all. The Gaelic word for 'colour' is 'dath', and it has been suggested that although the name was apparently usually written as McIlriabhach (the 'bh' in the middle of the word is silent, as about half of all Gaelic sounds seem to be), it may actually have been spoken to include the word for 'colour'. This would give Mac il'an dath riabhach (the son of the lad with the grey hair), and so Dath-riabhach, which in English sounds 'Darrach'. This complicated story also involves the disappearance of another sound, the 'ee' sound which is part of dath-riabhach, which sounds, 'da-ree-ach'. It sounds a very far-fetched explanation, although the idea of 'colour' may have another pedigree, as we will see shortly.

It has often been suggested that since the McIlriachs were actually MacDonalds, and found themselves living under Campbell control, they might have thought it wise to go for a change in name. The story is supposed to go like this: a Jura McIlriach was walking home, aided by his stout oak walking stick, when he suddenly stopped and said, 'Is darach mo bhat agus is Darach mi fhein' (oak is my stick, and from now on Oak shall be my name). The Gaelic word for 'oak' is 'darach'.

Since the shift from the old name does not seem even to begin until 1733, and since the Macdonalds were driven out of the island in the mid 1600s, the need to make changes seems to be coming far too late to be of any real service to the families concerned. In any case, to be of some effect, such a shift would have to be carried out swiftly and by common consent, and the historic reality is of a change which lasted over many, many years. Donald Budge added, I think with his tongue in his cheek, that it would be amusing after all this dispute if 'Darroch' turned out simply to mean 'man of Jura or Dura', being simply 'Durach' shifted by the changing of a vowel and the adding of an extra 'r'. This of course must be a fancy! After much investigation, we may have to face the fact that any real 'explanation' of the loss of 'McIlrioch' and its replacement by 'Darroch', seems likely to be impossible to retrieve after the passage of over 250 years. It may be easiest simply to accept it as something which happened, which local people of the day would have found perfectly natural, and which they could easily have explained.

BLACK

People called Black were until recently known as Mac-ille dhuibh (son of the black-haired lad). There is no reason to think that the Blacks of Jura did not derive their names as directly from the Gaelic as the Buies and Darrochs did. They do seem to have been long native to Jura, having been in Lergiebreac and Sanaig in the distant past, where ancient tradition credits them with having found a gold treasure trove. The Blacks appear in every list of names in the eighteenth and nineteenth centuries, and family representatives continued right on into the twentieth century.

The intrusion of the word for 'colour' in the name Darroch has been mentioned. J. F. Campbell's, *Popular Tales of the West Highlands*, records how a discontented poetess from Mull, with no love of nearby Jura, had a clever and punning satire on the island and its principal families. She said:

The worst lot in the world, and the worst colours on earth are there;
Yellow, black, and grizzled.

In the original Gaelic it goes:

Diu rath an domhain, 'us diu dath an domhain ann,
Buidhe, dubh, 'us riabhach.

The phrase which translates as 'the worst characters', or 'the worst bunch', 'diu rath', sounds exactly like the name Jura. There is a hint in this story of the ancient use of the word 'dath', colour, in association with the ancient names of Jura, as mentioned above.

MACCRAINE

Another surname which seems to have an ancient lineage in Jura is MacCraine. Certainly the story of the longevity of the family, and the history and stories surrounding Gillour MacCraine go back to beyond the visit of Martin Martin in 1694, for he said that Gillour, who lived to a great age, had died about fifty years earlier, i.e. about 1650. He was reputed to have been extremely ancient at the time, so was evidently alive during the sixteenth century. Stories of Gillour will be told in the appropriate place.

There is an interesting theory about the origin of the name. Raghnall, son of Somerled was a twelfth-century hero of the Clan Macdonald, who set it on the path to the Lordship of the Isles. For a Macdonald to call his son Raghnall was to hark back to the great days of grandeur, when the family were at the peak of their power. The genitive and vocative of Raghnall is Raighne. MacRaighne may be the original form of MacCraine and being a Macdonald name it fell in status as the Campbells grew in power. The name could also mean 'son of a sow', 'Mac crain'. This version of the name would be a ribald Campbell jibe at Macdonald rivals. Early versions may have been spelt MacCrainie. Early emigrants to North Carolina certainly spelt their name this way.

THE FRANCISCAN MISSION

It was in 1624 that one of the strangest episodes in the history of Jura took place. It is known as 'The Franciscan Mission', and against all the odds it gives us our first glimpse into the names of some of the people living on the island in the early part of the seventeenth century. The event is described in detail in the chapter on Church History. Suffice it to say at this point that Fathers Hegarty and Ward were involved in secret baptisms and conversions of the residents of Jura.

The Vatican recently released a complete account of this mission, and the published papers give lengthy lists of the names of converts from each of the areas and islands visited. The list for Jura runs to forty-two names. This is more than Hegarty's record of twelve baptisms but less than his list of 102 converts. Since one name, Christina Muireadh, is recorded as 'baptizata', the others are presumably converts. This small list of names predates the first Presbyterian baptismal register in Jura by eighty years, and is our first and only record of the names of ordinary people living in the island in the seventeenth century. Hegarty noted that he had baptised, 'ex eo rudi populo'. The names present an intriguing problem of disentanglement and translation as they are Latinised forms of the Gaelic names in use at the time. Here is the complete list as published:

In Insula Duirod

Daniel Cheoin, insulae dominus
Joannes Coilin
Alexander Cheoin, nobilis
Joannes Giollabuidhe
Maria Muireadh
Donatus Giollabuidhe
Nola Giollabuidhe
Gillatius Mocreadh
Maria Giollasuathnaidh
Severinus Cheoin
Aphrica Cheoin
Daniel Cneill
Aphrica Gobann
Reginalda Cnocoill
Christophorus Lageir
Christina Biocoir
Christina Kay
Maria Canoil
Maria Gabann
Gillatius Kay
Joannes Giollaceir

Columba Dubhuy
Fiacrius Fergusa
Catarina Guaret
Daniel Muireadh
Mora Dubhuy
Catarina Muileachluynn
Columba Baotodh
Christina Muireadh, baptizata
Aphrica Muirioson
Christina Alexandri
Columba Guaret
Columba Gilliosa
Joannes Gillasacbny
Columba Cuynidh
Catarina Cnocoil
Chistian Clery
Catarina Chemuis
Daniel Vosdin
Gillatius Fergusa
Dubfusa Breitnuidh
Daniel Coicside

We will now examine the surnames alphabetically, and suggest some possible modern equivalents:

Alexandri — MacAlastair
Biocoir — MacVicar
Breitnuidh — Mac a Bhreatnaith, Galbraith
Canoil — MacConoil, MacDhomhnuill, MacDonald
Cheoin — MacIain, hence MacDonald.

Note: five instances of the name 'Cheoin' are present including the Island's Chieftain, (Insulae dominus) and Alexander (nobilis) presumably his son.

Cnocoill — This may be another form of MacDonald
Chemuis — MacSheumais, Jamieson
Clery — Mac a Chleirich, Clark
Cneill — MacNeill
Coicside — difficult, possibly MacShithich, Keith
Coilin — MacGille Eathain, MacLean
Cuynidh — MacCoinnich, MacKenzie
Dubhuy — MacDubh shithe, possibly MacPhee, or Black
Fergusa — Ferguson
Giollabuidhe — MacGillebhuidhe, Buie
Giollaceir — Mac Gille chiar, Kerr
Gillasacbny — Gillasacbuy, Gilleasbuig, Gillespie
Gilliosa — Gille Iosa, Servant of Jesus, Gillies
Giollasuathnaidh — MacGilleSheathainich, as previously explained
Gobann/Gabann — Smith
Guaret — MacGuaire, MacQuarrie
Kay — MacKay
Lageir — Kerr, as above

Mocreadh	probably Moireadh, Currie as above
Muileachluyn	probably MacLachlan
Muireadh	MacMhuirich, Currie
Muiriosan	Muirgheasan, Morrison
Vosdin	McVastane, MacMhairtinn, MacMartin
Baotodh	this remains difficult, a further note will follow.

The list thus resolves itself into members of twenty-four families, many of whom bear familiar names. Some appear in the eighteenth-century baptismal register: Black; Buie; Clark; Gillies; McMartin; McNeill; Shaw.

Many others turn up again in the nineteenth century: Currie; Ferguson; Galbraith; Jamieson; Keith; Kerr; MacAlastair; MacKenzie; McLachlan; Morrison. It is not surprising that the name Macdonald did not survive the coming of the Campbells, nor that there should be no one of the name of Campbell on the list. A number of names which later became common in Jura are also absent. There is no mention of McIlirioch, McCraine or McDougald.

One hundred years later in 1724 the Presbytery of Kintyre found on a visit that there were 600 catechisable persons on Jura. We cannot guess what the adult population was in 1624, but surely the forty-two on the Franciscan list must have been less than 10 per cent of the people. It is impossible to say to what extent the list provides a cross-section of the families in the island.

The people recorded bear a variety of Christian names which will also be examined.

Male names:	Daniel, Joannes, Columba, Alexander, Donatus, Gillatius, Severinus, Christophorus, Dubfusa, Fiacrius, Reginalda.
Female names:	Maria, Nola, Aphrica, Christina, Catarina, Mora.

Comments on men's names:

Daniel	a commonly used form of the present Donald.
Joannes	John.
Columba	simply Calum.
Alexander	no comment.
Christophorus	no comment.
Severinus	still a common Italian name. Did Father Hagerty import it from Rome?
Dubfusa	Duffus.
Fiacrius	Fiachraidh was a common Gaelic Christian name.
Gillatius	this is unknown but may be derived from 'gille' (lad).
Donatus	could this be 'given' and hence illegitimate?
Reginalda	This may be a girl's name, the female form of Reginald.

Here amongst the men's names we see little sign of the coming of the most abundant Christian names of the next century. John, Donald and Alexander are here, but there is no sign yet of Neil, Malcolm, Duncan, Archibald, Angus, Alan, Dougald, or Gilbert.

Comments on women's names:

Maria	Mairi or Mary.
Nola	Fionnghal (white shoulders), perhaps later Finwall.
Aphrica	Oighrig, Effrick, Euphemia, Effie.
Christina	Christine.
Catarina	Catherine.
Mora	Mor, later Marion.

It seems strange that the Christian names of the women in the list prefigure the later names of Jura women so closely. The five commonest women's names in the eighteenth century are Catharine, Mary, Mor, Finwall and Christine, with Effie in eighth place. All of these are here in the Franciscan list.

Here then is the complete Vatican list more or less as it would appear today:

In the Island of Jura

Donald MacDonald, Island Chief	Calum Black
John MacLean	Fiachraidh Ferguson
Alexander MacDonald, Chief's son	Catherine MacQuarrie
John Buie	Donald Currie
Mary Currie	Mor Black
Donatus? Buie	Catherine MacLachlan
Flora Buie	Calum *Baotodh?*
Gillatius? Currie	Christine Currie
Mary Shaw	Effie Morrison
Severinus MacDonald	Christine MacAlastair
Effie MacDonald	Calum Smith
Donald MacNeill	Calum Gilies
Effie Smith	John Gillespie
Reginald MacDonald	Calum MacKenzie
Christopher Kerr	Catherine MacDonald
Christine MacVicar	Christine Clark
Christine MacKay	Catherine Jamieson
Mary MacDonald	Donald MacMartin
Mary Smith	*Gillatius?* Ferguson
Gillatius? MacKay	Duffus Galbraith
John Kerr	Donald Keith

Some problem names remain, (in italics above).

Baotodh, has been suggested as 'simpleton' or 'idiot', as in village idiot, from Dwelly. However, the record of the Mission includes long lists from Islay and Colonsay, and there we find other versions of the name: Beotadh; Biatadh; Buatadh. These leave the meaning open, and a continuing puzzle.

Gillatius (sometimes Gillasius), occurs twenty-two times in these records.

Donatus occurs twenty-one times. In the Arran record Donatus occurs as the third son in the chief's family. This throws the suggestion that it might mean 'given', or hence 'illegitimate', into confusion, and suggests instead a common name of the day.

CONCLUSION

Surely it is by strange paths that this record of some of the people of Jura comes down to us and gives us a glimpse of those who lived on the island 375 years ago. Although there was already trouble brewing between the Macdonalds and the Campbells, the 'insulae dominus' in his home at Sanaig can hardly have foretold that he would be driven out of the island, quite possibly within his own lifetime, and certainly in the time of his son Alexander. No doubt he could command the respect and the following of many on the island, and the people on the list must surely have been those who were prepared to follow him away from the infant Reformation, and back to the Church of their ancestors. Each is doubtless marked by a cross on the wall of the King's Cave, and all made the long journey to the remote shore of Loch Tarbert, to be shriven, blessed and reconfirmed by the bold Friars Hegarty and Ward.

Not all the families represented on that day left Jura, for the Buies and Shaws, the Blacks and the Clarks would still be there when the minister of the Reformed Church began again to record the baptism of their children, eighty years later in 1704. What happened to all the others? Did many of these folk, loyal to their chieftain and faithful to their own religion, leave Jura with the Macdonalds, and prefer to try their fortune somewhere away from the dominance of the Campbells? We will never know the answer to these questions, but the author, who lived for twelve years among Buies and Shaws, and Blacks and Keiths, many of whom had Christian names like Effie and John, and Katie and Calum, cannot help but imagine that these distant folk could not have been all that different from those he has known himself.

We must make what use we can of this information, for a complete silence now falls on the inhabitants of Jura, and lasts almost unbroken for seventy-five years to the turn of the century. Only one Jura resident is recorded during this period, and he is the infamous member of the Clark family who assisted Campbell in gaining access to Macdonald's house. His story is told in 'The Coming of the Campbells', where Geit a Chlerich (Clark's acre) was the reward of his treason.

Lachlan MacLean of Lochbuie, complaining in 1697 of mistreatment at the hands of some enemies, mentions three more MacLeans who actually live in the parish of Jura: Hugh MacLean in Ardlussa; John MacLean in Lagg; and Hector MacLean in Scarba.

With these slight records our information about people living on the island at the end of the seventeenth century comes to an end.

14

Coming of the Campbells

It would seem that the Campbells originated in the Kingdom of Strathclyde, and were of high rank. The former name for the Campbells was Clann O'Dhuine from an early ancestor of that name. Duine's son was one Diarmid, hence the popular adoption of the style Clan Diarmid for the Campbells, whose surname is a translation of 'crooked mouth' from another ancestor marked out by that peculiarity.

The first of the name on written record is Gillespie, who was granted lands in Menstrie in 1263, but several generations earlier the clan had become established in Argyll through the marriage with an heiress on Lochaweside, and it was this area that became their base. Initially the family was subordinate to the local dynasties of the MacDougall Lord of Lorn and the MacDonald Lords of the Isles. Sir Colin Campbell was killed in a skirmish with the former in 1294. From him, subsequent chiefs of the clan took the title MacCailean Mor, Son of Great Colin, which is held by the Duke of Argyll today.

The family's support of Robert Bruce brought them a great deal of land and gave them the power base on which to grow, initally at the expense of the MacDougalls and then of the MacDonalds. Indeed it was the Campbells whom the Scottish Crown mainly used to control the power of the Lords of the Isles.

In the mid-fifteenth century the Campbell chiefs moved their headquarters from Innischonnel on Loch Awe to the waters of Loch Fyne at Inverary. In 1470 marriage and a financial deal brought them the prestigious Lordship of Lorn. Their territory continued to expand. Acquisition of Kintyre from the forfeited MacDonalds in 1607 was followed in 1615 by the purchase of Islay by Campbell of Calder or Cawdor. This was probably a disaster for the island of Islay, for Sir John Campbell of Cawdor was reckless in accumulating lands in widely separate parts of the country and found it impossible to manage any of his properties well. The combination of mismanagement and national hardships such as years of grain failure resulted in poverty on Islay, and great financial difficulties for the Campbells. By the end of the seventeenth century matters had deteriorated even further. Famines occurred in Islay and on the mainland, and Scotland herself was generally poor.

We have now set the scene for the involvement of the Campbells in a much less important conquest that of the thinly populated Island of Jura.

This important chapter in the island's history appears to have started when the Earl of Argyll sent across to the Island of Jura, as his baillie, first Ronald Campbell of Barrichbeyan and, at a later date, Duncan Campbell of the House of Lochnell.

The Campbells of Barrichbeyan were connected with Jura for half a century, but, although they were granted wadsets of land, and rights of hunting and

122

forestry, it is doubtful if they ever had a permanent residence on the island. However, the Campbells of Lochnell were determined to take over the island, and added lease to lease until they effectively controlled the whole of Jura with the sole exception of the part at the north called Ardlussa. For nearly 300 years, from the middle of the seventeenth until near the middle of the twentieth century, most of the island was in the possession of this family.

Little is known of the Campbells of Barrichbeyan who became the first Campbell baillies of Jura. They are mentioned in the *Manuscript History of Craignish* where we learn that the Campbells of Barrichbeyan later became the Campbells of Craignish. They were not welcomed in Jura, and there was considerable strife between them and the Shaws of Jura, with whom they were connected by marriage. Donald Campbell of Barrichbeyan had a son called Ronald, who inherited his father's lands, and also gained land as dowry on his marriage to the daughter of the Constable of Inverary. Ronald added considerably to his estates, and received the occupancy of the castle of Craignish from the Earl of Argyll. Ronald of Barrichbeyan had four brothers: John, Archibald, Alexander and George.

The connections with Jura are detailed. The brothers had a sister who owned Maolbuy in Scarba, the island to the north of Jura, and in the Parish. She married one of the Shaws of Jura. Her brother George owned Ballichlavon in Islay, and his daughter married the Rev. John Darroch, the minister of Jura.

The lands in Jura for which Ronald Campbell received wadsets, all passed on to the Campbells of Lochnell when they became the Campbells of Jura. The names of these lands can still be easily recognised today: Knockbreck, Ardfin, Brostill, Strone, Auchaleck, Sannaig, Cracaig, Knocknafeolaman, Kilearnadil, with the isles of Fraocheilean, Islandrish and Glasheilean.

The fight which took place between the Campbells of Barrichbeyan and the Shaws of Jura is recorded in the *Manuscript History of Craignish*:

This Ronald Roy had four brothers: John, who was afterwards killed in Jura by the Macilliheanichs or Shaws of Jura; Archibald Roy; Alexander and George. In resentment for the slaughter of John Dou, for so his brother was named, being black-haired; Ronald encounters a cluster of the Shaws whom he had been long looking for, and in revenge slew in one morning fifteen of them, not sparing the chief of them although at the time married to his own sister, viz. the proprietor of Maolbuy in Scarba, who it seemed by one expression procured his own death; for when he saw the rest of his friends slain, is said to have cried out, 'Ronald, is not little John Dou's death sufficiently paid?'

The other being dipped in rage and blood made answer:

'If not it shall be,' and with the words lends one blow and finished him. A Remission for this slaughter, under the great seal, lies in the house of Craignish. After this action, Ronald, either being afraid of his neighbours, or feigning to be afraid, goes straight to the Earl of Argyll, and told him that his house at Barrichbeyan was no way sufficient to screen him from the nocturnal attempts of his enemies, and therefore entreated him that he might allow him the house of Craignish to live in, and that he would prove as efficient a chamberlain as the present one, whom he dispossessed, which possession his posterity have continued to this day. He had four sons and one daughter: Donald, John, Farquhar, and Archibald, his only daughter called Anna, all of whom in this order.

To avoid further slaughter, and no doubt considering discretion to be the better part of valour, Ronald set about contracting an agreement with the Shaws of Jura, in which both parties bind themselves to good behaviour.

The bond, somewhat abbreviated, runs as follows:

In Craignish on the twenty-first day of February in the year of God 1604.

It is appointed, contracted and finally ended and agreed between the parties underwritten to wit, Ranald Campbell of Barrichbeyan with consent and assent of his germaine brother Alexander, George and Archibald Campbell, and Ewir Macgillespic vic Ewir Bane of Lergonochy, and certain others their kin and friends on the one part, and Donald Shaw, Duncan Og, Gillechrist Gillecalleum, John Odhar and John Og, his germaine brother, also John Shaw, Gilliecallum his son, John Dubh his brother, Donald Og, Gilliecallum his son, Duncan Og his brother's son, on the other part.

In manner form and effect as follows; that is to say that inasmuch as John Dou Campbell, brother germaine to the same Ranald, was slain in the island of Jura by Angus Macdonald of Dunnyveg in the month of July in the year of God 1602, and since it was known that John Macdonald Shaw and Neil Macdonald Shaw were art and part in the slaughter of the same John Dou Campbell, in putting hands upon his body, holding him in hands, and taking his weapon from him, and striking him through the body with his sword and suchlike, manifestly knowing that Angus Macdunnachie Shaw and Neil Macdunnachie Shaw, were art and part in the same slaughter being allied to the same Angus Macdonald of Dunnyveg and committing rape and spoil within the Earl of Argyll's country, through which it chances that the same Ranald Campbell and his compliers to slay the same Angus Macdunnachie (Vicgilliechaynich) Shaw, father to the same Donald Macangus and his said brother, and so to slay the said Neil Macdonald vic dunnachie, brother's son to the said Angus:

Nevertheless both the said parties, because the said Donald Macangus and his brothers germaine, are sisters sons to the said Ranald; and both the said parties think it more necessary and kindly and commodious for their welfare, their familiarity, friendship, kindness and good neighbourhood be observed and kept among them in times to come and not enmity and fellony; Therefore the said parties have remitted and forgiven each other of the same slaughter, and the rancour of their hearts conceived against each other therethrough; the said Ranald Campbell for himself and brethren aforesaid, kind friends and assisters remit the fore names Macillehaynich (Shaw) and their heirs and successors forever, the slaughter of the said John Dou his brother, and all that may be imputed to them therethrough in the law or by the law.

And in like manner the aforesaid Macillehaynich for themselves, their bairns and successors, kind friends and assistants, remit the aforenamed Ranald Campbell, his heirs, brothers and compliers being art and part in the slaughter of the said Angus and Neil and all that may be imputed to them in the law and by the law.

Both the said parties bind and oblige themselves, their heirs and successors to be leal, true, and old friends to each other in all times coming, and to assist each one the other in all their lesum actions, causes and quarrels against all manner of men except the Earl of Argyll, their successors and surnames being excepted by the said Ranald and his aforesaids, and Maclean of Duart and his successors being except by the said Clan Macillehaynich.

And which of the said parties fail in fulfilling their part of this present contract shall pay the sum of 1000 merks to the parties fulfilling and keeping their part thereof.

The cautioners for the Clan Macillehaynich were Donald Campbell of Duntrone, Neil Campbell, Bishop of Argyll, John dow Maclean Vicsorley of Shuna, and Hector of Duart.

The witnesses were Archibald Campbell of Barbreck Craignish, Archibald Campbell Macgillespic Viceane in Kilmory, Donald riach Macdonald in Ardlaraich in Luing, John Macgillechallum viceana veckdonill, Donald Macgilliechreist vic larty, and Gillespic macane gorm vekdoull Craignish. The agreement was signed by Ranald Campbell of Barrichbeyan. The others made their sign through the notary, Dougall McArthur.

After the Campbells of Barrichbeyan, the Campbells of Lochnell arrived, also as baillies. These later became the Campbells of Jura. The situation in Jura at the time of their arrival can be gathered from the Commission given to Duncan Campbell on his appointment. This is dated 2 September 1661 and reads as follows:

To Duncan Campbell.

Loving cousin, You are upon sight hereof to go to Jura and Scarba and receive into your custody the arms, that is the swords, guns, pistols, dirks and other weapons of all and sundry the inhabitants of Tarbert, Camus, Ardlussa, Ardmenish, Knocktavil, Kenuachdrach, in Jura, and the isle of Scarba, and whatever persons, indwellers, tenants, subtenants, and their servants, there on the said lands and islands do surely and carefully make faith that they shall live peacefully and give obedience to the King's Majesty's laws, and in testimony thereof do deliver there arms as said is, and to your custody. You are to protect them in their persons and goods from all injury and prejudices to be done or offered by any person or persons whatsoever, and upon their performance as said is, thus discharging all persons, in commission of fire and sword, or in arms, by virtue of his lordship's commission to trouble or molest the inhabitants of the said lands in their persons and goods.

Fail not to do an exact diligence therein and that you secure the boats of Jura great and small that none of them be serviceable to the rebels now in arms against His Majesty's laws and authority, and that no cattle be ferried out of the said isles before the last of October next, as you will answer to the contrary. This is my advice at the desire of the Earl of Argyll.

Written and subscribed by me this second of September.

(J. H. Calder)

for Duncan Campbell, baillie of Jura

and all others whom it may concern.

It is clear that Duncan Campbell was instructed to take strong measures to pacify the island, and no doubt he carried out his instructions. He was the first of the family of Jura, and was born in 1596. He enjoyed the friendship of his kinsman and chief, whom he accompanied to the Battle of Inverlochy, where the Campbells were so nearly wiped out by Montrose, and at which his brother, the laird of Lochnell was killed.

Duncan Campbell was commonly called Dunacha Maol, or Bald Duncan. The charter chest contains letters to him and to his son John from Montrose, some of them from prison, previous to his death on the scaffold in 1661. In 1666 he received a commission from Archibald, ninth Earl of Argyll, appointing him baillie and chamberlain of the island of Jura, with the right of forestry and other privileges. He became a man of great influence, and came to be regarded as the chieftain of Jura.

There are few records from this early period, but these two survive:

In 1655 'Jura harboured sev'rall fugitives from church censure.'

In 1685 the Jura Baillie was to 'suffer none to reside there without testimonialls from the paroches they lived in.'

Previous to his coming to Jura, Duncan had been factor for the Earl of Argyll in 'Loyng and Netherlorn' and on his arrival in Jura he took up residence in Sannaig in south Jura, which had previously been the home of the MacDonald chiefs of the island.

Local tradition in Jura long treasured the story of the coming of Duncan Campbell, and the tale is recorded here as told by Donald Budge:

> When the power of the Macdonalds of Islay was finally broken and their lands made over to the House of Argyll, the first Campbell, in order to obtain possession of Jura, was obliged to raise smoke from the house in Sannaig, which was the residence of the Jura branch of the Macdonalds.
>
> This had to be accomplished by a certain date. He waited his opportunity, and arriving in Jura, found that Macdonald had gone deer hunting after barricading his house so as to debar entry during his absence. Campbell, being unable to enter, asked the assistance of a Jura man named Clark. Together they climbed up on the thatched roof, and Clark lowered Campbell down the wide chimney in a creel. Campbell thereupon lit a peat fire, and raising the necessary smoke, made his way out by the door.
>
> 'What do you want in payment for this day's work?' asked the new owner of Clark.
>
> 'As much land as I can turn with the cas chrom in a day's work'. [The cas chrom is the long-handled foot-plough of the islands.]
>
> 'You shall have that, my good man,' said Campbell, 'and if you had asked more, you would have got it.'

Macdonald from the hill saw the smoke rising from his home, and knew that his lands were lost. He did not even return to his home, but made straight for Faolin Ferry and left the island never to return. The man Clark received his payment for his day's work as he desired. It can be seen to this day, a small field enclosed by a turf dyke. It is known as Geit a Chleirich, and if he and his descendants had held on to it, no one could have deprived them of it.

Duncan Campbell, his son John, and his grandson Archibald styled themselves, the first, second and third of Sannaig. Dunacha Maol died in 1695 in his ninety-ninth year, and is buried in the family vault in Jura, where the inscription on his gravestone is still clearly legible to this day.

John Campbell, Duncan Campbell's son, succeeded his father, but was evidently actively involved in the affairs of the region during the years of Duncan's great age. John was entrusted with important commissions, not only in Jura but elsewhere, as, for example, in a transaction he was entrusted with on Argyll's behalf in Colonsay.

A letter, dated October 13th 1689: 'Argyll to John Campbell, son of the baillie of Jura. 'He had been informed that the said John Campbell had collected some money and forty cows from the tenants of Colonsay of their rent for 1688, and ordering him to sell the cows to the best avail, 'the loss being always to the tenantis' and to send the money to Edinburgh.

In a more serious vein is the letter he received some years earlier. The Macleans of Duart had forfeited their lands, but although the chief and his son had been killed, other members of the family still struggled to hold on to their lands, which included Coll and Tiree. Argyll and the Crown demanded action, and demanded it from John Campbell. In 1678 John Campbell accompanied the Earl of Argyll in an expedition against the Macleans of Mull, and lost some of his men in a skirmish.

In January, 1679 he received the following:

Commission by Archibald, Earl of Argyll, to Alexander Campbell of Lochnell, to send John Campbell, son of Duncan Campbell, baillie of Jura, with fifty men from those under his command, to the isles of Coll and Tiree, receive the arms of the inhabitants, and give protection to such as should render obedience.

The order is signed 'Argyll', and appended is an order signed by Alexander Campbell to draw out fifty men from the company under his command, with a sergeant and a corporal, and to proceed to the execution of the above Commission.

Ten days later a further order was sent to John Campbell:

Warrant by Archibald, Earl of Argyll, to John Campbell, son of Duncan Campbell, baillie of Jura, to proceed to the house of Moy with six rott [six companies of six men] of men, to take the house and apprehend the person of Lachlan Maclean of Lochbowie and bring him to Duart,

signed Argyll

On 28 July 1679 there came further instructions:

Order by Archibald, Earl of Argyll, to John Campbell, son of the baillie of
Jura, to convey to Duart a kist and two small coffers belonging to Mr Hector,
then lying in the house of Moy.

Signed Argyll

Some light is shed on these events by the fact that Lachlan Maclean of Lochbuie
later complained to the Privy Council about the treatment he had received at the
hands of his son Hector and others:

Complaint by Lachlan Maclean of Lochbuie.

Contrary to all law and order, when the complainer out of affection and
kindness to his son Hector MacLean, his eldest son, and for payment of his
debts had not only secured him in the fee of his whole estate, but put him in
actual possession of most of the same, reserving for an aliment to himself and
family, Glenbar, Mugart, Rosehall, Croagan, Druimtain, etc with the manor
house and castle of Moy at the head of Lochbuie, John Campbell, cousin
germain of Lochnell, Hugh Maclean in Ardlussa, John Maclean in Lagum,
Hector Maclean of Kilmany, Scarba, Campbell of Lochnell, and his said son
Hector MacLean, having combined to ruin and destroy the complainer, and
take from him what he had reserved, they on January 1679, came to the castle
of Moy, all armed with swords, pistols, dirks, hagbuts, etc, with three or four
score men likewise armed in their company, they set upon him and robbed
him of his arms, money, papers, and everything he had with him, and carried
him by force to the castle of Duart, where they kept him prisoner for five or
six months – and entering his house they stole also his whole furniture, char-
ter-chest and papers, and barbarously thrust his wife downstairs and out at
the gate, with the whole family, and discharged her to stay within any part
of the lands or that country. They also took away 500 cows and other cattle,
six-score horses and mares, 1200 sheep and goats, and other goods belonging
to him and his tenants, conform to the inventory produced; and having dispossessed the complainer, they masterfully maintain the possession, and to
prevent him from sheltering there, they put the said Hector, his eldest son, in
possession of the said castle and lands.

Charge having been given to the said Hector Maclean, Hugh Maclean in
Ardlussa, John Maclean in Lagum and Hector Maclean of Kilmany, Scarba,
and none of them compearing, the Lords ordained them to be declared rebels.

We note that John Campbell was not among those who were so declared. Perhaps
the fact that Argyll himself sat on the Privy Council had something to do with
the exclusion of the name of 'the son of the baillie of Jura.'

In 1681 John Campbell was appointed governor of Aros Castle. This had been
the stronghold of the Macleans of Mull, and John was there for at least ten
years. Trouble with the Macleans seems to have continued. There are instructions
dated 1690 signed by Sir Colin Campbell of Ardkinglass, relating to supplies and
equipment for the garrison under the command of John Campbell, governor of

Aros, with instructions as to what action to take against Macleans who have not delivered up their arms or taken the oath of allegiance.

Duncan Campbell's early years as the Baillie of Jura were evidently extremely turbulent and it is hard to get a clear picture of what was happening in the business of the control of the land itself. It is in the year 1683 that we suddenly encounter *Ane Minute of the Rental of the Isle of Jura given up by Duncan Campbell of Sannaik*; a document which gives a clear picture of the various personalities involved in the control of the island. Here we find Duncan Campbell himself, and his son John; the Earl of Argyll and the Laird of Caddell. Here are Colin Campbell, the Baillie of Colonsay, and Hector McLean of Torloisk. Amongst the various tenants is the Rev. John McSween, who we will later meet at length.

Unrest certainly continued to be rife in the Inner Hebrides. No doubt there were still many with a deep allegiance to the Jacobite cause. At any rate the Duke of Argyll raided Jura in August 1689 and arrested men who were apparently unprepared to take the oath of allegiance to King William. It was the following year, in 1690 that another episode occurred in which Jura merits a special mention.

The background is the campaign being waged by King William to secure the kingdom against another period of Catholic government. Reduced to its simplest form, William's attitude to Scotland was a determination that it should not become a recruiting ground for the Jacobites and a second front for Louis XIV. He had little real interest in the problems which the Revolution had brought to the Scots Parliament. If he thought anything at all of the Highlanders it was that they were troublesome savages. Various Scottish statesmen believed that the Highland clans should be forced to submit, and Duncan Forbes of Culloden proposed coercion by threat. He advised the king that nine strong garrisons should be built in the Highlands, the strongest being at the site of Monck's fortress at Inverlochy. Hugh Mackay of Scourie, a Highlander from the west coast of Sutherland had served many years in Holland with the Scots Brigade, and had brought his Scots back to England with William of Orange.

Mackay crushed a Highland uprising by Thomas Buchan and Alexander Cannon, and was given orders by the Privy Council to take the men and supplies he needed and build a new Black Watch garrison at Inverlochy.

Mackay worked quickly. In addition to his advance on the central Highlands, he planned a diversion up the west coast. Captain Thomas Pottinger, commanding the sloops-of-war *Lamb* and *Dartmouth* at Greenock, was ordered to take aboard 600 foot soldiers under Major James Ferguson of the Cameronians and to sail at once for a summer rendezvous with Mackay at Inverlochy. On his way, he and Ferguson were to 'alarm the rebels' coasts, cut their communications with the islanders now in rebellion, and take away or burn all their boats, whether in the isles or along the coasts of the rebels on the firm land.'

Though they were not to make landings without certainty of success, they could help the Argyll Campbells in their assault on the Macleans of Mull. They were to take the surrender of any rebels who submitted, and to give them the full protection of Their Majesties King William and Queen Mary. They were also to behave themselves. 'The said major shall have special care his men be kept under exact discipline both as soldiers and Christians, to hinder cursing and swearing, and all other unchristian and disorderly customs.'

On 14 May 1690 Major Ferguson's expedition sailed from Greenock with materials for the fort at Inverlochy. The squadron consisted of the 32 gun frigate *Dartmouth*, their flagship; the Scots ship *Lamb*; three English warships; four merchantmen; and from 600 to 800 troops.

The squadron set sail and proceeded to raid the islands. Houses, corn and cattle were destroyed. They were at Gigha on 17 May, Cara the following day, and at Colonsay and part of Jura on the 19th.

They sailed on to Mull, and burned areas round Lochbuie and Aros, but the Macleans had gathered 600 men near Duart, and Ferguson, obeying his orders to take no risks, had the Privy Council order Argyll to raise 600 Argyllshire men to join them. Meanwhile the ships dispersed to raid smaller islands.

They visited Coll, where Pottinger took prisoner the episcopalian Dean Fraser of the Isles. They were at Rum, and Eigg on 2 June. There they found only one old man, and, after vainly awaiting the inhabitants submission, visited Canna on the 6th. They then sailed on to Skye. 'Upon some Islands,' wrote Pottinger, 'the soldiers have left scarce a beast nor a Hutt to shelter in.'

Unfortunately three men from the *Dartmouth* were killed in the landing on Skye, and a fourth was caught and hanged. A boat's crew from Eigg who happened to be in Skye were involved and Pottinger and Ferguson decided to have revenge only on Eigg, rather than on the Macdonalds of Skye.

They returned to the island on 12 June. Although the fighting men were still absent, the other inhabitants, apart from a few who had fled on a second-sighted man's deathbed warning, were there, unsuspecting. The troops and sailors burst upon them and committed murders and rapes, unchecked, and even condoned by the commanders. The inhabitants were Catholics, and one of the massacres a Catholic priest described may have happened here: discovering their religion from their rosaries, the soldiers bound people to the stake and slaughtered them.

Surviving logs omit all mention of the massacre, and Pottinger's guilty conscience made him write an extraordinarily hypocritical letter, claiming to have killed only eight Highlanders in the whole campaign so far. 'Those under protection shelters the woman and Children to whom the Souldiers were strictly charged not to molest, either in person or apparrell.' Yet Mackay had strictly forbidden any harming of women and children, even when rigorously laying waste the most defiant rebels' islands, and Pottinger clearly feared exposure. An isolated major atrocity might not be noticed, but a series of them would have been, and, after such a letter, would have blighted Pottinger's career, even outside Scotland.

No exact details of what happened on Jura have survived these accounts, and we cannot be sure how many people were molested or slain, or even if any at all lost their lives. However there may be a remote and strange connection from America. 'Alexander Clark was a man of Jura who emigrated to North Carolina in the early waves of such journeys in the mid-eighteenth century. In the log he kept in his new country he gave some account of his background, and this has survived and been preserved by his descendant, Lt-Colonel Victor Clark of Dallas, as follows:

His ancestors, particularly his grandfather, had suffered much in the wars that had desolated Scotland, and fell heaviest on the Presbyterians. Being constrained to flee for his life, his grandfather took two of his sons and went to Ireland, and saw many trials and sufferings, which were brought to a close by the Battle of the Boyne, that decided the fate of the British dominions. Returning to Scotland after the peace, he sought his family. Leaving the vessel, he ascended a hill that overlooked his residence, and gazed in sadness over the desolation that met his eye. To use his own words: 'but three smokes in all Jura could be seen'.

Not a member of his family could be found to tell the fate of the rest. They had perished in the persecution. He returned to Ireland to find his cup of bitterness, overflowing as it was, made still more bitter by the death of one of his two sons. After some time he returned and spent the rest of his days in Jura, having for his second wife one whose sufferings had been equal to his own. Her infant had been take from her arms, its head severed from its body in her presence, and used by a ruffian, twisting his hand in its hair, to beat the mother on the breast till she was left for dead. Gilbert, the only surviving child by his first wife, returned with his father to Jura, and there lived and reared a family. One of his sons, settled in Cumberland County on the Cape Fear River.

When the author was working in North Carolina he encountered this story, and is ashamed to say that he gave it small credence, not at that time being aware of the 1690 campaign.

No doubt the story has problems of accuracy. The Battle of the Boyne was six weeks after the visit of the fleet to Jura, although it could doubtless take longer than that to rebuild if there was 'nor a Hutt to shelter in'.

However, the accounts of American emigrants often turn out to be based on real events, and perhaps this story should take its place in Jura's history. If so it may be put together with a story collected in Jura in the early years of the twentieth century. The story goes like this:

A sailor from a vessel at anchor at Small Isles Bay, pointing to a ridge behind the church, said to the great-grandfather of one of the Clarks of Keils, 'Is that the Long Rig?'

'It is,' was the reply.

'Are you sure that is the Long Rig?'

'It is, and I've seen that Rig that you could go to your knees in men's blood in it.'

The Long Rig, or Long enclosure (goirtean fada), lies high on the hillside above Small Isles Bay. No doubt the ship bringing Clark back from Ireland would also have put in to this bay, the best and safest anchorage, and even in the seventeenth century one of the centres of population of Jura from which several major settlements could be seen.

Perhaps it was on 14 May 1690 that the Long Rig ran knee deep with blood. Certainly there are no other historical accounts of massacres since the earlier clan battles spoken of previously.

We return to John Campbell, who survived these troubles, as contemporary documents show, for there are some dated 1691 giving accounts of pay due by the Earl of Argyll to John Campbell, governor of Aros, for himself and his ensign, servant, piper, porter, corporal, and twenty soldiers, from November 1690 until September 1691. John Campbell died in 1736. He did not live as long as his father, being only ninety–five years old when he died.

It was during this first quarter of the eighteenth century that the political situation referred to earlier in Islay came to a head. By 1717, Patrick Anderson, managing the estates for Cawdor, could report that there were many troubles with tacksmen and with the cattle plague. In May, he wrote to his father that he

> was grieved to find the place in so dismal a condition. Those that were rich and had great flocks had lost more than the half, and the small tenants are next to beggary. You'll scarce believe me when I tell you that I cannot get so much butter and milk in this place as serve my tea and the muttons are not worth the eating and it's with difficulty we can get as much bread as serves us. I would really have thought it impossible Islay could have been brought to such a low pass, but if it please God to send fair weather I hope what crops they'll have will be good which will in some measure keep the poor people from starving.

Although we have no similar contemporary accounts of neighbouring Jura, we must assume that, when fertile Islay was so hard hit, the comparatively marginal lands of Jura must have suffered the same privation. Two years later things were not much better. 'There was not one cow out of Islay. Not thirty were droveable. There is no money in this country just now.'

Apart from these local difficulties the writing was on the wall elsewhere for young John Campbell of Cawdor. He was apparently in financial embarrassment outside Islay, and his lawyer was soon urging him to sell property to clear some of his debts. In December 1721 he was being hard pressed again, and urged to consider selling off lands especially in Argyll, though not in Islay. In 1722 young John Campbell of Cawdor had entered into some form of financial negotiation with Daniel Campbell of Shawfield, to whom he had written in the following terms:

> I had the favour of your last post by your son. He is gone to Glasgow for a few days, and when he returns I expect to receive the £1500 which your obliging care has furnished me with.
>
> You may be perfectly easy about the people from Islay and Jura. Having gone so far with you, I shall, you may be assured, think myself bound in honour not to make any bargain till you and I meet.
>
> Jura is the door to Islay, and I shall reserve it accordingly.

In dealing with Daniel Campbell of Shawfield, young John Campbell of Cawdor always seems to have been at a disadvantage. He appears to have been trying to negotiate to lease Islay to Daniel Campbell for up to twenty-one years, but his affairs reached the point where he could not resist being bought out.

Desperate for ready cash, and unable to raise any in London, young John

Campbell ignored his lawyers and met Daniel Campbell of Shawfield there. The latter, with the advantage of age, and certainly with more business experience, managed to conclude what was to him a good business deal.

A wadset of Islay in 1723 mentions 'an agreement between the said John and Daniel Campbell, in which Daniel Campbell had advanced and paid John Campbell £6000 and £500 per annum, and John Campbell bound himself to repay the said sum, with interest. For Campbell's security he agreed to deliver a wadset to all his lands for twenty-one years or longer until the £6000 was repaid. He also granted to Shawfield the rights to redeem other wadsets granted in the past on Cawdor property in Islay and Jura.

Three years later, the Islay arrangement had changed in character from a lease to an outright sale. The terms were clear and wholly to the advantage of Campbell of Shawfield:

The disposition follows on a contract of wadset, dated 3 August and 7 October 1723, whereby the said John sold for £6000, with power of redemption, 'all and whole of his lands and estate lying within the islands of Islay, as in the 1614 charter, with the addition of Knockransaill, Ardaright, Ardalisyn, and Ardgarie and Jura'.

'The said Daniel became bound to pay £6000, over and above the previous £6000, as the price of the right of reversion of the said lands, and John thereby renounced the right of redemption and the feu-duty of £200.'

John Campbell retained his Cawdor and Pembroke lands, and went on to enjoy a full parliamentary career before dying in Bath in 1777. Almost the whole of Islay, and a large part of Jura were acquired by Daniel Campbell for not much more than £12,000.

Daniel Campbell of Shawfield and Islay was born about 1670. His mother had Islay connections. In his twenties he went to New England and became a shipowner and merchant. On his return to Scotland he built up an export business with Sweden, exchanging American tobacco for iron ore. He also became involved in the slave trade, became a collector of customs at the new Port Glasgow and one of the early Scottish financiers. In 1702, when just over thirty he was elected to the Scottish Parliament and held the seat for Inverary. He was in favour of the Act of Union in 1707, and continued to sit as Member for Inverary in the United Parliament. Meanwhile he had purchased the Lanarkshire estate of Shawfield on the banks of the Clyde between Glasgow and Rutherglen. He finished building his fine house, Shawfield, in 1711.

In 1725 an increase in the Malt Tax was passed by Parliament, and Campbell voted for it. This tax on ale and beer was so unpopular that the people of Glasgow became enraged about it, with the result that a mob broke into Shawfield and destroyed Campbell's furniture and household effects. Campbell was not in residence, and had removed valuables beforehand, even requesting General Wade's help in anticipation of trouble. However, the civic heads of Glasgow were held responsible, it being suspected that their sympathies were with the mob, and that they did not bother to control them. These dignitaries were seized by General Wade and his soldiers and lodged in the jail at Glasgow Cross, and then sent to Edinburgh under military escort, for trial. Campbell, having applied to

Parliament for compensation, the City of Glasgow was ordered to pay him the sum of £6080, which, with other damages, amounted to £9000. Campbell of Shawfield later admitted that this compensation money later formed part of the price he paid to Calder for Islay and Jura.

Campbell of Shawfield was now the outright owner of much of Jura, and the various wadsets held by the Baillies of Sannaig from Campbell of Cawdor now passed to him. This situation, however, did not last long. We may well suspect that he was less interested in Jura than in Islay, where he and his family had ample opportunity to embark on various improvements, and sixteen years later he sold most of his Jura land to the Campbells of Sannaig.

We conclude with a brief account of the generations of the Campbells of Jura as they serve to give us a time-line through the next centuries:

Duncan Campbell, first of Sannaig.   b. 1596, d. 1695
John Campbell, second of Sannaig, his son.   b. 1641, d. 1736
Archibald Campbell, third of Sannaig.   d. 1764

Archibald Campbell succeeded his father in 1736, inheriting his wadsets, baillery and forestry in Jura. In 1739 he purchased the fee simple, or outright ownership of all the lands in Jura owned by Campbell of Shawfield, with the exception of Tarbert and Ardmenish. After this purchase the Campbells of Sannaig came to be called the Campbells of Jura.

It was during the time of Archibald Campbell that his younger brother Duncan wrote an interesting letter which has survived:

Memorial for Duncan Campbell, Younger of Jura. Anent Smuggling.

The Isle of Jura in the shire of Argyle lyes near the western Ocean, Ships coming to Britain from the West Indies, Sweden, Denmark, Norway, etc, frequently put in at the Harbours of Whitefarland, McDougall's Bay, Small Isles and Dalyaile (Lowlandman's Bay) of Jura, sometimes to the Number of Twentie at a time, it being the first good harbour they can put into.

This repair of Shiping [sic] occasions much smuggling to the defrauding of the Revenue from Ireland, Isle of Man, etc. which can be sufficiently attested by Colin Campbell, Commander of one of his Majesty's Yachts, and Andrew Crawford, Commander of his Majesty's wherry of Greenock, who have frequently made seizures, in and about this Island, as well as by several others if necessary.

It would therefore be greatly to the benefit of the Revenue, that a fitt person was appointed properly authorised to prevent these practices.

The Memorialist, who's father has a property in that Island, to whom the Harbours thereanent belong, who resides in it, and who with great conveniency to himself and advantage to the Revenue, could easily occupy that office is humbly suggested as a fitt person to occupy it. [The word used here twice is not 'occupy', but is difficult to read; it looks most like 'accente', which might be an archaic form.]

The Memorialist has only further to observe that he is the only young man of any character in the shire of Argyle, who has not been taken notice of, and honour'd with some publick office, altho' he has to say that he and his predecessors, have always behaved loyally. In the 1745 His father and he did their utmost service to his late Majesty. They brought considerable numbers of able-bodied Highlanders, mostly their own Tenants in the Island of Jura – Volunteers to the Town of Inverary, for the service of the Government, over and above the quota furnished by the shire, whereof as Heretors they also bore their part, and these Volunteers cost a considerable expence to the Memorialist's father, of which he was never reimbursed.

These facts if necessary can be attested by all the Gentlemen of Argyleshire.

This letter contains the only reference known which relates to the involvement of people of Jura in the '45.

Since military service is mentioned, it can be noted here that a document exists which gives a list of the men available for military service in Jura in 1799. This is entitled: 'List of men in the Parish of Jura liable to be balloted', and comes from 'The Minute Book of the General Court of Lieutenancy of Argyll, 25th October, 1799'.

Those named number only twenty-two individuals, and their names will appear later.

To resume the list of the Campbells of Jura:

Archibald Campbell, fourth of Jura. b. 1744, d. 1835

He added to his estates by purchasing Tarbert in 1794; Ardmenish in 1800; Kenuachdrach in 1801; from Campbell of Shawfield, and Craignish, Scarba and the Garvellochs from the Duke of Argyll.

James Campbell, fifth of Jura. d. 1838
    Son of the above

Colin Campbell, sixth of Jura. b. 1772, d. 1848
    Brother of James

Archibald Campbell, seventh of Jura. b. 1808, d. 1851
    Son of the above. An advocate, and laird of Jura for only three years.

Richard Dennistoun Campbell, eighth of Jura. d. 1878
    Brother of Archibald. He sold the estate of Craignish, and eased rents
    at a time of hardship.

James Campbell, ninth of Jura. b. 1818, d. 1901
    Brother of Richard.

Colin Campbell, tenth of Jura. b. 1851, d. 1933
    Son of James. Married in 1876, Frances Monteath Sidey.

Charles Graham Campbell, eleventh of Jura. b. 1880, d. 1971
It was Charles Campbell, who, finding the estate a heavy liability, sold
    his part of the island in 1938.

The chapter was a long one, lasting nearly 300 years.

15

North Jura

When the Campbells came to Jura they found that the northern part of the island was in the possession of the Macleans of Duart and Lochbuie. Their chief stronghold was the castle of Aros at Glengarrisdale on the north-west coast, of which today nothing remains. The Macleans obtained the upper half of Jura when John, first Lord of the Isles, gave it in marriage to Lachlan Lubanach Maclean on the occasion of his marriage to his daughter Mary.

In due course two septs of the Macleans divided the north of Jura between them. The account of an early battle told in the *Manuscript of Craignish* seems to predate this separation since the Macleans of east and west coasts are treated as one group by their enemies. The story will be told here.

THE MEN OF LOCHBUIE AND THE MEN OF CRAIGNISH

The Macleans of Lochbuie possessed the northern end of the island of Jura. They were in the habit of raiding Craignish and carrying away spoil. They carried away cattle and at times went to Craignish at the time of the ripening corn. They destroyed the crops and carried away corn to Jura in sacks, to be used for their own planting.

Campbell of Craignish sent messages to the Macleans to cease from their plundering, and that if they did not cease, the men of Craignish would raid their land in return. The Macleans paid no heed but continued to raid Craignish as before.

A party of men of Craignish crossed over to Jura and they and the Macleans fought at a place called Cnaimhe Dubha (Black Bones), near to Barnhill, about five miles from the Macleans' castle at Aros. On that occasion the Craignish men were defeated, but they came back again in their war galleys or birlinns, to resume the fighting in Jura. The day was misty and although the Macleans had posted watchmen, the Craignish men were able to pass unperceived. A man who was tethering a horse was the first to meet them. It was believed at that time of those who were going to carry out revenge or some deed of daring, that unless they slew the first enemy who met them, their venture would fail, so they killed the man, although he had done them no harm.

They came upon another man in a bay near to Ardlussa, and him they bound hand and foot, and left him. It was a deserted places and infested with midges, and it is said that the bites of the midges caused his death. The spot was ever afterwards called Camus na Meanbh chuileig (Bay of Midges). The Craignish men returned again to the house of the watchman, but his wife happened to see them coming, and she hid her husband in a secret place, and although they searched for him they failed to find him. They continued on their way to Glengarrisdale to surprise the Macleans at Aros Castle. When the Craignish men had departed, the watchman said to his wife, 'I fear that these Craignish men will come upon my kinsmen unawares, I must try to slip past them and give warning to my companions at Gengarrisdale'. He set off, but was detected by the men of Craignish, who immediately killed him and continued their journey.

The Macleans and some of the Macfies of Colonsay had been competing in putting the weight, and had their weapons at some distance from them, piled together at a spot which was afterwards called Clach nan arm (Rock of the Weapons). They themselves were resting after their efforts on a hillock nearby, little suspecting that their enemies were anywhere near.

Their womenfolk were on the shore gathering shellfish, and seeing the approach of the enemy tried to warn their menfolk by calling to them to beware. The Macleans, not being able to see the approach of the men of Craignish, did not understand the cries of the women, and thinking that they were just being playful, laughed at their efforts to warn them.

Finally the enemy came in sight, which seeing, the Macleans ran to lift up their weapons, but the men of Craignish intercepted them and fought and slew them.

There were twenty men between the Macleans and Macfies and of these the Craignish men killed eighteen upon the field. One of the Macleans swam to sea, toward a small island in the Sound of Corryvreckan, and escaped. One of the Macfies swam across the bay which was there, and got ashore near to a cave which he entered. He was seen, however, by the Craignish men who followed him and killed him. That cave is now called Uamh mhic a phi (Macfie's Cave). His body was never buried and his bones were to be seen for a long time after.

It was the man who escaped by swimming to the small island in the Corryvreckan, who afterwards made his way to Mull, and told the tale of the disaster.

The following story was recorded by Donald Budge, and is one of his 'John Dewar' tales.

According to the records of 1603, Duart held various lands in Jura. Using their contemporary names these were: Kinuachdrach, Ruantallain, Glen na Muc, Tarbert, Lagg and as far south as Ardmenish. According to the same records for 1615, Lochbuie held in the name of Hector Maclean, male heir of Murdoch of Lochbuie, the two and a half merk lands of Ardlussa and Barnhill. These records indicate the way in which the Duart lands surrounded the Lochbuie lands, and restricted the Campbell lands very much to the southern part of the island.

Following upon their success in gaining the lands of the Macdonalds of Islay, the Earls of Argyll were anxious to oust the Macleans of Duart and Lochbuie from their lands, and acquire them themselves. The Macleans had always been loyal to the exiled Stuarts, and it was this loyalty which brought about their downfall. They fought at Inverkeithing in 1652; they fought under Dundee at Killiecrankie in 1689. As we have already seen, the Campbells had government warrant to make war on them at the beginning of the seventeenth century. However, their ultimate success came through finance rather than by force of arms.

The Maclean chiefs had incurred heavy expenditure in maintaining large numbers of fighting men, and this resulted in their being burdened with heavy debt. Argyll took the opportunity of purchasing the debts of the Macleans, which debt, when assessed by Argyll some years later, amounted to almost fabulous sums. Argyll proceeded to press the Macleans for payments which were impossible for them to meet. In the end the Macleans lost practically their whole estates to the Argylls. The forfeited property of the chief of Maclean enabled Archibald Campbell, first Duke of Argyll to add to his other honours the title of 'Lord of Mull, Morvern, and Tiree'. Almost too insignificant to be mention was his acquisition of much of the northern part of Jura.

All this seems to indicate a bloodless coup, but the change over to the possession of the house of Argyll did not take place without strife and bloodshed. Here are two examples:

> On 27 July 1620, Hector McNeill of Taynish made complaint to the Privy Council that he had been employed by the friends of the House of Argyll, who were acting for the young Lord Lorn, to plant the Isle of Jura with good tenants and see them suitably settled; that he was interrupted in the work by Charles Maclean, brother of Hector Maclean of Duart, who came to the island with a number of mastiff dogs, chased away the cattle and terrified the new tenants, and that the said Charles Maclean had threatened to return with a large force.

For this Hector Og and Charles his brother were both proclaimed rebels.

An abridged account from the Acts of Parliaments of Scotland records a second instance:

> Act and Decreet in favours of Murdo MacLean of Lochbowie against John McAllaster Roy alias Campbell & others:

> Anent the criminal libel summons raised and pursued before our Sovereign Lord and Estates of Parliament at the instance of Murdoch MacLean of Lochbuy, and Lachlan MacLean of Kachellie, against John McAllaster Roy alias Campbell, baillie of Colonsay, Neill McAllaster vic Fatrick alias Campbell of Torrobase in Ila, Malcolm McInroy in Corronbeg in Craignish,' and others, 'the said defenders, with guns, swords, bows, dorlocks, culverins, pistols and other weapons invasive, came under silence and cloud of night to the lands of Glengarrisdale in Jura, belonging and pertaining to the said Murdoch MacLean of Lochbuy, and there in the year of God 1647 and on one or other months of the same year, the said defenders most cruelly and barbarously murdered John McGilliechallum vic Donnalduy, John McCharles vic Alaster, Donald McAngus vic Ean, Donald McGilliechallum vic Comall, John McKnelduy & Donald McKenlduy, tenants and servants to the said Murdoch MacLean, all living quietly and peaceably at their own homes exercising their lawful calling and vocations, – and the said defenders having been lawfully summoned to this Court action, and not compearing, – the King's Majesty with consent of the said Estates of Parliament, finds, declares, and adjudges the aforesaid persons, defenders, to be fugitives and rebels against our Sovereign Lord's laws and authority, – and ordains them to be declared rebels and put to the horn and all their moveable goods to be escheated and inbrought to His Majesty's use.

It seems clear that in those days it could not be taken for granted that you could live quietly and peaceably in your own home – not at any rate in the north of Jura.

The properties of the Duart Macleans in due course passed into the possession of Campbell of Shawfield, and it was thus that Archibald Campbell, fourth of Jura was able to purchase them between 1794 and 1801. From this time on the Campbells of Jura owned the entire island together with the northern isles of the Parish, with only the enclave of Barnhill and Ardlussa remaining outside their holdings. The Macleans of Lochbuie, however, fared better in their long struggle with the Campbells, and were able by compromise to hold on to their Jura lands until they were able to finally part with them by the peaceful way of sale and purchase. Accordingly, in 1737, Donald McNeill of Colonsay, son of Malcolm, first of Colonsay, bought the estate of Ardlussa from John Maclaine of Lochbuie. An abstract of the Minute of Sale is dated 11 January and records the sale between:

> John Maclaine of Lochbuy and Donald McNeill of Colonsay, whereby said John Maclaine of Lochbuy dispones to the said Donald McNeill the two merk land of of old extent of Ardlussa, and the two merk land of old extent of Knockintaull (Barnhill), with salmon fishings, etc. in the parish of Killearndill in Jura. Donald McNeill of Colonsay binds himself to pay the sum of 26,000 merks Scots as the price of the above subjects.

As a result Ardlussa was McNeill property for a century and a half.

As we did in the case of the Campbell lands we will follow the ownership of the northern part of the island to recent times.

About 1773, on the death of Donald McNeill, Colonsay and Ardlussa passed to his son Archibald, who, having no heir, sold Colonsay and Ardlussa in 1805 to his cousin John McNeill, tacksman of Oransay. John McNeill sold the estates to his son Captain Alexander McNeill, who also acquired the island of Gigha through his wife. In 1846 Captain McNeill sold Colonsay to his brother Duncan for the sum of £39,980.

Captain McNeill, his wife and two daughters were drowned with the loss of the Liverpool steamer *Orion* in 1850. His son, John Carstairs McNeill had a limited succession to Ardlussa as a result of debts on the estate. The trustees found it a heavy liability. It was tried as a sheep farm, but made no profit, it was equally unsuccessful as a deer forest, and was then re-stocked with sheep.

In 1874 Ardlussa was sold to Mr Walter Macfarlane, who ran the estate as a sheep farm. He also opened up and worked a slate quarry at Inverlussa, for which that community's present houses were built. The slate was found to be of poor quality and production ceased.

In 1902 Mr Macfarlane sold the estate to Mr Alexander Crossman, and in 1913 he purchased the farm of Kinuachdrach from Campbell of Jura. This finally brought all the land north of Loch Tarbert under one ownership. Mr Crossman made many improvements, and the stone bridge over the River Lussa is named after him.

In 1919 Lord Astor bought the entire estate and also purchased from Colin

Campbell of Jura the estate of Tarbert, which includes Corrienahera, Lagg, Gatehouse, Ardmenish, Ardfernal, Knockrome, and part of Jura Forest – in fact, the whole island as far south as the Corran River.

In 1928, Mr Hargreaves-Brown purchased the Ardlussa estate from Lord Astor. This transaction produced the final arrangement of land ownership which obtained in Jura up to the Second World War.

IV

Early Visitors

16

Accounts by Visitors

The three Statistical Accounts of Jura were written, as was commonly the case, by the resident Parish Minister of the day. The first comes from 1794 by the Rev. Francis Stewart; the second from 1845 by the Rev. Alexander Kennedy, and the third from 1955 by the Rev. Donald Budge. These three ministers appear to have been the only residents in Jura ever to have written any account of the island, and their views take on an appropriate importance in consequence.

All the other descriptions of the Parish we have come from the writings of various historical visitors, and in this chapter we will review the contributions of the early visitors to our knowledge of the island as it was, and try to assess their relevance to this entire study. *The First Statistical Account* will be included.

The principal historic accounts of Jura are as follows:

1549	Dean Monro, *Western Isles of Scotland and Genealogies of the Clans*
1694	Martin Martin, *A Description of the Western Islands of Scotland*
1764	The Rev. Dr John Walker, *Report on the Hebrides*
1774	Robert Jameson, *Mineralogy of the Scottish Isles*
1776	Thomas Pennant, *A Voyage to the Hebrides*
1794	The Rev. Francis Stewart, *First Statistical Account*
1818	William A. Daniell, *A Voyage around Great Britain*

DEAN MONRO

The first account comes from Archdeacon Donald Monro, otherwise known as 'High Dean of the Isles'. He was Parson of Kiltearn, but was transferred to Lymlair on account of 'his ignorance of the Gaelic'. His *Western Isles of Scotland and Genealogies of the Clans*, dates from 1549, and predates the writing of Martin Martin, Jura's next literary visitor by almost 150 years. It thus gives a unique glimpse of the island in the mid-sixteenth century, and since it is quite short, it appears here in full with a suggested translation. The text used by R. W. Monro is reprinted, with variants in the British Museum manuscript given in italics:

Narrest that Ile layis Diuray ane uther fine forrest for deiris, inhabite and manurit at the coist side, part be Clandonald of Kintyre, part be M^cgillane of Doward part be M^cgillane of Loche of Boy, and part be M^cdufifithe of Collinsay, and Ile of twenty-four mile of lenth, lyand from the south-west to the north-eist twelve mile of sea from Gighay above-written, and ane myle from Ila quhairin thair is two lochis meittand utheris throw the mid-ile of salt water to the length of half myle. And all the deiris of the west part of the forrest will be callit be tynchells to that narrow entres, and the next day callit west again be tynchells throw the said narrow entres, and infinit deir slain there. Part of small woods in it. This Ile, as the Ancients alledges, sould be called Deray,

143

taking the name from the deiries in norn leid, quhilk hes given it that name in ault tymes ago. In this Ile their is two gudes Raidis and safety for schippis; the ane callit Lubnalenray (Lubnaleirey), the uther Lochcerbart (Loche Terbart). Foiranent uther is the greatest hills thairin (are chieflie) Ben quheillis, Ben senta corben, Ben noir (Ben cheilis, Bin senta, Corben, Ben an noyre), in Ardlayfasay, Ane chapell sumtyme the paroche kirk Kilernadill. The watter of Laxay their, the water of Udergane, the watcr of Glengargaster, the water of Knokbrek and ill caray avin villi. (Knockbraich, Lindill, Caray, Auanbilley.) All this wateris salmond slane on thame. This Ile is full of noble Cows with certain fresche water Lochis nocht mekle of profeit.

Narrest this Ile be twa myle lyis ane Ile callit Scarbay. Betwixt thir two Ilis thair runs ane stream above the power of all sailing and rowing with infinite dangeris callit Arey brekan. (Corybrekkan) This stream is eight myle lang, quhilk may not be hantit but be certain tydes. This Scarbay is four myle land from the west to the eist, ane myle braid, and heich Roche Ile inhabite and manurit with some woods in it.

Translation with notes:

Nearest that Isle[1] lies Jura, another fine forest for deer, inhabited and manured at the coast side. Part is held by Clandonald of Kintyre.[2] Part by MacGillan of Duart; Part by MacGillan of Lochbuie; and part by McPhee of Colonsay. An Isle twenty-four miles in length, lying from the south-west to the north-east. Twelve miles by sea from Gigha, mentioned above, and one mile from Islay.[3] Wherein there are two salt water lochs meeting each other through the middle of the island to within half a mile.[4] And all the deer of the west part of the forest will be brought by an encircling movement to that narrow entry, and the next day brought west again by the same movement, through the the same narrow place, and an infinite number of deer will be slain there.[5] There are some small woods in parts of the island.[6] This Isle, as the Ancients allege, should be called 'Deray', taking its name from the word deer in the Norse language, which has given it that name in olden times.[7] In this Isle there are two good Roads with safety for ships.[8] The one called Small Isles Bay,[9] the other Loch Tarbert. Opposite Loch Tarbert are the greatest hills in the island. Principally, Beinn a' Chaolais, Beinn Shiantaidh, Corra Bheinn, and Bein an Oir.[10] In Ardlussa a chapel formerly. The parish kirk Kilearnadill.[11] The River Lussa is there; the River of Glenbatrick; the River of Glengarrisdale; the River of Cnocbrec; Liundale, by the Cairidh Mhor; the Corran River.[12] All these rivers have salmon taken on them. The island is full of noble cattle,[13] with certain fresh-water Lochs of not much value. Nearest Jura, two miles distant lies an Isle called Scarba. Between these two islands there runs a stream in which it is impossible to sail or to row without infinite danger, called Corrybreckan. This stream is eight miles long, and cannot be handled except at certain tides.[14] Scarba is four miles long from west to east, and one mile broad. It is a high rocky island inhabited and manured, with some woods.[15]

[1] The previous island considered was Islay, evidently also a 'deer forest'. It is fascinating that here in the days of the Lords of the Isles, Jura is principally renowned as a

'deer forest', a hunting preserve for local Royalty, for at this time the Lords of the Isles were virtual Kings in these islands.

2 The owners of Jura cited by Monro agree with the land charters of the day to the degree that presumably the southern part of the island was owned by MacDonald of the Isles, while the north was owned by the MacGillans of Lochbuie and Duart. The charters do not record a connection with the McPhees of Colonsay.

3 Monro's physical description is accurate.

4 It is interesting that Monro sets the small inlet of Tarbert Bay against Loch Tarbert as the second of 'two salt water lochs' meeting to within half a mile.

5 Monro's description of the deer hunts is full of interest. Professor W. J. Watson believed that the term 'tinchell' meant the body of men, sometimes numbering thousands, who drove the deer into a stockade. The Rev. Donald McLean, Minister of the Small Isles, wrote about 1796, describing a similar procedure. What did he mean by 'infinite deer'? And if deer were actually herded and slaughtered in large numbers by this 'unsporting' method, was there a traditional 'stalking' and hunting procedure going on as well.

6 By this date, Jura is no longer a wooded island. Exactly as at the present date 450 years later, the only natural woodland is in small local copses.

7 Monro seems to be in no doubt as to the derivation of the name of Jura. He can give the name as 'Diuray' in his introduction, and relate this to 'Deray', which is actually quite impressive.

8 A 'road' is a place where ships can ride at anchor.

9 'Lubnalenray' is 'Lub na h-Eileanraidh' (Bay of the Islands). The termination 'raidh' is a collective, similar to 'rookery' or 'heronry'. Thus 'Small Isles Bay'.

10 The names of the three Paps and their fourth 'companion' are quite easy to disentangle.

11 As is discussed fully under 'The Church'. There should be a new sentence starting at 'In Ardlussa'. This marks the end of a list of the hills, and the beginning of a fresh list of the churches. Ardlussa, at the north end of the island does not belong with the Paps at the south.

12 The Rivers. The word 'lax' is Old English and Norse for salmon. 'Ardlayfasay' may have been 'Ardlay-lasay' so ultimately 'Ardlussa', with Laxay as 'Lussa'.

'Udergane' is a difficult problem, which is helped by the fact that there is also a small island in Monro's list called Ellan Uderga. Udergane is in a list which includes the main rivers, so must be a considerable stream. Its island is probably quite small. Entering Loch Tarbert on the south coast, is Glen Batrick, as the OS calls it; but this is at variance with local pronunciation. Gleann a' Bedirig. This is supported by Gen abedrig on Mackenzie's map in his 1776 Atlas. Locals say the 'real meaning' is 'a' Bheith dhearg' (The Red Birch), which gives 'Gleann na Beithe deirge' in the genitive. If we insert an 'e' we then have 'Bhederga' which is close to 'Bheit deirge'. This may have once been a Gaelicism for Old Norse 'beit', pasture + 'eyrvik', gravel bay.

In Monro's day the distinction in script and print between 'U' and 'V' was not rigid, so his 'U' may represent 'Bh' which is 'V' in Gaelic. So 'veterga' could become 'Uderga'.

'Glengargaster' is a reasonable approximation to Glengarrisdale, probably Norse, 'Godfrey's Dale'. Knockbreck is unchanged.

'Lindill Caray'. This reproduces the River of Liundale, which is close to the ancient and famous weir in the next glen, The Big Weir, or 'Cairidh Mhor'.

'Avin Villi', The Corran River runs into the northern part of Small Isles Bay which is called Loch na Mile on OS maps. The river is called 'Abhuinn Meill' by Pont. This could represent the Norse 'fjall' or 'fell' (A-Mheall) which would be a suitable name for the river draining the Paps, and would give its name to the Bay into which it runs.

13 The island has long been associated with Highland cattle – indeed the original black Highlanders were here on the island long ago. Did Monro see 'black Highland cattle' on Jura, and think they were 'noble'? It is an attractive idea!

14 This is the earliest mention of the maelstrom of the Corryvreckan. It is generally believed that the name was transferred from the whirlpool just north of Antrim, after Adomnán's time. The name is evidently well established by the sixteenth century.

15 This is an accurate description of Scarba, and easily recognisable.

Before we leave Monro's physical descriptions we should note the interesting work done by Malcolm McArthur, who has, as we have seen, rescued from another part of Monro's text a list of islands which turns out from Nos 37 to 52 to be the names of islands around Jura.

Monro makes a unique contribution to our study of Jura.

As has been said, his account predates the next account of a visitor by almost 150 years and earlier historical references to Jura are rare. We have noted John of Fordun's mention about 1400, which gives the name, the approximate length and says it has few inhabitants. Apart from this, our information is restricted to lists of names which appear on Land Grants and Charters. The Macdonalds are still in control of the island, and only the Bond of Fostering at Camustack in 1520 predates Monro's visit.

It is fascinating then to find so much that is accurate and still recognisable. If his central comments are extracted and put together we get the following general description:

Jura is a 'fine deer forest'. It is inhabited and farmed only along the east coast. It features conspicuous hills, notable rivers and bays and one great sea loch, all of which are named and described. It is partly wooded. It produces great numbers of deer which are driven to slaughter by a co-operative practice. It produces salmon, and is full of fine cattle.

It has a chapel and a parish church. It has famously dangerous waters to the north. The Macdonalds hold the main part of the island and the McLeans and McPhees hold the north.

Apart from the fact that he finds no room to mention the inhabitants, Monro's account is a masterpiece of accuracy and economy, and we are most fortunate to have it.

PONT AND BLAEU

As far as written accounts are concerned, Dean Munro is our only sixteenth-century source, and we have to wait nearly 150 years for Martin Martin. However, we can be certain that Jura had another visitor between 1583 and 1596. He left no journal, but the evidence for his visit survives in his Atlas. Timothy Pont

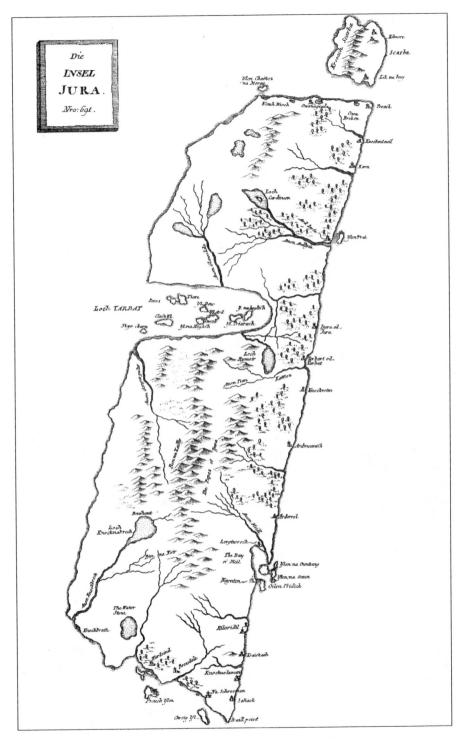

Map 14. The Blaeu map of Jura (German edition).

travelled through Scotland compiling maps which primarily located places where people lived, within a framework of rivers, streams, lochs and hills. He died soon after 1610 and did not see his maps published. The entire collection was purchased from Pont's heirs sometime before 1629 by Sir James Balfour of Jenmylne, Fife, who intended to publish them. However, by 1631, Balfour was in contact with Joan Blaeu in Amsterdam, who had learned of the manuscripts. After various difficulties, Blaeu's engraved collection was printed as an Atlas in 1654. There were well over thirty maps, which included one of Islay and another of Jura. J. J. von Reilly's 'Die Insel Jura' (1791) is much later than the beautifully coloured reproductions which hang on the walls of the homes of many Jura enthusiasts, but the basic map remained unchanged through the years, and this edition has the benefit of clarity.

As can be seen, Pont did a good job with the general shape of the island. The east coast is well drawn, although he seems to have missed Lowlandman's Bay. Perhaps he conflated it with Small Isles Bay, which he calls correctly 'The Bay of Meil'. The Corran he calls 'Avon Meil.' His west coast is understandably featureless, and he has difficulty with the complex shape of Loch Tarbert, although he does make a very brave attempt at the various islands in the loch, giving them all recognisable names.

As far as hills, lochs and rivers are concerned, Pont names a region, 'The Papes of Jura', although his ranges of hills do not pick out the main features. He has names for 'Bin na Noir', 'Ben na Kailly,' and 'Benishaut,' which seem to stand for the individual Paps. There is a good impression that the land north of Tarbert is richly endowed with lochs, and Loch Cardinan is named not far from the present Cathar nan Eun. In the south Loch Knockbreck is accurate, although The Water Stone is a puzzle. Loch Rymoir is wrongly placed on the south side of Loch Tarbert, since it stands for Loch Righ Mor, on the north.

Several rivers are named. Apart from the Corran, Knockbreac has its own river, and the Lussa is shown as Avon Ardlysa, an accurate name. The Glenbatrick burn on the west coast is called Glengargaster, and is misplaced south from Glengarrisdale. The reader may puzzle over many other features on the map.

It is in his settlement names that Pont is most impressive. Many names from the fifteenth- and sixteenth-century land charters appear. Knockbreac has been mentioned. Nardoind is Ardfin, and Brosdale is well placed. Na Schroonen is Strone, and Sanack is Sannaig, both in about the right place.

Knockuolaman, for Knocknafeolaman has slipped south of Krachach, or Crackaig, and it and Kilaridil, for Kilearnadil, have become separated from the Bay. Naynten remains a puzzle, although Lerguvreck is in exactly the right place by the mouth of the Corran. Arderrol and Ardmeanish, for Ardfernal and Ardmenish are in the proper relative positions, although looking strange without the great bay. Knockroim has slipped too far north for Knockrome's place beside Ardfernal.

Lagg and Tarbert have become conflated, with Kames, or Camus, which is Lagg appearing below the river with the puzzling name. Many people have guessed tha the place-name Jura, which appears on the coast north of Tarbert, being pretty well in the middle, may have started out as a general label for the whole island. Ardlysa is named at the mouth of its river, and Karn appears clearly and in the correct place, as it does in the Sasine of 1757, and Langlands Map of 1801. Knockintavill, Troach and Ouanagiala complete the list as Barnhill, Kinuachdrach and Owenegall. Pont's map is a constant source of delight to all students of Jura.

MARTIN MARTIN

Martin Martin (*c.*1660–1719) came from Skye. He graduated MA at Glasgow University and took a medical degree at Leyden, and he was either factor, tutor, or physician to the MacLeods of Dunvegan. His *Western Isles of Scotland* was the first published account of life in the Hebrides. According to Boswell, it was this book, given him as a child, which inspired Dr Johnson to visit the Highlands in 1773.

Martin's account of Jura contains physical descriptions, material on the health and behaviour of the people, and customs and beliefs. As noted above, some of his topics are dealt with in the appropriate chapter. Comments and notes follow. Martin Martin gives us a physical description which adds to Monro's:

PHYSICAL FEATURES

The Isle of Jura is by a narrow channel of about half a mile broad, separated from Islay. This isle is twenty-four miles long, and in some places six or seven miles in breadth.

The isle is mountainous along the middle, where there are four hills of a considerable height. The two highest are well known to sea-faring men by the name of the Paps of Jura.[1] They are very conspicuous from all quarters of sea and land in those parts.

Loch Tarbat on the west side runs easterly for about five miles, but is not a harbour for vessels or lesser boats, for it is altogether rocky.

There is a large cave, called King's Cave on the west side of the Tarbat,[2] near the sea; there is a well at the entry which renders it the more convenient for such as may have occasion to lodge in it. About two miles further from the Tarbat, there is a cave at Corpich,[3] which hath an altar in it; there are many small pieces of petrified substance hanging from the roof of this cave.

Within a mile of the Tarbat there is a stone erected about eight feet high.

About four leagues south from the north end of this isle, lies the bay Da'l Yaul,[4] which is about half a mile in length; there is a rock on the north side of the entry, which they say is five fathom deep, and but three fathom within.

About a league further to the south, on the same coast, lies the small isles of Jura, within which there is a good anchoring place; the south entry is the best; island Nin Gowir must be kept on the left hand; it is easily distinguished by its bigness from the rest of the isles. Conney Isle lies to the north of this island.[5]

There is a place where vessels used to anchor on the west side of this island, called Whitfarlan, about 100 yards north from the porter's house.

[1] True, but the Paps of Jura have long been considered to be three in number.

2 Martin Martin refers correctly to the place of the narrow crossing as 'The Tarbat', although we now spell it 'Tarbert'.

3 Corpach Bay is more like eight or nine miles farther on than the King's cave. There no longer seems to be an altar, and no conspicuous stalactites.

4 Lowlandman's Bay is well described, with An Dunan to the north, and the approximate sound of 'Gaal', the 'foreigner' or 'invader'. The depth of water is also quite accurate. Martin Martin seems to have a general interest in the safety of shipping, safe anchorages and passages, and their absence, interest him.

5 Not so clear, if you enter the Bay by the most southerly passage, Goat Island is on your right. The other mentioned is Rabbit Island.

Martin seems to have had little time for what might be called the 'Natural History' of Jura, and the following brief comments are the full extent of his interest:

The hills ordinarily have about 300 deer grazing on them,[6] which are not to be hunted by any without the steward's licence.

There is variety of land and water-fowl here. The river of Crockbreck afford salmon, but they are not esteemed so good as those of the river Nissa. The shore on the west side affords coral and coralline. There is a sort of dulse growing on this coast of a white colour.[7]

The natives gave me an account, that some years ago a vessel had brought some rats hither, which increased so much that they became very uneasy to the people, but on a sudden they all vanished; and now there is not one of them in the isle.[8]

In Conney Island there are black and white spotted serpents; their head being applied to the wound is by the natives used as the best remedy for their poison.[9]

6 Monro spoke of 'infinite' deer being slain. Martin's sample seems too small.

7 There are no longer conspicuous coral or coralline deposits in Loch Tarbert. Martin probably saw red seaweeds bleached white by the sun about the high tide mark.

8 The common rat is common on Jura at the present time. This is the brown rat (Rattus norvegicus), although it is not of epidemic proportions. It may be that the invader may have been the Ship Rat (rattus rattus), and that its immigrant population sustained a sudden crash, perhaps through sickness or change of climate.

9 The only 'serpents' in Scotland are the adder (vipera berus), although there are some records of Grass snakes in the south-east. Adders are extremely common on Jura, although the present writer has never seen one on any of the Small Isles. The adder has a dark zig-zig mark down its back, which might give rise to the 'black and white spots'. Contemporary folk tradition has no record of applying adder's head to the place of the bite, although many old people have told the author of being bitten in the fields during their childhood, without lasting ill effects.

Martin Martin sums up the religious situation of Jura in a single paragraph:

There is a church here called Killearn, the inhabitants are all Protestants, and observe the festivals of Christmas, Easter, and Michaelmas; they do not open a grave on Friday, and bury none on that day, except the grave has been opened before.

Presbyterianism had been re-established in 1690, and the minister at the time of Martin Martin's visit was the 'Late Episcopal Incumbent', the Rev. John McSween. It is surprising to find the seasons of Christmas, Easter and especially Michaelmas being observed. Perhaps this was under the continuing influence of an Episcopalian clergyman. The burial practices also seem to hark back to an earlier respect for Good Friday. No doubt these patterns would shortly disappear.

Martin Martin also records a tradition regarding the derivation of the name 'Jura', as follows:

> The natives say that Jura is so called from Dih and Rah, two brethren, who are believed to have been Danes, the names Dih and Rah signifying as much as without grace or prosperity. Tradition says that these two brethren fought and killed one another in the village Knock-Crom, where there are two stones erected of seven feet high each, and under them, they say, there are urns, with the ashes of the two brothers; the distance between them is about sixty yards.

This is an intriguing contribution, in view of the fact that many students believe that the derivation of the name Jura comes from its early form as 'Diura', and the Norse language, thus meaning 'Deer Island'. Martin Martin's story has survived in the folklore of the island to the present day, and has the further detail that when passing between the two standing stones at Knockrome people speak of passing 'between the Two Juras'. It seems not surprising that the local community should try to incorporate the ancient standing stones, which date from the Bronze Age, about 4000 years ago, into their oral traditions. The story may well enshrine an early Viking story of brothers who fought and killed each other, and the titles Dih and Rah may indeed be primitive. The connection with the two stones must come much later, and of course the possibility of urns beneath them turns out to be unlikely in the case of standing stones.

It seems that we are quite entitled to have both stories surviving side by side.

Martin Martin records also, 'Jura is the Duke of Argyll's property, and part of the Sheriffdom of Argyll.'

Martin Martin devotes the biggest proportion of his account of Jura to material relating to its inhabitants and their welfare. In this area, he corrects the earlier lack of such comment by Dean Monro. His views are to be found in the Chapter on 'Longevity', but a brief general comment appears here.

> The natives here are very well proportioned, being generally black of complexion and free from bodily imperfections. They speak the Irish language, and wear the plaid, bonnet, etc., as other islanders.

The dark complexion Martin observed is somewhat puzzling, especially if he contrasted it with other islanders. He uses the word 'Irish' to mean 'Gaelic'.

Dr Johnson refers to Martin as 'a man not illiterate', but censures him for 'some inaccurate observations', and that 'he has often suffered himself to be deceived'. In other parts of his *Description of the Western Isles* he is much concerned with 'second sight' and other supernatural and superstitious occurrences, from which his writing about Jura has largely escaped. He gives us a unique and vivid picture of the island and its people, the only one to have survived from the seventeenth century.

JOHN WALKER

John Walker (1731–1803), was born and educated in Edinburgh. He entered the Church and was minister of Glencorse, Midlothian (1758–62), Moffat (1762–83) and Colinton (1783). He was an Honorary MD of Glasgow, and was made DD of Edinburgh in 1765. He was Professor of Natural History in Edinburgh from 1779 until his death. He was sent to report on the Hebrides in 1764. He was a botanist, and published many botanical papers. He actually collected botanical speciments on Jura. The caricature from John Kay's *Original Portraits* seems to show a man of mature years, but he was only thirty-three years old when he made his famous ascent of the Paps of Jura.

Dr Walker begins his account of Jura with a fairly detailed physical description: 'Adjacent to Ila, lies the long extended ridgy Island of Jura, remarkable over many countries for the Height of its Mountains.' He computes its length and breadth, and gives an estimate of 115,200 English Acres.

The Proprietors are Campbell of Jura, McNeill of Colonsay, the Duke of Argyll and Campbell of Shawfield.

Walker's account of the hills is of interest:

> The Mountainous Ridges occupy the middle of the Island, and run from End to End, rising still higher and higher, as they run from the North-East, till at last they terminate in four Peaked Mountains, of a great Height and of a similar shape. Two of these stand close together, and bound the westerly part of the Island. They are much higher than the others, and are well known to the Sailors who frequent the Deucaledonian Sea, by the name of the Paps of Jura.

This description is, of course, not accurate. As we have already seen, the three Paps of Jura range from 2407ft to 2571ft. The two westerly hills, Beinn an Oir and Beinn a' Chaolais, being first and third in height, while the easterly Beinn Shiantaidh is the second. Walker continues with a dissertation on the alignment of Islay and Jura which he theorises is at right angles to the rest of the Hebrides, while conforming to the general rule, worldwide, that offshore islands extend in the same direction as their neighbouring continents. 'Deucaledonian', presumably the Second Scottish Sea, is a word which seems to have disappeared from use over the centuries.

> The Climate of Jura is very different from that of Ila, and not near so mild, though in its immediate neighbourhood. The Lofty Mountains with which Jura is crouded from End to End, occasion this remarkable Difference. Upon these the Snow resides, till Summer is far advanced, and in all Seasons of the year distress the Island with boisterous Winds and impetuous Floods.

Dr Walker visited Jura at the end of June, and presumably never saw the 'snow-covered Paps'. He was no doubt accurately recording answers given to him by local residents in answer to his questions about their weather? The Hebrides were just emerging from the famous 'Little Ice Age.' During the period

1550–1700 there occurred the second post-glacial oscillation of climate. Arctic pack-ice returned to Iceland, the Hebrides were scourged by storm, cold summers, and repeated failures of harvest.

The Island of Jura contains about 466 Inhabitants so that upon the above supposition of its consisting of 115,000 Acres, it contains 246 Acres for each Inhabitant. A most melancholy Proportion. To find a Parallel to it, we must go to the Wastes of America.

Webster's census of 1755 gives 1097 as the number of souls in the island. Walker's number is so far out that it seems he may have been considering only adults. Since we do not know what his criterion was, we will remain unclear about this. His calculations about the ration of land to each inhabitant are amusing, but surely hardly very fair. After all, he himself says that most of the island is mountain and moor. Since most of his other concerns will appear elsewhere, we are left in this Chapter with his comments on the Parish, and with his famous 'Experiment'.

THE PARISH

This extensive Island makes only a part of the Parish of Jura, which also comprehends Scarba and number of small adjacent Islands, and those of Colonsay and Oransay, which are six or seven Leagues distant. The common people are extremely ignorant nor is it possible they can be otherwise in their present Situation. Most of the Children grow up without being taught to read, which was not the Case formerly, when there was a School supported here, upon the Royal Bounty. But some years ago it was withdrawn without any Reason given, though there are few Places where it could be of more benefit. The utmost assiduity of a Minister is here altogether insufficient for the Instruction of the People. There are two places in Jura, where they assemble for public Worship, which are ten Miles distant from each other by a Road which cannot be travelled on horseback, but the Minister has neither Church, Manse nor Glebe. The Islands of Colonsay and Oransay he can only visit twice a year, and the other smaller Isles are cut off from one another by very hazardous Channels. In a Parish of such Extent, so much dispersed and all the Parts of such difficult and dangerous access, it is not to be expected, that Religion can subsist in a very prosperous State. These and many other Inconveniences to which the Minister of Jura has always been subjected, have occasioned this Melancholy Circumstance, that the Sacrament of the Supper, has never been but once dispensed in the Parish, during the present century. Few instances, it is to be hoped, are to be found in Christendom.

Dr Walker's account of the parish will come to mind frequently when we come to look at the history of the Church in Jura.

Dr Walker intended to use the information he gained from his travels to publish two separate works. *Report on the Hebrides*. and *Natural History of the Highlands*. The material we have so far studied comes from the first of these two books. The 'History of the Island of Jura' was one of the few sections Walker appears to have completed of his *Natural History of the Highlands*. It contains long sections on 'Eddies and Whirlpools', the 'Paps of Jura Experiments' and sections on plants and fossils, not included in the *Report on the Hebrides*.

THE EXPERIMENT

In 1764 it had not yet been determined what was the relationship between atmospheric pressure and heat. Gabriel Fahrenheit had discovered that the boiling point of water varied according to atmospheric pressure. Marain had found that the point at which water boiled was greater at the foot than at the top of a mountain. Walker wanted to settle the relationship exactly:

> Being desirous to survey the prospect from the height of these mountains, and in hopes of discovering upon them some singular plants and fossils, I resolved to attempt getting to the summits of the two highest, called the paps of Jura, though made acquainted by the people of the country of its being no easy undertaking.
>
> The execution also of two experiments, at so great a height in the atmosphere, made a considerable part of the design. The one was, to measure the height of the highest mountain, by performing the Torricellian experiment at its base, and upon its summit; which we chose rather to do, being provided with a proper apparatus for the purpose, than to trust to a portable barometer carried to the top of the mountain.
>
> The other experiment was to be made with the thermometer. Several years ago, M. Mairan and the other French academicians, discovered by experiments, that boiling water is not of the same degree of heat at the top of a mountain that it is at the bottom; but, by the thermometer, is visibly colder upon the mountain, than upon the plain. An additional and important fact, however, remained still to be discovered. What is the height of the column of air that corresponds to the fall of one degree of the thermometer in boiling water? The great height of this mountain in Jura, and our proposed mensuration of it in the exactest manner by the barometer, at the same time that the thermometrical experiment was performed, gave some hopes of solving this curious question with some degree of precision.
>
> Upon the 27th of June, we filled a barometer at the shore of the sound of Ila, at seven o'-clock in the morning; and being placed at the level of the sea, the mercury stood at twenty-nine inches and seven tenths. At ten o'-clock it stood at the same height, when we set off in order to ascend the mountain, which is one continued steep from that part of the shore. Some Highland gentlemen were so good as to go along to conduct us. And a box with barometrical tubes, a telescope, a large kettle, water, fuel, provisions, and a couple of fowling-pieces, loaded seven or eight servants.
>
> The first part of our progress lay through deep bogs, from which we sometimes found it very difficult to extricate ourselves. We then came to a chain of small but steep hills, where the heather struck us to the breast, and which were cut everywhere with deep glens and gullies, which we could not have ascended on the opposite side, without the assistance of the junipers and strong

heather, with which they were covered. We next travelled along the rocky skirts of three or four extensive hills, and came to a small gloomy lake, at the foot of the highest mountain. Upon this side, which was to the south, we found the ascent impracticable, being so abrupt and full of precipices, which obliged us to make a circuit to the east. Here we had before us a very steep and continued ascent of about one thousand five hundred feet of perpendicular height, and composed entirely of loose rocks and stones. They lay upon the side of the mountain, like a great stream, and upon the least motion, gave way all about us, which made our progress both tedious and dangerous. With great difficulty, we made our way against these hurling ruins of the mountain; and at last, after an ascent of seven hours, with excessive fatigue, we gained the summit.

It was now five o-clock in the afternoon, the day was serene, not a cloud in the firmament, and the atmosphere uncommonly clear; so that the view we now enjoyed, of the earth and the seas below, made us forget the toil of our ascent. Every way we turned we had a prospect of sea and land, as far as eye could reach. The sea in many places running out to the sky, and in others, terminated by lands and islands of various shapes, forming a very singular and grand horizon.

On one hand we had a thousand hills; the whole alpine country of Argyle-shire; the ancient Albion. Here only, our view was intercepted, and that only by mountains at the distance of above fifty miles. In another quarter we saw distinctly the whole of the Hebrides, and Deucaledonian ocean. Southwards, the vast promontory of Cantire lay under our eye; and beyond it; in one view, all the west of Scotland rising to the great mass of mountains in the head of Clydesdale and Nithsdale; in another view, the spiry summits of Arran, and the whole Irish sea, with its shores, to the Isle of Man. From the south to the west, the north of Ireland lay as a plain before us, further than the eye could reach. The impetuous strait between the Mull of Cantire and the Fair Head, with its lofty cliffs, was at hand; through which the Irish sea is filled every tide by the pouring in of the Atlantic. The promontory of the Giant's Causeway appeared near and distinct; and beyond it, the high land of Inis-huna, the north extremity of Ireland; beyond this, to the Hebrides, nothing but air and ocean.

The emotions in the mind of the beholder, arising from the grandeur of this scene, are not to be excited by any description. The extent of prospect from this mountain is indeed surprising, not much under three hundred miles, south and north. But the curvature of the earth is here greatly overcome by the elevation of the spectator, and the great height of the distant lands. Nothing else could render the Isle of Skye and the Isle of Man at the same time visible. At three such views, the naked eye might extend from the one extremity of Britain to the other. To stretch the eye over so many different seas, over such a mutitude of islands, and such various countries, in different kingdoms, is perhaps a scene that can nowhere be beheld in Europe, but from the summit of Jura.

During the time that our fire was kindling, we constructed a barometer, when the mercury stood at twenty-seven inches and one tenth. Fahrenheit's mercurial thermometer was then put into the boiling water, in a kettle which was made for the purpose, and, after many repeated immersions, was found to stand constantly at two hundred and seven degrees. We left the summit of the mountain at seven o'-clock, and left it indeed with regret, having been so much delighted. We descended, not without some difficulty and danger, upon the west side, where the mountain is very abrupt; and about midnight arrived upon the sound of Isla, at the place from which we set out.

Here again we repeated our experiments. The same barometric tube was filled, and at one o'-clock in the morning, the mercury stood at the level of the sea, at twenty-nine inches and seven tenths; the same height precisely at which it stood the preceding morning at seven o'-clock. And, as the air and weather had been altogether serene, without the least perceptible alteration during the intermediate time, there was reason to think that we had now the altitude of the mountain with as great exactness as it could be by the barometer. We at the same time put the thermometer into boiling water, and after repeated immersions, it was observed to stand constantly at two hundred and thirteen degrees. The thermometer employed, was one constructed by Professor Wilson at Glasgow, and we were therefore assured of its accuracy. The water carried to the top of the mountain, was from a pure perennial spring on the shore of Jura; and the water of the same fountain was employed in the repetition of the experiment.

From these experiments, therefore, it appears that a column of air of the height of this mountain, is equal to two inches and six tenths of mercury. And assuming Dr Halley's calculation of ninety feet for each tenth, the perpendicular height of the mountain turns out to be two thousand three hundred and forty English feet above the surface of the sea, which is just three hundred feet less than half a measured mile.

The difference in the heat of boiling water at the summit, and at the bottom of the mountain, appears from these experiments, to be equal to six degrees in Fahrenheit's thermometer. And the height of the mountain, divided by this number, gives three hundred and ninety feet for each degree.

This account of Dr Walker's expedition is fascinating for many different reasons. His party chose a long and arduous route to the top of Beinn an Oir. It seems likely that they set off from somewhere near Cnocbreac, but they may have initially been landed in Whitefarland Bay at the present day Inver. After their experiments were finished they had to set off roughly north-east towards the foothills of Beinn a' Chaolais. The west-facing lower slopes of this hill are, as Walker described, cut with deep gullies and glens. They would have come in due course to the main valley between Beinn a' Chaolais and Beinn an Oir and made their way up to the 'small gloomy lake', 'rough, or wild lochs' (na garbh lochanan), As they discovered, there was no route up from that aspect, and they had to work round to the east, finally climbing on to the broad ledge between Beinn an Oir and Beinn Shiantaidh. Even then they do not seem to have found an easy path, and climbed to the summit up extensive scree slopes.

The party were poorly advised, and one wonders if the local folk they persuaded to come as their porters had any more idea of what they were doing than Walker had. If they had been content to climb Beinn a' Chaolais, some 150 ft lower, they could have made their way up into Glen Astaile, up the Beinn Mhearsamail ridge and had a straightforward if energetic climb to the top. As it was they seem to have taken seven hours for the ascent. We would nowadays advise inexperienced walkers to allow say, three hours from the Corran Bridge, up the Corran River to Loch an t-Siob, with direct access to the route Walker finally found. The route is of the order of four miles, so not an easy saunter in the hills, but not the marathon experienced by Walker's party. In fact, as we are told, they spent a couple of hours on the summit, and left at seven; finally reaching their starting point at midnight; fourteen hours after they set out. There were the experiments to complete, and this was accomplished by one in the morning. We are left to wonder where they spent the rest of that June night. They were lucky to have been travelling in exceptional weather, and only about a week after the Summer Solstice It didn't get pitch dark at all that night. If they were given a bed for the night it can surely only have been at Cnocbreac, and it was probably poor lodging indeed!

Walker's report of the prospect from the summit of Beinn an Oir at 5.00 pm on 27 June 1764 is quite remarkable. He explains that the sky was completely devoid of cloud, and the atmosphere uncommonly clear. The features he details within 30 or 40 miles are commonly seen, but Walker is confident not only of the Giant's Causeway and the high land beyond on the mainland of Ireland, but also of the Isle of Man. To the north he is equally sure of the high tops of the Cuillins of Skye. He seems conscious of the unusual nature of these observations, and that he is indeed compassing 'not much under 300 miles, south and north'. The Isle of Man is some 130 miles from Beinn an Oir, although the Cuillins are perhaps no more than 90. The author has been on the top of the Paps a number of times and has never been confident of seeing much beyond the near coast of Antrim, with Rathlin Island in the foreground. *Whitaker's Almanack* gives 66½ miles as the maximum distance to an object at sea-level from the top of Beinn an Oir. One is, however, presumably entitled to add the allowable distances from mountain top to mountain top. Snaefell in the Isle of Man is 2034 ft high, giving it a permissible range to sea level of 59 miles. This gives a theoretical maximum visible range from the top of the Paps to the top of Snaefell of 125 miles; the actual distance is about 124. Thus, while treating Dr Walker's enthusiastic description with a touch of scepticism, it is impossible to say that he could not have seen the Isle of Man.

By these criteria, the Cuillins should be an easy object, while Ben Mhor, on South Uist, at the same height as Snaefell, and some 24 miles closer to Jura than it, should also be capable of observation. Perhaps Dr Walker was not aware that it was a possible target.

The Paps of Jura themselves are a famous landmark, and the distinctive group of peaks makes them easy to identify from a great distance. Contemporary references list them as visible from all the above distant places, and the author has seen them clearly from high-rise flats in Glasgow some 65 miles away, so perhaps we should not try to dim Dr Walker's glory, and his evident delight in a very rare treat at a time of quite exceptional seeing.

There is an interesting modern note to complete this topic:

The well-known Scottish naturalist and author, Seton Gordon, has a vivid account in his *Hebridean Memories*. Chapter XV is entitled 'Hekla: Peak of South Uist', and describes one day, 23 October 1922, when the author set off to climb the mountain. Hekla is the second highest peak of South Uist, and at 1988 ft it is 45 ft lower than Beinn Mhor. The day seems to have been one of great clarity, and the author describes the view from the summit:

Hills at an incredible distance were clear. A little to the east of south the mountains of Mull stood out against the cloudless horizon. Of these hills the most distant from Hekla is Duin da Ghaoith, which rises from behind Torosay, not ten miles from Oban. By the map the distance from Hekla to Duin na Ghaoith is some eighty-five miles, yet even at this great distance it could be seen that the twin tops of the hills were powdered with fresh snow. Bearing slightly more to the west one saw the long island of Coll; and behind it the Ross of Mull. West of that again was Tiree with its three hills. Almost directly behind Coll rose the Paps of Jura, plainly visible. Now from Hekla to the Jura tops, just over 100 miles of sea, hill and islands extend. It seems almost unbelievable that hills of no great height; they average just under 2500 ft, could be seen at so immense a distance, yet the Jura hills are unmistakable.

Seton Gordon here confirms Dr Walker's account of exceptional visibility, and must have experienced a similar day of clear seeing. The attention of the author was recently drawn to a letter in *The Scots Magazine* of November 1999, which is quoted here:

Dear Sir,

Many years ago I read in Seton Gordon's book *Hebridean Memories* that in crystal-clear winter conditions he saw the Paps of Jura from the top of Hecla in South Uist. This seemed to me to be bordering on the impossible.

Saturday, 21st August had exceptional clarity in the air here as I set off to ascend Hecla, armed with my binoculars. As one would expect under such conditions, the panoramic vistas over the Minch to Neist Point, the Cuillin, Canna and Rum were excellent. As usual Ben More on Mull stood proud in the distant south-east, with the equally distinct Beinn Talla and the hills of Torosay to the left. Lonely Tiree's massive radar dome shone radiantly under the strong summer sun, and relatively near at hand to the north-west were St Kilda's mighty crags.

Focussing my binoculars on the dark, low outline of Coll, punctuated by its gleaming beaches of white shell sand, my hearts almost missed a beat when there, just to the left of Beinn Feall, stood the unmistakeable Paps of Jura, looming in the background like three big, dull-grey currant buns. Now from the South Uist hills to the bens of Jura is a distance of some 108 miles, and as the late Seton Gordon himself said, it seems almost unbelievable that such hills could be seen at so immense a distance. My curiosity was indeed satisfied at last.

Alan M. Boyd, Grimsay, N. Uist.

We return to Dr Walker's expedition, and to his scientific reason for it. We must admire his determination to carry his experiments to their conclusion. His equipment did not allow him to get very accurate results; 2340 ft is some margin away from the true height of 2571 ft. Still, a 10 per cent error may be considered quite an achievement in his day. Walker was only two tenths of an inch out at sea level, 29.7 in. instead of 29.9 in., and about the same amount out at the top. He was using Dr Halley's constant of 90 ft per tenth of an inch of mercury, and this also led him astray. There is not a simple constant for this factor, but the true figure is nearer 100 ft per tenth inch than Halley's 90.

His second experiment gave a difference between 213° at sea level and 207° at the summit; a difference of 6°. His experimental error here was considerable. The boiling point of water drops by 1.8° for every rise of 1000 ft, although over a rise of many thousands of feet this figure also turns out not to be a true constant. Walker was close to the correct boiling point at the top of the Pap, but for some reason he was a full degree out at sea level, where he might have expected a reading of 212°. His estimate of the height was also inaccurate so his figure of 390 ft per degree of height was some distance out. The true figure is about 555 ft per degree.

By his visit and his account of it Dr Walker made an important contribution to our understanding of Jura in the eighteenth century.

ROBERT JAMESON

Robert Jameson's account of his visit to Jura in 1774 is extracted from his *Mineralogy of the Scottish Isles* (1800). Jameson made his tour of the Inner Hebrides and other Scottish islands in the summer of 1774 along with a friend, Charles Bell, who made the drawings and sketches. These were later engraved by R. Scott of Edinburgh. They travelled from Edinburgh by the 'Livingston Road' to Glasgow. From Glasgow they chartered a boat which took them to Ailsa Craig, calling at Greenock and Largs on the way down the Firth of Clyde. On leaving the Craig they set sail north to Lamlash on Arran, travelled round the island and sailed from Brodick to Rothesay on Bute and returned to the mainland via Cowal. Eventually they reached Loch Sween, and were not very impressed with what they saw before them. Jameson writes:

> We now descended from the mountains to the sea-shore, where we observed an old, gloomy ruinous building, called Castle Sween, situated in a wretched-looking country. Even the few inhabitants we saw had something so melancholy and depressed in their appearance; their miserable huts were in such unison with the scenery as to occasion in us an unusual lowness of spirits. We hastened, therefore, from this spot, and crossed a small ferry, and then walked about three miles to the shore opposite the island of Jura. We were fortunate in getting a boat, in which we passed to the island of Jura.

The 'small ferry' referred to must have taken them across Loch Sween to Danna Island where they probably hired a boat. Alternatively, they may have walked round to Keills where there was a ferry to Lagg on Jura. Jameson begins his chapter on Jura by giving a general description of the size and appearance of the island, as others did before him, and he comments that: 'None of the Hebrides present such a mass of ragged barrenness. The hills are often grey and bare; and the scanty portions of the lower ground which are cultivated, seem ill managed.'

Jameson then gives a detailed account of the geology of the island. This is the first such description, and refers to some of the rock specimens found by John Walker, to whom he dedicates his book. Jameson climbed the Paps, and gives another enthusiastic description of the fantastic panoramas to be seen on a clear day. Jameson toured round Islay, and later returned to Jura by the ferry boat at Port Askaig. He gives a detailed account of the geology around Ardfin, and then continues up to the inn at Craighouse. Here he observes:

> The harbour of the Small Isles Bay is rendered pretty safe by three or four small islands that defend it from the violence of the sea. It will admit vessels of several hundred tons: yet, as the island and the neighbouring country are but thinly populated, few vessels are to be seen enlivening this solitary scene.

Robert Jameson's visit to Jura ended when he sailed north from Small Isles Bay to continue his journey and visit other Scottish islands. Although his geological observations were important, he wrote very few comments on the social situation in the island at the time. His final comments about Jura are:

> Having found it very inconvenient to examine the west and northern parts of Jura, Mr MacNicol, the Minister of the island, to whose kindness we are much indebted, procured a boat, and we sailed from the harbour of Small Isles to the island of Seil.

THOMAS PENNANT

Thomas Pennant (1726–98) was born in Flintshire in Wales. He was a landowner of independent means, who became a naturalist and traveller. His books were valued for their highly readable treatment of the existing knowledge of natural history. His *British Zoology* (1766) stimulated zoological research, particularly in ornithology, in Great Britain, and his *History of Quadrupeds* and *Arctic Zoology* were also widely read. His travel books presented valuable information on local customs, natural history and antiquities. He went on many tours: Ireland in 1754; the continent in 1765; Scotland in 1769 and 1772. He seems to have visited Jura in 1772, and the account of that visit is to be found in his *A Voyage to the Hebrides*.

We pick up his journey as he approaches Jura:

> The remainder of the day is passed in the sound of Jura. About twelve at noon a pleasant but adverse breeze arose, which obliged us to keep on towards the North, sometimes tacking towards the coast of lower Knapdale, black with heathy mountains, verdant near the shores with tracts of corn; advance towards

upper Knapdale, rugged and alpine; I am told of a dangerous rock in the middle of the channel.

About one o'-clock of June 30th receive notice of getting into the harbour of the Small Isles of Jura, by the vessel's touching ground in the entrance. On the appearance of daylight find ourselves at anchor in three fathoms and a half water, in a most picturesque bay, bounded on the West by the isle of Jura, with the paps overshadowing us; and to the East, several little islands clothed with heath, leaving narrow admissions into the port at North and South – in the maps this is called the Bay of Meil.

Land on the greater isle, which is high and rocky. A boat filled with women and children crosses over from Jura to collect their daily wretched fare, limpets and periwinkles. Observe the black guillemots in little flocks, very wild and much in motion. Mr Campbell, principal proprietor of the island is so obliging as to send horses:

Land in Jura at a little village, and see to the right on the shore the church, and the minister's manse. Ride Westward about five miles to Ardfin, the residence of Mr Campbell, seated above the Sound of Ilay.

Pennant is always ready to describe what he sees, and his picture of Knapdale is vivid. His 'dangerous rock in the middle of the channel' is presumably Skervuile, which at that date did not have a lighthouse on it. The boat scraped the bottom getting into the bay. Despite having the whole island unexplored before him, Pennant still wishes to land on Goat Island, where he notes the gathering of shellfish. The water around Goat Island still has black guillemots. Archibald Campbell, the fourth, is thirty-two at this time, and has been in control of the island for twelve years.

Pennant spots both church and manse on the shore. This has always been a tantalising observation. The present church was not completed until 1777, and the former manse was nowhere near it. He may have been seeing a former church on Carn an Searmonaich, some distance north of the modern one. By this date the laird has moved from the ancient dwelling of Sannaig, and is living at Ardfin, which continued to be the family seat until the Campbells left the island in 1938.

Jura, the most rugged of the Hebrides, is reckoned to be about thirty-four miles long, and in general ten broad, except along the Sound of Islay; it is composed chiefly of vast mountains, naked and without the possibility of cultivation. Some of the South, and a little of the Western sides only are improveable. As is natural to be supposed, this island is ill peopled, and does not contain above seven or eight hundred inhabitants, having been a little thinned by the epidemic migrations.

Although there have been previous visitors, we can never be sure whether those who come later have had the benefit of reading the accounts of the earlier ones. Pennant's general comments are unremarkable. Webster's census of 1755, twenty years earlier than Pennant's visit, gave a population of 1097, while Stewart's *Statistical Account*, twenty years later gave 929. Pennant's upper estimate still seems a little low. One would not expect it to be lower than

Stewart's. He is, however, aware of the effect of the emigrations, which he calls 'epidemic':

> The very old clans are the Macilvuys and the Macraines; but it seems to have changed masters more than once; in 1549, Donald of Cantyre, MacGuillane of Doward, MacGuillayne of Kinlockbuy, and MacDuffie of Colonsay were the proprietors: MacLean of Mull had also a share in 1586. At present Mr Campbell by purchase from Mr Campbell of Shawfield; Mr MacNeile of Colonsay; Mr Campbell of Shawfield; and the Duke of Argyle divide this mass of weather-beaten barrenness between them. In 1607 Jura was included in the lordship of Cantyre, by charter, dated the last of May, then granted to Archibald, Earl of Argyle.

We now know that Pennant had read Dean Monro, for he quotes him accurately. He must also have researched his 1586 and 1607 charters.

Pennant goes on to speak of farm produce. His comments on fruits; dyes, quadrupeds and birds follow:

> Sloes are the only fruits of the island. An acid for punch is made of the berries of the mountain ash; and a kind of spirit is also distilled from them.
>
> Necessity hath instructed the inhabitants in the use of native dyes. Thus the juice of the tops of heath boiled, supplies them with a yellow; the roots of the white water lily with a dark brown; those of the yellow water iris with a black; and the Galium verum, Ru of the islanders with a very fine red, not inferior to Madder.
>
> The quadrupeds of Jura are about a hundred stags. Some wild cats, otters, stoats, rats and seals. The feathered game, blackcocks, grouse, ptarmigans, and snipes. The stags must here have been once more numerous, for the original name of the island was Deiry, or The Isle of Deer, so called by the Norwegians from the abundance of those noble animals.

In another place, on his expedition to the Paps:

> Cross on foot, a large plain of ground, seemingly improveable, but covered with a deep heath, and perfectly in a state of nature. See the Arctic Gull, a bird unknown in South Britain, which breeds here on the ground: it was very tame, but, if disturbed, flew about like the lapwing, but with a more flagging wing.

The sloe or blackthorn is not plentiful on the island at the present time, but may have been more abundant in the past. Rowan berries still have domestic uses, although it is doubtful if they have been distilled for a long time past. Mercer has an extensive list of local dyestuffs, and all of Pennant's appear there. Galium verum is Our Lady's bedstraw. Conservation workers in Speyside have recently experimented with this plant. The active agent is the skin or sheath of the fine roots, and the scraping is a tedious business. However, the resultant red dye is all that could be hoped for.

Pennant seems not much interested in Jura's wild life. Unless the population of red deer has plummeted, his 100 stags cannot be correct. His note of the ancient derivation of Deer Island shows that he is somewhat perturbed to find so few. At the end of June he would not have seen them very easily for himself as they would have been on the higher ground. Perhaps his local source was unreliable. Wild cats are absent now, and during living memory, and do not occur in the game bags of last century. If indeed present in 1776, they have long been gone. Otters, stoats, rats and seals are still plentiful.

Blackcock and grouse are present, but not abundant. There are persistant and persuasive reports of occasional ptarmigan on the top of the Paps, which are really too low and too far south to be ideal for them. Walker spoke of snow-covered Paps. Pennant's ptarmigan would reinforce the picture of snowier winters. Snipe have always been plentiful.

It is a pity Pennant does not show more interest in the birds of Jura, for his observations of nesting Arctic skuas is accurate, and indeed they breed still on the flat moorlands around the base of the Paps. We are left with this record and his black guillemots to put with some game birds. He could have recorded many more if his interest had been more engaged.

Pennant goes on to discuss longevity, illnesses, and further farming matters. His remaining concerns follow:

The Parish. The parish is supposed to be the largest in Great Britain, and the duty the most troublesome and dangerous: it consists of Jura, Colonsay, Oransay, Skarba, and several little isles divided by narrow and dangerous sounds; forming a length of not less than sixty miles, supplied by only one minister and an assistant.

Alexander Hossack had been Minister in Jura for ten years by this time, and it is interesting to have confirmation that he has so far prevailed in his battles with the heritors that he has now got an assistant.

Superstitions. Some superstitions are observed here to this time. The old women, when they undertake any cure, mumble certain rhythmical incantations; and, like the ancients, endeavour 'decantare dolorem', to sing sorrow away. They preserve a stick of the wicken tree, or mountain ash, as a protection against elves.

Pennant is hard pressed to come up with any exotic superstitions on Jura. Only the Rowan tree, which is universally a good omen, gets a mention:

Isle of Fruchlan. After dinner walk down to the Sound of Ilay, and visit the little island of Fruchlan, near to the shore, and a mile or two from the Eastern entrance. On the top is a ruined tower of a square form, with walls nine feel thick; on the West side the rock on which it stands is cut through to a vast depth, forming a foss over which had been the drawbridge. This fortress seemed as if intended to guard the mouth of the Sound; and was also the prison where the Macdonalds kept their captives, and in old times was called the castle of Claig.

It seems clear that Pennant is enjoying the hospitality of Mr Campbell at Ardfin. On his after-dinner visit to Claig Castle he must also have had the benefit of a small boat, and perhaps a servant to row him across. Am Fraoch Eilean (Heather Island), is close by, but still needs a boat. Claig Castle is one of Jura's few medieval monuments and has been looked at in that connection. Pennant's description is accurate, and no doubt also reflects the traditions of its use, held by local residents more than a hundred years after the Macdonalds departed.

The Paps of Jura. After a walk of four miles, reach the Paps. Left the lesser to the South East, preferring the ascent of the greatest, for there are three: Beinn a' Chaolais, or the mountan of the sound; Beinn Sheunta, or the hallowed mountain; and Beinn an Oir, or the mountain of gold. We began to scale the last, a task of much labour and difficulty; being composed of vast stones, slightly covered with mosses near the base, but above all bare, and unconnected with each other. The whole seems a cairn, the work of the sons of Saturn; and Ovid might have caught his idea from this hill, had he seen it:

> Affectasse ferunt regnum celeste Gigantes,
> Altaque congestos stuxisse ad fidera montes.

Gain the top, and find our fatigues recompensed by the grandeur of the prospect from this sublime spot. Jura itself afforded a stupendous scene of rock, varied with little lakes innumerable. From the West side of the hill ran a narrow stripe of rock, terminating in the sea, called the 'Slide of the Old Hag'. To the South appeared Ilay, extended like a map beneath us; and beyond that, the North of Ireland; to the West, Gigha and Cara, Cantyre and Arran, and the Firth of Clyde, bounded by Airshire, an amazing tract of mountains to the NE as far as Ben-Lomond; Scarba finished the Northern view; and over the Western ocean were scattered Colonsay and Oransay, Mull, Iona, and its neighbouring group of isles; and still further the long extents of Tirey and Col just apparent.

On the summit are several lofty cairns, not the work of devotion, but of idle herds, or curious travellers. Even this vast heap of stones was not uninhabited; a hind passed along the sides at full speed, and a brace of ptarmigans often favoured us with their appearance, even near the summit.

The other Paps are seen very distinctly; each inferior in height to this, but all of the same figure, perfectly mamillary. Mr Banks and his friends mounted that to the South, and found the height to be two thousand three hundred and fifty-nine feet; but Beinn an Oir far over-topped it; seated on the pinnacle, the depth below was tremendous on every side.

The stones of this mountain are white (a few red), quartzy and composed of small grains; but some are brecciated, or filled with crystalline kernels of an amethystine colour. The other stones of the island that fell under my observation, were a cinereous slate, veined with red, and used here as a whetstone; a micaceous sand-stone; and between the Small Isles and Ardfin, an abundance of a quartzy micaceous rock-stone.

Return by the same road, cross the Sound, and not finding the vessel arrived, am most hospitably received by Mr Freebairn, of Freeport, near Port-Askaig, his residence on the Southern side of the water, in the island of Ilay.

Pennant seems to have taken the same route to the top of Beinn an Oir that was followed by Dr Walker twelve years earlier. If he was indeed staying at Ardfin, he took horse along to Feolin Ferry and then went a mile farther to Whitefarland Bay by water. Archibald Campbell of Jura is now thirty-two years old, and has actually decided to climb the Paps with his house guest. We would know nothing of this from Pennant himself, but many years later we hear of it from Lord Teignmouth on his visit in the 1830s. It is almost sixty years later, and Campbell, who died at the age of ninety one in 1835 is a very old man. He spoke to Teignmouth of Pennant: 'Speaking of Beinn an Oir, the highest of the Paps, he observed with shame, that he had never reached its summit till he accompanied Pennant. Pennant he assured me, descended much more happily that he ascended, on the strength of a glass of whisky.'

Pennant is somewhat fanciful in his emotional response, and gives us the quotation from Ovid.

This comes from *Metamorphoses*', Book 1, lines 152–3. The sense is better if the quotation starts at line 151: 'Neve foret terris securior arduus aether.'

Frank Justus Miller's translation follows:

And, that high heaven might be no safer than the earth, they say that the Giants essayed the very throne of heaven, piling huge mountains one on the other, clear up to the stars.

Pennant notes carefully Scriob na Caillach (Slide of the Old Hag), mentioned already in Geology, and later to crop up in folk tales. Pennant has no exceptional distances to record from the summit, but the day must have been clear, for he has no difficulty with Northern Ireland or Ben Lomond, although he makes it clear that Tiree and Coll are 'just apparent'. Both Ben Lomond and Tiree are about 55 miles from the Paps. Ben Lomond is over 3000 ft high, but Tiree, at sea level is still 10 miles inside Whitaker's practical limit from Beinn an Oir. Walker's experience is reinforced as exceptional.

Pennant notes substantial cairns, and a red deer hind and some ptarmigan in July and records how Mr Banks and his friends climbed Beinn a' Chaolais and found it to be 2359 ft high. It is James Macdonald, in his *The Agriculture of the Hebrides* (1811), who establishes that Pennant's 'Mr Banks' is, in fact, Sir Joseph Banks, the eminent explorer and naturalist. He is home from plant-collecting trips to Newfoundland and Labrador, and from going round the world with Captain Cook. Two years later he will become President of the Royal Society. From Thomas Pennant's casual comment we learn of perhaps the most eminent person ever to have visited the Isle of Jura.

Banks was a close personal friend of Pennant, who includes Banks' description of his visit to Ailsa Craig in his own *Voyage to the Hebrides*. Twelve years after Dr Walker, had it become commonplace to take a barometer up such a hill, and simply read the height off a now available pre-calculated scale? James Macdonald credits Banks with the figure of 2420, rather than Pennant's of 2359. Modern measurements give 2407 ft for Beinn a' Chaolais, so Sir Joseph is out by only 13 ft. Walker, remember, was out by 230 ft. Of course, Banks may have been taking such measurements all over the world.

Pennant gives us some comments on mineralogy. He still has no information about metamorphic rocks, but recognises some of the constituents of quartzite, and can readily distinguish it from the slates and other rocks of the coastal belt.

This outing evidently marks the end of his stay on Jura, and he spends the night on Islay. When we take the above account together with his other observations on the native people and their way of life, we have another most individual view of the island. As well as having fortified him with whisky, Archibald Campbell records with a note of displeasure to Lord Teignmouth, sixty years later, that Pennant 'derived his information too much from the lower classes'. If this is indeed so, then we have good reason to be thankful, for it was not always that these 'lower classes' spoke freely to strangers, and it seems that while accepting the hospitality of the Laird, Pennant's sympathies may well have been with the common people.

It is likely that it was as a result of Joseph Banks' presence on Pennant's trip to Jura that the paintings by J. Clevely, came about. Banks regularly took a group of artists with him wherever he went, and Clevely was certainly in his retinue.

FRANCIS STEWART

Jura was the Rev. Francis Stewart's first charge to which he was Ordained in 1791. He had been rejected for the island of Gigha the previous year on account on his weakness in the Gaelic tongue. He is conscious as he undertakes his contribution to the *First Statistical Account* (1794) that he has not been very long on the island. He is also however determined to deal with the matter conscientiously, and his efforts result in a substantial document. It is not necessary to quote the *Account* at length, but we will pick out such matters as seem to give us new insights into the island.

Physical Description. This is, as one would expect, quite detailed, and lists by name the various islands which make up the parish. He continues: 'As there has been no actual survey, the length and breadth are not exactly ascertained. The appearance of the island is very romantic, and calculated to raise sublime emotions in the spectator's soul. There is a ridge of towering mountains, which run from South to North along the West side, terminating the prospect from the continent, and very often covered with clouds and darkness.'

The three Paps and Corra-Bhein are listed:

These peaks are seen from the continent of Argyllshire, and from part of Perthshire, from Buteshire, Ayrshire, Dumbartonshire, and, it is said, from part of Lanarkshire. They are seen at a great distance to the West, and are the first land which the sailors make coming in their direction from the Atlantic Ocean. There is very little vegetation on these peaks. Their summits and sides are covered over with fragments of stone, and exhibit a stupendous monument of the resistless force of time. The West side of the island is not fit for cultivation, it is wild and rugged, intersected with many torrents, which come rushing down from the mountains; and has been deemed so inhospitable that no person chooses to fix his habitation in it. All the inhabitants live on the East side of the island. Along the margin of the sea, on this side, the grounds are pretty level, but at a little distance from the shore there is a gradual ascent. The whole of this side forms no unpleasing scene. The coast is in several places variegated with bays and harbours and points of land. The arable and pasture grounds spread on a declivity before the eye and terminate a the base of those towering mountains, which form a romantic and awful background.

As one come recently to the island, it is as if his early impressions are still fresh. Stewart packs a great deal of information into this short paragraph. The landmark nature of the Paps is there. Their bare summits and scree slopes. The wild and remote nature of the uninhabited west coast, and the ascent from the cultivatable lands of the east coast to the central hills. However, we may be confident that no native of the island would call it either romantic or awful.

The air is pure and salubrious, as it is generally in the sea-coast, and in hilly countries. The clouds are, indeed often intercepted by the high hills, and descend in torrents; but we have constant breezes, sometimes brisk gales of wind to dry up the rain. The tops of the mountains are covered with snow a considerable part of the winter, but it seldom lies long on the low grounds.

Stewart's account agrees with earlier writers. He confirms that snow lies longer on the Paps 200 hundred years ago than it does today. He makes only a passing comment about wildlife on the island:

There are one or two herds of red deer traversing the mountains. We have plenty of grouse, some termagan and black game, but no partridge, no hare and very few rabbits. Among our birds of prey are the eagles, which build their nests in the inaccessible precipices on the West side of Jura, and prove very destructive to kids and lambs.

Stewart does not essay an exact number of deer. 'One or two herds' is his estimate. He also mentions grouse, ptarmigan and blackcock, which are not plentiful today. As a Lowlander, he expected partridge, but found none. The absence of hares is puzzling. Tradition says that the common hare was present in the nineteenth century, but shot out by the twentieth. The blue, or mountain, hare is abundant in the mountains to the present time, and was presumably on the island in the eighteenth century. Perhaps Stewart was not familiar with this animal. We would expect rabbits in a place where one of the offshore islands is called 'rabbit island', but they don't seem to be doing very well. Stewart makes no further attempt to comment on zoology or botany, a matter of some regret.

Stewart spends some time detailing the harbours of Small Isles Bay and Lowlandman's Bay, and the dangerous nature of navigation in the waters around the island, which he believes should be 'carefully examined and surveyed to see what improvements are practicable'.

Notwithstanding the excellence of these harbours, and that Jura is only a few hours sailing from the lochs where herrings are fished, there is no vessel above five or six tons burthen belonging to the island, and of these there is none employed in the fisheries.

In neighbouring Islay, where Campbell of that ilk invested considerable sums in setting up a fishing industry he found the local people reluctant to commit themselves to the sea-faring life. It appears also to have been so in Jura, although by the nineteenth century numbers of men become seamen on deep sea vessels.

As there was no register of births and marriages kept in this parish till within these few years, the author found it impracticable to trace back the matter as far as might be wished, but has gone as far back as the commencement of the parish records.

He records forty-six marriages and 134 births between 1787 and 1792.

There are several barrows through the island; there are also pillars, and castellums, or duns. There is one relic of antiquity of a singular kind. In more places than one, we can trace along the declivity of a hill, the ruins of a wall, that was once about four and a half feet high, terminating perhaps at a lake, or some very abrupt steep place. At the lower extremity of the wall there is a deep pit, about twelve feet in diameter at the mouth, and very much contracted at the bottom. This, the tradition of the country says, was a contrivance used in former times for taking the wild boar. The hunstmen drove him along the wall, till he took refuge at last in the pit, and was there made captive.

At the north end of the harbour called the Small Isles, there are the remains of a considerable encampment. On the side toward the shore there is a triple line of defence, with deep ditches. From the centre of the work the earth was scooped out to a considerable depth, in the form of three ellipses placed longitudinally, and thrown up in large mounds on the right and left. On the side toward the hills there were regular bastions formed all along, and at the east end, on a line with the centre is seen to be a pretty large mount which seems to have been a place of arms.

Local tradition retains no memory of either of these interesting constructions, and they seem no longer evident enough to be identified. Older-generation Knockrome crofters until recently pointed out traces of a long turf dyke and associated broad ditch which ran for some distance from south-west to north-east parallel to the existing main road at Doire a' Chlagainn (NR 574757). The feature was some 100 metres towards the sea from the road, and although recently only short stretches could be identified, the informants could recall when their elders could detect its course for some miles. It was supposed to be associated with some distant activity to control hunted animals.

WILLIAM DANIELL

The visitors of the nineteenth century have their impressions recorded later, but William A. Daniell visited the island about the end of the eighteenth century, and his account of his time there is recorded in *A Voyage around Great Britain*, published by Longman in 1818. His discourse on Jura follows:

The next object of investigation was the Ile of Jura, one of the most rugged of the Hebrides. There is a small harbour on the east coast between Lagg Ferry and the port of Small Isles, which will be noted, and it comprehends the summit of one of the Paps, which are distinguishable at a very considerable distance. The Laird of the Isle is Archibald Campbell, Esq. of Ardfin.

Daniell gives a detailed description of the Paps, but ultimately admits that, because of the poor visibility and the bad weather, he did not climb them. 'The coast of Jura, along the Sound of Islay, and on the western side, is rocky, the cliffs are in some places of considerable height.'

He discourses on the rugged west coast and the arable east coast:

Lagg Ferry, situated on the east coast, has a small but commodious pier, and a very good road extends from it through the island to a ferry on the south-west shore, opposite Port Askaig on the Isle of Islay. South-west of Lagg is the harbour of Small Isles, a capacious bay of about four miles in extent.

Presumably it is at this point in his journey that he paints, or has painted for him, the famous view of Small Isles Bay, which gives some valuable details. The excise house stands as it ever did, by the bridge across the mill burn. The smithy in later times would occupy the 'lean-to' on the near side of the house. One of the group of cottages which stood below and beside the mill still shows on the left of the bridge. The parish church is clearly to be seen along the shore. There are no other buildings in near proximity to it, and there is no sign of a manse. Only the left-hand Pap is exaggerated. The impressions of sailing craft in Small Isles Bay, and the dress of the folk in the picture are no doubt accurate enough. (Colour plate 18)

'The climate, owing to the prevalence of westerly winds from the Atlantic, is humid, but the air in general is so temperate as to be favourable to longevity.' Daniell here mentions Gillour MacCrain.

'The favourable influence of climate can hardly be said to be seconded by the habits of the people in promoting this duration of existence; they are not only exempt from the luxuries, but even from the comforts and conveniences of civilised life, and are exposed to all the diseases arising from defective clothing and scanty diet. But human nature accommodates itself more readily to privation than to excess, and hence it is that instances of longevity occur most frequently where the enjoyments of life are sparingly distributed.

Among the antiques of Jura may be mentioned some rude obelisks, eight to ten feet in height, which seem to have been the burial places of ancient warriors, since beneath such of them as have been thrown down, there has been uniformly found a small urn, containing ashes and some coins.

The mountains still afford shelter to several kinds of red deer, and here are also found abundance of grouse and black game. The high ground affords pasturage to numerous herds of sheep, and these, as well as the game, are exposed to the depredations of eagles. During the period of this tour, Dr Jura, the son of the Laird of the Isle, visited an eagle's nest near one of the Paps of Jura; it was about five feet in diameter, and there were two young ones in it. Near them lay a brace of moor game and a crow, as well picked as if they had come from the hands of a poulterer; there was a lamb also. His intention was to destroy the old birds if possible as well as the young ones, on account

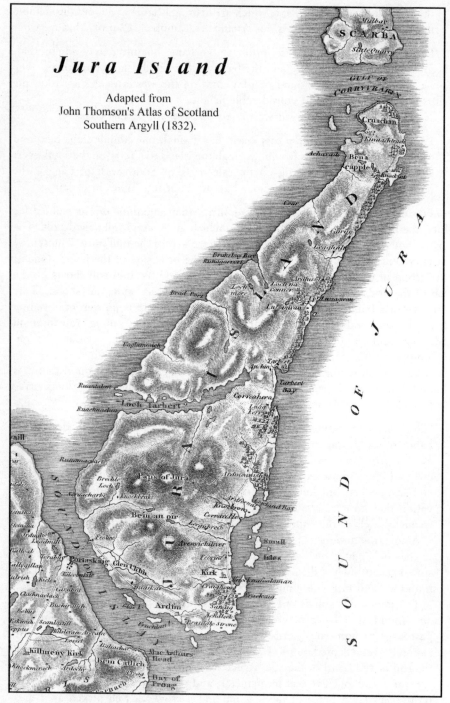

Map 15. John Thomson's atlas of Scotland – Southern Argyll (1832).

of the great havoc they make among the flocks. In conversing about the strength of these formidable animals, he stated, as a well known fact, that an eagle once took up a child which its mother had wrapped in a piece of flannel and laid down by a stook of oats (it being harvest season) and flew with it from Scarba to Jura. Some of the peope of Jura, observing the eagle descend, with what they supposed to be a lamb in his talons, hastened to the place where he alighted, and, to their surprise, found the infant unhurt, with the wrapping around it scarcely decomposed.

The tour was extended across the Sound of Islay.

Thus Daniell's visit ended, and with it this summary of visitors' accounts of Jura.

G. Langlands & Son produced their map of Argyll in 1801. The map shows only the east coast of Jura, but there has evidently been a great leap forward in map-making as the coastline and its settlements are now shown in a clear and accurate way. Ardfin lies off the map, but, from a point just to the east of it, the townships run up the coast in good order and in the right places. Here we see: Brosdale, Strone, Achaleck, Sanaig, Crackaig, Craighouse, Knocknafeolaman, Kirk, Manse, Feorine, Lergybreck, Corran House, Knockrome, Ardfarnall, Ardmeanish, Lagg, Corranaheran, Auchin, Tarbert, Lussagiven, Upper L., Ardlussan, Leaghalt, Carn, Knockintavill, Kinuachtrach. Scarba is shown, with Mulbuy and Kilmory and a slate quarry, and the 'Corrivichan' is clearly marked in the right place.

The map is a goldmine of information, and shows clearly how the various settlement names have become established by this date. Some names will change their spelling during the nineteenth century. e.g. Feorine to Feolin Farm; Leaghalt to Lealt; and some will disappear altogether, but G. Langlands & Son put them firmly on record.

Since Pont and Langlands have been mentioned, this is a good place to note the information available from later maps. In 1832 John Thomson's *Atlas of Scotland* was published. The map is self-explanatory. The general shape and main features are now pretty good, although comparison with the modern outline show that the northern part of the island is too narrow. Perhaps it was not so easy to get accurate measurements in that remote area. The names are consistent with Langlands.

By the mid-1800s, excellent charts are appearing, and *Anchorages on the East Coast of Jura* (1853), shows the associated land communities clearly, with each dwelling house marked individually. The 'swarm of inhabitants', to which Francis Stewart will later refer, can be clearly seen where Crackaig and Lergybreck, later completely depopulated, have each nine or ten houses.

17

Gulf of Corryvreckan

The great maelstrom of the Corryvreckan has been described in the early chapter on the sea surrounding the island. It had a great attraction for the various writers and visitors to Jura, and their various comments are gathered together here.

We are by now accustomed to beginning any chronological list of accounts of Jura with Monro from 1549. However, Monsieur D'Arfeville published in Paris in 1546 *The Navigation of King James V of Scotland round the Hebrides*, and gives an account of the Corryvreckan:

> Betwixt Scarba and Dura there is the most dangerous tide in Europe, because of the contrary tides which encounter there, and run betwixt the Mull of Kintyre and Ila, and, passing through a strait channel, it runs with such violence upon the coast of Scarba that it is thrown back upon the coasts of Dura with a frightful noise; In returning it makes a deep and roaring whirlpool, which hinders all ships to enter. If they unluckily get in there, they are in great danger of being dashed in pieces; but the safest time to pass that place is, either when the water is at the highest flood or lowest ebb. This passage is commonly called Corybrekin.

And now, after that intriguing early description, here is Dean Monro:

> Narrest this Ile be twa mile lyis ane Ile callit Scarbay. Betwixt thir 2 Ilis thair runs ane stream above the power of all sailing and rowing with infinite dangers callit Corybrekkan. This stream is eight myle lang, quilk may not be hantit but be certane tydes. This Scarbay is four myle lang from the west to the eist, ane myle braid, ane heich Roche Ile inhabite and manurit with some woods in it.

Monro does not describe a whirlpool, but instead quite accurately, a 'stream' eight miles long which is beyond the power of any sailing or rowing, and is infinitely dangerous. It cannot be handled but at certain tides. This is an excellent and concise account.

Martin Martin really goes to town on this subject and gives a lengthy account:

> Between the north end of Jura and the Isle Scarba lies the famous and dangerous Gulph, call'd Cory Vrekan, about a Mile in breadth; it yields an impetuous Current, not to be matched any where about the Isle of Britain. The Sea begins to boil and ferment with the Tide of Flood, and resembles the boiling of a Pot; and then increases gradually, until it appear in many Whirlpools, which form themselves in sort of Pyramids, and immediately after spout up as high as the mast of a little Vessel, and at the same time make a Loud Report. These white Waves run two Leagues with the Wind before they break; the Sea

PLATE 1. The Paps of Jura: the familiar view from above Lowlandman's Bay. *(page 6)*

PLATE 2. The Paps of Jura: from Port Askaig, across the Sound of Islay. *(page 6)*

PLATE 3. The Paps of Jura covered with snow. *(page 6)*

PLATE 4. Beinn a' Chaolais seen from the top of Beinn Shiantaidh. *(page 6)*

PLATE 5. The great raised beach of Maol an t'Sornaich on Loch Tarbert. *(page 10)*

PLATE 6. Scarba from the north tip of Jura. *(page 12)*

PLATE 7. The deserted island of Belnahua. *(page 12)*

PLATE 8. North-east along the cliffs the Garvellachs from Eileach an Naoimh. *(page 13)*

PLATE 9. Screes on the upper slopes of Beinn Shiantaidh. *(page 22)*

PLATE 10.
Dragonflies and damselflies of
Jura: the Common Hawker,
Aeshna juncea; the Golden-ringed
Dragonfly, *Cordulegaster boltoni*;
the Four-spotted Chaser, *Libellula
quadrimaculata*; the Beautiful
Demoiselle, *Calopteryx virgo*.
(page 34)

PLATE 11. The Marsh Fritillary Butterfly. *(page 34)*

PLATE 12. Artic Skua on Jura. *(page 40)*

PLATE 13. Red deer stag on Jura. *(page 42)*

PLATE 14. The cup-marked stone of Keils Glen. *(page 51)*

PLATE 15. The standing stone at Camas an Staca. *(page 53)*

PLATE 16. Kilearndale graveyard in the 1970s; the Cambell mausoleum at right. *(page 77)*

PLATE 17.
The grave of Eithne on eileach an Naoimh in the Garvellachs.
(page 78)

PLATE 18. Small Isles Bay: the William Daniell painting. *(page 169)*

PLATE 19. Jura Parish Church in the 1970s. *(page 234)*

continues to repeat these various Motions from the beginning of the Tide of Flood until it is more than half Flood, and then it decreases gradually until it hath ebb'd about half an hour, and continues to boil till it is within an hour of low Water. This boiling of the Sea is not above a Pistol-shot distant from the Coast of Scarba Isle, where the white Waves meet and spout up: they call it the Kaillach, i.e. an Old Hag; and they say that when she puts on her Kerchief, i.e. the whitest Waves, it is then reckon'd fatal to approach her. Notwithstanding this great Ferment of the Sea, which brings up the least Shell from the Ground, the smallest Fisher-Boat may venture to cross this Gulph at the last hour of the Tide of Flood, and at the last hour of the Tide of Ebb.

This Gulph hath its Name from Brekan, said to be Son to the King of Denmark, who was drowned here, cast ashore in the North of Jura, and buried in a Cave, as appears from the stone Tomb and Altar there.

As we might expect from a man of science, Dr Walker has a vivid account, but Pennant, whose description might have been lively, did not get to the Corryvreckan. Francis Stewart feels obliged to give a suitable account of the maelstrom in his *Statistical Account*. Lord Teignmouth also has a description. Donald Budge contents himself with recording the descriptions given by Martin Martin and the Rev. Francis Stewart. Budge also records the tradition set down by Alexander Kennedy but added his own comments:

It might be considered that the dangers of the Coirebhreacain have been exaggerated by different writers, both ancient and modern, but the following happening which took place in June 1951 will show that such is not the case.

On that day a Glasgow engineer, who with his wife has made his home in Lussagiven, crossed over to the mainland with his cabin cruiser the *Dewey Red* of thirty foot keel, and was returning to Ardlussa, having on board several barrels of paraffin and other commodities. He was accompanied by three others, some of whom were familiar with the Sound of Jura and its dangers since boyhood. On the journey the water pump of the motor engine seized and the boat had to be stopped. He proceeded to put the pump in order, a fairly simple operation for the skilled engineer that he was. The other members of the party were looking on, and at the same time keeping a look-out, when they suddenly noticed to their consternation that the boat had drifted into the swift-flowing tide-race, which would in a short time carry them right into the whirlpool of Coirebhreacain. They were still some distance from the pool, but knowing these seas as they did, they realised that there was only one thing to be done if they were to save their lives, and that was to crowd all four of them into the little seven foot dinghy, and leave the *Dewey Red* to her fate. Fortunately the sea was a smooth one, despite the strong tide, else they would not have lived to tell the tale. They abandoned ship and had the painful experience of seeing the fine vessel drift away to her doom.

The men reached land safely, but their vessel drifted out of sight, and was shortly afterwards swallowed into the maw of the Coirebhreacain. Not a board of her was ever seen again except one cask. What the whirlpool takes it holds.

The author has been in the habit of assessing the content and value of such accounts as the various foregoing descriptions. However, in the case of the Corryvreckan, the reader is probably in as good as position as any to weigh them up.

As Parish Minister from 1975–1987, the author had often to visit the northern tip of the island to escort visitors anxious to look at the maelstrom for themselves. The journey from Kinuachdrach was always of great interest, whether one followed the eastern seaboard walking on the heather high above the Sound, and finally climbing to the top of an Cruachan, at 650 ft, or whether one walked through the beautiful Gleann na Muc (Glen of the Pigs) and round from the Bay to look across to Scarba. On most occasions the spectacle would be disappointing, with merely the appearance of some small circling currents, and a general area of turbulence. On other days there would be a large area of confusion, and the impression that the area would be best given a wide berth. On one occasion late in February, the author was persistently urged by some out-of-season American visitors to make the trip, and arrived on the moorland path on a cold afternoon, walking into the teeth of a near gale-force wind. During the last mile, the party several times paused to gaze into the sky, to identify jet planes, which could be heard. It was only as An Cruachan was approached that it became clear that no planes were abroad! The roaring sound was coming from the Corryvreckan! The sight matched the sound, and the party was cast into a profound silence. Over a considerable area the phenomena described by the previous historic writers could be seen. There was no distinct vortex visible, as of a traditional 'whirlpool' structure, but the entire surface was in motion, with completely random and irregular waves and troughs. It was hard to estimate the difference in height between the tops and bottoms of these features, but the vertical scale seemed to be of several metres. Intermittently a discrete body of water would rise vertically above the surface with great force. It took the form of a vertical column which appeared to hang motionless for several seconds before falling back into the sea with a thunderous sound. These towers of water must have been many metres high. The visitors guessed as much as 15 to 20 feet. Watching them was like trying to watch salmon leap on a waterfall. As soon as one focused on one, the attention would be wrenched to another. The roaring noise did not seem to be coming solely from these features, but also from the streams of water which were entering the area from the Atlantic, and leaving it towards the Sound. These mighty rivers also had differences of level, and seemed to be generating a background noise. The consensus of the group, mostly Americans, was that no seafaring vessel of any size or construction could possibly survive in the area. One gave it as his opinion that the Commander of a contemporary US aircraft-carrier would be foolhardy to venture his ship in the vicinity. We watched in silence for over half an hour, until a sense of depression seemed to be replacing the initial one of awe and exhilaration. It was as if the human condition could stand only a limited amount of reminder of its frailty before despair ensured, and by common consent we came away.

Some years later the author was engaged in an exploration of the smaller islands of the Parish in a small sailing cruiser, and had occasion to sail through the Corryvreckan on a summer morning, with a light wind and at slack water. There was not the slightest presentiment of danger, and no evidence of turbulence or disturbing eddies. The little boat came through the fearsome place under sail alone, and without the need of its small outboard motor. A truly bewildering region.

Some days later a slightly foolhardy attempt was made to treat the Grey Dog in the same mannner, and he was evidently displeased. Quickly it snarled its way into a standing wave several feet high, which menaced the boat. Fortunately escape was possible, and relief ensued.

The entire region should be treated with the greatest possible respect, and the Clyde Cruising Club's *Sailing Directions* studied with care. The official account of the problems of navigation has already been given in full in Chapter Three. The author of this book can accept no responsibility for anyone foolhardy enough to venture too close to the great Gulf of Corryvreckan.

V

The Church

18

Early Ministries

There is no doubt that Jura and its accompanying islands to the north were close to the sphere of influence of the Early Christian mission centred on the island of Iona and led by St Columba in the sixth century. There is plenty of scope for discussion about the exact dates of the founding and establishment of the various Early Christian communities in these islands, but there is no doubt that the Garvellochs, Colonsay and Oronsay, and Jura and Islay, were all, in their different ways, the locations of Celtic Christian communities and churches.

The centuries of Viking influence did a great deal to confuse the simple lines of descent of the early churches of these islands, but the various later carved stones and monuments relate to times when the Viking influence had been overtaken by the kingly reign of the Lords of the Isles. The later buildings on Eileach an Naoimh on the Garvellachs, the Priory on Oronsay and no doubt the early Christian settlements of Kilearnadil, Kilmhoire and Kilchianaig on Jura, and Kilmory on Scarba, may all have distant foundations in the centuries immediately following Columba, but it seems reasonable to suppose that they were centres of Christian activity, work and worship in the fourteenth and fifteenth centuries, which is the period to which the carved grave slabs in the cemetery at Kilearnadil are assigned by the authors of the *Argyll Inventory*.

It was in the middle of the sixteenth century that Dean Munro visited the western islands, and described the Chapel at Inverlussa, known as 'Kilchianaig' and noted also 'the parish Kirk Kilearnadil'. At the time of his account Jura was firmly in the control of the MacDonalds, and under the sovereignty of the Lords of the Isles. There seems no information regarding whether the events of the Reformation of 1560 had any influence as far west as Islay and Jura. It is certain that Argyll and his family and followers were early supporters of the Reformation cause, while perhaps the McDonalds were more traditional and continued to accept the Roman Catholic order of things.

A mere fifty years after the coming of the Reformation in Scotland there is a faint rumour of its effect on Jura. The Rev. Colin Campbell is mentioned in the Argyll charter chest as having been Rector on Jura on 30 September 1614. Colin Campbell, of Blargour and Lakinmore, the son of Archibald Campbell of Kilmelford, was educated at Glasgow University and graduated MA there in 1611. As far as Jura is concerned, he is a shadowy figure, and it is doubtful if he ever did more than draw the vacant stipend of the island parish. He had a grant of the lands of Eileach Naoimh and Kilbrandon in the Garvellochs from Andrew, Bishop of Raphoe, in 1630. He was suspended in July 1645 and deposed before October 1647. He was admitted to the charge of Craignish before January 1617, so it seems unlikely that he had a long connection with Jura.

The Rev. Alexander McAlister, MA, however, was undoubtedly a minister in

179

Jura, for in the report by Thomas Knox, Bishop of the Isles, on the Diocese of Argyll and the Isles in 1626, Knox says that 'Jura, belonging to the Earl of Argyll is twenty-nine miles in length, four in breadth, a mountainous island having in all only twelve small towns, and pays to the bishop thirty pounds. They are served by Mr Alexander McAlester.'

This seems likely to be the same Alex. or Arch. McAlester who was admitted to Kilchoman in Islay in 1630. He was suspended in 1648 for associating with Royalists. In his defence it was allowed that he was forced to converse with the rebels in his congregation as his whole congregation had turned rebel, and that during the time of the rebellion he had continued in Islay, except twice. In 1652 he was returned to his charge, and was still minister there in 1660.

It is impossible to say how many years McAlister was minister of Jura, but he may well have been in office in 1624, a most significant date in terms of the ecclesiastical history of the island, for it was in that year that the Counter-Reformation arrived in Jura.

Until the recent publication of documents from the Roman Catholic Archives little was known of the activities of Catholic missionaries in Kintyre and Argyll in the early seventeenth century. However, we now know that four Franciscans led by Patrick Hegarty rowed across from Ireland to Kintyre on 14 July 1624. Starting in Sanda, they worked their way up Kintyre, visiting Arran and Gigha before finally reaching, Islay, Jura and Colonsay. No doubt the Reformation had had little effect on the day-to-day faith of the inhabitants of these western regions, and though under the law they were Protestant they would no doubt have been most willing to be re-admitted into the fold of the Catholic Church, and many were baptised. Patrick spent an uncomfortable time hiding in caves, and indeed was driven out of Gigha through the opposition of the minister, that island being too small to hide in. He also had to flee from Islay to Jura. Two more of the party, Ward and O'Neill, also got into difficulties. In 1649 Ward made a circuit of the southern islands, converting 327, and administering 1200 sacraments in caves and remote mountain shelters. Hegarty's earlier list had mentioned 206 converts in Kintyre, 119 in Islay, 102 in Jura and 133 in Colonsay. In Jura he baptised twelve, including the leading man on the island and his wife.

In 1971 John Mercer excavated Uamh Righ (King's Cave), on the north side of Loch Tarbert, and recorded over a hundred simple crosses engraved on the walls. Beneath the modern floor level was an area of level slabs, and a patch of paving. It is not hard to imagine this cave as the site of Fathers Hegarty and Ward's clandestine rites. The mission ended sadly. After a period of solitary confinement in a London prison, where his captors unsuccessfully tried to bribe him to reveal the names of Catholic chieftains, Ward was finally repatriated to Ireland.

Scottish Catholics around the Pope did not believe Ward's figures and no funds were awarded to continue his mission. Hegarty was caught in 1641 and was detained in various prisons for five years by those he called 'the Scottish Heretics'. He died a year later.

As we have already seen, the papers recently released give lengthy lists of the names of converts from each of the areas and islands visited. The list for Jura runs to forty-two names which have been studied in detail.

If Mr McAlister was translated to Kilchoman directly from Jura in 1630, he was in the island during Father Hegarty's mission, but no record survives of whether he was aware of it, or had any input into the business. When Mr McAlister left Jura in 1630, there followed a short Vacancy until the next minister arrived.

The Rev. John Darroch, MA was inducted into the parish in 1632. He had graduated from Glasgow University in 1625, and seems to have been minister in Jura until 1641 in which year he was translated to the parish of Southend, at the tip of the Mull of Kintyre. In 1644 he was brought before the authorities where he admitted that he had been guilty of 'being for long time preacher to the rebels', and was deposed from office. He was reinstated later in the same year, and died about 1648. John Darroch seems likely to have been a native of Jura himself, as Darroch is one of Jura's distinctive early surnames. There were men of Jura in the forces of Colkitto, who fought with Montrose, and it may be that John Darroch's sympathies were with the Macdonalds, and not with the Campbells, who by this time had taken control of the island.

After the departure of John Darroch in 1641, silence falls on the story of the Church in Jura. It is not known how soon the Presbytery of Kintyre was organised, but a new Minute Book was opened in 1656. There is no mention of Jura in the first few years of the Presbytery's business, but in that first year, one Andrew McDuffie, a resident in Colonsay was brought before the Presbytery to answer charges of immorality. He was instructed to give satisfaction before one of the ministers in Islay, 'because there was no Minister in Colonsay'. No minister in Colonsay means no minister in Jura either, since the two islands were the two halves of the same parish. We are entitled to deduce that Jura was vacant in 1656.

It was in 1661 that the Rescissory Act of Charles II restored Episcopacy to Scotland. Presbyterianism was cast down, but not destroyed. By an Act of 1662 all ministers who were not prepared to accept Episcopacy and seek recognition by patron and bishop had to give up their parishes. Rather to the surprise of the government some 300 did so. It was, of course, extremely difficult to find substitutes for so many, and the new Episcopalian 'curates' were not of the quality of the men they replaced. Many of them had probably qualified for the ministry in the usual way, but not previously found parishes of their own.

Acts were passed to strengthen the position of the new establishment; The Bishop's Dragnet (1663) required everyone to attend services conducted by the Episcopalians. The Scots Mile Act (1663) compelled 'outed' ministers to leave the districts they had served. The Conventicle Act (1670) was designed to put down the gatherings which resulted from the disinclination of the people to 'hear the curates'. All this led inevitably to persecution, to the Covenanters, and to the 'Killing Time'.

The Revolution Settlement of 1690 restored Presbyterianism in Scotland on the departure of James II and the arrival of William and Mary. The Episcopacy had lasted twenty-nine years. At the beginning of this time we may presume that the Parish of Jura, Colonsay and Gigha was still vacant. At least there is no news of any Presbyterian minister having to be 'outed'. But at some point during the succeeding years of the Episcopacy an Episcopal minister was appointed. It is at this point that we make his acquaintance. Before we take our leave of him, we will know him well.

19

The Rev. John McSween

We know nothing of where John McSween came from, or any details of his life before he settled in Jura. The Presbytery calls him, 'McSwine'. Martin Martin calls him 'McSwen'. His name on a Jura grave monument is given as 'McSween', so we shall adopt this latter as a conventional form of his name. We know that in addition to his office, he held wadset or tenancy of lands in Jura. He had a daughter Catharine who married Archibald Campbell of Campbeltown, the second son of Duncan Campbell, the first baillie of Jura. This couple are both commemorated on a fine grave slab in the Campbell Mausoleum in Kilearnadil Cemetery.

It was during Mr McSween's tenure that Jura was visited by Martin Martin, and he seems to have been impressed with him, and quotes him on several matters. He relates in some detail a description of an apparently mythical island to the south-west of Islay, and says, 'Mr MacSwen, present minister in the isle of Jura gave me the following account of it, which he had from the master of an English vessel that happened to anchor at that little isle, and came afterwards to Jura.' Later Martin visited Iona, and in his description of Relig Oran, he says:

> On the right hand within the entry to the churchyard there is a tombstone now overgrown with earth, and upon it there is written "Hic jacet Joannes Turnbull, quondam Episcopas Canterburiensis" (Here lies John Turnbull, former Bishop of Canterbury). This I deliver upon the authority of Mr Jo. MacSwen, minister of Jura, who says he read it.

In 1690, Presbyterianism was re-established, but it was the custom for Episcopal ministers who had given general satisfaction and were willing to continue in their ministries to be allowed to do so, and John McSween was one of a number in the Presbytery of Kintyre who did. Another was Patrick McLachlan of Kildalton in Islay. From this time on McSween is referred to as 'the prelatorial incumbent' or more usually 'the former episcopal incumbent' and we soon hear news of him.

The record of the Presbytery of Kintyre resumes in 1691. Its first meeting is in Campbeltown on 21 January, and it is in this meeting that Mr McSween first comes to our notice.

The spelling of all the forthcoming extracts of Presbytery has been modernised to make them easier to read. The word 'compear' which means a bit more than 'appear', being specifically 'to appear in court', has been retained. Here is our first Extract of Proceedings:

> The Presbytery, being informed that Mr John McSween, prelatorial incumbent in Gigha, Jura and Colonsay is guilty of frequent scandalous drunkenness;

negligence in discharging ministerial duties, and namely in exercising of discipline, examination, visitation, collections for the poor, uplifting those infirm; and designing to process him upon these heads do refer the matter to the next Synod now approaching, for advice anent the most effectual methods in processing him.

It seems reasonable to infer from this that John McSween has already been some time in Jura, for this list of crimes could scarcely have been accumulated in a short period. The charges have a 'ministerial' ring to them, rather than having been brought as a result of protests of parishioners. Perhaps the Episcopal incumbent was being visited by the bishop during the 1670s and 1680s, and a dossier recording his defaults may have been passed on to the Presbytery in 1690.

Some ninety years later in the 1760s, Archibald Campbell of Jura, while preparing a dossier to defend himself from having to give up some land in Jura for a manse and glebe, produces documentary evidence about Mr McSween: 'Mr John McSwine paid two years Tack on 5th December 1675 for his Glebe on Oronsay', and later, 'McSwine deponed in 1676 that he had been for six or seven years in possession of the Monastery of Oronsay as his Glebe and received rents and casualties for the same'.

This information puts John McSween firmly in his Episcopal office in Jura and Colonsay as early as 1673. The Synod took no action, and the next two years pass without further comment. It is at the meeting in Campbeltown on 26 April 1693 that we hear of him again. A further extract:

> Compeared Mr John McSween, Episcopal Incumbent in Gigha, Jura and Colonsay, declaring that the ground of his appearance was, partly a letter he received from Mr David Simpson, and partly of his own inclination to propose the matter following; viz; that he is overburdened with a troublesome charge of a parish so much scattered, which by reason of his present age and infirmity he is not able to make to manage, and that therefore he submits to the Presbytery their easing him of a part of the said charge, declaring his willingness to govern the rest of the charge as he shall be able. As also that said, Mr John McSween having signified his inclination to waive the subject of Mr David Simpson's letter to him, till another diet at which Mr David shall be present. As also that he inclined that the easing him of a part of his charge or of what part thereof, be remitted to the Synod. The Presbytery being straitened through Mr David Simpson's absence, and through want of any information from him, did condescend to waive that subject to another diet as the said Mr McSween desired. As to the other proposal, the Presbytery having signified that Gigha is the part that is fittest he be eased of, in regard that it may best be served with preaching and other ordinances from the continent of Kintyre, as by lands next adjacent to it, did remit him to address the Synod thereanent as he desired himself, and in the meantime recommend to the Moderator and to Mr John McLaurin to discourse him at more length after the presbytery be dissolved.

This Minute gives us quite a lot of information. It confirms the established size of the joint Parish. The provision of even the most basic ministry to these three scattered islands must have been almost impossible. It seems doubtful if the inhabitants could even have expected the benefit of clergy in the matter of the burial of their dead. It is noticeable that although now 'aged and infirm', John McSween is present at a spring meeting at Campbeltown. This is a daunting journey from Jura even today, and it is hard to imagine how it was accomplished 300 years ago. David Simpson was the minister of Kilarrow Parish in Bowmore, on the island of Islay. We don't know what his letter was about. It is impressive to note that the Presbytery, having accepted the need to reduce his parish, appointed its Moderator and another member to counsel John McSween after the meeting.

The Presbytery of Kintyre convened again in Campbeltown on 2 August 1693, and John McSween is again on the agenda:

Forasmuch as Mr John McSween, Episcopal Incumbent in Jura did not compear before the last Synod, conform to his express promise made judicially to the last meeting of the Presbytery, neither sent a letter of excuse to the Synod nor to this meeting, which the Presbytery constructs to be an evasion to postpone the process entered against him: Do appoint Mr David Simpson as being nearest to Jura, and Mr John Cumison as being nearest to Gigha (where the said Mr McSween sometimes resides), conjointly and severally, the one without prejudice to the other to summon him to the next Presbytery. And do instruct Mr David Simpson to have the materials of Mr McSween's libel and the proofs thereof ready, against their next meeting.

Once more we get some interesting information. Presbytery is getting a bit impatient with Mr McSween, and is now resolved to proceed. We note that he sometimes lives in Gigha. It is during this same meeting of the Presbytery that we hear of the other Espicopal Incumbent, Patrick McLachan who:

did leave the parish of Kildalton the week after Whitsunday last, and betook himself with his wife, family and goods to the Kingdom of Ireland where he hath taken a charge from the Bishop of Derrie, and did by a valedictory sermon take his leave of the parish of Kildalton. So plainly deserting the parish and the Church of Scotland.

The Presbytery now begin to make arrangements for his replacement. This gives us a fascinating glimpse into the religious world of the late seventeenth century.

It is not until 1697 that the Presbytery finally gets sufficiently organised to proceed against Mr McSween. It meets in Islay, at Kilarrow on 9 November 1697, almost seven years from the first intimation that there is a serious problem. The first mention of Mr McSween at this meeting gives intimation of what will become a continual difficulty:

The Moderator reports that he summoned Mr John McSween, Episcopal Incumbent in Jura, conform to the appointment of last Presbytery, by a line which he left at his dwelling house in the hands of (*blank*) McFaden. Archibald Campbell of Ardtalla, Mr David Sympson and Mr Dugald Campbell being present. The Presbytery therefore appoints he be called thrice at the patent door of the church. The said Mr John McSween being called, compeared not, nor sent any letter of excuse to the Presbytery. The Presbytery therefore appoints Allan McDugald, their Officer, to summon him for a second time to compear before the Presbytery of Kintyre to be holden at Kilarrow on Monday next, being the 15th Instant, with certification as officers. And the Clerk to give an extract of this Act and Summons to the said Allan.

The Presbytery continued its sitting, having a second session on 10 November, and a third session on 11 November 1697. In due course Mr McSween apeared:

Compeared Mr John McSween, Episcopal Incumbent on Jura, and being questioned why he compeared not the 9th instant conform to a citation left at his dwelling house, he answered that the boat was not at home he designed to ferry in, and so he could not come over at that time. The Presbytery holds the excuse relevant.

The Moderator in the name of the Presbytery laying to his charge several charges which by a 'fama clamosa' these several years bygone, he was alleged to be guilty of such as supine negligence in the exercise of his ministry, frequent drunkenness, imprecations, swearing, etc. as the libel drawn up against him doth more fully contain.

The said Mr John answered as to the first that he could instruct the contrary by his own, as to the rest he pleaded not guilty and craved a copy of his Libel, and time to consider it. The Presbytery after mature deliberation of what he said appointed Mr Archibald Keith, their Clerk, to give the said Mr John a copy of his Libel again, ten o' clock tomorrow, and allows him till Monday night at four o' clock in the afternoon, being the 15th instant to consider it.

The Articles of the Libel against the foresaid Mr John McSween are as follows:

1st It is alleged that he is guilty of supine negligence in the exercise of his ministry, particularly that for several years preceeding now; 1696, he neither catechised nor visited his parish.
2nd That he hath no ordinary collection for the poor on the Lord's Day.
3rd That he doth not regularly exercise discipline, that he hath not a session book, or records of baptisms and marriages.

2nd That he is guilty of frequent and scandalous drunkenness; particularly in July 1691 when he was infeft in his wadset lands in Jura did in Tigh a' Chorran, a Changehouse there, drink to excess and so scandalously swear that one (blank) NcVicRaoil, a profligate woman did reprove him for it.
2nd At another time he was so drunk in company with his cousin McSween and another gentleman of the name of Campbell, that he was carried by the said McSween and the said other gentleman from the Changehouse to his quarters in Balnile, which, when he noticed, said, 'What devil brought a Campbell here?'
3rd In Colonsay in presence of several gentlemen and others, after drinking of aqua vite to excess, and the bottle ending sooner than he desired, chapped

on it with his hand and said the devil put the bottom out of it.

4th Coming aboard a bark on the coast of Jura, was so drunk that he threw the silver dish overboard, and was on that account seized by the owner until he made satisfaction.

5th In July 1691 he was so drunk that he alleged the bushes were rebels and was carried from the shore by Austin Ross sometime in Lirabus in Islay and some others.

6th That one day landing in Jura he was carried out of the boat by one Charles McArthur an indweller in Kilarrow in Islay, and some gentlemen meeting him, and taking notice of his drunkenness, challenged him on it, at which he took up a stone, and throwing it from him, said: 'I pray God that stone be a witness against me in the Day of Judgement if I be drunk.'

To which the gentlemen replied; 'Poor man, you know not but it may be so.'

7th Another time, coming from Gigha on Saturday night, he drank all night, and on Sabbath morning he desired to be covered with many clothes, that he might sweat before the people did gather, as a cure of his drunkenness.

3rd That he is guilty of swearing, cursing, imprecations and rash judging, particularly by God and by his soul, as for instance at Ballathroy in Islay, the 15th July 1693, he swore by God, as also in the house of the deceased Hector McNeill of Ardealla, in prayer he did imprecate destruction on the Baillie of Jura, his family and children, at which two of his auditors, being stumbled, did remove.

2nd Likewise August 1693 he swore by God and threatened John Keir Campbell in Port in Elland that he would pray God to blow him up in the air, and moreover he affirmed the same day that Ballinaby was in hell, and this beside the particular instances in the preceding article of drunkenness at which time also he was guilty of frequent swearing.

4th That he is guilty of profane and irreverent behaviour in time of prayer. Particularly at the marriage of one Coll McDugald in Balloharly in Islay whom he married in his own house, and in the midst of prayer, a girl knocking at the door, he sisted, and ordered a person to go open the door, and, after her coming in, made a second pause, and desired the girl to sit beside himself, which made the auditors suspect he was intoxicate with the drink they drank immediately before the marriage.

And in the meantime appoints Allan McDugald their Officer to summon personally or at their dwelling houses, John McLean in Corrary; James Campbell in Kandrichet; Duncan Campbell in Small; Duncan McIntyre in Kilarrow; John Kier Campbell in Port in Elland; Charles McArthur, brother german to Mr Duncan McArthur of Drumurk; Colin Campbell, brother to John Campbell of Kirktoun; John Pyet in Airdinistill, and James Pyet his brother german there; Allan Campbell, brother to the Baillie of Jura; Adam McDugald in Keppus; Duncan McDugald in Carabus and Duncan McKellar in Jura. Witnesses to compear before the next diet of Presbytery, which is to be at Kilarrow in Islay on Monday next, being the 15th instant at four of the clock in the afternoon, to give their oath of verity in so far as they know or shall be asked of them, anent the Articles of the foresaid Libel given in against the said Mr John, to compear the said day and diet, to hear and see the said witnesses deponed and examined as said there.

There now follow some comments on all of the above material:

John McSween, having not appeared on Tuesday, 9 November, now arrives at the meeting on Thursday 11th. One would have thought that the season for such journeys was pretty well over by this time of year, but the Presbytery goes on undeterred, and for over a week. In a meeting of the Presbytery of South Argyll in the 1690s, there are eighteen parishes, each entitled to be represented by one Minister and one Presbytery Elder. Allowing for members to be unable to attend for various good reasons, one would hope for an attendance in excess of twenty. The sederunt of the meeting in Kilarrow in 1697 is only four. Namely: Mr James Boes, Moderator, a minister from Kintyre; Mr David Sympson, the minister of Kilarrow, Mr Dugald Campbell, another minister from Islay, and Duncan Campbell, the ruling elder for Kilarrow. Archibald Keith is co-opted as Clerk pro tempore.

Having dealt with various cases of discipline, the presbytery turns to Mr McSween. The Moderator declares a 'fama clamosa', which is defined as 'a notorious rumour ascribing immoral conduct to a minister or office-bearer in a church'.

John McSween says he can refute the charges of negligence without help. They would be in fact the least serious; and he pleads not guilty to the rest. He asks for a copy of the Libel, and the Presbytery give themselves until ten the next morning to make a copy for him. They say they will give him a copy 'again', implying that he has it already, and indeed if they wish him to make his defence the following Monday, one would think that he must already have had the Libel by hand delivery long before this date.

The Libel, now it is finally all out in the open, is a very considerable document, and it is evident that a lot of work has gone into drawing it up. It has been in existence for some time, and seems to be dated from the previous year, 1696. The numbering is a bit awkward, with first, second, third and fourth main categories, and with subsections also numbered first, second, third ... etc. (the main categories are in bold typeface.)

Here are notes on some points in the charges:

2nd 'infeft', i.e. in possession in his tenant lands. 'Tigh a' Chorran' (Corran House), a famous inn or change house, for changing horses, at the mouth of the Corran River. The profligate woman has two patronymics, 'nic', daughter of, and 'mhic', son of, where a female is concerned, so she is 'the daughter of the son of Ronald.'

2nd McSween had 'quarters' in Jura. He had of course no manse. 'Balnile' is a name which is unclear in the script, but neither it, nor any likely version of it can now be identified. Where he lived in Jura remains a mystery, but it was near enough to the change house to be carried home. It was also near to

Craighouse, nearly three miles from Corran House, A long carry! McSween's apparent loathing for the Campbells, who were the baillies, and no doubt also his landlords and paymasters may have caused some friction in the family since his daughter was married to the baillies' son!
3rd 'aqua vite', water of life, 'uisge-beatha', hence 'whisky', from an attempt to pronounce 'uisge'.

3rd There are of course scriptural warrants against 'swearing by anything'! A minister would not be expected to swear aloud, at least in public. 'By my soul' is a particularly fierce 'swear phrase' in the Gaelic; sufficient at any rate to be memorable. The imprecation of destruction against Campbell of Jura was evidently sufficient to cause two of those present 'to be stumbled'. Scripture says, 'thou shalt not cause the little ones to stumble!'
4th Prayer was considered sacrosanct, and conversation with God was more important than anything else. It was most unseemly for him to 'sist', or 'break into' his prayer for anything as mundane as someone knocking at the door.

There are to be thirteen witnesses. All of them except Duncan McKellar of Jura come from Islay. No one is called from Colonsay or Gigha, and all are witnesses for the prosecution. The entire case seems pretty well rigged against John McSween.

The Presbytery reconvened on Monday 15th as appointed and John McSween gave in a written paper entitled, 'Answers to the Libel against Mr John McSween'.

The contents are recorded in the Presbytery minutes as follows:

1st That he has exercised and used the function of his ministry preceding November 1696 by preaching of the Gospel, catechising of his parish, and visiting the sick, according to what strength and ability the Lord has bestowed upon him, without any supine negligence.
2nd That when any poor strangers that were not of the natives of the parish came to the parish, he caused to collect publicly for them in the church. And the elders and parishioners of the parish, by an Act of Session choose rather to maintain our own poor at their own houses and dwellings than make any public collection for them.
3rd That he does regularly exercise discipline and kept a session book for his whole parish since his serving the church, which book was with the rest of his books and plenishing in 1690 and was burnt in his house, and since that time he kept particular minutes with records for baptisms and marriages.

2nd But he altogether denies the second article concerning his drunkenness which is only a mere aspersion, and for instance, he was infeft in his lands in Jura long before July 1691, and that (*blank*) NcVicRuil, a very profligate person, was for her misdemeanours long before the year 1691 banished by Act of Session from Jura, and that he only allowed to the Notary and witnesses one peck of meal and some cheese for their maintenance, and went home himself without drinking to excess.

3rd The 3rd Article is altogether an aspersion and very unbecoming any Christian, but more especially any minister of the Gospel.

4th It is answered to the 4th Article that he ever did and does go to prayer with reverence and fear of the Lord, without any profane or irreverent behaviour, according to what ability the Lord bestowed on him, and that before Coll McDugald's marriage he did not as much touch aqua vite to his remembrance, nor use any such irreverent behaviour in time of prayer.

The Presbytery, considering the abovesaid paper, that it imports for the most part a denial of the whole Libel except the article of his not collecting for the poor, which he founds upon an act of Session which then he had not to produce, do therefore determine to proceed to the examination of witnesses.

Compeared Adam McDugald in Keppus; Duncan McDugald in Carrabus; John McLain in Corrary; James Campbell in Kandruchet; Alexander Campbell of Sorobus; Neil Campbell, his brother german and Duncan McIntyre in Kilarrow, the rest being either not summoned or at that time not compearing.'

All of these give evidence, and variously assert that they have seem him drunk or heard him swearing.

'The Presbytery then adjourned for a half an hour, and are to sit, in regard of the excessive lateness of the night, at Hugh Duff's house in the town, where all parties concerned are ordered to attend. The meeting is closed with prayer.

Later still on the Monday night:

The Presbytery maturely considered the depositions of the several witnesses and finding that the foresaid Mr John McSween is guilty of frequent scandalous swearing to that height that it was taken notice of by many, and challenged by a known profligate woman. As also that he is guilty of irreverent, profane and offensive carriage in prayer, particularly in stopping in the midst of his address to Almighty God, and taking notice of so frivolous a thing, as to desire the door to be opened to a person knocking at it, and again to stop and desire that person to come and sit down beside him, which certainly argues either (as was alleged in the Libel) his being intoxicate with drink, there being two marriages in the house that same day, before, and so no doubt drinking of aquavite as is usual at such occasions, or else a very profane and irreligious temper of Spirit.

Moreover, albeit his drunkenness was not positive in 'in terminis' proven, yet that his intemperance and excess in drinking was such as did engage him to more than ordinary mirth, speech, and indisposed him for doing or going till after sleep, and was taken notice of by spectators, which was scandalous and offensive in any Christian, and more especially in any who pretended to the ministerial function.

Likewise that he is guilty of imprecations, as also that he is guilty of scandalous lying, in swearing 'by his soul' that he would not marry a party, yet within one hour he actually married them.

Finally by his own confession he hath no ordinary public collections for the poor on the Lord's Day, contrary to the divine institution and practice of this church.

For the which causes the Presbytery after mature deliberation have Suspended, and do Suspend the said Mr John McSween, 'ab officio et beneficio' (from office and benefit), until the mid-summer Synod, which is to sit at Inverary on the third Wednesday of May next, 1698 years. To which Synod he is hereby summoned and appointed to go. And this without prejudice of what further sentence the said Synod or Presbytery shall think fit to inflict for the causes abovesaid, or when they shall have access to the examination of the rest of the witnesses who are now providentially out of the country of whom the Presbytery are credibly informed will prove the rest of the Libel. And appoint Mr David Simpson, minister of Kilarrow in Islay to intimate the said Act of Suspension at his Parish Church in Jura the 2nd Sabbath of December next, 1697.

Presbytery, considering that it is now late in the night, and being informed that the said Mr John is retired to his quarters refers the intimation of the foresaid Act till the next diet. Adjourns the presbytery till tomorrow at nine of the clock.

The seventh Session of the Presbytery Meeting is constituted the next morning, Tuesday, 16 November 1697:

Mr John McSween, being called, in order to the Presbytery's intimation of their act of suspension of him, gave in a paper, which was laid on the table till the said act was read, in which he appeals from the Presbytery of Kintyre to the Synod of Argyll, and protests against the sentence of the Presbytery, and gives his reasons of appeal, which are clear and appear soundly based.

The Presbytery remained completely unimpressed:

As also they find the said appeal unreasonable, being to the Synod, to which by their own sentence he is summoned and appointed to go. They therefore, notwithstanding of the said pretended appeal, hold firm and adhere to their own sentence, which they appoint their Moderator to intimate to the said Mr John.

Which being intimated to him, he insolently replied that he would make bold to preach, notwithstanding the said sentence.

We might be forgiven for thinking that it is all over now, bar the shouting, but the record of the Presbytery of Kintyre continues to give abundant evidence that this is far from the case. There are many more meetings which he is cited to attend: July 1699; October 1699; January 1700; March 1700; April 1700.

Of course John does not attend any of these. Next, however, at the Presbytery at Killean, 3 July 1700:

Mr James McVurich reports that he sent summonses to Mr John McSween which were delivered to him by John McLean, church officer, also that he summoned John and James Pyet. The said Mr John McSween and the witnesses foresaid being called and not compearing, the Presbytery appoints the said Mr

McVurich to summon them to their next diet with certification that in case
they do not comply that he deal with the magistrate that he interpose his
authority to oblige them to compear.

The said Mr James McVurich also reports that the said Mr John McSween
does administer the ordinances and marries, notwithstanding his being under
a sentence of suspension. The Presbytery therefore appoint the Moderator in
their name to write with the said Mr James to the baillie of Jura, that he
interpose his authority with the people of the said Isle that they receive none
of the ordinances of Christ at the said Mr John's hands, in regard he has
already been suspended from the exercise of his office for immoralities that
were proven against him.

Mr McVurich forgot to bring the execution of this summons with him to the
next Presbytery meeting so the matter was continued. More meetings were held,
in 1701 and 1702, with no result. Finally on the second of September 1702, the
Presbytery actually convened on Jura itself, at Kilearnadil, with four ministers
and two elders. They have a backlog of individual cases of discipline to deal
with, and of course they plan to continue the process of Mr McSween:

Mr James McVurich reports that he intimated the appointment appointing
John McLean to summon Mr John McSween, late Episcopal Incumbent in
Jura to appear before the presbytery, and the several witnesses appointed by
the last Presbytery to be summoned.

Mr John McSween, being cited did not compear. The Presbytery having
sent their officer to his dwelling to summon him afresh to the Presbytery, finds
that he withdrew himself on purpose to shun the Presbytery. Therefore the
Presbytery design, notwithstanding of his wilful absence to proceed to the
examination of witnesses, and to that effect appoint their officer to cite the
said witnesses at the most patent door of the church, which was done accordingly.

Compeared Gilbert McIlbhuy in Leargiebreack, and being deponed and
purged of partial counsel and malice declared that Mr John McSween christened
a child of his since the Act of Suspension was passed against the said Mr John.

Compeared Archibald McIlbhuy in Knockrome and being deponed and
purged of partial counsel and malice declared that he was present when the
said Mr John baptised a child to the said Gilbert McIlbhuy.

Compeared Archibald McIlbhuy in Ardernadil and being deponed and purged
as aforesaid declared that Mr John McSween christened a child of Neil
McGhoyll in Ardmeanish.

The said Neil McGhoyll compeared being deponed and purged as aforesaid
declared that the said Mr John McSween christened a child of his since his
suspension.

Compeared Donald McNamoill in Kill deponed and purged as aforesaid
declared that the said Mr John McSween baptised a child since his being
suspended.

Compeared Angus McIlbhuy in Leargibreak deponed and purged himself as
aforesaid. Declared that Mr John McSween married him with Isobel McNeil

now his wife since the time of his suspension, and that he was witness to several baptisms administered by him.

Mr James McVurich having lectured to the people, and after having done, the people being desired to remain till the sitting of the Presbytery, and being called were interrogate if Mr John McSween exercised any part of the ministerial function amongst them since the time of his suspension. They all judicially declared that he both baptised and married as formerly he did before his suspension.

The Presbytery having appointed their officer to cite Mr John McSween late Episcopal Incumbent of Jura, afresh at the most patent door of the church, and he compeared not. The Presbytery considering that he was summoned to many Presbyteries and several Synods, even since his suspension, and execution of the said summons returned endorsed, and particularly to three Presbyteries before this Presbytery, finds that he is guilty of contumacy, as also the Presbytery having considered his whole Libel, and the probation thereof from July, also finding that since being suspended he has exercised his ministerial function in baptising and marrying persons, as was proven by the depositions of the parents of the children baptised, and persons married and several witnesses present thereat, which evidence his being guilty of contumacy.

Therefore the Presbytery after mature deliberation think that he ought to be deposed, yet considering the paucity of their number, and that the ministers appointed by the Synod to associate them at this Presbytery are not present and that the deposition of a minister is a matter of great importance. Therefore the Presbytery delays passing the sentence of deposition against the said Mr John McSween to the said Synod which is to hold and sit at Inverary the second Wednesday of October in the year of God 1702.

The Presbytery continue to summon Mr McSween without success throughout 1702, until their meeting on 5 February 1703, when:

The Presbytery having received the execution of the summons given in by Cuthbert Campbell, Presbytery Officer in that Parish to Mr John McSween, late Episcopal Incumbent in Jura; bearing that he did lawfully summon and charge the said Mr John McSween to compear before this diet of Presbytery with certification that the Presbytery having considered the said execution, did unanimously sustain the same as a legal execution, and did appoint the Officer to call the said Mr John McSween thrice at the most patent door of the church, and the said Mr John not compearing, the Presbytery did pass the following sentence:

In regard Mr John McSween, late Episcopal Incumbent in Jura has now been under process before this Presbytery these six years bygone, and was suspended by them 'ab officio et beneficio' on the account of his being guilty of scandalous swearing, imprecations, profane carriage in prayer, lying and intemperance; as the said sentence passed at Kilarrow in Islay on the 15th of November 1697 more fully bears. From which sentence the said Mr John did appeal to the next diet of Synod and did not compear thereat; nor afterwards, to call the said appeal, whereby he seemed to submit to the said sentence; and notwithstanding this, he continued to exercise the function of the Ministry by administering the Sacrament of Baptism, Preaching and Marrying, and other parts of the ministerial work, as was proven by the deposition of the parents of the children that were baptised, and the persons who were married, and several other witnesses that were present at these occasions. During which time of his irregular practices he was often summoned to sundry diets of this Presbytery and the Synod, from all which he did contumaceously absent himself, particularly from several diets of the Presbytery held in the Isles within his former Charge and adjacent thereunto: Namely from the Presbytery that sat in Gigha in April, 1700, and from the Presbytery that sat in Laggavulin in Islay in January, 1702. And from the diet of the Presbytery which sat in Tighnacreig in Jura, close by his dwelling house, from which he did absent, and left the place to shun the Presbytery [2 September 1702] Besides several other diets that he was summoned to, from all which he did absent without giving any excuse for his absence. By all which it appears that besides his former immorality, he did, and still does continue guilty of irregular administration of the ordinances; gross contumacy and high contempt of the Judicatory of this Church; For the which cause the Presbytery, after mature deliberation Have Deposed, and by these presents Do Depose the said Mr John McSween from the sacred function of the ministry from henceforth, as a person every way unworthy to preach the Gospel and take the care of souls, and appoint Mr James McVurich, minister of Kildalton in Islay to intimate the sentence at the Parish Kirk of Jura on Sunday of this month and to make report.

This finally is the last historical reference to John McSween, and we hear of him no more. The first complaint was recorded against him at Presbytery on 21 January 1691, and he was finally deposed on 5 February 1703, a little more than twelve years later.

In April 1693 he was complaining of being aged and infirm. We have no record of his date or place of birth, but he had a daughter who died around the 1720s at the age of sixty-three, so he could well have been born in the 1620s. He could have been appointed to Jura at any time during the 1660s, 1670s or 1680s. He comments that he was in Jura 'long before 1691'. Indeed it seems unlikely that he would have been invited to 'stay on' as the former Episcopal Incumbent if he had only recently come to the island. It is also noticeable how little enthusiasm there seems to be amongst the parishioners of Jura or Colonsay to prosecute the charges against him, although much later they are willing to testify to his continuing activity. Even later they seem to have been willing enough to have their children baptised, and themselves married, while surely knowing that he was suspended. This all tends to suggest that he had been long in the island and was well known to them, and even respected and acceptable. His daughter grew up and married Archibald Campbell, the second son of the baillie, so presumably they were both living in Jura for some time. Perhaps his wife was also living there. We may presume she died, from the complete absence of any mention of her, and the general impression given that he lived alone.

No doubt he was managing his own finances on his tenanted lands. He would surely not have continued to get Teinds, or support from Duncan Campbell (Bald Duncan), the baillie, who he seems to have detested. Duncan Campbell died in 1695 aged ninety-nine, after John had been suspended. It is thought-provoking to wonder if John McSween conducted his old enemy's funeral, for the baillie was most certainly buried in Jura.

John had some sheep of his own, and may have been doing quite well from farming. We might guess that he would have had to be in his late sixties to be complaining of age and infirmity, and so would be finally leaving the islands at an age which might have approach eighty years.

It is fascinating to speculate on whether John McSween's behaviour would have got him deposed in today's church? We are more tolerant of 'swearing', although ministers who swear in public certainly raise eyebrows. Public 'deprecation' of local worthies would still be unacceptable today, and might, if complained about have the culprit brought 'before the Presbytery'. Frequent helpless intoxication in public places would still no doubt be his downfall, and could easily cause a 'fama clamosa' in today's Church.

If, as we may suspect, he was a widower, he may have developed a liking for whisky in the lonely years after he lost his wife. Certainly his drinking seems to have made him 'merrier than usual' and 'more talkative', so perhaps his parishioners were tolerant of his 'weakness', although a minister who was regularly 'carried home' must have occasioned a good deal of comment. John McSween may have had positive features which we know nothing about. He may well have been a fine preacher, or helpful in time of sorrow. He certainly knew Church Law, and was correct in many of the legal points he made. His original trial was completely unjust. He had no legal representation. He seems not to have been allowed to cross-examine witnesses. He was not allowed to call any witnesses to character, although there was spontaneous and unplanned support from a man of Ardlussa (the only local parishioner who spoke), which was disallowed.

His application to appeal to the Synod was not allowed, although it was of course completely proper, and it is not surprising that he was reluctant to appear before the Synod, which he may well have expected to rubber-stamp the findings of the Presbytery. In fact the Synod appear to have felt the need for much more proof than the Presbytery obtained, and keep referring this awkward case back to the Presbytery for further witnesses to be heard and evidence taken.

Indeed, after the decision to suspend him from office on 16 November 1697, John McSween never again set foot in a Church Court. He was able to continue in his unofficial role for over five years before his final Deposition.

Today we see John McSween only through the anecdotal evidence of the charges against him, most of which were never supported by witnesses, nor stood up in court, he may have been a nightmare to deal with when drunk, but perhaps we may still have a sneaking regard for him, and a suspicion that he may well have been a most likeable rascal.

20

Neil Campbell

It was during the latter stages of John McSween's case, that the parishioners of Jura and Colonsay have heard of a possible future minister in the shape of the Probationer Mr Neil Campbell. In due course Neil Campbell was ordained to the Ministry in Jura. Everything looked set fair for a new start to the ministry in the Islands of Jura and Colonsay, although we might need to be a little cautious regarding the future commitment of the Heritors to the Standard of Living of the new minister.

We know that Neil Campbell was the son of Alexander Campbell of Raschoille and that he had a son called Donald, who also went into the Ministry. Donald was married to Mary, the daughter of Archibald Campbell, one of the Campbells of Jura, and became minister, first of North Knapdale, and later of Ardnamurchan.

We are fortunate that Neil Campbell's baptismal register survived. He appears to have opened this record in March 1704, a year after his ordination, and he maintained it until 1734. The next records from the parish do not start until 1811. The existence of such record books seems to be largely a matter of chance. We will be studying later the evidence of residents in Jura at the beginning of the eighteenth century.

Neil Campbell holds the record for length of service in the Ministry in Jura, for he was still minister of the parish in what appears to be the year of his death in 1757. He was the minister through both the Jacobite Risings, and during the first of the Jura emigrations to North Carolina, and yet he left little impression on the history of the island, and once more we will be dependent almost entirely on the Presbytery of Kintyre minutes to hear anything at all of his affairs. There are many entries over the years, and we follow the development of the main themes; which turn out to be: his problems about his living, manse, glebe and stipend in addition to his health problems and the Presbytery's problems with him, concerning his absence from their meetings.

Neil Campbell's problems about his manse and glebe start within six months of his Ordination.

Presbytery at Inverary, 16 October 1703:
> Mr Neil Campbell, having addressed the Presbytery anent his want of a Manse and Glebe, or any compensation for them from his parishioners. The Presbytery in answer thereto have appointed the Brethren of Islay to deal with the Heritors and people of the Isles of Jura and Colonsay, that they would as soon as possibly they can, provide their minister in a Manse and Glebe, and in the meantime that they would grant him sufficient compensation in lieu of them to continue, aye and till he be provided.

Presbytery at Inverary, 27 May 1704:

Compeared Mr Neil Campbell, minister of Jura and Colonsay and represented to the Presbytery that although he was informed that there was a Glebe belonging to his parish lying in the Isle of Oronsay, yet he is not put in possession of the said Glebe (by reason that the Proprietor of the said Isle of Oronsay denies that there is any such Glebe there, and will not give him possession of it) and has got no compensation for it from his parishioners, nor a Manse, which he likewise lacks. And therefore craved that that the Presbytery would lay down a method for evicting the said Glebe and for procuring some compensation for the meantime. The Presbytery, taking this affair into their consideration did appoint the ministers of Islay to make special enquiry anent the state of the Glebe, and to summon witnesses before the Commissar of the Isles to take deposition on the said affair. And in the meantime that they deal with the Heritors to give sufficient compensation., and to make report.

Presbytery at Campbeltown, March 1705:
Neil Campbell craved a visitation to right his many greivances.

Presbytery at Kilarrow, 20 August 1705:

Mr Neil Campbell addressed the Presbytery to deal with the Heritors and others of the parish of Jura and Colonsay in order to obtain a Glebe which he has lacked since his ordination, and has got no compensation for it. The Presbytery, finding that the Baillie of Jura and Milcolm McNeill of Colonsay are at the place, and called them before them and presented the said affair to them. In answer to which the said Milcolm McNeill in the name of the inhabitants of Colonsay offered freely to pay the said Mr Neil their proportion of any reasonable compensation for a Glebe, and that duly, aye and while the parish make up a legal Glebe to their minister. The said Baillie being desired to condescend to the same for his interest in Jura, he refused the same, alleging that there was a Glebe in Oronsay to which the minister of the parish had a right. Whereupon Milcolm McNeill protested that he was willing to give his minister a sufficient compensation for his Manse and Glebe in proportion to his interest, and therefore cannot be legally prosecuted for any deficiency or expenses of Law that may follow thereupon, upon which he took instruments.

The Presbytery, considering the unwillingness of the inhabitants of Jura to give their minister a Manse or Glebe or any compensation for the same, in conformity to the obligation of their Call; appointed Mr John Campbell to write to the Synod's Agent to pursue them in the terms of their Call.

Presbytery at Kilmichael, 15 October 1705:

The Presbytery, considering that the minister of Jura and Colonsay has neither Glebe nor Manse, do resolve with their first conveniency to design a Glebe in the said parish, and in the mean time appointed the ministers of Islay in conjunction with him to pursue the parishioners before the Commissar of the Isles, or any other Judge competent for a compensation for Glebe or Manse to him for the present and bygone years since his ordination.

Presbytery at Campbeltown, 15 September 1707:

> Compeared Mr Neil Campbell minister in Jura and presented an address showing that he has laboured under several heavy grievances, particularly that his charge is very spacious and discontiguous, there being four distinct places of worship in three islands at a considerable distance therein. As also that he lacks a Manse and Glebe and his stipend is not sufficient for his maintenance in a charge wherein he is exposed to so vast expenses, in his travelling from island to island. And craving that the Presbytery might either remove his grievances or grant him an act of transportability from his present charge. The Presbytery having read and considered the said address did refer the same to the Comittee of Synod.

We are now in a position to see where Mr Campbell's problems lie. At a time when the stipend of a minister came from the teinds, a small proportion of the rents that the tenant farmers were paying annually to the landlord, and normally a very modest sum, the provision of a manse and glebe were vital to his survival.

The manse was always, and still remains today, the minister's greatest perquisite. It meant that he had a tied house provided at no expense, and usually maintained for him. In the absence of such a house, the minister and his family would either have to build, purchase or rent a house or lodgings, and most would be quite unable to do so.

The glebe was equally vital. It was supposed to provide sufficient land to enable the minister largely to maintain himself by raising livestock or growing crops. From the income of the glebe he would be able to pay farm servants to do the work on his land. The manse would normally have a complete set of farm buildings, comprising a barn, a byre, a stable, a calf house, a gig shed, a dairy, as the present manse on Jura has to this day. This establishment should make the minister virtually independent of his parishioners' support, and this contributed to his freedom to Preach the Gospel, without fear or favour. Mr Campbell's plight is genuinely a serious one. He is a married man with a family, and we have to this day no idea where he was living on either Jura or Colonsay.

The landowners in Jura and Colonsay are each holding the other responsible for his maintenance, and in this battle Campbell of Jura would expect always to come out on top, with the support of the powerful Campbell family. If they do not have the actual goodwill to provide the manse and the glebe, which either of them, both being wealthy, was well able to do, it will be hard for the Church to find any way to compel them to comply with its wishes.

They may hold meetings of Presbytery and Synod, and threaten the lairds with the Civil Courts, but both McNeill and Campbell know that they are in no danger whatever. The ordinary parishioners no doubt feel that if the men to whom they pay their rents will not do their part in housing their minister, they themselves can hardly be expected to do anything.

We should note that the promise to ferry the minister between his different islands free of charge appears never to have been honoured, at least it is not being honoured by 1707.

By our last extract, only four and a half years after his ordination, Neil Campbell is already, for the first time, requesting permission to leave Jura and

Colonsay and find another parish somewhere else. At this point in the church's history, this permission to be transported is not a mere formality. It is a permission which can be withheld, and in Neil Campbell's case it most definitely is withheld.

Note that Neil informs us that he conducts worship on three islands; not only Islay and Jura but also on Scarba, and that services take place in four places of worship. Presumably we here have reference to Kilchattan in Colonsay; Kilearnadil in Jura, where the ordination took place; Kilmory in Scarba; and most probably Kilchianaig at Ardlussa. These extracts give us our firmest evidence that the ancient church of Kilearnadil was still in use in 1707.

The Presbytery record will also tell us of the problems that Neil Campbell is having in attending the Presbytery meetings:

Presbytery at Southend, July 1705:
Neil Campbell was written to anent his absence from every Presbytery since his Ordination in 1703, except those at Inverary.

Presbytery at Campbeltown, March 20 1707:
Mr Campbell, being present, was interrogated about his non attendance at meetings.' He said that he had been in Colonsay and could not attend. This was accepted, but he was instructed to be more constant hereafter.

Presbytery at Campbeltown, July 12 1709:
Mr Neil Campbell being present, was interrogated anent his absence from all the diets of the Presbytery since last October, answered that he was kept away by the storminess of the season till April, and that his wife being valetudinary [unwell] he could not leave her. He was admonished to attend in the future.

Presbytery at Inverary, June 11 1712:
Mr Neil Campbell being present was interrogated anent his absence from Presbytery for the past three years. He replied that in harvest and winter he could not attend by reason of storms and the circumstances of his family. This was sustained, but he was told to endeavour to come more often.

Presbytery at Campbeltown, 26 April 1714:
Mr Neil Campbell, being present and being interrogated about his absence from the Presbytery these two years bygone, answered that as to the winter diet of Presbytery he could not attend by reason of the storminess of the weather and in the summer was necessitated to leave Jura and transport himself and his family to Colonsay.

Presbytery at Inverary, 11 August 1716:
Mr Neil Campbell being called to account for his absence these past two years, answered that his tenderness, his great distance, the confusion of the times and some things that fell out with respect to his family hindered his attendance. He was admonished to attend, especially in the summer.

Presbytery at Inverary, 12 August 1718:
Mr Campbell was interrogated anent his absence for the past two years; he answered that in winter it was not possible to attend; in summer he was in Colonsay and did not know the dates of the diets. He was enjoined to be at more pains to keep himself informed via the Islay brethren.

Presbytery at Inverary, 10 June 1720:

Mr Campbell being present; Presbytery expressed itself in no way satisfied with his absence these many years except when he meets them sometimes at Synod; in regard that he was frequently admonished at former occasions and that he did faithfully engage to attend their meetings in the summer season, and to wait the diets of Communion; and seeing that notwithstanding of all former admonitions, and leniency used towards him, and his own former engagements, he always continues to absent himself both from the diets of Presbytery and of Communion, to his own great loss and prejudice.

Therefore the Moderator is appointed sharply to admonish him, with certification that if he does not attend more punctually for the future they will proceed to further censure. And the Presbytery appoints him to have a Presbyterial Exercise on Romans 8:3: 'Who shall separate us ... etc.', and that notwithstanding of Mr McLean's having an exercise on hand at present, in regard the Presbytery seldom has access to meet with the said Mr Neill, and that he have the same in readiness to deliver it at the Presbytery to meet in April 1721.

Presbytery at Inverary, 7 August 1722:

Mr Campbell being present was again interrogated for his long and constant absence from diets; gave the excuse that he is very valetudinary. The excuse was sustained.

Presbytery at Inverary, 6 August 1726:

Mr Neil Campbell being called to account for his long and continued absence from the diets of the Presbytery, and for having the presbyterial exercise so long on his hands undelivered; answered that the Vastness and Discontiguousness of his Large and Spacious Charge, and his frequent Bodily Indisposition hindered his attendance. And he being removed, these excuses were considered, and the Presbytery could not but sympathise with him, under his Insupportable Greivances in his Charge, but in the meatime could not be satisfied with his constant absence, and his having the exercise so long on his hands. And the Presbytery appointed the Moderator to signify the same to him and to admonish him to attend Presbytery more frequently.

Presbytery at Tarbert, 5 August 1727:

Mr Neil Campbell being called to account for his constant absence from the diets of the Presbytery answered that his circumstances, through his grievances and bodily indisposition were such that he could not attend, and being likewise interrogated as to why, all the time of his being the minister of Jura and Colonsay he never did administer the Sacrament of the Lord's Supper; to which he answered that he was discouraged from attempting such a work in regard he found little appearance of the reality of Religion amongst them, and that he has no constitute eldership in his parish. And he being removed, and these excuses considered, the Presbytery were very much dissatisfied with them. And the Moderator appointed to intimate this to him, and to enjoin a due administration of the Sacrament of the Lord's Supper, and a more regular attendance on the dyets of Presbytery in time coming.

Presbytery at Campbeltown, 10 August 1733:

> Mr Campbell, being present was called to account once again for his continued absence from diets of Presbytery; this time for the past six years. He answered as he had on many occasions before, and was delivered of censure by the Moderator.

Here then we have an account of Neil Campbell's relationship with the Court of the Presbytery of Kintyre; the organ of Presbyterian Government which he had taken his oath to support. He attended only eleven times in a period of thirty years, and was held to be negligent in the matter. Indeed the Presbytery became increasingly frustrated by him over this long time.

Presbyteries nowadays usually meet monthly, with a break in the summer and at Christmas, amounting to nine meetings per year. The meetings of Kintyre in the eighteenth century suggest a regular monthly diet, with no breaks, held in various locations to further local business in the various parts of its huge area.

Almost all Neil Campbell's visits were to one of the summer meetings, usually in August. Only twice did he attend in the spring, and never at any other time. His summer visits took place on alternate years, and from the internal evidence it is clear that Mr Campbell had arranged his life to spend his six and a half months in Jura and his five and a half months in Colonsay on alternate seasons in successive years, and that his biennial visits to Presbytery occur during the summers he spent on Jura. It also seems that he timed these visits to take in both the Presbytery Meeting, and the meeting of the Superior Court: the 'Synod', which would meet several times a year, and comprised a group of the Presbyteries in a wider area. Mr Campbell may have been nervous of continually avoiding the Synod, for its powers of discipline were greater than those of the Presbytery.

The nature of the journeys he was required to make is interesting. He attended Campbeltown four times, and Inverary six times. One meeting he went to was at Tarbert, Loch Fyne. To reach Campbeltown he would probably have taken a local boat from Small Isles Bay to Tayinloan, the mainland port for the island of Gigha. This is a considerable voyage of about 18 miles. He would then have posted the further 17 miles to Campbeltown.

Inverary would be a different kind of journey. He would go up the length of Jura to the Kinuachdrach Ferry, 19 miles north of Craighouse; over the short crossing to Crinan; about five miles, and then by land to Inverary, 30 miles. Tarbert would have been a good deal shorter for Mr Campbell. If he could have got a boat from Craighouse to Kilberry, about 12 miles across the Sound, the road round Knapdale to Tarbert is no more than about 13 miles.

With fair weather – and appropriate tides – by no means a foregone conclusion – all of these journeys would have occupied an entire day, with little likelihood of arriving in time for the proceedings on the day of setting out, and lodgings to be paid for at the end of it. Meetings, as we have seen in the matter of John McSween could literally go on for several days, so a diligent commitment to the work of the Presbytery could occupy the best part of a week, once a month throughout the year, and involve considerable expense. Note that the three ministers of Islay, facing similar journeys, appear regularly on the sederunts of meetings on the mainland throughout the years. Attendance at Presbytery seems to have caused them no difficulty.

Mr Campbell makes several references to his time on Colonsay, complaining that he cannot possibly attend, starting from there; and indeed it is true that to start his journey from Colonsay would add two extra days to the venture. On the other hand, the Presbytery of Kintyre met intermittently, though infrequently, on the neighbouring Island of Islay, and he never attended there even once during the thirty years.

Mr Campbell was no doubt completely disillusioned with the Presbytery of Kintyre who had supported and encouraged him in engaging with the ministry of the Parish of Jura and Colonsay, with promises that 'all would be well', and had completely failed to deliver on the central question of his livelihood. Indeed, without a Manse or Glebe for thirty years it is a serious puzzle to consider what he and his family lived on. Perhaps, like John McSween, he leased land on both islands, and farmed for profit to maintain himself. A letter in the Campbell of Jura Papers from 1767, writing about the possible Glebe in Oronsay says: 'certain it is that Mr Neil Campbell, who died only lately and was succeeded by Mr Hossack, lived all his life upon the island of Colonsay, upon a farm of Mr McNeil's and had a beneficial Tack from him'. Our only clue, but probably a good one!

From the astonishing episode of his reluctance to offer Communion in his parish we conclude that he was equally disillusioned with his parishioners, who show, 'little appearance of the reality of Religion amongst them', and it is quite startling to discover that by 1727 he has not a single Ordained Elder in either Jura or Colonsay; so no kirk session; and hence of course, once more, Jura and Colonsay refer no cases of parochial discipline to the Presbytery; there being no kirk session to refer them.

Neil Campbell frequently tells us that, first his wife, and then he himself are in poor health, and the Presbytery seems occasionally to be moved by his evident indisposition. However, they are in general unimpressed by his years of non-attendance, and his absence from the meetings and also from their, probably annual, celebration of Communion not only grieves them but they feel it is all 'to his own great loss and prejudice'. He has in fact cut himself off from his colleagues. He is not even sufficiently in touch with his nearest neighbours on Islay to learn from them of the dates of the Presbytery meetings, and although the evidence may seem slight, he seems cut off from his parishioners as well. It is no small matter to withhold the Sacrament of Communion from an entire congregation for thirty years, and to refuse to Ordain any Elders.

But then, Neil Campbell is truly between the devil and the deep blue sea. The Presbytery either cannot or will not secure him an adequate livelihood, but at the same time, they will not allow him to move elsewhere. If he simply resigns his charge, he will not obtain a 'Presbyterial Certificate', and without one he will not be able to take another charge, and it is likely that being a minister is the only thing he can do. His plight is appalling, and in consequence the spiritual want of his neglected people may be similar.

His visit to the Presbytery at Campbeltown in August 1733 is his last personal attendance at a meeting, and we hear nothing more of him until 1749, sixteen years later.

Presbytery at Campbeltown, 14 June 1749:
 Mr Neil Campbell sent a letter to the Presbytery representing his incapacity by reason of his age and infirmity to discharge the ministerial work or any part of it, and devolving his charge upon the Presbytery and begging them to consider the deplorable situation in the islands of Jura and Colonsay.

This letter the Presbytery deferred and sent on to the Synod with no action.

Presbytery at Inverary, 1 August 1749:
 Letter from Mr Neil Campbell representing that by reason of the frailties and infirmities of old age he is not able to discharge the duties of his office any longer. And therefore craving that the Presbytery would accept of his demission and permit him to leave the island. The Presbytery, being informed that he still continues in the exercise of his office did resolve not to agree to his demission till they have further information concerning the reason and causes offered by him for demitting his charge.

The matter is moving towards its conclusion, but still with painful slowness, and with little grace on the part of the Presbytery.

Presbytery at Campeltown, 18 April 1750:
 The Presbytery, being informed that Mr Neil Campbell, minister of Colonsay, did in winter last leave the said island and hath not yet returned, and being further informed that he is now in a tolerable state of health, did appoint a letter to be written signifying their displeasure with his conduct, and requiring his immediate return to his charge, or give in a formal demission reserving the half of his stipend during his life.

So now Neil Campbell has given up Colonsay and is continuing to live in Jura, and presumbly continuing to preach there.

Presbytery at Southend, 20 July 1750:
 Mr Neil Campbell returned answer to the Presbytery letter that he discharged his office faithfully while in health, but now that he is turned very valetudinary. That he was obliged to retire for his health and that he is willing to give up 200 marks of the stipend for the assistance of those that supply there [i.e. Colonsay] and expects that Presbytery will apply to get that island supplied as other islands are.

The matter continues for a further year:

Presbytery at Inverary, 2 August 1751:
 The Moderator reports that he settled with James Campbell of Ratehellie, nephew to Mr Neil Campbell, who presented a Commission from the said Mr Neil, empowering him to transact with the Presbytery, and obtained an obligation under his hand for the payments of 200 marks yearly out of the Stipend of Colonsay towards the supply of the parish. The tenor whereof follows:
  Dear Sir. In consequence of the power granted to me by my uncle Mr Neil

Campbell, I agree to pay the sum of 200 marks Scots money out of the stipends of Colonsay towards the support of an Assistant to be employed by you, to supply the said Island of Colonsay, and that yearly during the incumbency of the said Mr Neil Campbell, and the same to commence for the current year, and that in case the island is supplied agreeable to the concert I had with your Presbytery here at this time. I also promise to draw upon Colonsay to pay to Mr Charles Campbell, minister in Jura, five pounds sterling for supplies given by him to the said island. Signed James Campbell.

Here is evidence that Neil Campbell has not only left Colonsay, but that he is employing another minister to preach in Jura. By November 1751 matters have moved on:

Presbytery at Campbeltown, 13 November 1751:
The Moderator reports that he got no reply to the letter to the Committee anent Neil Darroch, and in regard that the said Neil has officiated in Jura since last August, the Presbytery agree that a letter be sent to the Committee and Society acquainting them that he has been employed in Jura since last August and desiring them allow him that quarter's salary.

Presumably Neil Campbell has now left Jura, perhaps to live with his family on the mainland. We know nothing of his date or place of death, and indeed he is never again mentioned either in the Presbytery minutes, or anywhere else. Donald Budge, in his account of the ministers of Jura concludes that since his demission is not recorded by Presbytery he remained technically the minister of Jura until the parish became vacant through his death. Certainly there is no further mention of his ministry during the years 1751 to 1759, and no mention of a record of supply for Jura or Colonsay during these years. The most likely position is that Neil Campbell, having left Jura about 1751, continued to make arrangements for supply preachers, whom he would have partly paid out of his stipend, and who may well not have been dependent on their church salaries. Had his demission been recognised by the Presbytery, or had he died in these intervening eight years, the Presbytery would have been bound to respond by trying to arrange that the vacant parish be filled by a new incumbent. Their argument from silence is compelling, and the first we hear of a successor to Neil Campbell is in the minutes arranging for Mr Neil Macleod's Ordination in 1759. This would indicate a possible demission by death by Neil Campbell sometime in 1758, and a ministry of fifty-five years. In the absence of any Kirk Session on Jura, there could be no question of the survival of a Kirk Session Minute Book, so the only thing that Mr Campbell has left to us is his record of the baptisms he administered in Jura between 1704 and 1734.

It seems sad that he could have been there so long and apparently given such little satisfaction to anyone that his ministry was not marked by any testimony which has survived.

21

The Church in the Early Eighteenth Century

Before leaving the affairs of the Church on Jura during the first half of the eighteenth century there are some other matters to consider which we learn of through the minutes of the Presbytery of Kintyre.

JURA PARISH CHURCH

There is an almost complete lack of information regarding the main place of worship on Jura before the erection of the present building in 1777. From the age of the grave slabs in the present graveyard at Kilearnadil we can be confident that the island's oral tradition that this was the location of the medieval church is reliable. There are, however, no remains of the early building, and even some disagreement about where it actually stood. There are persistent traditions on the island about another church and another place of worship at Carn an Searmonaich (Preaching Cairn) on the ridge above the modern Primary School. Pennant on his famous visit to Jura saw on his boat trip to the shore in Small Isles Bay, 'to the right on the shore the church and the minister's manse'. The present church and manse are separated by about three-quarters of a mile, and could not have been so described. Some brief notes in the Presbytery Minutes are the only thing which may cast light on the mystery of the second church of Jura.

Presbytery at Inverary, June 1706:
> The Presbytery appointed Mr John Campbell to write to the brethren of Islay with their first convenience to go to Jura, that they might with the minister and gentlemen of that Parish condescend upon a convenient place for building a meeting house in that Isle.

Presbytery at Campbeltown, 24 December 1735:
> The Presbytery received a letter from the Commission informing them that they appointed some of their number to wait on Shawfield anent a new erection in Jura, and desiring the Presbytery to enquire into the real rent of the said lands. The Presbytery appoint the clerk to write to Mr Spence that they suspect he has all the papers relating to the parish, and that it is not practicable for them to hold a visitation there in the winter months, but as soon as possible they will send an account to him of what is done in that affair.

Presbytery at Campbeltown, 25 February 1737:
> The Moderator reported that the clerk had written to Mr Spence about the new erection in Jura and did besides send a transcript of the report of the committee appointed in the year 1724 to perambulate the island. He asks for up to date figures for rents and heritors.

Presbytery at Campbeltown, 20 April 1737:

> Mr Neil Campbell wrote, representing that Shawfield as a proprietor of part
> of Jura sometime, signified his willingness that a place should be designed for
> a Manse and Glebe, and that the last time he was in the island he was displeased
> it was not done, and craved the Presbytery's advice. The Presbytery appointed
> Mr Charles Stewart and Mr Scott to write to Shawfield upon the head, and,
> if he signify his willingness that they hold a visitation there and design a proper
> place for a glebe and manse.

The 1706 minute is the only mention at that time of the need for a replacement
church. It is termed a 'meeting house'. There is complete silence in the Campbell
of Jura Papers. It is just possible that a simple building was erected shortly after,
in response to the fact that the ancient kirk may have become derelict. The whole
thing may have been done very informally and on a small scale, and in view of
the minister's lack of contact with the Presbytery, it may have passed unnoticed.
There are folk tales of builders erecting a kirk which was regularly demolished
again each night by local folk because some objected to its location.

A 'new erection' is mentioned again thirty years later in 1735 and 1736. If
Campbell of Shawfield, who still had some lands in Jura, had a hand in all this,
the records might well have escaped the archive of the Campbell of Jura Papers.
By these later days the accredited modern church is only forty years in the future.
Whenever and wherever the intermediate church was built it was of short duration
and presumably was unsatisfactory in the long term. In the complete absence of
hard evidence, mystery will continue to surround this early building.

The last minute indicates that Shawfield took a passing interest in the question
of the manse and glebe, and that he had actually visited the island and been
annoyed that nothing was done. He might well have been a better ally than
Campbell of Jura, but probably no longer had sufficent legal foothold on the
island to take any initiative in the matter. No further interest by him is recorded.

PRESBYTERY'S PERAMBULATION

The Minutes of Presbytery record a 'perambulation'. This notable journey was
undertaken during Neil Campbell's ministry, and the record of its instruction
follows:

Presbytery at Campbeltown, 15 September 1724:

> The Presbytery of Kintyre, taking into their serious consideration that the
> Islands of Jura, Scarba, Colonsay, Oronsay, Gigha and Cara do lie all at a
> great distance, some of them from the continent, and also from one another,
> and that there are a considerable number of people inhabiting the same, many
> of whom have great scarcity of Gospel Ordinances dispensed to them, and
> that others have much peril of their lives when passing from Island to Island
> for the benefit thereof; and the Synod of Argyle, having in the year 1722 found
> it needful that two ministers should be settled there in the meantime; though
> these Islands would require three; but there being no sentence of the Judges
> competent in that matter which is now found necessary.

> The said Presbytery do hereby nominate and appoint Mr John Campbell,

minister at Kilarrow in Islay, Mr Neil Campbell, minister in Jura, Mr Neil McVicar, minister at Kildalton in Islay, and Mr Neil Simpson, minister in Gigha, together with Malcolm McNeill of Colonsay, John Campbell, Baillie of Jura, Hector McNeill of Gullcahile and Archibald Campbell of Ardmore, ruling elders, as a Committee to perambulate the bounds of the foresaid islands and to consider the distances of them from one another, the number of people in them, and other circumstances; and how the said Islands should be divided into ministerial charges and parishes and where the churches should be; and that as soon as possible they go about their work and report to the Presbytery.

In view of the fact that it was already very late in the season for such voyages, it is surprising to find that the Committee undertook their task at once, and were able to bring a Report to the Presbytery in Campbeltown in December of the same year. The Report follows here in full:

The committee named with relation to the new visitation reported that they had met, and that divers of their number having frequently travelled through the islands of Jura, Scarba, Colonsay, Oronsay, Gigha and Cara, and the other small islands, were well acquainted with the length and breadth and circumstances of them and discoursed the most knowing of the inhabitants concerning the disjunction of these islands into different parishes and the situation of the Church.

[The Report starts with details of Gigha and Cara, which were at the time part of the Parish, but these are not relevant to our study, and are omitted.]

That the Isle of Jura is from south-west to north-east in length twenty-four miles, and those so long that in just measure they would make upwards of thirty, and the roads rough, ragged and impassable for the most part, that not above ten miles can be ridden without difficulty and hazard. And in it are eight waters of so rapid a current that at some times they cannot be passed, there being no bridges. And many have perished in them. The Isle is in breadth commonly five or six miles. The number of catechisable persons in it about six hundred. Two stated places of worship at a great distance from one another and from many of the inhabitants, which obliges the minister for the conveniency of the people to preach at several other places, they not being able to travel to the stated places, especially the aged and children. The heretors are the Duke of Argyll with rent five hundred merks, the Laird of Calder, whose lands in the Isle are wadsetted to John Campbell of Sannaig, Colin Campbell of Carsaig, a minor, and Donald McLean of Iarboll. Their rent is two thousand one hundred and thirty merks. Alndeth McLean of Lochbowy whose rent is five hundred merks. The whole rent of the Isle is silver rent. The Teinds are five hundred and ninety six merks, two parts payable to the minister and the other to the Bishop.

North of Jura is Scarba at four miles distance. Here is the Gulf or Whirlpool of Corrievreckan, a sea so raging and dangerous that it cannot be passed but at a low ebb in very good weather and by persons well acquainted. This island is in length three miles and in breadth two. In it are sixty catechisable persons who can never attend public worship in the stated places for it in the parish.

The heretors are the Duke of Argyll. His rent is one hundred and twenty six merks, and Allan McLean of Kilmory. His rent is also one hundred and twenty six merks, all silver rent. The Teinds are forty eight merks.

North of Scarba lies Lunga at two miles distance, and in the passage likeways a most raging whirlpool, Beallach an Choin-ghlais, not to be attempted but at certain hours of the tide in very easy weather. In this Isle are thirty catechisable persons. The heretor is the said Allan McLean of Kilmory. The rent one hundred and twenty six merks. Teinds are twenty merks. Its length is two miles, its breadth one.

North of Lunga is Belnahuaimh at two miles distance. A sea passable only in easy weather at some certain times of the tide because of a very strong current called Caolis Nabrain. This island is about a mile in length and as much in breadth. In it are sixteen catechisable persons. The heretor the said McLean of Kilmory. The rent twenty merks and no Teinds.

West from Belnahuaimh is Garve Ellachmore at a distance of eight miles and a very dangerous and strict current. 'Tis about two miles in length; the breadth one; the number of catechisable persons is eighteen. The heretor, John McLachlan of Kilbride. Rent ten merks and Teinds payable to the Bishop.

West from Garvellach more is Eilean Naomh at a mile distance and a very strict and dangerous current. 'Tis about a mile in length and half a mile in breadth. There are families in it. The heretor is the said Mr McLachlan of Kilbride. Rent fifty merks. No Teinds.

West from Jura in the main Ocean lie the Isles of Colonsay and Oronsay at a distance of Seven Leagues from the place of landing. This dangerous sea is called the Linne Tarshin. The two isles are divided by a small Sound. The length of both, eight miles, the breadth two miles and a half. The catechisable persons four hundred. One place of worship at the centre. The heretor Malcolm McNeil of Colonsay. The rent sixteen hundred Pounds Scots money. Teinds included which are two hundred and eighty pounds money foresaid, of which two hundred pounds are paid to the minister and eighty to the Bishop. The Distance at which the minister of Jura and Colonsay is at from the seat of the Presbytery and Synod may be easily known from the account given above of the distance at which the minister of Gigha is from the same. (Eighteen miles from the Gigha landing to Presbytery and forty four miles to Synod; in which there are upwards of eight miles of a desolate mountain of exceeding bad road.)

And this large tract under the inspection of the minister of Jura of about forty miles in length and thirty in breadth is an intolerable charge for one minister, who in passing and repassing between the islands is put to insupportable charges and frequently windbound for ten or twenty days. Yea, sometimes for a Month or Six Weeks, and for the most part miserably accommodated to the great prejudice of his health. From all that, it appears that this charge cannot in any tolerable manner be supported without two ministers. One in Jura and another in Colonsay and Oronsay, and the small isles in the north and north-west of Jura to be annexed to the parish of Luing and Seil in the Presbytery of Lorn, to which they lie most contiguous. And that the islands of Gigha and Cara should be disjoined from the parish of Jura and erected into a distinct parish by itself.

The Presbytery, having heard and considered the above written report, and the verity of the same, and circumstances of the aforesaid islands therein being well known to them; they did approve of the report, and desire the Procurator and Agent for the Church to carry on all procedures needful to make the same effectual, and do humbly recommend the foresaid disjunction and new erection to the Right Hon. the Lords for Plantation of Churches and all Judges Competent and persons having interest as a matter in which The Glory of God, Good of precious souls, the health, safety and ease of many persons are much concerned.

This report is a mine of information. Its description of the length of Jura has never been bettered; 'twenty-four miles, and those so long that in just measure they would make upwards of thirty!'

The population figures are helpful, and those of the smaller islands most revealing.

In due course Gigha and Cara were disjoined as recommended, but then, as still today, the church found it hard to make boundary changes which crossed Presbyteries as well as parishes, and the northern islands were never attached to Luing and Lorn. Indeed, having expressed some concern for the minister's workload, and even for his health, the Presbytery did nothing about it for the next forty-four years or so.

CATECHISTS
The question of Catechists in Jura and Colonsay rises again in the 1730s and 1740s.

Presbytery Minutes of 5 November 1735:
> The Committee and Society for the Propagation of Christian Knowledge sent a letter acquainting that James Muir in Colonsay is continued Cathechist and Schoolmaster with £8 salary. Patrick McArthur is in Jura with £6 salary sterling. John Logan, Itinerant Preacher is Commissioned to preach in Jura from Whitsunday to November ensuing.

April 1737:
> Mr Neil Campbell represents that Mr Patrick McArthur, Catechist in Jura has his salary so far reduced that he cannot possibly subsist on it and will be obliged to demit for want of aliment, and craves that the Presbytery supplicate the Committee for an augmentation.

April 1742:
> Report that Mr Daniel Campbell is to continue as preaching Catechist in Jura with £20.

November 1745
> Duncan Thomson is commissioned to be Catechist in Jura.

It is interesting that various roles seem to overlap here. The SCPK have a schoolmaster who is also a catechist. John Logan is an itinerant preacher, presumably covering the five and a half months when Neil Campbell is in Colonsay. Daniel Campbell is a catechist who is also a preacher. As always there is a chronic shortage of funds on Jura.

A final note on 'the times'. Jura and Colonsay were perhaps too remote to be greatly affected by the upheavals going on in Scotland during the years in question although Neil Campbell in August 1716 gives, as part of his current excuse for non-attendance, 'the confusion of the times'. No doubt a reference to the aftermath of the 1715 Rising.

22

Neil Macleod and Alexander Hossack

NEIL MACLEOD

The next minister in Jura and Colonsay was the Rev. Neil Macleod. He was born in the Isle of Skye and educated at Aberdeen where he graduated in 1728. He was for a time Royal Bounty Missionary in the Outer Isles, after which he was admitted to Jura in 1759.

These were the days of 'Presentations' to vacant charges in the church, and Mr Macleod was presented by the Duke of Argyll. Neil Macleod was admitted to the 'United Parishes of Jura and Colonsay' on 21 April 1759, by 'ordination'. The place of the Presbytery meeting to ordain him is given as Taynacraig (Craighouse), so there is no clue here as to where the actual service took place. The place of assembly and worship of the people has a 'patent door', as is usual in such ceremonies, but the minutes do not tell us exactly where it is. The place of worship for the ordination of Neil Macleod in 1759 remains a complete mystery.

Silence now descends on the new ministry, until, three years later in 1762 we find yet another Presbytery minute which gives us some idea of how the land lies:

Presbytery of Kintyre at Campbeltown, 3 February 1762:
> Presbytery, taking under consideration the distressful situation of Mr Neil Macleod, Minister of Jura, as laid before them by his letter, agree to hold a visitation in Jura in summer next, and meantime sustain his excuse for absense.

There is a lack of evidence about what is happening, and this is the only minute which gives us any insight into the situation. It does look very much as if nothing has changed since Neil Campbell's departure. Indeed, Neil Macleod must have written a letter of complaint, similar to all those written by his predecessor, complaining that he has neither a manse nor a glebe.

His entry in the *Fasti* tells us that, in 1762, Neil Macleod married Elizabeth Campbell, the daughter of Archibald Campbell, of Jura. He was the grandson of Duncan Campbell, first of Sannaig, and had the title, third of Sannaig.

Neil Macleod had a son from this marriage, also called Neil Macleod. Neil Macleod died in 1786, and is buried immediately in front and to the side of the Campbell of Jura Mausoleum, together with his wife Elizabeth.

ALEXANDER HOSSACK

Alexander Hossack was educated at Marischal College and King's College, Aberdeen, where he studied between the years of 1754 and 1758. He was ordained as the next minister of Jura in 1766.

The Minute Book of the Presbytery of Kintyre records that the minutes of the proceedings of the Prebytery are missing from the record from 4 March 1762 to

18 June 1771. This fact is recorded in March 1797, although the minutes themselves resume on 29 July 1776. The missing period covers the time of Alexander Hossack's arrival on Jura in 1766, and the next few years while he is involved in litigation with Campbell of Jura. It will be instructive at this point to pay some attention to the relationship between the Campbells of Jura and the Presbytery.

John Campbell, second of Sannaig, was an Elder of the Church, and as a Presbytery Elder was present on the Perambulation of the Parish in 1724 at the age of eighty-three. Until his death in 1736 at the age of ninety-five, it was this old man who was so stubbornly resistant to Neil Campbell's appeals for help in the matter of his manse and glebe.

By the time Archibald Campbell, third of Sanaig succeeded his father in 1736, the minister was apparently already a broken man, but it would be Archibald who would continue the family tradition of non-co-operation with the Rev. Neil Macleod until his death in 1764.

Archibald Campbell, fourth of Jura succeeded his father while he was only twenty, and a minor. He was twenty-two when Neil Macleod died, and when Alexander Hossack became minister of Jura. It was a most unexpected discovery when the the Campbell of Jura Papers turned out to contain Extract Minutes of the Presbytery of Kintyre, dating from the missing period, and written by, and signed in the hand of, Archibald Campbell. It seems unlikely that such a young man was holding the important position of Clerk to the Presbytery, and abusing it to the extent of withholding important records so that they remained absent from the Kintyre Minute Book. Indeed, not only Minutes pertaining to Jura would have been in the missing records. It seems likely that young Archibald Campbell obtained the record and made copies for his own use.

When we come to the legal battles between the Laird and the Minister, we should remember that while we cannot put an exact age on Mr Hossack, Archibald Campbell was in his early twenties throughout the entire proceedings.

Alexander Hossack certainly wasted no time in setting matters to rights regarding his 'living'. He may well have written letters in a similar vein to his predecessors during the summer of 1766, and by October he had persuaded the Presbytery to convene in Jura.

At Kilearnadale in Jura, 26 October 1766:

Anent the visitation appointed to be held here the 15th current, the members being detained at Gigha and Islay by contrary winds and stormy weather could not meet before this day, and, finding that they cannot now proceed to business, adjourn till tomorrow.

Mr Hossack reports that he did duly intimate the diet of visitation conforming to its appointment, and the Presbytery officer gave in an execution bearing that he had cited these discreet, honest men of the said parish; viz Duncan Campbell; Dougald Bowie and John Mackay; and Angus Taylor, land surveyor, to give them their assistance in the matters after-mentioned. Then the Heritors, honest men, and surveyer above-mentioned, being called; Compeared Archibald Campbell of Jura and the honest men and surveyer above-named.

The Moderator, having enquired of the said Heritor and such of parishioners as were present, if there was a manse, glebe, and grass for their minister in the parish of Kilearnadale. It was found there were none. It was further enquired if there were any church lands in the said parish, near to the Church. Archibald Campbell of Jura answered that he knew of none, but it was found by the testimony of the parishioners present that there was a field not far from the place of worship containing a piece of ground called 'The Bishop's Dale'; another piece of ground called 'The Beddal's Glebe', both contiguous to a well called 'The Bishop's Well', all lying in the town and lands of Kilearnadale on the other side of the water, which they find to be the property of Archibald Campbell of Jura, presently possessed by Donald Black and other Tenants.

Thereafter, they, with the honest men and land surveyor did proceed to the designation of a glebe as the law directs, and did pitch upon the ground most contiguous to the Church; but Jura having represented to the Presbytery that that was the ground on which he intended to build his own house, they passed from it, and went over to the other side of the water. Then the said Archibald Campbell of Jura protested against the Presbytery's proceeding to design any part of his ground for a glebe, in regard there was of old a glebe in Oronsay in the parish of Killeran, which is united to this parish, and took instruments in the Clerk's hands. But the Presbytery, finding after all the enquiry they could make there was no evidence appeared to them that there was any such glebe, and finding that no minister of this established Church ever had been in possession of any glebe; they did proceed to the designation and visitation as the law requires. And Angus Taylor, land surveyor did measure out half an acre for building thereon a manse, yard, and office houses for the use of the said Alexander Hossack and his successors in office; and did also measure out four acres lying next to the seat of the manse, and gave in his report in writing as follows:

'Being summoned by you and at your desire, and in the presence of the Presbytery, I have surveyed arable glebe ground in the parish of Kilearnadale to the extent of four acres, three roods and ten falls. The quantity desired was four acres and two roods, but as the ground is interspersed with bushes of briers, brushwood, rocks and cairns of stones, together with the surface or contents of the high road passing through the same to the length of seven and a half chains and statute breadth being thirty-six falls or thereby. I conclude that the whole ground bearing crops is only four acres and two roods which was the quantity required. *Sic subsc.*

Angus Taylor, land surveyor

As also the Presbytery, with advice foresaid, did design as much pasture ground lying next adjacent to the glebe as will graze a horse and two cows; which glebe and grass are bounded as follows:

Viz. by the march dyke of Foiline on the north; by the sea on the east; by the water of Killearnadale on the south; by a line drawn along a little bank and in a straight line from thence to the march of Foiline as marked and meithad (*sic*) in the presence of the Presbytery on the west.

Then the Presbytery did assign the foresaid glebe and grass to belong to the present minister and his successors in office in all time coming with foggage, fewel, feal and divote out of the grounds next adjacent with free ish and entry thereto. Then the Moderator in the name of the Presbytery gave infeftment to the said glebe and grass to the said Mr Alexander Hossack by delivering of earth and stone. Then the Presbytery proceeded to deliberate on the estimates given in by the tradesmen upon oath at the last visitation of this parish upon the 21st day of May last; bearing that the sum of one hundred and fifteen pounds sterling would be necessary for building and completing the church in this division of the united parishes of Jura and Colonsay; which being considered by the Presbytery, they did approve thereof, and according thereto did appoint and determine that the aforesaid sum of one hundred and fifteen pounds sterling should be wared out and bestowed for the end above-mentioned and that they did and hereby do stent and decern the whole Heritors of the said united parishes of Jura and Colonsay in the said sum of one hundred and fifteen pounds money foresaid to be paid by them conforming to their received valued rents in manner following:

Viz His Grace the Duke of Argyll	£29 1/5 Rents and £15 19/2¼
Archibald Campbell of Jura	£122 18/7 Rents and £67 9/7¾
Donald Macneil of Colonsay	£103 17/4 Rents and £57 0/5¾
Daniel Campbell of Shawfield	£20 Rents and £10 19/6¾
Murdoch Maclean of Kilmory	£10 1/1 Rents and £5 10/4¼
Robert Stevenson of Belnahua	£1 Rents and 10/11¼

And the Presbytery considering that the foresaid designation or decreets if called in question, a process of this nature cannot be issued without trouble and expences. Therefore they did and hereby do decern the whole Heritors and wadsetters of the said united parishes in the sum of twenty pounds sterling money to be paid by them according to their received valuations towards defraying the necessary expenses that have been already, or may be hereafter incurred. And the Presbytery appoint and ordain the foresaid Mr Alexander Hossack and Alexander MacNeil, Brother to Colonsay, collectors for uplifting and receiving the sums above decerned.

The arrival of the Presbytery in Jura is actually quite surprising, and we should note that other matters have already been put in hand regarding the proposed building of a new church and of the manse. We are told that an earlier visitation took place on 21 May, when tradesmen gave estimates on oath. It may be that on that occasion Mr Campbell was invited to put land at the disposal of the Presbytery for church, manse and glebe. At that stage his co-operation may have been requested, and hoped for, but it is evident that it was not forthcoming.

The Presbytery at its next meeting in October may already be anticipating an objection from the laird. The Minute records an important disagreement, and it is evident from the formal evidence that the Presbytery's decisions will meet continued opposition.

The fact that Mr Campbell was involved in a confrontation which challenged his complete authority in the island seems to have made a deep impression on those present, for an account of the incident survived in the oral tradition of the community and was recited to the Rev. Charles Robertson by Malcolm Darroch of Keils about 1913.

The story he recorded goes as follows:

The manse was built and the glebe defined in the time of one of the Campbells known as Sean Ghilleasbuig; 'Old Archie'. An agent from Edinburgh lost patience with the criticisms and objections of Campbell and turning on him said: 'Bheirinnse mach e ged a b'ann eadar do bheul's do shroin.' ('I would have the land though it were between your mouth and your nose.') This Gaelic idiom may have something of the force of the English idiom: 'Though it were in the teeth of your opposition.'

One of the Jura men present asked Campbell; 'Am buail mi e?' ('Shall I hit him?')

'Cha bhuail, cha bhuail,' replied Campbell. ('Don't strike him, don't strike!')

The man who asked this question was related to the Blacks of Keills. The informant recorded that 'the agent's name was Hossack.'

The story records the event as an important one, and it retains, although inaccurately as to Mr Hossack's role, an important name from the past. So Alexander Hossack's name survived in memory for 150 years.

The exact location of the 'Bishop's Dale' and the 'Beadle's Glebe' are lost. The former church site is also gone, but it may have been somewhere on Sron an Tobair (Nose of the Well), and not at Carn an Searmonaich. An investigation on the ground using modern techniques might confirm the site, although the building seems to have been very short-lived.

There may have been a footbridge over the Minister's Burn at the public road, although it shoals over shingle where it runs to the sea, and can still be forded there. A crossing higher up where the meeting must have taken place could be a perilous and deep wade, although it is appealing to think of the ministers, possibly gowned for the meeting, gathering up their robes to cross away from Campbell's preferred field. If Mr Campbell did in fact have a plan to build to the south of the burn, he could well have continued to do so with no interference from the manse. The burn no doubt had alder and willow scrub along its banks then, as today. He would, however have wanted the decent fields behind the foreshore, which are well drained raised beach, and he would also have known that the bay in front of the manse was one of the best on the whole island for attracting great strandings of kelp after storms. This 'sea-ware' was to be the source of a long-running dispute between the minister and the laird.

Archibald Campbell marshals his arguments and communicates with his lawyer, and with the Court of Session. The Campbells were already well-established litigants by this time, and continued to be so until they left the island 170 years later.

He protests that the Presbytery have been both hasty and high-handed in seizing his land and produces a detailed piece of research intended to prove that the proper manse in the united Parish of Jura and Colonsay is at the site of the former Priory in Oronsay, and that he can produce documentary evidence to show that the Rev. John McSween actually had possession of this land as a glebe for a time about 1673.

His real objection is in his 'memorial' to his lawyer, where he makes it clear that he had planned to build a house of his own on the spot pitched upon by the Presbytery. It should be noted that after all this was over, in due course he chose a superb site when he built the present Jura House on one of the finest spots and the finest farms on the island.

It seems that neither the Presbytery nor the Lords Ordinary were very impressed. Perhaps they felt that the matter of the Oronsay Glebe was ancient history, and no doubt the Presbytery was able to adduce many years of non-co-operation from the Campbells throughout Neil Campbell and Neil Macleod's ministries.

Within a short time there is a 'Horning' issued against Campbell in the amount of the money he has been ordered to pay for the various erections. A 'Deed of Horning' was the terminology for being summoned to pay a debt.

By 3 February 1768, Campbell and the other Heritors have fallen foul of the Lords of Council and Session Commissioners appointed for the Plantation of Kirks and valuation of teinds, on an entirely different matter; namely; for not having paid the minister's stipend.

The 'Act and Commission' of the Court restates their own version of the description of the united parishes, first recorded at the 'Perambulation' by Presbytery in 1724. After the description of the parish, the 'Act and Commission' continues:

> The Minister's charges in going through his Parish; attending the Presbytery and for his paying Ferries, etc. must of necessity be very heavy and expensive and to conclude all, he has neither Manse, Glebe nor Grass, nor any place of domicil, neither is it in his power to have any comfortable lodging in the said Parishes except in Colonsay's house. And tho' the fund for Teind is very considerable as appears by a rental of the Stock and Teind of the said united Parishes therewith given out and holden as repeated 'brevitatis causa'; extending to no less than Nine Hundred and Ninety Eight Pounds, Eleven Shillings and One Penny Sterling. Notwithstanding whereof the pursuer was but meanly provided for his Service of the Cure of the said united Parishes; his present Stipend being only Seven Hundred Merks (£466 13/4); according to his best information. But he having no legal compulsitor to operate payment of his Stipend and having recovered only Seven Pounds Sterling or thereby of two years Stipend, he could not condescend on the precise quantum payable to the minister of the said united Parishes. Therefore the Lords of Council and Session Commissioners appointed for Plantation of Kirks and Valuation of Teinds, ought and should augment the foresaid Small Stipend and modify settle and appoint a constant and local Stipend in money and victual to be paid to the pursuer and his successors in Office; Ministers serving the Cure at the said United Parishes. Suitable to the extent of the Teinds and weight of the Charge and expense of the times and grant a Sufficient Allowance for furnishing the Communion Elements and establish as Locality of the whole payable by the

Heritors, Feuars, Farmorers, Tennants, Wadsetters, Liferenters, Factors, Chamberlains, Occupiers and Possessors of the Lands and others Intrometters with the Rents and Teinds of the said united parishes. Beginning the first year's payment thereof for the Crops and Year of God One Thousand, Seven Hundred and Sixty Seven and yearly thereafter in all time coming at the terms of payment following: Viz. The money at Whitsunday and Martinmas yearly by equal portions and the victual betwixt Yule and Candlemas yearly after separation of the Crops from the Land.

Here at last it sounds as if the minister of Jura is going to get justice at least in terms of his stipend, and it may be in contemplation of this letter than Archibald Campbell realises that he would be better to offer some kind of compromise in the whole question of his responsibilities for the ministry in Jura.

Letters and minutes fly to and fro between Campbell and the Lords Ordinary, who then appoint the minister of Kilarrow in Islay, John Woodrow, and Duncan Shaw, a tacksman in Islay to represent Mr Hossack, and suggest that they should meet with Archibald Campbell of Jura. The laird has apparently offered three properties on Jura as alternative sites for the manse and glebe, and has given assurances that he will allow land to be designated of equal quality and quantity on either Crackaig, Feoline, or Knocknafeolaman, if only the Presbytery will depart from their plan for Kilearnadail. Presumably the minister has hopes that this meeting will resolve the impasse, and no doubt he is not yet committed to the fact that his land and his house have to be on the lands designated. After all, building has not yet started, and there is as yet no sign that Campbell is going to pay for it, so presumably Mr Hossack has not yet entered upon the land the Presbytery gave him the previous year.

He would no doubt be unhappy with Crackaig, for, although by the 1841 Census it supported nearly fifty souls in more than a dozen dwellings, it was always a windswept corner and the ground was harsh and infertile. In its favour, it was only about two miles from the Church.

Feolin Farm was every bit as good land as the piece the Presbytery wanted, and adjacent to their choice, so no doubt Mr Hossack would have been quite content with that.

Knocknafeolaman has taken on an almost legendary quality in modern-day Jura since there has been no community there since early in the nineteenth century, and modern residents are unsure exactly where it was. The name survives as a little hill above Craighouse in the 1888 Ordnance Survey map. The high eminence of this location is now occupied by a Telephone Relay Station, and it is a stiff climb up from the shore. This may help to explain the outcome of the arranged meeting, for which we are fortunate to have an account minuted by the minister himself, and in his own hand, as follows.

At Craighouse in Jura, 10 May 1768:

The which day Baillie Archibald Graham of Islay and Donald Campbell of Ardmenish, on Mr Campbell of Jura's part, and Mr John Woodrow. Minister, and Mr Duncan Shaw, Tacksman in Islay on Mr Hossack's part, met in obedience to an Interlocutor of the Lords Ordinary's obliging Mr Campbell to excambe [exchange], the Glebe designed by the Presbytery of Kintyre, and design another equal to it in Quantity and Quality, considered upon any of the farms of Feoline, Crackaig or Knocknafeolaman, any lawful day before Whitsunday last. As appears by the Minutes agreed by Jura's Council.

But Mr Campbell, still willing to harrass the Minister, would not allow the foresaid gentlemen to obtemporate [yield obedience to], the Order of the Courts only for shifting matter, and pointed out a spot of ground, quite ragged and barren and ill to labour, on a great Eminence, very much exposed to wind and weather. The worst Situation for Manse and Office Houses in the whole Island. Besides building on such a height as would put the Parish to vast expenses, and the Minister and his successors in office to immense trouble, by carrying manure etc. up such a steep hill, and at a distance from the Shore, which is no small inconvenience to one living in an Island, and who has nine other Islands to go to.

Jura told the Referees: 'Design that for the minister, and if he does not take it, let him want!'

This spot is on the remotest and barrenest part of Knocknafeolaman, of little service to Master or Tenants at present.

But the Minister, agreeable to the terms of the Minute and Interlocutor desired Mr Campbell to let the Arbitrators design a Glebe on this same Farm of Knocknafeolaman, contiguous to the Shore, and equally convenient for building on with what the Presbytery designed.

But 'No!', says he, 'That would take away a part of the farm which I do not choose to part with.'

Then he was desired to let the Judges design a Glebe upon the farm of Crackaig, or Feoline.

His answer to this was that he would allow the designation of the Presbytery stand rather than have a Glebe designed upon Crackaig, Feoline, or any part of Knocknafeolaman, except the spot already described.

Thus Jura expressed himself and acted contrary to the Earnest Order of the Courts, which injured the Minister not a little by keeping him out of the quiet possession of a Glebe the Courts entitled him to, and the minister cannot help saying that Jura acted in this affair contrary to his word of honour, Obligation and the Obedience due to the Courts, in not designing a Glebe for the Minister as he agreed to once; and the Lord's Ordinary's Interlocutor past accordingly finding the Minister entitled to the possession of his Glebe before Whitsunday last.

But Jura being quite absolute and despotic in Jura found means to evade the appointment made upon him by the Courts.

The Minister at this meeting at Craighouse in Jura insisted that Jura and his party would commit to writing what passed that day, but this Jura and they absolutely refused, as if they were not answerable for their Conduct elsewhere

There being no Notary Public on the spot and nothing done, the Minister took no further step than telling them what he had represented in this paper, that he would lay this greivous treatment before the Lords, and that justice could be obtained there whatever would happen in a remote Island used hitherto to arbitrary measures.

Sic subscribitur: Alex. r Hossack

N.B. It is hoped now the Courts will find good cause from the foresaid considerations to affirm the Decree of Presbytery, which seems more agreeable to Jura than implementing the late order of the Courts, and oblige Jura to pay what expenses the Pursuer has been at in this Process.

Various documents indicate that after this bad-tempered meeting Archibald Campbell decided that there was nothing to be done but make the best of it, and accept that the Land at Kilearnadil was going to be the Glebe. At least he no longer makes any overt protest about the locality, although he continues to 'harass' the minister.

We have a letter from 15 December 1768, which indicates that he has objected to the boundary on the seaward side of the glebe, and has asked that the glebe should stop at the road, leaving him in possession of the seashore. Here is the letter which gives a ruling on the matter:

> 15th December 1768. The Lord Ordinary, having considered what is above set forth, finds that the ground designed by the Presbytery of Kintyre is to continue to be the Glebe and Grass Lands thereto belonging with these variations, that in place of the public High Road of the Island of Jura going through the said Glebe that the same shall go close by the Sea side, agreeable to the line marked out by the said James McAllester as mentioned in his report, signed by the said Lord Ordinary of this date as relative hereto, and of consent finds that the Charger and his Successors are entitled to a ninth part of the Sea Wrack or Manure on the Shore opposite to his Glebe, the remainder to belong to the said Archibald Campbell, and with these variations finds the Letters orderly proceeded and Decorous. Signed, Alexr. Boswell.

Generations later we find the Campbells still contesting the matter of seaweed in front of the glebe with each succeeding minister, although no doubt each new incumbent would be unaware that he was inheriting this age-old argument as well as the rest of his parish. With eight-ninths of the sea ware from the bay, the laird was doing pretty well, but on the right occasion the little bay can accumulate countless tons of seaweed, so no doubt the 'ninth part' would be sufficient to fertilise the glebe, although how such a fraction could be accurately calculated is now a mystery.

By 16 July 1771, Archibald Campbell is still being 'Put to the Horn' to pay his proportion of the amounts decreed in respect of the building of manse and church, so presumably is still resisting the Order of the Court, but the manse was finally constructed in 1774 – 'so inefficiently,' says the Rev. Francis Stewart, eighteen years later, 'that it now needs repairs'.

The church was completed the next year 1777, but there is an indication of 'meanness' there also for later we hear, 'there is no place for a bell, and it was never seated'.

Despite the matters of glebe, manse and church being settled, the question of the stipend runs on and on, with no doubt continuing bitterness between the two parties.

The documents concerning this matter are many and various. There are: Decreets of Modification; Answers and Queries, Valuations of Teinds, Observations on Expenses; and many more. Two documents however stand out from the rest and may act as an adequate summary of the entire encounter between the determined minister and the 'despotic' laird. The first is as follows:

25 July 1768: Teind Cause: Lord Elliock, Reporter. Condescendence for Mr Alexander Hossack, minister of the United Parishes of Jura and Colonsay; Pursuer:

The minister, in order that the heretors may not have it in their power to contradict what he shall condescend upon with regard to what the state and circumstances of these parishes are. He produces an exact copy of the report of the committee of the General Assembly appointed by them to visit the western isles. [a copy of the perambulation follows again]. Many inconveniencies, to which the minister of Jura has always been subjected, occasion this melancholy circumstance, that the sacrament of the Lord's Supper has been but once dispensed in the parish during the present century.

The minister further condescends, and says, that these parishes lie upwards of sixty miles from the seat of Presbytery, which is at Campbeltown, and about the same distance from Inverary, the seat of the Synod.

The situation of these parishes makes them perhaps the most expensive for a minister to follow his duty of any parish in Scotland; and its having so many ferries to cross, requires a great part of a stipend of themselves, without anything else, and these often very dangerous to pass.

The expense of passing and repassing from Jura to the parish of Colonsay is 16s Sterling; from Jura to the seat of Presbytery, coming and going £4 Sterling; from Jura to Keills, the place of landing to go to the Synod, 6s Sterling; from Jura to Scarba, one of the places of worship; going and coming, 5s Sterling. These for a small sample of ferries, although there are numbers of other ferries, fresh waters, etc, which the minister must be at a great expense in crossing and recrossing in the course of his duty, which he is very much inclined to do, if a proper subsistence was provided for him; and cannot compute the whole expences of crossing and recrossing ferries, etc. below £25 Sterling.

There is neither Manse, Glebe, nor Church in this parish; although application has been made for these, yet it has not been in the minister's power to obtain them.

The stock and teinds of these parishes, conforming to the scheme of the proven rental, adjusted in process, amounts to £900 18/10d Sterling, the fifth part whereof for Teind is £180 3/9d money foresaid.

From these circumstances, the minister hopes the Lords will be of the opinion, that serving the cure of the said united parishes of Jura and Colonsay is fully as weighty and expensive as that of Ardnamurchan, where their Lordships were pleased to give 2000 merks of stipend to the minister, with the burden of 500 merks to an assistant preacher. If their Lordships are of the opinion, that the state and circumstances of the united parishes of Jura and Colonsay require an assistant preacher to be given to the minister, the pursuer is ready to give such security to that assistant for the stipend to be allotted to him as the Lords shall judge proper.

In the mean time the minister being noways provided of any stipend whatsomever, nor of no place of residence, he hopes it will appear absolutely necessary to your Lordships, that he should be provided of a stipend suitable to the extent of the teinds and circumstances of the parish, that so he may be enabled to do what of his duty he is capable;

And if their Lordships shall afterwards be of the opinion, that for the good of the people, and prosperity of religion in these parts, an assistant preacher ought to be given, whatever way their Lordships shall please to devise to secure that assistant a decent living, the minister will cheerfully acquiesce.

In respect whereof, Etc. Alex. Hossack

In connection with Mr Hossack's appeal, Archibald Campbell is represented by one 'Ilay Campbell'; no doubt both his lawyer and a relation, and, as we shall see, a man of wit and wisdom.

Ilay Campbell produces 'Answers' in the Teind Cause to be reported to Lord Elliock, and these answers are dated 26 July 1768. After due consideration, Mr Hossack seems to have been given a further opportunity to enlarge on the matter of his expenses, and in consequence, Ilay Campbell produces a more complete argument, which enters the records as 'The Petition.'

15 November 1768; Teind Cause; Unto the Right Honourable the Lords Commissioners of Teinds. The Petition of Archibald Campbell of Jura:

Humbly sheweth that in the process of Augmentation, Modification and Locality at the Instance of Mr Alexander Hossack, Minister of Jura, against the Heritors, your Lordships, of this date, pronounced the following Interlocutor:

On Report of the Lord Elliock, Ordinary, and having considered the Condescendence and Answers, the Lords, modify, decern and ordain, the constant Stipend and Provision of the united Parishes of Jura and Colonsay, to have been for the Crop and Year of God, 1767, and yearly thereafter, in time coming, 2000 Merks Scots Money for Stipend, and £30 Scots, for furnishing the Communion Elements, with the Burden always of 800 Merks Scots yearly, to be paid by the Pursuer to an assistant Preacher or Helper in the said united Parishes; and decern and ordain to the same to be paid yearly to the Pursuer, and his Successors in Office, Ministers serving the Cure of the said United Parishes, by the Titulars and Tacksmen of the Teinds, Heritors and Possessors of the Lands, and others, Intromitters with the Rents and Teinds of the said united Parishes, out of the first and readiest of the Teinds, Parsonage and Vicarage of the same, beginning the first Year's Payment thereof, from the said Crop and Year of God 1767, and so forth yearly thereafter in all time coming, at the terms of Whitsunday and Martinmas yearly by equal portions, and declare, that the 800 Merks allotted for the said assistant Preacher in the said united Parishes, shall only subsist till a new Erection takes place in the Island of Colonsay; and remit to the Lord Elliock to hear parties upon the Security to be taken from the Pursuer, for payment of the said 800 Merks to the said Assistant, and to prepare a Locality, and to report.

Though the Consequence of this Interlocutor is to throw a very heavy Burden upon the Petitioner, who is in a Manner the only Heritor in the Island of Jura, he would be far from repining at any Judgement of your Lordships, in a Matter of this Kind, were he certain that the Facts on which it proceeded, had been fairly and fully represented to the Court. But upon looking into the printed Condescendence for the Pursuer, he had Reason to believe, that the Case was otherwise. The Facts are there greatly mis-stated, and the supposed Difficulties of the Charge are magnified in a most uncommon Degree.

The Pursuer seems to have relied chiefly on a Report of the Committee of the General Assembly, who some time ago visited the Western Isles; which Report bears: (the report follows again). The Reports of this Committee of the Clergy, who made a Jaunt to the Western Islands, are not always very accurate; and this is one instance of the little Pains they have taken to be informed. It is true, the Island of Jura is twenty-four Miles long; but it is not true, that through its whole Extent, the Island is covered with inaccessible Mountains. One side of it is plain and accessible, and there the Inhabitants reside. The other Part of the Island is indeed inaccessible, but for that very Reason, it is not inhabited, and the Minister has no more Occasion to set his Foot upon that Side, than he has to travel to *Japan*.

Neither is it true that there are 466 Inhabitants on this Island. The real Number is not above 300. The Minister will have no Occasion for the future, to preach in different Places of the Island. A good Church is now ready to be built, the Money, having been already awarded by the Presbytery for that Purpose. A Manse and Glebe have also been designed; no less than twelve Acres of Ground have been allotted for the Glebe, and the Petitioner has again and again offered to accommodate Mr Hossack with a House and other Conveniencies, till his Manse is fully completed.

In none of the Islands composing this Parish, has the Minister any occasion to preach, except in Jura, Colonsay and Scarba. The Custom has been, to preach four Times in the Year in Colonsay and twice in Scarba. The Fact is that the other Islands are more properly Rocks than Islands, with scarcely a living Creature upon them.

The Libel too mentions thirteen Rivers which the Minister has, at Times, occasion to pass. Ten of them are Rivulets, which the Minister at most Places may step over; The other three are very seldom impassable, and there are Bridges about to be built over them.

But the most extraordinary Averment was, that the Expense of Crossing Ferries, in the Course of his Duty, was not less than £25 per annum.

The Expense of passing to Colonsay, and repassing, he computes at 16s Sterling; that of going to Campbeltown to the Presbytery, and returning, £4

Sterling; crossing to Keills, in order to go to Inverary, the Seat of the Synod, 6s Sterling; going to Scarba, and returning, 5s Sterling.

Even this Calculation would amount to less than the one half of £25. But the true Fact is, that he has the Packet -Boat to Kintyre for 1/6d, when he chooses to attend the Presbytery, which he has no occasion to do often. The expense of crossing for Inverary, where he has still seldomer occasion to go is likewise a Trifle. And as to ferrying over to Colonsay, and to Scarba, in order to preach, this generally costs him nothing; the Inhabitants considering it as there Duty to ferry over their Minister 'gratis'. Scarba is not above a quarter of a mile from Jura; And, upon the whole, it is a mere Jest to pretend, that he is at any Expense for Ferries.

The Plan on which he has been pleased to make his Computation, is, in the first place, That he must give punctual Attendance on Presbyteries, Synods, Etc. And secondly, That he must freight a Vessel on purpose, every Time he ventures himself upon the Waves, in place of taking his Passage in the Ferry-boats.

One material Circumstance, to be attended to by your Lordships, is, that there is no Place in Scotland where living is so cheap as in this very Island of Jura.

A good Slaughter-Cow can be bought in it for forty or fifty Shillings; a Sheep for three or four Shillings; Kids below one Shilling each; and Lamb, Veal, Poultry, Etc. in proportion.

There is also great Abundance of Sea-Fish of all kinds, which the Minister may have at the Expense only of sending his servants to catch them. The Island lies contiguous to Kintyre, Knapdale, and Islay, the most plentiful Countries in Argyll-shire for Meal, which is therefore had at a cheap Rate in Jura. No Company resorts to the Island. The Minister is put to no extraordinary Charge of any kind. In short, if your Lordships adhere to your Interlocutor, he will have the most comfortable, the easiest, and the best Living in Scotland; few Highland Lairds will stand in Comparison with him.

It is believed what chiefly induced your Lordships to pronounce this Inter-locutor, was a similar Judgement in the Case of Ardnamurchan; but the Circumstances of that Parish were extremely particular. It consisted of the five Countries of Ardnamurchan, Sunart, Moidart, Arasaig, and Morhir, lying in two different Shires, Argyle and Inverness. Ardnamurchan and Sunart alone extended, due east and west, about thirty Miles, and in Breadth betwixt six and seven Miles, intersected by a high Ridge of Mountains, both sides of the mountains very populous, and containing three different Places of Worship. Moidart was proved to be eighteen Miles long, five broad, and mostly inhabited by professed Papists; Arisaig fourteen miles long, seven broad, separated from Moidart by an Arm of the Sea, and inhabited by 380 professed Papists; Morhir fifteen Miles in Length, separated from Arisaig by inaccessible Hills, containing a Number of Papists, and the whole of these Countries intersected with Arms of the Sea, Ferries to cross, travelling very bad; and, in short, it appeared to your Lordships, to be such a Parish, that no one Minister could possibly undertake the Charge of it.

Such were the Circumstances of Ardnamurchan, as appearing from the Excerpt produced by the Pursuer in this Process; and it is submitted, how far they are in any shape applicable, or can afford any Rule for the Decision of the present Case. The Petitioner did signify his Willingness, from the Beginning, to acquiesce in a reasonable and decent Stipend, and made Offers to Mr Hossack, which some of his own friends approved of; And indeed he himself never dreamed of asking anything near to what your Lordships have given.

May it therefore please your Lordships, to alter the above Interlocutor, and to allow the Pursuer no more than what shall be thought a reasonable Stipend, all Circumstances considered.

According to Justice, etc ...

Ilay Campbell

This fascinating document brings to an end our records relating to the conflict between Alexander Hossack and Archibald Campbell. Francis Stewart in the *Statistical Account* of 1794 is able to declare, 'The Stipend is 2000 merks, out of which the minister pays, in terms of the decreet of augmentation, 800 merks to his assistant in Colonsay.'

So here a quarter of a century after the Hossack debate, his efforts to secure an end to the troubles which had haunted his predecessors have evidently continued to bear fruit. The splendid stipend, based on that of Ardnamurchan is now established as the 'rate for the job'.

The last mention in our records of the Hossacks is on 15 February 1790, when a document in the Campbell of Jura Papers records the 'State of the Account between Archibald Campbell of Jura, and Mrs Helen Hossack, relict of Mr Alexander Hossack, Minister of Jura, and her children'.

23

Later Ministries

ALEXANDER STUART

Mr Hossack's successor in Jura was the Rev. Alexander Stuart. Mr Stuart, born in 1755, was the son of Andrew Stuart, farmer of Park, in the Parish of Killean and Kilchenzie. We know little about him, except that he was educated at the University of Glasgow, licensed by the Presbytery of Kintyre in 1780, and was admitted to Jura in 1786. Five years later he was translated to his native parish. He died on 22 December 1798. Two of his sons, Robert and Charles, were army officers and fought at the Battle of Waterloo. Mr Stuart compiled the *First Statistical Account* of the parish of Killean and Kilchenzie. No parish records survive from Mr Stuart's time, but there are some Minutes of Presbytery, which tell an all-too-familiar story, as follows:

The Presbytery of Kintyre at Campbeltown, 26 March 1788:
A Petition from Mr Alexander Stuart, Minister of Jura, setting forth that he had some time ago represented to the Heritors of the Parish the state of his Manse, and want of Office Houses, and that the said Heritors had agreed to cause the necessary reparations of the Manse to be made, and Office Houses to be built, and they had bestowed the sum of £125 10/6 for the purpose of repairing the said manse, and building Office Houses, as appears by an account under the hands of Will Fairlie, Mason, and John McTavish, Wright, and Henry Ireland, Slater. The greater part of the Heritors had expressed a desire to have a Decree of Presbytery passed and interponed for making any part of this said sum as yet unpaid effectual.

Craving therefore that the Presbytery would pass a decree for the said sum. And the Presbytery do stent and descern the Heritors of the Parish to pay the sum of £125 10/6 Sterling, according to the different proportions which refer to their respective valuations.

Presbytery at Campbeltown, 21 July 1789:
Petition from Mr Stuart, Minister of Jura that in addition to the sum decerned, there are other charges found necessary, and that in consequence the Heritors desired a visitation to Jura, for the purpose of taking the whole under consideration, inspecting the work done, and declaring the Manse and Office Houses sufficient.

The Presbytery of Kintyre at the Church of Jura, 25 August 1789:
Mr Alexander Stuart reported that he had duly warned the Heritors of the Parish of Jura and Colonsay to be present this day, and the said Heritors being called; compeared Archibald Campbell of Jura. James Fraser, Wright, and Thomas Spadin, Mason were summoned to attend. The said tradesmen, being called, compeared, and having given their oath 'de fideli' were desired to repair to the Manse and Office Houses of the Minister of Jura to examine the

same, to compare them with the estimate with which they were furnished and to report.

There was produced a reference from the Kirk Session of Jura anent a Scandal of Adultery raised and propagated against Dugald McArton, one of the Elders of the Parish. The Presbytery remits the affair to the Session with an instruction to them to punish Neil Darroch and Dugald Gray, mentioned in the reference as calumnators or slanderers unless they shall prove that the scandal raised and propagated by them is well founded.

Mr Stuart asked that, as the Court of Teinds had given by their decree provision for an Assistant Preacher in his Parish, the Presbytery should give their advice as to the place or places where the Assistant ought to be employed. The Presbytery, after hearing Mr Stuart and Mr Campbell of Jura on the subject, and reasoning on it, gave it as their opinion that the Assistant ought always to reside and officiate on the Island of Colonsay, except when the Minister of the Parish shall judge it for edification to call him occasionally to some other stations within the Charge.

James Fraser and Thomas Spadin, above mentioned returned and made their Report. They had gone to the Manse and Office Houses on the Glebe of Jura and examined the repairs and buildings mentioned in the estimate delivered to them by the Presbytery. They are of the opinion that the sum of £125 10/6 mentioned in the estimate, if it is faithfully laid out and exhausted, is good and sufficient. Mr Stuart produced an account of £2 sterling paid for making out the estimate, and also another of £2 sterling charged by James Fraser and Thomas Spadin for their attendance at this time, which with the sum already mentioned amounts in all to the sum of £129 10/6. Which sum the Presbytery to stent and decern the heritors of Jura to pay immmediately to Mr Stuart, and crave the Lords of Council and Session may be pleased to interpose their authority for rendering this decree effectual.

The Presbytery went thereafter to the Manse and Office Houses forementioned, and having viewed the same and heard the opinion of the tradesmen as above, they unanimously agreed to declare the said Manse and Office Houses free, and sufficient, upon all which Archibald Campbell Esq. of Jura, in his own name and that of the other Heritors took instruments and craved extracts. The said Mr Campbell of Jura represented that the Parish Church of Jura needed some repairs and craved the Presbytery to decern for the same. The Presbytery appointed James Fraser and Thomas Spadin to prepare an estimate of the said repairs and give it in at the next meeting.

As often seems to be the case, the Presbytery Record here is fragmentary and incomplete, and this is all we have. It seems as though the manse, built as recently as 1774, is now, only fifteen years later, needing a substantial amount of repair. Indeed the cost of the entire Building in 1766 was estimated at £157, and here we see Archibald Campbell required to bear his share of the new renovations, amounting to £129. It seems as if the later comment from the *First Statistical Account* of 1789 is relevant here: 'The Manse was built about eighteen years ago. New Office Houses were built and the Manse was repaired about four years ago, but so insufficiently, that it needs new repairs.' It may well be that the major part of the £129 was devoted to the 'New Office Houses'. The Office Houses attached to the 'New Manse', built in 1840, comprised: 'The Barn; The Byre; The Stable; The Gig House; The Calf Shed; The Dairy; The Boiler House; The Wood & Peat Shed.'

No doubt these would have been accepted as the standard requirements, based on the existing suite of buildings from the previous century. It seems as if the victory of Alexander Hossack in the matter of the building of his manse may have been for himself and his successors a 'hollow victory'. Perhaps the £157 voted on in 1766 was truly insufficient to complete the range of buildings which would have been necessary for his family to live in comfort, and effectively to farm the glebe.

In 1790 we hear of the appointment of Mr Patrick McRuer, a Preacher in Campbeltown, to be Assistant in Colonsay, provided the Presbytery are satisfied that he has sufficient Gaelic. Later minutes indicate that Mr McRuer gets into some difficulty, but the volumes of minutes from 1794 to 1796 are missing, so apart from the use of 'heavy' language, like 'unwarrantably negligent' and 'absenting himself for so long and so frequently' and of his 'misconduct', we have nothing but tantalising hints about the real problems.

FRANCIS STEWART

From 1791 until 1794, the Rev. Francis Stewart was the minister of the parish. At his 'Trials for Licence' on being Ordained to Jura, considerable stress was laid upon the necessity of his being proficient in the Gaelic tongue. The island of Gigha had rejected him as a candidate the previous year on account of his weakness in the Gaelic.

From Jura he was translated to Kilchrennan and Dalivich. He died in 1832. Our chief interest in Mr Stewart is that he was responsible for compiling the *First Statistical Account* of the Parish of Jura, and has consequently has given us a sharp picture of the island in 1794.

DONALD MACNICOL

After Mr Stewart left, the parish remained vacant for two years. The Rev. Donald MacNicol was called to the parish in 1796. He had been born in Craignish, and educated at the University of Glasgow.

Presbytery of Kintyre in Campbeltown, 9 August 1801:
Donald McNicol, Minister of Jura and Colonsay represented that several grievances existed in his parish, the Removal of which rendered a visitation of the Presbytery necessary, particularly the want of a Church in the Island of Colonsay, the Reparations which the Church and Manse of Jura stand in need of, and the Insufficiency of the Grass Ground which he enjoys for the proper support of Four Soums to which he is entitled. [A 'soum' was pasture for one cow.]

And, as appeared by a letter from Mr McNeill of Oronsay and Malcolm McNeill, acting for Col. McNeill of Colonsay, they desire him to apply for such a visitation with a view to having measures taken to build a Church in Colonsay. Presbytery found this reasonable.

Mr McNicol said, that notwithstanding the frequent admonitions given, and complaints made respecting the conduct of Patrick McRuer, Assistant Preacher in Colonsay, he continued still to give much grounds for complaint against him for his great and culpable neglect of duty in his station by reason of his non-residence in the Island of Colonsay,. and his frequent and long-continued absence from his Charge. Presbytery decided to enquire further, and summon him to attend.

It seems that despite the changing personalities, the problems of the parish of Jura and Colonsay remain fairly constant. Difficulty in attending meetings and difficulty in persuading the Heritors to be more open and generous in their dealings with the church.

Presbytery at Campbeltown, July 1803:
The Moderator was appointed to write to Mr McNicol recommending him to attend the next meeting of Presbytery or send a sufficient apology for his habitual absence, and also to give a particular state of the facts respecting the Assistantship in his Parish.

Ultimately in 1804 there is a lengthy investigation of the problems in Colonsay, which is outside this remit, although a letter from Patrick McRuer of 28 January 1804 to the Presbytery of Kintyre indicated that all was not well.

Mr MacRuer here reveals, not only his continuing dificulties with housing in Colonsay, but the fact that the laird has embarked on a campaign to have the assistant become a fully ordained minister, presumably as a prelude to an application to have Colonsay erected as a separate parish with its own church, manse and minister.

The new church in Colonsay was finished at Scalasaig in 1802, but it would be another sixty years before Colonsay was disjoined from Jura and erected into a 'Quoad Omnia' charge with a minister of its own.

During Donald MacNicol's ministry the endless saga of alterations and improvements to the church and manse in Jura continued. He won some rounds and Campbell won others.

Donald MacNicol was translated to the parish of Kilfinan in the Presbytery of Dunoon on 20 December 1811. He died, unmarried, in 1830.

ARCHIBALD MCTAVISH
On 6 May 1812 the Rev. Archibald McTavish was admitted to the parish of Jura and Colonsay. He was educated at the University of Edinburgh, and Licensed by the Presbytery of Lorn. In 1814 he married Mary MacFarlane, the daughter of the Rev. John MacFarlane, late minister of the Parish of Kilbrandon in the Presbytery of Lorn. He had a son called Dugald in 1814 and another named Duncan Archibald in 1818. A brief inscription on a stone grave-slab near the Campbell of Jura Mausoleum records only these words: Colin Campbell and Neil, son of Rev. Archibald McTavish.

We have no background to the story behind this stone. Presumably Colin Campbell was one of the sons of Colin Campbell, sixth of Jura. Perhaps this was a family disaster involving the untimely death of two friends.

Archibald McTavish went to Kildalton Parish at Port Ellen in Islay in 1823. He died in Glasgow in 1857.

ALEXANDER KENNEDY

The Rev. Alexander Kennedy who followed Mr McTavish, was minister of Jura and Colonsay from 1823 to 1849. He was educated at the University of St Andrews, and married in 1818, Ann, the daughter of Donald Maclean, a surgeon of Mull. Of their family, Mary, their daughter, born in 1819, married in 1840, Archibald Fletcher, tacksman of Kinuachdrach in Jura, and Ann, born in 1823, married the Rev. Donald MacFarlane, minister of Killean. Many important events took place during Mr Kennedy's ministry on Jura.

In 1835 the ministers of Islay and the minister of Jura and Colonsay petitioned the Presbytery of Kintyre to apply to the General Assembly to disjoin them from the Presbytery of Kintyre, and erect a separate Presbytery, to be called the Presbytery of Islay. The General Assembly of 1836 granted the petition, and disjoined the Parishes of Kilarrow, Kildalton, Kilchoman, Kilmeny, Oa, Portnahaven, and Jura and Colonsay, and formed these seven parishes into a new Presbytery, which they called Islay and Jura, with its seat to be at Bowmore.

In 1840 the major split in the Church of Scotland, known as 'The Disruption' took place. Mr Kennedy's role in this matter will be considered later, but the record shows that the established church on Jura and Colonsay remained part of the Church of Scotland, and it is some years before we hear of the activities of The 'Free Church' in the Parish.

In 1843, the government of the day required the compilation of the *Second Statistical Account*, and once more it was the parish minister who found himself writing about Jura. He tells us in some detail of developments concerning the church of Jura:

> The parish church of Jura, built about sixty-three years ago, was at first roofed in, furnished with doors and windows, seated in part, but never fully finished. For many years during the writer's incumbency it was allowed to fall into a miserable state of disrepair. It is now otherwise, considerable sums of money having been expended upon in in the course of the last year. A spacious vestry, a gallery and comfortable apartment for the accommodation of the Jura family, were furnished, chiefly at the expense of Mr Campbell of Jura. The passages were paved with freestone slabs from the quarry of Airdantallin near Oban. The interior of the church of Jura now exhibits such an air of comfort and elegance, as is surpassed by no other in the islands of Argyle. The sittings are free. A new manse and office houses, with garden wall, were built last year, and are now occupied by the minister.

No doubt there will have been the usual difficulty in persuading the heritors to agree to the improvements to the church, and to the complete rebuilding of the manse, but the Presbytery records do not furnish us with the same blow by blow accounts of this new phase of building as we had in former times. It is interesting that part of the improvement to the church went on the laird's gallery, and for the private 'retiring room' with fireplace and chimney for the laird's family. Here his servant could come early on a wintry Sunday, and make a fire. Perhaps the Campbells could have short breaks from the full duration of the minister's sermon. It is interesting that in the present century, when the estate was changing hands, it was suggested by their lawyer to the departing owners that it might no longer be in the spirit of the times to advertise the 'retiring room' at the parish church as a useful selling point, and it was left out of the sale specification. The room has in recent times become a gallery for local photographs.

The church of which Mr Kennedy was so proud lasted largely unchanged for the next ninety years. The main entrance was in the east wall, and there was an outside stair leading to the north gallery.

The church in this form saw out the First World War, and during the present author's incumbency it was still well remembered by several older members of the congregation. So clear were their memories that an artist living on Jura in the 1970s, was able to reconstruct an impression of the pre-1922 church. The church was a charming building, with pews on three sides, and a precentor's box below the central pulpit. A north and south gallery faced erach other, with the laird's loft in between.

We return now to Mr Kennedy. On the completion of the new manse, the laird seemed reluctant to issue a suitable certificate of occupation, and Mr Kennedy and his family moved out of the old and now ruinous house without an official hand-over. When Campbell learned of this he wrote a typical letter expressing his severe displeasure. Mr Kennedy wrote back with disarming courtesy, and his letter follows:

Sir,   Jura Manse, 24th June 1842

In reply to your letter of yesterday, I beg leave to state, that the absence of all comfort, and the presence of many inconveniencies and discomforts drove myself and my family from the Old Manse.

It is true that we have entered the New One upon the Evening of Tuesday last, 21st. This step I have not adopted without due deliberation and must of course, be prepared to abide by any consequences which it may involve.

I regret much that I have unconsiderously and unintentionally given you cause of offence, and remain, Sir,

Yours most obedient Servant,
Alex. Kennedy
Colin Campbell of Jura, Esquire.

Mr Kennedy did not live long to enjoy the comforts of his new manse, and died in 1849. He is buried in Kilearnadil Cemetery, but the location of his grave is no longer known. A fine early photograph survives of Ann Kennedy, his widow, with one of her daughters.

Mr Kennedy's manse remains standing to this day, and the author lived in it with his family for twelve happy years. It has a fine setting in the middle of the glebe and in front of Glas Bheinn, and looking out across 'the Minister's water' to the islands of Small Isles Bay.

LACHLAN MACKENZIE

The next minister was the Rev. Lachlan MacKenzie who was in Jura from 1850 until 1876. It was during his time that the island of Colonsay was finally separated from Jura and given its own minister.

As far as the Free Church was concerned, there seems to have been no great demand until new members settled on the island. By 1864 however, local subscriptions had raised enough money to build a church, and land was granted at Lergiebreck for the new building. Worship was largely under the control of lay catechists, or (Ceistearan), the last of whom, Ceistear McKay, left the island in the 1930s. Visiting preachers continued to hold services at Lergiebreck Kirk until well after the Second World War. The last service was held in 1968. It was Ceistear McKay who was on one occasion concerned with absenteeism from the Sunday School. There had been a ceilidh at Knockrome on the previous Saturday night. These events were held in a notable long barn, and Sandy Buie remembered well sitting behind the piper's legs and watching the fun. The following day Ceistear McKay arrived at Knockrome, and took his stance outside the barn. He raised a hand and declared: 'It's Satan's Synagogue!'

Lachlan MacKenzie's ministry seems to have been uneventful and he died in office. His gravestone is in Kilearnadil Cemetery and bears the inscription:

Erected by the parishioners of Jura in loving memory of their beloved pastor: Rev. Lachlan McKenzie   1876   77

ANGUS MCCUAIG

The Rev. Angus McCuaig, the next minister of Jura, belonged to Port Ellen, in Islay. He was educated at the High School and University of Glasgow, and was inducted to the Parish of Oa, on Islay in 1871, after which in 1876, he was translated to Jura. He died in office in 1903, and is buried in Oa in Islay.

The records of his ministry are not extensive, but the continuing story of problems with church property surfaces again in his time. Now we are dealing with the new Presbytery of Islay.

Presbytery of Islay and Jura at Bridgend, 30 June 1855:

The Committee appointed on 29th April to inspect and report on the state of Jura Church reported that they had visited on the day appointed with qualified tradesmen; viz John Keith, Joiner, Bowmore, and Donald McGilvray, Builder, Bowmore. James Campbell, Esq of Jura attended the meeting.

The Report follows: The seats are shaky and uncomfortable and will require to be removed and renewed. The seats in the Area will need to be removed and a new deal floor put in. A new pulpit will need to be put up and the Precentor's Desk renewed. The inside of the walls are damp and will need to be lathed on straps and plastered and lined. All the doors and windows will require to be overhauled and painted with two coats best oil paint. The whole inside of the church will need to be whitewashed and the front of the galleries cleaned and varnished.

The outside of the west gable will need to be picked and recast with lime

cement, also the stair. The whole outside of the walls of the church will require
. to be whitewashed with lime.

And there is much more; all accepted by the Presbytery; which adds its own
requirements and demands that the floor be lifted and the earth dug out.

Then they accept a petition from Mr McCuaig that he has no WC or bathroom
in the manse, and that the whole house is damp through defective drainage. We
don't have the figures for the work on the church, but it was certainly all carried
out.

This meeting led to a similar visit to the manse in 1877, when D. & J. McGilvray, Builders of Bowmore, submit estimates for a long list of repairs and
improvements, including the installation of a contemporary water closet. The bill
is £115, and falls now to James Campbell, ninth of Jura, who appears to have
paid with a good grace.

Mr McCuaig was a man well over six feet tall, abounding in energy and good
humour. At the time of the author's own incumbency on Jura in the 1970s, there
were still several aged inhabitants who remembered Mr McCuaig, and he features
in several 'Tales' which will be reprinted later.

The Kirk Session inserted a minute in their records at the time of his death,
which reveals the sense of loss felt at his departure: 'They will remember with
gratitude and affection his manly presence, his inspiring words, his unbounded
generosity and kindliness of heart towards themselves, the members of his
congregation, and all the other inhabitants of the island.' Angus McCuaig's wife
was Jane Macdonald. They had a son Duncan, born in Oa in 1871, who died
in his eighth year. The were also renowned for having nine daughters.

DONALD JOHN ROBERTSON

The Rev. Donald John Robertson followed as the next minister of Jura in 1903.
He was born at Breakish, in Skye, in 1870, and educated at the University of
Glasgow. After several assistantships he came to Jura, which was to be his only
parish. In 1910 he married Sarah, the daughter of Angus Mackay and Julia
MacPherson. Angus was a keeper on Jura. It would have been difficult for a
local girl to become the 'lady of the manse', but Sarah did it with ease, and
survived her husband for many years.

Donald John was the minister during the First World War, and moving
photographs survive of his prayers with the departing troops. (Plate 10)

He took an active part in local government, and served first on the School
Board and Parish Council, and later on the District Council. He was interested
in education and was himself a fine Gaelic scholar. In 1922 he was largely
responsible for the modernisation of the church. The north and south galleries
were removed, and the seating turned at right angles to the former plan.

It can easily be imagined what excitement this whole enterprise caused. The
church was closed for some months. The chief cause of the renovation was decay
in the roof and galleries. At any rate the roof was removed and the beams with
the wooden dowels replaced. Much spoil was carried away to the burning; the
dry laths from the old lath and plaster ceiling being particularly in demand. The
old north and south galleries were taken away completely with their access

stairways. The main door was turned into the second of the existing windows, and a new door was opened in the south wall, sheltered by a small entrance porch. The pulpit and precentor's box were removed as were all the old pews, and to compensate for the loss of so many seats with the removal of the galleries, the whole church seating was turned at right angles, forming the present chancel, and the existing seating plan. A new pulpit was installed, and a fine new communion table was presented by Mr Robertson, the minister. This table remains in use today. Oil lamps were given by the minister's wife, and they too continue in use, converted to function as electric lamp holders. The reconstruction provided a suitable opportunity for the erection of a War Memorial Tablet, and this was unveiled on the occasion of the re-opening of the church in December 1922.

Donald John Robertson was the minister when the rift between the Church of Sotland and the Free Church was finally healed in the settlement of 1929, at which time churches and church affairs passed out of the control of the Heritors and into the control of the Church of Scotland General Trustees. The actual site of the church was transferred by certificate of the Sheriff dated 25 February and recorded 14 March, both in 1929.

At this time the Local Architect recommended that as well as repairs estimated at £21 10/– being carried out, the heritors should be asked to provide a lavatory at an estimated cost of £130, and to erect a boundary wall facing the main road with two gateways in it, and to form a path to the church at an estimated cost of £170. Mr Robertson deprecated putting these proposals before the heritors as he stated that they had, within the past three years, entirely renovated and improved the Church at a cost of £1500. The General Trustees accepted the view of the minister, and in submitting their claim to the the Heritors they provided for the sum of £21 10/– in respect of repairs to the church. The claim in respect of repairs to the manse and manse outbuildings was £184 5/– making a total claim of £205 15/–. The Heritors maintained that £100 of these repairs were not their responsibility and offered the sum of £150, plus £15 for architect's fees in lieu of the repairs required. This amount was accepted by the General Trustees.

It was pointed out by the Heritors that there were in the laird's room in the church, five Hepplewhite chairs, a mahogany table and cover, a small carpet and a looking glass, while in the Jura proprietor's pew there were five Hepplewhite chairs, one armchair and a strip of coconut matting. The Heritors claimed that these items of furniture belonged to the laird and were not to be considered in the ownership of the Church.

This correspondence seems typical of so many items during the previous hundreds of years, and with it the financial responsibility of the Campbells of Jura for the church and its affairs finally comes to an end.

Mr Robertson was keenly interested in the cultivation of trees and woodland, and shelter belts of trees were planted by him on the boundaries of the glebe.

He died in office in 1947 after a ministry of forty-four years. He is buried in Kilearnadil Cemetery. A memorial tablet to him on the wall of the church pays him the following Gaelic tribute:

Uasal, iriosal, blath. (Gentle, modest and warm-hearted.)

DONALD BUDGE

The Rev. Donald Budge followed Mr Robertson. He was born at Dunvegan, in Skye and educated at the University of Glasgow and Trinity College, his first church was Crichton Memorial, Old Cumnock where he served from 1932 to 1949, with a break as a Forces' Chaplain from 1940 to 1945. In 1936 he married Eleanor Bradford Melchior of Virginia, USA.

Donald Budge was inducted to Jura in 1949, and remained until 1964, when he retired. He was responsible for further improvements and modernisations to the church resulting in a bright new chancel and a light and airy appearance. The church still looks much as it did in Mr Budge's day. (Colour plate 19)

Mr Budge used his glebe to good effect and became a breeder of Jura Highland Cattle, for which of course he is especially remembered by the estate and farming community. The time had arrived for yet another Statistical Return, and Donald Budge wrote the third Return in 1955. He also wrote the only book ever to be solely devoted to the island, which he entitled *Jura: an Island of Argyll* and which he published privately in 1960.

The parish had further ministries in more recent times: the Rev. John Mair, from 1965 to 1971, and the Rev. Donald McDonald from 1971 to his death in 1975. The author was inducted to the charge in 1975.

We have studied the history of the parish church of Jura in some detail, not only because it has its own intrinsic interest as a result of the colourful characters who passed through its ministry, but because it reveals a good deal about the community life of the island, and in particular of the role of the landowners through the centuries.

VI

The Eighteenth Century

24

People in the Eighteenth Century

At the start of the eighteenth century, Jura was a remote part of a Scotland at peace under the rule of King William, and still with its own Parliament, although the Union would come within seven years. Jura was now in the firm control of the Campbells who had had thirty-five years to establish their ownership of Jura and were now the legal superiors of all the lands with the exception of the far north, still held by the McLeans of Lochbuie.

The Church of Scotland was well established, although the 'former Episcopal Incumbent', the Rev. John McSween, though deposed by the Presbytery, was still on Jura and carrying on an illegal ministry which would continue until he was finally 'outed' to make way for the Rev. Neil Campbell, who was ordained to the parish ministry on 10 April 1703. At the very turn of the century the activities of Mr McSween, and the meetings of the Presbytery would reveal the names of a small group of individual residents on Jura. The detail of the proceeding has been studied, but only a handful of Jura names are recorded.

One Duncan McKellar was a witness at the 1697 Trial. There was an Archibald Campbell in Ardlussa at that time, and 'the daughter of Ronald's son' (NcMhi-cRaoil,) the famous and profligate woman at Corran House.

By 1702 various residents are called to give evidence as to baptisms and marriages, conducted by John McSween about the turn of the century.

Gilbert McIlbhuy had a child baptised in Lergybreck; Neill McGhoyll had a child baptised in Ardmenish; Donald McNamoill had a child baptised in Keils; Archibald McIlbhuy of Knockrome and Archibald McIlbhuy of Ardfernal were witnesses. Angus McIlbhuy of Leargiebreack was married to Isobel McNeil.

In 1702 the Presbytery dealt with some cases of discipline concerning people of Jura: More McPhaul; Neill McMillan; Donald Og McIlheaonich and Archibald Campbell of Ardlussa.; John McIlbhuy; Catharine NcIlriath and Rachel Campbell of Knockrome; in 1703, Arthur McConnerich; Effie NcPhaul; in 1707, Archibald Campbell, Former Surgeon; Malcolm McIlheny and Katharin McKinnis in Kinuachdrach; and in 1708, Malcolm McIlheny and Katharin McIlpheder of Kinuachdrach. Neil McMillan; Mary McPhail; Donald Og Shaw; Catherine McIlraith; John Buie.

The Christian names and surnames of these people will occur again and again as we have the opportunity to study a better sample of the population. At this time Neil Campbell was taking up his responsibilities as the minister of Jura and Colonsay, a role he would fulfil for more than fifty years. One of his duties was the baptism of the children of the residents of his parish, and as he was required to do by church law, he kept a record of all such baptisms. This record has survived, and provides us with our first systematic body of information regarding the names and some of the circumstances of the people of Jura. We will use the rare survival of this document to build on previous records of the inhabitants of Jura, and to carry our study of the population forward to the nineteenth century, where we will find the residents recorded formally in Statutory Registers and Census records.

We will also use this record to have a first serious look at the settlements in the parish where people were spending their lives and earning their living.

BAPTISMAL REGISTER, 1704–34

Neil Campbell's record starts in March 1704, the year after his ordination and continues with some consistency until August 1724. There follows a break until January 1726, and another between December 1726 and January 1731. The record concludes with a baptism in May 1734.

Here are the number of baptisms in each of the years in question:

1704	28	1711	22	1718	19	1725	0
1705	18	1712	24	1719	24	1726	14
1706	25	1713	23	1720	21	1727–1730	0
1707	34	1714	32	1721	15	1731	1
1708	28	1715	16	1722	21	1732	3
1709	36	1716	32	1723	23	1733	14
1710	10	1717	22	1724	16	1734	8

Until the record becomes a bit uneven near the end of the period, Neil Campbell was baptising an average of about twenty-three children per year.

The record covers the whole of the island of Jura, and includes a number of baptisms from Scarba and Lunga, and one from the Garvellachs. Colonsay, which was also Mr Campbell's responsibility must have had its own record, as it does not feature in this one.

In view of the endless disputes about how the minister should allocate his time between the two islands, one might have expected him to be baptising in Jura during only one half of the year. The record does not bear out any such pattern. Indeed, it seems more likely that Neil had an assistant in Colonsay, for he seems to have been free to baptise on every month, with the exception of September, when he may have been in the habit of leaving the parish for a regular holiday.

He performed no baptisms between August 1712 and February 1713, and a similar pattern appears between 1715 and 1721. Since no great backlog of christenings seems to occur at such times, it may be that the people of Jura were now free of any pre-Reformation fears for unbaptised children, and were not making very urgent demands on the minister to baptise immediately after birth.

The earliest research into this baptismal register was done by Dr Scott Buie, of Fort Worth, Texas, who is a descendant of an early Buie emigrant from Jura. Scott's database was a valuable first stage in the study of this important document. The author's transcript of the complete register is available on Jura.

The dates themselves raise more questions as to what was actually happening. In eighty-three cases no exact date is recorded within the month in question. In others a group of baptisms recorded on the same date covers places so widely spread that it seems impossible that they could have been conducted on the same day. Baptisms in Scotland at this date were usually performed in the home of the family concerned. It may well be that Neill did not carry his precious register about the islands on horseback, and filled it in only after the event, either from his notes or his memory. The dates in the record may do no more than note the date when he actually made the entry. No date at all within a month might then indicate his uncertainty as to the exact day on which he performed the baptism.

Since we have no one to ask, what can we deduce from the register as it has survived?

There are records of the baptisms of some fifty children whose names are not contained in the register. In some cases not even the sex of the child has been recorded. These gaps raise all kinds of questions about the circumstances surrounding the baptism of children three hundred years ago. Did the child in question die in early infancy so that a name was not chosen or given? Tradition on Jura suggests that still-born children were never baptised, and were always buried without benefit of clergy, but there must have been many deaths in the immediate post-natal period. Although such ideas may be intriguing, the record reveals that the absences of an accurate note of names and sexes are grouped in quite limited periods in certain years, e.g. there are thirteen such baptisms in February, April, June and July 1721. It seems likely that someone other than Neil Campbell was conducting these baptisms, perhaps while the minister was at work in Colonsay. This substitute minister was simply omitting to record the information which Neil Campbell invariably noted down during the first fifteen years or so of his ministry. The unknown substitute compounds his errors by also omitting the exact date of the baptism much more frequently than did the minister.

The inconsistency in the record reveals more about the bad practice of the officiating clergyman than about any tradition or custom among the community. Within the group of poorly recorded names there are some where the Christian name is absent, but the sex of the child has been recorded. While one would expect some pattern here of similar numbers of boys and girls, in fact, only three male infants have no name in the register, while there are fifteen such entries against female infants. This is so far from the expected statistical situation that one is tempted to ask if something was going on here? Was it generally less important to record the names of little girls? Again there is a preponderance of such records in the time of our unknown assistant.

Gaps in the record of personal details relating to the parents are somewhat different. There are a number of records where the names in the entries have not been decipherable; however, there are a considerable number of straightforward omissions. These tend to be the Christian names and less often the maiden names of the mothers and wives. The names of the fathers are almost always recorded. Indeed there seem to be only three genuine gaps in the male record, although of course some names are hard to read. The women's names are presumably quite accessible, indeed it has often been possible to fill them in where missing by comparison with the record of baptism of another child to the same family. Perhaps the minister thought it was significant to be sure that he had accurately recorded the full name of the father, but was simply less concerned to record the name of the mother. The considerable number of blanks, nearly sixty in the original total of 529 entries tends to support this conclusion.

What information can be obtained from the record itself? We will consider such matters as family distribution throughout the parish, Christian names and surnames, and any additional social data.

RESIDENCES IN THE BAPTISMAL REGISTER

Neil Campbell's baptismal register gives us our first opportunity to look at the communities of Jura in association with people who are actually living in them. Previously they have been mentioned only as lists of lands with rentals or valuations, or as the residences of various individuals appearing to give evidence in civil or church courts.

The register presumably does not give a complete list of the places where people were living in the parish, but only of where they were giving birth to children. Doubtless there were other dwelling places where young families with small children were not living. This question will be considered at the end of the list. The full list of the places mentioned in the baptismal register follows: Knocbreac; Ardfin; Brosdale; Strone; Auchivelick; Sannaig; Crackaig; Trianintorran; Craighouse; Knocknafeolaman; Keils; Kilearnadil; Erine; Lergiebreac; Corran House; Knockrome; Ardfernal; Ardmenish; Camus; Corrynahera; Tarbert; Ardlussa; Knockintavill; Kinuachdrach; Isle of Scarba – Kilmorie; Isle of Scarba – Mulbuie; Isle of Lunga; The Garvellachs.

PEOPLE OF THE BAPTISMAL REGISTER

Neil Campbell's baptism register is at its most complete between the years 1704 and 1724, inclusive, during which period baptisms were administered to the children of 228 couples on the mainland of Jura. If the more or less complete years of 1726 and 1733 are taken into this figure, the total rises to 248. If every family in the entire record is counted, we have evidence of the existence of 273 couples on Jura, Scarba, Lunga and the Garvellachs.

No record exists of what happened to these people during the years in question, although we will be able to follow a small number, e.g. as they later leave the island, and in one case, we have a gravestone record of the death of someone in the baptismal register. It seems reasonable to assume that most of the young adults having children about 1704 and onwards, would be still alive and resident on Jura twenty or so years later. These parents and children can therefore be used as a rough guide to the population, and can be considered as a 'running total'.

By the later years of the register, the children who were baptised in the earlier period had reached their twenties, and were thus capable of having families of their own.

In 1724 the Presbytery of Kintyre made a famous 'Perambulation of the parish', and members visited Jura, Scarba and Lunga. The visitors recorded figures for the number of 'catechisable persons'. The details are as follows: Jura, about 600; Scarba, 30; Lunga, 16; Belnahua, 16; The Garvellach Isles, 18 – which gives a total of 680 adults. It seems likely that persons catechised at this time were adults of child-bearing age.

Neil Campbell's baptismal register records the presence of 546 catechisable adults during the period from 1704 to 1734. However, it is evident that this includes many who were not of adult status during the first fifteen or so years of the record. We have tentatively identified some sixty or so who would have grown into that status by the early 1720s. Indeed by 1733, the annual total appears to be in the region of thirty new parents. No doubt if the baptismal register were complete, we would have similar figures from 1725, 1727, 1728, 1729, 1730 and 1731. Something of the order of 250 maturing adults would thus be added to the total of those who are in a sense 'double entries'. The register is concerned only with the young adults of child-bearing age, and makes no mention of those who were already mature by the time the register was getting under way. The baptismal register records a total of 1072 individuals, and provides us with much information which we would otherwise not have.

Perhaps the most obvious information provided by Neil Campbell's book is the names of many of the people residing in his parish in the first thirty-four years of the eighteenth century. We have the surnames of the fathers of children, and husbands of wives, and in many cases we have the maiden names of the mothers and wives of the same families. Not only do we have these names, but in many cases we know where the families were living in the island. We also know by what Christian names, and sometimes even by what nicknames they were known in their community. Some family names are relatively abundant and widespread, others are confined to one area, and yet other names occur only rarely. It would be interesting to be able to understand something of what all this reveals about the life of the people concerned, and this will be our task in the ensuing pages.

We will start with the major families. There were thirty-three families with the family surname of McIlirioch (including one Darroch). This was by far the most abundant surname in the sample. It was variously spelt, but the name has already been studied at length. Next came Shaws, represented by twenty-seven families. Five family surnames are represented by more than a dozen families: McArthur, 18; Buie, 19; Campbell, 16; McLean, 15; McDougald, 15. These seven family groups account for 143 of 273; or 52.4 per cent, just over half the family surnames in the parish.

A considerable number of family names follow which are represented by more than three families: McNamoile, 9; Lamont, 8; Clark, 7; McPhail, 8; McGhoile, 7; Thompson, 6; McCranie, 6; McCleisich, 6; McPhetruse, 5; McInne, 5; Black, 5; McCallum, 4; Gillie, 5. These thirteen family names account for eighty-one families, or 30 per cent of the total.

The twenty family groups so far listed account for 82 per cent of the family surnames which occur in the baptismal register.

There remain those family surnames represented by either three occurrences, or two, or a single mention. There are thirty such names, only one being a family surname which does *not* start with the patronymic 'Mc' – the single family of Fergusons.

Of the remaining 'Mc' names, there are six where there are three families of the same name: McBhrion, McCartna, McDuffie, McIlphedir, McKay, McNeill.

The six where there are two families of the same name are: McGoun, McIlhavish, McIllemichell, McInriver, McLaortrich, McPhaden.

The remaining seventeen names are each represented by one single family: McCalrid, McEachen, McEnlea, McEnrich, McIlerand, McIllis, McIllmartin, McIloran, McIlvoil, McIlvra, McInleadh, McIntyre, McIsack, McKianalich, McO'Shenoge, McPherson and McVurich.

One record has no known surname. These forty-nine records account for the remaining 18 per cent of the total.

Allowing for understandable variations in spelling, the island parish of Jura has fifty different surnames in use during the period in question.

As we try to compare this population profile with the tantalising glimpse of the island at the time of the Franciscan Mission a hundred years earlier, we see that the Buies, Shaws and McLeans are still more than holding their own. Of later Jura names, only Black and McNeill seem to have survived, although there are still representatives of MacKay, Gillies, McIllemartin, and Ferguson from the 1624 list.

McArthurs and McDougalds have become well established, and, as one would expect, the Campbells are present in some force.

MAIDEN NAMES

The family surnames of the children who were baptised are identical with the surnames of the fathers of each family. The mothers of the children import into the picture their own maiden names, which in many cases we know from the baptismal register.

In some cases the surnames of the parental couple are given as the same. Where the surname is uncommon, such as McO'Shenoge, it seems likely that the mother's maiden name is not known, but where both mother and father are called Campbell it should be remembered that a John Campbell may in fact have married a girl called Mary Campbell. This introduces a random factor into our study of parental surnames, however, the maiden name is evidently frequently given quite accurately, and since it represents the name of the wife's family it adds another dimension to our study.

Here are listed the numbers of recorded maiden names of wives in the family surnames in the numerically dominant families: McIlirioch, 18; Shaw, 22; McArthur, 17; Buie, 14; Campbell, 17; McLean, 20; McDougald, 8.

With the exception of the low entry for McDougalds these wives' maiden names are reasonably well in agreement in frequency with the family names of their husbands. There are, however, some surprises in the less numerous names: For instance, there are sixteen Clarks; twelve McPhetruses; and ten McDuffies in the female sample, far more than would be expected from the male family names.

Again in the mothers there are small numbers of names which figure in the middle range of the fathers' surnames: McNamoile, 8; Thompson, 5; McPhail, 5; McNeill, 5; McGhoile, 5; McPherson, 4; McCranie, 4; McCleisich, 4.

Other maiden surnames with only two or three examples mirror the infrequent male surnames: McCallum, 3; McCalrid, 3; McCallum, 3; Lamont, 2; McEnlea, 2; McIllmartin, 2; McIlpheder, 2; McLand, 2.

Single examples are also often identical with the male family names, establishing the presence of two families of each name providing the parents for children at this time: McCartna, McGoun, McIllmichel, McIllis, McIlvoil, McIlvra, McInnes, McPhaden and McVurich.

It is interesting to find a considerable number of surnames appearing as wives' maiden names which do not appear as the family names of their husbands. These each appear only once: Cargill, Livistine, McCalken, McCambridge, McColly, McIlghlass, McInvine, McIver, McMillan, McNiven, McOlonaich, McQuarie and McSwine. While McVastane and McLugash, both new, appear twice.

The total number of surnames for the wives of the families is only 245, but an accurate total cannot be relied on, for many names were evidently not entered in the original record.

SUMMARY

In all about seventy-five different surnames make their apearance in Neil Campbell's baptismal register, either as the names of the infants and their fathers, or as the maiden names of the mothers. The vast majority of these arrive with absolutely no pedigree whatsoever, and those few of which we have previous knowledge are easily summarised.

There are the archaic names of Mac-ille-bhuidhe, Mac-ill-riabhach, and Mac-ill-heanich (Buie, Darroch and Shaw), which occur in ancient legend and early history.

The names go through a variety of changes to arrive at their eighteenth- and nineteenth-century forms. The Franciscan Mission has Giollabuidhe and Giolasuathanaidh, for Bui and Shaw, and the early Presbytery minutes a few years before the baptismal register have McIlbhuy and McIlheaonich as slightly earlier forms.

The Clarks and the McNeills were also in the Franciscan Mission, although we may ask if the less common names in its lists such as Gillies and McMartin may have left the island to be replaced by new representatives later. The Clarks were certainly present at the arrival of the Campbells.

Written evidence of the Gaelic form Mac ill dhuibh, later Black, is missing, but the Blacks of Jura are no doubt an ancient line, as are the long-lived McCraines or McCranies.

Budge is confident that the Keiths are also ancient. The original name is likely to be MacCithich, the clan in Jura being known as Clan ic Cithich. He believed that the brothers Iain MacKeith and Donald MacKeith who fell at Colkitto's last fight at Dunaverty in 1647 were probably Jura men. The name is absent from the baptismal register, but may give us an interesting pointer to the fact that a number of such names may well have been present throughout the period of the book, from 1704 to 1734, without there being a birth to celebrate during the time.

A woman called Mary McOlonaich was married to Hew Black, and had six children by him in Crackaig. The old story of the 'Murder Glen' laid the blame at the door of a farmer called MacOlonaidh (thought by Budge to be Olafson), of Strone in the time of the second baillie of Sanaig.

The process of converting the Gaelic names of Jura folk into English no doubt went on over a considerable period. In a number of cases the component of the name which disappeared quite early was the 'Gille' (lad, or boy, or servant), which tended to extend the patronymic 'Mac', so 'Mac-ille', 'McIll, or 'McIl' – son of the servant of someone. We can see this being lost in a number of Jura names.

Other names may have simply been anglicised, e.g. McNamoile undoubtedly disappears, but in due course there are MacMillans in Jura. This name derives from Mac-ille-mhaoile (son of the servant of the tonsured or bald one).

Others may be errant forms of well known names, or even simply not clear or well spelled, e.g. McInleadh, or McEnlea may be forms of McKinlay, or Finlayson.

There are quite a number of saints' names: MacilleMichel, MacilleMartin, Mac a'Bhrione, McIllePheder, McPhetrus, McCambridge (servants of Michael, Martin, Brion, Peter, and Ambrose). Similarly the common McCleisich, is a form of MacCleish, and goes back to MacGill Iosa (Gillies), the son of the servant of Jesus.

The McGouns of Jura are surely Mac a'Ghobhainn, the son of the blacksmith.

McLaortrich comes from Mac Fhlaithbheartach (the generous ruler) so MacLafferty and McLarty

Similarly: McIlvoil; from Mac Gille Mhaoil to MacMillan
              McIlvra; from Mac Ghille bhrath to MacGillivray
              McIhavish; from Mac Ghille Sheumais to Jamieson
              or Mac Ghille Thomhais to Thomson, and
              McO'Sheoge; from O'Sheannaigh (sean, old).

All this sets us up for a quick survey of the 504 surnames which occur in the Old Parish Register of Baptisms, either as the surnames of fathers or the maiden names of mothers, as they occur in order of abundance:

McIlirioch (Darroch)	53	Bui (Bowie)	33	McPhail	13
Shaw	49	Clark	24	McDuffie	13
McLean	35	McDougald	23	Thomson	11
McArthur	35	McPhetrus	17	McCranie	10
Campbell	33	McNamoile	17	McCleisich	10
				Lamont	10
McNeill	8	Black	5	McCartna	4
McCallum	7	McIlpheder	5	McCalrid	4
McKay	6	Gillies	5	McPherson	4
McBhrion	3	McPhaden	3	McKellar	2
McEnlea	3	McIlhavish	2	McLand	2
McGoun	3	McIllis	2	McLaortrich	2
McIllemichell	3	McIlvoil	2	McVastane	2
McIllmartin	3	McIlvra	2	McVurich	2
McLugas	3	McInriver	2		

The following twenty-five names occur only once each:

Cargill	McEachan	McInnes	McKianalich
Ferguson	McEnrich	McIntyre	McMillan
Livistine	McIlerand	McInvine	McNiven
McCalken	McIlghlass	McInvoil	McOlonaich
McCambridge	McIloran	McIsack	McO'Shenoge
McColly	McInleadh	McIver	McQuarie
			McSwine

Many of the above have been dealt with in the text. The derivation of others will no doubt occur to the reader.

DISTRIBUTION OF FAMILIES

McIliriochs, or Darrochs occur throughout the island, appearing to radiate from a strong centre in Tarbert, Corrynahera and Lagg. Buies are centred strongly on Knockrome and Ardfernal.

It will be remembered that Shaws of Jura were involved in a blood feud with the Campbells of Barrichbeyan on the mainland to the north of Jura in the early seventeenth century, and it is interesting to find Shaws, 100 years later, still well established at Ardlussa, Barnhill and Kinuachdrach, with further members in Scarba, and a mention from the Garvellachs.

If it was possible to present a set of maps for each family name, they would show the settlements occupied by the major families:

McArthurs (18) from Cnocbreac right round to Tarbert.

McDougalls (15) with five families in Brosdale, but otherwise well spread.

McLeans (14) spread evenly throughout the island.

Campbells (17) with single families in each of the southern farms but absent from the Keils/Kilearnadil and Knockrome/Ardfernal crofting townships.

Of the less numerous families, some are concentrated in one community: e.g. McNamoiles in Kilearnadil and Keils; Thompsons, all at Ardfin; Lamonts at Corrynahera; McCranies at Knockrome; McPhails around Sannaig and Crackaig; McGhoiles and the Blacks in the south.

A few family names have no clear pattern of distribution, e.g. Clark, Gillie, McCleisich, McInne, McPhetruse, McCallum, McNeill, McKay, McIlpheder, the McCartna.

One of the most tantalising puzzles in the Register is the presence as previously noted of a large number of family names represented by a single family, or at most by two families. Some of these names are restricted to the north, e.g. from Barnhill and on to Scarba and Lunga: McIntyre, McKianalich, McIlvoil, McEnlea, McIllemichell, McBhrion, McInriver.

Five names occur only in Ardlussa: McLaortrich; McO'Sheoge; McIloran; McIllis; McIlerand; with a single McInleadh in Tarbert.

Ardfernal, Knockrome and Ardmenish have examples of McGoun (two), McCalrid, McIlvra, McDuffie (two), McPhaden, while Kilearnadil has a McEnrich; Knocknafeolaman a McIsack; and Ardfin and Brosdale have the single McIlhavish and McIllemartin families, and Ferguson. The solitary surname 'McVurich' is of unknown locality.

There seems no simple explanation for the presence of these families on Jura at this time, nor for their distribution throughout the island. By the time we have more systematic information about the names of the island's residents in the baptismal registers of the early nineteenth century and the first National Census in 1841 these strange surnames have all disappeared from the island, although the milling family of McIsaac is established at Miltown, and may connect back to the solitary record of John McIsac and Mary Campbell in 1704, also living at the mill site in Knocknafeolaman. Certainly Budge believed these McIsaacs were early arrivals.

Fergusons return to the island by 1841, but seem to have been absent before.

We will be examining the nineteenth-century population in detail in due course, but we may note briefly here than many of the families numerically dominant in the early eighteenth century are still the most common names in the nineteenth, e.g., by the 1841 census, McDougall, Darroch and Shaw are still the three most numerous families, with Campbells, Buies, Keiths, Blacks, and McCranes still very evident.

CHRISTIAN NAMES

When studying detailed information from the nineteenth century one is struck by the conservative choice of Christian names for the children of Jura. This trait was well established by the early eighteenth century.

If we consider the Christian names chosen for the infant boys during the years of the baptismal register we find that four names account for more than half of those which occur: John, Donald or Dod, Duncan and Archibald; with 45, 42, 27, and 27 occurrences accounting for 66 per cent. For girls names, the four most popular were Mary, Finwall, Catherine or Katherine, and More (or Mor); with 51, 36, 35 and 30 occurrences each, which accounted for 68 per cent of all the names.

In each case, it is not necessary to expand the selection very much in order to account for an overwhelming percentage of all the names chosen. A further six boys' names will take the total to 85 per cent, and a further five girls' names will take their total to 91.5 per cent. These are: Neill, 15; Malcolm, 13; Angus, 8; Gilbert, 7; Dougald, 5; Alexander, 5; and Margaret or Margrat, 18; Christine, 16; Ann, 14; Effie, 7.

The complete list is increased for boys by the incidence of seven names which occur only a few times: Hew or Aobh, 5; Niven, 3; Lauchlan, 3; James, 3; Hector, 3; Patrick, 2: Charles, 2. The following eight boys' names each occur only once: Alan, Coll, Finla, Kenneth, Michell, Murdoch, Petrus, William.

For girls, the five infrequent names are: Florence, 4; Janet, 3; Isobel, 3; Euffine, 3; Lizie, 2. The following eight girls' names each occur only once: Anaple, Beag, Catriona, Gillise, Marryon, Merran, Merron, Rachel.

All these names seem to be more or less uniformly distributed between the various families, with abundant and infrequent names cropping up at random in the various surnames.

The Shaws had a predilection for John and Neil. There were nine John Shaws and six Neil Shaws in the register.

The McIlliriochs certainly liked Donald. There were six Donald McIlliriochs, anticipating the appearance of even more Donald Darrochs in the nineteenth century. The McLeans also seemed fond of the name Donald.

The Franciscan Mission reveals a number of Christian names in use 100 years before the baptismal register. The girls' names prefigure many of the commonest names in the register: Mary, Finwall, Effie, Catherine, Christine and Mor are all there.

Some of the commonest boys' names are missing, but John, Donald and Alexander are present among the re-baptised.

A few notes on the derivation of some of the Christian names in use may be of interest:

Anaple	Anabla and Anable also occur as are old forms of Annabel, from Amabel (loving).
Beag or Beg	a shortened form of Beathag, a common old Gaelic Christian name, probably from Beatha (life), but possibly from Church Latin, beatus (blessed).
Ben Mhic	a puzzle, possibly suggesting a re-marrying widow?
Euffien	this and Euphan were old Gaelic forms of Euphemia, nowadays usually Effie. Originally from the Greek (of good report).
Finwall	Finwall is a variant of Fionnghal, probably from 'fionn' (white), and 'gall' (stranger), so the fair haired stranger. The doubled 'ff' has no special significance other than a writing habit. The name seems to have been gradually replaced by Flora in the mid-eighteenth century through an uncertain association.
Granie	an ancient Irish king of Tara called Cormac man Airt had a daughter called Grainne, who appears in many legends. The name was taken up in Scotland, and became popular. There may have been an association 'gradh' (love).
Mor	Mor, or its variant More, was a Christian name in its own right. It was translated into English as Sarah, and, at least in Jura, as Marion.
Marion	there are various forms in the register of Marion, e.g., 'Marran', 'Merron' and 'Marryon'.
Dod	this is used as a diminutive form of Donald. Dod is a separate Scottish name in the north-east, where it is a familiar form of George, but not here in the west.
Ard	this is a diminutive form of the name Archibald.
Finla	this is an early form of Finlay, the Gaelic for 'sunbeam'.
Sorlie	this is a common Gaelic name derived from 'Somhairle', a form of Somerled, the great Chieftain of the Isles.

OCCUPATIONS

Neil Campbell felt it was desirable to record the occupations of various residents as he baptised their infants. In the case of his own son Donald and his daughter Mor, he took the trouble to record that their father was 'the Minister of Jura and Colonsay'.

In the case of the children of Archibald and Barbra Campbell, in 1722 and 1723, he recorded that the father was 'the Younger of Sanaig, Baillie of Jura.'

In the field of agriculture we presume that most of the fathers were tenant farmers or crofters, but at a lower level of subsistence he recorded that: Neil Buie, of Ardfin, and Donald Shaw of Kinuachdrach were 'cottars', as also was Janet Campbell of Ardlussa, an unmarried mother.

In view of the lack of general information about the group called 'tacksmen', it is interesting to note that the father of an illegitimate child is the servant of 'Ard Campbell, tacksman of Kinuachdrach'. This Archibald Campbell is recorded as being 'of Lochhead'; usually taken to be Inverary. He lived away from Jura, but held tack in the island.

Malcolm McNeill of Ardmenish is recorded as being a herd. Weavers and tailors were also worthy of note: William Bui of Lergiebreck and Hector Bui of Knockrome; Duncan Bui of Knockrome; Donald McLaortrich of Ardlussa are all recorded as weavers.

John Shaw of Knockintavil; Alan McPherson of Knockrome and Gilbert McIlirioch of East Corran House are recorded as tailors.

Of other occupations, Gilbert Bui of Lergiebreac is a smith, and John McArthur of Knocknafeolaman is a miller. Donald Shaw of Tarbert is a merchant. Patrick McArthur of Knockrome is recorded as a catechist.

ILLEGITIMACY

Neil Campbell takes great pains to record the circumstances of the birth of any child not coming from a properly married family. There are twenty-four such records. The rate of record of illegitimate births accordingly runs at 9 per cent, or just under one in ten children born. The father is generally identified by his job or by his location. The mother is frequently identified as a servant to some local person, usually on the farm on which the father works.

The baptism of Mor McNeill in 1707 records that the parents were unmarried at the time of the child's conception. Malcolm McNeill, the baby's father was then 'servitor to Mr John McSwine', the former minister, which locates him still in Jura at that time!

Several fathers seem to have lived off the island, e.g., John Campbell, father of Charles Campbell (1709), came from Ballinabie in Islay.

John Shaw, father of Neil Shaw (1712) was the son of Neill Shaw in the Garvellachs, while Catherine McQuarie, the child's mother was a servant in Scarba.

John Roy McArthur, father of Mary McArthur in Tarbert in 1717 had apparently left a wife in Mull. The child was 'represented by his brother Charles McArthur of this parish'; the mother was daughter of the deceased Dushee Shaw in Tarbert. This case is recorded in the Minutes of Presbytery, where the child is listed as having been 'born in foulness in Tarbert, with her mother being there. She upon oath fathered on a man who lived in Mull, and came for a start to this Isle and fled away to Ireland, having left his own wife in Mull.' The date of this event is 1717, and there is in fact one Charles McArthur, living in Tarbert at this time and having children by his wife, a McIlirioch, in 1718, before moving to Lagg. Here is another tantalising reference to 'Dushee' as a Shaw Christian name.

In a similar case, John McEachan was baptised in 1719. Hew McEachan, the baby's father, appears to have been resident in Morvern.

Duncan Campbell, the son of the tacksman of Kinuachtrach, appears to have fathered two infant girls by his father's servant, baptised in successive months in 1720.

Other snippets of information may be gleaned from the register:.

Hector McLain of Kilmorie in Scarba was baptised in 1706 by the Rev. John Darroch, minister in Craignish. John McIlmichell of Brosdale was baptised by Mr John Campbell, minister of Kilarrow in Islay.

It is also intriguing to find the minister recording the death of the husband and the status of the wife and mother as 'relict of the deceased'. This occurs in the case of Neill McLain (1708), in Camus; Gilbert Clark (1716), father died last year in Inverary; More and Neill Bui (1716), where the father drowned in June last.

The death of the mother 'in childbed' is also recorded, in the case of Mor McDougald in Strone in 1709 and Euffine McIlpheder in Crackaig in 1716.

Even more odd is the record of an unnamed McIlirioch infant born in 1721 to Mary Clark and Duncan McIlirioch, 'begotten by her former husband on death bed'.

RE-USE OF A CHILD'S NAME
It has long been the custom in Scotland to keep alive the Christian name of a child who died bearing a chosen family name by re-naming a subsequent child with the same name.

In the baptismal register there are twelve examples of this practice:

Buies of Lergiebreac with two sons called Donald;
Buies of Knockrome with two sons called Donald;
Buies of Erine with two sons called William;
Buies of Ardfin with two sons called Donald;
Lamonts of Corrynahera with two daughters called More;
McDougalds of Brosdale with two daughters called Mary;
McIliriochs of Tarbert with two sons called Ard;
McIliriochs of Tarbert with two sons called Duncan;
McIliriochs of Camus with two sons called John;
Shaws of Tarbert with two daughters called Catherine;
Shaws of Knockintavill with two sons called Angus.

What may easily be forgotten is that the register here reminds us of the tragic early deaths of twelve infants, whose names had to be perpetuated by this practise.

The author encountered a fascinating variation of this custom in a previous parish in Glasgow, in the form of reversing the chosen name and using it for the next infant in its reversed form; as in 'Agnes' to 'Senga', and in the parish of Jura, 'Sarah' to 'Haras'.

The survival of the baptismal register is a rare bonus in the investigation of the social structure of Jura in the eighteenth century.

Neil Campbell appears to have no longer maintained his baptismal register after 24 June 1734. After all this time we cannot be sure why we have no further record of baptisms. The minister may in fact have become disinterested in his involvement in the baptisms of the new-born children of the parish. But he may equally may well have kept a record of subsequent events, which record may simply not have survived. As we look back to his ministry in the early eighteenth century, we must be grateful for the wealth of information which it has preserved for us; and for this intimate glimpse into the life of the community of which he was for so many years the parish minister.

SECULAR RECORDS

When we turn aside from Neil Campbell's baptismal register we find we are somewhat cast adrift in the first quarter of the eighteenth century, for as far as indivual residents on the island are concerned, records are thin on the ground.

In due course we will encounter the question of emigration, for the first sailing to North Carolina of ordinary residents of Jura comes in 1739, only five years later than the end of Neil Campbell's record. However, the whole emigration question will be dealt with later.

We do have some idea about the size of the population of Jura at this time. The Rev. Francis Stewart, the author of the *First Statistical Account* of the parish in 1794, records an earlier detail: 'According to Dr Webster's report, the number of souls in 1755 was 1097.'

Webster's figure was for the whole parish and so included Jura and Colonsay. Fraser Darling has calculated suitable proportions, and allocated Jura as 658. In 1794 Francis Stewart recorded 929 souls, an increase of 271. Stewart counted Scarba, Lunga and Belnahua separately, so we have to add Scarba, 50; Lunga, 29; and Belnahua, 132. Stewart's total thus becomes 1140. By 1801 the National Census has 1202. This is a further increase of 62. The population was rising steadily at this time towards its maximum at about 1840.

For information about this period we are almost completely dependent on the Campbell of Jura Papers, which are lodged in the Scottish Record Office. Many documents at this time concern events surrounding the death of Archibald Campbell the third of Sannaig in 1764.

The Campbell of Jura Papers contain a thirty-four-page document entitled 'Inventory of Grounds of Debts found in the Repositories of the deceased Archibald Campbell of Jura'. A similar, related document is an 'Inventory of Stocks of Black Cattle', also from 1764

The debts inventory shows outstanding payments of various kinds of rent due to Campbell of Jura. It gives long lists of the names of people and the places where they reside.

NAMES FROM THE INVENTORIES

Three different clerks appear to have compiled the 'Inventory of Debts', which results in some consensus as to how they represented the names of the people. It is interesting to note changes in practice since Neil Campbell's day. The clerk who wrote the 'Inventory of Stocks' has some different spellings of his own.

McIlirioch has now settled down to being 'McIlriach', the first 'i' having disappeared. The 'stocks' list has 'McIlreoch'.

Bui has now acquired its terminal 'e', the form which persists to the present day. The 'stocks' list still has a 'McIlvuy.'

Clark seems now to be spelt 'Clerk', close to the original 'Cleirich'. This will not persist, moving to the 'a' form by the end of the century. The 'stocks' list already has 'Clark'.

The McMillans seem to have split into two almost equal groups, half of whom have the name spelt, 'McNamoile', while the others spell it, 'McNamolie', with one quite distinct, 'McNamulie' in Keils.

McCraine and McCrainie both occur. There will be no unanimity about this name for some time.

McCartan, McClersich, McGuile and McPhetrish may be more 'up to date' versions of McCartna, McCleisich, McGhoile and McPhetrus.

The 'Inventory of Debts' only gives us a very small sample of personal names, and of course makes no mention of the far north at all. Nevertheless a dozen or so surnames still predominate in this small sample, and they are largely those which were numerically dominant in the baptismal register; viz: McIlriach; McNamoile; Buie; Campbell; McLean; McArthur; Shaw; McCraine; McPhail; Black; Clark; McDougald.

These account for 75% of the names in the inventory. Of the remaining twenty-two surnames which are mentioned, many feature in the earlier list, eg: McCartan; McCleisich; McEachern; McGhoil; McInnis; McKay; McNeil; McPherson; McPetrich; Thompson.

Nine make their appearance for the first time: Graham; Gray; Henderson; Lindsay; McNiven; Mustard; Paterson; Reid; Smith. There is no obvious link beween these names.

Additional names in the 'Inventory of Stock' call John Ferguson, 'John ban' and give a McIlreoch whose Christian names are 'Callum Chrom'.

RESIDENCES

Most of the main townships in the island appear in these inventories. Ardmenish has a separate ownership, and the far north and the northern isles are not of course mentioned, although there is a note regarding Knockintavill, as follows: 'Bundle 17th. Contains accounts betwixt the defunct & Colonsay and the people of Knockintavill, whereby it is supposed ther's some money due the defunct, but its impossible to ascertain the sums.' Ffeolin now appears the site of the ferry, and has a small shop (Hector Buie, merchant).

OCCUPATIONS

There is a record of another of that elusive group called tacksmen: William Campbell of Ffeolin.

Five of the men are now designated, 'farmer'. Four of these work at Sanaig, which is the administrative centre of the Campbells' kingdom, and presumably these men work directly for the laird on his own 'farm'; from which work they may take their title. The fifth farmer is at Knockbreac, and there seems no obvious reason for his appellation.

Fourteen men are described as 'tenant', and three are listed as 'cottars'.

'The Inventory of Stocks' adds three herds to the basic list.

Various occupations are given. As in the baptismal register there are weavers; one at Sannaig and one at Ardfernal, and there is a tailor at Brosdale.

There is a carpenter at Brosdale, another at Knockrome, and a carpenter and miller combined at Tarbert. There is a smith at Lergybreck, and at Brosdale there is also a joiner, distinguished from the allied trade of carpenter.

A boatman puts in an appearance, living at Knocknafeolaman.

The innkeeper at Lagg is mentioned and another is located in Tarbert, although there is no other evidence of a change house or inn there. As mentioned above there is now a merchant at Feolin Ferry.

Six women appear in the list, one of whom is described as 'widow'.

There is an interesting footnote in bundle fifteen:

Accounts betwixt the defunct and the Crew of a Wherry, which he and they had in company, from which any claim due to the defunct can hardly be ascertaned till further light is got into the matter.

A few years later than the two inventories comes another 'Campbell of Jura' document. This is a *Scheme of the Valuation of the Lands belonging to Archibald Campbell of Jura lying within the Parish of Jura* (1770).

This list seems to select a tenant from each of the townships and let him stand as an example of the others. It often says: 'The Croft possest by Duncan McDugald and others.' Seventeen men of the island are thus selected. Eleven have already featured in the 'Inventory of Debts'.

Six new names appear: Duncan Mcileroy (who may be a McIlrioch) in Brosdale; Duncan McArthur and John McDugald in Crackaig; John McIlerioch in Foaline (which may be Feoran); Donald Campbell of Ardfernal and Neil Shaw of Lagg. One Robert Agey makes his appearance in Lergybreck and in Knocknefeolaman. Robert Agey appears in other later documents.

Although only listing a small number of the residents of the island, the inventories of 1764 bring our study of names and places forward into the second half of the eighteenth century.

In the study of 'The Coming of the Campbells' it was noted that a list of men available for military service exists for 1799. This comes from a period when there is little evidence of the names of individuals on Jura, so the complete list, with names, places of residence and occupations appears here.

Dond McDougall Ardfinn, labourer
Dugd McDougall Brostill, labourer
John Darroch Brostill, tenant
John Black Sanaig, labourer
Archd Buie Crakaig, boatman
Thos McArthur Knocknafeolamane, labourer
Archd McDougal Keills, tenant

Dond Brown Brostill, labourer
Dugd McDougall Junr Brostill, labourer
John Ferguson Brostill, tenant
Archd McDougall Sanaig, fisher
John McPhaile Knocknafeolamane, weaver

James McPheden Knocknafeolamane, dyer
Dond Buie Ardmenish, carpenter

James Grant Craighouse, exciseman
Neil Shaw Lagg, ferryman
Angus Shaw Ardlussay, shepherd
Dond Shaw Auchintarbert, labourer

Dushee Shaw Lagg, ferrymen
Alexr McDougald Auchintarbert, weaver
Alexr McKeorin Speanane, fisher
Angus McDougald Knockerom, weaver

This sample of twenty-two men of military age is of course tiny, but it is interesting to see the usual names cropping up, and exciting to find a 'Dushee Shaw' at Lagg. The name evidently persists. The occupations are much as one would expect, but James McPheden is the first and only dyer we will encounter. Only 'Speanane' is a surprise, and doesn't connect with any known Jura place-name. Perhaps Alexander McKeorin, was not living on the island at the time

There is one further source of evidence about the people who were living in Jura in the eighteenth century and it is to be found in the three graveyards on the island. A number of gravestones reveal the presence of inhabitants who were living in the island before 1800. It is seldom possible to connect these gravestone inscriptions with other documentary evidence. The striking exception is in the person of one Neil McNeill, buried in Inverlussa Cemetery, who appears in the baptismal record for 1715.

25

Life in the Seventeenth
and Eighteenth Centuries

Let us now consider such evidence as will enable us to investigate the relationship between Campbell of Jura and his tenants.

As we have already seen, when Duncan Campbell arrived on Jura in 1661 with a commission from Calder at the behest of the Duke of Argyll to disarm the inhabitants of the north of Jura, to impose a legal peace on the whole island, and an embargo against the export of its livestock, it marked a turning point in the life of the island. MacDonald, the island's chieftain, left, possibly accompanied by some followers. The people who remained had few choices; they could go with the chief, and hope to find somewhere where the old way of life was still going on; they could go to the lowlands and seek work; later, they would have the option of emigrating; failing all these, they could remain and become rent paying tenants of the new landowner.

A substantial number certainly did remain, although it is difficult to be sure how many.

How did these people survive on Jura? It was no doubt all a matter of money. Funds-seeking landowners exacted rents, and also took over much of the land and farmed it themselves. How were these rents established, and how were they paid? For that matter, what was the value of the land the Campbells held, and how had it been established?

For centuries Scottish kings had been making land grants in the Highlands and Islands, grants which probably had little effect on the clan chiefs or their subjects. In 1494, James IV made grants to Lochbuie; the 2½ mark lands of Ardlussa and Knockintavill, and in 1508; an eighth part of Ardfernal and an eighth part of Knocknafeolaman, also 2½ marks.

In 1510 Duncan Stewart of Appin got lands in Jura from James IV; the five marklands of Ardmenish, Lagg, Tarbert, Kinuachdrach, etc; part of the old ten marklands; received from Duart against a debt of 4500 marks.

In the mid-1500s, Mary Queen of Scots granted lands in Jura to Macdonald of Dunnyveg. Each of the farms, or pairs of farms listed is valued at 16/8: Ardfernal and Knockrome, Feolin and Lergybreck, Kilearnadil and Auchichtovys, Knocknafeolaman, Crackaig, Sannaig, Auchaleck, Strone, Brosdale, Ardfin, Knockbreck.

It is difficult to know if these arbitrary valuations gave any guidance in the latter part of the next century when the question of a valuation confronted the Duke of Argyle.

In trying to find out what life was like for the ordinary inhabitants of Jura after the Campbells took control of the island we are fortunate in finding contemporary accounts in the Campbell of Jura Papers. These are some of the most significant:

1666 Extract registered Contract of Wadset between Archibald, Earl of Argyll, and Duncan Campbell.

1683 A Minute of the Rental of the Island of Jura given up by Duncan Campbell of Sannaig.

1694 An Extract registered Contract between Alexander Campbell of Calder, and John Campbell of Ardfin in Jura.

1751 Valuation of the Shire of Argyll.

1764 Rental of Archibald Campbell's Jura Estate for Crop and Mart.

1764 Inventory of Grounds of Debts found within the Repositories of the deceased Archibald Campbell.

1764 Inventory of Stocks of Black Cattle, Horses, Mares, Sheep and Goats, farm Boles Seed Corn, Bear etc. on the different farms in Jura possessed by the Defunct.

1764 Inventory of the Roup and Sale of Black Cattle and others belonging to the Deceased Archibald Campbell of Jura.

1770 Scheme of Valuation of the Lands belonging to Archibald Campbell of Jura lying within the Parish of Jura.

1754 Note of the Outstanding Rents owed to Archibald Campbell by Persons Intending to go to North America.

The central theme with which many of the above documents are concerned is money. The Campbells had to raise it from the tenants in order to support their capital investment. The people needed it to pay rent and other taxes, and for various articles they could not get by barter.

We consider first the position of the Campbells. It should be remembered that their papers reveal that Jura was only one of their financial and land-holding interests; they also had considerable interests in Islay and on the mainland.

1666: CONTRACT OF WADSET

Five years after being sent to Jura, Duncan Campbell obtained a wadset from the Duke of Argyll for 17,000 merks. A wadset is essentially a form of mortgage, exchanging the use of lands for the loan of a capital sum, subject to reversion.

One merk is 13/4 Scots or two-thirds of £1 Scots The rate of exchange is One Pound Sterling to 12 Pounds Scots. Thus 17,000 merks is £11,333 6/8 Scots; or £944 8/10½ Sterling Argyll had the right to redeem after nineteen years. Duncan Campbell and his heirs became bailies, chamberlains and foresters of Jura.

1683: The Rental of the Island of Jura given up by Duncan Campbell of Sanaig
Seventeen years have passed. The wadset still remains from Argyll to Duncan Campbell, and the figure is reconfirmed as 17,000 merks. However Argyll has 'desponed the Superiority' to the Laird of Caddel who becomes Campbell's superior and to whom he pays 20 merks of feu duty. He also now has a Tack

from Argyll for Strone and Auchaleck which pays rent which he pays to Caddel. Duncan Campbell still has only these limited lands under his direct control: Cnocbreac, Ardfin, Brosdale, Strone, Auchaleck, Sannaig, Knocknafeolaman, Kilearnadil, Feolin Farm and Lergybreck.

These lands comprise the whole of the island south-west of a line drawn across from the mouth of the Corran River, with the exclusion of an enclave consisting of the township of Crackaig, owned by Colin Campbell, the Baillie of Colonsay. He also has a tack from Argyll for Ardmenish, with Kinuachtrach and Mulbuie in Scarba, along with his holding of Crackaig; Colonsay has Knockrome and Ardfernal. Tarbert and Lagg are wadset by Argyll to Hector McLean of Torloisk, and his widow Catharine Campbell. Hector McLean is Duncan Campbell's father-in-law. The Episcopal incumbent John McSween and other tenants pay rent to Duncan Campbell, as do the tenants of Kinuachtrach and Mulbuie.

Ardlussa and Knockintavill are not mentioned in this document.

The total rental payable on the lands for which Duncan Campbell paid his 17,000 merks wadset; or £11,333 6/8 Scots, is £680 pounds Scots per annum.

The total rental payable on the lands for which Colin Campbell of Colonsay paid £5000 Scots wadset is £300 per annum.

A multiplier of £16 13/4 or 16.666 applied to each of these two rentals gives the capital sum of the wadset paid. Thus the annual rental could be expected to pay off the wadset in seventeen years, leaving over two years rent as clear profit before the redeeming date of nineteen years. The total rental payable on the lands for which McLean of Torloisk paid 6000 merks wadset, or £3333 6/8 Scots, is £400. For some unknown reason this gives a multiplier of £8 6/8 or 8.333, exactly twice as profitable as Campbell's terms.

The rental figures for the various townships seem to have been settled as 'round numbers' in Pounds Scots, based on the ancient values of the lands.

1694: Contract between Campbell of Calder and Campbell of Jura

Calder has become superior to John Campbell of Ardfin, in place of Caddel. No figures for rent are given. The 1683 group of lands is listed, with permission to improve them by augmentation (increase of rents): Cnocbreck, Ardfin, Brosdale, Sannaig, Knocknafeolaman, Kilearnadil, Feolin and Lergybreck. Campbell still has a separate tack for Strone and Auchaleck. This tack for Strone and Auchaleck is mentioned as 200 merks, which is the same as the rental for 1683. However he is now paying feu duty for Knockrome, Ardfernal, Lagg and Tarbert, as well as the enclave of Crackaig. This feu duty seems to be 33 merks, or £22 Scots with an option to reduce to £20 if he redeems Crackaig from Archibald Campbell, who is apparently living in Crackaig.

1751: The valuation of the Shire of Argyll

In this document the old values of the lands are mentioned again, eg, as 1¼ merklands or 8/4 pence lands etc. The current rents are now in pounds sterling. There seems to be no general rule about what has happened to the 1683 rents. Of those listed for 1683, six seem to have gone up; seven have gone down and a few have remained the same. The document calls these figures 'The Valued Rent', and covers the entire Shire of Argyll.

1764: Rental of Archibald Campbell's Jura Estate for Crop and Marts

We turn now to the busy year of 1764 when Archibald Campbell died. In this note of rental we begin to see how Campbell's finances connect up with those of his tenants. The properties listed are: Cnocbreac, Feolin Ferry and Change house, Ardfin, salmon fishing and islands, Brosdale, Strone, Sanaig and Auchaleck, Crackaig, Knocknafeolaman, Craighouse Change house, Wauk Miln and Meal Miln, Keils, Feolin, islands of Ploda and Ellanconan, Lergybreck, Change house of Tighchorran, Knockrome, Ardfernal, Lagg, Change house of Lagg, Croft of Lagg, Corrynahera and Auchintarbert, Tarbert.

This amounts to seventeen townships in all, with four change houses, two mills, two sets of islands as well as salmon fishing.

The rentals are now calculated in sterling money and have certain regular components:

Silver Rent: apparently set by the laird, and capable of 'augmentation'.

Teinds: the Scottish form of 'tithes' for the support of the church; established by the 'Teind Court'. By this date the teinds have become quite arbitrary, eg, for rents from about £20 to £40 rent they are £2. They are generally £1 for smaller rents. In Jura papers the word is spelt 'tiend'.

Cess: a small tax, imposed by government, often set at 2/6 in the pound.

Wedders: a wedder or wether is a castrated male sheep, the term occurs with the adjective 'kain', meaning rent paid in kind. A wedder is worth 4/– in 1764.

Fowls and dozens of eggs: a hen and twelve eggs seems to be a unit of tax worth 6d.

Grassum: a lump sum paid by some tenants on entry to a lease or feu or for the renewal of a lease.

Oats and Bear: oats and barley may be required as rent. 'Bear' or 'bere' is the old Scots form of barley, often called 'four-rowed barley'. The modern form is 'two-rowed'.

Grain is measured by the boll. One boll equals six imperial bushels. A bushel equals a dry measure of eight gallons (2219.36 cu. in.). The statutory bushel is a cube a little more than a foot in its length of side. A boll fills a rectangular box about 3 ft long by 2 ft wide by 2 ft deep. Such a measure of oats or bear is worth about 10/– sterling. A boll of good barley is worth 13/4 at this time. There are four 'firlots' to the boll, and four 'pecks' to the firlot. Innkeepers and the miller pay rent in grain.

The liberal sprinkling of one third and two thirds of a penny sterling can be quite puzzling. This arises from the fact that the old merk scots is still in use alongside the later sterling:

4 bolls bear @ 10 merks per boll equals £2 4/5⅓ sterling
1 merk is two-thirds of £1 scots; thus 4 bolls at 10 merks equals £26 13/4 scots
To convert to sterling, divide by 12; thus Two Pounds Four Shillings, Five Pence and One Third of a Penny Sterling.

Here is an extract from the Valuation showing the returns for Knockrome and Corran House:

Knockrom under Tack to Tenants 16shs. Land	Silver rent	£24	4	5				
	8 two year old Wedders @ 4sh. each	1	12	:				
	Tiends	2	:	:				
	Cess	1	4	:				
	24 fowls & 24 doz Eggs @ 6d for each fowl and dozen of Eggs	12	:		£29	12	5	
	N.B. They are bound to perform 34 days Service of one man & 4 days service of a man & horse					£211	2	10
Changehouse of Taychorran	Colin Agey, Tacksman pays of Silver rent	£3	:	:				
	Excise	15	:					
	16 Bolls Barley Solt to him by his Tack which he received this year out of Sanaig of crop 1764 @ 13/4		£10	13	4	£14	8	4

There are many fascinating entries in this document, for example:

The 'wauk miln'. The wauk or waulk mill was for the purpose of 'wauking' or pounding flax. Walker reported: 'The people of Jura have borrowed a little of the linen manufacture of Islay. They have as yet sown little flax, but are furnished with lint from Islay, and the yarn they make is exported to the Clyde.' Did their linen work bring in some hard currency to the township? There seems no evidence, but presumably it must have made a profit.

In the passage reproduced we find Colin Agey the tacksman, who is the innkeeper at the changehouse of Corran.

In another entry we find 'grassum yearly, as they have no tack at Crackaig.' The exact reasons for grassum, and the calculation of the amount seem unclear.

There is reference above to duty work. Knockrome tenants are bound to provide thirty-four days' service of one man, and four days' service of a man and a horse. This matter of 'duty work' or 'borlanachd' was a bone of contention all over the Highlands, and remained in force in Jura until the early years of the twentieth century; probably longer than anywhere else. Based on the likely number of tenants involved, duty work could result in spending almost a complete week working for the landowner.

Even the small islands brought an income: 'pasturage of the islands in Small Isles Bay; Pladda and Eilean nan Coinein (Rabbit Island), annual rent of £5'. Although the grazing there is pretty rough, and the settling and maintenance of livestock on these islands is always troublesome.

The total rent per annum entered on the 1764 list is £530/5/1⅔

1764: Inventory of Grounds of Debts found in the Repositories of the Deceased Archibald Campbell

Archibald Campbell died in January 1764 at the age of eighty. His son was only twenty and 'curators' had to be appointed due to his 'minority'. These curators appointed to deal with the estate on his death no doubt wanted to get a clear account of all his affairs. Their 'List of Bills' runs to thirty-four pages. The Jura accounts consist of just over twelve pages of these, collected in bundles.

Only a third of Campbell's outlay is concerned with Jura, which puts his business interests into perspective. There are 106 individual names of Jura residents listed as being in debt to Archibald Campbell at the time of his death.

The total amount outstanding is £487/6/10. The average owed per debtor is a little over £4 10/– which is considerably more than one year's rent for most tenants.

The majority of the bills date from April or May of the previous year, 1763, but the amounts do not match probable rent figures, and do not seem to relate to outstanding rents. Campbell may have been supplying grain or seed grain and seed potatoes on extended credit, probably to see his tenants through bad seasons for loss of livestock or poor harvest.

A number of substantial accounts go back to 1759 and 1760, so they have been outstanding for four or five years. A dozen or so of these older bills are for 'strength horses'. These particular accounts are always for round sums, e.g., £10 or £6. In view of the fact that commentators remark that the Jura horses are extremely small, it may be that more substantial animals were brought in from the mainland for the heavy tasks such as ploughing, while native horses did the routine lighter work. Stewart, 1794, says 'the horses, though hardy, are a very diminutive breed'.

On the other hand, in view of duty work of 'a man and a horse'; these sums could be financial penalties for the non-completion of strength work with horses.

Within the bundles is the account of Christian McNamoile, a widow in Keils, who is paying off a small debt. There is a note about a possible 'free house' for her.

John Gray, the innkeeper in Lagg has run up a debt of £24 15s – a considerable sum.

There is also one single record of 'herezeld'. This was the ancient custom whereby the laird would arrive after the death of a male householder tenant, and claim 'damh ursna'; 'the beast nearest the door'; or 'the best beast', from the widow. This animal he would take away. The transaction was originally an indication that he had put himself under an obligation to maintain the widow until her own death, but the custom degenerated until it became merely a 'perk' for the laird. The custom was outlawed by parliament in Scotland in the early nineteenth century, but as usual, carried on longer in Jura than anywhere else.

The list of debtors includes one called 'tacksman' at Feolin Ferry; three termed 'farmer'; all living at Sanaig, the home farm of the Campbells. Ten men are called 'tenant'. There are two cottars and one widow. There are a variety of other occupations: a boatman, three carpenters, an innkeeper, a joiner, a tailor, a miller and two weavers.

Christian McNamoile, Mary McNeil, Catherine McLean, Katharine Ferguson, Ann McCranie and Ann McIlliriach are presumably all widows, although only Catherine McLean is given the title in the list. Nine men appear again six years later in the 1770 valuation.

We have now moved forward some thirty years from the end of Neil Campbell's baptismal register, and here in the list of debtors we have another sample of Jura names. They hold few surprises: Blacks, Buies, Campbells, Clerks, Darrochs (McIlriach is also still in use), McArthurs, McCraines, McDougalds,

McLeans, McNamoiles, McPhails and Shaws all still predominate, with only a few newcomer names. The men's Christian names have also remained largely the same.

1764: Inventory of Stocks of Black Cattle, Horses, Mares, Sheep and Goats, farm Boles, Seed Corn, Bear, etc, on the different farms in Jura possessed by the Defunct

This is an extraordinary document running to ten pages, which gives a complete account of all the domestic animals on the part of Jura under the control of the Campbell family.

We will look first at the Cattle. Jura's cattle are always referred to in old documents as 'black cattle', by which is meant the 'kyloe', or primitive cow of the Scottish hebrides, which lies behind the breeding lines of the present day 'Highland cattle', familiar from the moors of Scotland. The modern Highlanders are a reddish-brown colour nowadays, but the earliest form was black in colour, and black Highlanders have been bred until the present century in Jura. The Rev Donald Budge records in his own book on Jura his own enthusiasm as a cattle breeder and gives some early details about the Campbells of Jura and their cattle. He implies that the family was engaged in improving the stock by selective breeding, but 1764 seems a little early for such activity on Jura. Walker in 1764 says: 'The Jura cattle are low in size and do not reap the profit that might otherwise be expected.' Francis Stewart says: 'The small tenants in general overstock their ground, so that the black cattle are rather small and inferior to those of Islay.'

The terms in use for cattle in these eighteenth-century documents are as follows:

Stot	a castrated bullock
Stirk	a yearling bull
Heifer	a young female
Quey	a heifer that has not yet had a calf
Cow	a female
Tydie	a cow with calf
Yell	a farrow or barren cow, not pregnant at present
Bull	a male

Here is a brief summary of the complete document:

Tarbert	Corrynahera park		221
	Tarbert		566
	The Muir		595
	In the Muir (not Strath)		200
	(cows, heifers stots)		
Ardfin	Corrynahera & Tarbert		400
Knockbreck	Stots	75	
	Stots from Ardfin	75	150
Ardfernal		125	
	Stots from Ardfin	12	137
Sannaig & Achaleek		93	
	Stots from Ardfin	4	97
Ardfin			192
	Total Cattle		2,558
Total Horses all ages & sexes			193

Sheep 3 flocks (numbers not given); flock of 70; flock of 82;
Goats 4 unspecified flocks; flock of 65

Only a few farms in Campbell's Jura are named in this Inventory. There is no mention of many of the biggest townships; e.g. Strone, Crackaig, Knocknafeolaman, Feolin, Lergybreck, Knockrome, Lagg. All these were tilled and pastured, and their farming tenants certainly all had cattle. This curious situation prompts the question, what is actually happening here?

The inventory was recorded as at 14 January, but there is continual reference to Hallowday. 'Hallowday' or 'All Hallows' was 1 November. The inventory here is recording the 'gathering' of the great majority of the cattle in the island on the two neighbouring pastures of Corrynahera and Tarbert. These farms are just north of Lagg, with its cattle ferry to the mainland. Corrynahera is steeply sloping ground bounded on the east by the rocky shore of the sound of Jura, and on the west by a steep rocky hill face leading to the bogs of the inner island. There is no trace of early cultivation, and probably no more than a few potatoes were grown there. Tarbert, while somewhat flatter, and possessing some good grassland around the bay, is also fairly inhospitable moorland.

This seems a somewhat remote place to muster the bulk of the islands beasts. Dean Monro in 1549 spoke of the driving of deer at this 'narrow entry', and 'infinit deer slain there'. There may have been a long memory that this was where cattle could be gathered and controlled between Loch Tarbert and the sea. It may well be that the inaccessibility of Corrynahera and Tarbert, some six to twelve miles north of the most intensively farmed parts of the island would make it less likely that the animals would find their way back south and make a nuisance of themselves on the outbye and inbye lands of the townships.

The numbers at such a muster could not always be accurate, and the word 'about' is in frequent use in the document. Beasts out on the moor and not able to be rounded up are estimated on four different occasions at the round number of fifty.

The gathering would be to enable the stock to be identified and sorted as far as possible. Cattle may have been branded or horn marked for individual tenants, and the landlord's large personal stock would have been established. This done, the beasts destined to be kept inside to winter in the tenants homesteads would be brought home. These would be the milk cows carrying unborn calves and with their current calves at heel. Perhaps there would also be a heifer or two for future replacement as milk cows. The stots, heifers and stirks, together with the bulls would remain on these northern parks and on the moor throughout the winter, and take their chances. It was then and there that mortality would occur, and with it the success or failure of the next sale.

Stewart says: 'In winter the pasture is insufficient to support them, and by want of dry forage a great part of the produce of the island is lost in that season by the death of the cattle.'

Knockbreck, a small isolated township on the west coast is also wintering 150 stots, half of them from Campbell's farm at Ardfin.

The number of animals at Ardfernal, Sannaig and Auchaleek presents something of a puzzle, for these farms are surrounded by many others, quite similar, whose cattle are evidently at the gathering to the north. The 300 hundred or so beasts here include every example of age and sex, but not of sufficient numbers to account for all of any category on the island. They may have included some of Campbells own beasts, but later in 1764 he sold more than three times their number. The reason for these stocks is probably no longer accessible.

Seed Corn is counted as part of the inventory, and that barley is mentioned as well as bear.

Bear, the four rowed variety was sown as an infield crop throughout the western isles. It was better adapted to acid soils than two-row barley, and withstood weather conditions better. It could be sown three or four weeks later than barley, allowing time for soils to dry out, but it still ripened up to three weeks earlier. It could be ground into 'meal' if necessary. It did well on raised beach soils, of which the Jura fields are typical, where there was seaweed available as manure. Barley was generally cultivated only in the more fertile parts of Scotland and it is somewhat surprising to find it growing in Jura. Many references fail to differentiate between two-row barley and four-row bear, and many writers use the word 'barley' when they plainly mean 'bear'. It can only be clearly distinguished when, as in this document, both words are used alongside each other.

John McIlriach of Ardfernal, and John Ban Ferguson; Neil McPherson; Donald McCraine and Glbert Clark of Sannaig, are all described as 'farmers' in this or the 'debts' papers. Presumably the same label should be attached to John and Malcolm McNamoile; Archibald McLean and Alexander Campbell of Ardfin. All of these appear on the 'List of Debts' owing substantial amounts, and seven of them appear twice, with the second entry relating to 'strength horses'.

Only people of this particular status seem involved in the inventory of seed corn, and obligation to 'the farm', 'the family' and 'the house', all of which references are somewhat cryptic.

Two members of the community appear with their nicknames: John Ferguson is John Ban, or fair-haired John, while Malcolm Darroch of Ardfin, is Callum Chrom McIlreoch, or 'crooked, or bent, or hunchbacked Calum'.

As we have seen the inventory produced a total of 2562 cattle on the island.

In due course the public roup of 1764 revealed that Campbell's own personal stock of black cattle numbered 1075.

These figures are in agreement with the record of the Rev. Alexander Kennedy, writing the *Second Statistical Account* some eighty years later, who says: 'There are from 1000 to 1200 head of black cattle annually sold out of the Island of Jura. One half of these by the tenants; average value £5 sterling. The other half consists of four year old stots and heifers sold by Mr Campbell of Jura and Captain McNeill, younger, of Colonsay, average value at the present prices, £10 sterling.'

1764: The Record of the Public Auction of all of Campbell's stock of cattle, and sheep and goats

The circumstances of the Public Auction or Roup were as follows: Campbell of Jura was in the process of buying part of Jura from Campbell of Shawfield, when Shawfield died in 1764. Shawfield's executors called on Jura to complete the payment of the purchase money. Before this could be done, Archibald Campbell of Jura died, to be succeeded by his son Archibald, who was only twenty years old, and thus a minor. Campbell had appointed 'curators' to his son, from among his friends. To meet the claims of Shawfield's executors they decided to sell some livestock: 'The whole black cattle, horses, mares, sheep and goats which belonged to the deceased Archibald Campbell.'

Inventory of the Roup and Sale of the Black Cattle and others belonging to the deceased Archibald Campbell of Jura, sold by Publick Roup upon the Lands of Tarbert, Corrienaheira, etc., upon the 21st May 1764 years in Consequence of the Sheriff Depute of Argyle's warrant for that effect of date the 5th May 1764.

Stots and the prices of each	*Purchasers' names and designations*	*Price*		
40 carried at £2 14 0 each	John Gillies of Duchra	£108	0	0
41 at £3 6 6 each	Alex. McNeil of Oronsay for Dunolly	136	6	6
40 at £2 11 0 "	" "	102	0	0
40 at £2 12 6 "	John McAlester at Ronnachan	105	0	0
40 at £2 11 0 "	William Campbell of Glenfalloch	102	0	0
60 at £2 15 0 "	Neil McKellar of Daille	165	0	0
60 at £2 16 0 "	Arch. Fletcher, younger, of Bernice	168	0	0
20 at £2 16 0 "	John Gillies of Duchra	56	0	0
24 at £1 16 6 "	John Campbell, Tacksman of Cadiltoun	43	16	0
40 at £1 10 0 "	Alexr. McKenzie in Corrilorn	60	0	0
39 at £1 13 4 "	Archd. Campbell, of Lochbuy	65	0	0
20 at £1 11 0 "	John Campbell, Tacksman of Cadiltoun	31	0	0
41 at £1 17 0 "	John Gillies of Duchra	75	17	0
44 at £1 14 0 "	John Campbell, Tacksman of Cadiltoun	74	16	0
	Rouped at Tarbert on 21st May 1764	£1292	15	6
Cows				
41 at £1 17 6 each	Charles Young, Drover in Glasgow	£76	17	6
41 at £1 18 0 "	" "	77	18	0
80 at £2 4 0 "	Peter McKellar, Drover	176	0	0
12 at £2 4 0 "	" "	26	8	0
Heifers				
30 at £1 10 6 each	Archd. Campbell, Son to Jura	45	15	0
10 & a Bull £1 7 0 each	Archd. Campbell, Ardmenish	14	17	0
9 & a Bull £1 10 0 each	" "	15	0	0
12 at £1 13 6 each	John McLean, Tacksman of Octofad	20	2	0
1 Bull	John Campbell, Cadiltoun	2	15	6
1 Bull	Archd. Simson, Tacksman of Culabus	2	12	0
1 Bull	Colin Campbell, Tacksman of Eorabus	2	0	0
2 Bulls	Duncan McLellan, Lergchonich	1	19	0

13 two-year-old stots at £1 7 0 each	Donald McNeil of Colonsay	17	11	0
13 two-year-old stots at £1 2 6	" "	14	12	6
		494	7	6
		1787	3	"

Here is a summary of the results of the Roup:

Cows	176		
Tydie Cows	81		
Yell Cows	2		
2 yr old Queys	7		
Heifers	61		
Stots	549		
2 yr old Stots	134		
Stirks	57		
Bulls	8		
Total	1075	Total Paid	£2144 16/

Young Archibald Campbell bought back some of the stock to rebuild the herd, as follows:

49 – Heifers & 2 Bulls; 9 – 2 yr old Heifers; 31 – 2 yr old Stots; 57 – Stirks; 14 – Tydie Cows; 2 – Yell Cows; for which he paid £204 14/6.

He also bought all the sheep and goats at the sale, amounting to 58 goats and 56 sheep for which he paid £19 19/–.

The only other beasts to remain on the island were two tydie cows bought by Robert Agey, of Corran changehouse, and two similar cows bought by Gilbert McIlriach of Ardfernal.

Despite the public notice, no horses were sold at the roup.

This document is of interest because it gives a complete set of contemporary values for every conceivable kind of cow that can be offered for sale. It is an artificial guide to Jura's annual cattle trade, as the estate is here involved in selling the entire stock, completely different from the annual situation in which the farming tenants are involved.

The Campbell stock had a heavy preponderance of male beasts. Indeed 355 female animals were sold and 720 male. He was able to put up for sale 550 stots, which by their prices must have been half three year olds and half four year olds. Campbell was evidently following a policy of keeping back his bullocks to fatten for at least two years longer than his tenants could afford. It is interesting to consider how he arranged to feed this number of large animals without their being a drain on his tenants' lands. No doubt the proportion of various ages and sexes of cattle in Campbell's herd was quite different from that in his tenants' herds. With investment capital behind him, Campbell could afford to wait to sell his animals at a profit, a luxury not available to the ordinary people.

1770: Scheme of Valuation of the Lands belonging to Archibald Campbell in the Parish of Jura

This Scheme is only six years later than the rental list of 1764, but presents a very different appearance. Archibald Campbell, fourth of Jura is now twenty-six years old, and no doubt very much in charge.

The scribe who drew up the valuation took the trouble to identify one or more of the farming tenants in each township. The result is sixteen named tenants. Of these, nine have already appeared in the list of debtors from 1674. These are: Donald McIliriach of Brosdale; Archibald Campbell of Strone; Duncan McArthur Snr. of Crackaig; Alexander McDougald of Knocknafeolaman; Donald Black of Keils; Archibald McCranie of Knockrome; Dugald McDugald; Gilneave McIlriach; and John McIlriach of Lagg.

Between 1764 and 1770 the method of valuation seems to have been changed, either on young Campbell's initiative, or by a change in the law.

The money rent has been reduced, and a sum is now allowed for various practices carried out by the tenants, which are now seen as privileges which have a definite monetary value.

These are: cutting wood on the pursuer's estate; the use of his ground; peeling bark for tanning their leather; burning fern to make Fern Ashes; and cutting seaweed or wrack fit for kelp.

The sums assessed for these, and various other monies payable by such as innkeepers, etc, are now deducted from the gross rent for the purpose of calculating the teinds, which are now set at one fifth of the gross rent. The tenants are thus paying a reduced silver rent, but it is brought back to its previous level by having these 'deductions' added back on to it. The amount due has not changed, but the gross total for the island is much less, as follows:

Campbell's gross income with all allowances	£420	8/6
Teinds; now declared as one fifth of the gross	£84	1/8
With deductions for services, etc., the income can be re-calculated as	£271	5/7
Teinds at One Fifth	54	5/1

This piece of 'creative accounting' brings a saving on Teinds of £29 16/7 . 'Cess' appears to have been discontinued by this time, although 'kain' payments of wedders, hens & dozens of eggs continue. As with earlier documents, the 1770 valuation has many insights into the situation at the time. There follows an extract which gives some examples of typical entries:

'The Six Shilling Land of the Town of Lagg & Ferry thereof possest by Gilneave & John McIleriochs, Malcolm & Neil Shaw, Dugald McDugald & Archibald McCloisigh – of money rent	14	10
Six two Year old Wedders at 3/– each		18/–
12 Fowls & 12 doz of Eggs at 5d for each Fowl & doz of Eggs		5/–
of Teinds		16/8
	18	9/8

Deductions

The rent of the Ferry of Lagg	£3		
The privilege of cutting woods of the estate for the use of the ground & for making Fern ashes & cutting wreck fit for kelp & peeling Barks for Tanning their Leather ⎫⎬⎭	£3		
		6	
			12 9/8

The two shilling Land of Lagg with the Change house and malt Barn thereon – of money rent		5	
2 two year old kain muttons at said conversion		6/–	
		5 6/–	

Deductions

The rent of the Change house & small Barn	£2 7/6		
The privilege of Cutting woods on the Estate for the use of the ground & for making Fern Ashes and Cutting wreck fit for kelp & Peeling Barks for Tanning his Leather. ⎫⎬⎭	£1		
		3 7/6	
			1 18/6
			15 4/8

The Land of Kille possest by Donald Black & others of money rent		22	
8 Two Year old Kain wedders at sd. conversion		1 4/–	
16 Hens & 16 doz Eggs at said conversion		6/8	
of Teinds	1	1 3/4	
		25 4/–	

Deductions

The value of the liberty of Cutting woods for the use of the ground & of Stripping Barks for Tanning Leather & of Cutting Ferns & making ashes thereof & of wreck fit to make Kelp	£2 10/–	
The rent of the Glebe or Loss to the ground by its being taken off	£7	9 10/–

1754: A Note of the Rents outstanding to Campbell of Jura by those intending to Emigrate to North Carolina

This document is part of the process against the emigrant tenants, which we will study in connection with the chapter on emigration. It gives us the names and circumstances of some individual farming tenants. Their share of the township in which they live is recorded, and details are given of their individual rents. This eighteenth-century document actually focuses on individual people:

Angus McIllirioch has one-eighth of Brosdale
Duncan McGheil has one-eighth of Strone
Duncan McArthur; John McDuffie and Iver Mackay have each one-eighth of Crackaig
while Dugald McDougald has one-quarter of the same Township.
Donald Clerk has one-quarter of Keils, while Archibald Clerk has one-eighth, and Gilbert Clerk has a 3/– teind and John McIlpheder has a 1/– teind.

Donald Black has one-half of Feolin
Donald Lindsay and Donald Buie each have one-half of Lergybreck.
Hugh McLean and John Cargill have each one-sixth of Knockrome, while John
    McIlrioch
and Archibald McCraine have one-eighth.
Gilbert McIlrioch has one-eighth of Lagg.
Archibald McIlrioch has one-sixteenth of Corrynahera.

For the first, and only time in the eighteenth century we can set the individual rent of a tenant alongside the rental of his entire township, and make some kind of estimate as to how many tenants there were.

Here, for example, is the rental of a tenant who holds one-eighth of the town of Brosdale.

			A	B
Angus McIlrioch	Silver rent	£2 10/–	£20 0/–	£22 0/–
	Teinds	4/2	£1 13/4	£2 0/–
	Cess	2/6	£1 0/–	£0 19/3
	1 kain wedder	8 kain wedders	8 wedders @	£1 12/–
	2 hens 2doz eggs	16 hens & 16 doz eggs	24 hens etc. @	12/–

A 8 times his rent;
B Actual rent of Brosdale 1764

The actual rent from the 1764 Rental comes from nine years later than the action against Angus McIlirioch. Everything except the value of a 'tribute sheep' seems to have gone up a bit.

The List of Debtors for 1764 gives us thirteen names for Brosdale. This includes a tailor, a carpenter, a joiner, and one female name (probably a widow). One would expect also that Brosdale might have several cottars.

Taking our records for Angus McIlriach together with all the other evidence we may conclude that the 'eighth' tenancy may indeed represent the presence of eight actual farming tenants in Brosdale.

We can apply a similar process for Strone which would also appear to have eight tenant families, Crackaig appears to be a little larger.

By comparison with the tentative rentals we have available, a rough estimate of the number of tenant families in each township would be as follows:

Cnocbreac	6	Keils	10
Ardfin	8	Feolin	4
Brosdale	8	Lergybreck	4
Strone	8	Knockrome	10
Sanaig & Auchaleek	8	Ardfernal	10
Crackaig	10	Lagg	6
Knocknafeolaman	10	Corrynahera	8
		Tarbert	12

This would give a possible total number of farming tenant families in Campbell's Jura of 122 in 1764.

The above list suggests sixteen farming townships in Campbell's part of Jura. We must add: Ardmenish, Auchintarbert, Ardlussa, Knockintavill and Kinuachdrach, which were not under Campbell's control. This would bring the number of farming townships we know of in the 1760s to twenty-one.

Francis Stewart records in 1794 that there were fifteen farms in tillage and twelve in pasturage on the main island; or twenty-seven in all. There are many possible explanations for the discrepancy in numbers. Stewart probably discriminated between linked farms like Sannaig and Auchaleek. Since the change houses had lands attached, he probably considered Feolin Ferry; Craighouse and Corran House as farms. Auchintarbert was probably also distinct from Tarbert in his eyes. A number of new settlements had appeared by the time of the 1841 census, and any of them may have featured in Stewart's list. Dainskeir; Camustac, or Dunans may have arrived. Certainly Camustac was an ancient dwelling. He may have still discriminated between Keils and Kilearnadil. We are unlikely to be able to say which of these names were the active farms he recorded in the *Statistical Account*, but there are plenty of candidates for his twenty-seven townships.

Stewart records 204 families on the island. Our missing townships above would add another 50 or so to our farming tenant total, bringing it to perhaps around 170.

Campbell's List of Debtors in 1764 contains the families of seven tradesmen. There is also a miller, a smith, and four innkeepers. There seem also to be an unknown number of cottars. There are also widows and elderly former tenants. The number of families is thus approaching Stewart's 204.

Stewart suggested fifty to sixty souls in some of the bigger farms. Eight tenant farmers in a township would mean sixteen adults plus their children at approximately four per family, or forty-eight souls plus the sundry non-tenant people, which approaches Stewart's figure.

According to Dr Webster's Census of 1755 the total population was then 1097 souls. By the *Statistical Account* of 1794 this had fallen to 929; a drop of 168; presumably largely as a result of the emigration of which the Rev. Francis Stewart complains.

Since the population decreased during the forty years after Webster's census, one would expect a proportionately higher number of families in 1755 than Stewart's 204; perhaps 240.

We return now to the question of black cattle, and to the inventory and cattle roup of 1764.

The 1500 cattle left on the island after the sale of the Landlord's herd, would have been divided very roughly into three categories: 500 cows, either in calf or capable of having calves; 500 stirks: the beasts born the previous year (stirks are both male and female); 500 stots and heifers two years old. The figures we have been looking at would produce a result of about nine or ten cattle beasts for each tenant family in our estimated 170, or a herd of about 80 to 100 in a township.

Thus an individual family's cattle holding would be a target of three cows in calf with their three stirks, together with two heifers kept as replacement cows, and three stots or heifers being fattened to sell at two years old. The township bulls would be held in common at a ratio of about one bull to every twenty-five cows.

PLATE 1. The Gulf of Corrievreckan: Scarba below; Jura above. *(page 15)*

PLATE 2. Kilearndale graveyard early in the twentieth century. *(page 77)*

PLATE 3. Jura House: the home of the Campbells of Jura. *(page 106)*

PLATE 4. Craighouse as seen from the pier *(l–r)* 'Torran Mhor'; Inn steadings; Craighouse Inn; distillery; Mill; Smithy; Excise House and shop; Ballard on the hill above. *(page 108)*

PLATE 5. An early view of Caigenhouse. The 'cock and hen hotel' at the right. The one-legged man is Parnell. *(page 108)*

PLATE 6. Keils about 1920. The dog looks hopefully in at the window. *(page 109)*

PLATE 7. Mary Campbell's cottage in Keils. *(page 109)*

PLATE 8. The paupers' cottages at Ardfernal. *(page 111)*

PLATE 9. Lagg. The new road winds up the hill past the village. The stackyard is full at the former Ferry House. *(page 112)*

PLATE 10. Rev. Donald John Robertson prays with the departing troops in the First World War. *(page 232)*

Sheelins in JURA and a distant View of the Paps

PLATE 11. *'Shielings on Jura.'* drawn by one of Joseph Banks' artists, during Pennant's visit to Jura in 1772. *(page 375)*

PLATE 12. *'Deer stalking on the Bens of Jura'* by Gourlay Steele. *(page 405)*

NEIL CLARK   ANGUS MACKAY
Gamekeeper   RICHARD CAMPBELL OF JURA
Laird   ANGUS MACKAY, Jr.

PLATE 13. 'The Jura Car' in use at Jura Forest Lodge. Angus McKay and John Clark. *(page 408)*

PLATE 14. *'Pioneer'* at Craighouse Pier. *(page 444)*

PLATE 15. Puffer off-loading coal at Lagg Bay. *c*.1930. *(page 447)*

PLATE 16. Lohn Lindsay of Lagg of Lagg post office with his pony and trap at Caigenhouse. *(page 449)*

This would mean that a family would be producing three two-year old beasts for sale each year; at a price of about £1 10/– each in 1764; giving an annual income from cows alone of £4 10/–.

The cash requirements for rent for such a family were between £3 and £3 10/–, so the great majority of their cash income would go out directly on the rent.

At the date of the inventory there seem to have been over 200 horses on that part of the island under Campbell's control; so perhaps 250 on the whole island. Thomas Pennant, visiting at this time records that about 100 horses are sold annually, although since no horses were sold at the roup, we have no idea what a young horse fetched at the time. Still, it would be another small sum in cash to add to the cattle.

The presence of the wauk mill confirms the visitor's accounts of flax, so there may have been some income from the linen work.

Virtually everything else in the local economy seems to have been a matter of payment in kind, or payment by barter. Later, the kelp industry got under way, and although Jura people were unable to earn large sums by the sale of the product – the laird claimed to own all the kelp on the island – they were able to earn wages in the process of gathering and kilning the weed.

Income and expenditure for the average farming tenant family in the mid-eighteenth century seem to have been very closely connected. There can have been little margin for error, and a poor harvest or a severe winter could have spelt disaster.

26

Emigration

By the latter part of the eighteenth century it became widely known that large-scale emigrations were taking place from the Highlands and Islands of Scotland, and that great numbers of settlers were arriving in Canada, Nova Scotia and the American Colonies.

When Dr Samuel Johnson visited the Western Isles in 1773, he was greatly distressed to witness the large emigrations which were going on:

> Some method to stop this epidemic deserves to be sought with great diligence. In more fruitful countries the removal of one only makes room for the succession of another; but in the Hebrides the loss of an inhabitant leaves a lasting vacuity; for nobody born in any other part of the world will choose this country for his residence; and an island once depopulated will remain a desert.

As far as the island of Jura is concerned, as we have seen, it was seldom visited by people who had any interest in making public what was happening. The island was not easy to get to, and no doubt Campbell of Jura found it easier to manage without the interference of 'strangers'.

Not until the production of the *Second Statistical Account* in 1794 do we get a glimpse of what has evidently been going on for some time. The minister, Francis Stewart had only been inducted to the parish in 1791, and was faced with writing the account only two or three years after his appointment. He gives the population of the main island as 929, and follows this with his comments:

> As the present incumbent has not been long in the parish of Jura, and as he has not been able to procure former examination rolls, it is out of his power to give a statement of the population prior to the date of his own survey. Emigrations to America have proved, once and again, a drain to this island; but, in the present mode of management, it may be said to be still overstocked with inhabitants. Near half the farms in the island are in pasture, and require very few hands to manage them. Of course, the great body of the people live in the farms, which are in tillage. In some of these there are between fifty and sixty souls. Such a swarm of inhabitants, where manufactures, and many other branches of industry are unknown, are a very great load upon the proprietors, and in a great measure useless to the state. The slightest survey of the situation of the people shows how much improvements in farming, and the introduction of industry, are wanted. *The spirit of emigration is still powerful in the island, and requires considerable alterations to extinguish it.*

Francis Stewart is, of course, responsible for the account of Colonsay also, and he has an interesting comment to make in this case:

A few emigrated from Colonsay to America, summer 1792; but in summer 1791, a considerable proportion of the inhabitants crossed the Atlantic. Those who remain give out that they are waiting only good accounts from their relations, and a proper opportunity of being transported to the other hemisphere. Pity it is that such numbers should bid farewell to their native country, when there is so great a demand for useful citizens; and their situation might be rendered more comfortable at home.

A little earlier than Francis Stewart, the *Scots Magazine* of August 1768, reports: 'between forty and fifty families have gone from the island of Jura for Cape Fear in Carolina to settle thereabout and in Georgia.'

In August of the following year the same source tells us that the *Mally* sailed from the island of Islay for North Carolina full of passengers to settle in that province, and it is said that this is the third or fourth emigration from the shire of Argyll since the conclusion of the late war (i.e. in 1763). In February 1771, comes news that 'Upwards of 500 souls from Islay and the adjacent isles prepare to emigrate next summer to America'.

No doubt the movements of which Francis Stewart was writing must have had a great impact on the life of the island, but by the time of the author's residence on Jura in the 1970s, there seemed little trace of these events in the folklore of the island. No stories or anecdotes surfaced in his extensive periods of listening and collecting. A new initiative in this matter came from members of the communities of North Carolina, loosely located around the city of Fayetteville in that State. With strong traditions of a Scottish Highland ancestry in their families, and in some cases with family documentary evidence, these people entered into correspondence with residents on Jura, and in due course a considerable number came across the Atlantic to visit the island they identified as the birthplace of their ancestors. It is in the nature of things that in such a parish as Jura, the minister holds a pivotal role in these matters, and most of the American visitors found themselves directed to the manse, where many hoped to fulfil their expectations of being able to study records which would reveal their ancestral birthplaces, and perhaps even the presence of contemporary 'cousins' living on the island.

Some of these early encounters were a little confusing for the local people. The author well remembers the look on the face of an elderly and dignified member of the Buie line in Jura, as he was embraced by a gentleman from North Carolina who also bore the name Buie, and greeted him warmly as 'cousin' with a southern drawl that gave the word an exotic flavour.

The author began regular journeys to Edinburgh to copy out Statutory Registers of Births, Marriages and Deaths, and other nineteenth-century census records so that the visitors would be able to do at least some basic research while actually on the island of Jura.

An examination of Donald Budge's book revealed that he was well aware of the emigrations, and once put on the scent, some Jura residents entered into research with a will, soon revealing that, at least in the case of the nineteenth-century emigrations, they had no difficulty in establishing their relationship with those who had departed. Residents such as Miss Katie Darroch were a fund of such information. However, the impetus and the energy seemed to be located on the other side of the Atlantic, and people like Dr Scott Buie, and Lt-Colonel Victor Clark began serious efforts to investigate the 'Argyll Colony'. Family histories, Abstracts of Records, Directories of Residents, and Periodicals on the topic began to appear in considerable numbers, and the 'Highland Scots of North Carolina' appear now to have been thoroughly researched.

We can now push the story back more than fifty years before Francis Stewart's account, and a summary of the present state of the investigation follows.

NORTH CAROLINA AND THE HIGHLAND SCOTS
North Carolina was England's only colony during the Elizabethan age. In 1584, explorers sent by Sir Walter Raleigh reached the area now known as Roanoke island, and so, a year later, he sent a colony to settle there. For various reasons the English were not able to return with supplies for some five years, and when they finally did get back in 1590 the colony had vanished. It has since been known as the 'Lost Colony'. North Carolina developed slowly, partly because of its lack of good harbours, and partly for political reasons. In 1663, when King Charles granted the colony to several creditors who had assisted in his restoration to the throne it had something more than 500 persons living in it.

By 1730, people from Wales began settling along the west bank of the Cape Fear River, in what would become known as the 'Welsh Tract'. From this time forward North Carolina experienced tremendous population growth, from about 36,000 in 1729 to some 300,000 by 1776. Most of this extraordinary increase in numbers was the result of an influx of immigrants from other colonies and from Europe, filling the Cape Fear Valley, and spilling over into the back country. A good part consisted of perhaps as many as 50,000 Highland Scots.

A major reason for this immigration must be the effective governorship of Gabriel Johnston, a Lowland Scot and graduate of St Andrews University who served as Governor of North Carolina from 1734 to 1752. He felt it would be good for the future of the Cape Fear Valley for it to be settled by large numbers of Protestant Highland Scots, so he began writing enthusiastic letters to friends in Scotland inviting them to come to a land where there were two crops each year, free land grants and possible exemption from taxation for a time.

It is true that three Highland names are mentioned in the Land Grant Records of North Carolina before the time of Governor Johnson. Hugh Campbell, William Forbes and James Innes had land grants in what is now Cumberland County in 1733, but it is most likely that this was a purely speculative venture and it is doubtful if any of them ever actually set foot in America.

What is certain is that Governor Johnston's letter reached the ears of Argyll tacksmen such as Duncan Campbell of Kilduskland, Neill, Hector and Archibald McNeill from Gigha and Kintyre, Coll McAlester and his sons Hector and Alexander of Islay, and, of special interest to us, Alexander Clark of Jura.

These were all prosperous men, who were concerned at the undercutting of the tacksman's position on the Duke of Argyll's estate, as well as the depression in cattle prices in the mid 1730s, and were thus prepared to take a serious look

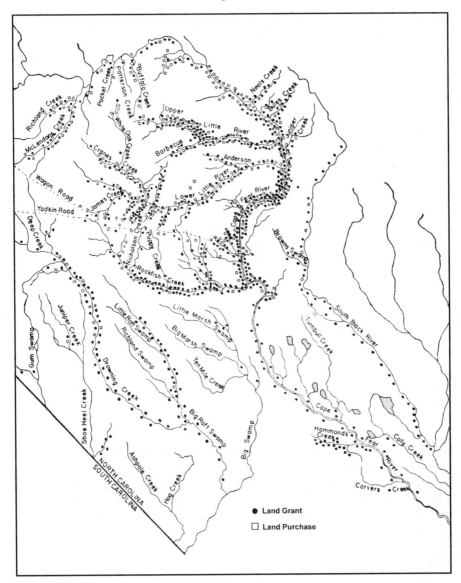

Map 16. Land grants and purchases secured by Highlanders on the Upper Cape Fear
River in North Carolina.

at good opportunities elsewhere. They took Governor Johnston's letters about
North Carolina seriously enough to organise a committee to visit the Cape Fear
Valley in 1736.

It is probable that this committee may originally have had its attention drawn
to North America by Captain Hector MacNeill, a merchant shipmaster, who
sailed for many years to places as far away from one another as Boston and
Africa and elsewhere. He had written to his brother Neill (one of the Argyll

committee) in early 1736, encouraging the bringing of a colony to New England, but the Argyll committee decided on North Carolina, probably because of Governor Johnston.

The committee liked what they saw in Carolina, returned to Argyll, and by 1739 brought a substantial colony of friends and relatives with them back to the Cape Fear River.

Some 350 emigrants sailed from Campbeltown in July 1739 on the *Thistle*, guided by Neill Du MacNeill (Black Neil of Ardelay) and landed in September, most likely in the port of Brunswick. The Argyll Colony travelled up the Cape Fear Valley some 90 miles upstream from the port of entry to the heavily wooded country which would become the heartland of transplanted Highlanders in Carolina. This section was then known as Bladen County, but in 1754 was set off as Cumberland. It was centred on what is now Fayetteville, but was then two small adjacent trading towns, Campbeltown and Cross Creek.

The question should be asked why the settlers undertook the long and arduous journey upriver. The story goes today among their descendants that their Highland Scots ancestors were literate and well read, and could read the sign displayed on the jetty which said 'Better Land Upstream'; whereas the present inhabitants of Wilmington are the descendants of those illiterates who could not read the sign and stayed put, knowing no better. It is a delightful story, but almost exactly the opposite of the truth. It would have been more true if the sign had read 'Poorer Land Upstream, but all that's left'. In fact, the rich bottom lands of the lower Cape Fear were much superior to the sandy hills of the upper valley. The explanation is simple. Earlier English and Welsh colonists had already taken up the fertile land along the lower Cape Fear, and the Highland Scots had no option but to go upstream to an area where land grants were still available.

The Argyll Colony was a success by any measure. The emigrants were given substantial Land Grants by 1740, relief from taxation for ten years, a financial grant from the Colonial government, and several of them (including Duncan Campbell, Daniel McNeill, and Dugald McNeill) were immediately appointed Justices of the Peace for Bladen County. Word of their good reception was not long in reaching home, and a door was opened through which untold thousands of Highland Scots would come for nearly a century.

THE FIRST JURA EMIGRANTS

We now return to Jura to see if Alexander Clark of Jura managed to persuade any of his fellow countrymen to embark on the *Thistle*. Were Jura families amongst the '39ers', as they are often known? We have to accept the fact that if our information had to be derived solely from records surviving from the eighteenth century here in Scotland, we would be completely unable to answer this question. Such scanty population records as we have make no mention of the departure of colonists in 1739. Indeed local records of emigrations are rare from this period. However, in the United States, the descendants of the Highland colonists have done a vast amount of research into their own family histories, and this has resulted in numbers of well authenticated studies revealing the genealogy of families which originated in Argyll and its offshore islands. Here we find Buies, Clarks, Shaws, and many others, and here we find people who proudly trace their ancestry to the island of Jura.

Of the 350 souls who were allocated berths on the *Thistle* only fifty-two names have been generally agreed as authentic members of the party. These fifty-two, all men, no doubt represent families, as in later manifests, wives and children of heads of households seem to be regarded as 'chattels' and not recorded by name. Women who are recorded later seem to have been single females travelling alone.

There seems now to be a generally accepted list of those for whom there is some firm evidence that they actually arrived in 1739, and subsequently settled and received land grants.

This complete list now follows:

The Argyll Colony 1739

1	Thomas Armstrong	27	Hector McNeill (Carver)
2	Alexander Clark	28	Neill McNeill (Long)
3	John Clark	29	Nathaniel Smylie
4	Archibald Clark	30	Matthew Smylie
5	Alexander Colvin	31	James Campbell
6	Alexander McAlester	32	Malcolm McNeill
7	Col. McAlester	33	Torquil McNeill
8	Hector McAlester	34	Will Stevens
9	James McAlester	35	Daniel McNeill
10	John McAlester	36	John Cameron
11	Alexander McKay	37	Daniel McDuffie
12	Hugh McLaughlin	38	Gilbert Patterson
13	James McLaughlan	39	Black Neill McNeill
14	John McPherson	40	Dugal Stewart
15	Archibald Buie	41	Patrick Stewart
16	Duncan Buie	42	Malcolm Clark
17	Daniel Buie	43	Miles Ward
18	Hugh McCranie	44	Samuel McGaw
19	Murdoch McCrainie	45	Daniel McDougald
20	Duncan Campbell	46	Archibald mcGill
21	Archibald Campbell	47	Neill McGill
22	Edward Connor	48	John Smith
23	Neill McNeill	49	Neill McNeill (Little)
24	Hector McNeill	50	Arch'd Buie (Gum Swamp)
25	Archibald McNeill	51	Dugald McNeill
26	Lachlan McNeill	52	Hugh Ward

Our interest in these first Jura settlers of North Carolina leads us into a fascating area of research. Can we firmly establish Jura as the birthplace of some of these '39ers'?

The list of fifty-two families contains a number of well-known individuals whose origins are known, and who come from elsewhere than Jura. These are not our concern. They are the McAlesters: Alexander, Coll, Hector, James, and John; Alexander McKay of Kintyre; The McNeills of Gigha: Archibald, Daniel, and Black Neill; John Smith from Knapdale; Duncan Campbell of Kilduskland, and Captain Archie Campbell.

Next it seems reasonable to eliminate men whose surnames do not appear in any collection of Jura inhabitants, and in particular are absent from our best source, the Old Parish Register of Baptisms from 1704 to 1734. This group consists of Thomas Armstrong, Alexander Colvin, Hugh McLaughlin, James McLachlan, John McPherson, Edward Connor, Will Stevens, John Cameron, Gilbert Patterson, Dugal Stewart, Patrick Stewart, Ward Miles, Samuel McGaw, Hugh Ward.

About those who are left on the list, opinion differs a little as to which names are definitely of men who came from Jura. American research dovetails neatly with the Old Parish Records of Baptisms, in a number of cases. The author is reasonably happy to consider the following thirteen adults and two children as Jura-born members of the '39ers'.

1 Alexander Clark.   Alexander Clark and his wife Finwall McLean had a son John, born in Crackaig and baptised on 5 June 1724. Clark family history researched by Lt-Colonel Victor Clark, gives Alexander's father as Gilbert and his wife as Flora McLean. The name Flora generally replaced Finwall in the mid-eighteenth century.

   Lt-Colonel Victor Clark's research contains earlier family recollections, especially concerned with events after the Battle of the Boyne in 1690. These events are recorded elsewhere. This is the man who went on the scouting party of 1736 and must be responsible for the recruitment of the emigrants.

2 John Clark.   The son of Alexander; as confirmed by American family history.

3 Archibald Clark.   Also a son of Alexander; also from family history. Gilbert Clark, a son of Alexander, presumably too young to be recorded on the sailing. Daniel Clark, also Alexander's son, and too young to be on the list.

4 Archibald Buie.   There was an Ard (Archibald) Bui in Knockrome in 1726 when he and his wife had a son Duncan baptised. His wife was a McCranie, but her Christian name has not survived. Their son Duncan is a confirmed '39er' who would have been thirteen years old at the time of the journey. It is widely believed that Archibald and his wife also were in the 1739 party. Archibald Buie of Ardfin was baptised in 1705, so would have been thirty-four years old in 1739. He was the eldest son of Neil Buie and Christine McPherson. He could well have been the emigrant Archibald, appearing also as an infant, in which case we would have a record of his parents.

5 Duncan Buie.   A confirmed emigrant, he was born in Jura in 1724. He lived at first with his family on the Upper Cape Fear River, near Buies Creek, and acquired land in 1750. About 1755 he moved to the Barbeque Creek area and became an Elder in Barbeque Church in 1765. He was known for his piety and knowledge of Church doctrine. During the revolution, probably for political reasons he left Barbeque, and settled near Raeford's Creek, opposite Bluff Church. He died in 1819 in Cumberland County.

6 Hugh McCrainie.   Aobh or Hugh, and his brother Murdoch McCraine were baptised in Knockrome in 1704 and 1707. Their parents were Ard McCranie and Ann McLaine.

   When Hugh grew up he married Catherine Bui, and they had a daughter Merron, baptised in Knockrome in 1733 when Hugh was twenty-nine and his brother Murdoch was twenty-six. Hugh, and presumably his wife and family are confirmed members of the '39ers'. Hugh was allocated a 500 acre land grant in Bladen Count, North Carolina, on 4 June 1740.

7 Murdoch McCranie.   Another definite '39er' – see history above.

8 *Daniel McDuffie*. Baptised in Knockrome in 1722, he was the son of Duncan and Margaret McDuffie. (Donald seems to be the original form in Jura of what often turns into Daniel in the USA.) Duncan and Margaret turn up as common names amongst their descendants.

9 *Torquil McNeill*. Married to Catherine McKellar and lived at Ardlussa in the north of Jura. They had four children who appear in the Baptismal Record: Florence, baptised 1711; Donald, 1713; Neill, 1715; Lauchlan, 1728. At the time of the emigration Torquil would have been in his late forties, and his four children in their twenties. Torquil and Catherine may well have been '39ers', together with their sons Neill and Lauchlan who were twenty-four and twenty-one years of age in 1739.

10 *Neill McNeill*. A possible '39er', as a son of the above Torquil.

11 *Lauchlan McNeill*. A possible '39er' as another son of the above Torquil.

12 *Neill McGill*. Neill McGhoile and his wife Ann McDuffie had two daughters late in the period of the baptismal register – Margaret in 1731 and Katherine in 1734. They would have been eight and five in 1739, and their father and mother could well have been in their late twenties. They were living in Crackaig and Brosdale. Neill McGhoile could very well have been a '39er' from Jura.

13 *Daniel Buie*. The same thing can be said about Buies called Donald. Daniel seems to have been less common in Argyll at the time, and we may suspect as mentioned above that many North Carolina Daniels started as Donalds in Scotland. There are at least three Donald Buies who would have been about thirty years of age in 1739, and could well have been married with young families who would not show in the baptismal register. As in the case of Archibald, above, it seems very likely that Daniel Buie was a Donald Buie from Jura.

While the above research contains a good deal of speculation, the author believes that the Jura contingent on the sailing of the *Thistle* probably contained the above thirteen men and their wives and children – a group of perhaps fifty among the 350 who sailed. Alexander Clark seems to have been able to persuade about a dozen heads of families to join in the great adventure. There may have been more, but it is unlikely that we will be able to confirm additional members at this time.

Five of the families appear to have come from the large and overcrowded crofting township of Knockrome. Clark himself came from Crackaig, a township a little north of Campbell's seat at Sannaig. He may well have been a tacksman in the island, although there is no independent evidence of this. Neil McGhoile also came from Crackaig.

The McNeills of Ardlussa would probably have had family connections with the McNeills of Kintyre and Gigha, and may have been influenced by the McNeills leading the journey. The remaining Buies may have come from Knockrome, nearby Lergiebreac, or Ardfin.

A further name on the list of confirmed '39ers' is in some dispute, and will be mentioned here:

Archibald Buie. Here we have a person testified to as being a '39er' by the addition of the identification 'Gum Swamp' to his name at No 50 in the list. I am indebted to Dr Kelly's *Carolina Scots* for the following note:

Archibald Buie first acquired land on Gum Swamp in Cumberland County by land grant in 1765 and the compilers think that he was also called Archibald Buie of Cypress Swamp in the very early records. He lived within the Barbeque District of Cumberland County but also owned land in Moore County. In 1765, he was named an elder at Barbeque along with Duncan Buie, Gilbert Clark and Daniel Cameron, who were all noted to be pious men and devoted to their duties as elders. Archibald married Catherine Shaw, also of Cumberland County. It is generally accepted that Archibald was born in Jura, and came to North Carolina as a young man.

However, Dr Kelly suggests he may have been born between 1735 and 1740. If so, then he could have been on the *Thistle* as a child, but could not be part of the passenger list as an individual. It seems more likely that he crossed over later; indeed as a young man, perhaps around the late 1740s.

It may be of some interest to note that we do have a suitable Archibald Buie in the baptismal record. He was baptised in Ardfernal in 1734, the son of Donald Buie and Margaret McIlirioch.

There is some evidence to show that the *Thistle* sailed north from Campbeltown and called at the island of Gigha to embark the contingent from Gigha, Islay and Jura. The people of Jura were accustomed to sail to Gigha, which is in sight of the island, and was for long a part of the huge scattered church parish of Jura.

It is understandable that citizens of the United States with a lively interest in their Scottish roots should have been especially curious about the very first settlers to arrive from their ancestral islands and mainland territories. By contrast with the concerted interest in the '39ers', information about the subsequent sailings to include colonists from Islay and Jura is much more vague. There are continual hints in the literature that there was another sailing in the following year, 1740. The most that Dr Douglas Kelly will say on this matter is, 'it is possible, though not yet established, that another significant number joined them as soon as 1740.' It may be that confusion has arisen in this area from the fact that the '39ers' did not receive their Land Grants until 1740. This may have given rise to the idea that those who are recorded in 1740 actually arrived in that year.

Tantalising new scraps of evidence continue to turn up. The following, for example, concerns a lawsuit from the records of a Sheriff Court.

This suit is to recover twelve protested bills of exchange originally made payable to Captain Robert Arthur, Commander of the *Diamond* of Glasgow, at various places in western Scotland between 26 March and 8 April 1740. The total of the bills, amounting to £124 16/– appears to represent fifty-two adult passages to America. The full fare was then £2 8/–. The bills were payable on 20 May 1740, and all were endorsed over to Archibald Campbell, merchant of Oban, who brought suit to recover the sums. The names and addresses appear largely to be connected with Kintyre, but the twelfth and last bill concerns the Island of Jura, and is as follows:

1740, April 8th. Jura Note to Arthur £24 sterling.
Donald McQuean in Knockinlasell (Knockintavill)
Donald McInnish in Ardmeanish (signed with mark)
Angus McInnish in Ardlussa
responsible for 10 passages (£24 sterling), of which
£16 12/– was paid in part of the bill at Gigha on July 17th, 1740.

The registration of these protested bills was made at Inverary and authenticated on 5 September 1740.

The acceptors of the bills may or may not have been passengers themselves. The Old Parish Register has no note of McQueens in Jura, but there are three McInnes families in Ardlussa, and one near Ardmenish in Ardfernal in the early years of the century.

This suit may be evidence that the *Diamond* sailed for North Carolina in the spring of 1740 with a complement which included ten adults from Jura.

THE ARGYLE PATENT

In 1738, 1739, and 1740, three groups of families, totalling 472 persons set sail from Islay under the Captaincy of Lauchlan Campbell to New York. They emigrated as a result of the invitation of the Provincial Governor of New York Colony, who offered 1000 acres of land to every adult and 500 acres to every child who paid passage. For various reasons the contract was not kept by the Governor. In 1764, a large number of colonists, led by Alexander McNaughton, succeeded in securing a grant of 47,450 acres, known as 'The Argyle Patent', in the township of Argyle, and in parts of the towns of Fort Edward, Greenwich and Salem, in Washington County.

Unlike the sailing to North Carolina, the New York venture was very well documented, and Captain Campbell published detailed lists of the men, women and children who crossed under his command. The families listed have names which relate readily to the population of Islay, and until recently anyone studying the neighbouring island of Jura was little interested. However, the presence of the Baptismal Register of 1704–1734 in Jura has made it possible to search for Jura connections, and one or two have been found: Dugald Thomson and his wife Margaret McDuffie are listed on the June 1739 sailing with 'Archibald, Duncan and Christie and and his Brother's Daughter and four children'.

The Old Parish Register of Jura has an entry for 'Dougald Thomson and Margrat McDuffie, with a daughter Mary (1714) and a male child (1721) baptised at Ardfin'. It seems certain that this is an Argyle Patent family.

Patrick McArthur and his wife Mary McDougall are listed on the July 1738 sailing from Islay, with, 'Charles, Colin and Janet his three children.' In the baptismal record we have a family consisting of Patrick McArthur and Mary McDugald with a son John (1733) baptised in Knockrome. Patrick McArthur is said to be a catechist.

The Jura records are incomplete from 1726 to 1734, so the children who sailed with them might well not have been recorded. This is a very strong connection with the Argyle Patent.

One further Argyle Patent family is of interest: 'John McGilvrey and Catarine McDonald his Wife; Hugh, Donald, Bridget and Mary his four children'. These all sailed from Islay in November 1740. There are no Jura records relating to this family, but an American descendant is confident from his family history that they came from Jura.

THE 1754 SAILING

The records of North Carolina do not record a general list of emigrants, and seldom refer to individual ships by name. One such list does survive in detail from 1767, and this would be our next evidence of Jura folk involved in the emigration were it not for our own familiar source: the Campbell of Jura Papers. Here we discover that in the summer of 1754 a ship called the *Mary*, out of Glasgow, anchored in Small Isles Bay, and it was brought to the notice of Archibald Campbell that sundry Jura people were planning to set sail for America. Campbell, the third of Sannaig was at this time seventy years of age, having had to wait to succeed his father until the age of fifty-two in 1736. John Campbell, his father, had reached the age of ninety-five.

Archibald was always quick to take offence at any sign of insubordination, and went to law at the drop of a hat. He evidently decided that the intending emigrants were about to sail for the New World leaving their outstanding rents unpaid and immediately sought a warrant from the Sheriff in Inverary to arrest them and to sequestrate their effects. Two fascinating documents survive from this incident. The first is a comprehensive list of all the residents who have signed up to sail. The second is a complete account of Campbell's process at law, which lists in detail the outstanding payments due by all those who are paying tenants.

That we have this fascinating and rare record is due not only to Campbell's meanness, but also to a considerable stroke of good fortune, for the documents concerned come from a very small number of papers which disappeared from sight for a time and, having resurfaced, were acquired by the National Archives of Scotland, and are now reunited with the entire collection.

The two documents now follow in transcript; the list first and then the legal paper.

To assist in future discussion I have added a reference number in the left margin in *italic*.

A Note of the people intending a voyage for Cape Fear in North Carolina and the amount of their accepted Bills to Neil Campbell, 20 May 1754

A list of Men, Women and Children that go for America

1	Gilbert McIlriach, tenant in Lag; five beds seven souls	7
2	Archd. McIlriach, tenant in Corinahera; three beds four souls	4
3	John McIlriach in Knockrome; three beds	4
4	Archd. McCrainie; three beds there	4
5	Hugh McLean; six beds there	7
6	Alexr. McDougald; there; four beds	4
7	John Cargill (McGuile crossed out); five beds there	6
8	Don. Cargill (McGuile crossed out); three beds there	3
9	Hugh McGilriach, servant there; two beds	2
10	John McCrainkein, svt. Ardfernal; one bed	1
11	Katherain McLean; servt. in Corran House; 1 bed	1
12	John Shaw in Knockintavill; 5 beds	6
13	Don^d. Linsie three beds; Lergiybreck	4
14	Don^d. Buie, smith; 3 beds	5
15	Don^d. Black in Feolin; 3 beds	5

16	Arch^d. Clark in Kiles; 5 beds	6
17	Dond. Clark in Kiles; 5 beds	5
18	Gilbert Clark in Kiles; 3 beds	4
19	John McIlpheder in Kiles; 3 beds	3
20	Archd. Roy Black svt. there; six beds	6
21	Christine McLean svt there; one bed	1
22	Margaret Bowie, cottar in Knocknafeolaman; three beds	3
23	Dugald McNamoile, shoemaker in Erin; four beds	4
24	Duncan McArthur in Crackaig; five beds	6
25	Ivar MacKay in Crackaig; two beds	4
26	Dougald McNamoile there; four beds	6
27	Duncan Black tenant in Sannaig; eight beds	10
28	Duncan McGuile tenant in Sroine; three beds	3
29	Angus McIlriach, tenant in Brostile, junior; three beds	4
30	Alan McDugald in Brostile; three beds	4
31	Archd. McIlriach in Knockbreck; three beds	4
		137

32	Hugh McRaine, svt in Ardfernal	(altered from)	139
33	Alexr. McDugald; Sannaig		
34	Malcom McIlriach; Ardfernal		
35	Neil McGoun in Lag his daughter		
36	Katherine McDugald		

On reverse, faintly: (37), Cath McNamoile; (38), Giliand McArthur
The reverse also has two columns of figures in '£s'; with alterations.

CAMPBELL'S ACTION AGAINST THE INTENDING EMIGRANTS

At Inverary the Seventeenth day of June Seventeen Hundred and fifty four years. Anent the Petition given in and presented to Mr Archibald Campbell, Writer in Inverary, Sheriff substitute of the Sheriffdom of Argyle For Archibald Campbell of Jura. Humbly Shewing That Where Neil Campbell, Master and Owner of the Ship called the 'Mary' of Glasgow having prevailed on and entered into certain Articles with the persons after named who are Tennants and possessors of the Petitioner's Lands and Estate after specified, to leave their native Country and to Transport themselves, Wives and Children to Williamstown of Cape Fair in North Carolina. Animo remanendi. That the said Tennants being resolved to ship themselves on board the said Neil Campbell's Vessel now ready to receive them and lying in the Small Isles of Jura. And that on or before the Twenty seventh of June current, Notwithstanding they have not legally and timeously renounced and Yielded up to the Petitioner their reserve possessions after specified of his Estates, whereby they are not only lyable in payment to him of the Current Year's Rent of their possessions, With the Cess and Teind, due by each of them in manner after specified:

[There follows a complete account of the tenants and their outstanding payments. We have already looked at the rents in the previous chapter, but here give only the names and farms.]

5 Hugh McLean for his possession of 1/6 part of the Petitioner's Town and Lands of Knockrome.

7 John Cargil pays the like Rent for another sixth of the possession of Knockrome

3 John McIlrioch pays for one eighth of Knockrome possessed by him

4 Archibald McCraine pays the like rent for another eighth part of Knockrome

  6 Alex^r. McDougall pays the like rent for another eight part thereof

 13 Donald Lindsay pays for his possession of ¼ part of the Petitioner's Lands of Lergybreck

 14 Donald Bowie, Smith pays for another fourth thereof

 29 Angus McIlrioch pays for his possession of 1/8th of the Petitioner's Lands of Brosdale

 28 Duncan McGheil pays for one eighth part of the Petitioner's Lands of Strone

 24 Duncan McArthur pays for his possession of 1/8th part of Crackaig

 39 John McDuffie pays the like rent eighth part thereof

 25 Iver Mackay, the Petitioner's ffarmer pays for his possession of one eighth part of Crackaig

 26 Dugald McDougald alias Macamaile pays for his possession of a fourth part of Crackaig as the Petitioner's ffarmer

 17 Donald Clerk in Keills for his possession of a fourth part of the Petitioner's Lands of Kilernadale

 18 Gilbert Clerk pays for his possession of a three shiling teind thereof

 16 Arch^d. Clerk pays for his possession of one eighth part thereof

 19 John McIlpheder for one shilling land thereof

 15 Donald Black, ffarmer in Ffeolin pays for one half there

  1 Gilbert McIlrioch pays for his possession of one eighth part of the Petitioner's lands of Kaim

  2 Archibald McIlrioch pays for his possession of a sixteenth part of Corynahera

Extending in whole to the sum of Seventy Three pounds one shilling and eight pence Sterling money. And Moreover by the forenamed Tennants their relinquishing and deserting their possessions at such an unseasonable time as this of the Year. The Petitioner will be under the necessity of keeping up the Neighbourhood. With the other possessions of the said lands to prevent the samen's becoming totally Waste. Whereby he must necessarily expend and deburse the sum of (*left blank*) Sterling money And seeing the Petitioner is willing to depone that the whole fore-named Tennants are now in Meditatione fuge bye their being about to go abroad to Cape Fair as aforesd.

  Compeared the above Archibald Campbell, the Petitioner, Who, being solemnly sworn Deponed that the whole persons above complained upon have entered into a Contract with the above Neil Campbell to Transport them and their ffamilies to Cape Fair in America, And that they are actually preparing to ship themselves aboard the Said Neil Campbell's Ship Which is now lying to receive them at the Small Isles of Jura, And this was the truth as he should answer to God, ... The Sheriff granted and Warrants to the Officers of the Court & their Asssistants To apprehend the persons of the several people complained upon in the said petition, And to incarcerate them within the Tolbooth of Inverary, Therein to remain Ay & While

It can readily be seen from the above document that it was Campbell of Jura's normal practice to pursue people with whom he had a grievance to the full letter of the law, and no doubt his action would have resulted in the voyage of the *Mary* either being aborted altogether, or taking place at least without its complement of Jura passengers. However, the outcome seems to have been very different.

As far as can be ascertained from other contemporary documents, McNeill of

Colonsay had an interest in this matter, as he was related to Neil Campbell, the master of the *Mary*, and had invested in the passage. It appears that he decided to settle the outstanding rents due to Campbell by the intending colonists; to the tune of £73 1/8. The warrant became void, and the ship duly sailed for the New World. Its arrival there was not recorded, and we do not know how many of the passengers arrived safely, or whether or where they obtained their land grants.

It is here that yet another strange fragment of history survives and can be tied into our story. The McAlesters of Loup on Islay were mentioned earlier. Letters indicate that Coll McAlester may have been in Wilmington, North Carolina as early as 1736, where he is said to have kept a tavern for several years. According to family tradition he was one of three brothers who emigrated together. Colonial records show that four McAlesters were in North Carolina by 1739, and list James, Hector, Alexander and Coll. Hector soon went back to the island of Arran and never returned to Troy, his plantation on the Upper Cape Fear River, though for more than thirty years, as his letters show, he talked of doing it. Alexander also returned to Scotland for a short time, but went back to America and spent the rest of his life near Wade, a town about twelve miles north-east of Fayetteville. When a group of Scottish Presbyterian settlers in this area organised the Bluff Church in 1758, he was named as one of the ruling elders. This family later became involved in the War of Independence, and were part of the complex story of Flora and Allan McDonald. A number of letters written by one brother to another have survived as the McAlester Papers, and the earliest has a direct bearing on our story:

Hector McAlester to Alexander McAlester   Moniquill, Isle of Arran
                                                          June 26th 1754

My Dear Brother,
Your favour of the 24th April per Capt. Munay came to hand about eight days ago, and it gives me infinite pleasure that you are all well. It's not in my power to express my grief for the death of my Aunt, who was more like a mother than Aunt to us ...

I wrote you several letters these two years past, by way of Virginia, signifing my intention of seeing you and other friends in that Country, but have always been balked for want of an opportunity to Cape Fear, as it would be much out of my way to land anywhere else with passengers, and am resolved after my long absence to make the Colony the better of me, by bringing with me as many as I can, and had indeed this year twenty or thirty families engaged besides young folks, and would have got a ship from Clyde, were it not that the Merchants of Campbeltown promised to furnish me a vessel from their town and when I went there the beginning of May in order to Contract with the owners, I was unluckily disappointed, and so were they, for they engaged with twenty or thirty passengers for Philadelphia, two days before I came to town. Had that not been the Case they would have their full complement with me for Cape Fear.

I sent the bearer Neill Munrow instantly to Jura, hearing that Capt. Neill Campbell was disappointed of some passengers he expected there, desiring him, if that was the case, to run in to Campbeltown harbour and I would engage to get him his Complement, but it seems he gets from Jura as many as he can accommodate. Were I to go this year and leave those engaged with me, it would be a loss both to me and the Colony there, as several of them are judicious honest people.

The owners of the Argyle Snow of Campbeltown have promised to have that vessel in readyness for me any time twixt the month of March and July next and on that I have fixed since I could do no better and have got all my people settled for this year. Mr Neill McLeod whom the Colony wanted over to be their Minister, was to go with me, and as he is a very popular man amongst the Commonality, would encourage numbers to leave this Country. So you'll not fail to advise to write pressingly for him again. He is a good preacher and full master of the highland tongue, and am sure would please all parties.

Much more follows about what goods and freight will be most profitable, and what news there may be of his estates in Carolina. He ends: 'I have little news to give you. The lairds here are much afraid to have their lands waste, and give strange Character of all that Country, but you should all write home the best encouragement you can with truth give.'

Here then we have a personal account of Neil Campbell's visit to Jura, and confirmation that he got on board there as many passengers as he could accommodate. Together with McAlester's letter, we also have, courtesy of Archibald Campbell's legal action, another glimpse of members of the community of Jura in the middle of the eighteenth century. As on previous occasions we will give some thought to the people on the list, and to what we can learn from their personal details.

THE 1754 EMIGRANTS

There are thirty-nine named people in the full list. A number of family names we would expect to find, and indeed they are well represented. There are: three Blacks; two Buies; two Clarks; two McArthurs; three McCraines; four McDougalds; seven McIlriachs; three McLeans; three McNamoiles.

A number of other names we have encountered earlier in the century have a single representative in the list, e.g., Lindsay, McDuffie, McGoun, McGhoil, McKay. There is only one Shaw in the list. We would expect more.

John and Donald Cargill, one of whom holds a sixth part of Knockrome, are set down plainly on the list as McGuile. The 'McGuiles' are roughly crossed out and 'Cargill' is written above. The legal hand which included John in the list of debtors calls him simply 'Cargill'. Perhaps this is another example of a name in the process of change.

Only five of the intending emigrants are women: we have a Margaret, a Christine and three Catherines (Cath, Katherain and Katharine). Even with such a tiny sample these Christian names provide no surprises.

The thirty-four men also tend to traditional Christian names. There are six Donalds and six Johns, followed by five Archibalds, one of whom is 'Red Archie'.

There are three Duncans and three Hughs, and two each of the common Gilbert and Alexander. Alan, Angus, Dougald, Malcolm and Neil are all represented, as is the Christian name Iver, which is absent from the Old Parish Baptismal Register as is the difficult to read 'Giliand' or 'Giliard'.

The homes of the intending travellers fall naturally into district groups: ten are from the Campbell's heartland between Ardfin and Craighouse (Brosdale, three, Strone, one, Sannaig, two, and Crackaig, four); nine are centred on Keils (Knocknafeolaman, one; Keils, six; Feolin, two); thirteen are from the north end of Small Isles Bay (Lergybreck, two, Corran House, one; Knockrome, seven; Ardfernal, three); four are from Lagg (Lagg, three, Corrynahera, one).

The extremes are represented by one from Knockbreck and one from Knockintavil. The two names scrawled on the reverse of the list have no location noted.

In general terms we can say that the intending emigrants come mainly from crofting townships which we already know are suffering from overcrowding, e.g. Brosdale, Crackaig, Keils, Knockrome, Ardfernal and Lagg.

THE WOMEN

Christine McLean, of Keils and Katherain McLean, of Corran House are both servants and are travelling alone. Margaret Buie, a cottar of Knocknafeolaman had an allocation of a single berth, but is listed as a party of three souls. She is presumably accompanied by two babies. Cath McNamoile's, name is added to the reverse with no details. It is possible that she was a dependant of Dougald McNamoile of Crackaig, who is travelling in a party of six souls. Katherine McDugald, of Lagg is the only member of the party with a recorded relationship with another member, and is the 'daughter of Neil McGoun', also of Lagg. There is no record of the number of beds in his party.

THE MEN

Of the thirty-four men listed, only John McCrainkein, a servant from Ardfernal appears to be travelling alone. There are no details given for Hugh McKraine, Ardfernal; Malcom McIlriach, Ardfernal; Alexander McDougald, Sannaig; or Neil McGoun, as these names appear to have been added to the foot of the list as additional entries. The same can be said of Giliard McArthur, whose name is on the reverse of the document.

John McDuffie, of Crackaig is in a quite anomalous position as he is included in the detail of charges as tenant of an eighth part of Crackaig without in fact being mentioned on the original list of intending passengers. This is a curious situation, whose explanation will ever remain out of our reach.

The remaining twenty-seven men on the list are travelling as heads of families, and their requirements for bunks on board are set down together with another figure which is twice mentioned as 'souls'.

Only Hugh McIlriach of Knockrome is making the journey with his wife but no children. The other twenty-six men are all accompanied by their wives and a varied number of dependants.

In eleven cases the couple are accompanied by one, two, three or four dependants, all of whom require berths, so that the number of berths and the number of souls is the same. The simplest explanation would be in terms of young married couples with children of such an age as to be unable to sleep with their parents. The parties travelling in this fashion look like this:

Father and mother with one child	three families
Father and mother with two children	three families
Father and mother with three children	three families
Father and mother with four children	one family

In seventeen cases the couple appear to be travelling with children who require individual berths, but also with infants who are counted as 'souls' but do not require separate accommodation. In these cases the numbers for 'beds' and for 'souls' are different. These varied families emerge from the bare statistics much as one would expect. If we call the party member requring a berth a 'child', and the one not needing such a berth a 'baby', the families look like this:

Father and mother with one child and one baby	eight families
Father and mother and one child and two babies	one family
Father and mother and two children and one baby	five families
Father and mother and two children and two babies	one family
Father and mother and three children and one baby	one family
Father and mother and three children and two babies	one family
Father and mother and four children with one baby	one family
Father and mother and four children with two babies	one family

In view of our lack of detail about the last six entries, and John McDuffie, we simply do not have sufficient evidence to be sure how many people actually sailed on the *Mary* in 1754.

We may guess that the people for whom we have no detailed information were probably typical of all the others. Thus, Hugh McCraine, Alexander McDugald, Neil McGoun, Gilaird McArthur and John McDuffie were most likely all married emigrants, leaving with their wives and families. If we accord them each two children and one baby we will equip them with the average family size of all the others.

The complement of the entire party then would have been as follows:

Unaccompanied women	4
Unaccompanied men	1
Women with dependants	1
Married men	33
Wives	33
Children	65
Babies	28
	165

Perhaps the last thing we can investigate before leaving the 1754 emigrants is whether, as with some other eighteenth-century people, we can identify any of them as infants that Neil Campbell baptised and which event he recorded in his baptismal register.

The picture which we have revealed of the typical family to sign up for the voyage to Cape Fear is of a young married couple with two or three young children. Since Neil Campbell was baptising babies from 1704 until 1734, the infants of his period would have been from twenty to fifty years of age in 1754. Bearing in mind the fact that Neil Campbell's record was incomplete, one might still hope to make some connections between his infant baptisms and the adults who purposed to emigrate on the *Mary* in 1754. Examination of the list reveals the expected situation and the usual range of options.

The baptismal register contains no suitable candidates for thirteen of the names on the list: These are: Gilbert McIlirioch (1); John Cargill (7); Hugh McGilriach (9); John McCrainkein (10); Donald Lindsay (13); Archibald Clark (16); Donald Clark (17); John McIpheder(19); Archibald Roy Black (20); Ivar McKay (25); Dugald McNamoile (26); Duncan McGuile (28). Katharine McDugald (36) of Lagg appears to be the daughter of Neil McGoun (35). If so we have no suitable record for her, but see note below under Alan McDugald (30).

At the other end of the process we have some common names for which we have too many candidates in the register; e.g., for John McIlriach (3), we have nine possible names; for Donald Buie (14), we have six; and for Malcolm McIlriach (34), we also have six possibilities. Our three emigrants seem very likely to have come within this pool of names, but there is of course no way of sorting them out.

We have four people on the list where there seem to be three candidates in the register: Alexander McDougald (6) and (33) (we have two men of this name), Christine McLean (21) and Duncan McArthur (24). They may bear examination for likely connections:

Alexander McDougald. One of our two was on the extras list, so we do not know his origin. The other came from Knockbreck. The register has one born in Brosdale in 1706 which seems too early for a young man with two children. The other two were born in Lagg in 1714 and 1718, which makes them thirty-six and forty, but some distance removed from the community of Knockrome.

Christine McLean of Keils. In this case there is a likely connection with one born in Feolin in 1722. This Christine would be thirty-two, and from a nearby community. One of the other possibles comes from the north of the island, and the other would seem to be too young.

Duncan McArthur of Crackaig. Again there seems a possible candidate born in Knocknafeolaman in 1726. The other two being likely to be too old.

Five names on the list produce two possible matches from the register:

Archibald McIlriach (of which name there are two on the list; one of Corryna-hera (2) and one of Knockbreck (31)) The register has one born in 1720 in Ardmenish, and one in 1717 in Tarbert. The Tarbert child would be thirty-seven years old in 1754, and from a related part of the island to the Corrynahera man.

Hugh McLean of Knockrome (5). There are two Hugh McLeans in the register, but from unrelated parts of the island and probably resulting in candidates who would be older than likely.

John Shaw of Knockintavil (12). There are two John Shaws in the register. One from Knockintavil, aged forty-seven in 1754, and one from Ardlussa, aged thirty-eight in 1754. In terms of age and locality either of these could very well be the emigrant.

Margaret Bowie (22) of Knocknafeolaman. One Margrat Bui was born in Knockrome in 1721, and would be thirty-three at time of sailing. It is intriguing to find that the other Margrat Bui, born in Knockrome in 1733, and only twenty-one at time of sailing, is one of only three families in the register who seem to spell their names 'Bowie'. It would be pleasant to feel that here we have found our young single Emigrant, who is given as a 'cottar' in the sailing list. This would of course give a different scenario of her being a young unmarried mother with two small children. If she was in fact a widow, then her married name would not be accessible.

Angus McIlrioch (29)of Brosdale. There is only one Angus McIlirioch in the register, as an infant. He was born in Lagg in 1716, and thirty-eight at the time of the sailing. However, our emigrant Angus is noted as 'Angus Junior', and we do have an Angus McIlirioch fathering a child in Brosdale in 1726. The emigrant Angus has two holdings in Brosdale, but only one child. He would be in his late forties in 1754, but with only a wife and a single child. Perhaps Angus of Brosdale had a son, later, in the register gap years, his first child did not live. He would then be the 'Angus Junior' of our list.

There remain six names on the list for which the Baptismal Register produces a single possible match. These connections are by no means certain to relate to the real people involved as we have seen the incomplete nature of the baptismal record. They vary in attractiveness depending on age and place. Here is the complete set of six:

Donald Black (15) of Feolin. There is one Donald Black in the register, born in Crackaig in1710, and forty-four at the time of the sailing. He would perhaps be of a suitable age to be the Tenant in Keils of Legal Action, with a wife and three children.

Gilbert Clark (18)of Keils. There was a Gilbert Clark born in Feolin in 1716,. At thirty-eight years of age at the time of the sailing, he could well be the tenant of the three shilling land in Kilearnadil, and have a wife, one child and an infant.

Duncan Black (27)of Sannaig. There was a Duncan Black actually born in Sannaig in 1720. He would be thirty-four at time of sailing. The continuity of name and place is attractive, but our emigrant is the father of eight children and might have been expected perhaps to be a little older.

Alan McDugald (30) of Brosdale. There is only one Alan McDougald in the register, born in Knocknafeolaman in 1718.

Hugh McCranie (32)of Ardfernal. Aobh McCranie is likely to be Hew McCranie of Knocknafeolaman and Crackaig. Fathering children in 1721 and 1723 this Hugh would now be in his fifties – perhaps a bit old to be our emigrant.

Cath McNamoile (37) (no location) There is one Katharine McNamoile, who was born in Knocknafeolaman in 174, and who would now be twenty years old.

Note: Katharine McDugald (36). The last two entries on the List appear to be:
(second last line)   Neil McGoun in Lag; his daughter
(last line)   Katharine McDugald

It is evident that this information can be interpreted to mean either that Katharine McDugald is Neil McGoun's daughter (continuing from the line above) or that Neil's daughter is listed, but un-named, and Katharine is a separate entry. If the second, we should note that Alan McDugald, born in Knocknafeolaman in 1718, had a younger sister Catherine, born in 1724. She could be sailing with her brother!

The reader is in as good a position as anyone else to decide whether the suggestions above reveal that the list of those 'to go for America' contains people we have already encountered earlier in the century in Neil Campbell's records.

There is no record of the arrival of the *Mary* at Wilmington, and so no confirmation of how many passengers disembarked. The information relating to this 1754 sailing has only been available for study for about ten years, and there has probably not yet been enough time to bring all the enthusiasm of the American genealogists to bear on it. Land Grants, and personal identification with some of the names we have studied may yet reveal what happened to some of the '54ers'. They may yet become as famous in their own right as the '39ers'.

THE 1767 SAILING

We will in due course be examining various records of individual emigrant families which indicate various sailing dates after 1739, however, we will complete this part of our emigrant study by looking at the only other eighteenth-century sailing of which we have a comprehensive list of passengers from Jura. The vessel concerned was the *General Wolfe* and she docked in Brunswick, on 4 November 1767.

While there may have been many routine recordings of the names of immigrant passengers on such ships, this landing is the only one to have come down to us from the eighteenth century. The local authorities listed the name of each passenger, together with the number and sex of his dependants, and, most importantly for our interest, their place of origin. A note of the amount of Land Grant awarded completes the list. It appears to have been at the rate of 100 acres per party member. There is no indication of berth requirements, and consequently we are left to make up our own minds as to whether the list of children includes, or does not include young infants.

The Minutes of Official Proceedings records: 'On November 4th, 1767, there landed at Brunswick, North Carolina, from the Island of Jura, Argyllshire, Scotland, the following families and persons to whom were allotted vacant lands, clear of all fees, to be taken up in Cumberland or Mecklenburgh, at their option'

Whether this Minute refers to the complete complement of the vessel, all of whom came from Jura, or only to a part of a larger passenger list is not clear.

Here is the Complete list of Passengers from Jura on the *General Wolfe*:

Name of Family	Children Male	Children Female	Total	Acres to each family
Alexander MacDougald and wife	1	1	4	400
Malcolm MacDougald and wife		1	3	300
Neil MacLean and wife	1		3	300
Duncan MacLean and wife			2	200
Duncan Buea (sic) and wife	1		3	300
Angus MacDougald and wife			2	200
Dougald MacDougald and wife	3	1	6	600
Dougald MacDougald and wife	2		4	400
John Campbell and wife	1		3	300
Archibald Buie and wife	1		3	300
Neill Buie			1	100
Neill Clark			1	100
John MacLean			1	100
Angus MacDougald			1	100
John MacDougald			1	100
Donald MacDougald			1	100
Donald MacDougald			1	100
Alexander MacDougald			1	100
John MacLean			1	100
Peter MacLean			1	100
Malcolm Buie			1	100
Duncan Buie			1	100
Mary Buie			1	100
Nancy MacLean			1	100
Peggy MacDougald			1	100
Peggy Sinclair			1	100
Jenny Darach			1	100
Donald MacLean			1	100

Here then we have emigration seen from the North Carolina standpoint, and it is full of surprises. There are twenty-eight entries in the complete list.

Ten consist of married couples with or without children, but eighteen refer to single persons apparently travelling alone; thirteen men and five women.

In the 1754 sailing, of the thirty-one familes for whom we seem to have detailed records, only four were travelling alone. What were all these single men and women doing? Were they genuinely unattached? Or was there possibly a cut-off age for male and female children accompanying their parents, so that some of these were 'teenage' members of the married couples at the beginning of the list? The way that the Land Grants are distributed to each of these eighteen single persons seems to suggest that they were in fact each solitary individuals.

It is even possible that there were some deaths on the crossing, and that some of these single folk had set out from Jura as married couples, only one of which survived to the New World. As has so often been the case, we are never likely to get any additional information to give us answers. The names represented in the 1767 crossing are quite different from previous samples of Jura surnames, at least in their relative abundance. Family surnames are as follows:

MacDougald	11
MacLean	7
Buie	6
Campbell	1
Clark	1
Darach	1
Sinclair	1

It will be remembered that in 1754 the McIlriochs were the dominant family name, with MacDougalds in second place, while Blacks, McArthurs, McCraines, McLeans and McNamoiles, were all present in third equal place, with Buies and Clarks bringing up the rear. In this list the Blacks, the McArthurs, the McCraines and the McNamoiles are all absent, while the McIlriachs are represented solely by Jenny Darach. There is no mention of any Shaws.

In terms of Christian names, the men's names are perhaps what we would expect from Jura:

Alexander	2	Angus	2	Archibald	1
Donald	3	Dougald	2	Duncan	3
Malcolm	2	Neill	2	John	3
Peter	1				

Of these, only Peter is in any way surprising.

Of the five women's Christian names, only Mary has been previously common. It is quite surprising to find two Peggys, a Nancy and a Jenny.

The party contains ten male children, and three female children; a total of thirteen children distributed in ten families, and an average of 1.3 child per family.

The 1754 party had eighty children distributed among twenty-nine families, an average of 2.75 children per family. In the absence of any supporting evidence of any kind it is evidently impossible to deduce what exactly was happening at this time, and what kind of families were on the move.

With earlier eighteenth-century inhabitants we have tried to make some connection between individuals and entries in Neil Campbell's Baptismal Register. Thirty-three years separate the emigrants of 1767 from the last year of the Register in 1734. It may seem like a forlorn hope to try to connect the 1767 emigrants with any entry of their baptism, but there happen to be two promising late entries. In each case they are the only example of their name in the Register:

Archibald Buie. One appears as the son of Donald Bui and More McIlliriach, baptised in 1734 in Ardfernal.

Donald McLean. One appears as the son of Hugh McLean and Margaret McArthur, baptised in Knockrome in 1733.

These men would be thirty-three and thirty-four years old respectively, and could well be emigrating in 1767.

There are also two sets of brothers in the baptismal register, who would match names in the emigrant list. They also would be in their fifties, but may still be worth a mention. They are:

Alexander McDougald and Malcolm McDougald. Sons of Hew McDougald and Catherine McIlirioch of Lagg, baptised in 1714 and 1716.

Duncan McLean and John McLean. Sons of Malcolm McLean and Rachell McArthur of Crackaig, baptised in 1712 and 1716.

With this brief excursion into speculative reconstruction, our study of the *General Wolfe* passengers is concluded. It would be good to know a little more about the Land Grants and settlement of this group of Jura emigrants, and some information may yet be available through North Carolina research.

SUMMARY

It becomes clear that if it were not for the remarkable survival of Archibald Campbell's attempt to prevent the sailing of 1754, we would have no individual records of people who emigrated from Jura in the eighteenth century. We would know of this important social event only in the most general terms, through such accounts as Francis Stewart's, where the social effect of large scale emigrations is lamented. In view of the fact that we have been able to examine only three actual shiploads of emigrants; from 1739, 1754, and 1767, it is hard to escape the general conclusion that there must in fact have been far more crossings than these to underlie such comments as: 'emigrations have proved a drain to the island' and 'the spirit of emigration is still strong'.

THE POLITICAL SITUATION

By 1773 the Government was becoming concerned. The Customs Board wrote to the Controller in Campbeltown:

> There being frequent rumours of persons emigrating or removing from different parts of this country to America we recommend you to obtain the best intelligence you can as to the truth of such reports respecting what of that kind may have happened in the precinct of your Port, or within your knowledge, and to lay the same before us in all the circumstances distinguishing the number of men, women and children which may have been embarked for such Purposes in your Precincts within two years past and the inducements held out to them and the means used and by whom to engage them to leave their native country. You are from time to time to inform us of any future circumstances of the kind which may occur.

The Collector replied on 23 February:

> There have been no vessels cleared out of this port for any part of America since the month of July 1771. We have heard of several people taken on board ships for America in different Lochs within this district. Enquiries have been made from all offices in different parts, but we have found it impossible to give numbers, much less distinction of men women and children in the years 1772/73. Emigrations much more numerous in 1769/70 and numbers sent for those years.
>
> With regard to motives. These are various. One cause assigned is the Heritors have raised the rents of their lands perhaps higher, considering the state of

the tenants who are well versed and skilful in agriculture and have not abilities to carry on improvements; than they could well pay; tho' we do not find that many tenants who were in possession of lands have gone, and believe by much the greater part of the number that did go were people in low or desperate circumstances who expected their conditions would be better there than here.

We are told that some people who have gone to America years ago ... write enticing letters to their friends at home to follow them, representing the great plenty of provisions, cheapness of living; low rents and goodness of the soil, with other flattering motives perhaps exaggerated as arguments to induce them to go to that part of the world.

On 2 September 1775 the Board sent a cutting from the *Edinburgh Courant* of 30 August. They had a report that two vessels were lying at Gigha, ready to receive emigrants to Cape Fear from Kintyre, Knapdale and the circumjacent islands, and that they would sail as soon as they got beds fitted for 150 in each vessel.

The people engaged to go over are in high spirits and seem in no way intimidated on account of the many informations they receive concerning the commotions in the British Colonies and the danger of Emigrating at this time. The Lord Advocate states through the Board, that though the Government has not yet prohibited Emigration to America it must be discouraged. Postpone clearing out orders for such ships. Use best endeavours to prevent sailing and state fully to those concerned all present circumstances.

Two days later: 'The Lord Advocate reports that there have been many embarkations of His Majesty's Subjects in this country for America, and some of them with money, arms and ammunition, which may afford aid and support to His Majesty's Rebellious subjects in the several colonies in America.'

After the war emigration slowly resumed. In response to a request from the Board, the Controller reported on 15 May 1788 that there had been only two ships in the previous four years. On 3 September 1791, the Board enquired regarding a considerable number of people from Colonsay about to embark in Islay for North Carolina. British Manufactures were threatened:

You are particularly to guard against any tools or utensils used in the woolen and silk trade, or made use of in the Iron and Steel Manufactures being exported to foreign parts, and to prevent the seducing of artificers or workmen employed in these manufactures to go into parts beyond the seas. No countenance is due to emigration.

Malcolm Campbell, the Islay officer, reported that the ship had come to Islay and then gone on to Colonsay 'to take in the passengers with all their effects which consist only of wearing apparel, as they are poor people who have been deprived of their farms by their landlord, and they will not be stopt going by him'.

The Master had refused to go to Campbeltown to make the necessary declaration, but stated: 'The ship would take 150 full passengers to be landed at Wilmington in North Carolina.'

It was later reported that the ship was the *General Washington*, James Miller, Master; and that she had the following passengers: from Islay, nineteen men; twenty-one women, thirty-one children. From Colonsay twenty-eight men, twenty-eight women and eighty-six children. From Mull, four men; four women and twelve children. From Jura, one man.

This was accompanied by a claim from Mr Campbell for expenses incurred, and a Protest by him against James Miller taken before Archibald McNeill of Colonsay, 'for all harm, damage or detriment that may arise from his refusal'. The Board agreed to meet the expenses, but warned, 'In future the Collector is to avoid incurring expense where the improbability of rendering effectual service shall be so apparent as in the present case.'

FURTHER EVIDENCE OF EMIGRATION IN THE EIGHTEENTH CENTURY

We will turn now to the scattered references which emerge from family research in the United States, and encounter not only more individuals of Jura origin, but some indications when further sailings may have taken place. Our principal sources will be *Directory of Scots in the Carolinas* by David Dobson, and *Carolina Scots* by Douglas Kelly

The *Directory of Scots* has five puzzling entries whose source is the North Carolina Archives, and which have in common only that the men listed 'emigrated from Jura, Argyllshire, to North Carolina, before 1764'. It is not clear why 1764 is a 'cut off date' in this connection. Is it that they appear on Land Registers in 1764, and must therefore have arrived somewhat sooner? This remains to be discovered.

The entries are as follows:

Malcolm Buie emigrated with his family from Jura to North Carolina before 1764
Alexander Clerk emigrated with his family from Jura to North Carolina before 1764
McCraine emigrated from Jura, Argyllshire to North Carolina pre 1764
Colin Shaw emigrated from Jura to North Carolina before 1764.
A merchant in Cumberland County, North Carolina *c.* 1764
John Shaw emigrated from Jura to North Carolina before 1764.
Brother of Colin Shaw, a merchant.

In the five cases above, before 1764 certainly does not mean '1754' as our 1754 list does not contain any of these families. Buie, Clark, McCraine and Shaw all figure largely in the Baptismal Register, where there is a Malcom Buie born in 1716; an Alexander Clark who appears in the register as the husband of Finwall McLean and father of John Clark in 1724. There are no Colin Shaws in the register, but two John Shaws as infants, and nine as fathers.

If these people stimulated active and successful family research on the part of their American descendants one would expect to find them in Professor Douglas Kelly's recent and informative work, *Carolina Scots*. This book lists a Malcolm Buie who was born in Jura *c.* 1735, and came to the Upper Cape Fear region with his brothers, Archibald, John and Neill, where he married Ann McCraine (or McRainey) daughter of Hugh McCraine and Catherine Buie, *c.* 1760. The North Carolina family research does not give an exact date for the arrival of this family, but there is insufficient room for a family of four boys in the Buies of 1754. This Malcolm Buie was too late for the register, but if Archibald was his *younger* brother, there is one such in Ardfernal in 1734.

On Alexander Clark, Colin Shaw and John Shaw, Douglas Kelly's book is silent. (The *Directory* lists this Alexander Clark as distinct from the significant one in the '39ers'.) Colin Shaw will shortly emerge from obscurity as party to some rare and well-known letters.

The above little group of references seems to point to another 'sailing' sometme between 1739 and 1764 about which we have no other information.

John McLean. We turn now to Dr Kelly's important 'McLean Family'. This is the story of 'Sober John' McLean'. He was known as 'Sober John' because of the leadership he gave on the Tory side in the Revolutionary War. He apparently remained sober while his other compatriots became inebriated, and thus he could be entrusted with difficult tasks, such as handling prisoners of war. His career is well recounted in the book, and he must have been an intriguing man.

The relevant entry is: 'Sober John McLean was born in Jura in 1730 and emigrated with his father, Hugh McLean, and mother Margaret McArthur to Cumberland County, North Carolina in 1749. The parents of emigrant Hugh McLean were John McLean and Katy Buie of Jura. Sober John McLean married Effie McCranie, daughter of Hugh McCranie, Sr and Catherine Buie. John McLean died in 1793 and his wife Effie in 1810.'

The Baptismal Register contains some promising references to this family:

There is an entry for 'Hugh McLean and Margaret McArthur in Knockrome, where they had a son, Donald, baptised in 1733'.

'Sober John' does not appear in the register, and neither is there any mention of Hugh's parents, John McLean and Katy Buie. Since there are no other records of this period in Scotland, these most valuable details must come from internal family research in North Carolina. Such records are rare indeed!

Knockrome at this time also contains a couple called 'Hugh McCrainie and Katherine Bui' with the note of their daughter Merron's baptism in 1733. We have suggested him as a second generation entry, and as the same person as 'Aobh' McCraine, the son of Ard McCranie and Ann McLaine, and baptised in Knockrome in 1704'. Again, our records do not show a second daughter, 'Effie'. Indeed from local Scottish records we have no independent evidence that this family actually emigrated at all, which they plainly did.

Note that there is a cross-reference in Dr Kelly's book to another daughter of these McCrainies, as the Malcolm Buie, mentioned above, married their daughter, Ann McCraine, *c.* 1760. It seems unwise to be sceptical about any North Carolina Family evidence, and a claim to know the exact date of an ancestor's arrival in the new country should be taken seriously. We therefore have a reference to a definite crossing in 1749.

We will now study some further emigrants from Jura researched in *Carolina Scots* and the *Directory*:

Kenneth Black. Born in Jura, *c.* 1730. Family tradition says he had brothers called Archibald, John, and perhaps Hugh. They obtained land grants on Big

Rockfish, in Cumberland County. Kenneth married Catherine Patterson, who, with her mother and brothers was born in Argyll, and emigrated *c.* 1748. The Blacks must have emigrated to North Carolina some years before the Revolution, *c.* 1770. They might have been on the suggested crossing of 1768, as they certainly were not on the *General Wolfe*. Kenneth lived latterly in Moore County, near the modern town of Southern Pines. He was a friend to Alan McDonald of Kingsborough, husband of the illustrious Flora, and it was to Kenneth Black that Flora appealed for help when her house was burned in 1777 at Killegrey, and it was his house that Flora's daughters were vsiting when the rude soldiers ripped their silk dresses with their swords. Kenneth Black was murdered by the American soldiers under Colonel Alston soon after the Piney Bottom Massacre of 1781. His widow lived on their land for some forty years after his death. They had a family of five, with typically Jura names: Archibald, Hugh, Malcolm, Effie and Margaret.

Daniel McNeill. Son of one Archibald McNeill, who died in 1746 in Jura. He emigrated to North Carolina around 1760, and probably settled in Hoke Country. We have no suitable names for the family in the Baptismal Register, and he wasn't on the 1754 or 1767 sailings, so we have here another emigration date *c.* 1760.

Neill McNeill. Born in 1771 at Ardlussa in Jura, the son of Hector McNeill and Margaret Darroch. He landed in Wilmington, North Carolina in 1792. He left a brother Malcolm in Scotland, and had another brother, Laughlin, who drowned at sea on the way to America. He first lived at Bluff in Cumberland County. In 1799 he married Sarah Graham, known as 'Prettie Sallie'. He was captain of a river boat on the Cape Fear and later bought a farm in lower Cumberland County south of Big Rockfish Creek on Chicken Road. He was an elder of Big Rockfish Presbyterian Church and died in 1858. They had ten children, known as 'The McNeills of the Bridge'. For many years and well into the twentieth century, one of the family homes was called Ardlussa. Modern descendants are in touch with Jura.

Daniel McLean. As we study the records we have of the early emigrants, we constantly realise how fragmentary is the picture we piece together. Many of the early families were evidently closely intermarried, and names frequently occur which we may suspect strongly are of native Jura folk, but for whom the actual evidence is missing, e.g. The McAllester family had a vital role in the '39' sailing, and are often called 'The Second Argyll Colony Family'. They are also important for the valuable collection of family papers which reveals a great deal about the early colony. Alexander McAllister, son of Coll McAlester and Janet McNeill (all original settlers), was married to Janet Buie (probably one of the Jura Buies). Their eldest daughter was Flora McAllister, and she married one Daniel McLean, who is recorded as being the son of John McLean and Katie Buie of Jura. Flora was born in 1782, and she would have married in the early 1800s. Her older brother and younger sister married in 1809 and 1802 respectively.

There are two John McLeans on the 1767 crossing, either of who could have married Katie Buie on arrival and had a family of suitable age for Daniel to have married Flora McAllister. As so often, the story gives tantalising hints of a more complex picture, and leaves the question of whether Daniel McLean was born in North Carolina or Jura open.

Piper Archie. Archibald Buie, 'The Piper', and his brother John Buie, are generally believed to have been born in Jura. Piper Archie first appears in North Carolina records in 1755 when he bought ninety-one acres of land on the north-east side of the north-west branch of the Cape Fear River in Cumberland County. Later tax records show him living in the Barbeque district. He died in 1806, unmarried, and left his property to the children of his brother John. John's wife's name is unknown. His sons Malcolm, Archibald and John moved to Georgia in the early 1800s. Beyond saying that these two must have arrived prior to 1755 we have no information about the date of their emigration. There are no suitable candidates in the baptismal records. There are a number of traditional stories concerning 'Piper Archie'.

Daniel Ray. Born in Jura in 1763. His wife, born in Islay, was called Margaret, but her maiden name is not known. They emigrated to North Carolina in 1792. In 1812 he was a farmer in Cumberland County with a wife and six children. He died on 9 March 1826 and is buried in Longstreet Presbyterian Cemetery, Fort Bragg, Hoke County, with his wife, and two of his daughters; Catherine and Mary. The Cemetery at Longstreet is full of 'Rays' and, more than thirty gravestones survive. Ten of these deceased were born in the eighteenth century, although no emigration dates are given.

Daniel's birthplace in Jura is actually inscribed on his tombstone, so there is no doubt about his origin, but his name is a puzzle, for it appears nowhere else in Jura records either before or after the emigration. Among the many other settlers called Ray is one Angus Ray who was born about 1785 and settled in Robeson County with his family. His wife is called Mary, and she was born about 1800 in Jura. They have six children in the US census of 1850: Margaret, Laughlin, Sally, Neill, Angus, and an infant. Mary Ray, native of Jura, is likely to remain a mystery.

John Buie. The family history of Neill Buie Jr of Cumberland County, North Carolina, seems to have been in some dispute. The accepted situation now is that he was born in October 1769 in Cumberland County and that his father was John Buie who had emigrated from the isle of Jura in 1768. In view of the date of birth of his son, this John Buie must have been an adult at the date of his emigration, but he was not on the *General Wolfe* in 1767

We come now to a group of emigrants known only from their gravestone inscriptions in various cemeteries in North Carolina:

Archibald Campbell. Born in Jura during 1750, he married Sarah (1780–1835). He died on 28 June 1853 and is buried at Campbell Cemetery, Anderson Creek, North Carolina. There is no further family history or date of emigration.

Malcolm McLean. Born in Jura, *c.* 1797. He died in North Carolina on 1 November 1862 and is buried in Union Cemetery, Carthage, Moore County.

Flora McLean. Born in Jura, *c.* 1823. She died in North Carolina on 23 April 1867 and is buried in Union Cemetery, Carthage in Moore County. No other information.

Neill McNeill. Born in Jura in 1784. He married Sarah (1784–1860). He died in North Carolina on 17 September 1857, and is buried in Phillips Cemetery, Raeford, Hoke County. No other information.

Hugh McDougald. Born in Jura, *c.* 1753. He died in North Carolina on 27 February 1827, and is buried in Longstreet Cemetery, Fort Bragg, Hoke County. No other information.

Malcolm McPhail. Born in Jura in 1771, and died in North Carolina on 1 June 1851. He is buried in Longstreet Cemetery, Fort Bragg, Hoke County. No other information.

John McPhail. Born in Jura in 1776, and died in North Carolina on 2 October 1852. His gravestone records that he was 'a resident of this country for the last thirteen years of his life'; so he arrived in 1839. He is buried in Longstreet Cemetery, Fort Bragg, Hoke County.

Neill McPhail. Born in Jura in 1819, and died in North Carolina on 24 March 1898. He appears on the baptismal record as having been baptised in 1819; the son of John McPhail and Mary Campbell of Knockrome. He is buried in Longstreet Cemetery, Fort Bragg, Hoke County.

Hugh McPhail. Born in Jura on 6 May 1827, and died in North Carolina on 21 December 1852, aged twenty-five. He does not appear on the baptismal record. His gravestone records 'He was a consistent member of the Presbyterian Church'. He is buried in Longstreet Cemetery, Fort Bragg, Hoke County.

The *State Archives of North Carolina* contain a vast amount of information on people who were evidently Scottish Immigrants. There are Lists of Taxables; Records of Land Grants; and Abstracts of Wills. Tempting though many of these sources are, there are usually of no practical help in our particular quest since they do not firmly identify the place of origin of those mentioned.

For example: 'Abstracts of Wills; 1754–1863; Cumberland County; North Carolina', contains numbers of Wills made out by people with Jura names, e.g. Buie, 11; Clark, 19; McCraine, 5; McDougald, 5; McLean, 18; McNeill, 37; Shaw, 14. It is likely that many of these relate to people from Jura for whom we cannot establish firm connections. However, the entire collection contains one single emigrant, new to our enquiry, who takes the trouble to record his place of birth:

Neill McNeill. Died 25 August 1853. Recorded June 1858.

'I Neill McNeill, a native of Jura, Argyleshire, Scotland, but a citizen of Cumberland Co,. for the last 61 years, being now in my 83rd year.'

Listed in his will are: his wife Sarah; his sons, Hector McNeill and Neill J. McNeill; and his daughter, Janet McDonald. His grandchildren are mentioned but not named. Also mentioned are children of his son Alexander or Sandy, and grandson George Hector. As can be seen this will gives us a birthdate for him of 1775, and an emigration date of 1797, when he was twenty-two years old. This comes from the period of our greatest ignorance about Jura residents.

EMIGRATIONS OF THE NINETEENTH CENTURY

It will be seen that the list of emigrants known only from their gravestone records has led us out of the eighteenth century and into the nineteenth. We will now look at the 'second wave' of emigrations which took place during the first half of the nineteenth century.

Dugald MacArthur has helpful comments in his *Some Emigrant Ships from the West Highlands*:

> One important point to remember is that up to 1815 emigration was voluntary, and carried out against the wishes of the Highland landowners. After 1815, emigration was different in that much of it was forced, as against the earlier voluntary movement, but it too went in waves caused by the failure of kelp after 1820; the minor potato blight of 1836–37, and the complete failure of 1846–47. The Highland and Island Emigration Society helped with passages to Australia from 1852–57, while many lairds helped to pay for passages to America right up to 1880.
>
> Up till the Passenger Act of 1803, no government agency on either side of the Atlantic was consistently responsible for recording the departure or arrival of emigrants. After 1803 the Customs Officer was responsible for seeing that the provisions of the Act were complied with, but the shipping agent or contractor was able to find a way round the regulations.
>
> 'Emigrant Recruiters' were operating quietly on the margins of society. One of the more notorious of these agents, Archibald McNiven of Islay, claimed to have transported between 1821 and 1832, 12,000 Highlanders to Cape Breton; Nova Scotia mainland; Prince Edward Island and Upper Canada. Other reports credit him with 16,000 by 1840.

The Chief Enumerator for Jura for the Second National Census, held in 1851 was the Rev. Lachlan McKenzie, the Parish Minister. He attaches the following note to his Census Return:

> The different enumerators of Jura have submitted their enumeration books to me for my inspection. The only remark I deem it necessary for me to make regarding them is that any decrease in the population of the Parish of Jura since 1841 is to be attributed to the Emigration of a considerable number of families to the United States of America and Canada, and to the removal of a few families and individuals to Greenock and other towns of Scotland.

Once we pass the time of the first census in 1841 it becomes easy to quantify what Mr McKenzie is observing. The total population for the main island of Jura in the 1841 census was 1158. By the 1851 census it had dropped to 943; a loss of 215 men women and children.

The figures for households are similarly revealing. In 1841 there were 210 households; ten years later there were 17 – a loss of 35 families during the ten years.

The 'Spirit of Emigration' complained of by Francis Stewart in 1794 is evidently very much alive again, but once again, in this new century the detailed documentary evidence remains slight.

It is interesting that the Campbell of Jura Papers include forms sent to the island in 1853 for would-be emigrants to complete. These seem to have remained unused as a result of the conditions included. Applicants

> must have been in the habit of working for wages; single men cannot be taken unless they are sons in eligible families; single women with illegitimate children can in no case be taken, nor if over thirty-five; nor if more than two children under seven in family, or three under ten, or in which sons outnumber daughters; nor widowers and widows with young children; nor if in the habitual receipt of parish relief; nor if liabilities exceed assets.

It is hardly an attractive picture, and the survival of unused forms is not surprising.

We turn then to such evidence as we have for individual Jura families who emigrated to North Carolina in the nineteenth century. We are indebted to Dr Kelly once more for three well-documented family groups, and we will start with them:

Murdoch Ferguson. Born in Jura in 1750. He married Mary McDonald, who was born in 1765, and they had eight of a family: Daniel, Norman, Neil, John, Murdoch, Sarah, Nancy, and Rachel. The first five children were born in Scotland, for the family emigrated to North Carolina about 1802. They settled just south of the present town of Cameron in Moore County, and are buried in the McDonald Cemetery between Cameron and Vass. Murdoch Ferguson died in 1830, and his wife in 1825. There are many descendants.

Fergusons were thin on the ground in Jura in the eighteenth century. There is one family in Ardfin in 1733, when Alexander Ferguson and Cirstin McGhoil had a daughter Katherine baptised. The name is absent from the early part of the nineteenth century. We do not know if Murdoch even grew up and married in Jura before he and his family emigrated.

Angus McInnis. Son of Malcom McInnis and Catherine Campbell, he was born on 15 February 1785, near Inverlussa on Jura. Family research suggests two previous generations. His first wife was Mary Shaw of Jura. He was a sailor until he left Scotland for America somewhere around 1820. He left with his wife and four children: Duncan; Isabel, Archibald and John. They were accompanied by his wife's sister, Flora Shaw.

They came first to Quebec, then to New York and thence by ship to Wilmington, North Carolina, and on up river to Fayetteville. Angus purchased land in the Rockfish area just west of Fayetteville and farmed there, raising five children by his first wife and six by his second wife, Margaret McEachern. There are many descendants. Angus McInnis died on 21 October 1849, and is buried in Longstreet Cemetery. His gravestone has an inscription recording his birth on Jura. Mary Shaw died about 1825 and is buried in the same graveyard.

The Shaws and the Darrochs. Duncan Shaw and Janet Campbell of Lagg must have been married in the early 1800s. They are known to have had eight children: Janet, Ann, Malcolm, John, Neill, Katie, Sarah and Janet. Neill and Sarah appear in the Baptismal Register in 1810 and 1813.

Ann Shaw, b. 1807, married one *John Torquil Shaw* (known as Torquil) in 1827. Torquil Shaw was the son of John Shaw and Flora McDougald. His father drowned on a cattle boat in Scotland. Torquil and Anne Shaw emigrated to North Carolina in 1829 with their oldest son John, and settled in the Flat Branch Community in Harnett County.

Torquil had a sister Margaret who married Daniel McDougald and emigrated to Prince Edward Island, Canada. His sister Annie emigrated with him and lived with him until her death.

Torquil and Anne had ten children of whom only three married. Gilbert, born in 1837 was the great-grandfather of Angus Shaw, of Harnett County, whose son Tom Shaw has been a prime mover in establishing modern links with his ancestral line from Jura.

Anne Shaw's sister Janet Shaw, b. 1811, married Alexander Darroch in 1828, and they had five children: Angus, Mary, Donald, Janet and Nancy (died aged twelve).

Alexander Darroch and Janet Shaw emigrated from Ardfernal in 1847, and settled in the Old Darroch place in Moore County, Settle River Township, near Mount Pleasant Church. They were received into membership of Cypress Church in 1848 on a 'Certificate of Transference' from Jura Parish Church. Anne and Janet's brother Neill Shaw also emigrated and settled in Cumberland County. He was known as 'Joe Neill Shaw'. He did not marry.

Alexander Darroch and Janet Shaw also have descendants who have visited Jura, and researched their proud Scottish ancestry. Dennis Cameron has had a fine memorial tablet erected to his ancestors. He has also researched another branch of his Jura forebears:

It is interesting how much information begins to emerge when a North Carolina family begins to tackle the problem with enthusiasm.

The emigrants Anne Shaw, Neill Shaw, and Janet Shaw had a brother John, whose wife's name is unknown, but who had a family who all remained in Scotland. Neil moved to Greenock. Mary married a McCraine but had no issue. Ann married a Darroch and became the grandmother of several extremely significant residents of Jura this century.

Their brother Duncan, known in Jura by his Gaelic title 'Dunacha Sha', was unmarried, but was, most unusually, a most determined correspondent, and we possess no less than nine letters from his hand, written by him to two of his American cousins. These were Angus Darroch and Janet Darroch (married name Thaggard), the children of the above Alexander Darroch and Janet Shaw, Janet Shaw being his aunt. These letters have been treasured by their North Carolina descendants as heirlooms, and will be studied later.

Donald and Isabel Black. Married in 1835, they lived in Keils with their children Mary, Duncan and Anne. They are gone from Jura by the 1851 Census, and are believed to have emigrated about the same time as the Darrochs in 1847.

William Macdougald. A respected family of Campbells in Lumberton, North Carolina, have evidence of an ancestor called William McDougald, born in Jura about 1800. William is an uncommon Christian name in Jura, but there is a William McDougald who married Catherine Buie in 1831. The family lived at Lergiebreck. They emigrated to North Carolina in October 1839. Family history has a lively sketch of William McDougald:

> After a long and useful life he died near Swann's Station, Moore County in 1874. He became early in life a subject of converting grace, and connected himself with the Church in Jura, where his father and grandfather were ruling elders. Soon after his arrival in North Carolina he set about repairing Barbeque Church, which had become vacant, and was instrumental in securing the services of Rev. Colin McIver, and was soon Ordained as an Elder in Barbeque Church.

More anecdotes about his remarkable life follow.

There was a son Dougald McDougald, who was born on 5 July 1832 in Jura, and was seven at the time of his arrival in North Carolina. His descendants have also researched the family.

Neill McNeill. The McNeill family of Delaware have researched their Jura ancestors. Neill McNeill, was born in Jura in 1784. He married Marion (or Sarah) McDougall, also born in 1784 in Jura. They lived in Lussagiven and had two daughters baptised while they lived there: Isabella, in 1815 and Margaret in 1817. They emigrated to Cumberland County, North Carolina, about 1819, and settled at Raeford where four further children were born. These were: Roderick, John Duncan, Janet and Anna. Neill McNeill died on 17 September 1857, and Sarah died on 25 November 1860. They are both buried in McCaskill Cemetery near Raeford, which is now in Hoke County. John Duncan was the direct ancestor of the contemporary descendants.

It is surprising how quickly the well-documented instances of emigrants in this second wave begin to peter out – e.g., the McDougalds of Statesboro, Georgia, have clear family tradition for Jura ancestors called Archibald McDougald and Dougald McDougald. These would have been brothers who emigrated about the mid-nineteenth century. There are a number of suitable candidates in Jura records, but it has proved impossible to be certain exactly which of these are the direct ancestors of a family which is enthusiastic about its ancestry, and has visited Jura to pursue it.

Very rarely the need for an American family to treasure early documents as heirlooms has given us another insight into the mid-nineteenth century. As in the case of John Darroch and Catherine McLean. Here we have not only the Last Will and Testament, but, uniquely in the case of Jura, we have the Certificate of Transference of church membership from the Kirk Session of Jura Parish Church. Transcripts of these documents now follow:

Certificate of Transference of Church Membership.
The Bearer John Darroch and his wife Catherine McLean are Natives of this Parish. They have intimated to us their intention to emigrate to America with their young and interesting Family of two sons and two daughters. John

Darroch is by trade a Cooper, but some years since came to succeed his father Michael Darroch, late a respected Elder in this Parish, and a Tenant in the Farm of Lergybreck. He is a Cousin German of General Darroch of Gourock. He is sober, honest and industrious. He is a member of the Established Church of Scotland; was admitted to sealing Ordinances in this Parish; and is Hereby recommended to all such as may have it in their power to forward the Temporal and Spiritual Interests of himself and Family.

Given in name and by Authority of the Kirk Session of Jura and Collonsay this 10th day of July, 1841 years.

Alexr. Kennedy, Minr. of Jura & Collonsay, Moderator
John Campbell, Elder and Session Clerk.

Subjoined is an Authenticated Extract from the Record of Births and Marriages in this Parish of the ages of the Members of the Family.

John Darroch and Catherine McLean were married 19th Dec. 1819.
Their daughter Janet was born 24th Oct. 1820.
Michael was born 1st February 1823
Sarah was born 25 July 1825
Donald was born 26 April 1828

Jura, 10th July 1841; John Campbell, Elder and Session Clerk, Parish of Jura & Collonsay.

Notes: 'cousin german', a full cousin, or first cousin; 'sealing Ordinances', instruction and admission to the Sacraments, as a church member.

We have now emerged from the lack of evidence of the eighteenth century, and have some records which bear on this family. The Old Parish Register of Marriages records the ceremony in 1819. The baptismal register records the baptisms of Janet and Sarah. The family are still living in Lergybreck at the time of the 1841 census which shows John Darroch, Catherine McLean, Michael, Marion and Donald. Ages are given as fifty-four, fifty-two, eighteen, sixteen, and twelve. Janet would seem to have been absent. The census taker calls Sarah, Marion.

Neither this certificate nor the Will indicate anything about the actual emigration, but the Will completes the story:

The Last Will and Testament of John Darroch

'In the Name of God. Amen.

I, John Darroch, Planter of the County of Harnet, being old and in a declining state of health, do see fit to make this my last Will and Testament.

Firstly I give and devise all my land to my son Daniel Darroch and my daughter Sarah Darroch; Sarah's Dividend or her half is to include my Dwelling and the Buildings adjacent.

The Balance and residue of my goods and chatels I give and bequeath to the aforesaid Children with a reservation hereafter to be made.

Again to my Daughter Janet Darroch I give and bequeath two Cows.

I nominate and appoint my son Daniel Darroch, Executor of this my last Will and Testament; Witness I set my hand and affix my seal the day of April in the year our Lord, One thousand eight hundred and sixty /1860/ in presence of Neill McLean. John Darroch (seal)

We see here a very good example of a puzzling question in the matter of Christian names among the emigrants, referred to previously. It appears that many of the men called 'Donald' in Jura, become 'Daniel' in North Carolina. The name 'Donald' continued to be popular in Jura, and continues to the present time, while it more or less disappears in the States. Why 'Daniel' should have become the transatlantic version of this name remains a question which has not been satisfactorily answered.

As our reliable sources for Jura emigrants dry up we realise that we have information about only a tiny fraction of the great number of people who left Jura and settled in North Carolina between 1739 and 1850. We are reminded of the likely depth of Jura residents when we use North Carolina records and lists which show the presence of people who sound as though they probably originated in Jura. Here, for example, are names of men from the Cumberland County Tax list of 1755 who seem likely to have Jura connections: Archibald Buie, Donald Buie, Duncan Buie, Gilbert Buie, Alexander Clark, Archibald Clark, John Clark, Neil Clark, Duncan Clark, Hugh McCrainie, Hugh McDougald and Dushee Shaw.

These are some men of Harnet County who served in the War of Revolution in 1780: Captain Daniel Buie, Duncan Buie, John Clark, Captain Neil McCrainey, Archibald McDougald and Neil Shaw.

Much later we have a list of Harnet County men who fought in the Civil War of 1863: Archibald Black, John Black, Daniel Black, Neil Buie, Angus Darroch, Daniel Darroch, Malcolm Darroch, John McDougald and Gilbert McDougald.

Before we give some consideration to other destinations for Jura people seeking to leave the island we must make some comment on:

THE BLUE FAMILY
People in North Carolina with the family surname Blue are numerous and influential, and a number of people of the name emigrated from Argyll. The name is probably an anglicisation of some form of McGuirmins. The Gaelic word 'gorm', 'blue', may have been involved with a saint such as St Goram. These Blues emigrated from Knapdale, but have always claimed that they came also from the north end of Jura as a result of their close ties with the MacNeills of Colonsay who came to own Ardlussa in 1737. A number of these well-researched families assert that their ancestors were born on Jura, lived there and emigrated from there, and it would be a bold person who would deny the claim. It is, however, strange that there is not one single reference in any document relating to Jura of anyone of the surname Blue ever having set foot on the island. This fact evidently is no embarrassment to the Carolina Blues, who are in no doubt whatever that they come from Jura. To everyone else it remains an intriguing mystery.

CORRESPONDENCE

We conclude our study of the North Carolina emigrations with a look at various documents which have survived and come to hand. First, the fifteen letters which have been preserved.

We have knowledge of only four eighteenth-century letters between Jura emigrants and Jura residents, and all were written to Colin Shaw, Merchant of Cumberland County, who appears in the *Directory of Carolina Scots* and has already been mentioned.

Two of the letters, dated 1764 and 1770, are from Donald Campbell of Ardmenish. One is from Duncan Shaw, in 1773 recently moved from Jura to Port Askaig in Islay, and one is from Angus Shaw, innkeeper at Lagg, and dating from 1789. It seems just possible that since these letters are well known in the North Carolina Archives, and, the first is dated 1764, it may itself be sufficient reason for the *Directory* to say that Colin Shaw emigrated before 1764.

In view of their great rarity, these four letters are reprinted here:

Mr Colin Shaw, Merchant, Cumberland County, North Carolina July 31 1764

Dear Collin,

I received the last of your two letters to me two days ago from Inverary. I am very glad to hear of you and the rest of your brothers welfare, and also the welfare of your sister. I find the rest of your brothers has entirely forgot me, but I wonder of John, your brother, for he promised to write me often before now, so that I may say as you observed 'out of sight, out of mind'.

As to news; the bearer Neil McArthur will inform you of all the news of the country; your grandmother is dead a long time ago; the old and young Bailie are dead, and no one but the youngest to the fore. The country is in a good way; your friends in Ardlussa are all very well and the rest of your friends in the country are well. As I find by your letter to Neil McArthur that you are in a good way of living and thread back and forth to Jamaica and other parts, and as that is the case, I would be glad if you saw it would profit you and it would be in your way to come to Scotland. Then I would be glad to have the pleasure of seeing you in this part of the world; as written in your first letter to me. I find you was informed that I was married to a woman from Islay who is a [obscure] of yours and all your brothers as well as I am.

Now Collin, if you don't think it convenient to come, and I hope you will, do me the favour to let me know the conditions of your brothers and sisters living in particular, and the conditions of the whole of the rest of the Jura people. My son Archibald is not at home, and if he was he would write you. I desire you may remind me kindly to all the Jura people who was my good neighbours.

My wife and I joins in our compliments to you and all your brothers and your sister. The same to Hugh McLean and his family, and Malcolm Buie and his family and Donald Paterson's son, and all the McCraines, and tell them I am very well, and wants to hear the same accounts of them; and tell them I have killed a deer this same year in the muir of Tarbert, and I am,

Dear Collin, your friend and humble servant,
    Donald Campbell.

To Collin Shaw of Cumberland County, North Carolina. Ardmenish, Jura,
Aug 22nd 1770

Sir,
I received the favour of your kind letter by Mr Campbell of Baliole in which
you are so kind to let me know of your welfare. I'm glad you have done so,
and it gives me pleasure to know that you are in a thriving state, and sincerely
wish you much joy in your married state, which was a good reason for your
not seeing your friends here at the time you proposed coming to see us, and
you may believe there are but few that would rather see you in a flourishing
condition than I, and how soon you may renew and pursue your resolution
in letting us have the pleasure of seeing you here.

The bearer Archibald Campbell, son to Ronald Campbell, Bailie's son, who
is married to my eldest daughter; goes together with their small family of
bairns to America to try their fortune there. Their luck in this country has
been but very indifferent, which obliges them to go to your corner of the Globe
to try what chance they may have there. Though their luck here be bad, it
cannot be said that it's owing to him or her, both of them are industrious in
their way of life. He writes a good hand, and I make no doubt he shall be
careful and honest in any trust that providence shall think proper to put in
his way. They go to a foreign country, with a family of small bairns, without
money, or acquaintances, but I have great reliance on your friendship, and I
earnestly entreat and beg it of you as a favour that you may give them you
advice and assistance, and have them put on some footing of having bread,
and indeed I make no doubt you shall do what you can for them. I recommend
them to all my friends and acquaintances there. As I'm in a hurry I cannot
write them all, but beg you offer them my sincere good wishes. You desired
me to let you know what sort of goods from your country would suit best
for this country. As I am not very well acquainted with these things may I
recommend you for intelligence to the bearer and to my nephew Archibald
Simson, who also goes to America in the same ship with my son-in-law, and
brings goods with him to sell there. Your Uncle-in-law, Neil McCraine is very
tender and hard of hearing, but has effects. His daughter was contracted on
Saturday last to Donald McDugald, Jura's Servant. All your old friends in
general are pretty well. My wife and I join in compliments to you and Mrs
Shaw, and believe me to be,
    Dear Sir; Your assured friend, Donald Campbell.

To Capt. Colin Shaw in Cumberland County, North Carolina,
    In favour of Alexander Campbell, Esquire of Balole.
                                        Port Askaig, 21st Sept. 1773

Dear Cousin,
Having this opportunity of Mr Campbell, Balole, I have thought it advisable
to write to know whether you are in life or not. I long very much to hear of

you, also my friends there, and in particular from you, who can inform one of them, also in General. I do assure you I would not begrudge the postage of letters at any time that one or more of my friends would take the trouble of writing to me.

On Whitsunday last was Twelve months I came to live to this Port and thank God my wife and family enjoy a pretty good state of health. Mr Campbell who I understand is very fond of you, and speaks much in your favour, in most company, can inform you of the news in general of this Country. Please write and let me know which of our friends are in life and who are not, and such as pleases to write me of them that they may let me know how to Direct for them. Mrs Shaw joins me in love and compliments to your Mrs Shaw and also my friends there whom you have occasion to see or be in company with, and I am,

> Dear Cousin, Yours most Affectionately,
> Duncan Shaw.

Mr Coline Shaw, Cumberland County, N. Carolina, N. America.
For favors of John Darroch.

My Dear Friend,
Let it not in the least surprise you that I give you this trouble, as all are writing to their friends, I think it a duty to write to you as mine; though we are unacquainted; our predecessors were, and so may we in manner, though we are at such a great distance. I doubt not but you remember my father and family, but I refer you to the bearer for that and all the news of this island, who will tell you all about us, that you would wish to hear or know. I would wish with all my heart that we had here such an opportunity to hear from you next year as you have to hear from us this year; that is, from a friend on the spot that we could depend upon, as you have many from us, and especially the bearer, to whom I hope you will be kind even on our account, if not for your own. But since it is the case that you will not come any of you here, I do really expect that you will in answer to this, write a particular account of the country and of the friends there, and especially your own way of living, and now assure yourself that I will with pleasure pay postage, and am with esteem, your sincere friend and very humble servant,

> Angus Shaw
> Lagg,

Jura,   Direct to Angus Shaw, Innkeeper at Lagg, Jura, and let me
July 9th, 1789 know punchually how to direct to you as I am at present at
                a loss for that.

Although the contents of these four letters seem on the face of it somewhat humdrum, they deserve publication for their antiquity, and for the glimpses they give us of how people were thinking in Jura about the friends and family who were for ever lost to them in the Colonies.

Donald Campbell's first letter makes it clear that Colin Shaw has recently been in correspondence with him, and that consequently he has a good deal of 'news' about the emigrants.

He still complains however that those he believed were most loyal are not prepared to write to him.

He gives up to date information about Jura, its laird and all friends and relatives. He expresses a desire that Colin will return on a visit, but one gets the impresion that he has no real expectation that this will happen. His closing paragraph gives us some insight into the close-knit community on Cumberland County of which we know so little. We hear of Hugh McLean and his family, Malcolm Buie and his family, Donald Paterson's son, and all the McCraines. The group of people listed in the *Directory* along with Colin Shaw, as emigrating 'before 1764' includes a Macolm Buie, and an unknown McCraine. We may be getting a reference to them here. Neil McArthur is carrying Donald Campbell's letter at the end of July 1764, so presumably we have a firm date of a sailing around this date. We should also note that Colin Shaw is not only a Merchant in Cumberland County but plies for Trade between North Carolina and Jamaica, and 'other parts'. Presumably the deer killed in the muir of Tarbert was poached!

Donald Campbell's second letter is mainly a testimonial to Archibald Campbell, his son-in-law. We learn that his nephew Archibald Simpson emigrated on the same boat in 1770. Colin's wife is evidently a McCraine, for her uncle Neil is frail and deaf, but quite well to do. Note that this letter gives us another firm sailing date around 22 August 1770

Duncan Shaw's brief letter makes it clear that Colin is his cousin, and that he and his wife would be glad of a general résumé of which of the emigrants are still alive and which are not. It is of some interest that he has left Jura, and now lives at Port Askaig. Was there much commerce between the islands at that time? We have little information. Mr Campbell of Islay is bearing the letter, and this gives us another definite date for a sailing in September 1773.

Angus Shaw is also commending another 'letter bearer', although he doesn't mention his name. He is loosing a bow at a venture, for he doesn't actually know Colin Shaw. He suggests that his predecessor at the inn in Lagg knew Colin's predecessor, although whether in Jura or North Carolina is not clear. Was Colin Shaw the innkeeper at one of Jura's other change houses before he emigrated 'before 1764'? He doesn't appear on any of Campbell of Jura's rent lists. Again there seems a great thirst for some description of what life is really like in North Carolina, and of his own 'way of living'. It looks as if we have found another firm sailing date here at 1789.

The Campbells of Winston-Salem in North Carolina have a treasured letter sent to Alex Campbell's emigrant grandfather. William Campbell apparently emigrated with his brother Alexander. The family history is confident about their Jura birthplace, but they escape the 1841 Census, and do not appear in the 1810 Baptismal Register. The author of the letter, John Campbell, the Schoolmaster of Knockrome, is fifty-one at the time of the 1851 census. He also was born too early to be caught by the Baptismal Register, and his parents would have escaped note at the time of their wedding. The emigrant Campbell brothers are evidently amongst the group for whom there are no statutory records in Jura. They presumably went to North Carolina in the 1820s or 1830s. John Campbell left his mark on Jura, in the shape of a record of employment, of some local letters, and a gravestone in Kilearnadil cemetery.

He will reappear in our consideration of Education on Jura. His letter is a very remarkable one, and appears here in full:

Knockrome, 18th August 1857

My Dear Brother,

I had your last letter which you sent last year, and in reply to the same, wrote you about this time last year, but you nor Sandy did send no answer, tho' I wrote to you both at the same time. I was used in the same way by them at Missisippi. I hope on receipt of this you will write to me and tell me how you all are, because I am anxious about you. I now enjoy good health; but I had a bad turn of the cough the beginning of last Summer. I suppose it was an influenza and not the effect of cold, because many others were then complaining as well as I was.

John Darroch is now married to a Jura girl; the youngest daughter left by *Alastir MacAilein* that was in Brosdle. I had them both here last April. I was glad to see the poor man, having not seen him for nearly six years before they took a snug room in Greenock. He is just now in the West Indies, and his wife expects him home about the end of this month.

The crop here looks well, but the blight is come upon the Potatoes; however it is expected they will turn out better than last year. A wire fence is now set in the muir above this farm; the poor people are now reduced to very narrow limits, yet there is no abatement in the rents. The Landlord would rather we would all go that he might reduce the whole to a sheep farm.

I hope on receipt of this you will write to me, and tell me how you all are; give me also some account of friends and acquaintances there; but specially tell me how little Sandy is coming on.

With kind love and best wishes to yourself and your wife.

 I remain, My Dear Brother,

  Yours very affectionately, John Campbell

Here is the letter we would expect from a very sophisticated man, with a keen awareness of what is happening in his own world. He gives us a clear indication that the wave of settlers from Jura is no longer confined to North Carolina and Georgia, but has now reached as far as Missisippi. There is no trace of the John Darroch he mentions, either in Jura or Greenock. It is interesting to note that the blight is still a serious problem long after the most severe attacks of 1846 and 1847. We note also the encroachment on to the traditional common lands, which will emerge in evidence when the Crofters Commission arrives in 1894. Also that John Campbell is bold enough to set these things down in a letter.

There is, in this letter, a wistful yearning for 'information'; about the writer's kinfolk, now lost to him. The reference to the progress of 'little Sandy', is particularly moving.

The Shaws and Darrochs, whose emigration history has been given in some detail, had, as has already been mentioned, a cousin called Duncan Shaw, who was a cooper to trade, who remained unmarried, and looked after his mother, Catherine Darroch Shaw until she died in 1884.

Duncan Shaw, known locally by his Gaelic name, 'Dunacha Sha', lived alone in one of the pauper's houses in Ardfernal until his death in 1901. He was well remembered by old residents of Jura until the 1980s. One recalled visiting him when a child, he had had a leg amputated in his later years; indeed his letters speak of early lameness, and on being given the Gaelic greeting, he was wont to reply that 'he was well, but rolling about like a seal on Lowlandman's Bay'.

He seems to have been a determined correspondent, and nine of his letters to various family members in North Carolina have survived. From his references to emigrant family members, and his news about family and friends in Jura, it was easy to construct a comprehensive family tree which put the American descendants firmly in touch with their not-so-distant cousins in Jura.

Dunacha Sha's American letters span from 1872 to 1889. In his letter of 1872 he mentions about fifteen relatives and friends, and their spouses and families, while referring to a considerable number of relatives in North Carolina. The full text of these letters would occupy an unreasonable amount of space. Here are some selected passages which may reveal something of Dunacha Sha's interests:

You may tell your father that Hugh McDugald in Knockrome lost his four daughters since May last (1874), and they were going up daughters, and one of them was married, and it is a sad story, and a heap of men departed this life the year ago.' (The Statutary Register of Deaths records, Marion (13); Christina (22); Mary (24); Margaret (18); all dying in 1874, a tragedy indeed. Also five young men dying in the previous year.)

If you see Dugald Kennedy, kindly tell him that John and his family are all well, and that he wonders very much how he ceased writing. Accept my thousand compliments for yourself and husband, and I need not tell you how pleased I am always to hear from you. I may mention you are the only one of my friends in that part of the country who are mindful of me in writing. Although placed in humble circumstances myself, I always endeavour to answer any word that comes from friends who are far from the land of their birth. I will be delighted to get your own and husband's likeness along with your family.

I intend sending a newspaper per post along with this note to let you see some of our Scotch news. We intend to get a land bill passed in Parliament for us in a short time. There is an awful turn out in the Highlands for a reduction and fixity of tenure and the like of that. There was a commission through the Highlands already and a Royal Commission likely will be again. They had to put some of the men-of-war to some of the Northern Islands already. Likely you would hear about the war between Great Britain and the Arabs before this and at present.' (1885)

I have to let you know that we have a grand deer forest on the island of Jura, and some of it is leased to an Englishman named Mr Evans. He is a very kind gentleman. He built a nice house for me, with one room, a kitchen and closet and loft. So you see that I would need a housekeeper to keep it in proper order.

I had a few letters from sister Janet from Canada lately. She was well. Give my respects to your sister and brother. I always like them, although I have never seen them. I am wondering if all your family is red-headed?

I may state here that the highlands is very dull and hard up at the present time. (1887) Trade is very dull in the towns, low markets and very little work to be found. It is not very easy to live at the present time. I intend sending a newspaper to you in a short time and you will find some of the news there better than I can give you.

Your cousin Neil Darroch sends you his kindest regards and his wife Mary McColl is at this moment sitting at my fireside, and she wishes to be remembered to you. She also sends you her love, and begs me to say if you have forgotten the time you were running about the houses here, and she nearly took your thumb off! She has a large family and they are all doing for themselves now.

Remember me to Uncle Neil. It is hardly worth while to call him an Uncle. I wished him in my letter to cousin Janet to write; but he has never done it!

It always affords me great pleasure to hear from any of my friends on the other side of the Atlantic. I am here alone, an old Bachelor, and likely to remain so. (1889) However, I have a reason to be thankful. I always enjoy good health, the greatest blessing on earth.

I was very glad to hear that you have so much land. 300 acres will keep you very comfortable. I wish I had some of these grand things you mention.

John Kennedy was pleased to hear about his brother Dugald. He did not hear anything for a long time prior to your letter. All we Jura people take a great delight in hearing from our friends in America. You cannot send us too much news.

Your cousin Neil is always going about, but is failing very fast. He is getting quite an old man. He is also troubled with rheumatism, a complaint very prevalent in Jura. A great many of the old people have it.

We have a beautiful summer and the crops look well; a long way over last year at this time. Prices are good, and on the whole things are in a flourishing state.

With these extracts from the letters of Duncan Shaw of Ardfernal, we bring our study of the eighteenth- and nineteenth-century emigrations from Jura to North Carolina to a close.

We have accumulated a quite reasonable number of eighteenth-century emigrant sailings. By adding all the various references and claims to dates we now have crossings in 1739, 1748, 1749, 1754, 1760, 1764, 1767, 1770, 1773, 1789, 1791, 1792 and 1797. We should also remember that, having arrived initially in the region of Fayetteville, in what we now often refer to as 'The Valley of the Scots', the families of these Jura people did not stay in the same place, but moved away south and west to settle in many other States. They can now be found as far away as Texas, and their numbers are impossible to calculate.

We conclude the story of Jura folk in the United States with the episode of Neil Lindsay.

Neil's family tree can be seen in detail in the families of the twentieth century. He was born at Lagg in 1862, one of the nine children of Archibald Lindsay and Effie McGilp. His grandfather John Lindsay was the post-runner at Lagg. Neil was also the nephew of the famous Hugh Lindsay, who won a piping competition in Inverness in 1845. He also became a fine piper in his turn.

Neil followed the family tradition and worked as a postman in Jura. However, at some point in his twenties he went to San Francisco where he became a significant member of the Scottish community. Everything we know about the next few years comes from Neil's scrapbook, which he kept from about 1890 onwards. From this we learn that he had met I. S. R Tevendale, another native Scot, and reputedly the finest piper in the United States. Tevendale had a drinking establishment at 536 Sacramento Street, where Neil served the customers. A cutting states:

Tevendale's; the characteristic resort for Scotchmen and others who appreciate good things to drink, has been remodelled and thoroughly refurnished, interior and exterior. The improvement is a pleasant surprise to old-time patrons, and the place is one of the best of its class in the city. Neil Lindsay, so widely known to the customers of the house, has purchased an interest in the business. This makes a hot combination, for Tevendale and Lindsay are the two most famous pipers in the Scotch colony.

The establishment was soon renamed, as another cutting makes clear:

Those who enjoy a delicious mixed drink, should drop into Tevendale & Lindsay's, 536 Sacramento Street, and get a pleasant surprise. There will be found inviting quarters and all that is necessary is to call for a 'Neil's Patent,' and the man in the Scotch cap will do the rest. You can't find out how it is made, but that makes it all the more attractive. Try one.

The various cuttings in the scrapbook tell us a good deal about Neil's role in California:

The well-known bagpiper, Neil Lindsay, cut a wide swathe at the Sacramento Scotch games last week. Neil, being a boy of 'buirdly' build, wore the philabeg to such perfection; dirk, sporran, plaid and all; that he got away with the first prize for 'the best dressed Hielandman'. Some say that his 'cairngorm' dazzled the eyes of the judges.

Another is headed 'The True Sportsman':

Among the Highland Pipers, who led the Jubilee procession at the chutes, the most conspicuous for elegance of attire, martial bearing and skill in piping was Neil Lindsay, who otherwise bears an illustrious record. Born in the Isle of Jura about thirty years ago, Mr Lindsay for some time carried Her Majesty's mail in the Highlands of Scotland. He is now Pipe-Major of both the Caledonia and Thistle Clubs of this city, and has been offered the same position in a Scottish regiment, now stationed in Aberdeen. For several years he has carried off first prize for 'best-dressed Highlander', also in many competitions for piping.

Occasionally Neil seems to have been 'robbed'; as in the following:

Kissing goes by favor in California, and that is the reason why Neil Lindsay was not awarded the first prize as the best dressed Highlander on the ground at the picnic of the Caledonian Club at Shell Mound last Thursday. It is well known to all true sons of Scotia that his real Lindsay tartan, his solid silver ornaments set with cairngorms of the first water, his sporran, hose, shoes, and Glengarry, all mounted with heather, thoroughly corresponded, and formed, all together, the handsomest costume in California. These are the facts, in spite of the judge's decision, and Lindsay, if he did not get the prize, gets the credit for having been the best full-dressed Highlander at the picnic.

A great number of cuttings from the local press continue to hammer home Neil's dominance in both piping and Highland costume. The frequent stories reveal the intense interest in the 'Highland Games' of a huge number of expatriate Scots:

Scots in Kilts at Shell Mound. Many Clans Represented at the Caledonian Club Games. The Thirty-Second Annual Gathering of the Society.

The shrill music of Neil Lindsay's Scotch bagpipes, attuned to 'Cameronians South' was heard yesterday morning at Shell Mound Park, calling the lads and lasses to their national games and dances.

Since this cutting was dated 1897, the paper puts the first such event at 1865. Neil's scrapbook contains details of the traditional events of a Highland Games, and many records of the achievements of the Scottish Highland emigrants in immensely high-profile tug of war contests.

He himself is frequently portrayed, and photographs and cartoons abound.

On 19 April 1906, Neil's American adventure came to an end, as the San Francisco earthquake wiped out Tevendale & Lindsay's, with the destruction of Sacramento Street. Neil came back to Jura, where Sandy Lindsay, an elderly crofter living in Caigenhouse, took him into his home. Both of them were apparently convinced that they were distantly related but neither seemed very sure in what way. The author has been unable to make the connection either. In due course Sandy died, and left his croft land and house to Neil, who married Mary McIndeor, of Islay. In time they had a daughter called Effie, who married Dan McDougall and became a notable Jura personality in the twentieth century. Neil Lindsay, the new owner of Sandy's house in Caigenhouse, named it Frisco, and it bears its name proudly to the present day.

AUSTRALIA AND CANADA

The passage to Australia took roughly twice as long as that to America, but the

Figure 3. Neil Lindsay at the Highland Games in California.

chances of safe arrival were considered to be much greater. However, there was still a general preference among Highlanders for Canada instead of Australia. This was based on two considerations. Firstly, they had relatives in Canada who sent back favourable reports and, secondly, there was a distinct aversion from the fact that convicts were associated with Australia.

Our proven connections with emigrants to Australia are pitifully few:

The MacLeods. The MacLeods of Mount Pritchard, New South Wales have compiled an excellent family tree which traces their line of descent to the Rev. Neil McLeod, minister of Jura after the long-serving Neil Campbell. Neil MacLeod was minister of Jura from 1759. He died in 1786 and is buried in Kilearnadil. He married the daughter of Archibald Campbell of Jura, and his children and grandchildren became widely scattered. Neil MacLeod was not himself a native of Jura, however, since his wife was Elizabeth Campbell of Jura, the family line is an authentic one.

Alexander MacDougall. Allan MacDougall of Sydney has a clear and proven ancestral connection with Jura, as his father Alexander emigrated late last century. Alexander McDougall's sister Janet was the mother of the recent family of Shaws in Ardmenish, so a close relationship remains with the island.

Janet Lindsay. Keith Wakeling of West Hobart has been tracing his family tree, and following one Janet Lindsay, who was transported to Van Diemen's Land along with her brothers Angus and Donald. His investigations reveal that there were thirteen members in the Lindsay family and that they came from the isle of Jura. Janet and her brothers were convicted for 'sheep stealing' in the year 1849. Janet Lindsay seems to have been 'alias Currie'.

Unfortunately, although there are a number of families of Lindsays in Jura at the time of the 1841 Census, there are none with the names Janet, Angus or Donald. There were two boys, Donald and Angus Lindsay born at Lagg in Jura in 1817 and 1819 to Archibald Lindsay and Flory Darroch. There is no mention of Janet, and the family seems to have left the island before 1841. This promising story looks like a dead end.

With this tiny sample our information about Jura folk in Australia comes to an end. There must of course be many more.

The situation is slightly better in connection with Canada, and here is a small collection of examples of which we can be confident:

Angus McPhee and Jane Buie. Jane Buie was born in Jura, and baptised in 1813, the daughter of Duncan Buie and Ann Buie at Ardfernal. It is believed by the researcher that Angus McPhee also came from Jura, but the couple were married in Colonsay in 1840, so he may well have been a native of that island. This seems born out by the 1841 census which shows them in Killcattan in Colonsay with Angus' parents Donald and Catherine McFee. Angus and Jane have a one-year-old child called Donald at that time. They left Colonsay about 1849 and emigrated to Ontario. Angus died *en route*. Thelma Collens of Oakville, Ontario, has traced this family. Jane Buie was her great grandmother.

Neil Shaw. Born in 1720 on Jura, the son of Neil Shaw and Rachell Clark of Kinuachdrach. He left Jura and met Catherine MacInriver, who had been born in 1728 in Inverary. They were married in 1751 in Kilmartin, and had six children: Mary, Malcolm, Annabella, Duncan, Katherine and Merrion in the 1750s and 1760s. They emigrated to Prince Edward Island, Canada, in 1770. Mary Shaw married one William Lawson, originally of Monzie, Perthshire, and they have a descendant called Sue Jorgenson in Southern California, who has done the investigation.

John Buie. This story starts with the solitary entry in the baptismal register for Archibald Buie, son of John Buie and Jannet Livingstone, baptised on 29 February 1813 in Ardfernal. Other children followed: Christina (1828) and Sinclair, born in Bowmore in 1840.

The family emigrated about 1852 to Arran Township, Grey and Bruce Counties, Ontario, Canada. The local 1871 census for North Bruce shows:

John Buie, Sea Captain, aged ninety, Presbyterian Old Church, living with Neil Darroch (forty), Christina Darroch (forty) and children Archibald (eight), Mary (five) and Jessie (three) His wife Jannet had died in 1857, aged sevety-four and is buried in Henderson Cemetery. His daughter Christina married Neil Darroch in 1860 in Canada.

Neil Darroch was one of the children of Niven Darroch and Mary Buie, who were married in Colonsay in 1823, and may have been born in Jura. This family seems to have emigrated at the same time as the Buies. Captain John Buie's granddaughter Jessie is in a neighbouring farm. He himself died in 1874, aged ninety-three. Dr Neil Watters of Ontario is a great-great-grandson, and has done this research.

Neil Darroch and Catherine Buie. The 1841 census for Jura shows Neil Darroch and Catherine Buie living in Lergybreck with their children. The baptismal register lists nine children between 1819 and 1836, three of whose names appear twice, the first named in each case presumably dying in infancy. The family disappears from Jura before the 1851 census and are lost to view.

However, Thelma Collens, of Angus McFee history (above), has found a gravestone in Duntroon Pioneer Cemetery, Nottawasaga Township, Simcoe County, Ontario:

By grateful children to perpetuate the memory of a loving father and mother, Neil Darrach and Catherine Buie born in the island of Jura, Argyleshire, Scotland, the former in 1789 and died Aug 31, 1860, the latter born 1799, died June 27, 1865. They had emigrated to North Carolina in 1842 and re-emigrated to Canada West in 1857.

Here we have a rare account of people who had moved twice. This also may have been quite common, but the evidence is missing.

Colin and Euphemia McFadyen. Colin McFadyen and his wife Euphemia McInnes were born on Islay in 1805 and 1815. At some point in the 1850s they came to Lagg in Jura where Colin is listed as 'Ferrymen and Farmer'. The 1861 census shows his ten children, ranging in age from twenty-six to five years, as follows: Finlay, Catherine, Donald, Charles, Colin, Margaret, Malcolm, Ann, Duncan and Archibald. By the 1871 census they have left Jura, and we know, from Mrs Helen Norman of Kincardine, Ontario, that the family emigrated there in 1864. They settled in Kincardine Township, where Mrs Norman, their great-granddaughter still resides. Her account of the family gives fascinating details about the times and lives of eleven children and their descendants, also an interesting account of the parents:

> Colin McFadyen was a Sea Captain. He owned his own boat. He carried mail, provisions and people back and forth from Jura to the mainland. On Jura, the McFadyens rented Laird Campbell's estate, on which they ran 600 sheep. The Laird owned Lagg House, a hotel, which they operated for him. Alcoholic drink was not served at Lagg House. The family lived in the hotel. As there was no future on Jura for his seven sons, Colin decided to emigrate to Australia as some of his brothers had done. Euphemia had a brother, Archibald McInnes at Iroquois, Ontario, and another brother at Mount Forest, Ontario. Euphemia won out.
>
> Colin McFadyen brought his nephew Colin Fletcher to Canada with him. He became a minister at Seaforth, Ontario. Ahead of him had come his brother, Donald Fletcher, also a Presbyterian Minister, and their sister and her husband. Colin's sister, Mrs Peter Fletcher, remained in Keppols, in Argyll with her son Edward.

Annie Shaw. Some references are more vague than others. The reference to Annie Shaw comes solely from a newspaper cutting of an Obituary:

> Early Friday morning, Dec. 17th 1920, Mrs James McGlennon passed away at her home in Colborne. Before her marriage she was known as Annie Shaw, and was born on the Island of Jura, off the coast of Scotland in the year 1844. When nine years of age she came to Canada with her parents, the late Mr and Mrs James Shaw, who were for many years residents of Lakeport. Here she married the late James McGlennon, who died in September, 1915.

The report goes on to detail her ten children, and to describe the funeral service. Joseph B. Comstock of Claremont, California is a great grandson of Mrs McGlennon, and informs us that her husband was from the Isle of Man, and that they met in Canada.

In terms of Jura records, Anne Shaw was baptised in Ardfernal in 1844, the daughter of James Shaw and Janet Darroch. There is a record of an older sister Flora. In the 1851 census James Shaw and Mary Shaw are living in Ardfernal, where he is recorded as being a seaman. He is in Lussagiven with his mother in 1841, already a seaman, and Mary Darroch is also still single in Ardfernal. The 1851 census shows more younger children: Nancy (six), John (four) and James and Mary, infant twins. The funeral notice mentions Anne's brother, Captain John Shaw, and also a sister, though only by her married name, and Captain

James Shaw, another brother, so it seems likely that the whole family left in 1853.

John McPhee. Our information about John McPhee also comes from Thelma Collens, who indicates the record of his birth in the baptismal register for 1 December 1814, where he was the son of Malcolm McPhee and Ann Paterson of Crackaig. The family seems to have lived in Brosdale for some time and Duncan, Neil, Jean and Mary, were all born between 1814 and 1826.

There is no sign of them in the 1841 census, and since John McPhee married Hester Galbraith in Colonsay in 1845, it may be that the family went back to Colonsay, from where, with the surname McPhee, they may have originated. John McPhee and his wife emigrated to Ontario in 1847, and we are fortunate to have a newspaper account of his life from the *Paisley Advocate*, 27 June 1907, from which these extracts are taken:

Mr John McPhee, the oldest of the pioneers of this settlement, passed away on Monday afternoon. Mr McPhee was over ninety-two years of age and had retained his vigor and vitality until quite recently. During the winter he began to fail, his visits to town became less frequent, and a few weeks ago ceased, for he was as a sheaf on the canvas, already cut down, and soon to be gathered by the great harvester.

Mr McPhee was born on the Isle of Jura, Argyleshire, Scotland on November 29th 1814, and came to Canada in 1847, the year after his marriage, settling in Mariposa Township. The land in that section having already been taken up, Mr McPhee decided to find a homestead elsewhere, and late in November set out for the new lands in the Queen's Bush. In company with the late Angus Galbraith (presumably his brother-in-law), he came from Victoria County, their route lying from Mariposa to Orillia, taking boat from there to Owen Sound, and walking from the landing place to their destination on the Elora Road North. Mr McPhee did not bring his family until 1854, and the bush was still in its original state of wilderness, so that it was impossible for the wagon to get farther than Invermay. The journey from there to Paisley was walked by Mr and Mrs McPhee, he with a pack on his back, and she with a baby in her arms, and two or three little children trudging bravely beside her. Thus began the home life in Bruce, which was destined to extend to the end of the span allotted to them to be together on this earth. Mrs McPhee, whose maiden name was Hester Galbraith, predeceased her husband about thirteen years. The family are: Angus, on the homestead; Mrs Dugald Campbell of Zion City; Mrs Andrew Neelands of Sarnia, Ontario; John of Crookston, Minn; Neil of Grand Rapids; Alex of Vancouver, who is home at present. The funeral takes place on Wednesday afternoon to Rusk's cemetery, and the services will be conducted by the Rev. J. O'Neill, of the Baptist church, with which congregation the deceased has long been identified as a member and office holder.

THE HUDSON BAY COMPANY LETTER

During the 1820s there were many employees of the Hudson Bay Company who had come from Scotland. The company was gaining power with its trading, commerce and exploration in the new world. Young men would sign on with its ships when they called in at Scottish ports to take on supplies. Many of the emigrants kept in touch with their families in Scotland by writing home, and mail would be directed out to them. There were probably difficulties in the delivery of these items, and a considerable amount of undelivered mail simply got put into storage. In 1974 more than 200 letters were shipped from the company's headquarters in London to Manitoba in Canada. Mrs Judith Hudson Beattie, the keeper of the company archives in Winnipeg has conducted modern research into these letters. More than forty Scottish addressees are among them, and the collection turns out to contain a single solitary letter written from the Red River Settlement [modern day Winnipeg] to the island of Jura. The letter is written from Red River and is dated 18 October 1824.

It was addressed to: Alexander Buie Carpenter North Britain Jura Argyll Care of the Hudson Bay House, Finch Church Street London

It is perhaps understandable that this letter did not arrive. The significant word 'Jura' does seem rather hidden in the address, and may have conveyed little to the company employee responsible.

The writer is one James Livingston, who appears to come from Islay, since he refers to the 'Parish of Kilmeny'. He is married to Sally Buie, Alexander Buie's sister. He addresses Alexander Buie as 'Brother', but is presumably his brother-in-law. A considerable number of Jura girls seem to have got married to lads from Islay, and there are many such records.

As far as the addressee is concerned, a suitable Alexander Buie and his wife Sally Black, appear in the censuses of Jura, where he is recorded as a carpenter and also as a boatbuilder. He had several children, and lived in Feolin Farm and Ardfernal, before retiring to live at Dainsgeir. He had attained the age of 102 years when he died in 1889. His parents, and thus those of his sister Sally, were John Buie and Catharine McCallum.

James Livingstone writes in a clear hand and has a good vocabulary, but his considerable confusion with grammar and spelling makes reading his letter quite a challenge.

> Dear Brother, I take this opportunity to let you know I am in good health at present, and all your friends (*are also*)
>
> I received your letter on the 16th of this month.
>
> In the meantme there are men going to the States of America, so I write these few lines to let you know about trades. [*A deleted line comes here; referred to below as an error!*]
>
> They're all good. Any trade is good, from the tinker to the clerk.
>
> Carpenters from 5 shillings to 6 per day, and labourers; 3 shillings per day. I made a mistake up there!
>
> I send this letter away with those men. Whether you will get here or not you will want to know what I am doing. I am sometimes farming and also working at all trades.
>
> This summer Hugh and I built a church. To let you know the truth I am

not earning much money because I have made a family, and I must stay about them; but a man that is single; he will not be one day idle if he chooses to work every day.

Winter and summer is all the same. There is plenty of work.

For me, I cannot leave the house. I have 5 cattle and a crop, and for that I must stop at home; but I still would not exchange, this day, with the best farmer that I left in the Parish of Kilmeny.

You heard about War being here, but there is no such a thing here since we came.

I will advise you to come as quick as possible. Not you alone, but as many as you can take with you, and (*do not think*) for to take anything with you from that place for you will get everything here cheaper than with you.

A pound of tobacco for 3 shillings and every kind of goat's cheese;

a yard of blue cloth; 5 shillings; a pound of tea; 5 shillings;

a 3 point blanket; 12 shillings; a gallon of Rum; 12 shillings;

a bushel of wheat; 5 shillings.

No more about this; but when you will get this letter you will send another to Lochbuie and let them know that we are all in good health.

No more at present; only I wish that you would have the courage to come!

But mind which way you will come! Mind that you will not engage with the Company or Colony. I am out free!

Now I have some more to tell you yet. James Donald and Hugh; we are Constables.

No more at the same time. No more, only my kind compliments to you and to all my friends as you know them.

James Livingston and Sally your Sister.

To judge from his long life in Jura, Alexander Buie and his family were not to be persuaded to join the Livingstons in Canada, and we have no information about what happened to James and Sally. With these few references to Jura pioneers, we bring our brief study of records relating to the emigration of Jura folk to Canada to a close. We know there was a considerable settlement in Prince Edward Island, and have many rumours of other places, but hard evidence is not easy to come by, and these few accounts must suffice.

SETTLEMENT ELSEWHERE IN SCOTLAND

While people were leaving Jura for the Colonies, we must not think that all others were simply prepared to remain in the island and cope as best they could. During the nineteenth century there would have been many who were dissatisfied with their lot, and who decided to go elsewhere and see if they could do better. It was known that many of the ships sailing for the New World would depart from Greenock, on the Clyde, so no doubt a number of Jura folk decided to leave the island and head for Glasgow and hence for Greenock, in the hope of a passage to North Carolina, Canada, or Australia. Some may have obtained such transport, but it is evident that many did not. Perhaps initially disappointed of their prime objective, many settled in the Clyde ports and found employment.

In the 1970s the author found research into these mainland settlements difficult to pursue. However, modern technology has advanced the cause of population research, and it is now possible to analyse the census of 1881 for the whole of the British Isles, and discover the location and personal details of people by their place of birth.

Such an analysis has now been done, and reveals that in 1881 there were well over 550 people living in Great Britain who were born on Jura. The settlement pattern is concentrated in Scotland, as there are only two families in England. These are: Dugald Taylor (25), born on Jura, his wife Elizabeth, from Helensburgh, and their two small daughters living in Sunderland, where he was a barman. Malcolm Shaw (51) lived at Chatham, in Kent, with his wife Louisa Susan, and his twenty- and sixteen-year-old sons. His wife came from Chatham and the boys were born there. He was a shipwright and they were both riveters. Apart from these two, England and Wales appear only because Jura men are aboard ships in the ports of Falmouth, Cardiff and the Isle of Man. They will be looked at later.

In Scotland the general pattern which appeared thirty years earlier in Greenock is maintained. Only a very small number of married couples have left Jura together. Indeed the complete total is only thirteen. They mostly bear traditional Jura names. There is one family each of: Black, Clark, Darroch, Fletcher, Keith, Lindsay, McCraine, McDonald, McGill, McLean, McNeill, Rankin and Shaw. Four settled in Argyll and the rest in Lanarkshire. This bears out the contention that those who married on Jura generally did so because they had expectations of being able to go on living there.

It is also not surprising to find that the census shows only a small number of children who were born on Jura. The total is forty-six. Some of these were the children of the thirteen families above. Others were born on Jura while their parents lived there pursuing their employment. The families have now moved on. So there are Jura-born children living in Arbroath, where their father is the lighthousekeeper on the Bell Rock light. Another lighthousekeeper's children live on Tiree. A catechist and teacher, formerly on Jura, now lives in the Small Isles with his Jura-born children. A gardener in Stevenston and another in Largs have also spent some years on Jura, where their children were born.

The people who left Jura and are to be found living in Scotland as adults of various ages were, by and large unmarried girls and boys. Of these some eighty or so girls are still unmarried at the time of the census, the majority being between fourteen and thirty-five. There are far fewer unmarried men at the same time, in fact only about fifteen.

The girls and women are in all the usual expected jobs. Their employment pattern looks like this: general servants, 18; domestic servants, 21; kitchen maid/housemaid/table maid, 4; housekeeper, 5; cook, 9; laundress, 2; washer woman, 2; dairymaid, 5; farm worker, 4; dressmaker, 5; factory, 4 (printfield, spooler thread mill, machinist, cotton winder); shop woman, 1.

There are eight young unmarried men who are farm servants. There are two labourers, an apprentice grocer, a ferry assistant, a carter, and a twenty-nine-year-old Free Church minister.

The success story seems to centre most on those who left Jura as unmarried

young people, but who found work elsewhere in Scotland, and found also wives
and husbands. These are mostly settled families by 1881, ranging from young
couples to aged couples and widowed individuals. It seems to make little difference
whether it is the husband or the wife in these families who comes from Jura,
the occupations of the head of household seem very similar.

Twenty-six occupations seem statistically important, and are set out here.
Either a Jura boy has found the job and married a local girl, or a Jura girl has
found a local boy with the occupation and married him.

Employment	Husband from Jura	Wife from Jura
Agricultural Labourer	1	2
Boatbuilder	2	1
Blacksmith	3	4
Carpenter	6	2
Carter	4	6
Coal Merchant	1	2
Crofter	1	1
Dairyman	2	2
Distillery Worker	3	3
Engine Fitter	2	1
Farmer	11	9
Fisherman	4	6
Gamekeeper	1	2
Gardener	5	2
Joiner	8	8
Labourer	13	25
Mason	1	4
Merchant/Grocer	2	3
Policeman	5	4
Shepherd	11	3
Ship's Carpenter	7	2
Spirit Merchant	1	2
Slate Quarrier	3	5
Storekeeper	1	3
Tailor	1	2
Turner	1	1

There are a large number of other occupations available. Jura men are to be
found working at the following jobs (one each unless otherwise specified): brewer;
boilermaker; cab proprietor; clerk; custom's officer; cooper (2); draper; physician
(2); fireman (2); herd; grain storeman; hammerman; cattleman; commercial
traveller (2); iron moulder (2); ironship builder; lock keeper; laundryman; minister
(Free Church); minister (Parish Church); painter (3); pastry baker; publican;

porter; plumber; shipwright; steamboat agent; steam boatman; stevedore foreman; warehouseman; water man; watchman.

Jura women have also married men with a different variety of jobs as well as those in the shared list above: artist; butcher; calico printer; carrier; dyer; hotel keeper; lodgekeeper; plasterer; ploughman (2); plumber; railway brakeman; riveter; roadman; sailmaker; school superintendent (ladies); teacher; tinplate worker; van driver; yacht master.

As well as the above there are of course a number of old people who have presumably remained in their chosen community and not returned to Jura. A number of these are in various 'combination poorhouses', and some are in lunatic asylums.

The 1881 census gives detailed information about the families of all of the above. Their home addresses are known, as are full details of their occupations, the birthplaces and ages of all their children, and similar details about other relatives or visitors who may be in the house at the time. This would be in itself a fascinating study, and no doubt will be followed up by people anxious to trace their Jura ancestry.

There remain two significant areas of interest.

First it seems important to pay some attention to the powerful tradition in Jura which associates its men with seafaring, and which gives rise to the term 'Mariner's Row', for Caigenhouse, and many claims of the numbers of retired ships' captains who lived there in the early years of the twentieth century. In this regard the census gives us an interesting picture of what was happening on the seas around Great Britain. There follows a list of the vessels which had native-born Jura men as members of their crew on census day in 1881. Only the Jura crew members are noted:

The Clyde	Anderston	*Rose*	Able Bodied Seaman:	Alan MacDougall (24)
		Chevalier	Ordinary Seaman:	James MacDougall (25)
		Shamrock	Carpenter:	Duncan Darroch (44)
		Cedar	AB Seaman:	Malcolm MacDougall (24)
	Tradeston	*Inverary Castle*	AB Seaman:	John Shaw (20)
		Amethyst	AB Seaman:	Dugald Clark (23)
	Blythswood	*Staffa*	Sailor:	John Buie (26)
	Greenock	*Cartsburn*	Mate:	John Fleming (46)
		Chesapeake	Engineer:	Duncan MacDougall (47)
		Flying Dutchman	Master:	Duncan Keith (30)
			AB Seaman:	James McCraine (27)
		Flying Sylph	AB Seaman:	John Darroch (19)
	Rothesay	*Bute*	Carpenter:	Neil Shaw (51)
		Argyle	Mate:	Malcolm MacInnes (43)
	Cumbrae	*Lancelot*	Seaman:	Angus Brown (33)

Caledonian	Fort	*SS Lochiel*	Chief Mate:	John Darroch (32)
Canal	Augustus			
	Fort William	*Pioneer*	Seaman:	John MacDougall (25)
			Fireman:	Norman MacLean (37)
	Oban	*Gondolier*	Master:	John McKechnie (39)
Tobermory		*Nyanza*	Steward:	Duncan McLarty (43)
Stornoway		*Clansman*	Stevedore:	Angus Shaw (25)
Stranraer		*Flying Foam*	Master:	Alexander MacDougall (42)
Isle of Man Ramsay		*Flying Huntress*	Master:	John Lindsay (32)
			Mate:	Neil Darroch (32)
			AB Seaman:	John Blair (22)
Falmouth		*Flying Kestrel*	Master:	John Campbell (45)
			Mate:	John Rankin (40)
			Ordinary Seaman:	John Campbell (21)
Cardiff		*Cape Wrath*	Carpenter:	Archibald Lindsay (38)

There were presumably other Jura men on the date of the census who were actually on the high seas, and not accessible to the census-takers.

Some twenty other seafarers were on land and at home on the date of the census.

Angus Clark (35), Master Mariner; John McNeill (36); Master Mariner; (both in Govan); Hugh McDougall (37); Ship's Captain; John McPhail (39); Ship Master (both in the Barony, Glasgow.)

The census shows many ordinary seaman; such as: Alexander Darroch; Islay; Angus Shaw, Donald Shaw; Kilfinan; David Campbell; Dunoon; Donald Darroch; Barony; Angus McDougall; Wigtown; Donald McDougall; Row; James McDonald; Belville St Greenock; Allan Rankin; Malcolm Rankin; Regent St Greenock; Archibald McLarty; Glasgow; Duncan Darroch; 69, Dale St Govan: Neil Darroch; 24 Washington St Glasgow; Neven Darroch; 115, Stobcross St., Glasgow; Hugh McGill; 17 Piccadilly St Glasgow.

Many others are associated with the sea in other ways, but the above list gives good reason to see why retired mariners might arrive home in Jura in such numbers that Caigenhouse could be called 'Mariners' Row'.

The last matter which concerns us here is where the people we have looked at from the 1881 Census were actually living in Scotland. The census-takers were operating on the basis of old Church Parishes, and some of the names they use are rather obscure, especially in Argyll, however, these have been deciphered and modern township names substituted. The numbers which follow represent either individuals living on their own, or as lodgers with other families, or families in their own right:

Tiree	2
Colonsay and Oronsay	3
Islay (various parishes)	31
North & South Knapdale	24

Craignish, Glassary & Kilmartin	25
Island of Mull	8
Oban and surrounding area	32
Dalmally & Tyndrum	4
Inverary	2
Kintyre	7
Cowall Peninsula	14
Bute & Cumbrae	7
Largs, Ardrossan and South	13
Dunbarton (various communities)	19
Port Glasgow, Inverkip, Paisley	19
Renfrew and nearby communities	12
Greenock, all areas	86
Glasgow (Govan, Barony, + others)	132
Lanark (Hamilton, Bothwell, etc.)	6
Edinburgh, Leith, Bathgate, Boness	9
Borders (Selkirk, Peebles, etc.)	6
Angus & Fife	3
The North & North-west	12
Central (Falkirk, Sitrling, Perth)	8

It is not surprising to find the people who left Jura concentrated in Argyll, and in the industrial area around Greenock and Glasgow, but as the map will show, small numbers of Jura-born folk are scattered quite widely, if thinly, across Scotland. Here we leave the people of 1881.

CONCLUSION

In 1794 Francis Stewart observed, 'The spirit of emigration is still powerful in the island, and requires considerable alterations to extinguish it.'

Such alterations would have had to comprise a better standard of living for the inhabitants. Opportunities for the young people to find gainful employment on the island. Investment in its economy, and the promotion of some kind of independence for the people. No such alterations took place.

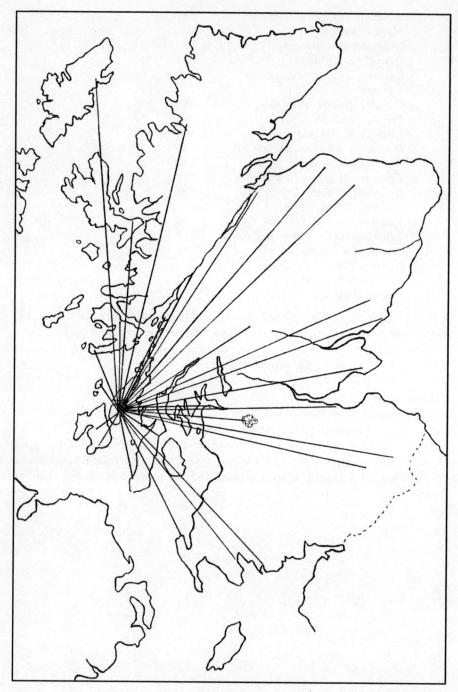

Map 17. This map shows the pattern of settlement of people born in Jura shown by the census of 1881.

VII

The Nineteenth Century

27

People in the Nineteenth Century

Since there were no systematic population records during the eighteenth century, an attempt to accurately construct a picture of the people living in Jura at that time was inevitably bound to fail. While the 'Old Parish Register of Baptisms' and various tenancy records gave a rough impression of the general situation, and a number of individuals could be placed in their island setting with some certainty, many gaps remained throughout the period.

During the nineteenth century the situation changed dramatically, at least from 1841 when the first national census recorded everyone living in each parish in the nation. This practice was followed every ten years, and the censuses to 1891 are all now open to public inspection and analysis. In addition to this valuable source, Statutory Registers of Births, Marriages and Deaths were begun in 1855, and constitute a national archive open to public inspection until the present day.

Here are the figures for the population of Jura, starting with Walker's 1775 census:

1755 1801 1811 1821 1831 1841 1851 1861 1871 1881 1891 1901 1911
658 1202 1157 1264 1312 1320 1064 1038 943 931 717 625 570

The decline in population continued through the twentieth century, and will frequently be discussed.

The combination of statutory registration and the censuses from 1861 onwards makes population reconstruction from this date a fairly straightforward matter. However, the first two censuses are not backed up by a register of deaths, making it difficult to account accurately for the disappearance of names from the census records before 1861. Missing people may have left the island, but it is impossible to be certain that they have not died there, and now lie in an unmarked grave. Few gravestones from this period survive. There are only some fifteen inscriptions from these years in the three Jura graveyards.

Further difficulties arise with the 1841 census. Although from 1851 the information becomes detailed and reliable, the first national census gives the impression of being something of a beginners exercise. Married women are mostly given their husband's names, thus losing the valuable information about maiden names. Most adults' ages are rounded *down* to the nearest multiple of five. Thus people are thirty-five, or fifty, or eighty-five.

The baptismal register was an important source for the early 1700s, having survived between 1704 and 1734. Subsequent records have long been missing, but the baptismal register from 1810 surfaced again and continued unbroken through the century accompanied by a very simple minister's record of marriages for the same period. These records give population information which reaches back thirty years before the first national census, and can be taken in conjunction with it.

It is with this baptismal register that our study of the nineteenth-century population will begin.

THE BAPTISMAL RECORD

There are 1074 individual entries of baptism in the baptismal register from 1811 to the end of 1841. The year 1841 has been chosen as the date when the baptismal record can be linked to the first national census. The present population study proposes to consider the northern islands of the parish as a separate matter, so baptismal entries for Scarba, Lunga, Belnahua and the Garvellochs are deducted from the total. There were sixty-eight baptisms here during the period in question. This figure is greatly influenced by the forty which took place among the slate workers of Belnahua from 1818 onwards. The baptisms in the northern islands have been deducted, with the exception of four families who moved to mainland Jura during the period in question. There were also eleven entries which provide insufficient evidence to establish who is involved.

When this is taken into account, the corrected total of entries for mainland Jura is 999.

Detailed study of this record with a view to collecting all the baptisms for a single family under one entry produces a total of 290 different families whose infant arrivals are recorded in the register.

This register will be used as a source for a study of the people of Jura during the early part of the nineteenth century, however it should not be forgotten that in the first instance it was a record of the administration of the sacrament of baptism on the infant or older children of the families who were living on, or who arrived to live on, Jura.

The minister recorded the name of the child, the name of the father and the maiden name of the mother. The exact date the baptism was performed was noted, as also was the place of residence of the family. In some cases where the baptism came long after the birth, the date of birth was also noted. Several children might be baptised on the same day, and the note 'E. D.' (*'eodem die'*); is set in place of a date. Sometimes the date is simply blank, and it is necessary to assume that the baptism took place on the date of the previous one. If only the minister's record had come down to us, it would set its own limits on our study. However, we are fortunate in the occurrence of the first national census in 1841, which gives us a valuable benchmark to set against the baptismal record of the previous thirty years.

Everyone present on the day of the census was recorded, including of course all the children. The census taker was unaware whether they had been baptised or not, and it was no part of his remit to record this fact.

A comparison of the records in the baptismal register with those in the 1841 census is most intriguing. Many families who appear on both the census and in the baptismal register have some children present on the day of the census who are in the baptismal register alongside others who are not. The ages given frequently bracket the two categories. The presence of infants in the baptismal register who do not later appear in the census is easily explained by the likelihood that they have died in the interval, and certainly there is a great deal of evidence of child mortality from this period. But what of the children who are present in the census, but who are not in the baptismal register?

It is impossible at this distance to penetrate the actual circumstances in which a succession of ministers recorded these baptisms. The Rev. Donald MacNicol was responsible for the years 1810 and 1811, until his translation to Dunoon in December 1811. Archibald McTavish was Jura's minister until 1823, followed by the Rev. Alexander Kennedy. When baptism records are entered against the names of people present in the 1841 census an intriguing situation is revealed. A considerable variety of circumstances appear in which children were apparently not baptised. Some of these are easy to understand. Where it is the first child, or the first few children in the family who are unbaptised, and baptism then starts and is continued, it may well be that this record indicates an approximate date of the arrival of the family on Jura. The earlier children may have been baptised in their previous parish.

In 1841, the year of the census itself, the record is patchy, and it may be that, depending on the date of birth of the baby, it was not possible to arrange a baptism before the census took place.

It may be that the gaps in the baptismal record were not due to the neglect or dilatoriness of Mr Kennedy, but to the fact that certain islanders were refusing the 'Sacrament' at the hand of the 'Parish Minister'. Although it was many years before the Free Church became established on Jura, children may well have been being baptised informally in an underground movement which did not result in an entry in the baptismal register. This is, of course, highly speculative, but it is most interesting that when Lachlan MacKenzie arrived in 1850, he immediately began a campaign to make good any omissions in baptisms during the previous incumbencies. The nature of the record changes dramatically about 1855, and entire families appear with dates which must be dates of birth, rather than a record of when the baptism took place. Some of these baptisms go back to the 1820s. Even after Mr MacKenzie's efforts the census of 1841 shows about 125 children within the population who were never baptised.

BAPTISMAL RECORD FAMILIES

We have seen how from the date of the rediscovery of the baptismal register in 1811 to the year of the first census in 1841, 290 families had one or more children baptised on the mainland of Jura. It might have been expected that a family on Jura in the early part of the nineteenth century, once settled and producing babies, would stay in the same community or dwelling house during the time of the family's early development. The baptismal record shows that this is not the case. During the thirty years between 1811 and 1841, about one-fifth of the families moved at least once. The actual number was sixty-three. Of these, twenty-one moved twice, while three moved house three times and one moved four times during the period. These family movements seem to occur throughout the island. There is a good deal of movement within closely related communities, e.g., the farms in the south: Ardfin; Brosdale; Dunans and Crackaig; or the communities around Craighouse Inn. There is also movement between the townships of Keils, Feolin, Lergybreck, Knockrome, Ardfernal and Ardmenish. However, there are also movements from one end of the island to the other. Two families move between Kinuachdrach and Crackaig, while Tarbert, Lagg and Lussagiven see movements to Brosdale and Knockrome, as well as amongst themselves. As one might expect, half a dozen of the families who move twice return to base after a period somewhere else.

NAMES IN THE BAPTISMAL RECORD

A fairly detailed analysis was conducted of the surnames and Christian names of the people whom records showed were living on Jura during the eighteenth century. An update will reveal how the situation has changed.

Both the surnames of fathers and the maiden names of mothers have been studied. This gives a name pool of 580 surnames. We are fortunate that the baptismal record takes pains to record the mother's maiden name in virtually every case.

Ninety-two different surnames occur in the 290 families of the baptismal record.

Three long established families are now numerically dominant in the population. There are seventy-one parents called Darroch; seventy called McDougall and sixty-two called Shaw.

These three family groups account for almost exactly one third of the population sample.

If we add in the Campbells (37) and the Buies (35); then the 'Big Five', with 275 individuals account for over 43% of the adult parents in Jura between 1810 and 1841.

The detailed study of adult names in the baptismal register one hundred years earlier allows us to see how the population has altered. At that time Darroch and Shaw were the most abundant names, with Buie coming a close third.

McArthurs, Campbells, McLeans and McDougalds all followed closely, with these seven families accounting for just over half the family surnames in the island. This group contains the 'Big Five' of the nineteenth century although the McDougalls have grown at the expense of other names to become the second most numerous. In the early 1700s the McDougalds came at number six.

The next eight names in the nineteenth-century register have from twenty-two to thirteen representatives. These families are: Black, Lindsay, McLean, McEachern, McPhail, McArthur, McCraine and McNeil. This group accounts for a further 21 per cent of the total.

Blacks, McLeans, McPhails, McArthurs, McCraines and McNeils all had a significant presence in the early 1700s. The Lindsays are now well established, with twenty individuals in the register, although the first Lindsay did not appear in documents until 1764. Budge believed them to be an ancient Jura family, first coming to operate the Lagg ferry. Although there is a single McEachan (sic) in the 1704 register, there were no McEacherns, although a John McEachern appears at Feolin in 1764. However, by the 1800s there are sixteen McEacherns in the baptismal register.

The next group consists of those eleven names which appear from ten to six times: Keith, 10; McPhee, 10; McGilvray, 10; McColl, 9; McLeod, 9; McAlister, 8; McInnes, 7; Rankin, 6; McArtan, 6; Livingstone, 6; McDonald, 6.

These eleven families account for a further 14 per cent of the total. All but two are making their appearance for the first time. There is a single McCartna in the 1704 baptism register and a McCartan in 1764. There is also a single McIlvra, presumably also McGilvray. There are five families of McInnes in the early record. None of the remaining names features anywhere in the eighteenth century.

The appearance of John Keith of Knockrome in the first year of the rediscovered record in 1810 is particularly interesting. We noted in a previous chapter that Budge adduces evidence of the family's ancient connection with Jura. The 'nil returns' from the various records of the eighteenth century was certainly not conclusive evidence that there were no Keiths on the island then. The new baptismal register establishes their presence with nine fathers, although, perhaps strangely, only one mother!

We have looked so far at twenty-three surnames from the 1810 to 1841 baptismal record. People with these names account for 79 per cent of the 634 parents in the record.

There remain sixty-eight different surnames in the record. These are listed by their number of occurrences:

5 times: Fletcher, Gray, McFarlane, McNiven, McPherson, Smith.

4 times: Brown, Clark, McCallum, McCannel, McFadyen, McGill, McIsaac, McKellar.

3 times: Gillies, McGregor, McIntyre, McLarty, McMillan, McVean, Paterson.

twice: Grant, Kennedy, Lammont, McCormick, McDuffie, McKay, McKeory, McLellan, Turner.

The parental names in the baptismal register are completed by the thirty-eight further surnames which each occur only once:

Blinkison, Blackwood, Brodie, Buchanan, Cameron, Carlyle, Carmichael, Conley, Crichton, Currie, Dryden, Duffie, Galbraith, Halliburton, Hamilton, Harkness, Head, Johnstone, Kerr, Lamond, Matelane, McCalman, McCorquidale, McEwen, McIriosh, McLaine, McLauchlan, McTavish, McVorran, Park, Sever, Sinclair, Spears, Spence, Stevenson, Sutherland, Thomson, White.

Within this catalogue of names are a few who probably represent a continuation of families established in Jura in the previous century.

The McNamoiles, later called McMillans were represented by nine families in the 1700s. The Lammonts had eight families and the Clarks seven. There were five Gillies and four McCallums; three McDuffies and three McKays. The McLartys of 1800 may be the continuation of the McLaortrichs of former days, as no doubt are the McFadyens, or McPhadyens, the modern form of McPhaden. The McIntyres, McPhersons and McNivens of the 1800s may or may not be continuous with the single inhabitants with these names a hundred years earlier. The names are common, and families may have come and gone. As an example, Ann Thomson of Corran House in 1813 was married to Harry Hamilton. Both were incomers and had no connection with the considerable number of Thompsons who lived on Jura in the early 1700s, who seem to have disappeared.

One family we can be sure of: John McIsack and his wife Mary Campbell lived at Knocknafeolaman in 1704, where their son Donald was born. The McIsaacs remained the millers to the estate throughout the next two centuries, and in 1898 we find John McIsaac giving up the occupancy of the mill and the millership. The name McIsaac occurs frequently in the very early historical records of Argyll. One of them, spelling his name MacIosaig, signed the Ragman Roll in the time of Edward I of England, and in the year 1544 one John MacIsaac was chamberlain to the estate of Craignish. The miller's family retained a dwelling at Milltown, and descendants remained on the island until recent times.

We are now in a position to review the comparison between the names in use on Jura 100 years later than our earlier study. A number of prominent families occupy a similar position after 100 years: Darrochs, Shaws, Campbells, Buies, McLeans and McPhails.

Some surnames are more abundant at the end of the hundred-year period: McDougalls have moved up from seventh position to second; Blacks from eighteenth to seventh; McCraines from fourteenth to eighth and the McNeils from twenty-seventh to thirteenth.

Some have become less dominant: the McArthurs have dropped back from third to fourteenth. The McMillans from eighth to forty-second. The Clarks from tenth to twenty-fifth.

A number of names have survived with only a few representatives, and with similar numbers apparently to those they had a 100 years earlier. These probably represent a modest but continuing presence: Gillies, McDuffie, McCallum, McFadyen, McIsaac, McLarty, McPherson,

Some names are now substantially present in the 1800s, although they were either absent altogether, or only marginally present in the 1700s. These are: Lindsay, 20; McEachern, 16; Keith, 10; McGilvray, 10; McPhee, 10; McColl, 9; McLeod, 9; McAlister, 8; Livingstone, 6; McDonald, 6; and Rankin, 6.

One feature which has changed dramatically is the nature of the names themselves. In the 1704 Record there are only nine family surnames which do not begin with 'Mc'. If the most abundant twenty names are discounted, as in the lists above, the remaining surnames contain only one name which does not start with 'Mc' (Ferguson).

The vast majority of these 'Mc's have now disappeared without trace. Some of them were important groups in the eighteenth century, although many of the names sounded somewhat exotic to our ears. Names no longer in evidence in the nineteenth century are: McBhrion, McCalken, McCalrid, McCambridge, McCleisich, McColly, McEnlea, McEnrich, McGhoile, McGoun, McIlerand, McIlghlass, McIlhavish, McIllemichell, McIllis, McIllmartin, McIloran, McIlphedir, McIlvoil, McInleadh, McInriver, McInvine, McIver, McKianalich, McOlonaich, McO'Shenoge, McPhetrus, McQuarie, McSwine, McVastane, McVurich;

Even more striking is the appearance in the nineteenth-century record of many names which do not contain the patronymic 'Mc'. Within the group of sixty-eight surnames which feature five times or less in the baptismal record there are twenty-seven which feature the 'Mc' prefix, and more than half of these are established by having several examples.

It seems reasonable to explain this change by the possibility that various agencies are now importing people to work on the island. Campbell of Jura has need of tradesmen and estate staff. The distillery is in operation. The ferries are working. Surely it is thus that people arrive on the island with somewhat unexpected surnames: Blinkison, Blackwood, Brodie, Buchanan, Conley, Halliburton, Harkness, Head, Matelane, Park, Sever, Spears, Spence, Sutherland and White.

There is one footnote on an odd phenomenon. It was noticeable in the 1704 Register than there could be considerable differences in the numbers of mothers and father with the same surname. There is one rather startling example in the 1810 Register, where there are twenty fathers called Shaw, but forty-two mothers with the same name. The minister's record of marriages during the same period produces an even more striking imbalance. Between 1811 and 1841 the minister conducted marriages in which ten men called Shaw were involved, while during the same period there were thirty-six brides of that name. Some explanation seems called for, but none is readily apparent.

CHRISTIAN NAMES

When the Christian names in use early in the eighteenth century were studied, it was remarkable how names were chosen by the families.

Twenty-five names covered the entire spectrum in the case of the boys, while only twenty-one girl's names were in use.

In the period from 1810 to 1841 the pool of names in use for the parents of the baptismal families has increased, no doubt due to the arrival of many more incomers. The total of male names has gone up to thirty-five, while that for females has gone up to twenty-five.

In the earlier century the four commonest boys' names in use were John, Donald, Duncan and Archibald, and now, 100 years later that situation still obtains. These four names accounted for 66 per cent of the entire list, and they remain at the top of the nineteenth-century list. However, in the nineteenth-century record, it is necessary to include the first six names to reach 66 per cent. It may be interesting to see the order of frequency of the commoner male names:

	1704–34	1810–41
1st	John	John
2nd	Donald	Donald
3rd	Duncan	Duncan
4th	Archibald	Archibald
5th	Neil	Malcolm
6th	Malcolm	Alexander
7th	Angus	Neil
8th	Gilbert	Dugald
9th	Dougald	Angus
10th	Alexander	James
11th	Hew/Aobh	Hugh
12th	Niven	Lauchlan
13th	Lauchlan	Alan

It is remarkable how consistent the two lists are after the passage of several generations. Of course, the 1810 list contains many names which indicate plainly incoming surnames, e.g., Bartholomew, Edmond, Harry, Hector, Samuel and William. The ten most numerous surnames of the fathers in the register amount to 176 individuals and, of these, all but ten have Christian names drawn from the thirteen names in the list above.

To complete the study, the following list takes the 1810 names on down the frequency occurrence from Lauchlan and Alan: Peter, 4; Murdoch, Samuel, William, all 3; Colin, Gilbert, Niven, Thomas, all 2.

The remaining names occur only once: Andrew, Bartholomew, Coll, Duffie, Edmond, Harry, Hector, Michael, Nicol, Robert, Rodger, Torquil.

When we turn to the names in use for girls in the early eighteenth century and compare them with the names of the mothers in the 1810 register, we find a similar situation.

The four most numerous girls' names in 1704 were Mary, Finwall, Catherine and More, or Mor. These four accounted for 68 per cent of all the names.

In the 1810 register Mary is still the dominant name with sixty-nine occurrences against thirty-seven for the next most abundant. Finwall has disappeared to be replaced with its more modern version of Flora or Flory, and Mor has also been replaced by its modern form as Marion or Sarah.

Catherine remains popular, but the picture of the four commonest names is changed by the increased popularity of the name Anne, which has moved up from seventh to second place.

The most popular four names now become: Mary, Anne, Catherine and Marion. Again it is necessary to broaden the group to the first seven names to reach 70 per cent of the total, an indication again of the prominence of the Christian names used by incoming families:

	1704–34	1810–41
1st	Mary	Mary
2nd	Finwall	Anne
3rd	Catherine	Catherine
4th	More	Marion/Sarah
5th	Margaret	Flora/Flory
6th	Christine	Margaret
7th	Ann	Isabella/Bell
8th	Effie	Christian
9th	Florence	Janet
10th	Janet	Effy
11th	Isobel	Peggy
12th	Euffine	Jean

Again the traditional families show the most conservative use of names. The remaining list, with numbers of occurrence, reveals the presence again of some evident incomers: Elizabeth/Betty, 8; Nancy, 6; Chirsty, 4; Jane, 3; Barbara, 3; Lilly, 2. The remainder have a single occurrence each: Susan, Sally, Rosanna, Meron, Ellison, Cicely.

CHILDREN

We have confined the above study to the names of the 580 parents who presented children for baptism during the years in question.

During this period over a thousand children were baptised. A small group have no name entered in the register. When these are subtracted there remain 999 records of baptisms on the mainland of Jura; 517 boys and 482 girls were christened.

An analysis of their Christian names shows little difference from the names of their parents. The eleven most abundant names chosen for boys in the period remain exactly the same as the eleven commonest names given to their fathers. The exact order is slightly different, with 'Neil' moving up from seventh place to third, and displacing Duncan, Archibald, Alexander and Malcolm.

The complete pool of Christian names has increased from thirty-three in the parents to thirty-eight in the sons, but twenty-seven names are common to both lists, and the increase comes from a few more less common names often associated with incoming families.

In the case of the mothers and their daughters the picture is very similar. Of the twenty-one names in use amongst the mothers, all but four are similarly in use amongst the daughters. The first fourteen names in ascending order of occurrence are common to both lists. Mary remains first by a large margin. Anne and Catherine are hard to separate in second and third place. Several of the remaining eleven names move up or down a little in order, but the changes are not significant.

Four of the single occurrences amongst the mothers, which we attributed to incoming family choices, have disappeared, but there is evidently a continuing influence from incoming families, and this produces twelve new Christian names. Helen occurs three times and Rachel twice. The other ten each occur once. Taken as a group they stand out in sharp contrast to the names of choice of the estabished Jura families, as will easily be recognised: Rachel, Elinor, Esther, Grace, Henrietta, Joanna, Julia, Kenallis, Miny and Nelly.

BAPTISMAL FAMILIES ABSENT FROM THE 1841 CENSUS

When all the records are brought together, there are 129 families in the baptismal register who leave no trace on the 1841 census. These have often complicated relationships, frequently with husbands remarrying after the death of a first wife. These families have been studied to see whether either parents or children are recorded in the Statutary Register of Deaths which started in 1855.

Five families, though absent in 1841, had children who died on Jura at later dates. These will be looked at later. The remaining 125 families who appear in the baptismal register simply disappear from Jura without trace before 1841.

The argument for searching for offspring on the island went as follows: The records where baptisms were recorded in the earliest years of the record (i.e., 1810 and the few years immediately following) probably relate to couples who have had the majority of their children in the years before the record starts. There are twenty-six families who had their last children in the years between 1810 and 1815. These baptisms would relate to children whose mothers might be in their late forties at this time. By the 1841 census the parents would be quite old, and might well be expected to have died. However, it was thought that their children could still to be living on Jura. This turns out simply not to be the case. They are all absent from the censuses of 1841 and 1851, and do not appear in the Death Register.

We might hope for confirmation of the deaths of these parents on gravestone inscriptions. However, the burial customs in Jura in the eighteenth and nineteenth centuries bear on this problem. In east coast towns and in urban communities one might expect to find a considerable number of records confirmed by gravestone inscriptions. These expectations are not well borne out in Jura, and for several reasons. Jura was remote and probably had no one resident on the island who could cut inscriptions. The population was far from prosperous, and an inscribed stone may have been too expensive for many to contemplate. However, there seems to have been a long-standing tradition on Jura of using an unmarked stone to record the position of a grave. A suitable boulder would be fetched from the surrounding moorland and installed at the head of the grave. This placed reliance on local tradition to record the location of all burials. In the earlier years of the twentieth century Mary Campbell of Keils was responsible for much of this information. She died, sadly, without recording her information. The torch was picked up and carried by Donald Black, who was often urged to make some permanent record of his knowledge. He, too, died without leaving a record. Mention has already been made of recent disturbance of the graves in Kilearnadil. There seems little doubt that the local early tradition of uninscribed stones was in place during the period in question, and goes some way to explain why so few inscribed stones are present.

Taking the three graveyards together, there are only fifty-three stones with legible inscriptions between 1800 and 1855, and only one in the eighteenth century.

As far as shedding light on what happened to any of our 125 baptismal families, only three stones have any relevance at all.

John Buie and Catherine McCallum buried their daughter Isabella in 1816, aged thirteen. There is a much later record of their having another daughter, Catherine, baptised at Knockbreac in 1832, after which they disappear from view.

Tarbert cemetery has the following inscription:

Here lie the earthly remains of Lachlin Darroch late farmer in Lagg who departed this life, 25th Dec A.D. MDCCCXXII aged 25 years to whose memory this stone is erected by his disconsolate widow and his affectionate father.

Lauchlin Darroch and Mary Shaw had a son called Colin baptised in Lagg in 1813, but again, apart from noting that they had a sad Christmas Day in 1822, the burial sheds no light.

One of the more unusual incoming names in the baptismal record is that of Ellison Park, wife of Thomas Grant. The couple are living in Miltown, and have infants baptised in 1828, 1829 and 1831. The children are named Thomas, William, Thomas and John Charles. The renaming of a second child after the first dies is a matter we will consider later. It seems reasonable to assume that Thomas Grant is associated with the distillery, either as worker, manager, or in an excise capacity. In this case there is a relevant gravestone in Keils, as follows:

Ellison Park – 1831 – 22
also her two sons – Thos. & Charles John Grant – 16mths & 19 days
erected by her husband – Thomas Grant
father-in-law Thos. Park.

Thomas and Charles John were both baptised on 5 March 1831. Presumably they were twins, and Ellison died as a result of complications during the birth. The previous Thomas had lived more than a year, and had his name inscribed on the stone. Note further confirmation of the family's mainland origins with the use of a rare 'double-barrelled' Christian name. Before 1841 Thomas Grant's appointment came to an end and he left Jura with William and the surviving twin, Thomas.

This ends our slight evidence for mortality as a cause of the disappearance of our group of families with children between 1810 and 1815.

The above group of fifteen or so seem to be a bit early to take their place in the 'second wave' of the emigrations. Although there is no firm evidence, it may still be a sound inference that many of these parents died on Jura before 1841, and that their children moved away.

Some baptismal register families have already been noted under 'emigration': William McDougall and Catherine Buie of Lergybreck; Jane Buie, the daughter of Duncan and Anne Buie of Ardfernal, who married Angus McPhee; John Buie and Janet Livingstone of Ardfernal; Neil McNeil and Marion McDougall of Tarbert; and Torquil Shaw and his wife Ann.

Some familes may just have 'passed through', like Ellison Park above-mentioned. We have seen that Thomas Grant and his wife came to Miltown to work, probably at the distillery, and left, either, disheartened, or at the end of their tour of duty.

When studying the surnames and Christian names of the baptismal register families we were able to guess at incomers with some ease, and here they are again in our 125 group.

From their surnames we may suggest that they came to the island to work on the estate, in the distillery, or for some special purpose. They may not have liked Jura, and may very well not have stayed long. Even in recent years there have been examples of culture shock when distillery workers from Glasgow have been somewhat shocked as what passes for 'amenity' on a Hebridean island, and more than one family didn't stay too long.

Bearing all this in mind we have a few families to nominate whose disappearance before the 1841 census may be simply explained as 'moving on'.

Bartholomew Blinkison and Elizabeth Sever with William,	bap. '36
Nicol Black and Isabella Crichton with Margaret,	bap. '39
Neil McKellar and Barbara McCannel with William,	bap. '38
Robert Cameron and Anne Shaw with Dugald,	bap. '38
James Grant and Ann McCalman with Donald,	bap. '10
Samuel Smith and Anne Campbell with Anne,	bap. '37

Donald Buchanan and Nancy Shaw with Flory,	bap. '14
Donald Carmichael and Betty McIntyre with Peter Robert,	bap. '17
Harry Hamilton and Ann Thomson with Thomas,	bap. '13
Archibald Carlyle and Mary McEachern with Dugald,	bap. '14
John Currie Harkness and Isabella McLean with Thomas,	bap. '39
William Halliburton and Rosanna Conley with Elinor Isabel,	bap. '40
Peter Speirs and Isabella McDougall with Jane,	bap. '20
Dugald McCormick and Catherine McCorquidal with Mary,	bap. '10
Edmond McAlister and Janet McLeod with Nancy,	bap. '21;
Alexander,	bap. '22
Archibald McCallum and Anne Head with Archibald,	bap. '37;
Isabella,	bap. '37;
Neil,	bap. '35.
Samuel McMillan and Jenet McNeil with Hector,	bap. '15;
Flory,	bap. '16;
Marion,	bap. '19

It is noticeable that several of the seventeen young men appear to have married local girls.

Anne Shaw, Anne Campbell, Nancy Shaw, Mary McEachern, Isabella McLean and Isabella McDougall could well pass for Jura lasses. The record of marriages kept by the minister shows that six of the above couples married on Jura. It is also significant that all but the last three couples had only a single child during their stay on the island, and even these three had their children during a period of no more than four years.

BAPTISMAL RECORD FAMILIES IN THE 1841 CENSUS

The 1841 Census records 211 separate households on the main island of Jura. Of this total, 156, or 74 per cent, contain people known already from their presence in the baptismal register. Some of the remaining fifty-five households have evidently arrived on the island only recently, and have no records of baptisms. Others are elderly or belong to categories less likely to appear in a register of baptisms

The most numerous household in the census consists of a married couple with their various children. These families may be living on their own, or with a variety of other relatives, and various unrelated people.

There is a further group of households which we would now call 'single parent' homes, where either the father or mother is absent through death. There are a few 'sibling' homes, where brothers and sisters live together, and a few elderly women, more or less on their own.

These are the constituent families which comprise the 156 containing people who appear in the baptismal register from 1810 to 1841.

Families with two parents in the house	115
Families with a single parent in the house	26
Houses with brothers and sisters	7
Houses with sons and mothers	4
Houses with elderly women	4
	156

Within these homes are many grandparents and grandchildren, together with lodgers and various kinds of servants. The composition of these families can be studied in the complete census record.

CHILDREN AND YOUNG PEOPLE

Frequent reference has been made in this study to 'children', and so far this term has been used loosely to refer to people whose parents are actually living in the house. This can give rise to some confusion if we call thirty-year-old men and women living in the home of sixty- or seventy-year-old parents 'children'. We will now call everyone over twenty an adult. No doubt twenty-one would be a more logical age, but remember that the 1841 census rounds ages to the nearest multiple of five, so people who are twenty-three or twenty-four will show up as twenty. We will also separate those younger than twenty into 'young people' and 'children proper'.

Since 'children' can evidently be away from home and working in various capacities at twelve, thirteen, and fourteen years of age, it is something of a problem to define a cut-off age between the two groups. We will choose fifteen years as the first age for 'young people', and call boys and girls 'children' up to fourteen years. It might be preferable to choose sixteen rather than fifteen but the rounding down principle means that many young people recorded as fifteen, will in fact be several years older.

Discounting young people and children not members of the head of households family, but living in the house, this gives the following situation:

Children living in their parents' houses	348
Young people living in their parents' houses	54

It is in a matter like this that we see the limits of the single snapshot image provided by the national census. The number of children in a family is not frozen at one date, any more than the presence of the parents can be relied on to continue.

Families with very small children will presumably go on to have more, and families with only 'young people' present have presumably had others at an earlier date who have now left home. Both situations are capable of further study.

The population is sampled again ten years later in the census of 1851. A number of the two-parent and single-parent families have left Jura by this time. Indeed, of the 141 households concerned, thirty-one have left, while 110 remain in some form ten years later. Many have had further children during this period.

All these families, who we know of already through the baptismal register continue to have between them a total of ninety-four further children in the following ten years, many of whom of course continue to appear in the minister's record as they arrive.

Although the census record allows us to look forward, the baptismal register allows us to look back. In the 156 families we have studied many people are mention in the baptismal record who do not appear at all in the 1841 census. The total number of these 'missing persons' is 225!

This seems a remarkably large number. As we have seen already, this group contains many mothers and fathers who have died by 1841. There are many 'young people' in the list and it is impossible to know if they died young, or grew up and left the island.

IN THE 1841 CENSUS BUT NOT IN THE BAPTISMAL REGISTER
Fifty-five households remain to complete the study of the 1841 census. These are the people who do not feature in the baptismal register, so there will be a little more detail of the make-up of these families. Twenty-eight families are built around a married couple. There is an expected spread of ages. Eleven of these couples are living with no children of their own present, although other folk may be in the house. The remaining eighteen families have between them forty-six children, and seven young people of sixteen and over.

Fourteen of these houses have no one in them but the parents and the children, but the remaining fourteen homes have the usual complement of other people living with them. There are thirty-three in all.

There are the usual lodgers: three agricultural labourers, four female servants, and one each of the following: schoolmaster, teacher, joiner, apprentice joiner, cottar.

There are nine members of extended families including grandchildren and other relatives. There are thirteen people of unknown relationship including children and visitors.

What of the twenty-seven remaining households?

There are five single women living alone, three of whom are registered as paupers. Their ages are: (50); (60); (60); (72); and (76).

Three mothers and one father live alone with children: Mary Shaw (55) with James (25) and Donald (15); Mary Darroch (45) with Donald (10); Catherine Buie (39) whose married name was McDougall, with Mary (16), Catherine (12), Anne (10) and Merron (8).

Joseph Brown, a 45-year-old road contractor lives with his son Malcolm (15).

There are two 'sibling' homes and two with single occupants: John Shaw (15); Neil (12); and Duncan (10); three brothers; John Shaw (20) with Margaret Shaw (15), probably his sister; John Darroch (16), lives alone, as does Duncan McEachern, Smith (20).

Ronald Bell (20, Archibald Bell (15) and Angus Shaw (20), occupy a house at Lussagiven. All three are drainers, and may be in temporary accommodation while working.

There are eleven households where the relationships are not self-evident: two have men as 'head' and nine have women. They are here for inspection:

Colin Morison (45) with Colin McPhadyen and Alexander McPhadyen (8) and (6) and with Mary Buie (53) also in the house. Sounds like his mother under her maiden name?

Neil McDougald (40) with Mary Campbell (60) and Jannet Campbell (70)

Mary McDougall, Cottar (25) with Anne McDougall (9) Possibly an unmarried mother with a young child.

Marion McDougall (35) with Flora McDougall (25) and Neil Lindsay (7) Her sister and the sister's son?

Catherine McArthur (45) with William McLean (12) and James, Malcolm and Alexander McAllister (45); (15) and (14).

Catherine McNeill (48) with Duncan Bell and Ag. Lab of unknown age; Anne McEachern (21).

Mary McColl (50) with Marion Shaw (30).

Catherine McDougall (50) with Marion Stewart (15) Caterine Shaw was 'Widow McDougall' and a cottar in 1835.

Catharine Shaw (65) with Catherine McFadyen (25), Archibald McNab (30) and Colin McFadyen (35).

Mary Shaw (74) with Anne Shaw (27) and Anne Lindsay (5), probably her daughter and grandchild.

Catherine Darroch (90) with Bell Campbell (48) and Mary McColl (9).

This brings the total to fifty-three, and leaves only two further entries.

Living in Jura House are Isabella Campbell (50) and her son John (20) and daughter Augusta (7).

Isabella was the wife of Colin Campbell, sixth of Jura, and daughter of Richard Dennistoun of Kelvingrove. John is the youngest of their five sons. Archibald, Richard, Colin and James were his older brothers. There were seven girls. The census-taker found six other people in the house: Eleanor Silani, governess (25); Betsy Smith (35) Flora McGregor (25) Jane McIntosh (25) Elizabeth Young (30); all female servants, and William Lambert (35), a servant.

The last of the entries is from Ardlussa and appears to represent the site of the half-built Ardlussa House. There are thirteen tradesmen present: Donald McDougall (50), joiner; Hugh McDougall (20), journeyman wright; Archibald McDougall (18), wright's apprentice; William Hill (25), journeyman wright; Ronald Bell (47), journeyman mason; Archibald Bell (18), mason's apprentice; Neil Martin (27), journeyman mason; Hector McLean (70), quarrier; David Crawford (66), quarrier; John Shaw (32), quarrier; Hugh Black (40), labourer; Duncan McIntyre (35), plasterer; Gilbert McEachern (30), journeyman mason.

This completes an analysis of the fifty-five families which remained in the 1841 census. They were selected solely because they did not contain anyone who featured in the baptismal register. Some of the reasons why this is so should be self-evident. The married couple families contain a number who by their surnames were evidently recent arrivals. Here are some of the names: Armstrong, Barrie, Brown, Greenlees, Grieve, Lyon, Mill, McEwen, Rutherford, Scott, Smith, Thomson and Taylor.

The various reasons why none of the above families appear in the parish baptismal register, are now probably beyond our reach.

NOTES ON THE 1841 CENSUS: 'CHILDREN' 'INCOMERS' AND 'OCCUPATIONS'

Population Breakdown for 1841

Various population statistics from the 1841 census:

Children up to the age of fourteen years, living in their own families	439
Children up to the age of fourteen years but not the parent couple	81
Total to the end of their fourteenth year	520

Young people aged fifteen to nineteenth, includes 'rounded down
to fifteen' with their own parents　　　　　　　　　　　63
Young people aged fifteen to nineteen living with families on the island　30
Total of those we have deemed 'Young People'　　　　　93

For the population as a whole, the 'rounding down' principle means that decades have to run from the multiple of five upwards. The 1841 census then goes like this:

Children	510
Young People	93
20 – 29	148
30 – 39	152
40 – 49	101
50 – 59	72
60 – 69	45
70 – 79	25
80 – 89	7
90 +	1
Total	1154

There are several unidentified entries which bring the formal total to 1158.

INCOMERS

The census-taker made an effort to establish who was an 'Incomer', and designated varous people as not being native to the island:

The Sutherlands of Feolin Ferry.
Eleanor Silani, Governess; English.
Alexander McAlister, smith in Brosdale; Irish.
Margaret McEachern of Strone.
John Mill and his whole family; brewer in Craighouse.
Donald Darroch, the cooper's wife and three children.
The two Lamonts who live with the schoolmaster in Small Isles Schoolhouse.
The Minister.
Robert and Alexander Scott, masons working in the manse.
James McGregor, hand loom weaver of Knockrome; Irish.
John McDonald, tailor, Knockrome.
William Thomson of Corrynahera and his whole family.
James Scott of Tarbert and his whole family.
John McLennan and Finlay Finlayson; Ag. Labs. of Tarbert.
Thomas Armstrong of Ruantallain and his wife.
Thomas Grieve of Lussagiven and his whole family.

No doubt the people above came to the island from elsewhere. The problem is that we also know of far more people in the census who we are equally sure did not come from Jura, but the census gives no indication that this is the case.

By the time of the next census matters seem to have become a bit more organised with regard to places of origin, and the census taker seems to have recorded the birthplace of anyone not born on Jura. A number of the people mentioned were also in Jura ten years earlier, in 1841. From this source we can see that there was an active relationship with the nearby mainland, for there were wives from Craignish who married men from Lagg and the north. The schoolmasters came from Craignish and Knapdale. A shoemaker also comes from Knapdale. The Lagg innkeeper came from Inverary, and the miller came from Kilmeny in Islay. Indeed quite a number of folk came from Islay, and a few from Colonsay. James McGregor's Irish ancestry is pinned down to County Antrim, and even as early as 1841 there are shepherds on the island who come from the Borders: James Scott from Roxburgh, and Thomas Armstrong from Dumfries. Other shepherds come from Glassary, Dalmally and Mull.

We must be grateful for this small input from the later census, but aware that we are left with a great lack of information about the real nature of the 'incomers', and this is all we are going to get.

OCCUPATIONS
No notice has so far been taken of the fact that in addition to designating someone as the 'head' of each household, the census-taker also often sets down the occuption of that individual. The most numerous designation is 'tenant' and there are forty tenants listed.

This may be a reasonable moment to mention that the Campbell of Jura Papers have a list of tenants and cottars, dated 15 July 1835. This list amounts to seventy-five tenants, who can be found in Cnocbreac, Brosdale, Keils, Feolin Farm, Lergybreck, Knockrome, Ardfernal and Lagg.

Thirteen of these are mentioned in the baptismal register, but have evidently either died or left Jura before 1841. Fifty-six names on the list are also present at the census, but only forty of them are designated as 'tenant' on the day. Thirty-seven of the estate list are still tenants in 1841, although in three cases the son has taken the tenancy while his father remains head of the house. Six of the 1835 tenants are now called 'agricultural labourers'. One was the publican at Craighouse Inn, and remains so still. One or two are now working in other capacities, and four have no description at all.

Forty-two heads of household have no other designation than 'head' in their entry. Their occupations are simply a nil return. Was the census-taker always careful to find out what people's status actually was? The estate list gives a further list, after the tenants, of people who are 'cottars'. There are forty-two cottars listed, twenty-six of whom are still on Jura in the 1841 census. The trouble is that the census taker list only five heads of family as cottars. Here we are on much firmer ground. Many of these people are readily recognisable, and the census gives several occupations for them, without mentioning their status as cottars. There are for example four hand-loom weavers, three tailors, three agricultural labourers. There is a shoemaker and a boatbuilder. The postman at Lagg, John Lindsay, is listed as a cottar in 1835, and is still delivering in 1841. Presumably he has not suddenly stopped being a cottar. A number of named widows are listed as cottars in 1835, but have no such designation in 1841

The matter of the cottars puts the list of forty-two household heads with no designation into some doubt. If we could be confident of the accuracy of these entries we might be tempted to think that here we are looking at a group of 'stateless people'; folk who do not even merit the designation 'pauper', and are hence not even supported by the 'Poor Fund', and survive only by the grace of the communities around them. This may indeed by the case in some instances, but the fact that it is possible to show that a number of these 'nil return' cases are actually people with some other definite status throws the reliability of the whole category into doubt, and makes assumptions based on it unsafe.

To return to the list of occupations, the next most numerous are the agricultural labourers of which there are thirty-four.

There are eight 'male servants' and one 'female servant'. There are two 'farm servants' and two 'farmers'. Eleven are 'labourers'. Ten householders are listed as 'paupers' and one as a 'pensioner'.

Of the 211 heads of households, there are fifty-five who have other clearly listed occupations: In alphabetic order there are: boatbuilder (3); brewer; cartwright (2); church officer; cooper; drainer; dykebuilder: excise officer; ferryman (7); foot post; gardener; grocer; herd (4); hand-loom weaver (4); joiner (3); miller; minister of religion; publican (2); sailor; schoolmaster (2); seaman; shoemaker (4) slate quarrier (3); smith (4); tailor (3); road contractor; estate proprietor.

This group contains the 'service industries' of the island, and they can be easily picked out. The island has its teachers, its publicans, its minister. The status of the church is emphasised by the presence of a full-time church officer. The island has a postal service. Joiners, smiths, cartwrights, drainers and dykebuilders keep the structures of the community in order. The miller deals with the 'bread of life', and there is a small shop in Keils. Weavers, tailors and shoemakers keep the population clothed and export their surplus. The ferrymen keep the island in contact with the mainland. An industry has arrived, in the shape of the distillery; and coopers, brewers, managers and excisemen will become a regular part of island life. Overshadowing everything and everyone, either benevolent or repressive, depending on your point of view, is the estate, for the island belongs to its owners, lock, stock and barrel.

Confronted with the unsatisfactory nature of the 1841 census in many of the above details, we turn to the census of 1851, and find a great many more details.

One or two of the 'catch all' labels, such as 'male servant' and some of the 'nil returns' give up some more information. Here we find a gamekeeper at Ardfin, whose McKay descendants know full well that that was his job. Duncan McLellan of Ballard turns out to be the distillery manager. There are also two distillery labourers in the vicinity. Mary Darroch of Ballard is a washerwoman in the 1851 census, and, quite excitingly Mary Darroch of Ardfernal is listed as the island's 'midwife'. She presumably goes some little way to rectify the obvious omission that at this time Jura has no medical man. A resident doctor will not arrive for very many years, and in medical emergency the doctor comes over from Islay.

Perhaps most intriguingly of all, the enumerators of 1851 seem not content with the label 'agricultural labourer', which the 1841 census uses on thirty-four occasions. In at least seventeen places the job is given more definition. In the southern part of the island there are shepherds (2), herds (2), cowherds (2), dyke builders (2), a drainer, and a ploughman.

That the northern end of the island is already turning into one enormous sheep farm is borne out by the presence of six shepherds and a grazier, all merely called agricultural labourers in 1841.

These notes bring to an end our study of the two primary documents we have available for the first half of the nineteenth century in Jura: the baptismal register and the national census of 1841. The complete text of the 1841 census is available on Jura.

28

Where People Lived
in the Late Nineteenth Century

The baptismal register of 1704 provided an opportunity to study the places where young families were living and producing children. Now, a century later, the register of 1810 gives a new picture. We are fortunate to have two maps from this period which are revealing in terms of the communities they mention. G. Langlands & Son's *Map of Argyll* has the east coast of Jura down its left margin, and John Thomson's *Atlas of Scotland*, published in 1832, has an excellent map of Jura in its 'Southern Part of Argyllshire'.

Several communities mentioned in the 1704 register do not feature in the 1810 register or in the 1841 census: the ancient township of Achaleek, or Auchivelick, near Strone, has gone, although both Langlands and Thomson show it clearly. Presumably it was deserted by 1841. The 1898 Ordnance Survey map shows one ruined building. The single reference to the puzzling Trianintorran does not recur. The move between Kilearnadil and Keils seems to have been completed, and Kilearnadil no longer appears.

Some eighteenth-century names have changed. Erine is no longer in use, replaced by Feolin, although both Langlands and Thomson still show it as Feorine. Camus is now being called Lagg.

Many earlier mainstream communities reappear, and have records from the earliest years of the register. Baptisms are recorded by 1812 from the following, all of which feature in the 1704 baptismal register: Cnocbreac, Ardfin, Brosdale, Strone, Sannaig, Crackaig, Craighouse, Knocknafeolaman, Keils, Feolin, Lergie-breck, Knockrome, Ardfernal, Ardmenish, Lagg, Corrynahera, Tarbert, Knockintavill, Kinuachdrach, together with Scarba and Lunga.

A number of residences appear for the first time in the 1810 baptismal register or in the 1841 census. Many have been discussed in the basic list of settlements in an earlier chapter, but some additional notes and details are provided here.

ARDFIN

It seems that the Campbells, who settled initially at Sannaig, and were known as the Campbells of Sannaig until 1739, must have moved their own residence to Ardfin some time after their purchase of the fee simple of the lands in Jura from Campbell of Shawfield at that time. Certainly various documents from the 1770s show them to be living at Ardfin, probably on the site of what became the estate home farm. This would agree with Lord Teignmouth's account of 1836:

The residence of Mr Campbell, the laird of Jura, is built on a weather-beaten eminence above the sea, a decent farm-house, surrounded with ramparts of peat. Mr Campbell is so attached to his present habitation that he has vowed to end his days in it, though he has built a house, in the modern style, near it, as a residence for his son.

The Campbell in question, was Archibald, fourth of Jura, who must have been close to death at Teignmouth's visit, as he died in 1835 in his ninety-first year. Jura House, was presumably then inhabited by James Campbell, fifth, an army doctor, who was laird for only three years. Jura House does not feature in connection with baptisms in the first half of the century. The next laird, Colin Campbell, married Isabella Hamilton of Kelvingrove in 1806, and it seems likely that their twelve children were born on the mainland with the assistance of Isabella's family.

Isabella is, however, present in Jura House at the 1841 census, although Colin was away at the time. She is there with a twenty-year-old son, John, and one of her daughters, Augusta, aged seven. There is an English governess, called Eleanor Silani, and five house servants. On the subsequent four censuses, a Campbell presence was recorded at Jura House only in 1871, when Richard Dennistoun Campbell was in residence. Though so dominant in the life of the island, the Campbells were evidently not permanently on the island.

BROSDALE

At the time of the 1841 census there were ten occupied houses in the township of Brosdale. The old community was at NR 490634 on a fine location directly overlooking the water, and with magnificent views of Islay and the distant Mull of Kintyre. However, it was only some 600 yards from Jura House, and evidently plainly visible through its windows. Local tradition relates that this did not suit Isabella Campbell, who insisted that the community be moved to a more suitable site. Her husband evidently complied, for between 1841 and 1851 all the dwellings but one in Brosdale were demolished and the residents resettled in 'New Brosdale'. By 1861 the last remaining house was gone in old Brosdale, and today the site reveals that the houses did not in fact fall down, but were deliberately reduced to ground level.

Mrs Campbell's plans resulted in eleven cottages at the new site. New Brosdale was north of the main road and lies in a dip in the ground which means it is unseen when approached until the last minute. By the same token there is absolutely no view from within the settlement, unlike the vistas which usually open up from traditional Jura townships.

The houses were planned to constitute 'a street', the only one in Jura to this day, with two rows facing one another across a central pathway. There was a well nearby, and the community was overlooked by a small round hill to the north with a dun on its top. In due course a school was established as well. Tradition also reports that the new settlement was cordially detested by the inhabitants who neither liked its location nor the formal arrangement of the houses. However, like it or not, the population remained. Old Brosdale had sixty souls in 1841, and New Brosdale had sixty-one in 1851. After a dip in 1861, there were eleven occupied houses with forty-seven inhabitants in 1871, and forty-five in 1881. The population dropped to twenty-eight by 1891, when the census recorded seven homes, and took the trouble to note the presence of four unoccupied houses. The new school was given the name Cabrach, and the 1898 Ordnance Survey map shows the whole settlement with this name. Deaths continued to be recorded from there until 1918. An elderly inhabitant remembered being taken by his father to make fuel deliveries there when a child. He recalled that it had suddenly occurred to his father that for the first time in his experience he was in a position to offload the sacks on both sides of the cart at once. 'We had one side of the cart down, and father told me to put down the other side as well. I did so, and the back fell off!' Could this be termed an example of 'culture shock'?

CAIGENHOUSE

Caigenhouse remains today a picturesque row of cottages stretching along the shore of Small Isles Bay. Two families have children baptised there in 1810. Gaelic speakers of Jura seemed to derive this name from 'caigeann' (a pair), as in 'a pair of houses'. However, it seems unlikely that there were originally two houses in the row. Certainly by 1841 there were seven small cottages, although the community grew to double that number by the end of the century. The other difficulty is that the 'house' portion of the name seems always to have been in the singular, which is odd if it connects with 'a pair'. Calum McArthur notes the narrow passage up the cliff, between the rocks just behind the houses, and derives the name from 'caigeann' (a rough rocky pass) and this should surely be accepted. The row becomes significant as comprising dwellings for various folk other than crofters. Indeed the 1853 chart attaches the label 'wrights' in bold type. It has evidently become known for the presence of various artisan families. The 1841 census shows two hand-loom weavers, a cartwright, a tailor and a shoemaker living in the row, so the name seems justified. Later it became known as 'Mariners' Row' from the number of retired seamen living there.

AUCHINTARBERT

Auchintarbert, 'Field of Tarbert', featured as a tenancy distinct from Tarbert in the valuations of the eighteenth century, often connected with Corrynahera, and at a time when Tarbert proper was not part of Campbell's jurisdiction. Now it appears as a distinct community in which families are living and having children; the first in 1813, and four contemporaneously in the late 1820s and early 1830s. Both Langlands and Thomson show this community as Auchin, which is probably a space-saving abbreviation.

The census-takers seem to have been uncertain of the status of Auchintarbert. The 1841 census credits it with a single dwelling. The same resident continues in this house but is simply lumped in with Tarbert in the 1851 and 1861 censuses. The name disappears completely in these and in the 1871 and 1881 censuses, but makes a surprising return in the 1891 census which credits the community with three dwellings. Important in its day, this township becomes a shadowy one in the nineteenth century. The statutory register of deaths does not mention it. Local tradition seems uncertain of its location, but the ruins can be seen just to the south of the path which leads from the road by the Tarbert standing stone to the headwaters of Loch Tarbert. This location would agree with the position on the two early maps. There is no indication of it on the 1898 Ordnance Survey map.

RUANTALLAIN

This appears as a residence in the baptismal register, with baptisms recorded for 1811 and 1829, and with a family having four children from 1833 to 1840. It then continues on in the 1841 census, and with two cottages through the succeeding five censuses to 1891.

Ruantallain was the most remote residence on Jura, located at the extreme western end of the north shore of Loch Tarbert. Ruantallain is the anglicised version of 'Rubh' an t-Salein'; here the 'd' of 'Rudha' (point of land, or promontory) has been changed into a 'b' on recent maps. The name simply means 'salty point'. It appears on the west coast chart of Captain Joseph Huddart in 1794, as 'Ruintalin'.

From the cottages, now semi-ruined, it is over nine miles of difficult walking to reach the road and the community of Tarbert, which would have been and is still, the nearest township. By boat, the seven-mile trip takes you through the 'narrows' of Loch Tarbert, a difficult and often dangerous passage, and indeed, impossible to navigate in adverse conditions of wind and tide. In 1811, when Gilbert McVean came to Jura to be a shepherd with his wife Jane McCallum, and had their daughter Christian, and then their son Peter, in 1819, before moving to Corrynahera, their home would have effectively been the only habitation on the west coast of the island. The holiday lodge of Glenbatrick, on the coast south of the loch, was not built until the following century, and the northern coastal township of Glengarrisdale, inhabited from 1851, was more than twelve miles away. By 1851 a second family had arrived, and from then on, and throughout the rest of the century there seem to have been two families at Ruantallain. One of the men was a shepherd to trade, while the other was a keeper. That the remoteness of such a dwelling could take its toll is borne out by the fact that Duncan and Janet McNeill's daughter, Ann, died there on her second day. The most recent record from Ruantallain is the death of Barbara Shaw in 1926.

ARDLUSSA

Ardlussa has of course been discussed in the earlier chapter, and continues to feature in the nineteenth-century baptismal register and in the 1841 census, where four dwellings are listed. In one of these the residents on the day of the census consist entirely of thirteen artisans. We have stumbled upon the building of Ardlussa House which was erected by the Right Hon. Duncan McNeill, Lord Advocate of Scotland, and brother of Captain McNeill of Colonsay, the proprietor of the northern part of Jura.

AN CARN

'Carn', as we call it (An Carn simply means 'the cairn'), is a ruined and deserted township at NR 681935. Carn was briefly described on the earlier list. The site commands a fine view of the sound of Jura, and has something in common with other elevated township sites such as Old Brosdale and Ardfernal. The township is well described in the Argyll *Inventory*, where an excellent plan is also provided. There appear to be six well-defined structures with various connecting turf dykes and small enclosures. Some distance away there is a ruined corn-drying kiln. Nearby on the raised beach is one of Mercer's mesolithic sites, while below the ruins there is a small bay with a cave which has produced finds of late medieval date. There are rock surfaces within the site which bear cup marks. Carn appears on Pont's map of about 1590, as 'Karn', with his small symbolic building indicating a community. Langlands, 1801 and Thomson, 1832, both show it clearly as 'Cairns'.

Carn is not mentioned in the 1841 census, or any subsequent censuses, and indeed it does not appear in a single surviving document. In the northern part of the island, owned by the MacLeans of Lochbuie and the McNeils of Colonsay, we do not have the kind of valuation and rental evidence we have for the part governed by the Campbells. However, we do have the Old Parish Registers of Baptism. Neither the eighteenth-century record from 1704 to 1734, nor the nineteenth-century one of 1810 to 1841 and beyond, records even the name of Carn, although in both registers there is ample evidence of baptisms of infants being born in all the small communites which lie to the north, south and west of it.

Mercer, in his archaeological paper on Carn's mesolithic settlement, states: 'Until the nineteenth-century clearance of the settlement of Carn, the main track ran along the cliffs.' In his book, he says, 'On Thomson's 1824 map, the north-easterly Cairns had been cleared and become ruined by 1868, and the road to it swung so as to pass a mile inland, putting resettlement out of the question.'

A close study of the Ancient Monuments Survey indicates that the entire site may have contained no more than three actual dwellings, and the other structures were likely to have been of agricultural significance. It seems possible that Carn had long been a small community, and this view is reinforced by the evidence that it produced no children during two periods of thirty years at the beginning of both the eighteenth and nineteenth centuries. It seems unneccessary to postulate the political action of 'clearance' to account for the disappearance of a township which may simply have aged and died.

29

Changes in Population
from 1841 to 1891

The total population of the main island of Jura at the 1841 census was 1158 souls. These men, women and children were living at the time in 211 separate households.

Ten years later in 1851 the corresponding figures are: total population, 943 souls, number of households, 181. This is a net decrease of 215 people and thirty households.

THE CENSUS OF 1851

What then does the 1851 census reveal about what has happened to the population? About 103 families remain in the same house and largely unchanged. Fifty families remain largely unchanged but move to another house on Jura. Nine elderly people are presumed to have died during the ten years. In six cases, one member seems to have died and others in the house moved away. Fifty-seven families or parts of family left the island by 1851.

Those families who left the island contain many who we had already nominated as being unlikely to stay by virtue of having incomer names, or because they seemed likely to be occupying specific jobs such as distillery workers. So we are not surprised to see the departure of families with surnames such as: Barrie, Bell, Greenlees, Grieve, Livingstone, Lyon, McArtan, McEwen, McGill, McGilvray, McLarty, Mill, Morison, Smith and Thomson.

It seems unnecessary to postulate that these people were forced to emigrate. It may have been simple for them simply to go 'back home' and seek fresh employment.

Not so the great majority who have completely 'mainstream' Jura names, and who often have considerable families: the Buies; the Darrochs (5 families); the Blacks; the Campbells (4); the Lindsays (3); the McPhails (3); the McNeils and the Fletchers (2 each); and of course the McDougalls (6).

It is here that we could look with confidence for emigrants, and for the continual enlargement of the colony in Greenock.

Where did they leave from? There was no single target area. One or two families left from each of: Cnocbreac, Dainsgeir, Ardfin, Brosdale, Crackaig, Miltown, Ballard, Caigenhouse, Keils, Feolin, Lergybreck, Knockrome, Ardfernal, Lagg, Corrynahera, Lussagiven, Lealt, Kenuachdrach.

To be sure there were six from Knockrome and four from Ardfernal, but then these had the largest 'swarm of inhabitants'.

That the population did not drop by nearly sixty families to around 150 households is due to the fact that some twenty-five families moved into the island during the ten years. Many of these came to take up vacant positions, as follows:

James Taylor (57) of Dumfries; his wife and family came to Ardfin where he was to be Farm Steward.

Donald Johnson (50) of Tiree came to New Brosdale with his wife, to be Gardener at the 'Big House'.

Colin Campbell (31) of Kilmore, came to Cabrach with his father and mother to run the new 'Society School' for the children of Ardfin and New Brosdale.

Archibald McConnell (30) was a drainer. He and his wife came to Dunans. He was probably coming back to Jura where he may have been born.

Flora Shaw (35) came to Dunans. She may have been working on the mainland.

James Audus (35) and English, came to Craighouse with his wife Christine to be the Exciseman.

Thomas Orr (30) came to be Distillery Manager.

Francis Edmonds (40), from England, came to Miltown with his wife Louisa, also to work for the Excise.

Duncan Cook (41) and his wife came to Caigenhouse. They came from Bute. He was a cutterman.

John McDougall (51) and his wife and four children came to Caigenhouse. He was an Islay man from Kilmeny, and would work on the land.

There was a new minister and his family at the manse.

Alexander Fletcher (32) came to Feolin, where he was employed as ploughman. He came from Bowmore in Islay.

Sally McDougall (51) moved to Knockrome. She became a cottar, and may have been coming home.

Neil Campbell (48) and his wife Mary appear in Knockrome to take up a tenancy. He was previously not known.

Other and similar, quite ordinary-sounding families came to Knockrome, Ardmenish and Lagg.

Two more shepherds arrived in the north end with their families. One came from North Knapdale.

A gardener arrived for the newly built Ardlussa House. Not a native Jura man, he was called Robert Sword, and came from Ettrick. His wife Mary was born in Fort William.

There is nothing very dramatic about these incomers. It is difficult to strike an exact balance on numbers of households between the 1841 and the 1851 census for there are many variable factors, but there seem to be about the right number of incomers at the end of the period, i.e., about twenty-eight.

Of course, much has been happening quite unseen during the ten years. There is not yet any formal record of deaths in the parish, so it is impossible to say what was going on in terms of the deaths of children, young people, or people in middle age. Many of the important but transient events in the lives of the local residents must remain hidden from us forever.

However, the account given here makes it quite plain that a process has begun which will continue into modern times. Namely, the dereliction and ruin of houses no longer required for local families who have been forced by a variety of circumstances to leave the island.

THE CENSUS OF 1861

We may take a similar approach to see what further changes have been taking place in the population between 1851 and 1861. The figures for the 1861 census are as follows: households, 162; and souls, 812. It can be seen that the decrease in number of households is only nineteen, but that actual number of people lost is 131. At the end of this ten-year period 101 families are found to have continued living in the same place as at 1851. Twenty-seven families remained on the island, but moved to a different place. Forty-one families moved off the island, while thirty-six moved in.

There are fifteen elderly people in the 1851 census who have disappeared by the 1861. It is a puzzling group, all of whom would have been over sixty by 1861, and some of them over eighty, and yet, although the Statutary Register of Deaths opened in 1855, only two of these people appear in it. Of course, some may have died in the four years immediately before 1855. The only conclusion for the others seems to be that they left the island in their advancing years to live with younger relatives somewhere else.

The number of families who remain in their own homes remains much the same between 1851 and 1861 as it did in the previous ten years, but the number who move somewhere else within the island has dropped sharply, from forty-eight to twenty-five. Perhaps the population is beginning to become more settled. Certainly the number of families moving off the island has dropped from fifty-seven to forty in this decade.

The people who move in and out continue to include families coming into employment with the distillery or the estates who don't settle down for long. Of the forty families who move away from the island during the ten years, fourteen had arrived between 1841 and 1851 and have now left again by 1861. Again one can almost predict that this would happen, and confirm it by many of their surnames: Tayler, Johnston, Audus, Orr, Edmonds, Cook, Fletcher, Campbell, McLean, McFarlane, Shaw, Leitch, Sword and McPhail.

Certainly one might have guessed that the Auduses, Orrs, Cooks, Leitches and Swords would not be long on the island. The remaining twenty-six families contain a few such as the Armstrongs, who, although present in 1841 and 1851, may not have deep roots in the island. Craighouse Inn has changed hands with the departure of the Fletchers.

In the main group who leave by 1861, there are certainly some well established Jura names, but one can sense the absence of the more dominant families like the Darrochs and the Shaws. There is only one McDougall and one Shaw in the group and no Darrochs. Indeed the list makes slightly strange reading: Black (4 families), Brown, Clark, Gillies, Gray, Keith, McAlister, McArthur, McConnel, McCraine, McDonald, McEachern, McFadyen, McKellar, McLean, McPhail, McNeil and Taylor.

It is almost is if the families with generations of tradition on the island are those who have found some *modus vivendi*, and are now going to 'stick it out'. This may seem a bit fanciful, but the idea has a certain appeal.

The families who move into the island during the ten years are also an interesting group. There are of course the people required to replace the short-stay incomers who have left. Here we have families with names such as Ferguson, Fraser, Gray, Grant, Johnston, McKerral, McKellar, McLellan, McPherson, Rutherford, Tant and Taylor.

However, there are groups of people with established island names also. Are they returning to the island, having heard that things are improving somewhat? Examples are: Black (2 families), Campbell (4), Darroch (2), Keith (2), McCraine, McDougall (2), McEachern, McLean (2), McPhail (2), Rankin and Shaw (5).

It is of interest that by the time of the 1861 census, the Statutory Register of Deaths has been in operation for six years. During this time seventy-six inhabitants of Jura have had their deaths recorded.

We now have some confirmation of the pattern of child mortality we have been looking at indirectly through the baptismal register.

Here we see the tragic events of a community which saw seventeen of its children die before reaching their tenth birthday. A further five young people died before the age of twenty-one.

Incomers in the 1861 Census

Since there have evidently been so many moves in and out of the island, and since the enumerators now seem to be taking great care with the birthplaces of anyone not native to the island, let us look at where the incomers have been coming from, and what they are doing.

The total comes as a considerable surprise as it amounts to 122, which works out at exactly 25 per cent of the total number of adults on the island. They come from a wide range of places.

There are thirty-nine from nearby islands: twenty-four from Islay; eleven from Colonsay; two from Coll; two from Gigha; and one from Mull.

There are many who have come from just across the Sound of Jura on the nearby mainland, and a few from Loch Fyne. These amount to thirty-four in all: six from N Knapdale; twelve from Craignish; five from S Knapdale; three from Glassary; one each from Danna, Luing, Kilmory, and Inverary, Lochgilphead and Ardrishaig. Only two come from Kintyre, with one each from Campbeltown and Kilcalmonell.

There is a group of seventeen from the region of the industrial west of Scotland: nine from Greenock and one each from Gourock; Rothesay; Kilchattan; Paisley; Neilston; Renfrew; Hamilton and Overtown. Edinburgh and Leith provide two.

The Oban region produces twelve. The place-names were household words in their day, but many have now declined, and are known only by their old parish names:

There are one each from Dalavich, Glenorchy, Kilbride, Kilbrandon, Kilchrenan, Kilmore and the isle of Kerrera.

There are five from Loch Ness, Inverness, Kilmallie, Kiltarlity (two) and Urquhart.

From further north incomers arrive from: Fearn and Kiltearn (two); and one each in Ross; Sutherland and Lewis.

The Borders have one each from Selkirk and Moffat and two from Roxburgh. There is one distiller from Rothes. A single family from England and two from Ireland complete the total.

It adds up to 122 families in all, who do a wide variety of things. It would be wrong to think that they did not penetrate into the old crofting townships because they are definitely there. In Keils and Knockrome where they are simply called farmers, and there are three of those. A number more work on the land in other capacities. One is an agricultural labourer and two are farm servants.

Ploughmen seem to come from Islay, and there are four of these. There is one herd, and there are five shepherds in the north, some from the borders.

Servant girls are in demand, and six are working on the island.

A number of skilled people come from elsewhere. A mason, a carpenter, a shoemaker and a weaver are all incomers, as is a slate quarrier. Boatmen and ferrymen also come from elsewhere.

Then there is the distillery. Although some mashmen/stillmen seem to be local, the manager, the excise staff (three, one retired); and at this time one stillman, come from elsewhere.

The professions all come into the island. The minister, the society schoolmasters, and now for the first time a catechist, representing the Free Church of Scotland, and an inspector of poor taking up his appointment. The innkeepers are from off the island, and there is now a general store in Milntown which is run by incomers.

At the north end there are fishermen: one salmon and one herring.

As the estates become more formalised, and adopt the grand Lowland style of living, new appointments appear which tell their own story. The grieve is now called the 'farm overseer'.

There is now a coachman, although the quality of the road leaves much to be desired. Keepers are now termed gamekeepers. The big houses have people with new titles: governess, housekeeper, housemaid, cook, chambermaid, dairy-maid, gardener, and even butler. There are several of some of these occupations on the island, for in the shadow of Jura House, the distillery manager and the minister also employ a cook. Dressmakers have also put in an appearance.

Recorded on the island at the time of the census is Archibald Campbell, an elderly 'sheep and cattle dealer' from Glassary. Also present are Ann McDougall (55), a pedlar from Kilchattan, and Alexander Fisher (28), a pedlar from Hamilton,

The census taker also noted at Lealt that Dugald McPhail (84), from Mull was 'going about dumb'.

THE CENSUS OF 1871

By this census the population of Jura has dropped again, but this time by considerably less. The total for 1871 is 753; down by fifty-nine on the figure for 1861. There are still 157 families, only five fewer than ten years previously.

Once more a solid proportion of families have been able to stay in their settled homes. There are 111 of these, and only twenty-one have moved somewhere else on the island, as against twenty-five at the last census. Some fourteen of these flittings have been made by families working on the land who have moved from one farming job to another and they have stayed largely in the same part of the island, e.g., a shepherd from Ardlussa has gone over to Glengarrisdale still to be a shepherd. A cowherd from Ardfin has gone to farm at Strone, probably, as a promotion.

Other moves concern professional appointments as we trace the various teachers from school to school. A new house has been built along the shore from Caigenhouse, to be the official home and office for the inspector of poor. It is called Holly House right away, and retains the name to this day.

Some elderly people have also moved; a number into designated 'paupers' cottages'.

This is the first census in which we have the benefit of a full ten years of the Statutory Register of Deaths, and for the first time it is possible to see the real effects of mortality in the community. It is surprising that for many of the events recorded in the register there is no evidence in the censuses. The ten-year period seems to give ample time for significant things to happen without their being recorded by the census-taker at all. However, among the settled families, and those who have moved within the island there have been fifty-seven deaths which the census does confirm. The biggest share of these occurred in people over sixty years of age. Only ten deaths occurred to people between thirty and sixty.

Not caught by the census, thirteen babies died at or near birth. Before they were a month old, three infants died. Before reaching their second birthday, another two, and subsequently five children who were less than ten years old died.

All the adults whose deaths are in the above records lived within families which continued in some form after they were gone. However, in each census we have looked at the people who simply disappear from one census and do not reappear at the next. These are candidates for leaving the island, and going off to some unknown destination. With the full death record available we can now record that twelve of the families missing from this census have disappeared because the occupant simply died. They lived either alone or with a companion, or young relative, and after their deaths the dwellings became vacant. This group sadly contains two young people living alone, who died aged twenty-five and fifteen.

The remaining families who leave before 1871 follow patterns we have become used to. A number have gone, having only arrived on the island in time for the 1861 census. They did not stay long. There are five of these families. The remaining seven had all been on the island during the 1861 and 1851 censuses, and in three cases as far back as the 1841. They give the impression of being people who have done their best to 'stick it out', but have finally come to the point which so many others reached ten or twenty years earlier, and have left.

They are replaced by the usual crop of new incomers. Some represent a change of face in the inn or the distillery. People such as William Waugh and Thomas Orr fit easily into our picture of short appointments. However, nothing can be taken for granted. John McKechnie comes as 'general merchant' to open the 'village store', and founds a dynasty. The same can be said for William Nicolson who comes to run Craighouse Inn with a background as a lighthouse boatman, born in Orkney, and this family also has connections with the island to modern times.

Some have evidently come as staff for the estate houses, and others to replace tradesman, such as Buie the carpenter and McKechnie the blacksmith. Others have mainstream island names and may have found their way back to an association with their kin on Jura.

Skervuile Lighthouse Station is now in place, and the census records: William Crow and his wife and five children from Tarbert; John and Sarah Wilson from Wigtown; and William and Mary Mill and their three children from Arbroath. These would be the first of an important group, many of them throwing thmselves heart and soul into the life of the island. One called Galbraith, became a church elder, and stories of his somewhat compliant personality survive until recent times.

THE CENSUS OF 1881
In the 1881 census the number of families is 158, and the total population is 766.

For the first time on record the population has not become smaller in the ten year period. There are actually thirteen more souls on the island, and the household total has increased by one. We must not give this too much significance, as the census contains a visiting ship. In the entry before Craighouse Inn, we find:

Naiad   73, 790 Glasgow Tonnage 43. Screw Lighter Coasting Trade.
                 Charles Brown, Master. Lying at Anchor, Small Isles, Jura.
                 Aboard were: Charles Brown, master (45), from Helensburgh
                 Archibald McArthur, mate (60), from Kirkmichael
                 John McLean, seaman (33), from Sleat
                 Alexander Graham, engineer (33), from Belfast.

Once again the population is much more settled than it was earlier in the century. Almost the same number of families continued to live on the island, and almost the same proportion of them moved to a different house.

There was a similar move in appointed people during the ten years. Teachers came and went, a new minister arrived. Distillery staff underwent a change as did lighthouse men. A good number of estate employees were also replaced. The statistics for deaths on the island were similar between 1871 and 1881 to those for the previous ten years.

One significant change in the island was the arrival of Henry Evans, who took a long lease of 'Jura Forest' in 1874. This area is bounded on the coast from north of the manse to the Corran River, and stretches inland into the Paps. It was long regarded as a deer forest in its own right, but now Campbell of Jura was prepared for his new tenant to erect buildings on it. Jura Forest Lodge was built, together with a number of dwellings for keepers, for a factor and a gardener. These dwelling are termed 'Lergybreck' by the census, presumably because they lie near to the old community of Lergybreck. However, it will be remembered that this township was 'cleared' by McLeod of Feolin, and the implication that these new houses are somehow continuous with the old is misleading. The early Jura Forest lease ran north of the Corran River on to what is now the Tarbert Estate, but after Evans' lease expired in 1904 the northern part was added to Tarbert.

Caigenhouse has continued to grow with four new dwellings bringing it to fourteen houses in all. The old community of Knocknafeolaman has long disappeared, and Ballard, which continued it for a time is now reduced to the blacksmith's house. However, the distillery now has several properties, and Miltown continues to thrive. By 1881, on the coast of Small Isles Bay, between the Craighouse Inn and Small Isles School there are now twenty-four dwellings. This community thus presages the development over the next hundred years during which time the island's population would become increasingly concentrated in what has now become called 'Craighouse'.

The crofting townships of Keils, Knockrome and Ardfernal remain remarkably stable during the ten years, although the latter two are showing the first signs of losing ground against the population of Keils.

Keils still has twenty households in 1881. However Knockrome and Ardfernal each have been reduced to thirteen.

THE CENSUS OF 1891

The 1881 census showed the great haemorrhage of population of the earlier years of the century slowing to a halt. Unfortunately during the next ten years the problem reappeared so that the statistics show a decline yet again.

The number of families in the 1891 census is 146, and the total population is 614. This is a loss of eleven homes, and 152 souls. From this time the population will continue to decline steadily.

The nature of the decline, however, has changed since the earlier years of the century. There is now very little evidence of families simply leaving the island to try life elsewhere. As in the previous census, about the same number of families arrived as left and most of these were short-term employees such as distillery workers and lighthousekeepers. The established families are even more settled than before, and even the internal movements, so typical of the earlier years have been dramatically reduced. Only about a dozen families moved to a different house in Jura, and there was family continuity in well over 100 houses.

Around 115 deaths occurred during the decade. The decrease in the number of occupied houses is due almost entirely to the death of an elderly resident, sometimes accompanied by the departure of a younger relative. At first sight it seems surprising that a decrease of only eleven households could result in the overall population going down by 152.

When the censuses of 1881 and 1891 are compared the reason became clear. The number of adults present in the upper age brackets remains nearly constant during the period:

	1881	1891
People in their fifties	63	66
People in their sixties	44	48
People in ther seventies	34	30
People in their eighties	12	13
People in their nineties	1	1

As we examine people under fifty the situation begins to change: there are seventeen fewer people in their forties in the island; there are nineteen fewer people in their thirties; there are twenty-four fewer in their twenties.

However, it is when we look at the youngest members of the community that we are struck by an important change. In 1881 there were 344 children and young people on the island. By 1891 this figure had dropped by ninety-six to 248. Of children ten years old or under; there were forty-five fewer after the ten year period.

The settled population is ageing rapidly. In the settled crofting townships there are very few yo ung families. In Keils which has declined through death from twenty to fifteen households there are only three families with as many as five children and only one of these has children younger than five years. There are fifteen children ten years old or younger. Fifty years earlier, the number was more than double that figure.

Knockrome has only a single family with small children in its ten homes and Ardfernal is in a similar situation. Many other townships on the island have few small children or none, and it is noticeable how often the larger family with younger children are those of people who have come but lately to the island. Distillery and lighthouse workers are generally young married couples with young families, as are incoming keepers, gardeners, shepherds and the like.

It seems that the island is already reaping the reward of the departure of so many young families and single young men to the mainland and elsewhere. While deaths in the previous ten years amounted to 115, marriages on Jura in the same period were only fifteen. The future begins to look bleak indeed.

We will never know if the various employers on the island took the population into consideration in engaging their new workers. In modern times the island has watched with hope to see if each new family would bring its quota of children of school age, and has felt somewhat let down if the new arrivals have plainly been unlikely to increase the school roll. This state of affairs may go back for some considerable time.

We will be studying the continuing decline when we look at the twentieth century.

30

Accounts of Conditions in Jura

Our first ideas about the general way of life of the Jura residents come from the writings of the small number of historical visitors whose accounts of the island have been recorded.

Only Dean Munro visited the island while the MacDonalds of the Isles were still in power. As the Franciscan Mission later makes clear there would have been a MacDonald living in Jura who would have been the island's chieftain. As we have seen, Munro, in 1549, is our first visitor by almost 150 years.

He makes it clear that the island is 'inhabited and manurit' at the coast. In other words the coastal strip is farmed. Although he calls it a 'fine forest for deer', and no doubt it was a hunting preserve for the Lords of the Isles, none the less, his description of great organised drives of deer into a narrow place by a great body of men seems to suggest a different activity to individual stalking with dogs or with bow and arrow. Perhaps the 'infinite number of deer slain' were salted down and eaten by the clansmen during the hard winter, or even consumed fresh in great communal feasts.

Munro tells us that all the rivers have salmon taken on them. Perhaps again the ordinary people had their share of this resource. He also tells us the island is full of noble cattle. The island has long been associated with black cattle. Did Munro see the forerunners of early black Highland cattle, and think them 'noble'?

Munro's account is nearly 150 years earlier than Martin Martin's visit, and we have only the most general idea of what life was like in Jura in the 100 years between his visit and the coming of the Campbells.

LIVESTOCK, CROPS, FARMING PRACTICE

As Munro makes clear, from the earliest days on Jura, cattle farming was a way of life. The hilly inland ground was more fertile than it is today, with grassland running far into moorland pasture where all is now heather and rushes. Jura had wide grazings and big herds of black cattle which would later be exported by ferry from Lagg Bay to Keills in Knapdale. In modern times the moors are largely empty, only the deer are everywhere. It is hard to appreciate that the scene was once different, with all the shallow glens green and thronged with cows and calves, and the moors dotted with shielings.

With wheat rarely ripening in the Hebrides, the chief crops were two-rowed barley, bere, oats, flax, and, no earlier than 1740, potatoes. Campbell, in 1774, added rye and hemp as Jura crops. Bere, a four-rowed bread-barley pulled up by the roots to avoid shrinkage yielded four to five times the amount sowed.

Various writers give excellent descriptions of the system in use, and although none is referring specifically to Jura the main argument no doubt applies exactly. Murray gives a general picture:

The land was divided into inbye and outbye. The inbye was sub-divided into arable and out-run, the latter making poor arable or good pasture. The outbye was coarse pasture; turf dykes might or might not separate the three divisions. This resulted in small, scattered, awkwardly shaped plots.

All manure was laid on the infield, which was tilled. The outfield was ploughable land, kept in grass and corn, and this was dunged by cattle, sheep and horses folded there for the purpose. The hill pastures were ranged by cattle, sheep and horses. There was no rotation of crops, and no sowing of grass for winter fodder. Lack of winter cattle-grazing meant autumn export, with the towns remaining animals being let onto the whole arable in winter. This ruled out winter crops.

To that account is now added this of T. Bedford Franklin:

The arable land or infield, was situated in the lowest ground that was dry enough to cultivate, and was ploughed each year. On it was lavished all the manure that could be collected. It was cultivated 'run-rig', that is, each tenant had rigs or ridges scattered amongst those of his neighbours, and different ridges were given to him by lot each year.

The rest of the holding or outfield, was rough pasture for cattle and sheep and received no other manure than the droppings of the animals that grazed it. Sometimes part of it was ploughed up, cropped for a year or two, or as long as it would bear anything worth harvesting, and then allowed to return to moorland pasture, while another portion was taken into cultivation.

There was practically no enclosed land, so the cattle were tethered during the summer, or trusted to the care of a herd who had great difficulty in preventing the hungry animals from breaking into the adjacent corn crops. In the winter the cattle practically starved, and by the spring, at the time of 'lifting to pasture' again, many of them literally had to be lifted from the byre to the grass by the joint exertions of the whole family. That more of them did not die was only due to their great stamina, but the result was that few were ever fat for sale, and the 'marts', or those killed at Martinmas, provided only tough and stringy salt meat for the family during the winter months.

This vivid description does not take account of the 'summer sheilings' which effectively took the cattle away from the cultivated fields, but otherwise sounds most realistic for Jura.

Another note is added by Ian Whyte:

The arable land, whether infield or outfield, was not divided up by permanent enclosures. Temporary fold dykes of turf were used to keep cattle on parts of the outfield, or to protect meadowland from livestock in summer, but in general there was no permanent barrier between the yards surrounding the township and the head dyke, which divided the arable from the permanent pasture. The head dyke was thus the most important division in the system. It protected the arable from the depredations of livestock. The open-field character of the arable land was necessitated by the communal nature of farming, and especially by the practice of turning all the livestock, belonging to several tenants and cottars, on to the arable after harvest to graze the stubble. In an era before effective undersoil drainage had been developed, the best way of draining the soil was to plough it ridge and furrow. Over large areas of Scotland the soils suitable for cultivation were boulder-encumbered clays derived from glacial drift. The land would be ploughed into a series of broad ridges, aligned approximately downslope, perhaps thirty to thirty-five feet wide and three feet high from furrow to crown. Water drained off the ridges into the furrows, and then downhill to field drains and stanks. This system tended to cause the parching of crops on the crests of ridges in dry weather, and waterlogging in the furrows in wet seasons. This is reflected by the fact that the traditional Scottish inch was calculated from three grains of bere set end to end: 'ane taken off the middle of the rig; ane off the syde and ane off the furrow', to make a fair average.

Potatoes were grown on ridges or lazy-beds, their outlines still to be seen all over the island. The seed potatoes were laid on manure upon last year's unturned ridges, two to four feet across, and covered with three inches of soil flung up out of one and a half to two foot wide furrows. Lazy-beds were fed industriously with seaweed, and yielded luxuriant crops, often being used also for oats and barley. They can still easily be seen on many hillsides in Jura.

The beasts required for winter food were slaughtered in autumn and the beef and mutton salted down. The rest of the beef cattle were turned out to fend for themselves, when they either lost all their fat, or in bad winters died in large numbers through lack of fodder.

Milk cows, often shared the people's houses, and, although confined to one end, this was often unpartitioned, for islemen often preferred to allow the cow a sight of the fire. The dung that accumulated on the floor in winter was carried out in wicker creels to manure the field, together with peat ash from the fire, and old sooted thatch from the roof.

The year's work was traditionally not begun until 10 March, following a comparatively idle winter. Other work, especially fishing, complemented the return from the land.

Lands were early valued as 'pennylands', which varied in size and pattern.

A turf or stone dyke, although often only an imaginary line, separated the arable from the hill pasture. The green pasture, so-called, was mostly ground too wet, or woody, or stony to be ploughed.

There is little specific information about cultivation on Jura itself, but the methods in the Inner Hebrides seem to have been reasonably standard and widespread. Tools were few: there were peat and turf cutters; harrow; potato digger; peat sledge; flail; horse baskets; cheese press and tubs. However, the principal tools were the cas-chrom (crooked foot, or foot plough); the cas-dhie-reach (straight foot, or ordinary spade) and the plough. The cas-chrom was superior to spade and plough. Ground dug with it gave a heavier crop, equal to ground twice ploughed; it could be used to cultivate either boggy ground or steep hill-slopes inaccessible to the plough. It accomplished almost double the work of a spade with the same labour.

PLATE 17. Katie Darroch, storyteller of Jura. *(page 509)*

PLATE 18. Donald McKechnie, the Jura Bard. *(page 514)*

PLATE 19. Neil Shaw and his mother at Inverlussa. *(page 513)*

PLATE 20. Kate Clark, Mr McCuaig's cook at Jura Manse. *(page 499)*

PLATE 21. Men of Jura about to leave to serve in the First World War. *(page 525)*

PLATE 22. The Long Rigs of Knockrome at harvest time. *(page 526)*

PLATE 23. Cutting oats at Lagg. Colin Campbell and the Lindsay girls. Angus McKechnie at right. *(page 526)*

PLATE 24. The dairymaids of Ardfin House. McDougall the postman at the left. *(page 526)*

PLATE 25. Bringing in the peat at Inver. *(page 526)*

PLATE 26. Donald McDougall, the blacksmith, with his son Dan. In the doorway is Captain McDougall – no relation. *(page 526)*

PLATE 27. Duncan Buie scattering guano at potato planting at Ardfin. *(page 526)*

PLATE 28. Colin Campbell with his son Charles Graham Campell. *(page 526)*

PLATE 29. Kate Buie, known as 'Kate Stramash'. *(page 535)*

PLATE 30. Angus McKechnie, holding the McLean skull. *(page 541)*

PLATE 31. Member of the Black family in front of their family home in Keils. *(page 534)*

PLATE 32. Charlotte Darroch at Knockrome with her pig. *(page 526)*

PLATE 33. Miss Campbell of Jura presenting the trophies at the Jura Show. *(page 531)*

PLATE 34. 'Grannie Darroch' of Feolin Ferry Farm. *(page 535)*

PLATE 35. John Macgregor and Kate Buie at Ardfernal. Katie Darroch's grandparents. *(page 537)*

PLATE 36. Four old men of Jura in the 1920s. Neil Buie, a gardener, d.1926 (73); Jimmy Shaw of the ferry d.1933 (86); Ian Rankin, former sea captain, d.1925 (87); Donald Stewart, a cooper, d.1929 (73). *(page 544)*

The cas-chrom had a six foot shaft of oak or ash, which had the lower end, naturally bent at an obtuse angle. Sometimes the head was a separate piece made fast to the shaft. It was about two feet six inches long, four or five inches wide, and shod with a six inch iron tip. A strong wooden peg projected eight inches from the right-hand side where the shaft and head met. The worker placed his foot on the peg and drove the head tip-first down into the ground with two jerks. A sideways jerk on the shaft threw a clod of earth about ten inches to the left side. On stony ground the lever was powerful enough to turn out boulders up to 200 pounds in weight. The cas-chrom worker moved backward, and twelve men working in a line could dig an acre in a day.

The cas-chrom, or the earlier straight spade were importantly used for lazybedding. Considerable areas of moorland and hill slope were thus made fertile.

The plough was a cumbersome wooden contraption in which the only metal was the iron coulter or soc.

Grain when ripe was early uprooted by hand, although later sickled or scythed. The grain was winnowed before being parched in the local kiln. The remains of the township kiln can be identified in most surviving crofting townships on Jura. In early days grinding was a daily chore for women and there were querns in every house. Two women milled, one rotating the upper stone and the other feeding in the grain. It took four hours to grind a bushel. Querns can still be seen lying near the back door of croft houses. Later, the laird established his own mill, and everyone was compelled to use it.

Martin Martin visited Jura in 1695, thirty-four years after Baillie Duncan Campbell established himself on the island by rule of law, backed up by force of arms. The Clan system was no more, and the land was owned by the Campbells, from the Duke of Argyll as ultimate superior, down through Cawdor and Shawfield to the lesser lairds of Jura. The ordinary people had become tenants and cottars, the lesser ranks being little more than serfs.

Martin gives us more details about the environment:

> The earth of Jura is brown and greyish on the coast, and black in the hills, which are covered with heath and some grass that provides good pasture for horses, cows, sheep and goats. The hills ordinarily have about 300 deer grazing on them, which are not to be hunted by any without the steward's licence. The rivers afford salmon.

The grass mixed in with the heath provided 'good pasture'; and Martin mentions 'horses, cattle, sheep and goats'. Horses would be needed for any kind of agriculture beyond cultivation by hand with such implements as the cas-chrom. Sheep would have been the old 'unimproved' breed, rather like the Soay sheep of today, which would have been milked on a daily basis. Goats are also important at this time. The island has in modern times been famed for its 'wild goats' which are no doubt a feral population based on earlier domesticated stock.

The people's cattle and sheep are evidently available for slaughter, for the inhabitants eat beef and mutton. The cattle produce milk, which is drunk and is also made into butter and cheese.

After Monro's early accounts of the indigenous wild animals, birds and fish, which he implies may somehow benefit the natives, all mention of stags and salmon now disappears as they become associated with the privilege of land-ownership and hunting and fishing.

Sea fish can still be caught. Indeed Francis Stewart in the *Statistical Return* (1794) lists: 'cuddies' (coalfish or saithe), 'lythe' (pollack), small cod, and a delicate fish called 'murloch' (a kind of dogfish). Oysters are mentioned in Loch Tarbert, but the Campbell of Jura Papers make it clear that they are a prerogative of the landowner. The loch also contains lobsters and crayfish.

Pennant, in 1776, observed women crossing over to Goat Island in Small Isles Bay to collect limpets and periwinkles, which he calls 'wretched fare'.

In recent times saithe and lythe have been caught in quantities off the rocks of Jura, and dried for use during the winter. Photographs taken in the twentieth century show the lines of fish hanging to dry in the sun. Mackerel are abundant in the inshore waters, and are caught with enthusiasm by recent inhabitants, although there is no mention of them in earlier times. There is no evidence that Jura folk ever indulged in serious offshore fishing.

It is intriguing to remember that it was in the 1760s that Campbell was involved in complex litigation with the parish minister, Alexander Hossack, and in evidence wrote: 'There is also a great Abundance of Sea-fish of all kinds, which the Minister may have at the Expense only of sending his servants to catch them.'

DIET

In 1637, the Franciscan Ward observed: 'the people generally use milk-foods, and, in summer, they have scarcely any bread.'

Martin Martin comments: 'There is no place so well stored with such a great quantity of good beef and mutton, where so little of both is eaten.' Only persons of high rank ate meat daily, or had three meals. All others ate two meals. Their normal fare was 'brochan' (oatmeal moistened with boiling water and butter), bread, butter, cheese, fish (salted in winter), salted beef and mutton in winter and spring, eggs and milk. Contemporary crofters believe that oats was the cereal crop best able to withstand the wet climate of Jura.

Brochan and bread were the staple diet in winter and spring. The local bread mentioned would be made of oatmeal flour, milled by the landowner's miller at the landowner's mill. Oat bread is heavy, but sweet tasting, and very filling. Barley bread was also common at this time. The bread in this diet was not then stripped of its vitamin content by over-refinement of the grain before milling. Martin says, 'brochan and bread used for the space of two days restores lost appetite.' Barley was also used, malleted wet in stone basins and then made into broth. The people drank no tea, coffee, or alcohol with their food, only pure water. The diet was ample and everyone had much exercise in the open air.

Martin mentions the potato as common in 1695. Although widely grown, it was in the beginning not appreciated as a food of value, therefore not intensively cultivated. However, from the mid eighteenth century as much as eight pounds of potatoes might be eaten a day, by every adult, eaten boiled with a little milk or salt.

Wild foods were probably eaten in greater quantity than was recorded, e.g., marine and land plants, shellfish, birds and rabbits. The islanders grew neither fruit nor green vegetables, but they did gather them wild.

By the late seventeenth century ale was being imported into the Western Isles and wine consumption had fallen by two-thirds. Brandy and whisky were drunk by everyone, 'to counteract the moist climate', but seventeenth-century 'whisky' should not be confused with the later, more famous product. Distilled from grain, usually oats, the spirit was variously named according to its alcoholic content: 'trestarig' (if thrice distilled), and 'usquebaugh' (from 'uisge', water, and 'beatha', life), (if four times distilled). Martin says that if any man exceeded two spoonfuls, 'it would presently stop his breath, and endanger his life'.

There was food value also in sloe gin and heather ale; the latter was made from two thirds young tops, one-third malt. Famines, when the potatoes failed, widened the food range; cattle were bled, for example.

Imported groceries were always costly compared to island incomes, and higher priced than on the mainland. Tea was a luxury until the late nineteenth century. MacDonald said in 1811 that the islanders probably ate a half to a quarter as much as the average Englishman.

Despite dirty conditions in the houses, children had a good expectation of life if they survived babyhood or later accident. Longevity was the rule and ages of eighty and ninety not uncommonly attained. The excellent state of general health, maintained without medical services, may be attributed in part to the natural environment of clean air and unpolluted earth; in part to clean living and simple diet. Martin records that mothers and wet nurses were abstemious and babies usually suckled till the end of the second year. They were bathed every morning and evening, some in warm water, some in cold. And the boys, incited no doubt by the great tales of the bards at ceilidhs, set out to make themselves hardy.

Plain fare and limited leisure brought their rewards. Not only was health generally good, but deformities of body and defects of mind were absent. In all his travels Martin saw no fat people nor any who looked starved. On the other hand, mainly because so little food was imported, the islands had no reserves to meet occasional famines when crops failed. In the notorious season of 1688, many people died of starvation in Skye.

REGULATIONS FOR TENANTS OF 1743
From 1743, some eighty years after Duncan Campbell came into control of much of Jura, there has survived a record of a series of regulations which were to be imposed on the tenants by the then landlord; Archibald Campbell. He had succeeded to his father John in 1736, and seven years later, this decree was proclaimed to the tenants. The document gives some idea of what Campbell was like as a landlord, and what it was like to be his tenants.

Memorandum of what things are to be proclaimed
to the tennants upon Sunday 9th of May, 1743.

Imp: They are to sett the half of their Potatoes in old land under the Penalty of five
  shillings sterling to each Person that shall be guilty of a breach of this Act, being
  the Staint upon each two pence of Land within the whole Bailirie.

Itt: They are to divide the Wintertown whenever the Crop is gathered for the first and second year of their Tack, and each Tennant to cleanse his Proportion of the same, under the Penalty of a Crown upon each twopenny land if it is not done within the 2nd year.

Itt: They are yearly to divide their Heath and cleanse the same under the Penalty above-mentioned upon each two penny during their Tack.

Itt: Every town within the whole Bailirie is to keep two sufficient Bulls for their Catle after this year, during all the remaining years of their Tack, under the Penalty of Two Pound Sterling to each Town that shall be guilty of a breach of this Act.

Itt: They are all to goe regularly to the shieldings under the Penalty of a Crown to each Person that shall stay for one day longer than the rest of the Neighbours.

Itt: They are all to cast their peats regularly as the Officer and any other two persons appointed by the Baillie shall direct them, under the Penalty of ten shillings sterling upon each 2 penny land.

Itt: They are not to keep or make use of any Schringeing Nets under the Penalty of five pound Sterling to each Person guilty.

Itt: Any person that is guilty of theft to the value of a sixpence is to lose his Tack and a fine imposed upon him according to his crime.

Itt: Any Person that is found guilty of bad Neighbourhiade is to loose the benefit of his Tack.

Itt: Any Person that shall putt any beaste unto any of the Isles without liberty is to pay a Crown for each beaste.

Itt: All the Towns below Ardmenish are to send eight Botles of straw to thatch the Miln and Smidy every two years during their Tack, and the Milner and Smith to thatch the same, and to send it to the Miln and Smidy before the eight Day of October.

Itt: Any Person that has Oversums is to put away the same before the first of June or to forfeit all the Oversums to the Master.
All the fines that shall be collected by any breaches of the things above mentioned to be equaly divided between the Master and the poor of the Parish.

It seems likely that this body of twelve regulations may have come as something of a shock to the tenants. We have no idea about existing legislation to which it was being added. Here are some comments.

Potatoes. It seems to have been the practice to grow potatoes on lazy-beds. The seed potatoes were laid on seaweed on the previous year's unturned ridges, and covered with soil flung up out of the intermediate furrows. The tenants evidently have to be discouraged from continually breaking new ground. Presumably they found they could get a better crop the first year they planted potatoes in fresh land. This regulation may have been an early attempt to get them to rotate their crops.

Wintertown. An obsolete term; this is to be divided after the crop is taken, and each tenant is to 'cleanse' his portion. The business of 'cleansing', or getting rid of pernicious weeds, was vital as a weed-infested field would produce no acceptable crop. This 'division' is a description of the runrig system. The reason for runrig strips was that a regular rotation of these strips between the various tenants would mean that each in turn got not only the best land, but the worst. The system was intended to be a fair division of the ground. In fact, local tradition says that it did not actually work like that. The good tenant did not bother to try to improve the land he was working on, because the following year someone else, and quite possibly a good-for-nothing rascal, would get the benefit. In the time of the present crofters' grandparents, the rotation of the rigs had already been abandoned in favour of each tenant retaining and working his own strips.

Heath. Dividing and cleansing the heath is more difficult to understand. It is not clear what was going on here, and why there was a penalty for non-compliance. Presumably the 'heath' is synonymous with the 'outbye' land.

Bulls. Since the provision of a bull is a drain on the township's pasture resources, it would seem to be fair that each township had to be responsible for its own bulls. It might also be too much of a strain on the neighbouring bulls if they had to serve cows outside their own herd.

Shielings. As we have already noted, it is rare to find written evidence about this practice. Since going to the shielings is a necessary discipline on all, and means the loss of woman power at a time when farm life is busy and demanding, there must be fairness about agreeing that everyone will set off for the shielings on the same day, and no one will get an advantage over his neighbours by remaining in the township longer than the others. It is the question of the date of departure for the shielings that is meant here, not the date of return. This also means that all the sheep and cattle are away from the arable land, and none are left behind, thus saving on cattle watching.

Peats. It is interesting to see that the responsibility for cutting peat is not simply a matter of personal inclination. The word 'cast' means to throw up and dry. 'Regularly' means 'by regulation', in other words, the peat banks are to be controlled by the baillie. There is 'the officer', a new functionary, who works together with two persons appointed by Campbell.

Schringeing Nets. The *Scottish National Dictionary* has various entries under 'screenge'. The relevant one is from 1825: 'screengin, a mode of fishing with small nets during the night'. Since contemporary residents of Jura have long memories of setting gill-nets along the shore in appropriate places to catch sea-trout and salmon, we may assume that Baillie Campbell is seeking to outlaw the possession and use of nets which would catch such game fish before they could run up Jura's rivers.

Theft. This regulation seems to be directed against petty theft among the townships. There seems no profit to the laird from this regulation. It may be altruistic, but it may reflect an awareness of the prevalence of this kind of small theft occurring in the community.

Bad Neighbours. This regulation is the most vague of the twelve. The word the secretary uses is difficult to read, but it looks like; 'Neighbourhiade'. This may be an early form of 'neighbourliness'. So a bad neighbour will lose 'the benefit of his tack'. This would mean he became essentially stateless, and no doubt would be forced to leave Jura. But how is 'bad neighbourliness' observed or proved? What does the crime consist of? What underlies the need for this new regulation?

The Isles. Rental Lists show that there is a set amount of rent payable for the offshore islands such as Pladda and Eilean nan Coinean. Unauthorised grazing there is evidently considered to constitute tresspass.

The Mill and the Smithy. Duty work does not put in an appearance in these regulations, but there is an indication of its ramifications in this reference to the thatching of the mill and the smithy. In general, one of the services which the landowner provided on an estate was that of milling.

The conversion of the island's grain crops into various kinds of flour had from time immemorial been a vital community task. The grain was dried in kilns and then ground in a rotary quern.

By the eighteenth century Campbell had built his own water-powered mill, and was binding the tenants to use it, and to pay the miller's 'dues' or 'multure'; a sixteenth of the grain in 1836. This 'thirlage' clause, like many other Jura regulations, hung on late in the island, and was still in force as late as 1916, in case the mill, though by then defunct, should be restarted.

The miller had the right to destroy such hand querns as he could find, but enough could be found to grind the relief maize of the 1840s famine, when water for the laird's mill seems to have been in short supply.

The fine eighteenth-century mill just beside the distillery gave its name to 'Miltown'. The latest mill, much of whose structure still survives, had a grain-drying floor, with a metal 'Saladin bed', which was heated from below. There was a 'wauk mill' nearby for the processing of flax. The miller leased the mill from the baillie. He supplied the machinery and the basic construction. The miller paid a rent for the mill and the croft which was usually associated with it. To ensure that he had adequate custom to meet his rents, the laird compelled the tenants to use only his mill. Tenants also had to help the miller to maintain the fabric of the mill, the dam and the lade. Here we have a record of the need to keep the thatch in good repair. The word for the quantity of straw is unclear.

In the nineteenth century the Knocknafeolaman mill was run by a family called McIsaac, who seem to have been brought into the island to take the position. Duncan McIsaac was the miller at the time of the 1841 census, but oral tradition says they came to the island about the end of the previous century. A remembered story records that all did not go smoothly in the matter of the mill.

It happened that Campbell fell out with McIsaac, and put him out of the mill, and put his own man in to do the milling. Campbell's man did not meet with the approval of the local tenants and they demanded a meeting with Campbell about the matter. When they met the Laird, he asked them outright what their grievance was.

The leader of the deputation spoke: 'Well,' said he, 'It's this way. The knot that is on the meal sacks when we come to collect them is not the same knot we put on them ourselves.

Th e upshot was that Campbell was forced to dismiss his miller, and have McIsaac back on his own job. The miller was helping himself to the tenants meal, but he couldn't copy their way of tying their bags.

The Blacksmith. The importance of the smith to the community is also stressed by the mention of the need to maintain the smiddy, or smithy.

Some of the customs which surrounded the work of the smith have been preserved. Ross, in the 1880s, records:

In one cottage I saw the occupant dropping burning peat through a small hole in the floor; below was a small chamber about two feet in diameter built of stones; about twenty inches deep and covered with a flat stone, like the upper stone of a quern. When the chamber was quite full, sods are placed over the hole. The resulting peat charcoal was used by the township blacksmith, wood being scarce and coal costly, and was said to greatly improve the quality of the iron. Each of the townships twelve tenants paid the smith fifteen shillings a year for his ready work, and the crofters must each provide his own fuel, blow the bellows and work the forehammer.

Soumings. The number of domestic animals kept by the various tenants was controlled, either by the laird or by agreement among the tenants. This was known as the 'soum', and the allowance was called the 'soumings'. Any animals over the agreed number are called 'oversoums'. This was a topic which caused endless disagreement, and even litigation between the laird and the tenants.

SUMMARY
It is striking to note that on two occasions Archibald Campbell, usually referred to as 'The Baillie', is also called 'The Master!' The owner was also frequently simply called 'Jura', or sometimes 'Old Jura'.

It would have been impossible for the tenants to resist this kind of autocratic legislation. Campbell's superiority was established by the Duke of Argyll, and his authority was supported by the Government, and if necessary reinforced by armed might. Doubtless the people were not capable of any kind of 'industrial organisation', and would have had no option but to conform or lose their tack, and with it their livelihood and position on the island. They would then become stateless and vagrant, and would be unable to avoid starvation for themselves and their families. It is hard to resist the impression that Campbell's attitude was patronising, and in general treated the people as if they were irresponsible children. Only contemporary inquiry, which we are in no position to make, would establish if he had any real justification for this position.

DR JOHN WALKER
In 1764, Dr John Walker, Professor of Natural History in the University of Edinburgh, visited Jura. The main reason for the visit was his experiment on the

Paps, but he had, as we would expect, a lively interest in everything he saw, and
he gives us a good deal of new information about the people of Jura: 'The people
live mostly on Milk, Butter, Cheese, Fish, Mutton, Venison, and use very little
vegetable aliment.' It is interesting to see that Walker believes they are able to
eat deer meat. Did he actually know; or is he surmising from the presence of so
many deer? Walker investigates questions of longevity. He disagrees with Martin
Martin in that he does not find the people to be in general more healthy than
in neighbouring islands, indeed he considers the reverse to be the case. He gives
reasons:

> In their Diet alone they differ; and to this may be ascribed any greater degree
> of mortality. Grain is here in greater scarcity than in the other islands, and
> the people lack gardens to supply them with vegetables. Of recent years the
> cultivation of potatoes has enlarged the proportion of their vegetable diet, and
> has added greatly to their health.

Here Walker is quoting the fashionable idea of the day that the ills of the
Highlands stem in part from their lack of vegetables. He writes about the
agriculture of Jura, but links his observations with his recommendations for the
improvements which he thinks could be made:

> The inhabitants sow as much barley and oats and plant as many potatoes as
> serve to support them. These crops they have upon the little plains by the
> seaside, but the whole of the arable land is very inconsiderable for of the
> 115,000 acres which the island contains, there does not seem to be above 15,000
> that have ever been cultivated, or that are capable of cultivation.

Walker considers that the people should change their farming policy. He
discusses the topic of the previous chapter:

> There is a particular product for every country, which its soil and climate and
> the situation with respect to a market point out. This however is frequently
> overlooked or neglected by the inhabitants, and another product adopted than
> what nature dictates. This is remarkably the case in the island of Jura.
>   The capital product is black cattle, but they are low in size and few in
> number, nor do they yield the profit that might otherwise be reaped from the
> island. In the low valleys there is indeed pasture for black cattle, but three
> fourths of the island consists of mountains and declivities too steep and abrupt
> for any black cattle to feed upon, and the grass they produce is too short and
> fine to afford them a tolerable pasture except in the height of summer. In
> winter the pasture is insufficient to support them and by the want of dry forage
> a great part of the produce of the island is lost in that season by the death of
> the cattle.
>   What the inhabitants of Jura should therefore wholly betake themselves to
> is raising of sheep. These cattle will thrive where cows and oxen must starve,
> and being far more hardy will go at all seasons of the year to such heights as
> are inaccessible to black cattle. The mountains of Jura are generally dry and
> green, with such a proportion of heath as is beneficial upon sheep grounds.

The sheep of this island may be driven to markets in Stirlingshire and Clydesdale at a small expense, and was the island fully stocked with them, under the management of skilful sheep farmers, I am persuaded that their wool alone, would amount to more than the whole profit presently obtained both in corn and cattle.

Walker also talks about manufacture:

The people of Jura have borrowed a little of the Linen manufacture of Islay. They have as yet sown little or no Lintseed, but are furnished with their lint from Islay, and the yarn they manufacture from it is exported to the Clyde. They send to Islay in exchange for the lint a considerable quantity of wool, some of which is of an exceeding good quality, and of a snow white colour, as the sheep are never smeared nor housed. But they manufacture no more of it than what serves for their own clothing.

We noted previously the presence of a flax industry. Walker considers they should give this operation up entirely, and concentrate on sheep and on spinning the wool themselves:

We have found above, that the inhabitants of Jura are mistaken in the product of their island, and they are, no less so, in the manufacture they ought to pursue. Neither their soil nor climate are well adapted for the production of flax, and the manufacture of it they ought entirely to resign to their neighbours in Ila. Their wool is what nature points out as the object of their industry. It is in sufficient plenty to employ all the labour in the island, and were they once trained to dress and spin it, their would find their labour much more profitably employed than it can possibly be in any branch of linen manufacture. In short, there cannot be a greater solecism in manufacture than their present practice of exporting wool and importing lint.

Walker further comments:

The shores of Jura afford a considerable quantity of seaweeds which are annually manufactured into kelp. The mountains abound with red deer and upon every farm there are large flocks of geese which live almost entirely upon what they pick up in the fields. No limestone, marle nor freestone have hitherto been discovered. Iron ore abounds in many places, and Sir Alexander Murray mentions his having discovered several veins both of lead and copper, but they are at present unknown to the inhabitants of Jura.

There are large rocks of the hone or whetstone upon the shore of the island of Jura, lying on the Sound of Ila, about three miles south from the passage at Portaskig. It is situated in plates or layers of different thickness. Some of them are coarse, and fit only for common tools, but others of them are capable of serving as whetstones for the finest razors and chirurgical instruments, and may be cut with a saw into any shape like wood. If quarries at this place were opened, the importation of hones from abroad might certainly be superseded.

Dr John Walker must be given credit for his observation and for his interest.

Underlying his comments is the implication that he is aware that the people are living in considerable poverty, and his suggestions are all intended to change their situation for the better. It may well be that the number of animals they could support was restricted by regulations imposed by the landlord, and that the changes he was recommending were not within their power to make. It seems clear that when the island began to carry a much larger number of sheep, it was because they were brought in by the landlord, and managed by his imported shepherds, and this new livestock brought no benefit whatever to the indigenous people of the island.

It seems unlikely that Walker had any political position from which he could commend his aspirations for the people of Jura to change their manufacturing habits in regard to flax and wool, or in connection with mining or quarrying. His suggestions were no doubt well intentioned, but it is not clear from the published account of his visit whether he actually wrote to Campbell of Jura to urge his opinions on the baillie. It seems certain that only Campbell could have taken any initiative in these matters on behalf of his tenants.

THOMAS PENNANT

The Welsh naturalist and traveller visited Jura a little later than Dr Walker, in 1776. In the midst of his keenly observed general description, he provides us with some interesting information about the lifestyle of the local people:

> The produce of Jura is about 300 or 400 head of cattle, sold annually at £3 to graziers who come for them. About 100 horses are also sold annually. Here are a few sheep with fleeces of most excellent fineness, and numbers of goats. In good seasons sufficient bear and oats are raised as will maintain the inhabitants, but sometimes they want; I suppose from the conversion of their grain into whisky. The chief food of the common people is potatoes and fish and shellfish. It is to be feared their competence of bread is very small. Bear produces four or five fold; oats three fold.
>
> Fern ashes bring in about a hundred pounds a year; about 200 tuns of kelp is burnt annually, and sold from £3 10/– to £4 per tun.
>
> Sloes are the only fruits of the island. An acid for punch is made of the berries of the rowan, and a kind of spirit is also distilled from them.

Shielings. We are also indebted to Pennant for giving us a detailed description of sheilings. This was late on his tour sailing north from Feolin Ferry towards Inver and Cnocbreac:

> See on the Jura side some 'sheelins' or summer huts for goatherds, who keep here a flock of eighty for the sake of the milk and cheeses. The last are made without salt, which they receive afterwards from the ashes of sea-tang, and the tang itself which the natives wrap it in.
>
> Land on a bank covered with sheelins, the habitations of some peasants who attend the herds of milch cows (cows kept for milk). These formed a grotesque group. Some were oblong, many conic, and so low that entrance is forbidden without creeping through the little opening, which has no other door than a

faggot of birch twigs, placed there occasionally. They are constructed of branches of trees, covered with sods. The furniture is a bed of heath, placed on a bank of sod; two blankets and a rug; some dairy vessels, and above, certain pendant shelves made of basket work, to hold the cheese, the produce of the Summer. In one of the little conic huts I spied a little infant asleep under the protection of a faithful dog.

This vivid description gives a unique picture of shielings on Jura, and we are fortunate that Pennant was interested in describing them. We are even more fortunate that the famous illustration has survived. In 1774 Pennant reported that Joseph Banks allowed Pennant's artist, Moses Griffith, 'to copy as many of the beautiful drawings in his collection as would be of use in the present work.' Another of Banks' artists was Charles Grignion, and it is possible that it was he who did the drawing, although it has also been attributed to Miller, based on the style of the painting. (Plate 11)

The Paps can be seen in all their splendour, with Corra Bhein and Beinn Tarsuinn to the north of the three Paps. Pennant locates his shielings near Cnocbreac on the west coast, and the artist would have found reasonably level moorland there where the settlement of huts could be sketched. He would have had to gain higher ground to get a suitable vantage point for his drawing of the Paps.

The conical and rounded huts are drawn with fine detail. The branches used for the frame protrude in wigwam style from the apex. The turfs that Pennant described are clearly seen. The rounded hut in the foreground seems somewhat dilapidated, and may show a hut from a previous year, not now in use. The distinguished visitors are evidently engaged in conversation with women, who are, as we would expect, the inhabitants. There is a small child being introduced to Pennant and a colleague, and two dogs play nearby. The doorway is clearly defined, and higher than in Pennant's notes, but the door itself appears to be constructed of birch faggots as Pennant describes. The ground appears to be of turf with some low birch scrub. There is no sign of the domestic animals for which the venture is undertaken.

The days of the shielings were until recently a vivid recollection among the older folk in Jura, and many locations could easily be pointed out. One recent inhabitant was always known as 'Donald Airidh', because he had been born at the shielings.

REV. FRANCIS STEWART

Thirty-two years after Pennant's visit the government commissioned a *Statistical Account of every Parish in the Land*. The date was 1794, and the person who got the job was the current clergyman, the Rev. Francis Stewart. Mr Stewart stayed only three years in Jura, and having been inducted to the charge only the year before the account, had, as he himself says, 'not been long in the parish'. He does his best in his account of his parishioners' way of living:

Soil and Produce. The soil along the shore is thin and very stony; towards the moor it is clayey, and in some places there is improvable moss. As the arable ground lies on a declivity in the neighbourhood of high hills, the water is constantly oozing down through it, and in many places, bursting out in little springs; so that it is what the low country farmers call 'spouty ground'.

The crops are oats, barley, potatoes and flax. There has been no trial made of artificial grasses, though there are some spots proper for them. Common peas, likewise are not raised here. Oats are, in general, a very unproductive crop, the greatest average returns are not above two and a half. Potatoes and barley are more productive, and, were the ground properly managed, might prove very valuable crops. The system of farming here has made very slow advances towards improvement, and is at least half a century behind that in many parts of the low country. The farmer does nothing to his grounds all the summer. Although there is plenty of limestone on the opposite shore of Knapdale, and in the adjoining island of Islay, and plenty of peat in Jura for burning lime, yet no person remembers a single trial made of that manure. The only manure used is the seaweed, which is to be had in great abundance, and gives one tolerable crop. This answers the contracted views of the farmer, who keeps the best patches of his ground constantly in tillage, and labours like one who is not certain of his possession beyond the present year. The farmers of this country are utter strangers to the mode of abridging labour. It is no uncommon thing to see twelve men and twenty horses at work in a farm which three men and four horses would, on an improved plan, labour to much better purpose.

The tame animals are cows, horses, sheep and goats. The small tenants, in general, overstock their grounds, so that the black cattle are rather small, and inferior to those of Islay. The horses also, though hardy, are a very diminutive breed. The sheep of Jura are remarkable for the fineness of their wool and the delicacy of their flesh. Were proper care taken to keep this breed from degenerating by mixing it with the Galloway sheep now introduced into the island; were it allowed to increase and cover the greater part of the island, Jura, in the course of a few years, might have very considerable returns from its wool, and transport annually the increase of its flocks to richer pastures on the continent, where the mutton would greatly excel that of the English or Low Country sheep.

There are several flocks of goats in Jura, but they are much on the decrease. They are not so profitable as sheep. They carry no fleece and their flesh is inferior.

The inhabitants of this island would find it in their interest to banish two-thirds of the horses which they keep; to rear fewer black cattle, and to extend their flock of sheep and goats. As there is very little meadow ground in the island, and the arable land makes such poor returns in oats, it ought certainly to be the grazier's object to keep such a stock principally as would shift for itself in winter.

Near half the farms in the island are in pasture, and require very few hands to manage them. Of course, the great body of the people live in the farms, which are in tillage. In some of these there are between fifty and sixty souls. Such a swarm of inhabitants, where manufactures and many other branches of industry are unknown, are a very great load upon the proprietors, and in a great measure useless to the state. The slightest survey of the situation of the people shows how much improvements in farming, and the introduction of industry are wanted.

Small quantities of slates have been quarried, and the colour and quality seem to be very good. Sand for glass manufacture and slate surely deserve attention.

What might be turned to great advantage is Jura's excellent wool. Were a few spinning machines introduced, and blanketing, and stockings manufactured, the hands that could be spared from agriculture and pasture would be usefully employed, and instead of being a dead weight on the proprietors, furnish an example of useful industry to their neighbours. The white herring fishery is an object which might be prosecuted with advantage from every corner of the parish. The harbours of Jura give it great advantage for large vessels, but through all the islands there are creeks for small fishing boats. Perhaps the best mode of encouraging the young men to embark in this undertaking would be for the gentlemen to join with them in fitting out a few boats of moderate size for that purpose. Should these boats be successful, they would be the means of circulating money, an article which from the absence of trade and manufactures is very scarce among the lower classes. The little sums introduced in this way would rouse a spirit of adventure and give new springs to every kind of industry.

Here, near the end of the eighteenth century, Francis Stewart confirms many of the facts and opinions of Walker and Pennant from thirty-five years earlier. Crops seem established as oats, barley, potatoes and flax. No fodder grasses are sown. No fertilising is undertaken except for the application of seaweed to the potato fields. No improvements whatever are undertaken for various reasons such as the absence of firm leases and the compulsory rotation of ground. The yield from arable crops is generally poor. Livestock remains as we have already considered; overstocked, and in consequence smaller than, and inferior to, the beasts on neighbouring islands.

Stewart mentions twice that the 'swarm of inhabitants' is 'a load upon the proprietors', although there seems no evidence that the laird subsidises the livelihood of the people.

Sheep. The old sheep Stewart describes were often household pets, with names, taken in at night, milked intensively. Jura may still have had a few in 1811. His observations on the sheep and goats of Jura are interesting, since after his time the question of sheep will become a major issue in the life of the island.

As he says, the predominant imported sheep was the Blackface. The mutton yield was multiplied several times by the change. A Blackface fetched 3s 3d in 1764, but had reached 7s 8d in 1792, and 11s 8d by 1824. Its fleece, coarse, averaged 2½–3 pounds in 1811, as did the Cheviot's. Blackface wool was 7d a pound, having risen from 3d in 1792; Cheviot was as much as 1s 8d a pound.

Here is an example of the management of these new flocks. In 1836 Tarbert had 3588 sheep and 902 new lambs, on 24,000 acres; or one sheep to five acres. Of these, 803 were then sold; 18 per cent each of lambs and adults, and including the 453, four-year-old wedders, or castrated males. This left 3581 in November; 86 rams, 1906 ewes, 1589 wedders, with 126 by then missing or dead.

At this date a Blackface was still worth only 12s with its wool down to 3½d a pound.

The 1854 Jura rules included the unsatisfactory, and since-abandoned, smearing of the sheep with a tar and butter mixture in October/November, against ticks (although these were not active again until the spring.) All the wool prices quoted are for 'smeared', or 'laid', worth only tw o-thirds 'white' wool.

Between 1860 and 1890 the Blackfaces were improved in yield, with an average sheep reaching 22s 5d and its wool reaching 6½d a pound. By 1892 Jura had 22,141 sheep, its peak; on a little over 56,000 acres; or one sheep per 2½ acres. But the animals were down to 19s 7d each, the wool to 4d a pound.

Following this slump, the various prospectuses offering parts of south Jura as sporting estates referred to sheep as to a blight – 'cleared' from Tarbert in 1901, from Feolin Ferry in 1936, and so on.

Goats. Stewart is also very familiar with Jura's goats. Goats were introduced into Scotland probably in the Neolithic. They were numerous in the eighteenth century. Pennant saw a flock of eighty, with shepherds near Feolin Ferry. They were kept for milk, cheese, and their wiry wool, and with hair left on, the skins made knapsacks and holsters. Reduction in numbers began about 1800, probably in response to the sheep boom. By the middle of the century there were not very many. An 1872 Ardmenish Crofter, leaving, handed over eleven nannies and their kids; twelve yearlings; ten yelds, or barren; and three bucks. Into the twentieth century a few were still pastured on islets such as Eilean nan Gabhard, Goat Island, in Small Isles Bay. In 1764 a goat fetched 2s 6d; in 1792, up to 10s; in 1872, 15s for a fine animal.

Several herds of wild goats still frequent the island. These animals are no doubt properly called 'feral', but no one seems very sure how the present populations relate to previously domesticated animals.

JAMES MACDONALD

Macdonald's *General View of the Agriculture of the Hebrides* (1811) includes an account of his visit to Jura. He addresses himself first to previous estimates of Jura's area, which he considers inaccurate:

> This gives 117 square miles, or 58,500 Scotch acres. Of these, little more that one nineteenth part, or 3000 acres are arable, i.e. under regular or occasional till-age. The old system of exhausting the ground by repeated white crops, without any regular rotation of grasses and green crops, prevails. Excepting what Mr Campbell has done near his place at Ardfin, and a little near the minister's manse, no part of this island exhibits any symptoms of advancing agriculture. Mr McNeill of Colonsay employs his share of the north end entirely under pasturage, and under the sheep farming system. Mr Campbell passes his time in the ancient hospitable Hebridean style, without any innovation whatever.
>
> A road is carrying on from the Islay ferry to the north-east of Jura which, it is hoped will be the signal for other improvements to the natives. They have

a vast deal of improvable soil, with a fine exposure, the finest and wholesomest atmosphere in this whole region, and considerable facility of procuring manures. With a little more industry, and the advantages of leases for their lands, as well as salutary regulations concerning their stock of horses, cattle and sheep, they might soon follow in the footsteps of their neighbours in Gigha, Islay and Colonsay, and remove the reproach often levelled against them of being a century behind the people of those well managed isles.

Considerable quantities of kelp; perhaps eighty or ninety tons, are annually made here; some fern ashes were formerly exported, but of late years that manufacture seems to be abandoned, owing to the decrease of the material which yielded it. Many tons of fine sand which form the bottom of some bays on the west side were used for glass manufacture, but this is no longer the case – that kind of sand being found nearer the towns.

Neither the crops or the livestock deserve any particular notice. Potatoes are cultivated with some care, pretty much in the same way as in Islay. They constitute four-fifths of the nourishment of the inhabitants.'

Macdonald's comments convey his impression of the neglected state of the island at the beginning of the nineteenth century.

LORD TEIGNMOUTH
Lord Teignmouth published his *Sketches of the Coasts and Islands of Scotland* in 1836. Here are his more general comments:

The bay of the small isles affords good anchorage for shipping. The surrounding shores and hills are cultivated but poorly, and without enclosures. A sheltered rock, at the entrance of a wooded glen, contains a decent public house, a mill, some cottages, and a little pier for boats. The innkeeper rents the largest arable farm in the island for £100, but declines improving it, as he has no lease.

All the corn used in the island is ground at the above mill, passing through the hands of the laird, who remunerates the miller, chiefly in the old style, for his work, by what is called multure, one-sixteenth of the grain which he grinds.

The little agriculture in Jura is in a very neglected state. No leases are granted. The island yields neither lime-earth, marl, nor calcareous sand. The farms are clustered together, on an average eight in number, each farmer having a separate plot of ground for corn and potatoes, and from four to eight cows grazing on a common pasture.

Lord Teignmouth spent some time on Colonsay, and was returned in Mr McNeil's boat to Loch Tarbert. On the passage up the Loch he comments:

The fishermen who catch the herrings and other fish which frequent Loch Tarbert, are from Isla, and take up their quarters in the caves, while their few boats afford the only proof of human inhabitants. The upper part of this Bay is connected with the lower by a passage of the breadth of a canal between high rocks.

So he passed the famous narrows and was landed at the head of Loch Tarbert.

It is here that he found himself able to record perhaps his best-known recollection of Jura:

> On landing and reaching a height, in the midst of the vast howling wilderness, for wind and rain augmented the dreariness of the scene, I perceived on a distant knoll a solitary black spot, which might have been mistaken by an unpractised eye for a sign, infallible to the sportsman, of the place of his wounded quarry; a collection of crows or corbies, employed in accelerating the death or devouring the carcase of the poor animal.
>
> It proved, however, on near approach, to be a band of mourners assembled at a rustic funeral, on an ancient and perfectly sequestered cemetery, distinguished by the ruins of a chapel. A grave was digging to receive the remains of a shepherd of the laird of Jura; and beside the coffin lay two others, containing the bodies of his children, one of whom had been buried two years, and the other one year, and were now taken up to make room for their parent.
>
> When the grave was closed, the mourners, sixty in number, attended by their dogs, which were very numerous, sat down on the ground, now thoroughly soaked with heavy rain, which had been falling for some hours, and the brother-in-law of the deceased invited me to drink a glass of whisky, and eat some oatcake. About twenty women and girls were present, among whom were the mother and daughter, accompanied by the sons of the deceased. The mother, nearly seventy years of age, sat fixing her eyes earnestly on the grave, in which were buried her husband, and children, and grandchildren, and just sipped the whisky which was first offered to her. The women seemed to dispense with this part of the ceremony, but the men and boys drank three rounds, according to custom; and abundance of oatcake was distributed. The repast was concluded with a prayer and thanksgiving in Gaelic, delivered by a brother-in-law of the deceased, who stood up in the midst of the circle, all present being uncovered.
>
> A man from Isla, whom I had asked whether prayer was ever offered on these occasions, replied with obvious suspicion as to the motives of the inquiry, and in a low tone of voice 'Yes, that is beginning; but it is Popish, and there are no Papists here;' at the same time he had no objection to the commencing and concluding with thanksgiving, which had taken place that day. He added that the brother talked all about the New Testament, which he could do very well, and that it was a great blessing to be able to read the Bible both in English and Gaelic.
>
> The mourners had assembled with the promptitude characteristic of their ancient obedience to any summons to a public occasion, for the deceased had breathed his last only the day before, at five in the morning. Friends had been instantly despatched in all directions to different parts of Jura and Isla, inviting the mourners to the grave at three the following afternoon. The corpse had been brought half the length of the island that day, and the Isla man, with whom I had conversed, had walked thirty miles since morning, and intended returning twenty miles more to the ferry of Port Askaig that evening. They had well earned the refreshment which was provided for them.

The ceremony was conducted with perfect order and solemnity; and the mourners returned to Tarbert, where boats awaited them. The little public-house in Lagg bay, where we landed and I took up my quarters, was well thronged; and my companions soon exchanged their demure looks for smiling and merriment; those who had far to return were induced to stay, and they continued drinking and singing till past midnight, making an uproar which prevented the possibility of sleeping. The mourners found their reception at Tarbert so pleasant that they remained the next day and assisting in restoring a bridge.

Teignmouth's eyewitness account is the only one we have of a nineteenth-century funeral on Jura and is full of fascinating detail. The distant group of mourners looked like crows on a carcass. Had the men put on black clothes? The family grave was evidently opened and closed by the friends and neighbours, a practice which continued in Jura until the 1970s. The parish minister, Alexander Kennedy, who had been in office for about twelve years seems not to have been present at all. The occasion was evidently religious in nature, for there was an opening and closing 'thanksgiving', and the brother had read the New Testament, presumably in Gaelic, and apparently spoken on it fluently.

Teignmouth's question about prayer, which raised the question of Roman Catholic practice may have been understood to mean 'prayer for the deceased' The Reformed Presbyterian Church did not, and still does not, approve of 'prayers for the dead', on the grounds that, by the time of the funeral, God would be assumed already to have the dead person in his own safekeeping, and further prayers for his or her welfare would be redundant. On the other hand, the question may have simply been a general one from someone who would have been used to formal prayers from the Prayer Book, and found their absence surprising.

Whisky, cheese and oatcakes were distributed at the graveside after an interment as recently as the author's incumbency in the 1970s and 1980s, so the practice is of long standing. It is also interesting to find women and girls present at the cemetery. In various parts of Scotland and at various times in the past it was not the custom for the women to go to the interment, but at this time in Jura there was evidently no barrier to their attendance, although most of them did not partake of the dram.

The custom of adjourning to a nearby hostelry after a funeral was, and still is, widespread in Scotland, and was evidently expected at this time. The distance from Tarbert to Lagg was only about two and a quarter miles by sea or land, and it was evidently considered preferable to go by boat. Although Teignmouth gives us a great deal of detail, he fails to put the matter of the relationships of the various family members beyond question. Exactly who is 'the mother, nearly seventy years of age'? On balance it seems likely that the dead shepherd is in middle age, and that the coffins taken up to make room for him are those of children who have died in infancy or early childhood. Surviving sons of his are also present. The 'mother and daughter' would then be 'his mother' and 'his sister'. Mother is gazing on the grave, which contains her husband (his father),

her children (his brothers and sisters) and grandchildren (his children and those of his siblings).

This leaves the question of the dead man's wife. Was she present, but not identified by Teignmouth? Was she dead, or absent for some other reason? Was she present as 'the daughter' of the mother, which would make the deceased shepherd her son-in-law, rather than her son? Teignmouth leaves the matter open for our speculation.

Apart from the fact that Martin Martin tells us in 1695 that the inhabitants of Jura 'do not open a grave on Friday, and bury none on that day, except the grave has been opened before', Teignmouth's account of a funeral from the 1830s is the only mention of the customs surrounding death and bereavement we have until early nineteenth-century traditions about the burial of strangers.

ALEXANDER KENNEDY

In 1845 *The New Statistical Account* was published in which the Jura entry was written by the Rev. Alexander Kennedy, the parish minister. Mr Kennedy, appointed in 1823, was by the time of writing well acquainted with his parish. Here are some of his comments:

> Since the last Statistical Account much has been done in the way of turning waste and pasture lands to the very best advantage. Considerable sums of money have been expended in making sheep drains in hill and dale, by which means several extensive tracts of land, where nothing but stunted heath, sprits, and underwood was to be seen, now present an improved surface clothed with verdant covering.
>
> Bridges have been constructed, comfortable farmsteadings erected, and throughout the whole extent of the parish, sunk fences with whin, black and hazel thorn hedges, substantial and well built stone dykes, judiciously laid out, now intersect the island of Jura. Judging from the progress already made, and from the zeal displayed by the principal proprietors in this work, it may not be too much to expect that, in a short time, the yearly value of the lands may be much enhanced, and the landlords amply remunerated for their outlays.
>
> Horses, though generally small in size, are exceedingly hardy and active. The breed of black cattle, the staple commodity of the country, is considered to be superior; it is reared solely for the market, at which it meets a ready sale; much attention is therefore paid by landlord and tenant to the improvement of it, the payment of their rents being made to depend upon the produce of their cattle; but few of the tenants send corn to the mill, the produce of their harvest (bear and potatoes excepted), being for the most part expended upon their stock, during the months of winter and spring. There are from 1000 to 1200 head of black cattle annually sold out of the island of Jura; one half of these by the tenants; average value £5 Sterling. The other half consists of four year old stots and heifers, sold by average value at the present prices; £10 Sterling. Previous to the year 1800, the island of Jura was stocked with the small white-faced Highland breed of sheep, which was highly valued on account of the flavour of the mutton, and the superior quality of its wool; at that time the black-faced breed was introduced, which in its turn is likely to give place

to Cheviots, now prospering in the extensive tenement of Tarbert.

The quantity of grain annually sown in Jura may fluctuate between 400 and 500 bolls of oats, and from 80 to 100 bolls of bear.

Having survived the Disruption of 1843, Alexander Kennedy doubtless is concerned not to upset Campbell, the heritor and his chief patron. His account details 'considerable sums of money expended in making sheep drains', and lists many other 'improvements'. As a result, he notes, 'the yearly value of the lands may be much enhanced, and the landlords amply remunerated for their outlays.' Whether the local inhabitants were also expected to benefit from these changes is not clear.

Kennedy, however, may reveal more than he intends. We can extract from his account. Black cattle are reared solely for the market, and landlord and tenant pay attention to the improvement of the breed. The payments of rent are made to depend on the produce of cattle. Little oats is available for milling as it is all fed to the cattle as winter feed. Between 1000–1200 head of black cattle are sold out of Jura annually. One half by the tenants at £5 per head and the other half by the laird at £10 per head. Cheviot sheep are now prospering in 'the extensive tenement of Tarbert'. (In this sense a 'tenement' is a holding by a tenant.)

FURTHER ACCOUNTS

We have looked at Jura through the eyes of those who visited it periodically through the eighteenth and early nineteenth centuries. After Kennedy's report of 1845 it seems that fewer of the people who came to look at the island subsequently recorded and published their impressions. Indeed, with the exception of bodies such as the Crofters' Commission and the Red Deer Commision there is a conspicuous absence of public comment from about the middle of the nineteenth century to the middle of the twentieth. Much was happening in Jura during this period. However, formal comment from visitors seems largely to dry up, and few impressions are recorded.

F. FRASER DARLING

F. Fraser Darling is an exception here and was, of course, an exceptional student of the Scottish Highlands and Islands. In 1955 he edited and published *West Highland Survey: an Essay in Human Ecology* from which we reproduce his view of Jura more or less in its entirety:

Jura. This island of 93,794 acres can scarcely be other than a problem. It is the largest expanse of that very poor rock, metamorphic quartzite, in the Highlands. Only an extremely narrow strip on the eastern side is of different rocks; hornblende, phyllitic and mica schists, and graphitic schist and slate. The island is over thirty miles long and is almost cut in two by a western sea loch, Loch Tarbert, but this loch-side holds no human habitation and it is trackless. The entire western side of Jura is trackless and uninhabited except at the south-west corner where there is a ferry house looking across the three-quarters of a mile of sound to Port Askaig in Islay. From Feolin Ferry the road goes round the south end of Jura and up the east coast to Ardlussa, from which place there is a track almost to the north point.

The surface of Jura is extremely broken and difficult to traverse. In the southern half of the island are the fine conical hills known as the Paps of Jura, rising to 2571 feet, with lower slopes to the sea clothed in blanket bog. The northern half of Jura does not rise about 1500 feet, but it is even harder to get about there. Small areas of birch scrub still exist in Jura, but for the most part the surface is poor blanket bog. The island is remarkable for the great lengths of raised beaches. The name of Jura means deer island, and it has a long history of being a hunting-ground rather than anything else. It is now divided into four forests, but it would seem that there is quite insufficient toll taken of the deer during the stag and hind seasons, and numbers are too high. The result is that what little crofting there is in the few townships on the east coast schists is much hampered by the depredations of the deer.

The human population is about 263, and as there is nothing but crofting and a little part-time work on the estates, the husbandry remains good. Proprietors have also given the crofters large soumings; up to fourteen cows in some cases; so that they have a rather better chance of making a living than in the small crofts elsewhere. There was once a distillery at Craighouse where the pier is, but it closed down in 1912, so the acre strips of the Craighouse crofts which then went empty, were taken over by the crofters of Keils, a township of thatched oval houses that preserves all the appearance of the traditional and romanticized Highland clachan. The hopelessness of Jura ever being much else than a deer forest is shown by the fact that the inbye ratio to total area is 1:135, and the tillage to total area 1:427. The tillage to inbye ratio is surprisingly high at 1:3.15.

One can see little other hope for Jura than an enlargement of souming to the crofters to whatever they can manage; and first of all an attempt to make a census of the deer (such as Henry Evans did for his part of Jura for many years in the old days), and to get the excessive numbers down to one to sixty acres, exclusive of calves of the year, which would mean about 1500 deer on the island as a continuing stock, yielding 250 carcases a year, and two thirds of the harvest should be of hinds. After some time it could then be judged whether a forestry project on the east side would be practicable.

Here then is the opinion of the most highly respected naturalist and ecologist of his day, writing in the middle of the twentieth century. It is a depressing picture. Studies in other chapters reveal how accurate and full of insight Fraser Darling's general assessment was. He could not have been expected to predict that the distillery would be reborn, although he was correct in foreseeing afforestation, and that the future for crofting was precarious. His was yet another voice to add to all those we have heard from the earlier past to declare that because of the hostility of their natural environment, those who wish to live on Jura have always been, and will always be, very much 'up against it'.

31

Life in the Nineteenth Century

REGULATIONS FOR COTTARS

In 1854 the local laws for Jura peasantry were enshrined in neatly printed blue leaflets; one for land-tenants or crofters, and one for hired men or cottars. Of these sets of regulations, we look first at that prepared for the cottars. It is a most remarkable document, and follows here as originally set out.

General Conditions and Regulations for the Cottars on the Estate of Jura, February 1854

1st   The Cottars shall possess their whole houses, and the arable land to be annually allotted thereto, by themselves and families, and are expressly prohibited from admitting or harbouring any other person or persons whatever, without the Proprietor's consent in writing.

2nd   Their entry to the houses and grazing shall be at Whitsunday, and to the arable land on the 1st of February preceding their entry to the houses. The Cottars shall have no right to the arable land allotted to them, after the removal of the crop, or be entitled to a waygoing crop. Cottars possessing for more than one year by *tacit relocation*, shall have no right to the same portion or piece of arable land as they cropped the preceding year, but only to such portion as may be allotted to them from year to year, by the Proprietor or his Factor, in the month of February.

3rd   The stipulated rent shall be payable to the Proprietor at the mansion-house of the estate, the first half-year's rent at Martinmas after their entry, and the next at the Whitsunday following; and in addition to the stipulated rents, such Cottars as the Proprietor considers able to do so, shall pay poor rates, and shall each perform twelve days' duty work, and attend the cutting and leading of the peats required by the Proprietor for his own use, according to the use and wont of the Estate.

4th   The Cottars shall labour, manure, and sow the arable land allotted to them respectively in a proper and suitable way, and keep such kind and number of stock only as shall be fixed upon by the Proprietor. Cottars keeping cows shall be bound to put at least the one-half of the arable land allotted to them under potatoes, and those keeping no cows the whole. Cottars keeping cattle or horses shall be bound to graze them, along with the Tenant's cattle of the farm on which they reside, or in such other place or way as the Proprietor may direct, and shall have no right to the hay growing on the land bordering on the portions of ground allotted to them respectively, and shall not break or cut up the surface of the ground for feal, divot, or any other purpose whatever.

5th   The Cottars at entry shall receive their houses under comprisement, and shall be bound to maintain and uphold them to their comprised value during their occupancy, or pay the deficiency, as shall be ascertained by the Birleymen or sworn Apprisers of the estate, on their removal. Nothwithstanding which, however, the Cottars shall be bound, at least once in every two years, or when required by the Proprietor or his Factor, to put on a sufficient and substantial coating of thatch on their houses, and Failing compliance with this requisition after six days notice, the Proprietor or his Factor may direct the same to be executed at the expense of the respective Cottars, which expense, as certified by the Birleymen of the Estate, shall be exigible from the Cottars at next rent collection. No doors, windows, partitions, lofts, nor any other article of furnishing, shall be removed or carried away by the Cottars on their removal.

6th   No Cottar shall keep a dog, nor more than one sow or pig, and the pig shall not be allowed to go at large from the 1st day of April until after the potatoes are dug, and then only on condition that their noses are securely ringed; and shall be bound to remove to a distance, or keep confined, their poultry during harvest and seed time; and shall cut and win the peats necessary for their own consumption only, in a regular manner, laying the sods or parings with the grass sides uppermost, so that no water may remain, and that in such place or places and manner, as may be pointed out by the Proprietor or his Factor, and shall, in particular, make no new openings.

7th   In case the Cottars shall manage or crop their land, break the surface of the ground, or cut peats contrary to the foregoing regulations, they shall pay £3 of additional rent to the Proprietor; and if they respectively keep more cattle, pigs, or bestial of any kind, than the number fixed upon by the Proprietor, then they shall respectively pay an additional rent of £3 for each horse, £2 for each cattle beast, £1 for each pig, and £1 for each dog or other animal, as well as 1s per day of additional rent for every sow or pig, or head of poultry, allowed to go at large without the Proprietor's consent in writing, contrary to the foregoing regulations. And in the event of the Cottars keeping and harbouring strangers in their houses, without the Proprietor's consent, they shall pay of additional rent, 2s per day for each stranger, and for every day they shall do so; and in the event of their not attending and performing the stipulated duty-work when called upon to do so, they shall respectively pay for each day's absence 2s And all these additional rents shall be considered not a penal, but as a pactional rent, payable at the next rent collection to the Proprietor, over and above compensating the Proprietor, his Tenants and Cottars, for any damage or loss which may have been sustained by him or them in consequence.

8th   The Proprietor reserves full power and liberty, in case of a Cottar keeping a dog, to destroy it, on giving the Cottar twelve hours' notice to remove the dog from the estate. The Proprietor also reserves power to remove any over-soums of cattle, horses, sheep, pigs, or other bestial, belonging to the Cottars found on his property, and to sell the same at such price or prices, and in such manner as he may think most advisable, with which sale the owners shall have no right to interfere or find fault, the Proprietor returning the proceeds of said sale to the owners of the animals so removed, but under deduction always of all charges and expenses attending the same, unless removed by the Cottars themselves from the estate after receiving ten days' notice.

9th   The Cottars shall be bound to remove from their houses, land, and other subjects let, at the expiry of their leases or minutes of sett, without warning; and in case they continue to possess after that period without a new agreement, they shall respectively pay double the stipulated rent and duty work until they do remove. Yearly Cottars, and Cottars possessing by *tacit relocation*, must give written intimation to the Proprietor or his Factor, of their intention to remove, on or before the 1st of February in the year of their intended removal, otherwise, in the option of the Proprietor, and without prejudice to his power to remove within the statutory period, they shall be held as Tenants for another year.

10th The Cottars shall be bound to suppress poaching and salmon-fishing, and to give all information and assistance in their power to the Proprietor and his Factor, for suppressing all tresspass, poaching, poachers, and salmon-fishing, not only within the bounds of their respective possessions, but generally within the whole lands and estate of Jura.

11th In the event of any disputes arising between the Cottars, in regard to any matter connected herewith, the Proprietor, and in his absence his Factor, shall act as sole Arbiter therein, and the decision pronounced shall be obligatory on both parties.

This dreadful document legislates for the group who have the least possessions, and very little ability to influence their situation. However, a very similar document was in force at the same time for full tenants, who might well be expected to be under a more liberal regime.

A study of the set of conditions for tenants, shows that they are in fact even more closely hedged around with rules than the cottars. It must be remembered that from the point of view of the Campbells, a tenant was capable of causing much more trouble than a cottar, and indeed the Campbell of Jura Papers show plenty of evidence that tenants could be difficult to control.

It may be worth remarking that the record of the meeting of the Crofters Commission in 1894 in Jura, which is recorded in full later, shows Miss Isabella Campbell attempting to show her family in the light of noble, kindly and benevolent landlords. *The Conditions and Regulations for Cottars*, had they been entered as evidence, would have told a different story. It may well be that this kind of document is not confined to the primitive social situation of Jura, but that similar sets of regulations could be found in many other parts of the Western Isles.

The various visitors whose accounts we have studied seem to have been aware that the common people of Jura were living in great poverty. There are well-documented examples of Highland lairds who did what lay in their power to help their tenants in such hardship. There is no evidence that the Campbells of Jura were interested in such a venture.

It seems unneccessary to give any detailed comment on the above regulations as the atmosphere they convey will no doubt appal any contemporary readers as much as it always has distressed the author. However one aspect of these is worthy of note.

DUTY WORK

To avoid twelve days' 'duty work' a crofter had to pay 4s a day, twice the wage paid by the owner to his employees. It is clear from the fines in the 1875 wages book that all able-bodied members of a crofter's family had to do the unpaid stint, in practice, of twenty days.

The question of duty work seems to have been a bone of contention over many years. It arises in the evidence given to the Crofter's Commission, and it was still fresh in the memory of elderly residents being interviewed about farming practices in the 1970s. The custom seems to have been fading away in the Hebrides by the end of the nineteenth century, but it may well have hung on in some form in Jura until the Campbells sold up and left the island in 1938.

The author was told of the custom of 'borlanachd', or duty work, by Norman McDonald, the farm manager of Jura House Estate, who clearly recalled that it was operated on the basis of 'tokens' which were handed out and returned. He felt that it was likely that some of the old tokens had survived, and gave permission for a search to be made. In the final event a cache of tokens was found in the ruins of an old desk. There were eighty-two of them. The tokens were rather corroded, thin, zinc discs; 27.5–28mm in diameter. Each one was counterstamped with a single letter or number about 8 mm tall. Individual discs numbered 1 to 7, although there was no example of the number 2, and only two of number 4. Others were individually lettered F, P and S.

No one could be found on the island who was able to give any indication of how the system operated. It is presumed that each token was for one day's work. The numbers might indicate different days, and the numbering may have been to counteract possible forms of cheating. Local folk gave it as their opinion that F, P and S probably meant 'Farm Work', 'Peat Work' and 'Seaware'. This is only conjecture, and the exact operation of the system now seems lost to us. Only the tokens survive, together with the fading memory of a resentful tenantry.

THE CAMPBELLS AND THEIR TENANTS

The Campbells' financial situation was strong because it was broadly based, with only a small part of their wealth concerned with the island of Jura. Indeed only about a quarter of Campbell's income came from within Jura. Miss Campbell speaks of her father and grandfather being forced to sell off their much beloved pedigree Highland cattle, because the herd was consistently making a loss. However, such a balance was completely artificial. The Campbells, had they chosen to do so, could have subsidised loss-making ventures in Jura from other interests elsewhere, but took the view that Jura had to pay its way.

The 1827–8 cash book of Archibald Campbell of Jura shows that just over £100,000 passed through the family's hands in that year. Analysis of the 1849 wages shows that his average male employee then earned £17 a year for a six-day week. The working day was from 6 am to 6 pm.

In 1811, MacDonald estimated the capital of a typical Jura tenant at between £5 and £12.

Virtually every tenant was in debt to the landowner for outstanding back rent, yet while his tenants lived in poverty, Campbell's household accounts reveal an expensive style of living. In 1814 Campbell spent £135 on a pipe of Madeira. In 1827 a silk handkerchief cost him 30 shillings. In 1845 he bought a musical box for £9. In 1846 Colin Campbell's yacht, *Red Deer*, cost £1476, and his grandfather's portrait £72. In 1849 Archibald Campbell, the seventh, was selling shoes to his workers at 9 shillings a pair. He seems to have been able to buy them for 2s 6d, which represented over a week's work to the buyers.

Evidence of benevolence is slender and intriguing. A note in 1834 says, 'Tobacco to be given away to Work people'. By 1835 Campbell's various rents amounted to about £4000 a year.

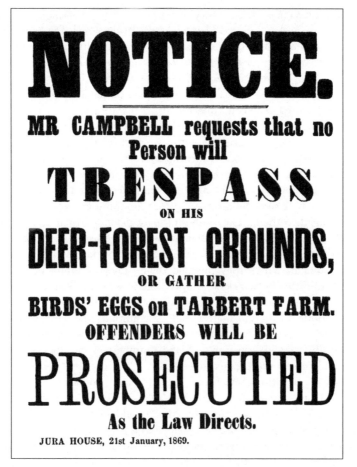

NOTICE.

MR CAMPBELL requests that no Person will

TRESPASS

ON HIS

DEER-FOREST GROUNDS,

OR GATHER

BIRDS' EGGS on TARBERT FARM.

OFFENDERS WILL BE

PROSECUTED

As the Law Directs.

JURA HOUSE, 21st January, 1869.

Figure 4. Poster suppressing poaching (1869).

Wages paid during the period are of interest. In 1792 a male labourer got 8d a day, but by 1811, probably because of the kelp, he was being paid 1s to 1s 6d.

In 1811 MacDonald noted that Jura 'tenants' paid £5-£20 per annum rent; and 'sub-tenants' got £3 per annum, usually in services or kind. By 1836 the forty-seven small-holdings at Ardfernal, Knockrome, Leargybreck and Keils were rented at from £4-£16 with the average about £9. The 1854 leaflet shows there was still rent in kind – 'the usual kain, according to the possessions they hold'.

Cottars could not keep a dog at all and crofters paid 5s a year tax on each dog after the first, or these could be destroyed, at the landowner's option, a right insisted upon at least to 1916. About 1854 the owner's game book lists all his dogs – Major, Parson, Walter and so on – and details his purchases such as babbery powder, hogslard and sulphur vivum for their treatment.

Regulations concerning suppressing poaching were reinforced by posters such as the one from 1869. It would be interesting to know which 'Law' Campbell is referring to when he says, 'As the Law Directs'.

THE KELP TRADE

The word 'kelp' and associated phrases like 'cutting wreck for kelp', have been occurring throughout these documents, and a word should be said on this subject.

'Wrack' or 'wreck' was the general term for seaweed, either washed up on the shore, or growing where it was exposed by the tide. Its use as a manure was known of ancient times, and fertility was maintained in poor ground by the application of rotted seaweed collected from the shore. The yield of oats and barley, and later potatoes, which could be gained by the use of seaweed was far in excess of that which was possible with any other form of manure. The question of the right to collect seaweed washed up by storms on the beaches, or to wade out and cut it from the lower shores was argued fiercely between landlord and tenants. The Campbells of Jura always maintained that the land between the tide-marks was part of their estate, and that anything growing on it or cast up upon it belonged to them. They unhesitatingly extended their claims to the bed of the sea offshore, and to the offshore waters themselves, although it seems likely that their success in upholding these claims was largely due to the remoteness of the area in which they pursued them. They certainly insisted that the cutting and collecting of 'wreck' was a privilege to which was attached a monetary value.

Kelp was quite a different matter. Kelp was initially the name given to any of the large brown seaweeds which grow in thick tangles offshore. However, it came to take on the specific meaning of the commercial product resulting from collecting and processing these seaweeds.

Kelp thus became the name for the alkaline ash produced by the burning of seaweed. The industry started in North Uist in 1735. Knowledge of it had been brought from Ireland to the Uists by MacDonald of Clanranald. The product was used in the manufacture of glass, soap, and linen. Large quantities of soda-ash needed for these industries were imported in the form of 'barilla' from Spain, France and Italy. Hebridean beginnings were small, but kelp-making spread to Harris, Lewis, Skye, Mull and Islay and Jura. In 1750 it fetched £1 a ton and this rose to £3 10/- a ton in 1755.

The seaweeds most commonly used were the wracks found growing between the tide-marks. These were knotted wrack (*Fucus nodosus*); serrated, or saw wrack (*Fucus serratus*); and bladder wrack (*Fucus vesiculosus*). Where they could be reached the oarweeds of the deep-sea tangles were also harvested. There are four main species of tangleweed living offshore from Jura: oar weed (*Laminaria digitata*); *Laminaria hyperborea*; *Laminaria saccharina*; and furbelows (*Saccorhiza polyschides*).

These are the weeds which grow below the low tide mark and are unpopular with yachtsmen, as they give 'poor holding' for anchors. They can be seen giving a dark tangled surface to bays such as Small Isles Bay at extreme low water of spring tides. They are torn loose from their 'holdfasts' by major seasonal storms and cast up on exposed beaches in enormous quantities, all round the island.

The seaweed was gathered at low water from boats and by wading, and the work lasted for a couple of months. The seaweed was cut by sickles and long hooks, and a rope of heather or birch was laid round the cut mass so that it could be hauled in as the tide came up. Then it was carried in creels to the foreshore where it was spread out to dry in the sun, being turned occasionally to stop it fermenting. When enough weed was dried to make about a ton of kelp, it was forked into the kiln; a trench 12–24 feet long by two or three feet wide and two feet deep. The more elaborate kilns had stone walls and a turf bottom, but much kelp was made on a flat rectangle of ground, marked out by stones. There the weed was set alight and kept burning with straw and heather for four to eight hours. It was a skilled job (often done by women), keeping the flames steady without letting in air, and the heat was intense. The fired weed, turned with long iron tools called clatts, reached a semi-fluid state, then cooled to a hard, brittle, resinous substance, transparent and many coloured. It was this finished product which was 'the kelp'. This material was broken up into manageable lumps and loaded on ships which came regularly to pick it up. These vessels were chartered by the proprietor. The ultimate buyers were not encouraged to visit the islands.

The work was physically hard and demanding, and not without its dangers. In 1799 the Oronsay owner said, 'Nothing but the very high price ... would induce any person to take the shore ... one of the worst and most precarious of occupations'.

Lumsden in his *Steamer Companion* (1928) explained to the traveller 'the great columns of dull whitish smoke ascending from the shore, and ... a strong disagreeable smell'.

The facts and figures of production go something like this. One ton of kelp could be won from twenty-two tons of wet weed. The chemical composition of the finished product was: potassium chloride 17%–25%; sodium chloride (common salt) 14%; potassium sulphate 10%–14%; sodium carbonate 4%–5%; iodine 1%–6%; a little magnesium sulphate; and much insoluble ash.

The market was heavily influenced by international affairs and the availability of other sources of supply. When Britain entered the Seven Years War in 1756 against France and her allies, and seized her colonial possessions in America and India, supplies of barilla dwindled and were cut off. The opening price had been about £2 5s a ton in 1740.

After 1756 the price rose steadily to £20 a ton, reaching a maximum of £22 during the American War of Independence (1775–83), when Britain was opposed by the whole of Europe. By 1769 Jura seems to have been producing 200 tons a year at about £4 a ton, although even in Jura the price would rise considerably during the following fifteen years. The price fell after 1783, but the Napoleonic Wars and their aftermath kept it to about £10 a ton until 1822.

Murray tells us that the bad news came with the Battle of Waterloo. The duties on salt and barilla were lowered in 1817 and 1822. This depressed the market for kelp, but when shortly afterwards the huge deposits of sulphate of potash at Strassfurt in Germany were exploited, the price of kelp dropped to £2 a ton. The bubble had burst and ruin faced everyone. The kelp trade was virtually ended by 1835. For sixty-six years the Hebrides enjoyed this bonanza in which the tacksmen and lairds all shared. The kelp revenues for the landlords were enormous, and even the ordinary people made some money.

THE KELP INDUSTRY IN JURA

The first mention of kelping on Jura is by John Walker in 1764, who writes, 'The shores of Jura afford a considerable quantity of sea weeds which are annually manufactured into kelp.'

Pennant in 1772 puts a firm figure on the production: '200 tons of kelp is burnt annually, and sold from £3 10/– to £4 per ton.'

The Rev. John Lightfoot, the author of *Flora Scotica*, accompanied Pennant, and made some informed comments on the kelp industry as a note on his botanical interest in bladder wrack:

In Jura the inhabitants dry their cheeses without salt by covering them with the ashes of this plant; which abounds with such quantity of salts, that from five ounces of the ashes may be procured two ounces and a half of fixed alkaline salts.

But the most beneficial use to which the *Fucus vesiculosis* is applied, in the way of economy, is in making pot-ash or kelp. The manner of doing it is this. The plant is collected and dried carefully on the shore in small heaps. When thoroughly dry, a pit is dug in sandy ground, about seven feet wide, and three deep, lined with stones. In this pit a fire is kindled with small sticks, and the dried Fucus is laid upon it little by little and burnt. When a sufficient quantity is consumed for the purpose, and burnt to a certain degree, it appears in the pit like red-hot ashes. The operator then (to prevent its being reduced entirely to ashes) with an iron rake stirs about briskly this hot matter from one side of the pit to the other, mixing it well together, till at length it begins to congeal and vitrify. The salts being now all melted, the matter is left to cool in the bottom of the pit, where, as in a mould, it concretes to a solid mass, called Kelp, which, when cold, is broken out of the pit, and carried to market for the use of the soap and glass-makers.

There is great difference in the goodness and price of this commodity, and much care and skill required in properly making it. That is esteemed the best which is hardest, finest grained, and free from sand or earth. The price of Kelp in Jura is £3 10s per ton, and about forty or fifty tons are exported annually from that island. So great a value is set upon this *Fucus* by the inhabitants of that place, that they have sometimes thought it worth their while to roll fragments of rock and huge stones into the sea, in order to invite the growth of it.

Francis Stewart says in 1794: 'The seaweed from which kelp is made grows abundantly on the shores. Before the general use of barilla, the kelp of Jura was a considerable addition to its rental.'

Stewart seemed to believe that the bottom had dropped out of the market as the result of the resumption of supplies of barilla, and that there was virtually no kelping going on in 1794. However, Macdonald, in 1811, also records: 'Considerable quantities of kelp; perhaps eighty to ninety tons are annually made here.'

Our informants give a broad picture of what was happening. At 200 tons a year, the Jura teams are making an average of four tons a week, although of course the job was seasonal in nature, being largely confined to the late spring. Murray's description suggests that the kelp should have been fetching much more than £4 per ton by 1772. It is in the Valuation of 1770 that we see the 'privilege of cutting wreck fit for kelp' being given a monetary value together with some other 'privileges'. In view of the fact that the production of kelp from the nearby island of Mull may have been about 750 tons, the small population of Jura seems to have been doing rather well.

One hundred years after Francis Stewart, in 1894, the Crofter's Commission sat at Jura. Miss Isabella Campbell gave evidence, and she herself raised the question of kelp. She says:

In 1868, Keils Glen was formed into part of the deer forest; the population was very considerably larger than it is at present. That was entirely owing to the kelp industry, which yielded the proprietor from £1500 to £2000, and when that was done away with, several hundreds of the people emigrated themselves, because there was no occupation for them. There was not a single eviction from this place.

The Rev. Malcolm Maccallum of the Commission followed up on this statement with questions which Miss Campbell answered:

Q. I think you said the proprietor made a large profit out of the Kelp?

A. It yielded from £1500 to £2000 a year.

Q. Was that a profit off the people's work?

A. The people worked at wages to him. He paid them wages for making the kelp.

Q. I was rather astonished at hearing that the proprietor got out of the labour of these people £2000 a year?

A. It was not out of their labour but out of the kelp.

Q. Did he not make that profit out of it? What did he contribute to it?

A. He paid them wages the same as anybody else pays a servant wages.

Q. He made that as a profit out of the labour of the people?

A. It was just like any other industry; it is just as if you had a coal pit and paid wages to the miners for working it.

Q. It was not a patriarchal system; it was just a commercial transaction?

A. Yes, it was simply a commercial transaction, the same as if there had been a coal-pit and wages were paid to the miners, and the people of Jura would be very grateful if the laird would employ them again in the same manner. The people emigrated of their own free will, because they found they could not live here.

Here then are the usual tantalising glimpses of what was going on in Jura, but a very clear picture of how the matter was viewed by the Campbells. It seems clear that there was a considerable kelp industry in Jura. It was plainly established by the 1760s and with fluctuations in quantity of production was certainly still going on in 1811.

One of Campbell's many actions at law concerned the taking of stones and other material from the foreshore of Jura. A number of local people gave evidence in 1881 on this matter, and the question of the kelp is mentioned.

Neil Lindsay, a mason, aged eighty-four, whose whole life was spent in Jura. Sixty years ago [i.e. 1821] he made kelp in Loch Tarbert. The kelp was sent to Liverpool at £20 per ton, and Neil sometimes went to Liverpool with it.

Angus McKechnie; a joiner, aged 77 years. Like Neil Lindsay he made kelp at Loch Tarbert and Ardfin 50 years ago.

Alexander Rankin; a labourer, aged 79. He spoke of kelp cutting, and of getting ropes round it and dragging it in at high water. The beds took years to ripen after being cut.

John Buie, crofter of Dainskeir; aged 85 years. As far back as 1816 he saw kelp taken.

Alexander McCraine; Church Officer, Caigenhouse; 70 years of age. He was at the kelp when he was fifteen. The furnace for burning the kelp was at Farellan.

Neil McPhee, a keeper, aged 64, said: 'My father got 6d a barrel for taking Loch Tarbert kelp round as freight.

Donald McArtin, an under gardener, aged 79, remembered kelp being taken from Cnocbreac and from Camustac.

A number of these men speak of the laird 'giving up' the kelp industry, and various other people taking it over: 'A man Watt from Greenock, and after him a man called Wilson.'

Angus Mackay, a keeper, aged 68 recalls that Wilson the kelp man lodged with him. In 1835 and 1836 at Knockrome he was out after otters when he saw the Islay man taking kelp with McCracken and Buie, the shore watcher.

As Macdonald suggests, by 1811, Jura seems to have been making only 80–90 tons a year, although the work continued in a smaller way until the 1830s. By this time new chemical processes had allowed the extraction of soda from common salt, and the value of both barilla and kelp slumped still further. By 1836 kelp was finished on Jura, for seaweed was once more being used as 'seaware' to manure the fields.

The Poor Law Enquiry of 1841 estimated that on Jura more than fifty men had been employed in the kelp. They would all have been assisted by various other members of their families.

There was a short resurgence of the industry in the 1850s when it was found that iodine, discovered in 1812, could be extracted from the laminaria oarweeds, but local people did not benefit this time, as the shores were leased to mainland kelp-makers. In due course better methods were found, and seaweed was not collected commercially after 1862.

Miss Campbell seems to be suggesting that the question of the kelp was relevant in Jura as late as 1868. It seems very unlikely that she was right about this. She also seems to have believed that it was solely as a result of the sudden drop in income from the loss of the kelp work that several hundred people emigrated. The matter was evidently more complex than her testimony implies, and evidently happened a good deal earlier than her account would suggest.

She was, however, not alone in her opinion. A Jura witness told the 1895 Red

Deer Commission that upon the kelp failure, 1830–40, 'several hundreds ... emigrated ... there was no occupation for them'.

Despite the fact that we cannot accurately compute how many families were involved in the kelp industry, and what effect the wages from the kelp had on their livelihood, we may conclude that the years of the kelp secured a better standard of living for many people on Jura, and that hardship undoubtedly resulted when they came to an end.

As has already been said, the kelpers were not allowed to work for themselves, but had to pass their produce on to the owners, who usually paid about 15 per cent of the value of the crop.

We do not know exactly what time in the long period of kelp production Miss Campbell was referring to when she said that the family made from £1500 to £2000 per year from the kelp. If the pay was indeed 15 per cent, the local people were earning £300 per year. Divided into the fifty families estimated by the Poor Board, each was making an additional £6. Since an independent source has said that a kelper on nearby Mull could earn £8 a year, we seem to be in roughly the the right area. A much earlier note suggests that in the 1750s a kelper could earn 7½d a week, at that time a fair wage.

In 1849 the Campbell cash book shows: 'for your daughter gathering weeds; 18 days at 4d a day; 6 shillings in all.' This may have been the rate for a young person, as it would produce only about £1 4s for a ten-week season. Duty Work for an adult was worth two shillings a day.

The general picture appears to be that at the various times when kelping was an option for an able bodied family it probably came close to paying the rent, thus allowing the tenant to live virtually rent-free. No doubt the families concerned became used to this additional income, especially because it came at a time of year when it was possible to find some time away from the land. Miss Campbell is no doubt speaking the literal truth when she says: 'the people of Jura would be very thankful if the laird employed them in the same away again.'

FERN ASHES

Another of the 'privileges' entered in the 1770 Valuation is the 'cutting of ferns to make ashes'. Presumably we are thinking here of bracken, which, when cut, wilted and then set alight, would create 'fern ashes'. At first sight this might be seen as an internal matter, creating a product which might enhance the fertility of the township's crops by being spread on as an additional manure.

However, Pennant in 1774 and Stewart in 1794 both speak in terms which make it clear that the product was exported.

Pennant: 'Fern ashes bring in about a hundred pounds a year.'

Macdonald: 'Some fern ashes were formerly exported, but of late years that manufacture seems to be abandoned, owing to the decrease of the material which yielded it.'

The ash yielded 'potash' for which there was for some time a market. It seems likely that Macdonald was right in thinking that the bracken could not stand the regular cutting.

POTATOES

The potato arrived in the Hebrides first in Uist in 1743. The crop spread quickly and by 1774 it had arrived in Jura and become the staple food. Our visitors have commented as usual.

By the latter part of the century people may have been eating as much as half a stone of potatoes each day, eaten boiled, with a little milk or salt.

Apart from the practice, much encouraged by the laird, of putting a lot of arable land under potatoes, the people of Jura brought previously unproductive moorland into cultivation by planting potatoes in lazy-beds. These areas were called 'feannagan' in Gaelic. *Dwelly's Gaelic Dictionary* says 'the term 'lazy-bed' applied to it in English, is merely a southern odium on the system of farming in Gaeldom, where soil was scarce, and where bog-land could not be cultivated any other way.' Lazy-beds were crofting's response to the acute shortage of cultivatable land and the general impoverishment of much of the land of Jura. They were created by digging drainage trenches with the cas chrom, and piling the extracted sods, 'soil-up', on a central strip. Manured with 'sea-ware', Collins' *Encyclopedia of Scotland* says 'considering the labour involved, only a seriously warped sense of humour can account for their being called 'lazy-beds'. Although long since abandoned, lazy-beds can be picked out quite easily on countless hill slopes on Jura.

WHISKY

The swollen population of the Hebrides, which by 1831 had reached 92,000, had been made possible less by the kelp industry than by the introduction of the potato. Further aid to the people of the Hebrides came in the last part of the eighteenth century from whisky. Whisky distilled mainly from barley had been the universal beverage of the isles from the middle of the eighteenth century. The arrival and success of the potato released large quantities of barley for distilling that had previously been required for food.

Pennant had already commented: 'In good seasons sufficient barley and oats are raised as will maintain the inhabitants, but sometimes they want, I suppose from the conversion of their grain into whisky.' The rise of the island's export trade in whisky may have been prompted by increase in rents.

Mainland grain shortages during the American and Napoleonic wars prompted the Commissioners of Supply to conserve grain by prohibiting whisky distilling in 1782, 1795 and 1797. The policy was inconsistent, for in other years they restricted legal distilling by a heavy licence duty of £9 on each gallon of still-capacity. Illicit distilling and smuggling throve on such bans and obstructions, and developed into a domestic industry of economic importance. Island farms and townships all had stills for home consumption, and in order to pay the rent these now turned to export. Tiree, for example exported up to 3000 gallons of whisky per year. By 1800, illicit distilling and smuggling in the Hebrides had had an extraordinary expansion. As operators gained in skill and experience, illicit whisky improved in quality until it became superior to the legal product. Legal distillers, faced with heavy taxation, duty of spirit, and competition from a better product, either went bankrupt or entered the illicit business. Until recently, Jura ancients would proudly point out the secret location of former community stills.

Copper stills of 10-gallon capacity could be bought complete with worm, arm and head for under £5 from Campbeltown. Since distilling took nearly a month and co-operative work, largely left to women, was needed among the families of a township. Many widows and spinsters distilled for themselves, or gave their service to local men, which encouraged early marriage. Co-operation was important, for if one operator was caught by an exciseman all shared the payment of the fine, and the confiscated still could be easily replaced. The net profits were around ten shillings a week for each still. In 1822, the price of whisky was ten shillings a gallon at 20% above proof. (Proof spirit is 57% pure alcohol.) But prices varied widely depending on scarcity and quality.

The smugglers, whose task was to ship the whisky to the mainland coast, and direct to Glasgow, were crofter-fishermen, who organised themselves in small bands. Both they, and the still operators, if brought to court, could rely on having sympathy, and some protection from the magistrates, who were the landowners. The excisemen in the islands had an impossible task. They were not Gaelic speakers, and they were usually without local knowledge. The land was without roads, and they were easily misdirected and confounded.

A local tale of Jura undoubtedly goes back to these days. Excisemen, looking for an illicit still at Gleann nam Muc, near Kinuachdrach, asked the women where the men were, and were answered honestly that the menfolk were at the Bay of Pigs. A verbal joke was played on them, making a play on words, since 'pig' was also used for 'still' in Gaelic.

Badly hurt by their loss of revenue, the government tried every way to end the trade except the right one. They tried charging a heavy licence fee on stills; they prohibited stills of under 500-gallon capacity; they imposed a high duty of nearly ten shillings a gallon. Everything failed. Finally light dawned. In 1822, they asked only a licence fee of £10 and cut the duty to a modest sum. They had found the answer. Many illicit distillers took out licences. Smuggling began to die away and had largely disappeared from Jura by the latter part of the nineteenth century.

Jura's first legal distillery was built in 1810, beside the cave in which its founder had for a long time practised without a licence. Falling eventually into disuse, it was leased to James Ferguson & Sons from 1875 to 1918, and modernised at a cost of £25,000. A feature was the lack of a steam engine, the sloping site allowing water and gravitation to do the work. The whisky was 'pure Highland malt', and by 1885 annual production exceeded 60,000 gallons. The buildings covered three acres, and in an enthusiastic contemporary description were 'visible for many miles around'.

The Rev. Alexander Kennedy, in the *Statistical Account* of 1843, could write:

There are two licensed public houses in Jura. Only a small proportion of the means of the parishioners is now expended in the deleterious practice of dram-drinking, and in spirituous liquors. Weddings, funerals, and public meetings, which at one period exhibited scenes of revelry and drunkenness in this parish, are now conducted in such a way as to show a decided improvement in the habits of the people. Illicit distillation of whisky, and other kinds of smuggling, which at one time were carried on to an alarming extent are now all but suppressed.

The island community was now having to deal with a devastating combination of changed circumstances, all of them hostile.

The 'overtime' income from the kelp had gone. The additional income from illicit distilling based on barley released for the purpose by the success of the potato as the staple diet had also gone.

The next tragedy was the appearance of potato blight. As in Ireland the sudden appearance of blight (*Phytophora infestans*) in 1845–6 spelt catastrophe. Overnight and throughout the Highlands and the Hebrides, the haulms wilted and the tubers rotted. Blackened fields and a nauseating stench heralded in the words of James Hunter, 'a human tragedy unparalleled in modern Scottish history'.

Compared with Ireland, deaths from starvation were few. There was a swift governmental response, and relief arrived quickly. The second report of the 1847 Free Church Destitution Committee included Jura as in need of help, and sent fifty barrels of Indian corn meal to Jura.

This seems almost the only direct evidence of the effect on the people of Jura, but the island certainly did not escape, and the blight came and went for a number of years. John Campbell's letter to Carolina, in 1857 says: 'The blight is come upon the potatoes, but it is expected they will turn out better than last year.'

Faced with these difficulties many left, and the island's population continued to decline.

OTHER OCCUPATIONS

Cloth. Until about the middle of the nineteenth century island women made their own cloth, of wool and flax. The dyestuffs were lichens and other plants. Spinning was by spindle and distaff, the wheel probably only appearing in the late eighteenth century. The government effort to establish weaving results in the appearance of hand-loom weavers in Caigenhouse and the crofting communities of Keils, Knockrome and Ardfernal in the 1841 census, and on through the century until about 1900. Even in 1911 the Highland Home Industries had workers on Jura, perhaps reviving tweed-making. Islay was renowned for its flax. Jura also attempted to grow flax for a time, although as we have seen, various commentators said it was a poor choice.

Thatching. The people thatched their own houses every two years by Jura rules, and at least up to 1912, each had to write a letter to the landowner about 20–24 July for permission to pull the heather, and another in September or October, to be allowed to cut the rushes.

In 1876 the cost of professionally thatching a large Jura farm's barn and stirk-house was estimated at £4 19s. This was made up as follows: two carts heather, 10s.; two men pulling heather, 4s; three men cutting rushes, 3 days, 18s;

three horses, carts taking home this thatch, 15s; one cart cabbers (poles or rafters), two men each, 4s; horse, cart for same, 5s; horse, cart, one day with two men for sods, 9s; three men three days thatching, 18s; two men one day putting on cabbers and sods, 4s.

Fishing. Inshore fishing for several well known species, and the taking of lobsters and crabs has already been mentioned, and the practice has continued to the present day. Commercial fishing on any large scale seems never to have made a great appeal to the native inhabitants of Jura, although the seas around the island were providing a living for many folk who came to the area to exploit the wealth of fish.

The success of the herring fishery based at Gigha led, in 1894, to the attempt to set up a quay and curing station at Cruib in Loch Tarbert to save the boats their frequent return journeys to the mainland. The company sought to do so under a 1770 Act which gave herring fishermen the right to use 100 yards above high watermark of unused land. In this case the 'recalcitrant fringe' was told by the lawyer that this meant only 'temporary use' and that regular pasturing might take the land right out of the Act; or the owner should bring his influence to bear on the 'Fisheries Board' to close the loch by a special by-law. The shooting tenant, who had written that the area would become 'a hell on earth' sank back in relief.

Shellfish had also long been part of the staple diet of the people. The collection of winkles from the rocks has already been mentioned. Other, more desirable molluscs were known to live in Jura waters, but the local people were not encouraged to make use of these resources.

Upon the sale of south Jura by the Islay owner in the eighteenth century, the latter retained the right to demand, in addition to 'four fat deer', some 6000 Jura oysters a year. The oysters are to be found in Loch Tarbert, inland of the 'Great Narrows', where in 1889 the employees of a Tarbert Loch Fyne merchant were caught, 'picking Oysters of the Rocks with small iron scrapers of chisels ... also wading knee deep and picking up the Oysters ... they were dredging the deep water ... at Chariidh Mhor ...' The owner sent at once to his hard-worked lawyer and obtained an interdict. Simultaneously, in a dispute with the Crown over his foreshore rights, Campbell was claiming the oysters were 'of little value'. The shooting tenant, who cared nothing for title, relaxed, writing happily, 'I believe we are in possession of the oysters.'

HOUSING

This may be a suitable moment to say something about the more permanent dwellings of the people of Jura in the seventeenth and eighteenth centuries. Throughout seventeenth-century Scotland the basic type of farmstead was the 'long-house', where people, crops, equipment and animals were accommodated under a continuous roof, often with a minimum of internal division. It is likely that descriptions which apply to mainland Scotland in the seventeenth century can be applied to Jura much later, and certainly well into the eighteenth century. In the kind of multiple-holding townships which existed in Jura at this time, such houses would not have been standing alone and isolated in the landscape.

A whole cluster of houses would have huddled together, with their cottar houses, kilns, peat stacks and corn yards.

Recent archaeological research indicates that stone-built houses in the Highlands and Islands of Scotland replaced previous turf-built houses over a considerable period.

Cruck-framing, where the roof was supported on a series of timber arches (crucks, or couples) was the standard building technique. The cruck frames could be formed from two massively curved pieces pinned together at the top, or may have been composite ones produced from several pieces of timber. They carried the weight of the roof down to ground level. The walls of early turf houses did not support the roof and could be quite flimsy affairs.

The cruck-framed roof structures of later stone buildings may have been the continuation of this earlier style of building, carrying on into buildings where the stone walls could have carried the roof without difficulty. Fine examples of such early long-houses have been reconstructed at the Highland Folk Museum in Newtonmore, based on detailed excavation of a nearby medieval township. We may infer a great deal about the vernacular buildings on Jura in the eighteenth century from these exciting examples.

Wattling was obviously widely used. Pennant illustrated an apparently 'Dalradian' (straight-gabled) house from Islay, but the gables seem to be wattled, with stone walls to the house. Pennant said that houses in Islay were: 'scenes of misery, made of loose stone; without chimneys, without doors, excepting the faggot opposed to the wind at one or other of the apertures.' He added; 'But my picture is not of this island only.'

James Robertson's paper was read before the Society of Antiquaries of Scotland in 1788. The relevant passage refers to north Argyllshire:

> The houses in which they live they call basket-houses. Their method of building them is this; they first make out both length and breadth of the house, then drive stakes of wood at nine inches or a foot distance from each other, leaving four or five feet of them above the ground, then wattle them up with heath and small branches of wood upon the outside of which they pin on very thin turf, much in the same manner that slates are laid. Alongst the top of these stakes runs a beam which supports the couples, and what they call cabers (thin rafters or scantlings stretching from wall-head to ridge-pole), and this either covered with turf, heath or straw.

It seems that there may have been more than one style of dwelling in Jura in the eighteenth century. It is not possible to be sure at what point stone buildings came into vogue, and whether they were customarily square-ended, or gableended, or whether the end of the building was rounded, leading up to a rounded or 'hipped' roof. The ruined township of An Carn at the north of the island, has been examined, and preserves indications both of gable and hipped roofs. The listed thatched buildings at Keils are cruck-framed and gable-ended.

With the arrival of new farming ideas, the stone-built 'Dalradian' cottage appeared, nearer to Lowland dwellings than to 'Skye' or 'Hebridean' types. This cottage, square-cornered, had a whole-length roof ridge, as opposed to other types' cut away roof-ends. The steep roof was covered with thatch, usually of rushes, sometimes of straw, heather, or bracken – this overhanging the long walls as eaves. Stapled down heather ropes, and later netting, were used to keep the thatch in place, themselves being further tethered by weights hanging over the walls. Windows were few and small, with the back to the wind more important than the face to the sun. A number of recent byres in crofting townships are the last of the island's Dalradian houses, with examples previously mentioned at Keils of special interest.

The interior plan of the earlier cottages included a byre, with the fire on a raised area in the middle of the main room. Some had a suspended wooden smoke-hood at one end. By the early nineteenth century, and aided by the vertical gable wall, modern type chimneys had come in. Lumsden's 1827 print shows a cottage with a chimney in Jura. The floors were beaten earth or clay, the main room's sometimes of wood. Jura dwellings between Lagg and Craighouse were first floored with concrete in 1892.

The thatched roofs were eventually replaced by slates or tarred felt or corrugated iron. This latter went on the roofs of incoming 1910 to 1920 tenants who were no thatchers.

Furniture. Ancient furnishings were simple. The main articles were closet beds in the eighteenth century. Earlier, in the sixteenth century, people slept on the ground on straw or, better, on heather, which they laid on the floor stalk down and leaf up. Heather gave a refreshing scent. A Latin record from the late 1500s says:

> This makes a pleasing bed, vying in softness with finest down. Heath naturally absorbs moisture and restores strength to exhausted nerves, so that those who lie down weary at night arise in the morning alert and vigourous. They all have not only a contempt for pillows and blankets, but choose to cultivate hardiness.

There would be a dresser and table; the meal and clothes kists; low chairs and stools, the latter three-legged, like the wooden-lidded pot hanging on a chain above the fire. At night the sooty walls were lit by the iron crusie lamp – a pan of oil seated on a drip bowl, with a wick of cotton twist or peeled rush. To light it, a spark from a flint set a charred rag smouldering. This ignited a home-made match and this the lamp.

Much later we have a precious description of a visit to an ordinary home. It comes from Lord Teignmouth's time on Jura in 1836, and follows here in full:

> The dwellings of the farmers are wretched, and those of the cottagers yet more so. One of these, by a lakeside near the sound, I entered at the invitation of an old woman, who addressed me in good English and with much politeness, apologising at the same time for its poverty and dirt. It was built under a bank forming one of its sides, and was lighted by a single small pane of glass. A hole in the roof served for a chimney; and nearly half the area was appropriated to a cow; the bed and some miserable furniture covered the little remaining room. It had been penetrated during the late storms by the water, which lay

a foot deep on the floor. We sat down, and the poor woman hoped I would excuse her appearance, observing that it was vain to wear clean clothes, which would be instantly soiled by the soot, and then offered me milk, cream, or tea. She conversed with sense, spirit, and even elegance, and with perfect ease, showing that she had seen better days; asked me the usual questions as to my arrival in Jura, and spoke of the Jura family and other lairds, like one who knew their history and characters, and had lived on equal terms with them. She informed me that she was seventy-four years of age, sister to a farmer in the Island, the oldest of Mr Campbell's tenants, who was ninety years of age, who lived at some miles distant, and allowed her the hovel which she occupied, and her cow for subsistence. He would give me a hearty welcome, she assured me, if I would visit him. Another of her brothers had been captain in the 42nd Regiment. She was born and had passed part of her life in Jura, had married, and on his death removed with her two sons to Bowmore, in Isla. One of them had held the commission of lieutenant in the army; the other had spent two years in Glasgow, attending the University, with a view to a liberal profession, and became, to use her own expression, a noble scholar. But ill health blasted his prospects, and he now lived with his mother. She was perfectly satisfied with her lot, only complaining of the uncomfortableness of her dwelling, and its being by no means proof against the violence of the storms. Her son read the Bible to her; and when the weather permitted, she attended Kilmenie Church, and passed the night in her brother's house. Her neighbours treated her with kindness, and rendered her any assistance which she required. The old lady bore a good character in the neighbourhood. In this island I found much of that genuine hospitality which characterises the lowest, no less than the higher classes of the natives of these regions. They invariably offer their visitors the best fare which they can command; and frequently it is with the utmost difficulty, and evidently to their mortification, that they can be persuaded to accept remuneration.

Lord Teignmouth's description suggests that his visit was made at Cnocbreac, the only community where there is a 'lakeside near the sound'. His hostess evidently did not survive much longer, for there is no sign of her in the 1841 census. Her aged brother must also have died by 1841. Her visits to church were made across the Sound of Islay, for Kilmeny Church is at Ballygrant. Teignmouth's account is significant both for what it tells us about the lady herself and about her circumstances.

COSTUME

It is impossible to get any direct evidence what people on Jura were wearing before the eighteenth century. No one seems to have written about them, and no paintings have survived.

Teignmouth's encounter with Campbell of Jura sheds a little light on the matter of dress:

Mr Campbell was born in 1744, and has spent his whole life in this island. The greatest misery, which he ever experienced, was the change of the national garb; he recollected every man in the island clad in the kilt. Speaking of Bein-an-noir, the highest of the Paps, he observed with shame, that he had never reached its summit till he accompanied Pennant. Pennant, he assured me, descended more happily than he ascended, on the strength of a glass of whisky, which he had prevailed on him to drink, a beverage to which the traveller expressed a dislike. Mr Campbell said of Pennant that he derived his information too much from the lower classes.

The laird whom Teignmouth describes is Archibald Campbell, fourth of Jura, who died on 18 July 1835 in his ninety-first year. Teignmouth's account was published in 1836, so it seems that he met Mr Campbell not long before the old man's death. He had in fact climbed the Paps with Pennant when he was a young fellow of thirty-two years, and probably would have made nothing of the adventure.

Campbell could scarcely have been aware of the Unclothing Act of 1746, since he was only a year old at the time. The Disarming Acts, forbidding the plaid and filibeg and all tartan came into force in 1747. It was not until 1782 that the Act was repealed, when Campbell was a man of thirty-eight years. John Prebble says there was no enthusiasm to return to the tartan or the kilt:

The old attachment to the Highland dress had died in a generation, the old patterns were forgotten; the wearing of the kilt was an affectation for gentlemen. It was not until forty years later, when George IV came to Scotland and dressed himself in a ridiculous uniform of scarlet kilt, plaid, bonnet, eagle feathers, broadsword dirk and skean dhu that a romantic and extravagant interest in the Highland dress was born. Was the old man simply romancing when he recollected every man in the island clad in the kilt?

Moses Griffith's illustrations to Pennant's journey in the mid-eighteenth century appear to show women in simple long dresses with sleeves, and possibly shawls and head scarves. An illustration in Islay shows a patterned dress with a horizontal diamond motif. The girls seem to have dressed like their mother, but a boy has a jacket and a bonnet. A man working in front of his cottage in Islay appears to be wearing trousers, and a waistcoat over his shirt. He also has a bonnet.

HUNTING

In the Middle Ages the right to hunt belonged to the Crown. The people who occupied the land were simply 'keepers'. As with the land, so the animals became gradually 'owned' by the island chiefs. The ancient tale of the arrival of the Campbells on Jura recalls that MacDonald, the island's chieftain had been hunting a deer on the hill when he returned to find Baillie Campbell in his house. Vestiges of the ancient practice lasted on into the nineteenth century. The Islay Campbells' superiority over Jura gave them hunting rights, and even later the mainland head of the Campbell, the King's Lieutenant, insisted on his ancient right to hunt over Jura. Up to 1800, agriculture and serious hunting kept the deer under control; indeed the increase of cattle prices from 1750 brought the deer territory to its smallest ever by the end of the eighteenth century.

By 1811 Campbell refers to his land as 'much hunted'. This was the time when the rich of the new industrial society were attracted by the social distinction of deer-shooting, organised in such a way as to be subtly flattering to them.

When the kelp failed, the laird of Islay wrote to Campbell in 1841 that 'at the rate now paid by Englishmen', Jura's shooting was worth £300 or £400 a year. Each drop in sheep and cattle prices let deer on to more land. The deer forest of 'Jura Forest' was established in 1868, and Mr Evans established his hunting kingdom at a substantial rent. From 1878, 25,000 stock-free acres were on a twenty-five year shooting lease at £900 a year. In 1888 the shootings for the whole island, excluding Mr Evans' 'deer forest' were worth £365 in the valuation.

Both the newly formed Crofters Commission and the Red Deer Commission accepted that the peoples' holdings had been whittled away, and that there was good land lost to farming. To make sure that no action was taken, the Highland Proprietors' Association was formed in 1885. Answering their questionnaire, Campbell and Evans wrote that the 64,500 acres they controlled held only three to fifteen acres of arable, but loss of these would utterly ruin the deer and sheep preserves. It seems the Association had primarily in mind that Highlanders could never cope with any more land, or would multiply terribly. Lochiel, the chairman at their main meeting, concluded: 'We are fighting this battle on behalf of the crofters.' (Loud applause.)

In spite of the recommendations of the Crofters Commission, nothing was done. In 1922, the Deer Forest Commission was called, reached much the same conclusions and was disbanded.

Between 1891 and 1911 the island's rents fell to half, with sheep and cattle grazing unlet deer preserves during the First World War. By 1922 prices were back at their 1891 level; 22,000 acres on north Jura were let at £855 a year.

Of course, great play was made by the Campbells at the Crofters' Commission hearing in 1894 of the fact that Henry Evans' 'deer forest' was benefiting the island in many ways. His own generosity to tenants was cited. The amount of money he spent on the island, and the fact that his venture gave employment to a number of families was noted. Indeed, by 1888, Evans was employing eight families, which made him the second-largest single employer in the island.

It was Henry Evans who in 1890 privately printed the result of his obsession with the Red Deer of Jura. The booklet was simply entitled *Some Account of Jura Red Deer* and ran to thirty-eight pages. Evans recorded everything he possibly could about the deer he was shooting – their ages, weights, numbers, breeding success, parasites, causes of death. He compared everything he could about their presence on the various parts of the island. It makes for dull reading, with its endless tables of weights and sizes. Only occasionally does he have any interesting general comments to make, e.g., he speaks briefly about the famous Jura 'Cromie':

> Cromie stags are very curious; it is said they exist only on Jura where certainly they are historical. Cromie in Gaelic means crooked. These Cromie horns slope backwards, and are altogether very remarkable. Some Cromie heads are beautiful. We have shot eleven cromies in twelve years. Five were seen in one day last year. Two were shot in 1890.

He also has a comment on 'hummels':

There is a small number of bald, or hornless stags in Jura. These animals usually carry a very high condition; they fight as eagerly as horned stags, sometimes beating off their armed adversary.

He is little interested in history, but notes: 'As for ancient history, I possess a fossil stag's antler, dug up in Jura gravel, showing Jura red deer to be prehistoric.'

The author is unaware if Mr Evans' mass of statistical information and endless recording of facts and figures is still of value to those who manage deer forests and farms nowadays. It seems unlikely. It seems evident that the business of hunting red deer on Jura was not only a matter of leasing out the right to shoot to wealthy clients, but became one of the reasons why the Campbells of Jura retained their control of the island during the nineteenth century.

It was certainly in line with enhancing the prestige of his position that Richard Campbell commissioned Gourlay Steele to visit Jura and paint the famous *Deer Stalking on the Bens of Jura*. Gourlay Steele was appointed Animal Painter for Scotland by Queen Victoria after the death of Landseer in 1873. This prestige ensured him a virtual monopoly of sporting commissions in Scotland. The painting gives us not only a portrait of Richard Dennistoun Campbell, eighth of Jura, but clear portrayals of three of his retainers. Angus McKay was his head keeper. His son lived at Inver. Neil Clark was at this time the caretaker at Jura Forest, so the hunt may have taken place on 'Forest Ground'. (Plate 12)

The business of the stalker or gillie is a highly skilled one, requiring an intimate knowledge of the ways of the deer, and not ignoring the place of all the other animals and birds of the hill and moor. The work is arduous and makes great demands on fitness and stamina. On the modern estate there is some kind of assistance provided by modern vehicles which can penetrate the remoter areas and bring the carcases down from the high ground. In former days the work was done by hand, and help came from the ponies kept by the estate. It is of interest that in this matter Jura became widely known for its horse transport. Alex Fenton records:

> The kind of sledge known as the Jura Car, with side struts fastened to the sides of a horse and their rear ends trailing on the ground, with a carrying platform linking the struts behind the horse, might well be considered a primitive survival. And so it is in a way, for slipes of this type go back to the Bronze Age, and are known from many parts of the world. They were illustrated by John Slezer in 1693 at Dunblane; Perthshire; and Arbroath in Angus; and appear to have been in widespread use in hilly areas. Yet the Jura Car, though a link; perhaps the last one; in a long chain of succession, was nevertheless made, as it survives, by estate joiners, to carry the deer shot by sporting gentry off the trackless hills. No equipment or tool can really be described as primitive, where it is obviously serving a purpose that more up-to-date equipment cannot serve, or at least cannot serve better. (Plate 13)

After the stalk is concluded the carcass has to be butchered. This takes place at the larder, and now, with the laird, or the guests no longer present, it may be possible for the staff to work at a more leisurely pace.

THE CAMPBELLS

When we consider how completely reliant we have been for our documentary evidence about Jura on the archive called the Campbell of Jura Papers, it is surprising how shadowy the members of the family appear from our perspective.

The Campbells of Sanaig were evidently fighting men of their day, involved in the pacification of their territory for Argyll. Later, as we have seen, they were leading their men in the '45.

The litigation concerning Mr Hossack in the eighteenth century gives us some unexpected flashes of humour, and reveals them as a well-educated and highly sophisticated family. It is intriguing to find Archibald Campbell, the fourth of Jura, as a very old man, expressing some strong feelings to Lord Teignmouth, but then he may have been prepared to be more open to one of his own class.

When we come to consider the work of the Crofters Commission we will encounter Miss Isabella Campbell, who was 'acting laird' at the end of the nineteenth century, and whose statements reveal a good deal about her family.

A rare glimpse of the Campbells of Jura comes in her time, as in 1899 the press records the Golden Wedding of her father and mother. In fact, two separate events take place. We will consider first the Jura one:

The Golden Wedding of Mr and Mrs Campbell of Jura. Rarely has a more successful or more sumptuous estate entertainment been held in the county than that which took place on the Jura Estate on the 3rd inst., in celebration of the golden-wedding of Mr and Mrs Campbell, the popular laird and his much-respected lady. On the actual anniversary of this happy event Mr and Mrs Campbell had been absent from home, and the popular rejoicings had therefore been postponed until the present occasion, when upwards of 220 guests assembled to offer their congratulations, and enjoy the hospitality of the laird. The extensive offices of the Home Farm were admirably adapted for an entertainment of the sort, one of the large barns being laid out as a supper-room, capable of seating 112 at one time; a second entirely devoted to dancing, and a third arranged as a tea-room, where also were laid out for inspection the very handsome presents already received by Mr and Mrs Campbell from the Jura people and other friends in March last. All the rooms wore a very smart appearance; the ball-room in particular being appropriately hung with stags' heads, coloured banners, and various floral decorations, and brilliantly lit with large pendant lamps. The proceedings commenced at 8.30, and dancing was maintained with unimpaired vigour to an early hour. Shortly before the supper-room was thrown open, glasses were filled, and the Laird in a brief, but expressive speech, described the keen pleasure he felt at seeing so many of his people gathered round him; and while heartily thanking them for all the extremely handsome presents they had given to Mrs Campbell and himself, he assured them that what he valued above all was the kindly feeling which had prompted the gifts; a feeling to which their presence there that night was a further and much appreciated testimony. The conclusion of the speech was the signal for prolonged and enthusiastic cheering for Mr and Mrs Campbell, coupled with expressions of every good wish for their long life and prosperity. Mr and Mrs Campbell, younger, of Jura, were unavoidably absent, but all the other members of the family were present, including Mrs Allan Gordon Cameron, of Barcaldine, and Mr Cameron, who wore the full Highland dress. In view of the fact that the organisation and superintendence of the festivities devolved entirely upon Miss Isabella Campbell, it is right to say that to her ready resource, unfailing tact, and indefatigable energy, the undoubted success of the evening was largely due.

The celebrations on Jura having been recorded, we now look at the previous party on the actual date of the Golden Wedding:

On the 9th inst. at 11 Cornwall Gardens, South Kensington, London, there was celebrated with much congratulations and appropriate festivities the golden wedding of Mr and Mrs Campbell of Jura; Mr James Campbell, fourth son of Mr Colin Campbell of Jura and Craignish Castle, Argyllshire, having been married to Mary, second daughter of Colonel Campbell of Cessnock and Treesbanks, Ayrshire, on the 9th March 1848.

This interesting and happy occasion had been awaited with very great interest by a numerous circle of friends and relatives in both counties, who accordingly signalised the eventful day by sending many costly presents, large numbers of floral tributes, and a host of congratulatory letters and telegrams. In the evening Mr & Mrs Campbell entertained at dinner a large family party, some of whom had travelled south specially to be present on the occasion. The table decorations were entirely composed of masses of golden-yellow flowers, and the guests entered the dining-room to the accompaniment of pipe music, the piper playing the spirited clan march 'The Campbells are Coming', which in bygone days so often stirred the echoes of far Lochawe. During dinner the health of Mr & Mrs Campbell was drunk by the assembled guests with Highland honours amid great enthusiasm.

On the afternoon of the day following, Mr & Mrs Campbell held a numerously-attended reception, at which the flowers and presents were displayed, inspected and admired. Conspicuous among the presents were a pair of exceedingly handsome solid silver five-branched candelabras, a solid silver coffee pot and milk jug, and an exquisite gold chain bangle, all subscribed for and presented by tenants and servants on the Jura Estate, with whom, by request, was included Mr Henry Evans, lessee of Jura deer forest, who, with the sympathetic tact habitual to him, desired to be associated as one of themselves, with the people among whom he has spent so many years of his life. The estate subscription was, we understand, promoted by Mr D. MacKechnie, whose long and faithful service with the Jura family peculiarly fitted him for the occasion; and the ready and liberal response he met with on all sides constitutes an eloquent tribute to the deserved and enduring popularity of the laird and his lady, with which they cannot fail to be deeply touched and gratified. Included among the other presents were: Gold and turquoise bangle from Miss Campbell, Miss J. H. Campbell, Miss M. Campbell, Miss C. A. Campbell, Mrs Cameron, Mr & Mrs Colin Campbell, younger, of Jura, and grand-children; gold and pearl brooch from Mr Adam Gordon of Balcardine, and twin grandsons; gold mounted claret jug and gold topped toilet bottle from Miss Meiklam; gold and silver fruit dish from Colonel McAlester of Loup and Kennox, and family; gilt mounted spirit bottles to Mr Campbell from the Misses Campbell and Mrs Cameron; gold stamp box and sketch from Mr & Mrs Denison; gold pin trays from Mr & Mrs J. Kingston Barton; pair of silver candlesticks and flowers from household servants; silver cream jug and muffineers from Col. Campbell of Treesbanks; gold mounted cut glass ink bottle from Mrs Marsden and Miss Campbell, senior of Jura; handsome flower glass and flowers from Mr & Mrs Gidey; silver sugar spoon and moustache brush from Miss Johnston; gold mounted liqueur stand, bottles and glass, from Capt and Mrs William Grant of Glenmoriston, Mrs Donald Beith, and many others. The celebration of the event at Jura, is, we understand, postponed till the return of the family.

Here then we get a revealing picture of the two lives of the Laird of Jura. He lives in two very different worlds, in his town house in South Kensington, with its household staff, and in his country estate in Jura. He has a considerable personal fortune, and estates and properties in a number of places. However, he maintains the public position that his estate in Jura must pay for itself. This posture was maintained consistently until 1936, when Charles Graham Campbell sold the parts of the island the family still owned. The family continued to live elsewhere in considerable comfort.

Throughout their long involvement with Jura, the Campbells rarely lost a legal battle, and they fought many. Only the eighteenth-century church stood against them, and only Mr Hossack emerged to some extent the victor. Successive generations of Campbells of Jura never forgot or forgave, and each successive minister found himself, to his surprise, the inheritor of their hostility to his office.

32

Wages

We have focused in our studies of the habits of Jura folk on those who have been earning their own living, largely from the land. These people have been tenants or crofters or sometimes cottars. They have lived in houses owned by the landowner and have paid rent for these and for the land which goes with them.

However, there are in the nineteenth century at least a number of people who work for the laird, and who are paid wages by him.

These families also live in property which Campbell owns, but they pay no rent. The rent is hidden as a sum which is deducted from their wages at source. It does not figure in any rates or calculations, although its presence may be noted as 'house'.

We have a detailed abstract of Campbell's payroll for the year 1879, when it consists of thirty men: Angus McKay (66), head gamekeeper; Dugald Buie (36), estate cartwright; John Darroch (50), cowherd; Alexander McKennel (33), ploughman; Donald Taylor (70), mason; Alexander Clark (50), shepherd; Neil Lindsay (80), Alexander Darroch (76), Donald McCranie (60), Donald McCartan (72), James McConnel (53), Neil Darroch (59), John Shaw (37) are all agricultural labourers; Donald Kerr and his son are shepherds; Neil Campbell is a coachman.

Four of the above men are 70 years of age or older, and Neil Lindsay is 80, but there is no evidence that they are in any way different from the others on the payroll. They are all evidently continuing to work. Some are shown as 'single men' and relatives of the above: Duncan Rankin (23), son of Sandy Rankin, Donald Darroch (43), son of Alexander Darroch, Archibald McCarten (31), son of Donald McCartan, and Malcolm McCranie (20), son of Donald McCranie, are all agricultural labourers; Alexander Clarke (18), a labourer, is the nephew of James McConnell; and John Darroch (18), a coachman, is the grandson of Marrion Darroch, a widow.

The remaining names are something of a mixture: Malcolm McCranie (54), unmarried labourer; Hugh McDougald (68), estate worker; John McDougall (69), cowherd; Sandy Rankine (76), agricultural labourer; Duncan McKay (26), son of Angus McKay, Head Keeper, is a keeper.

William Rutherford (76), from Roxburgh, is the Farm Overseer, and his name appears at the head of the Document as the man who pays the wages.

These men, with their various families, live at Ardfin, New Brosdale, Cabrach; Dunans, Crackaig, Sannaig and Caigenhouse.

After the above twenty-nine names appears the single name, Fletcher. This is Archibald Fletcher, the Farm Manager at Tarbert. He lives there with his wife and four children, and is very much on Campbell's payroll.

All of these thirty men are paid in cash for their work. The account shows the total money paid for the year 1879. In some cases, the weekly rate is noted alongside the annual total, and in one case a daily rate is shown. The weekly rates are shown in shillings, written in the conventional manner, familiar from 'pre-decimal' days, with the figure, followed by an oblique stroke and dash.

The amounts mentioned are 7/–, 8/–, 9/– and 10/– per week.

These rates generate an annual wage on the basis of 52 weeks' pay. There are no holidays: 7/– amounts to £18 4/– per annum; 8/– amounts to £20 16/– per annum; 9/– amounts to £23 8/– per annum; 10/– amounts to £26 – per annum.

The accounts show that one man, John Shaw of Crackaig, gets 1/6 per day and £23 8/– per year, so we know that 1/6 per day amounts to 9/– per week, which confirms that he works a six-day week.

Many of the wages are given as a 'per day' rate: e.g., 1/8 per day = 10/– per week; 1/4 per day = 8/– per week; and 1/2 per day = 7/– per week. Here we also find the blacksmith's rate as 13/– per week. The payroll gives £33 16/– per annum.

The payroll shows Hugh McDougall, the joiner, earning £40 6/– per annum. A 'note' explains that he gets 2/4 per day in winter, and 2/10 per day in summer. This works out neatly as £18 4/– for 26 weeks at 14/– per week, and £22 2/– for 26 weeks at 17/– per week. This is the highest daily rate on the payroll, but Hugh McDougall is alone among the employees in paying a rent for his house of £3 4/9.

The rate paid at this date to the largest number of employees is 9/– per week.

Nine men receive wages at this rate: five are agricultural labourers; a mason; a coachman; a labourer; and an unidentified man.

Four agricultural labourers are paid at the lowest rate of 7/– per week, and two are the only representatives of the 8/– per week rate.

The rate of 10/– per week is paid to the cartwright, the ploughman, the herd, one labourer, one agricultural labourer and a shepherd.

The blacksmith and Neil Campbell, another coachman, are paid at the rate of 13/– per week.

Angus McKay, Head Keeper, was paid £23 15/– but the reason for this odd amount is probably lost.

Alexander Clark, the Shepherd of Dunans, was paid £10 19/5 in 1879, another odd amount. William Rutherford was paid only £30, as estate overseer cum gardener. He was of course already 76, and may have been on 'light duties', so that his wage does not reflect his full responsibilities.

Archibald Fletcher was paid £50 for the year, which may have been an annual salary for his management of Tarbert, rather than a weekly wage.

These are the cash payments for 1879, but in addition to them there are a whole variety of allowances, all of which have a cash value which is set down alongside the wages. The allowances are paid to men with families. Single men living with their families evidently do not qualify. All of them are paid at the uniform rate of 1/6 per day; £23 8/– per annum, and there are no entries in their allowances columns.

Milk Allowance. Three families get an allowance for milk. The amount is £4 11/3 per annum. This is 1/9 per week or 3d per day. The gamekeeper, the ploughman and the coachman are those who get this milk allowance.

Meal Allowance. Five families get an allowance of meal, accounted in a similar way, at a rate of 17/– per boll.

For instance; Donald Kerr gets 13 bolls, so £11 1/–; John Darroch gets 9½ bolls, so £8 1/6; Dugald Buie, Alex McConnel and John McDougall each get 6½ bolls, so £5 10/6; The Jura boll was proabably 140 pounds.

Of course, we have no information about what exactly was being purchased. It may be that more was on offer than simply 'oatmeal' suitable for porridge or oatmeal cakes. Some quality of flour was doubtless on offer for bread, and some of the meal may have been of suitable condition to feed to chickens or even to domestic livestock during the winter.

Campbell is buying grain in bulk from the crofters, putting it through his own mill and selling it on to his employees. In this department he is supplying several tons of meal per annum.

Coal Allowance. The laird is also in the business of supplying coal to his workers. Thirteen of the married men get an annual supply of coal, with a recorded cash value.

For six families the year's allowance is £2 8/–, for five it is £4 and for two it is £5 12/–. The unit cost would thus appear to be 8/–, presumably for a standard weight of coal. These families have used 6, 10 and 14 such measures.

If there were only the 1879 accounts to go on the units of measurement would be a matter of guesswork. However, here also there is useful 'note' which records that the unit costs are for 'half a ton', so the families concerned are actually using 3 tons, 5 tons and 7 tons of coal in the year. This sounds like quite a lot of fuel, but it must be remembered that this will be the only source of power in the household.

Campbell's stock must be well over 50 tons per annum. Presumably it is he who contracts with the coal boat to make a delivery to the island. Many residents will still be relying heavily on their peat banks, but by no means all have access to peat by this time. For example, it seems from the coal allowances that the people of New Brosdale are not operating peat cuttings, and, indeed, in the laird's weekly employ it is unlikely if they would be given sufficient time off work to enable them to cut a supply of peat. No doubt Campbell is selling coal directly to many other inhabitants who increasingly come to depend on it for winter fuel.

Potato Allowance. One family, that of John Darroch, the herd, gets an allowance of potatoes, worth £2. This is the only entry under this heading, and there is no indication in the documents as to what weight of potatoes can be supplied for £2. Most employees must still be growing their own.

Livestock Allowances. The final allowance which applies to all but two of the married families concerns cattle and sheep. The accounts heading says simply 'Cow'.

Seven families get a credit of £3 10/–; three families get a credit of £5; one gets £7; one gets £10; one £12; one gets £15; and one gets £17 5/–.

It sounds as if Campbell is supplying livestock, and the setting the value against wages, but another useful note makes it clear that we are dealing here with 'keep' or 'feed' for animals, rather than animals themselves.

Donald Buie, the cartwright, gets 'the keep of a cow', and the smith, McKechnie, 'the keep of two cows', and thereafter throughout the list, the employees who have an entry under 'Cow' have a sum 'for cow's grass'.

Several men have entries headed 'braxy', e.g. £1 15/6. Braxy is an infection in sheep. A further entry reads 'one barrel braxy'. The barrel of braxy was a barrel of salted mutton from braxy sheep, an important perk at the time, as it was very low priced.

John Darroch, the cowherd at Ardfin, also had a large allowance against meal, and £12 set against his 'Cow' entry. An additional note appears over his total – 'keep boy and woman'. Indeed the census shows that in addition to his wife, Ann (14), Flora (11), Euphemia and Archibald (9) he gives lodging to Ann McCraine and Donald McDougall, both twenty-five years old and unmarried. Ann is in service, but there is no information about Donald. A further 'note' gives more detail here, and says, 'to keep a woman and a strong lad and to pay them himself'.

Donald McCranie and Neil Darroch earned each £1 in 1879 for hay cutting.

Since the rate was only 4d per day, and only a fraction of the usual rate, this work was presumably done in the men's 'own time'. They must have found two or three hours early in the morning or late in the evening, on top of their twelve hour day, and they must have engaged in this for ten weeks over the summer period – a hard way to earn 'overtime'.

Archibald McCartan earned an additional 7/– for sheep smearing.

Eight employee families have the fact that they have a 'house' noted in their wages although their is no actual cash amount set against this fact. Three families also have 'potato land', but this isn't costed either. Alexander Clark of Dunans has an entry: 'for herd and hogs, £6'.

There is also to hand a brief extract from the actual 'Cottars' Wages Books' from some thirty years earlier than our study, in 1849. This is just after the ten-year rule of Colin Campbell came to an end, and one year into the brief control of his son Archibald, seventh of Jura.

The extract concerns five men living in the newly established community of New Brosdale. All but one are agricultural labourers and all are married men with families.

Neil Lindsay (48) is a dyke builder, with a wife and five teenage children. Donald McArtan (46) has a wife and four children. Alexander Rankine (46) has a wife and six children. At the time of the 1851 census he has a 74-year-old aunt and a 40-year-old lady visitor in his house. Alexander Darroch (46) has a wife and five children. Peter Keith (61) has his wife, his grown-up son, Duncan, a ploughman, his daughter Ann, a house servant, and a small grandson in his house.

The wages and allowances are set out quite differently at this date. The number of days each man has worked appear. A six day week produces a complete year of 312 days. Our five men worked 323, 301, 313, 361 and 336 days.

Alex Rankine hit almost the exact year of six-day weeks, while the others varied. Alex Darroch put in almost an entire year, working apparently every day but four. It must have been possible for him to work and be paid on the Sabbath, which comes as a considerable surprise, since it has been widely accepted that

Sunday work was not acceptable in the Western Isles in the middle of the nineteenth century.

The actual wages earned were £17 8/–, £17 4/–, £17 11/–, £16 13/– and £16 8/–.

Unlike the later system, however, these figures represent the total earning capacity of the men concerned. This is the total income, at least as far as the employer is concerned, and all other aspects of the family's life which require to be funded are supplied by the landlord, and deducted from the wage. In some cases this means that no cash wage is paid at all. The situation is further complicated by the fact that all except Peter Keith are in arrears to the Laird, and some of this may be 'clawed back'; presumably by negotiation with the landlord or his agent.

We will look at the many allowances shortly, but here is the simple situation of debt and credit.

Neil Lindsay began owing 19/–, earned £17 8/0, was paid £1 3/–, ended owing 7/–

Donald McArtan began owing £1 18/–, earned £17 4/–, was paid nil, ended owing £1 12/–

Alex. Rankine began owing £3 4/–, earned £17 11/–, was paid 5/–, ended owing £1 13/–

Alex Darroch began owing £3 12/–, earned £16 13/–, was paid nil ended owing £4 9/–

Peter Keith began owing nil, earned £16 8/–, was paid £2, ended in credit 5/–

Neil Lindsay, Donald McArtan and Alex Rankine have all managed to peg back their arrears. Indeed Neil could hope to square his account the next year and still manage to get a little cash.

Alex Rankine also did well, paying back almost half his debt and still getting a tiny sum of money. Peter Keith seems to be managing, though it is interesting to see that he is not paid the whole £2 5/– to which he is entitled, and has a credit balance held back against hard times to come.

Alex Darroch is doing less well and ends the year behind by almost four months' wages, despite working almost every day in the preceding year.

It is interesting to contemplate the life of these farm workers with big families of growing children, who have to live out their lives at Ardfin with absolutely no hard cash in their possession, at least in the form of wages. The kelping boom is over and they can hardly be selling illicit whisky at this date. They may of course have some home-made goods for sale. Since they must be manufacturing their own clothes, there may be a small surplus. Other essential goods must be bartered for, yet it is hard to see what they can have to trade. These folk apparently all keep a cow for milk and dairy produce. Certainly they pay for grazing for it. Presumably they hope to breed its replacement, and sell the occasional calf. They will not be allowed to increase the number of cattle, and could not feed them if they did. We must remember that it is against this kind of background that people are leaving the island in large numbers.

Let us now see what it is that is swallowing up their small wages.

To start with there is no question, as at our later dates, that the house comes with the job, for each of the five families pays £3 10/– per annum for 'rent of house and grazing'. Thus approximately one-fifth of their earning power goes on the house and the keep for their cow.

There is also the question of sheep. Neil Lindsay and Peter Keith each have an allowance against one ewe, at 13/6 and 14/–. Donald McArtan and Alex Rankine get a supply of raw oats, doubtless for animals, for which they pay 2/6.

All five families have an allowance against wool, measured by the stone. A stone, where wool was concerned, was 24 pounds. The families get 3, 2, 3, 3½ and 2 stones each and pay: £1 10/–, 15/–, £1 3/–, £1 4/– and 15/– respectively.

Here we have housewives who are getting through a very considerable weight of wool. No doubt they spun and wove their cloth within the community. Some may have taken the process right through to the finished garments, although the community had its resident tailors who would presumably run you up some clothes and take their payment in additional wool. With as much as 70 pounds of wool coming into the house, there may have been a surplus for profitable sale.

We come now to the staple foods. Where in 1879 the laird is supplying only oatmeal, here, thirty years earlier, the people are buying four kinds of meal: oatmeal, brose meal, Indian meal and barley meal.

Indian Meal. This sounds as if it is the Indian maize which has been sent by the Committee on Destitution in response to the potato famine. If so, then it is not being handed out free to the starving people, but being retailed by the laird around 14/8 per boll. The five families get between 1 and 1¾ bolls apiece.

Oatmeal. They get between 7 and 11¾ bolls of oatmeal at about 17/6 per boll.

Brose Meal. This is presumably ground to the proper grade for making brose, which is simply boiling water added to oatmeal. The quantities vary from 1 to 1¾ bolls at about 14/8 per boll.

Barley Meal. We have already noted that barley bread was baked in Jura, and doubtless enjoyed. The quantities are quite small ranging from one eighth of a boll to three quarters of a boll at about 14/– a boll. The exact rates paid vary slightly from person to person, which is surprising. It may be that at this time the rates for the various meals were varying from shipment to shipment, and consequently it is impossible to get an exact tally for the amounts expended.

Each of the five families has a quantity of each of the four kinds of meal.

The allowances for food also include potatoes in each case, no doubt a vital commodity at this time.

If we add up the totals spent on meal and potatoes the family's outlays are as follows: the Lindsays, £9 16/–; the McArtans, £12 1/6; the Rankines, £10 19/6; the Darrochs, £12 16/–; and the Keiths, £8 19/–.

About three quarters of the outlays of these families on food materials supplied by the Laird goes on basic oatmeal. The percentages range from 68% to 85%.

It is interesting to compare this much earlier glimpse of the wage structure of Campbell of Jura's employees with the details we have examined from 1879 and 1888. Even although we would consider the later conditions to represent extreme poverty, the situation in 1849 would appear to be very much worse.

33

Tenants and Rents in the Nineteenth Century

Several documents have survivied from the nineteenth century which give some indication of what is happening in terms of numbers of tenants and what they were paying as rent.

From 1831 there are papers relating to an action for damages at the instance of Neil MacGilvray, a tenant in Knockrome, against Archibald Campbell of Jura. These say that 'previous to March 1831 there were twelve joint tenants in Knockrome of which Duncan McGilvray and three others held One Eighth each and the others One Sixteenth, then in March they were divided into twelfths each'.

From 1836 there is a curious hand-written document relating to Keils and Ballard:

Keils and Ballard are roughly supposed to be 740 acres.
Each Tenant has 10½ acres of arable land.
The total number of Cattle which should be kept in the farm are:
Cows; 25 to tenants; 15 to cottars. Total; 40
Young cattle; 25 1 & 2 year olds; 16 of which are the tenants'
Horses; 5; 4 to the tenants. Sheep; 20
Rent paid by township including cottars at Caigenhouse is £ (blank) Viz; 4 tenants @ £10 10/– 1 cottar @ £10 cottars @ £3 4/–
1836 On Farm of Keils 17 tenants & cottars paying a total Rent of £106 9/– 11 tenants paying £8 12/–; 2 @ £4 6/–; 4 cottars, 1 @ £1, 3 @ 15/–.

This Keils and Ballard note is full of useful details. The picture in Keils seems to be that there are twelve full tenancies, at £8 12/– rent. However, one of them is divided between two parties at half the rent. There are four cottars. This account agrees well with the first census five years later, which shows twelve men and their families as tenants. Hugh Black's son, Donald, has an independent tenancy by 1851, and this may be the family who share the rent between father and son. Neil Keith, Murdoch McCraine, Donald Black and Alex. Clark could well be the four cottars. A hand-loom weaver, a seaman, a labourer and a dyke-builder would be reasonable candidates. Malcolm and Ann Shaw, in their seventies, may have been 'annuitants'. Barbara Lindsay and Catherine McDougall are designated 'paupers', and Catherine Keith (60), and her wee grocer's shop may not have attracted a rent.

Also from 1836 a small table of Holdings and Tenants has survived which gives a picture of the numbers of tenants and cottars in a selection of the crofting townships in Jura. Ardfernal, Knockrome, Lergybreck and Keils produce a total of forty-seven tenants and four cottars

Patrick Fletcher, the publican at Craighouse Inn, is added with his rent of £120 along with the blacksmith of Miltown, Alexander McDougall. It is likely that by this date, Corran House is operating as a farmstead, rather than an inn.

The total rent available from these fifty-four tenants comes to £542 11 4¾; however, the full extent of tenancies in Jura is not covered by this brief table, nor by the previous note. Various lands in the south of the island are not listed, and there is no mention of Ardmenish or Lagg.

Another Campbell Document from 1835 gives what purports to be a complete list of tenants and cottars in Campbell's part of the island. This is a remarkable list, and perhaps better than any other document of the time, it gives a clear picture of the number of families who pay rents to the Campbells. Each is of course a 'head of household', and behind them lie their families.

This comprehensive list of all of Campbell's tenants amounts to seventy-five tenant householders, of whom three are widows; and forty-two cottagers or cottars, of whom eight are widows and one is a woman householder.

Here there is reference to 117 households of the total of 210 shown in the 1841 census.

The figures for 1836 suggest a possible average rent for tenants of about £9 and for cottars of about £3. If these are reasonable estimates, the families on the 1835 list must have generated over £1000 in rent per annum.

In 1850 a labourer in the Western Isles earned something between £5 and £10 per annum. Campbell of Jura was raising in rent an income more than 100 times that of one of his workers. At present-day average annual wages, the Laird's annual income from rents put him in the millionaire bracket.

A Rent List from 1879 and the Land Valuation return for 1888 have survived and gives a clear picture of what is happening in Jura at that date.

The forms list under 'Subject and Locality' most of the properties on the island, and other interests such as 'Shootings'. There is a comprehensive list of tenants which corresponds well with the information we get from the censuses. There is also a list of inhabitants and occupiers who are 'not rated', in other words, employed by various people on the island. They are also in the census by and large.

James Campbell still has a payroll of nineteen men. Henry Evans, employing eight men, has become the second-largest employer on the island. The farming tenants at Kinuachdrach, Tarbert and Lagg also employ between them two ploughman, two herds and a farm servant.

The figures which appear in the 'Valuation' in 1888 are directly related to the amounts paid in rent by the tenants in 1879, but are appreciably less.

Here is a selection of the amounts:

	1879 Rental	1888 Valuation
Ardmenish Tenant	£25	£23
Knockrome Double Tenant	£40	£30 10/–
Knockrome Single Tenant	£20	£15
Keils Tenant	£13 10/–	£10 16/–
Keils & Caigenhouse Cottars	£3 4/–	£3

The total valuation for the smaller tenants was less than the 1879 total rent by a similar margin, viz about £500.

The rental figures for 1879 contain several larger sums shown against individual farming concerns. These appear again in the valuation. The same column headings apply:

Feolin Ferry and Farm	£30	£25
Strone Farm	£100	£40
Feolin Farm	£90	£65
Lagg Inn, Ferry and Farm	£60	£40

The resultant calculation from a study of these two sets of information gives:

Total in Rent List: £826   Total in Valuation Roll: £616

The Valuation Roll works out at roughly 75 per cent of the 1879 Rental Value.

The total Valuation Roll for the island is a completely different matter, for here we find a substantial number of properties which do not figure in the Rent List at all. Here are the additional missing entries:

House and Farm Kinuachdrach	£150
House & Farm Tarbert	£500
House and Farm Crackaig	£60
Home Farm, Ardfin Sanaig, Dunan, etc.	£380
Croft House and Farm Corran	£40
Mr Evans' holdings:	
Lodge, Forest Lands and Interests Lergybreck	£1127 10/-
Other Hunting Interests:	
Shootings Kinuachdrach	£15
Shootings Tarbert	£150
Shootings Ardfernal; Knockrome; Ardmenish	£250

Of all over the above properties and interests James Campbell is the only Proprietor. Their total value is: £2672 10/-

The income from the above properties and interests is 25% higher than the Valuation as with all the smaller ones. We know, for example, that a few years later the annual rent on Jura Forest Estate is £1348.

If we add 25 per cent this would produce a gross income from the larger holdings of approximately £3340, which taken together with the £825 from the smaller tenancies gives a 'Grand Total' for the whole island of £4165 from rents alone per annum.

By 1890 a gamekeeper was earning about £45 a year, and a ploughman £24. Once more, the Campbells seem to be able to maintain their usual differential, taking in by rent about 100 times more per annum than the people who work for them earn. This enormous annual income of course takes no account of Campbell's profits from all aspects of his management of his estates.

It is hard to reconcile all this with the complaints of hardship made by Miss Campbell at the Crofters' Commission a few years later.

34

Longevity, Age and Death

It was Martin Martin on his visit about 1698, who first set down the belief that the people of Jura were extremely long-lived, and exceptionally healthy:

> Several of the natives have lived to a great age. I was told that one of them, called Gillouir MacCrain lived to have kept one hundred and eighty Christmasses in his own house. He died about fifty years ago, and there are several acquaintances living to this day, from whom I had this account.
>
> Baillie Campbell lived to the age of one hundred and six years, he died three years ago; he passed his thirty-three last years before his death in this isle ... Donald MacNamill, who lives in the village of Killearn at present, is arrived at the age of ninety years.
>
> A woman of the Isle of Scarba, near the north end of this isle, lived seven score years, and enjoyed the free use of her senses and understanding all her days; it is now two years since she died.

Dr John Walker about 1764 has his own comments:

> The people live mostly on Milk, Butter, Cheese, Fish, Mutton, Venison and use very little vegetable Aliment. Notwithstanding this they appear to be rather longer lived than many of their neighbours. The accounts of one Macrain who died here in the last century at the age it is said of 140, are still fresh among the inhabitants. The last Baillie of Jura was 87 and his father is said to have been 110. Several such remarkable instances of longevity I heard related but have not had the opportunity to find them sufficiently verified. We will not be far wrong however, in concluding from them that the inhabitants of Jura, are in general a long lived people.

A few years later in 1776, Pennant gives us his own version:

> The women are very prolific and very often bear twins. The inhabitants live to a great age, and are liable to very few distempers. Men of ninety work; and there is now living a woman of eighty who can run down a sheep. The account given by Martin of Gillour Mac-Crain was confirmed to me. His age exceeded that of either Jenkins or Par; for he kept a hundred and eighty christmasses in his own house, and died in the reign of Charles I. Among the modern instances of longevity I forgot to mention John Armour of Campbeltown, aged one hundred and four, who was a cockswain in our navy, at the time of the peace of Utrecht; and within these three years was stout enough to go out a shooting.

Francis Stewart in the *First Statistical Account* of 1794, says:

The inhabitants are very healthy, and many of them live to old age. A few weeks ago, died a lady at the age of 96. She retained the use of her faculties to the last. Till within a few months of her death, she could walk about with considerable vigour, could read the smallest print, or thread the finest needle without the help of glasses.

Alexander Kennedy in the *Second Statistical Account* of 1845 has nothing to say about the health of the islanders, but mentions the longevity matter:

The island of Jura has ever been proverbial for the longevity of its inhabitants. Instances are on record of many who attained the advanced age of 100 years, in the full possession of their faculties until the last.

Referring to Martin Martin's comments on Gillour MacCrain it is interesting to note that the old man became an important legendary figure in the folk traditions of Jura, and until very recently a number of heroic stories were still being told about his courage and wit in extreme old age.

Dr Walker has Gillour's age as 140, but Pennant records that the story was confirmed to him in 1776, mentioning the 180 Christmasses and saying that he died in the reign of Charles I. Martin Martin's '50 years ago' at 1645, falls within Charles' reign from 1625 to 1649.

Since anyone living for 180 years is impossible, it has often been suggested that there is a witty explanation, which would be in keeping with the nature of the stories that surround Gillour. The Gaelic-speaking nation kept Christmas on 25 December, and the Gaelic New Year on 6 January, for each of which the Gaelic word 'Nollaig' can be used. So Gillour could have kept two Christmasses each year, making ninety Christmasses in his own house.

This would, however, hardly have been sufficient to make his great age as memorable as it seems to have been, since ninety years was often achieved in the Western Isles. It may well be that Gillour was known to have been over 100 years of age, perhaps even at the upper end of human possibilities in the 105 plus bracket. In his time his contemporaries may have been well aware of this, but focussed on the continuous period of ninety years 'in his own house'; which is not to say that they did not know that he had been 'away at the wars' for fifteen years or so in his younger days. If we credit him with an age of 105, he was born in 1540, and would have been perhaps too old at fifty-eight, to have fought in the Battle of Gruinart in 1598.

The whole matter is easy to speculate on and impossible to prove.

However, one of Martin Martin's other 'records' is susceptible to proof. He gives Duncan Campbell, Baillie of Jura, an age of 106 at his death 'three years ago'. By Dr Walker's time his age has lengthened a little to 110. In this case we have a contemporary family grave monument which records his age as ninety-nine and his date of death as 2 May 1695. Martin's informants have added seven years, although the Baillie's age seems to have been a matter of public interest. The tendency to exaggerate is universal.

Martin mentions Donald MacNamill of Killearn, who is ninety years old. Presumably he would have been delighted to record the presence of someone of great age actually living on Jura at the time of his visit, but could go no higher than ninety at that time. This is not really at all surprising.

He concludes his longevity records with a nameless woman of Scarba who had been dead for two years, and had reached 140 years (seven score). This account also has to be discarded as being far outside the recognised human limits. No doubt there was a notable old resident in Scarba at the time, remembered for 'enjoying the free use of her senses and understanding all her days', but we know neither her age or her name.

In all of these considerations of longevity we are handicapped by a total absence of factual evidence. However, in 1855 Statutory Registration of Births, Marriages and Deaths started, and we can begin to study the population statistics of places such as Jura.

Of course, while the death register records the exact date of the individual's death, it can only base the 'age at time of death' on family evidence, and in matters of extreme old age this evidence may be no more reliable than earlier legends.

In all considerations of mortality and cause of death we will examine a period of 100 years. We will start at 1855 and conclude our study at 1954.

During this period the Statutory Register of Deaths records details of the deaths of 842 persons.

Infant mortality was very high with fifty-three babies dying, and 110 deaths recorded before the age of ten. The death rate was low from the twenties to the fifties; 104 people died in their sixties; 109 in their seventies; 189 in their eighties; and forty-three in their nineties.

Only three residents lived beyond 100 years in the 100-year period.

There is little to interrupt the life of a resident who reaches, for example, the age of 40. The deaths of those between forty and fifty, are similar to the numbers who died in their teens.

There is an even distribution of death rates after the age of seventy years. The years seventy to ninety seem to have an average of about eighteen per year during the 100 years in question. The likelihood of further survival does not seem to fall dramatically until a resident has passed his or her ninety-second birthday.

In the Jura community men and women reach these ages in almost identical numbers.

In terms of our discussion about longevity, the 100 years in question produced forty-six men and women who reached or passed their ninetieth year, but only thirteen who passed ninety-two.

There are no records for ages 99, 100 or 101, but there is one each at 102, 107 and 118. The relevant entries are:

Alexander Buie; pauper; widower; married to Sarah Buie; died at Dainsgear aged 102 in 1889; son of John Buie and Catharine McCallum.
Catharine McDougall; widow of John McDougall; slate quarrier; died at Kenuach-drach, in 1868; aged 107; daughter of John McLean and Margaret Cowan.
Mary McCraine; died at Lussagiven in 1855; aged 118; daughter of Donald McCraine and Mary McNeven.

It is unneccessary to question the validity of the records of Alexander Buie or even Catharine McDougall, but Mary McCraine produces quite another problem.

The gravestone at Inverlussa says she was a descendant of Gillour MacCrain and credits her with an age of 128 years at the time of her death in 1856. The stone inscription adds ten years to the age accredited by the death register.

The oldest authenticated centenarian in Great Britain in recent years was Miss Alice Stevenson, 1861–1973, who was 112. No other British citizen appears to have reached his or her 112th birthday. Our collection of early baptismal records for the eighteenth century stops before the range of dates where we might expect to find Mary McCraine. Presumably we must distrust the actual accredited age of 118. However, Miss McCraine was famously long-lived.

She was called 'Mairi Ribeach', or 'untidy Mary', because her hair was always straggly.

In Portnahaven in Islay, the author heard a saying about her from James McArthur:

"*Ciamar a tha thu?*" "*Tha mi gu math.*" "How are you?" "I am well."
"*Tha mi mar each mairi Reubach, Daonnan a dol mun cuairt.*"
"I'm like Mairi Ribeach's spindle! Always going round!"

She was thus a byword for longevity and hard work in her lifetime. In Jura the story survives that she asked to be taken to Inverlussa Church shortly before her death. She was carried into the church, and the congregation were amazed to see that she had the form and face of a small child.

We can be confident that Mary MacCrain, while not the holder of the UK record, was indeed a very long-lived woman. It seems that after our study, we may be able to agree with Dr John Walker's modest conclusion that the inhabitants of Jura have been in general a long-lived people.

HEALTH, ILLNESS AND CAUSES OF DEATH
Having studied the special question of longevity in Jura, we now record various observations of the historical visitors and their opinions on questions of health and disease.

As usual we must start with Martin Martin:

This isle is perhaps the wholesomest plot of ground either in the isles or continent of Scotland, as appears by the long life of the natives and their state of health, to which the height of the hills is believed to contribute in a large measure, by the fresh breezes of wind that come from them to purify the air; whereas Islay and Gigha, on each side of this isle, are much lower, and are not so wholesome by far, being liable to several diseases that are not here.

The inhabitants observe that the air of this place is perfectly pure, from the middle of March till the end or middle of September. There is no epidemical disease that prevails here. Fevers are but seldom observed by the natives, and any kind of flux is rare.

The gout and agues are not so much as known by them, neither are they liable to sciatica.

Convulsions, vapours, palsies, surfeits, lethargies, megrims, consumptions, rickets, pains of the stomach, or coughs, are not frequent here, and none of them are at any time observed to become mad. I was told by several of the natives that there was not one woman died of child-bearing there these past thirty-four years past. Bloodletting and purging are not used here.

If any contract a cough, they use brochan only to remove it. If after a fever one chance to be taken ill of a stitch, they take a quantity of ladywrack, and half as much of red-fog, and boil them in water. The patients sit upon the vessel, and receive the fume, which by experience they find effectual against this distemper. Fevers and diarrhoeas are found here only when the air is foggy and warm, in winter or summer.

There are several fountains of excellent water in this isle. The most celebrated of them is that of the mountain Beinbreck in the Tarbat, called Toubir ni Lechkin, that is, the well in the stony descent. It runs easterly, and they commonly reckon it to be lighter by one half than any other water in this isle; for though one drink a great quantity of it at a time, the belly is not swelled, or any ways burdened by it. Natives and strangers find it efficacious against nauseousness of the stomach and the stone. The river Nissa receives all the water that issues from this well, and this is the reason they give why salmon here are in goodness and taste far above those of any other river whatever.

The women of all ranks eat a lesser quantity of food than the men. This and their not wearing anything strait about them is believed to contribute much to the health of both the mothers and children.

Martin is as usual both interested and interesting. He has a very high opinion of the healthy environment in Jura, and takes considerable pains to give a comprehensive list of the ailments from which the inhabitants do not suffer. The Statutory Register of Deaths was not to start for another 150 years, but when it begins to record causes of death most of Martin's absent conditions are recorded, with the possible exception of 'surfeits'. There was seldom enough food to make that a problem. Consumption is by then a major killer, and childbirth also takes its expected toll. Martin was questioning the living and not the dead. It may be that he was receiving the treatment meted out so often by islanders of being told exactly what he wanted to hear. He had formed the opinion the island was healthy, and enquiries bore out his opinion.

Martin is fascinated by magic, and his account of the well is of great interest. Martin has his healing well rising in Bein Bhreac, whereas the ancient well 'Tobar Leac nam Fiann' rises on the south-east slope of the more northerly Ben Garrisdale, from where indeed its waters find their way down into the Lussa River. Martin knows it as 'Toubir ni Lechkin', and translates this as 'the well in the stony descent'. John Mercer calls it 'Fairies' Well', and excavated it in the early 1970s. He found water a few inches deep on glacial clay, covered by a neat cairn. In the earth were twenty Stone Age flints, either knapped by the well's first users or collected as charms by later people. There were twenty-four lumps of milky quartz and eighty pieces of crystal, probably from one or more balls, used as charms in the region up to the mid-nineteenth century. There were clay pipe fragments, a rivet, a buckle, four buttons (all copper), thirty-six lead shot, broken glass and china and a paste amethyst from a brooch. On the underside of the well's sill had been cut eight sets of initials, with dates up to 1869. In the water were half a dozen low-value coins, from an 1861 penny to a 1926 sixpence. Martin's well evidently had a long local history. The Ordnance Survey title would translate as 'Well of the Slab of the Giant', rather than of the Fairies. Martin Martin testifies to the well's significance about 300 years ago.

Dr John Walker also has comments to make on health. It seems likely that Walker has been able to read Martin Martin for he seems to give a deliberately contrary view, as if to correct Martin's errors:

> They are not remarkable however, for a greater proportion of health than their neighbours. Diarrhoeas and inflammatory fevers are rather more frequent here than in the islands where the inhabitants live more upon vegetable food, and the Smallpox is nowhere attended with greater mortality. The soil of Jura is extremely dry, especially in all the inhabited places near the sea. Nothing can be purer than the air; kept in perpetual motion by the mountainous nature of the country. The waters are most salubrious, and the manner of life of the inhabitants is the same as in the other islands. In their diet alone they differ, and to this may be ascribed any greater prevalence of mortality in the above diseases. Grain is scarce, and the people want gardens to supply them with vegetables. Of late years the cultivation of potatoes has enlarged the proportion of their vegetable aliment, and by pretty certain observation has added greatly to the health of the people.

As can be seen Walker is less impressed with the people's general health than Martin, although he agrees that the air and the water are excellent. Walker seems to imply that potatoes have now arrived, but have not been in cultivation for many years.

He goes on to give a very detailed description of the crippling disease caused by the 'fillun worm':

> Over the Highlands in general there are fewer people to be observed either lame or decrepit than in any other country perhaps in Europe. But in the island of Jura, the cripples are remarkably numerous, owing to a very singular disease with which this island is peculiarly infected.
>
> This disease arises from a Worm lodged under the skin, that penetrates with exquisite pain, the interior parts of the limbs. It is termed in the Gaelic language, 'Fillun', and is generally lodged either in the knees and ankles.
>
> It is first discernible very deep, as the patients themselves say, at the bones. Whether it really affects, or penetrates the bones, I could not positively learn, though it is not unlikely, from the extreme pain which it occasions. But in a little time it makes way through the cartilages, tendons and muscles and penetrates the skin, with several small ichorous orifices.
>
> The worm disappears soon after this stage of the disease, but when it is suffered to come to this length it never fails to cripple the patient for life. Both

men and women, children and adults, are equally subject to it. And the intense pain with which it is accompanied sometimes destroys the appetite and spirits and occasions death.

The worm itself is about half an inch long. It has a white head, with a sharp bony rostrum. And the body is a reddish colour, and of a compressed shape, with a row of feet on each side.

The only cure known for this disease is the root of a plant and the marrow cord of beef bones, or, if they cannot be had, they make use of goat tallow in its place. The root is pounded and mixed with the oleaginous substance and the mixture applied in the form of a poultice, as hot as the patient can bear it. The application of this remedy before the worm breaks the skin, kills it within and cures the patient. Yet even those who are thus recovered, most of them have their limbs to some degree lamed or distorted, and the disease is so frequent that there is not a farm upon Jura but there are two or three persons to be found who have suffered it.

The plant whose root is used for the cure of this disease is the Pedicularis palustris of Linnaeus, or Great Marsh Rattle, which has long been known as an officinal plant, but this remarkable virtue which seems to reside in it, has been discovered and known only by the inhabitants of the Hebrides. There does not seem to be any account recorded, either of the animal here described, or the disease which it occasions.

Pennant, mentions the same affliction on his later journey. His account does not seem to follow Walker's one:

I had some obscure account here of a worm, that in a less pernicious degree, bears some resemblance to the 'furia infernalis' of Linnaeus, which in the vast bogs of Kemi drops on the inhabitants, eats into the flesh and occasions a most excruciating death. The 'Fillan', a little worm of Jura, small as a thread and not an inch in length, like the Furia insinuates itself under the skin, causes a redness and great pain, flies swiftly from part to part, but is curable by a poultice of cheese and honey.

Walker and Pennant were not alone in recording the 'fillan'. Martin Martin, at the end of the seventeenth century, had recorded a case on Skye and another in the Outer Hebrides and added that the 'fillan' had been 'in several persons in the Isles'. James Robertson, a botanist touring the Highlands in 1767, while in Lochaber, heard of 'an animalcule that nestling in people's legs or other places causes exquisite pain'. As late as the twentieth century, Alexander Carmichael came across a man in Gairloch who had suffered from the 'fiollan fionn' (the white worm), and told him a charm 'against the worm'. Dwelly gives 'fillean' as 'a species of worm that breeds in the human head and neck, causing painful swellings'.

Whatever may be happening here, if Walker's description is at all accurate, this infestation was responsible for the crippling of a substantial proportion of the inhabitants. It seems to have caused excruciating pain and, in some cases to have led to death. The treatment was also pretty brutal. The condition apparently attacked men, women and children, and was treated only within the community, rather than by any formal medical attention.

It is difficult now to be clear about what the 'fillan' is or was. 'Filariasis' is a group of diseases caused by various nematode worms, generally called round-worms. In tropical countries roundworms can be responsible for serious diseases like elephantiasis and many other life-threatening disorders.

Walker's description does not sound appropriate to a nematode worm. These may be very long, but are usually of a very small diameter, even 'threadlike'. If Walker's 'worm' is based on an eye-witness account it cannot possibly be a nematode. The animal is about half an inch long, with a white head and a sharp bony rostrum. The body is white and compressed and it has a row of feet on each side. It sounds more like some kind of carnivorous grub. The parasites known as 'chiggers', which are mostly various species of mites, have larvae which burrow into human tissues. No such creature lives in modern-day Scotland, but one may have done under different climatic conditions in the past. It would be interesting to consider in more detail what the 'fillun' may have been.

Francis Stewart gives his own assessment of health and illness on Jura:

Diseases are few in number, owing, perhaps in a good measure, to the simple mode of living of the inhabitants. They are sometimes seized with inflammatory disorders; this seems to be occasioned by the lightness of their clothing, par-ticularly of their bed-clothing, which is not sufficient to keep up the perspiration while they are at rest. They are liable to those disorders which are occasioned by living much upon milk and fish. Of late, rheumatic complaints have become more general among the lower classes. We have had one dropsical case last summer, that proved fatal; several have died within the last twelvemonth of stomach complaints. There is no surgeon in the island and they never send for one, except in cases which are deemed extremely dangerous. A great proportion of children die in infancy, and many of the mothers, though of a strong constitution, recover slowly in child-bed. Both these circumstances seem to be owing to unskilful treatment, for there is not a single bred midwife in the island. The smallpox, in the natural way, carried off many children in autumn 1791. The people entertain no prejudice against inoculation, but grudge the expense of it.

The minister considers the people to be generally very healthy. He believes that their proneness to 'inflammatory disorders' is due to their getting chilled at night – an interesting theory. He also holds their diet responsible for ill-nesses. Stewart does record some actual cases – the first individual causes of death in the Jura record. There was one fatal case of dropsy and several of stomach complaints. Many children die in infancy and, although mothers do not actually seem to die in childbirth, they are slow to recover from it. Stewart seems to believe that this situation would be improved if there was a trained mid-wife for the island's confinements. Walker has noted the severe mortality from smallpox, and here Stewart confirms that it can cause a serious loss of life in an epidemic, as occurred in 1791. Inoculation, which he mentions as unpopu-lar, would in due course begin to take effect, and would contribute to the problem of over-population as a result of its effect in reducing the mortality in children.

The interesting opinions from visitors like Martin Martin in the 1690s and Walker and Pennant in the 1770s about the questions of health and disease in Jura, are not of course supported by any formal medical evidence. Francis Stewart's assessments are similar. From 1855 a reason or cause of death is recorded against every entry in the death register, and this gives us the opportunity to examine the diseases which caused the inhabitants to die from the middle of the nineteenth century.

CAUSES OF DEATH FROM 1855 TO 1954

We will examine the causes of death by Age Cohort, 1855–1954

Deaths of Infants before their First Birthday

The following are the reasons given for the death of infants before their first birthday:

Acute Laryngitis	Asphyxia	Bronchitis	Convulsions
Cough	Debility	Died at Birth	Gastric Catarrh
Heart Disease	Inflammation of Bowel		Intus susceptus
Liver Disease	Neglect	Premature Birth	Scarlatina
Stoppage of Bowels	Throat Disease	Unknown	Want of Breast Milk
Water in the Head	Weakness	Whooping Cough	

Deaths of Children from One to Twelve Years

During the 100 years sixty-five children died between the ages of one and twelve years:

Accidents (falls, burns, scalds, drowned)	Bronchitis		Consumption
Croup	Diphtheria	Disease in Chest	Eczema
Epilepsy	Gastritis	Heart Disease	Hydrocephalus
Inflammation	Influenza	Intus susceptus	Liver Disease
Lockjaw	Measles	Meningitis	Obstruction
Pneumonia	Rheumatism	Scrofula	Scarlet Fever & Scarlatina
Tubercular meningitis	Tuberculous peritonitis		Whooping Cough

Deaths between Thirteen to Nineteen

From 1855 to 1954 there were twenty-five deaths of those we would nowadays call teenagers. Causes of death are headed by six cases of tuberculosis. Here are the others:

Cephalagias congestiva	Cephalagia	Croup
Disease of Liver & Lungs	Haemorrhage from Gunshot Wounds	
Heart disease	Inflammation & Fever	
Inflammation of Abdomen	Influenza	Liver complaint
Measles & Meningitis	Pneumonia	Rheumatic Fever
Shot while Loading a Gun	Strumous disease	Ulcers
Water in the Head	Whooping Cough & Debility	

The list emphasises the hazards of life on a hunting estate, with boys of sixteen and eighteen dying of gunshot wounds in 1859 and 1915.

Deaths of People in their Twenties.

Between 1855 and 1964, fifty-six inhabitants of Jura died in their twenties. In this age group tuberculosis is by far the most significant cause of death. It appears under various titles: 'affection of lungs', 'consumption', 'phthisis pulmonaria', 'inflammation of the lungs' and 'tuberculosis'. Under these titles it was responsible for thirty of the fifty-six cases on the island.

The dates are of interest:

1855; 1858; 1861; 1867 (2); 1869; 1870; 1872; 1873; 1874; 1876;
1887 (3); 1889 (2); 1891; 1892; 1894 (2); 1897; 1898; 1900;
1907; 1911; 1912; 1916; 1920; 1927; 1946.

This shows a steady drain of young people, with some periods of intensity, like the nine deaths between 1887 and 1894. In the small sample from Jura there are exactly twice as many men in their twenties dying of TB as there are women. Here are the remaining twenty-six causes: bowel complaint; bronchitis; cold after measles; cramp; decline from childbirth; diabetes (2); died in childbed; disease of spine (2); epilepsy; general debility; head injury; heart disease; hepatitis; jaundice; measles with congestion of the lungs; meningitis; pain in the head; palsy; paralysis; pneumonia (2); sudden death; upset skiff; drowned.

Deaths of People in their Thirties. Once more in the thirties the main cause of death is TB. In this age group it is responsible for fifteen out of the forty deaths. The remaining causes are somewhat similar to those listed for the previous cohort.

Deaths of People in their Forties. Men and women in their forties died less frequently than any other age group. Only thirty deaths of this age group are recorded during the 100 year period. With nine records, tuberculosis is still the biggest single killer. Accidental death continues to figure, with three drownings and one death at sea. Deaths in childbirth are significant. There is also a single suicide. The other causes are not listed here.

Deaths of People in their Fifties. Forty-five inhabitants of Jura died in their fifties during the 100 years. Tuberculosis is no longer numerically significant by this age, with only three deaths, all men. The biggest single cause of death is now heart disease, under various labels, e.g. angina, fatty degeneration of the heart, myocarditis, valvular disease of the heart, coronary infarction, etc. There is also one record of cardiac failure after alcoholic excess. Heart problems account for eleven deaths, or a quarter of the group. Cancer makes an appearance in this group, and there is one death by 'acute opium poisoning'. The other causes are not listed.

Deaths of People in their Sixties. As one would expect, the 104 deaths for residents in their sixties are far more than for the middle years. Within these records there are six causes which account for 50 per cent of the deaths: bronchitis (6); cancer (stomach, abdomen, womb) (9); cerebral haemorrhage (7); tuberculosis (10); heart disease (13); paralysis and paralytic shock (6).

It may be of interest to note some of the other causes recorded: apoplexy (3); brain fever; died of burns (clothes on fire); disseminated sclerosis; drowned;

drowned (dead on shore); epilepsy; general creeping paralysis; gravel complaint; senile decay; softening of the brain (2); and sudden death (2).

Deaths of People Over Seventy Years of Age. The Statuary Register of Deaths contains 424 entries between 1855 and 1954, which relate to people who lived to 70 years and beyond.

The causes of death of many of these people come under the general category of 'Old Age'. Several descriptions were in use for the 210 deaths in this area: old age; senile decay; general decay; senility; debility; and extreme old age.

The other main causes of death in this age group are as follows: heart disease (34); cancer (various) (20); bronchitis (16); influenza (12); tuberculosis (12); paralysis (13); apoplexy (12); cerebral haemorrhage (9); pneumonia (7); rheumatism (6); asthma (5).

There remain some seventy deaths whose causes are not detailed here.

The circumstances of the registration of the deaths we have considered remains something of a mystery. There was only intermittently a resident General Practitioner on Jura during the twentieth century. Indeed, Dr Stewart Sandeman on his arrival in 1917 was the first permanent appointment. The Office of Local Registrar was established at the same time, but in the earlier years the death of a resident on Jura was registered in Islay. The Islay doctor may have seen the deceased as a consequence of attending the person in Jura while sick, and may thus have been able to render an opinion as to cause of death, however, local folk lore gives humorous accounts of the Islay doctor's reluctance to make 'house calls' in Jura, so the number of cases he attended may have been limited.

In a number of cases the Statutory Register bears the legend 'Certified' which appears to indicate that the body was actually examined by the Islay doctor after death. There may even have been occasional post-mortem examinations.

The medical opinion which accompanies the entry as a diagnosis of the fatal condition may have originated with the local midwife, who may have assisted in the 'laying out'.

This may go far to explain the considerable number of 'causes of death' entered in the register in 'non-medical' language.

It is also of interest to see the way in which an illness could slowly acquire new and more modern labels. We have considered tuberculosis, and heart disease undergoes a similar process. It is an uncommon cause of death from 1855 to 1900. In the 100 years under study, only twenty cases are recorded during the first fifty years, while forty-three are recorded between 1904 and 1954. And this is against the background of twice as many deaths in total in the first fifty years as in the second. 'Heart disease' is the most common description throughout the entire 100 years, followed by 'heart failure', but other diagnoses occur, e.g., angina, cardiac dilation, endocarditis, fatty degeneration, fibrillation and finally 'coronary infarction' makes its appearance.

Cancer is recorded in thirty-five cases, with 'tumour', and 'carcinoma' as comments. The perception that cancer occurs throughout the body is well borne out by the register, for a remarkable list of locations is recorded for cancer.

Childbirth. In view of Martin Martin's assertion that there had been no deaths of women in childbearing for the past thirty-four years, we should note that there were seven such deaths from 1855. These occurred in: 1856, 1861, 1870, 1873, 1874, 1890 and 1919, at an average separation of nine years.

Historic accounts listed the terrible effects of smallpox in the eighteenth century, but the Death Register does not record a single smallpox death after 1855. Influenza, on the other hand, was responsible for eighteen deaths.

Accidental Death. The list of twenty-one accidental deaths in the period in question seems a little surprising. The risk of accidental death on a Hebridean island would probably be thought of as quite low nowadays. Here are the details:

Four small children died of burns, scalds, a fall and drowning.

Two teenagers died in shooting accidents

Eight adults are recorded as having drowned. One was William Quiston, a seventy-year-old seaman, from the sloop *Janet*. A sixty-two-year-old man is presumed to have chosen walking out into the sea as his method of suicide. One forty-year-old woman drowned in a burn. One elderly man fell off the *Pioneer*, the paddle-steamer ferry boat. Men of forty, forty-four and sixty-one also drowned in unexplained circumstances. A twenty-four year old man drowned after the skiff he was in overturned. A forty-one-year-old man was lost at sea and no body was recovered.

Two elderly residents died after fatal falls, and two old people died of burns.

One twenty-three-year-old man died of an accidental head injury.

There was one suicide recorded on Lunga.

There were two firmly certified causes of death from Islay in the nineteenth century:

Cephalagias congestiva: a thirteen-year-old female in 1874

Podagra retrograda: a forty-seven-year-old male in 1857

Many of the other obviously modern medical terms appear after the arrival of a resident GP.

A contemporary medical man has provided a glossary to some of the terms which appear in the register. Some are tentative guesses, but may give some idea of the kind of things which lay behind the causes of death.

Here are a few, in alphabetical order:

Anasarca, subcutaneous fluid, or dropsy; Ascites, abdominal fluid;
Cephalagias congestiva, swelling of the brain; Cramp, possibly appendicitis;
Croup, fatal croup may have been diphtheria; Disease in chest, probably TB;
Disease of spine, also probably TB; Dumb palsy, stroke;
Genito-vesical fistula, leakage from the bladder; Gravel, kidney stones;
Intus susceptus, inversion of the bowel; Pain in head, sub-arachnoid haemhorrage?
Paralysis agitans, an old name for Parkinson's Disease; Podagra retrograda, gout;
Psoas abscess, TB of the spine coming to the surface in the groin;
Puerpural embolism, childbirth bloodclot; Pyaelia, septicaemia;
Scarlatina, scarlet fever; Scirrhus of the stomach, a hard tumour;
Scrofula or King's evil, TB of the lymphatic glands;
Strumous disease, Goitre, inflammation of the thyroid;
Syncope, unconsciousness from lack of blood to the brain;
Tabes dorsalis, syphilis, stage four; Throat disease, probably diphtheria;

Many of the more informal causes of death are found in the earlier part of the record. These are often puzzling, but behind each of them lies a human story of sickness leading to death, and often of family and friends helpless before the course of the illness. For example: apoplexy; bilious affection; brain fever; birth; catarrh; cold; constipation; cough; cramp; debility; decline; diarrhoea; fall; fainting fit; gangrene; general creeping paralysis; hernia; inward pain; lumbago; neglect; nervous exhaustion; pain in head; pain in side; palsy; piles; shortness of breath; stitch in side; stitch in breast; want of breast milk; wasting; water in head; weakness.

With these reminders of mortality we bring our study of the human frailty of the former inhabitants of Jura to a close.

VIII

Schools and Travel

XIII

35

Schools and Schoolmasters

The first indications of the existence of formal education in Jura come from the beginning of the eighteenth century. In 1638 the General Assembly of the Church of Scotland met in Glasgow and erected the Synod of Argyll, which was to consist of the territory that had formerly been the Diocese of Argyll and the Isles. The newly erected Synod immediately took up, along with its other duties, the task of establishing schools within the bounds.

The first mention of Jura comes with Alexander Buchan, who was at Ederlin in Glassary in 1699, and in Jura from 1700 to 1702. He then went to the remote isle of St Kilda, where he became well known as the author of *A Description of St Kilda, the most remote Western Isle in Scotland.*

In 1696 Parliament passed a new law making it compulsory for the heritors to provide schools and maintain the appointed schoolmasters. By 1698 there were twenty-five 'Fixed English Schools' in the Synod, including one for the parish of Jura and Colonsay.

In 1701 a group of men deeply interested in the educational needs of the Highlands, met in Edinburgh and set up *The Society for the Propagation of Christian Knowledge*, usually known as SPCK for short. The aim was 'the further promoting of Christian knowledge and the increase of piety and virtue within Scotland, especially in the Highlands and Islands, and the remote corners thereof'. Initially the directors outlawed the use of Gaelic, and insisted that all instruction be in English. This was a serious blunder, but was set right in 1767, when, not only did they encourage instruction in Gaelic, but also had the New Testament translated into Gaelic and distributed widely throughout the area.

Pupils were taught reading, writing, arithmetic and the elements of Christian knowledge. An attempt was made for a time to introduce a system of technical education, and courses were provided in agriculture, woodwork, and ironwork for boys; and spinning, knitting, weaving and sewing for girls. Later this attempt was given up.

The teachers were paid a small salary, between £10 and £20 per annum. Synod or parochial school teachers got from £6 to £11 2/2. There was usually a free house and a piece of land to keep a cow and grow potatoes, but the provision was fairly basic.

The records of the Society give some information about the schools on Jura:

Jura: Erected 1 May 1741. Duncan Thomson, master. sixteen boys, four girls. Proficiency in learning. Bible; Testament; Proverbs; Catechism; Writing, Arithmetic, Church Music.

From Reports on the Society's Schools in Jura
1774   Duncan Maclean, master. Salary £7. twenty-eight boys,

six girls.
1774–9   Thomas Davidson, master. Salary £10.
1780–81   John Fraser, master Salary £10.
1783   John Fraser, master Salary £10. thirty-five boys, three girls
1783   Spinning School, Mary Cameron. Salary £6.

Knockrome, 1796; Alexander Campbell, master. Salary £15 thirty-four boys seventeen girls. Alexander Campbell's salary went up to £17 in 1813. He remained until 1822. John Campbell was master from 1822 to 1841 at a salary of £17. Between 1809 and 1841, the numbers of scholars vary between forty-nine and seventy-nine.

Lord Teignmouth, visiting in about 1835, has education as one of his interests. He records:

> The parish church stands on the shore of the bay. It might be taken for a good school-house, and is used for that purpose. The master spoke English but little; he taught his scholars to read it, but confined himself to grammatical explanations, and made no use of catechetical instructions; consequently their lore could be of little or no advantage to them. The manse is near to the church. There is a parochial school here and another at Lagg. At the latter the master observed that the children learnt English more easily than Gaelic, and that therefore he taught it to them first; and certainly their proficiency did credit to his instructions.

Alexander Kennedy makes a brief mention of Education in his *Statistical Account* of 1845:

> Education: The maximum salary is divided among three parochial teachers, two in Jura and one in Colonsay. The defect in the act of 1803 anent parochial schoolmasters is, in this parish, amply provided against by the liberality of the principal heritor, Mr Campbell of Jura, who has expended a large sum of money in the erection of two commodious school-rooms, with accommodation for the teachers and their families. He has also allotted to each a garden and a small pendicle of land, sufficient to maintain a cow and to grow potatoes to serve their families. There are besides, two schools upon the establishment of the Society for the Propagation of Christian Knowledge, one in Colonsay, and the other in Jura. There are also three unendowed schools in the parish. Average income of the teachers is £12 per annum. The number of scholars attending all the schools is 347.

Another source of information about the schools and schoolmasters comes from the censuses of the 1800s. In 1841 there was a school on the shore between Keils and Caigenhouse, called Small Isles School. It seems likely that this was the first to be established on the island, and that the records from the eighteenth century relate to this.

In 1841 there were also schools at Lagg and at Lussagiven.

These three continued until 1851, although there is no appointee at Lagg at the time of the census. By 1851 a school has been set up in the vicinity of New

Brosdale. This is usually called 'Cabrach', and it is specifically listed as a Society School.

Another school has arrived at Knockrome. The original building remained in use for many years, and was known as the SPCK School of Burnside. The cottage was inhabited long after it ceased to be the school, and the ruin still stands by the road to Knockrome.

The five schools continue through 1861, but Lagg School seems to have closed by 1871 as the population in Lagg declined. Also by 1881 the northern school has moved to the new village of Inverlussa. The four schools of Cabrach, Small Isles, Knockrome and Inverlussa continue through 1881 and 1891. The northern school is now called Ardlussa Public School, and the new Knockrome School has been built between Knockrome and Ardmenish. In the early years of the next century Lussagiven Schoolhouse was turned into a stalker's cottage.

Some fifteen different names appear in the teaching posts in these schools between 1841 and 1891. They mostly have birthplaces far from Jura, and many appear in only one census. Here are some of the teachers:

In Lussagiven in 1871: Alexander Shaw (23) from Campbeltown; unmarried; a boarder.
In Knockrome in 1881: Lachlan McBeth (58) from Applecross.
In Inverlussa in 1881: Margaret Nicholson (23) from Portree.
Some may have been born in Jura, as for example:
Duncan Shaw, in Lagg from 1841 to 1861. Duncan was also the postman.
The Lussagiven School had Dugald McPhail (40) in 1841; Alexander McDougall (21) in 1851; Ann McKechnie (15) in 1861.
Knockrome in 1891 had Margaret Shaw (29) a 'Certified Teacher'.

Some stayed for some time. John McGillivray of Dunlichty was in Cabrach in 1871, 1881 and 1891, with his wife Jessie and five children by that time. He combined the role of inspector of poor with his teaching duties. He died in Jura in 1911 at the age of seventy-six, and he and his wife and three children are all commemorated on his gravestone at Kilearnadil.

Two men called Colin Campbell were teachers in the nineteenth century. The first was in Cabrach in 1851, but the second Colin Campbell taught in Jura in 1861, 1871, 1881 and 1891. He was called a 'Society Schoolmaster'. The later Colin Campbell was still only fifty-six in 1891 and may well have continued teaching for some time after that. He died in 1917 and is buried at Kilearnadil. His parents are remembered on a separate stone which he erected, and his own monument contains records of his wife and five children all buried in Jura. Colin Campbell's children lived into the 1940s and 1950s which reminds us how near we are to the teachers of the nineteenth century.

Many of these parochial schoolmasters were college men, still engaged in their studies, or working their way towards qualifying for the ministry of the Church of Scotland. In some cases they were 'stickit ministers', that is, men who, while good and able scholars, were not able by their preaching to secure a call to a parish. The majority of these teachers, both parochial and Society, were qualified to instruct far beyond the minimum required of them by the authorities.

Malcolm McNiven, who was parochial schoolmaster in Ardlussa Public School in 1891, taught Greek and Latin. He had the brothers Archibald and Alexander Shaw as pupils, and instructed them so well that, after some additional night class work in Glasgow, they were able to graduate in Arts and as Bachelors of Divinity, and enter the ministry, first in the United Free Church and, after the Union in 1929, in the Church of Scotland. Malcolm McNiven was a first-rate Gaelic scholar and taught Neil Shaw, who for over thirty years was secretary of An Commann Gaidhealach and, after that, President of that organisation.

We have already encountered one of the Society's schoolmasters in Knockrome. John Campbell, the author of one of the precious letters to American colonists to have survived, taught in other parts of the island as well as Knockrome until, and even after, his retiral half a century later. Among those who benefited by his teaching was the Jura Bard, Donald McKechnie, whose prose writings especially, in Gaelic, are classic examples of Gaelic writing and idiom, and this despite the fact that because he lived so far from a school he was unable to get any regular education. Mr Campbell had a bold and inquiring mind. An account of one of his exploits has survived:

John Campbell, at one time schoolmaster at Knockrome, and afterwards a tutor at Tarbert, when one of his pupils was mistress of the farm, was a man of excellent character, and a disbeliever in at least much of the superstition of the day.

In order to test the truth of current reports of unaccountable things heard and sights seen in 'An Uamh Dearg', he set out, and according to one account, taking a Bible with him, determined to pass a night in the cave. (The 'Red Cave' figures in stories to be found later.)

However, he was back before morning, and never gave any explanation of his failure to spend the whole night as intended in the cave. The mistress of Tarbert knew that he would tell her if he would tell anyone, and she took occasion to ask him. His reply was: 'I did a foolish deed that night, Mary, an act which I would not advise anyone to do, but what I saw I shall not divulge to anyone else.'

His original words in the Gaelic were: '*Rinn mise turn amaideach, a Mhairi, an oidche ud agus urd nach toirinn comhairle air neach air bith a dheanamh ach ciod a chunnaic mise cha'n innis mi do neach eile.*'

And that is all he was known to say on the matter.

This story connects John Campbell with Tarbert, where he seems to have been a tutor. In the census of 1861 he appears in the home of the Fletchers, who farmed Tarbert, He died there ten years later in 1871 at the age of seventy-three. It seems that Campbell of Jura had written to the retired teacher, suggesting that he ought to have gone to live with some of his relatives, rather than being a burden on the Fletchers. Mr Campbell's reply has survived:

Tarbert, 9th February 1871
My reason for not putting myself in my illness, under the care of a near relation, is that I would be stripped of my money or of any other property I might possess in one day; and then left to die under miserable neglect.

That Mr Fletcher's motive for taking care of me in my illness, is that consideration of by-gone services, and not my money or property, for what are both to him though they would be a hundred-fold more. His motive proceeded from the same noble principle with that of the Society I had the honour to serve for so many years, when they superannuated me for long past services.

I am under no obligation to any of my friends in Jura, and none of them has a right to intermeddle in any of my concerns.

Signed; John Campbell. Superannuated Teacher

upon the Establishment of the Society for the Propagating of Christian Knowledge.

It gives considerable satisfaction now to go to Kilearnadil Churchyard and look at John Campbell's gravestone, which reads:

John Campbell, Teacher at Knockrome, and one of the Elders of Jura, who died at Tarbert in Jura, 1871, aged 73

Erected by Rev. Lachlan MacKenzie & Archibald Fletcher of Tarbert.

Here we have a servant of Education and the Church who was not answerable to the Laird, and even in the year of his death was able to write a spirited reply to what he considered was Campbell's unwarrantable interference in his personal affairs. Just occasionally the Campbells did not get it all their own way.

The schools at Cabrach, Small Isles, Knockrome and Inverlussa all continued to the middle of the next century, although in modern times only Small Isles survived. The school buildings and their houses are all still standing.

36

Communication and Travel

Throughout history Jura has always been reached by sea. The various waves of prehistoric settlers probably favoured the short crossings from the mainland at the north end of the island. The camps of the Mesolithic hunters mostly seem to be on the north-east coast. At the time of the Columban Church there was no doubt a good deal of commerce between each of the neighbouring islands and in due course when the Vikings arrived, they also came by sea.

The earliest oral traditions of Jura tell of ancestral prototypes making raids on Colonsay in galleys powered by oarsmen, and the Macdonalds of the Isles evidently controlled the important sea routes such as the Sound of Islay, and have left monuments to that period such as Clag Castle.

Later tales tell of Jura's usefulness as a land corridor between Islay and the mainland. 'Una's Elopement', and the skirmish involving 'Colkitto', recorded later in the folklore collection, are such accounts, the first even making it clear that the 'overland route' was chosen because inclement weather made the voyage from the south of Islay to Craignish impracticable.

In early times the island was evidently a stepping stone to the isles to the north and west, and funeral parties made the crossing from the mainland to Tarbert, across Jura, before sailing to Iona from Corpach on the west coast.

By the late seventeenth and early eighteenth century we begin to get a picture of what travel was like in the region, at that time largely from ecclesiastical accounts.

By the Rev. John McSween's time the parish included Colonsay and Gigha, and his journeys there and to the mainland are recorded, often in connection with his well-publicised drunkenness.

At the beginning of the eighteenth century, Neil Campbell, the long-suffering minister, spent half the year in Jura and half in Colonsay, and is recorded as making journeys to the Presbytery at Campbeltown and Inverary.

In 1724 the Presbytery perambulation, recorded in the chapter on the Church, took place. This account concentrates on travel within the island itself and records, as we have seen, that 'the roads are rough, ragged and impassable for the most part, that not above ten miles can be ridden without difficulty and hazard. And in it are eight waters of so rapid a current that at some times they cannot be passed, there being no bridges. And many have perished in them.' The later 'Act and Commission' records that the terrain was 'in many places not Rideable with Rocks, Mosses and Thirteen Rapid Rivers running through it'.

In 1768, in his endless action against Campbell of Jura, the Rev Alexander Hossack gives some details of the conditions of travel.

The expense of passing and repassing from Jura to the parish of Colonsay is

438

16s Sterling. From Jura to the seat of Presbytery, coming and going; £4 sterling. (Presbytery was meeting at Campbeltown, so this was probably the crossing to Gigha.) From Jura to Keills. the place of landing to go to the Synod; 6s Sterling. From Jura to Scarba, one of the places of worship, going and coming; 5s Sterling.

In due course Campbell of Jura comes forward with his reply, which puts a different complexion on the above descriptions:

> The Libel mentions thirteen Rivers which the Minister has, at Times, occasion to pass. Ten of them are Rivulets, which the Minister at most Places may step over. The other three are very seldom impassable, and there are Bridges about to be built over them.
>
> The most extraordinary Averment was in the Expense of Crossing Ferries. The true fact is that he has the Packet-Boat to Kintyre for 1/6, when he chooses to attend the Presbytery, which he has no occasion to do often. The expense of crossing for Inverary is likewise a trifle. Ferrying to Colonsay and Scarba to preach costs him nothing, the inhabitants considering it their duty to ferry their Minister 'gratis'. The plan on which he has been pleased to make his Computation is that he must freight a Vessel on purpose, every time he ventures himself on the Waves, in place of taking his Passage in the Ferry-boats.

This dispute probably needs a bit of dispassionate judgement. First in the matter of impassable rivers. It is difficult to be certain how much water these various streams carried in the eigheenth century, but there is no reason to think that the rainfall was very different from the present. One curious fact about Jura is that the moorland which covers so much of the island is in a pretty constant state of saturation so that there is very little reserve to absorb rainfall. The effect of this is that many of the small streams turn rapidly into considerable torrents very quickly after rain, and return to being the 'rivulets' Mr Campbell speaks of quickly thereafter. The author lived beside 'the Minister's Burn' for twelve years, and on the great majority of days in that time an active adult could cross it more or less dry-shod without the use of the excellent bridge, where the stream fans out over the shingle near the shore. A pony would make nothing of it at all, and a stout pair of boots would get anyone across. However, after a period of very heavy rain, the little burn could turn into an impassable torrent, dangerous to livestock and to people, and treated by everyone with great respect. It seems that in the case of many of the rivers in dispute, Hossack and Campbell could have it their own way, depending on whether it had recently rained or not.

The Corran River and the River Lussa are both considerable, both meriting the title 'river', although both had ancient 'fords' used for horse and cart until recent times. The argument for the smaller burns applies here in a more serious fashion. When heavily swollen by rain, both of these rivers would make the postponement of a journey likely.

The Dainskeir Burn, and the one at Lergybreck could also be quite substantial hazards, but the others in the Presbytery's catalogue are definitely in Mr Campbell's 'rivulet' category.

The Presbytery assertion that 'many have perished in them' may well be quite valid. Jura lore tells of a drowning near the mouth of the Corran in the nineteenth century, and more recently an elderly lady who lived in Keils drowned in the Keils burn. How many more may have lost their lives attempting to cross in previous centuries can only be conjectured.

In connection with all of this we turn to Lord Teignmouth's account of 1836 relating to the funeral he witnessed at Tarbert in 1836:

> The mourners found their reception at Tarbert so pleasant, that they remained next day, and assisted in restoring a bridge which had been swept away by a torrent. It consisted of a stone embankment, in the centre of which an interval was left, just sufficient for the passage of the water at its ordinary height, beneath a covering of flagstones. About twenty men were employed, and it was amusing to see the leisurely manner in which they proceeded; spending the greater part of their time in contemplating each stone on its being deposited, and hesitating long before anyone volunteered to bring another to the spot. Nor were they at all discomposed by the conviction that all their labour must be renewed after the first spate which would infallibly, as they allowed, wash away every vestige of their rude structure. The expense of a few planks would have served the purpose effectually; but this definite mode of completing their work would not suit the loitering habits of the Highlanders, who habitually verify the old adage, that 'lazy people take the most pains'.

This is a curious account. It bears out the fact that small streams can undoubtedly prove difficult to cross after much rain, but oddly it indicates the presence of a substantial stone-built bridge or culvert at Tarbert. Several small burns run into Tarbert Bay and which one we are considering here is not made clear. The approach of the men in deliberating carefully before choosing each stone is certainly part of the tradition in dry-stane walling in Jura. It used to be said that once the man's hand had stretched out and taken hold of a stone, then that stone had to find its place in the wall. Indeed the tale was told of one proud man, who couldn't fit in a stone selected late in the afternoon, and carried it all the way home with him and back in the morning, lest he lose face by putting it down again. As with many of the jobs done by Islesmen, it often looks as if they are working slowly, or lazily, but the results are good, and on your return to a peat bank to see how the crofter has got on in your absence you are often amazed by his progress. It also seems possible that while the men were perfectly well aware that the bridge would not last beyond the next major storm, they may have also been aware that it might have been some years since it was last washed out, and might be some more before the next occurrence. Would a timber structure have been more durable? And where was the timber to be found? In any case the party was on 'free time', after a funeral, and this was probably a highly satisfactory communal project. Teignmouth's contemptuous 'loitering' and 'lazy' are probably ill-merited judgements, stemming from culture shock between respective backgrounds.

To return to the differing viewpoints of two other men who requently misunderstood each other. We are forced to conclude, albeit perhaps reluctantly, that Campbell is likely to be more accurate in the matter of ferries than Alexander Hossack, who has a point to make, and probably goes a bit over the top in making it. It is interesting to hear of a backet boat to Kintyre for 1/6. How frequent would this service have been? If only once or twice a week, Hossack may have felt it was too inconvenient to get him to and from the mainland to a meeting. He may have felt obliged to 'freight a vessel' to keep an appointment.

It is from this same period that we get some hard evidence about communications from the Minutes of the Commissioners of Supply. These relevant extracts span from 1744 to 1773:

1744. The people of Knockintavill of the Parish of Jura, with those of Scarba and Lunga, to work three days on the Quay of Kinuachdrach, under the inspection of Malcolm Buie in Kinuachdrach.

1747. The inhabitants of Jura and Scarba to work three days upon the quay of Kinuachdrach, and the slate quarriers and other inhabitants of Belnahua, with their tools, to work similarly under the inspection of Duncan Campbell of Lochhead and Robert Stevenson of Belnahua.

1748. Inhabitants of the Upper End of Jura beyond Tarbert and the island of Scarba to work upon the quay of Port-na-Lakersaig in Knockintavill. (the name of this quay has disappeared from maps showing Barnhill. 'Rubha na h-Acairseid'; 'rock of the anchorage'; can be found at the south end of the island.)

1749. Inhabitants of Jura south of Ardlussa to work upon the quay of Feolin, while those north of Ardlussa with the inhabitants of Scarba are to work upon repairing the Quay of Kinuachdrach.

1750. Inhabitants of Jura south of Ardlussa to work three days on the Quays of Kaimes (i.e. Camus, or Lagg), and Feolin, and the inhabitants of Jura north of Ardlussa, Scarba and Lunga to work three days repairing the Quay and Fank of Kinuachdrach.

1758. Representation by Archibald Campbell of Jura showing the necessity of a bridge over the Abhainn an Daimh Sgeir; (the Water of Dainskeir), Jura; appointed to obtain an estimate.

1762. As Ardfin, parish of Jura, is not a publick ferrying place, any further work at the harbour thereof is discharged.

1764. Petition of James Duncanson of Keills for a further £15 towards erecting a quay at the ferry place of Kilvickocharmaig, parish of North Knapdale; before answering this petition the Meeting appoint a committee to deal with the proprietors for removing the ferry from Keills to Barnashallig on the Knapdale side, and from Lagg to Ardlussa on the Jura side.

1765. A report given in by Dunardry concerning the proposed scheme of removing the ferry place between Knapdale and Jura. Dunardry to commune with Shawfield with regard to commuting the labour of 400 persons for making a road to the intended ferrying place in Jura.

The proprietors of Keills and Lagg are appointed to keep good boats and accommodations for passengers and ferrying cattle. [The northern ferry appears to have been unaffected, for in 1765 the inhabitants of Craignish were required to work on the road from Gartcharran to Aird.]

1767. Petition by James Campbell of Craignish and Duncan Campbell of Glendaruel.

It has of late been judged more convenient to have a ferry erected between Lagg and Keills for ferrying cattle brought from Colonsay, Islay and Jura, than bring them by the ferry between Kinuachdrachin Jura and Aird in Craignish; the latter ferry falling into disuse. The Petitioners ask the Meeting to fix upon which one should be the only ferry; the matter deferred to the next General Meeting.

These minutes tell us that 'Duty Work' could be forced on the inhabitants by this appointed body; The Commissioners of Supply, as well as by the landowner. They also give us some insight into which were the important ferries in the eighteenth century. Feolin Ferry never seems to have been questioned as the necessary link between Islay and Jura, and it remained the connection to the overland route across Jura for people in Islay.

The ferry at Kinuachdrach seems to have been vital in early times, and was of course the shortest crossing to the mainland. If the sheer distance is measured in statute miles, making no allowance for wind or weather or prevailing tides, this northernmost crossing is about four miles.

There was a permanent ferry boat stationed at Aird well into the nineteenth century. It was recorded in 1843 that the Parish of Craignish possessed a small vessel chiefly for ferrying to and from Jura.

The petition to move from the well-established crossing from Lagg to Keills, to a previously unheard of crossing from Ardlussa to Barnashalg was evidently not successful. The sea journey would have been increased by about a mile. This is the route which has long been followed privately by the Proprietors of the Ardlussa estate. It seems likely that the petitioners lived on the mainland, and were anxious to reduce the amount of road travel on their side of the Sound.

The Lagg ferry was always the best bet for traffic from Colonsay and the other islands to the west. The bay on the Sound of Jura at Tarbert was always sandy, shallow and unsheltered, and Lagg was only about two and a half miles south of the end of Loch Tarbert, whereas the quay at Ardlussa was about double that distance. There seems never to have been a strong tradition linking Colonsay to the north-west coast of Jura, although Bach Gleann nam Muc (the Bay of the Glen of Pigs) is a good enough anchorage, and leads to the shortest crossing of Jura you can have. It seems likely that the route would always take vessels too near to the influence of the Corryvreckan, and would consequently have been avoided. Some evidence for this route will appear in our study of the drove roads.

In connection with the proposed new bridge, it has already been noted that the Dainsgeir Burn is one of those smaller streams which can turn extremely nasty after heavy rain. Campbell of Jura seems to share this view and considers a bridge here is 'a necessity'.

The minute of 1765 gives the first real indication that a road is being considered on Jura. If approved, this work would require 'commuting the labour of 400 persons'; in other words changing their sphere of work from some other field to the business of the Jura road. This scheme did not in fact meet with approval, and the road had to wait for nearly fifty years.

By the time of these reports the West Kintyre road had already been constructed, but Jura had only foot and horse tracks; the best between Campbell's house and Feolin Ferry, this being the stretch interrupted by the Dainsgeir burn, where Campbell is so keen to get a bridge built.

From about 1800 the island was included in the country's general move to improve communications. The Jura road caused a lot of difficulty. In 1804 Langlands put forward a straight inland route from Feolin to Lagg, probably following the line of the old drove road, and ignoring the coastal settlements. Wilson proposed a 17 mile route with bridge designs, and it was this that was finally adopted. Wilson's designs and maps have survived. Telford built the road between 1809 and 1812 at a cost of £4330. This was a huge sum of money in those days. About 1814 Telford built Craighouse's old pier for £712, and Campbell contributed one half of the cost. Telford also built the piers at Feolin and Lagg according to Wilson's 1804 designs. All the piers and slipways built at this time were constructed almost solely for 'drove road' traffic. Campbell tried to get support for the extension of this road from Lagg to Kinuachdrach which was to cost a further £3000. Telford's own reports on the work record that Campbell placed milestones on the Jura road, and built a short road from Lagg to Tarbert Bay, at a joint expense with the Government of £800. That marked the end of the public road, with a short spur to the Jetty where boats came and went to Colonsay. This part of the road was completed in 1814, but most of the stretch north from Tarbert was not built until the First World War.

We know very little about the boats of this period. It is thought that the first weekly sailing packet between mainland Tarbert and Port Askaig dates from 1726, the date at which the Campbells of Calder disposed of Islay to the Shawfield Campbells. The 1787 Langlands map is embellished with the same three sailing vessels which are pictured off Dainsgeir in Lumsden's 1827 steamer guide. One of these may have been the island's packet boat, referred to by Campbell in his dispute with Mr Hossack, and bought in 1767 for £200. This ship carried passengers, mails and freight, and plied between Colonsay and mainland Tarbert by way of the Sound of Islay.

In 1826 communications were revolutionised by the advent of steam. John Ramsay purchased a paddle-steamer called *Waterloo*, launched in 1815, the year of the famous victory. This boat was 72 feet long, 16 feet in beam; had a gross tonnage of 90 tons and a nominal horse-power of twenty. Ramsay renamed her *Maid of Islay* and she began the Islay run in 1826, making a weekly crossing in summer from Port Askaig to West Loch Tarbert. This ship left Tarbert every Tuesday, having connected with the Glasgow to Loch Fyne steamship at East Loch Tarbert.

In 1827 a second vessel was acquired by Ramsay and his partners, and rather unimaginatively named *Maid of Islay No. 2*, the original ship being then renamed *Maid of Islay No. 1*. A sailing notice from March 1827 stated that No. 1 sailed from Glasgow each Tuesday bound for Islay, Staffa and Iona, and every Thursday morning for Portree, Tobermory, etc; No. 2 left West Tarbert on Tuesday afternoon, arriving at Islay the same evening, and returned to Tarbert on Thursday. Passengers leaving Port Askaig on Thursday would reach Glasgow the same night. This was a summer service only, No. 1 being laid up during the winter.

Campbell of Jura was extremely displeased by the arrival of this competition as, up until that time, he himself had supplied the ferries. He claimed the new boat was guilty of 'evasion or emulous contravention' of his ferry from Lagg to Keills, and wanted it stopped. Miss Isabella Campbell, giving evidence to the Crofters Commission in 1894 says: 'Mr Campbell, for the benefit of his people, keeps up three ferries and a meal mill at a great loss to himself.' Campbell's viewpoint on the matter is intriguing. Was it true that the ferries could not be made to pay throughout the nineteenth century? Until the arrival of steam, Campbell was presumably concerned with capital outlay and depreciation on fairly small sailing vessels, and with the payment of wages to their crews as the modest expenses. Is this another area where Miss Campbell gives a somewhat biased interpretation of what is going on in Jura?

We note that after 1830 the number of steamer sailings multiplied rapidly in the western isles so that by 1890 as many as eleven were entering Loch Dunvegan on the north-west coast of Skye, in one week. More called at Portree, and still more at the numerous ports of Islay. The new opportunities given by steamer, rail, and road transport encouraged the tide of emigration, which had slackened, even almost halted, around 1880, to flow once again and, to that movement, further impetus was given in the last decade of the century by the spread of education.

Jura's first pier suitable for steamers came about in 1884 as a result of the lease between James Ferguson & Sons, Distillers, and Campbell of Jura. In the lease agreement the distillers 'bind and oblige themselves at their own cost and expense, to erect and completely finish a good substantial pier, with a depth of not less than ten feet of water at the pier head at low water', and to 'erect a waiting-room and store on the pier, with road access and bridge, and all to be sufficiently wide to allow two loaded carts to pass at any point'.

We have the diary of a traveller who came to Jura on 25 August 1890. The day was a Monday. The *Fingal* evidently returned to Tarbert on the Tuesday. It set out on the Wednesday again, this time going directly to Port Ellen, from which Mary was able to return to Glasgow on the Thursday. It looks as though, as earlier in the century, in 1890 there were two steamers plying on this run, and giving two trips per week to Small Isles, Jura.

In the twentieth century and within recent memory probably the best loved of Jura's vessels was the *Pioneer*. (Plate 14) The arrival of the boat was an important event. There would be cattle to be loaded and sheep too. On the departure of the vessel there would be the ritual of 'Waving Her Away', when many of the local community would asemble on the pier. After the Second World War a variety of more modern ships were in use and MacBrayne's *Lochiel* is remembered with affection.

SHIPWRECKS

It would be pleasant to imagine that good seamanship and good fortune kept all the vessels on the various Jura crossings from disaster but this was certainly not the case.

1854 saw a shipwreck which could have had serious consequences, when the paddle-steamer *Chevalier*, built in 1853 by J. & G. Thomson of Govan, ran on to Iron Rock in the Sound of Jura and foundered. Iron Rock is not named on present day charts and maps, but can be safely identified as Skervuile (Sgeir Maoile), about two miles off Lowlandman's Bay, and still bearing its fine lighthouse. The *Chevalier* was 176 ft long and had a gross tonnage of 229 tons. She came to grief on 24 November, but remained on the rocks, with her decks only covered at high water, and her crew were able to reach safety. It is believed that her engine may have been salvaged. Some wreckage has been found just off the north-west of Skervuile, between the permanently exposed rock and a reef which only shows at low water. This may well be the remains of the *Chevalier*.

In the story of the the *Culzean*, we are faced with the most serious marine disaster to affect Jura. The *Culzean* was an iron sailing ship built by John Reid & Co., Port Glasgow, and launched in November 1871. Her tonnage was 1572 gross. She was 250 ft long, 40 ft of beam and 23ft of draught. Her mishaps began when she started a long voyage from Calcutta to Dundee. She had left Dundee in the summer of 1881, and was on the return trip when she was caught in a severe gale in the English Channel on 14 October. She lost her masts, and sustained other serious damage. She was picked up and towed into the Tyne for temporary repairs, then on to Dundee where she was unloaded. Her owners, John Kerr & Co. of Greenock, then arranged for her to be towed to Greenock for permanent repair. She left Dundee under tow by the Clyde Shipping Company Tug *Conqueror* in late November with seventeen crew aboard and a local pilot, Captain Duncan. The weather was atrocious, causing them to put into port several times. While making the hazardous passage through the Pentland Firth they had to shelter in Scrabster. Later, off Cape Wrath, they again had to seek shelter in Stornoway. The *Oban Times* adds: 'While the vessel was at Stornoway, a resident offered the use of a tow rope, but it was declined. The tug had previously lost a rope and had no spare rope on board.' It also recorded that 'the *Culzean* was being towed from Dundee to Greenock because the repairs could be done quicker and cheaper in the Clyde'.

They set off again, but only got as far as Tobermory in Mull before the weather became bad again. Finally the two ships reached the Sound of Jura on the evening of the 21st, and as they struggled past Iron Rock in heavy seas, the hawser broke, and the *Culzean* drifted off helplessly with no masts or sails. It was the last that was seen of the ship, of Captain Pirnie, his crew and the Pilot, Captain Duncan. Captain Morrison of the tug *Conqueror* had to fight to save his own ship, and keep position off the light of the Iron Rock, and heading into the sea until daybreak.

At first light they set off in search and found that the *Culzean* was reported to be on Jura, north of Lagg Bay, and under water, except for a small portion of the bow section. There was no sign of the crew. Wreckage was strewn along the shoreline, and was washed ashore on the mainland coast of Knapdale, opposite, and on islands at the entrance to Loch Sween. The bodies of the crew were washed ashore at various locations around the Sound over the next few days The heavily salvaged wreck lies a short distance south-east of the ferry slip in Lagg Bay.

The Board of Trade Enquiry found that before leaving Dundee, signals had been arranged between the master of the tug and the ship, which left the control of the vessel while under tow to the master of the *Conqueror*. The Court was clearly of the opinion that, taking into consideration the state of the weather, the Master of the tug was not justified in passing Crinan, but having passed it, and the gale increasing gradually throughout the day, the Court thought that the Master of the tug committed a grave error of judgement in not putting back before night set in. The Court considered that it would have been more prudent to have had two hawsers attached to the ship, and they attribute the loss of the ship to the breaking of the second hawser, whereby the vessel was driven ashore and became a total wreck with deplorable loss of life.

Thirteen of the men of the *Culzean* are recorded as having died in the Statutory Register of Deaths of Jura. It is not known if all the bodies were recovered. The drowned seamen were interred in Jura, at the expense of the Poor Board, but there are no grave inscriptions.

The loss of the *Culzean* made a deep impression on the people of Jura. A story survived which was told to the author. It seems that on the night of 21 November, a devout member of the congregation of the Kirk at Lagg was holding a Bible Study and Prayer meeting in his house, which was the old inn near the shore. As the worshippers were settling down to begin the service, a man's face was seen at the window, and as he seemed to be seeking admission, an extra chair was brought through, and someone was sent to the door to bring him in. However, on the door being opened, no one could be found outside, and the service went on without the stranger. It was much later in the night that it became clear to the community that a ship was going on the rocks, and there was no sleep that night. In the first light of dawn, parties of Lagg folk were searching the shore, where several bodies had already been found when they caught sight of what appeared to be a survivor, seated hunched over on a rock, with his face to the sea. However, when they approached the man it was found that he was dead already. The men from the Prayer Meeting confirmed that his face was that of the man who had been seen at the window the previous night.

War would later bring its own share of disasters. The cemetery at Tarbert has a sad inscription: 'A Sailor of the 1939–1945 War Merchant Navy Known unto God.' Kilearnadil has a similar stone, dated December 1941.

The far west coast of Jura may well have had naval casualties whose bodies were never recovered. One German seaman from the Second World War was found by Kate Johnson, of Uist, who lived at the remote croft of Glengarrisdale. Kate was a powerful lady, and carried the body across the island to report to the authorities. She was paid a small bounty for her trouble, and was later asked by a local inhabitant how she had managed such a feat of strength, and how she felt about it all. She was reported as having been unperturbed by the experience, but expressed some disappointment that there had only been the one sailor!

A much more recent episode, but one which falls just within the remit of this book, concerns the puffer *Stormlight*. In 1973 the *Stormlight* had been having a history of engine trouble. On Saturday, 15 December 1973, she again had engine problems while heading from Campbeltown to Oban carrying a large reel of underwater telephone cable for the British Telecom work at Loch Crenan. As bad weather was developing she put in for shelter to Small Isles Bay, Jura. At 7.10 p.m., in the darkness, the puffer hit the south end of Goat Island. The Islay lifeboat took off the crew and put them ashore at Craighouse, where they stayed overnight in the hotel. On Sunday morning, Graham Davidson, who was working in the distillery, took the crew back out to the *Stormlight* in Dougie Buie's double-ended outboard boat, the *Scout*. They got the engines going, but the *Stormlight* was hard aground in the cove next the Perch with her bow pointing out. She refloated on the rising tide, but in the rising southerly wind she pounded on the rocks until she rolled on to her port side. The bow section is all that is left. The rest of the hull has now rusted away.

Puffers were originally nicknamed because they used an engine that blew a puff of smoke up the funnel with each stroke of the engine. This changed when the surface condenser was invented in 1836. However the name remained. Puffers were built in two sizes, 66ft long to fit the locks in the Forth & Clyde Canal and 88ft boats to fit the Crinan Canal locks, which were approximately 88ft long by 22ft wide.

Before the Second World War all puffers were built in Scotland, but, during the war, sixty-three puffers were built for the Royal Navy. Most of these were built in Doncaster, Goole, Hull and Northwich. The *Stormlight* was the last of the traditional 88 ft puffers and was built by W. J. Northwick at Northwich. (Plate 15)

POSTAL SERVICES

Up until the building of the road, the people of Jura had to make their own arrangements to collect mail from the nearest post office which was at Port Askaig in Islay. The exact date of setting up this postal service is not known, but in 1760 the postmaster of Inverary is recorded as making up a weekly mail-bag for Islay, obviously following a much older tradition. Walker's *Economical History of the Hebrides* refers to the establishment of a post office, 'on the Sound of Ila' in 1767, and this was in fact opened at Port Askaig on 10 October of that year.

Following the completion of the Jura road in July 1812, Francis Ronaldson, the surveyor, established a post office at Lagg Inn, and arranged for an overland postal route from Lochgilphead via Keills sub-post office at the tip of the Loch Sween peninsula. Mails were ferried across the Sound of Jura to Lagg by undecked rowing or sailing vessels. Mail from Lochgilphead went to Glasgow and Edinburgh via Inverary, but in 1815 there was a new proposal by local landowners. The Marquess of Breadalbane, Campbell of Melfort and Campbell of Jura suggested that mail should be conveyed from Lochgilphead to Oban, thus forging a link with Central and Eastern Scotland, and this was approved by the Post Office. This route conveyed the mail from Islay as well as Jura and included a relay of two runners, one from Lagg to Port Askaig and the other from Port Askaig to Bowmore. The cost of these runners was borne partly by the Post Office and partly by the local people, but this was a highly unsatisfactory arrangement. In the autumn of 1825, the surveyor, Charles Reeves, visited Islay and reported that the islanders 'occasionally assume the control and make the posts subservient to individual rather than public accommodation'. The postal revenue of Islay alone had, by this time, grown to £260 per annum, and the Secretary advised that in future the Post Office should pay the whole cost of the runners.

It was evident to the Postal Authorities that from their inception, the *Maids of Islay* were carrying letters illegally. They would be put into the post at Tarbert, or even Greenock, depriving the Post Office of revenue at a time when letters were charged according to the distance they travelled. In 1833 the Post Office decided to send one post per week by steamer to Port Askaig as well as three by the traditional overland route via Keills and Lagg.

Jura's first postmark was a framed mileage mark inscribed JURA with the mileage beneath. The distance from London to Glasgow was computed as 513 miles, but the diemaker transposed the numerals so that the distance appeared as 153 miles, and a datestamp bore the legend, 153. Despite this glaring error this first postmark was allowed to remain in use till at least 1826.

Letters from Jura in the 1840s and 1850s invariably bear the Lochgilphead datestamp, testifying to the route taken by the mail at that time. The ferry from Lagg to Keills, however, had fallen into decay and was operating only intermittently. There may have been some attempts to use the shorter crossing from Craignish to Kinuachdrach, but the absence of a good road to the north of Jura probably made this impractical. However, in the mid-twentieth century, about the 1940s, Donald Darroch of Inver could remember hearing of mail being carried from Crinan directly to Kinuachdrach. The MacKinnons of Kinuachdrach still acted as part-time ferrymen until Donald's time, after the Second World War.

The old overland route finally came to an end in 1868, when the Post Office contracted with John Ramsay for a steamer service to Port Ellen and Port Askaig at £150 per annum. From this date Lagg would be served by a foot runner from Port Askaig at 14s a week. This was a retrograde step, as Jura had enjoyed a horse post for some eight years. The Jura post office changed its name to Lagg, and was apparently downgraded, since no datestamp thus inscribed was issued at that time. As a small concession, however, a foot post from Lagg northwards to Ardlussa was instituted in 1870 and increased in frequency in 1873.

As part of the new agreement between the Post Office and Messrs Hutcheson in 1876 their steamer from West Loch Tarbert to Islay was to call once a week at Craighouse. A shift of postal importance from Lagg to Craighouse resulted from this change, and a post office and money order office was established at Craighouse on 1 December 1876.

The horse post from Feolin Ferry to Craighouse and Lagg was restored some time after this. In 1888 an allowance was made for the lodging of the Port Askaig to Lagg mounted postman when detained overnight at Port Askaig. At the same time he was authorised to carry parcels weighing more than 11 pounds, an indication of the growth of the mail order business from 1885 onwards. A weekly foot post from Craighouse south to Jura House was introduced in 1892. The following year an allowance was paid for an assistant postman on the foot post from Lagg to Ardlussa, and in 1894 this was increased to three times a week.

Later in the same year a thrice-weekly foot post was established between Craighouse and Knockrome.

In 1901 the Lagg to Ardlussa post, which had operated only in the summer months, was made an all-year-round service. The re-arrangement of the steamer schedules in 1905 permitted the despatch of mail-bags from Craighouse at 9.30am on Tuesdays and Fridays. A weekly mail to the tiny island of Skervuile was instituted about 1900 for the benefit of the two men manning the lighthouse. It is of interest that the mounted postman of Jura shortly before the First World War was John Lindsay, whose grandfather had first operated the service half a century earlier.

The First World War had little effect on Jura's postal service. If anything, the island was better off, since it had the benefit of a thrice-weekly steamer on the Port Askaig route. In the 1920s, however, MacBrayne's schedules called for only two visits each week at Craighouse. (Plate 16)

After the Second World War, a motor maivan replaced the horse post. A further improvement came on 1 July 1947 when a third post office was established, at Inverlussa. Mail from Inverlussa was collected at 7.30 a.m. on Tuesdays, Thursdays and Saturdays to connect with the outgoing mail from Craighouse at 9.40 a.m. The continuing decline of the population led to the closure of Jura's oldest post office, Lagg, on 1 August 1963.

The information here has come from the Islands Postal History Series, and its detailed information is of general interest for the light it shines on the development of life in the island.

FURTHER COMMUNICATIONS IN THE TWENTIETH CENTURY

In 1952, Jura got its new pier. Duncan McKechnie of Craighouse represented Jura and Colonsay on the Argyll County Council for nearly thirty years, and worked tirelessly to bring about the modern pier. This concrete and iron pier enabled boats to call in practically any weather, and was opened by Mr McKechnie in May 1952, a few weeks before his death.

It was at this time, during the 1950s that the Fletchers of Ardlussa allowed Iain MacKechnie, skipper of their 36-ft motor launch *Lady Ailsa*, to oblige people by ferrying them to and from Carsaig. Apart from carrying the summer holiday-makers, the ferry, under Iain's command had sometimes to act as a seaborne ambulance and respond to all kinds of emergencies. One Old Year's Night Iain had to come straight from a dance to convey a woman in labour across the Sound of Jura. On another occasion in the 1950s Iain, along with Alaistair Shaw had to use the ferry as a salvage tug to save the Glasgow puffer *Raylight* from coming to grief in the Corryvreckan. The *Lady Ailsa* was also used to tow a cobble full of slates across the Sound. In 1958 the Ardlussa 'ferry' was augmented by the acquisition of a smaller motor boat, the *Caughoo*. Later in the 1960s and early 1970s, when Iain left Jura to take over the Gigha ferry, a 30-ft ex-naval pinnance, the *Fiona*, became the Ardlussa 'ferry boat'.

After periodic upgrading and modernisation of the nineteenth-century main road, new spur roads were built, one in 1951 between Knockrome and Ardfernal, and another in 1953 to the township of Keils from the main road.

In 1950–1 a telephone system was established so that the whole island from Inver Lodge to Ardlussa was in communication with the mainland.

Dramatic changes took place regarding travel and communication in the 1970s. The historic MacBrayne's service directly to Jura ended in 1972 with the withdrawal of the *Arran* steamship.

In 1967 a private company, Western Ferries, began operations in competition with MacBrayne's. In 1973 it provided a service from Kennacraig on West Loch Tarbert to Port Askaig, with a landing craft connecting to Feolin Ferry on Jura. Many inhabitants of Jura felt that the departure of the Arran would spell the death of the island. However, the cutting of that direct link with the mainland re-aligned all the island's commerce towards Port Askaig, and with a regular car ferry established between Feolin Ferry and Islay, the neighbouring island, with its larger population and community services, suddenly become accessible to vehicles from Jura. Alternatives to the traditional mainland services became an option. For example, secondary school education became available on Islay, although previously secondary school children from Jura had to go to boarding school at Oban. Although the road to Feolin Ferry lengthened the necessary journey to leave Jura, it suddenly became possible to leave the island by car on a daily basis, and indeed on more than one sailing each day. The traditional isolation of Jura began to be broken down, and a more cosmopolitan community began to develop.

In recent years consideration has often been given to projects to establish a car ferry between Lagg and Keils, on the line of the old Lagg ferry. This would create an 'overland route' to Islay from the mainland, through Jura. This has proved to be a controversial idea, and at the time of writing nothing has come of it.

In recent years a regular air service to Islay has had a major effect on rapid communication, and has speeded up things like postal services. Jura has its own airstrip, established by a small company in 1965, and this is available for small private planes, and for an air ambulance service.

As communication is an area in which modern change is extremely rapid, this may be a reasonable place to abandon any attempt to be 'up to date' in Jura's communication system.

DROVE ROADS

We have looked at the development of roads, ferries and postal services. Now we will go back once more in time and examine questions relating to the movement of livestock. In this connection we are bound to look beyond Jura to its neighbouring islands.

Islay was from earliest times among the rich grazing and farming lands of Scotland. The island is described in 1549 as 'fertile, fruitful and full of natural grassing, with many great deer, many woods with fair games of hunting beside every town'. The grasslands fed, even in these early times, large numbers of stock. As early as the latter part of the seventeenth century the sale of cattle from Islay for droving to the south appears to have been on a considerable scale. In the spring of 1680 Sir Hugh Campbell sold to Walter Scott of Langhope '1000 stots and cowes of the ile of Ila', and a few years later he writes to his factor that owing to disturbed conditions having interfered with the normal marketing of his tenants' beasts, he will 'raise a drov on his own wentur and giv the tenants a resonable pryce', though he has 'noe assurance nor probability of pryces in Ingland'.

The abundance of summer grass, but the absence of hay-making, which did not become common in the islands until after 1754, made it almost inevitable that much stock should be disposed of on the approach of autumn, and it is not surprising that when the latter part of the eighteenth century brought an awakening of interest in agricultural knowledge and statistics, the export of cattle from these favoured lands was found to be large. Pennant in 1772 estimates that 1700 cattle were then exported annually from Islay, though despite this many died in the spring from lack of food, while Colonsay and Oronsay sent 300 to market. At the time of the *Statistical Account*, the number sold each year from the parish of Kilchoman in the south-west corner of Islay was alone estimated at 800. Macdonald in 1811 gives figures showing the average number of black cattle ferried from Islay to Jura in each year from 1801 to 1807. These figures, kept by the tenant of the ferry at Port Askaig show that during this period the average number of beasts ferried annually was 2640. On the conservative estimate that only one-quarter of the total stock was sold off each year, Macdonald suggests that this indicates a cattle population in Islay of over 10,000 head.

The *Falkirk Herald* of 27 June 1900 refers to a notice published in the *Edinburgh Advertiser* of May 1779 by the Lairds of Islay to the effect that they have in hand:

> for disposal by small lots of eight or ten, between 2000 and 3000 of the largest and best of the true Highland breed which have never been housed in winter or summer; that being strangers to the gentlemen graziers of England they do not expect to be furnished with money or credit from them, but will at their own expense execute the commissions given and find careful drivers with the cattle and deliver them at Glasgow or Dumfries upon receiving payment of the original purchase money, 3% commission and the net expense incurred in ferrying and driving. The price of cattle is not stated.

The cattle owners of Islay, Colonsay and Oronsay followed the basic principle of sending their cattle to the mainland by the routes which offered the most grazing on the way and the shortest sea crossing.

The cattle from Colonsay and Oronsay would cross to north Jura, while those of Islay were ferried from Port Askaig over the Sound of Islay to Feolin Ferry. Contemporary Islay documents give some insight into the business.

In 1787, drovers from Islay 'complained of a lack of a fank for enclosing their beasts while waiting for the ferry at Port Askaig', and in that year it was decided to establish one on a site of sixty to eighty acres, an extent which shows that the droves must have been of considerable size. A few years later, James Hill in charge of the ferry was ordered 'to keep the paving of the slipway in good order to prevent damage to the cattle, and to regulate disputes which had arisen among the drovers about priority in ferrying their beasts to Jura'.

Problems with fanks and with the drovers were not the only difficulties to affect the transport of cattle from Islay to Jura, for the crossing was the subject of yet another piece of litigation between Campbell of Jura and Campbell of Shawfield concerning the fares Jura was entitled to be paid for the transport. This was a case which ran to countless legal documents and endless argument. As with so many of Campbell's legal wrangles there appears to have been no clear outcome to the dispute between Islay and Jura.

John Macculloch, who toured the Western Isles in 1824, described the scene at the crossing of the Sound of Islay:

> The shore was covered with cattle; and while some were collected in groups under the trees and rocks, crowding to avoid the hot rays of a July evening, others were wading in the sea to shun the flies, some embarking, and another set swimming onshore from the ferry boats; while the noise of the drovers and the boatmen, and all the bustle and vociferation which whisky did not tend to diminish, were re-echoed from hill to hill, contrasting strangely with the silence and solitude of the surrounding mountains.

Macculloch's description of the noise at the ferry would seem to be well founded, for only six years earlier the local Stent Committee found it necessary to give their attention to this very matter. Hitherto the allowance of whisky for the ferrymen had been unlimited, but, 'a surplus quantity being often found injurious to the cattle and the proprietors thereof', the allowance was in future to be fixed at one mutchkin (an English pint) for every thirty cattle ferried.

After crossing to Jura, the Islay cattle were then driven up the eastern shore of the island, through the rising moorland upward to Market Loch. Here they passed the night, and here the Islay droves were joined by the cattle which had been bought at the Jura market, held by the lochside. Care was taken to keep the droves well away from the farms and from the holdings of the crofters, and so, on the evening of the next day, the drove found itself at Lagg. Donald Budge reports that on arrival there they found 'the same gabbarts [barges] which had ferried them across the Sound if Islay, now waited, weather permitting, to transport them across the Sound of Jura to Keills in Knapdale'. It has not been possible to trace Mr Budge's authority for this opinion. It may be that he saw some source not available to the author. It still all sounds very strange. Did the fleet of barges used to get a few hundred beasts from Port Askaig to Feolin really see the last cattle landed, and set sail themselves down the Sound of Islay, round the treacherous channel at the south end of the island, and then up the east coast to Lagg, to keep a rendezvous with the animals which had trekked up the island in a day and a half? The beasts had to walk a bit less than four and a half miles to Market Loch, which they could manage the same day they were landed from the boats, as long as they were on Jura by about midday. The next day was a different matter entirely with a full 10 miles to get them to Lagg, and presumably no embarkation in the boats that night. Meanwhile the barges would have to make a passage of nearly 22 miles under sail and oar to reach Lagg Bay. It would be interesting to have the opinion of some experienced sailors as to the possibility of this having been the usual routine.

In a note to his *Agriculture of the Hebrides* which we have already studied, James Macdonald writes:

In former times the cattle exported from Islay for the mainland markets were never strong enough for the journey until the middle of June, the driest and best season of the year. They were then driven by herdsmen thro' Jura by a hill road, which went between the back of the farms, which are all on the eastern shore, and the mountainous ridge which occupies the middle and western parts of the island. They had freedom of pasturage 'gratis', during the journey. In consequence however of the late improvements in Islay, the cattle of its proprietors and tenants are much earlier ready for the market than June, and indeed are exported all the year round; and they are also much heavier and more unwieldy than they were in former time and consequently cannot travel along the hill road. The road now making, and of which one half is made by Government, is carried along the Easter shore, and Mr Campbell of Shawfield maintains that he is entitled to the use of it for the cattle of Islay in their passage through Jura, while Mr Campbell of Jura alledges that Islay is limited to the hill road only, which is practicable, as already mentioned, during the summer months.

The dispute about the roads was fierce one and many documents survive from it. One of the clearest is a note of advice sent to Richard Dennistoun Campbell by Mr Ranken, his legal adviser, writing from Edinburgh in May 1860:

My dear Sir,

I have carefully gone over the opinions of Lord President Campbell, and Mr Mathew Ross, and the case of the Marquess of Breadalbane, against MacGregor and others decided in the House of Lords, 14th July 1848, but not reported by Mr Sydney Bell till March 1850.

I am decidedly of the opinion that you cannot prevent any persons whatever from driving cattle on the public road.

The drove road in Jura is a burden in your title in favour of Mr Campbell of Shawfield, as proprietor of Islay and his tenants, and I do not think any other parties have a right to use that road without your consent. Your agreement with the Colonsay people might, and I daresay would operate as a bar against you now challenging it, insofar as they are concerned.

But you are not bound to give resting places, or grass, for the sheep or cattle passing along the public road; and if they cannot be driven in one day from the Sound of Islay to Lagg, that circumstance will operate practically as a bar to the use of the public road. The bestial cannot be *rested* even upon the road; and the parties driving them will be liable to interdict, and claims of damages, if they allow the animals to tresspass upon your lands on either side of the road, and to consume your crops or grass.

There is a good deal of light thrown upon the whole of this matter, in the opinion of the Peers who decided Lord Breadalbane's Case, and which you can peruse the first time you are in Edinburgh.

We have a favourable change of weather these two days past.

    I am, My dear Sir, Yours sincerely; J. H. Ranken

It has hard to find evidence to show whether the drovers continued to try the new road with their charges, or continued on the traditional route. They certainly often preferred to keep the cattle on moor or grassland with the complaint that made up road surfaces were hard on their feet. Indeed on many mainland drove routes cattle would be shod to prevent this wear and tear. Cattle on a long drive tend to fan out along many parallel paths, and it seems uncertain whether the drovers would be successful in keeping them on the new road even if they wanted to. Campbell's main complaint was probably that whereas the old hill path lay through poor quality uplands, the new road lay through his own farm land where the cattle would rob him of good grazing. North of Keills and the Corran River the traditional drove route and the new road may have taken more or less the same path and the problem may not have arisen.

All this question concerned the movement of cattle from Islay, but of course that was not the only departure point for the Jura drove road.

Cattle from Colonsay and Oransay were ferried from Colonsay to Ruantallain near the mouth of Loch Tarbert on the west coast of Jura. They were then driven to the ferry at Kenuachdrach, in the extreme north of the island, which of course went to Aird on the Craignish peninsula.

It seems unlikely that they were taken up the remote west coast. Most probably they were brought in along the north coast of Loch Tarbert to follow the easier route up the east coast.

Some Colonsay cattle appear to have been landed at Corpach Bay and driven along Cruaidh Ghleann and Glen Grundale to reach the east shore at Ardlussa. This crossing is no more than about six and a half miles in distance, but rises to 1000ft at the central ridge, so a considerable climb for the animals.

By either route is seems that by the time they reached the latitude of Ardlussa they were already on the east coast, and tradition suggests a 'stance' near Lealt. Occasionally Colonsay cattle seem to have been taken directly to the extreme north-west coast of Jura, and then ferried straight to the mainland, sometimes even through the Gulf of the Corrrievreckan. While this avoided the crossing of Jura altogether, the sea route must have been hazardous. The question of the right-of-way for Colonsay cattle also resulted in much litigation for the Campbells of Jura, this time with the McNeils of Colonsay. Finally, after more than one Court of Session action an agreement was arrived at and the dispute settled. The Deed of Agreement on this matter is dated 1 October 1838:

James Campbell, Esq. of Jura, heritable proprietor of the lands of Tarbert, Jura, and his heirs; consent and agree that the said Alex. MacNeill, Esq., younger of Colonsay and heritable proprietor of Ardlussa and Knockintavil, Jura, and their respective heirs and successors, shall enjoy and exercise an heritable and irredeemable servitude right and tolerance over the said lands of Tarbert, to the extent and effect of a right of passage; for all the cattle, sheep, and lambs; and the servants and attendants necessarily accompanying the same. The said cattle and other bestials, and servants shall land and embark, unless tides and weather will not permit, at Ruantallain in Tarbert, and proceed by the drove roads next to the lands of Ardlussa and Knockintavil, to the ferry at Kinuachdrach.

From the north end of Jura the cattle crossed to the mouth of Loch Craignish, and moving up the north shore of the loch, either continued up the Barbreck River towards Loch Avich and the crossing of Loch Awe, or more probably turned south-east at the head of Loch Craignish towards the west end of Loch Awe and the road over the Leckan Muir on the direct route to Inverary. The cattle which crossed from this Kinuachdrach to Craignish faced a passage only a little less hazardous than that at Kyle Rhea between Skye and the Inverness-shire coast. On the Jura side they were dangerously close to the tides and eddies of the Sound of Corrievreckan, while their route to Craignish took them past the north end of the perilous waters of the Dorus Mor, where the tide sweeps round the end of Craignish Point. The number of cattle which crossed by this route cannot be accurately determined, but as late as 1843 when the *New Statistical Account of the Parish of Craignish* was complied, it was recorded that the parish still possessed a small vessel chiefly employed in ferrying beasts from Jura. At that time it was estimated that each year 3000 sheep and 1000 cattle, including some from Colonsay, were ferried there on their way to the trysts. The *New Statistical Account for Jura* states that 'the number of black cattle annually sold out of the Island is estimated at 1000 to 1200'.

The men who accompanied the cattle to the markets were paid at the rate of one shilling per day and their food. The return journey they were expected to make at their own expense. Jura's last link with the cattle traffic of the old days ended with the death of John Maclean of Lagg in 1954. John Maclean spent all his life in Jura, as cattleman, shepherd, and later, stalker of the Tarbert estate. He could remember as a boy crossing over from Lagg to Knapdale with the cattle drovers, and receiving for his services the sum of two shillings and sixpence. He, too, had to make the return journey at his own expense, and this he made with no little trouble and anxiety, there being no regular service once the cattle had been ferried across. Mr Maclean was eighty-four at the time of his death. His memories were shared by old men of his own generation living in Knapdale, who also remembered in their youth the last remnants of a traffic already shrunk to a mere shadow of what it once had been.

On the Knapdale side of the Lagg ferry there are the remains of a cattle landing slip in Carsaig Bay and the stone landing pier at Keills still stand intact in a little bay facing south-west. Until recently there were still men alive who remembered cattle droves from Jura passing over that pier in their youth.

The Lagg crossing was indeed the route taken by the greater part of the Islay and Jura cattle to the mainland. The landing jetty at Keills still stands in a little bay facing south-westward down the Sound of Jura. The boats appear to have been mainly open, not decked or half-decked like some of those on the crossing of the Minch. They were single-masted, but with heavy oars to help in calm weather. The bottom and sides were thickly lined with birch branches. These, according to local evidence, were tied in bundles, the whole being secured by chains. As on the crossing from Uist to Skye, many of the beasts were thrown overboard in deep water as the ferry boats neared the mainland shore. Near to land the swimming beasts would be kept to the right heading by men in small rowing boats. In some of the larger boats it seems that a section of the gunwale hinged outwards to help the unloading, but cattle wearied with hours in the boat and smelling the grass of the shore would seldom linger, and once the leader took the plunge the rest would follow easily.

A hundred years earlier, James Hogg in his *Highland Tours* told of seeing two cows swimming, one exhausted with her side uppermost in the Sound of Jura:

> We were lost in conjecture where these cows could have come from, there being no other vessel in sight from which they could have made their escape. I could think of nothing more probable than that they were beasts which have lately been ferried from Jura, and were attempting to swim the Sound to their native isle, a distance, I suppose, not exceeding eight miles; but you know as much as I do.

Sometimes in calm weather the five mile crossing would take the full day, while the boats drifted with the strong currents of the Sound, the men laboured at the oars and the morning mist lingered on the Jura hills. In the days when the traffic was at its height, many boats would be employed, and here, where the most part of the cattle of Islay, Jura and Colonsay crossed, the ferrying took several days, the cattle already landed on the mainland resting and feeding in the rich pasture along the Knapdale shore till the ferrying was completed, and the drove ready to continue its long journey.

Mr Joseph Mitchell, Engineer to the Commissioners for Highland Roads and Bridges from 1825 to 1853, has recorded the following description of the crossing from Lagg to the mainland:

> On arriving at the Ferry, we found every corner of the Inn crowded with drovers who had been detained by the weather for several days, and were passing their time, as was their wont, in riotous and continuous drinking.
>
> We felt it was no agreeable sojourn to stay in the inn with these half-intoxicated and noisy people, for the very air was impregnated with an odour of whisky.
>
> We appealed to the ferrymen to take us across. At first they positively refused on account of the storm, but with some persuasion, and a handsome douceur, their scruples were overcome, and they prepared for the voyage.
>
> No sooner had the drovers, who had been so long detained, heard that the boat was to cross at our instigation, than they got excessively angry, talked in Gaelic long and loud, and insisted that we should take at the same time a cargo of their cattle. This the boatmen could not refuse, and eighteen cattle were put on board.
>
> The boat was of great width of beam, and the cattle were fastened with their heads to rings on the gunwale on each side. We had also the chief drover's pony, which stood in the middle of the boat. The wind was quite in our

favour, but it blew furiously, and the sea was high, but its severity we did not feel so much in the shelter of the harbour.

At last we cleared the land, and got into the channel. How the wind did roar, and how the cattle struggled to get their heads free! The extent of sail we carried was forcing the bow of the boat too deep into the sea, and there was fear of being swamped.

The men tried to lower the sail, which, in their agitation, they could not effect, and all looked helpless. On this the drover seized the helm, and with sharp and decisive words took the command of the boat. By his admirable steering he relieved her a good deal, and enabled the men to lessen sail. Still the boat flew before the wind and rolled heavily; every moment we expected would be our last. I grasped the stirrup of the saddle on the pony, in the hope that if we did go, the creature might swim ashore. On we ploughed our way in the midst of this furious storm. How admirably the drover steered! We had to take the narrow and rocky entrance of the harbour, a most difficult navigation; but the drover's sharp and distinct orders were promptly obeyed, and in no time he landed us in shelter within the little bay.

The time we took to effect the crossing; nine miles; was little more than half an hour. Although some forty years have passed since this incident, I shall never forget the Lagg Ferry, or the gallant Highland drover, who by his prompt and decided action was the means under Providence of saving our lives.

From Knapdale the drove proceeded by easy stages, averaging 10–12 miles per day. There may have been an interim gathering and sale at Kilmichael Glassary, before the long journey continued through Dumbartonshire and Stirlingshire, to Falkirk, where the great cattle trysts were held. For the cattle, however, Falkirk was not the end of the journey, for after changing owners at the Falkirk market, the long trek was continued right into central England, perhaps even as far as London.

The annual cattle and sheep drives must have constituted a major upheaval on the island of Jura, and few inhabitants can have been completely unaffected by them. However, the season was very short, and the number of days in the year occupied in this way must have been very few. No doubt the excitement was soon over and the island returned to its quiet routine for another year.

IX

The Crofters' Commission and the Isles of the North

37

The Crofters' Commission

The hardships in the Highlands and Islands which followed the 1745 Rising lasted well into the nineteenth century, when 'clearances' resulted in a huge depopulation of the entire area, accompanied by forced emigration and movements to the Lowlands. It seemed as if these terrible times would never come to an end, but by the second half of the century there were signs of resistance, and a distant promise of change.

The long agony of the Highlands and Islands finally came to a head in Skye in 1882 with the Battle of the Braes. Gladstone, then Prime Minister, began to sense the truth, that since 1746 there had been a gross dereliction of responsible government, both local and central. In 1883 he appointed a Royal Commission of six men under a Scot, Lord Napier, who ten years earlier had been Governor General of India. Their report when presented to Parliament within the year disclosed 'a state of misery, of wrong-doing, and of patient long-suffering, without parallel in the history of our country'.

This time Parliament acted promptly, for the tide of public opinion had changed in the past forty years. There was a strong and vocal national feeling that no men should have power from unjust laws to inflict such cruelties as the Highlanders had long been suffering. The result was the Crofters Holding Act of 1886. It gave all tenants who paid rent of less than £30 a year, fixity of tenure, and established a Crofters Commission to take over from the landowners the entire management of their crofting estates with power to fix fair rents. If a crofter stayed on, his croft descended to his heir, and his house, which was free of rates, could not be seized for debt.

In order to establish the true situation in each parish, the Crofters' Commission visited each locality and took evidence from all parties. In 1890 the Commission came to Jura, fixed fair rents for all the crofters, and wrote off a considerable proportion of outstanding arrears of rent. About two-thirds of each outstanding amount was cancelled, and an arrangement made to pay the balance in three instalments at the following three Martinmasses was agreed.

On 6 April 1894 the Commission re-convened in Jura. Internal evidence shows that there was a publicly declared agenda for the meeting. A 'notice convening the meeting' had been posted and 'an object of the inquiry' made clear. It seems that the chief aim was to inquire where there was any land on the island, not at that time within the croft system which could be used either to set up new smallholdings, or to increase the holdings of the established crofters.

However, there was a wider agenda also, and the meeting began by hearing general complaints from crofters, especially concerning 'boundaries'.

The thirty-sixth Sitting was convened in Craighouse in Jura on 6 April 1894. This consultation gives us a unique insight into many of the issues central to the life of the people of Jura during the second half of the nineteenth century, and to give the full flavour of the encounter some of it will be reported here verbatim. The Commission operated in a question-and-answer mode.

The Commission questioned seven men, six of whom had the status of crofters, while the seventh was a caretaker. Two of the men questioned came from Knockrome, four from Keils, and Neil Clark was from Lergybreac, which the Commission and witnesses always call 'Learganbreac'.

Although various Campbells have been materially concerned in the years under investigation, one, Miss Isabella H. Campbell, daughter of James, features prominently in the Commission's proceedings. She seems not to be mentioned in other documents, and Donald Budge, usually so interested in the Campbell family, gives no details. She is not buried on Jura in the family vault. If she was born near in time to her brother Colin, she would have been in her forties at the time of the Commission's visit. Miss Campbell mentions several relatives. She speaks of her father, her grandfather and her great-grandfather, also of her uncle and her brother.

Near the end of the hearing Miss Campbell says, 'I very much regret that my father was unable to be present today, and my brother also could not attend.' To which the Chairman replies, 'If I may be allowed to say so, I do not think their interests have suffered in any way by their absence.' An examination of the entire sitting is of great interest. Here only highlights will be given, and a variety of questions and answers and comments apear. The local crofters were examined in Gaelic through an interpreter. The witnesses words are in italics. The author's comments are in square brackets.

What were you asked to lay before us? *I was asked to say that we have scarcely any water for our cattle; and to speak about the boundaries we used to have.*

Were the old boundaries made narrower? *Yes. There was a wire fence put up which narrowed the bounds; of old we used to have liberty to go over to the back of the island.*

[We are strongly reminded of John Campbell, the schoolteacher of Knockrome, who wrote to North Carolina in 1857: 'A wire fence is now set in the muir above this farm; the poor people are now reduced to very narrow limits, yet there is no abatement in the rents. The Landlord would rather we would all go, that he might reduce the whole to a sheep farm'.]

What was done with the land that was taken from you? *Put into the deer forest.*

And is it the desire of the people of Knockrome, if possible to get the land back? *We do not ask to go to the back of the island, but if we got to the top of the hill that would do.*

What was the rent before you applied to the Crofters Commission? *A few years before the Commission came it was £15, but previously it was £20.*

And were the tenants also relieved of twenty days duty work by the laird before the Commission came? *Yes.* Was the work valued at £2? *I believe it was: but it was great slavery.*

[Duty work or 'borlanachd' had long been a bone of contention, hanging on in Jura long after it had been discontinued elsewhere. Cottars paid two shillings per day if they failed to attend, which amounts to £2 for twenty days. Tenants or Crofters seem to have done twenty days, while Cottars did twelve.]

What kind of fence is it that divides your pasture from the hill now occupied? Is it a deer fence? *It is a fence that keeps us out of the forest but does not keep the deer from going in, and a few of them were in our stackyard last winter.*

Would it be possible to add any arable ground to your holding? *There is a field above the schoolhouse here that could be utilised if we had outrun in proportion for grazing.*

Who occupies that field now? *We ourselves have it, but we have no power to change it from grazing.*

You have stated that you are desirous of getting more land. Do you know the hill of Dubh-Chreag? *Yes.*

[Dubh Chreag, the 'Black Rock' or the 'Black Cliff' will become significant in the paper. It is a hilly valley running from south-west to north-east about a mile south of the summit of Glas Bheinn. It is thin soil with purple moor grass. There will be a got bite on it in summer, but nothing else.]

Were the Keils tenants offered the whole of Dubh-Chreag? *Yes, but we would not be much the better of it.*

Did you ever get compensation from the laird for damage done by deer to your crop? *We had to be watching the deer, and we got 2s 6d a night for that; but there has been twice as much damage done to the crop as we got in compensation for watching.*

Did you hear the evidence given by the previous witness? *I caught cold keeping the deer out of my stackyard, so that I am somewhat deaf, and did not hear his evidence.*

Do you know any land outside what was spoken to here today that it would be desirable we should see in pursuance of our remit? *Yes.*

Where is there land that would be suitable for small holdings? *Sanaig and Strone.*

Besides Sanaig and Strone, do you know any other place that you think it would be desirable we should visit? *Yes, Learganbreac, north of here and Cnocbreac, on the west side.*

Are these places in your opinion localities in which new small holdings of a reasonable size could be made? *There are plenty of places in the island suitable for that.*

To Neil Clark. What is your occupation? *I am care-taker on the deer forest of Learganbreac.*

What is Learganbreac used for at present? *It is used for many a thing; for feeding sheep,cattle, horses and deer; and for people. There are five families in Learganbreac.*

[Well, just possibly, if he counts himself and Mr Evans' housekeeper, Martha Calder, from Biggar, who is in the new Forest Lodge. Then there is Peter McDonald and his family, from Fadderty, he is the new estate gardener. There is John Murchison and his wife. He is a Keeper for the Deer Forest and comes from Contin. Then Hugh McLeod and his wife, also a Keeper. He comes from Kincardine. It doesn't, on the face of it, look much like the crofting township of Lergybreck, and of the new community, only Neil Clark himself comes from Jura.]

Is it necessary to the deer forest to have Learganbreac along with it? *What would the deer forest do without it?*

In your opinion is there available land at Learganbreac for more crofters or for more residents than are there just now? *No, I don't think so. There used to be five families. Four crofters and a herd in Learganbreac, and there are five families there just now.*

[This is a straightforward lie, but who is to know?]

Were the deer done away with entirely, and the green patches or the good patches, devoted to crofters, would Jura as a whole, or would the people as a whole, be better than they are just now? *No, I don't think so.*

Why? *Where would they get work then, or how would those get work who now get it from the shooting tenant? The crofters could not give them work.*

Miss Isabella H. Campbell of Jura makes an Opening Statement:

I should like to say that Ardmenish, which has been referred to and which is now under four crofters, was in the proprietor's own hands formerly, and his factor lived there. In 1847, he made it a crofter township, and removed the crofters from Leargan-breac, distributing them on other parts of the estate where there were vacant crofts; and put his factor to Learganbreac, giving him a sheep stock and grazing his own cattle at Learganbreac. The laird had sheep all over the forest ground. Keils, Knockrome and Cnocbreac people's stock grazed along with the laird's stock, but simply as a privilege, not as a right; and as Neil Clark told you, he was the herd at Learganbreac, where the laird summered some of his cattle, and Clark usually went along with the shepherds to gather the laird's sheep on the forest ground. At Cnocbreac there were four tenants, and Neil Clark's mother, who was a widow, was also there; but these four tenants were at the same time herds to the proprietor and watchers of his salmon river there; and received their crofts as part of the wages they thus earned. When he removed them, only one left the island; the others got crofts in other parts.

[Miss Campbell tells the same story about Lergybreck as Neil Clark did. In fact it seems likely that he was carefully coached. Of the nine families in 1841 none were resettled in Ardmenish by 1851. Indeed three families had emigrated by then, forced off the island by the prevailing conditions. Of the six crofting families remaining in 1851, two left the island. One family broke up and was dispersed. One very aged couple went to retire to Knockrome. One moved into Corran House, and only John McDougall and his wife and grown up family went to a croft house in Ardmenish. Indeed, Ardmenish was a flourishing crofting township in 1841 with seven crofting families, and no sign of the laird's factor, who was in Feolin. There had been some moves by 1851, but Ardmenish still had six crofting families. By 1861 Ardmenish is down to five households, all continuous with the families of ten years previously, plus just the one family which has come from Lergybreck ... The account is a complete fiction.]

In 1868, Keils Glen was formed into part of the forest. Half of that was in the hands of the Keils' tenants; the other half was in the hands of the laird's own factor, who was removed at that time from Feoline, the home farm that is now let with the forest to Mr Evans. Learganbreac, as I said before, is now under the same number of people as there were before, viz: four families, and Neil Clark, who was the laird's own herd for the cattle. The population was very considerably larger than it is at present: that was entirely owing to the kelp industry, which yielded the proprietor from £1500 to £2000, and when that was done away with, several hundreds of the people emigrated themselves, because there was no occupation for them. There was not a single eviction from this place.

[Learganbreac is *not* of course under the same number of people as before. The new community there has nothing to do with the former community which was cleared quite ruthlessly. Miss Campbell assumes that the larger population then was 'due entirely to the kelp, and when it was done away with, the people emigrated themselves, because there was no occupation for them'. Notice how no one was responsible, except the people themselves. There was still not a single eviction!]

All I have to say in conclusion is, that up to the present day the feeling between the tenants and the proprietor has been a very friendly one, and I think, if you ask them, one and all would be sorry to see Mr Evans compelled to leave the island, although they may wish to get a little more land.

Is not the most evident way to enlarge their bounds seeing there was so much land available? *Did we not offer it, and was it not refused?*

Where is that? *It is contiguous to their holdings and can be easily seen from the road. It is where we have our own sheep and cattle.*

When, may I ask, was that offer made? *Six or seven years ago.* My brother wrote authorising it to be offered, but it was refused.

Did they assign any reason for refusing that offer? *No, I did not hear any reason.*

Or, in your opinion was there anycondition that would make it unacceptable? *There were no conditions whatever; they were to be given the grazing of Dubh-Chreag. There was not even a fence, and their stock would have gone a great deal further than the actual hill; in short. they would have come on to our ground very considerably.*

Is it not the case the Dubh-Chreag would not increase the value of their holding to any great extent? *Well, we consider it very good grazing for our own stock.*

Is it not under deer just now? *There are deer all over Jura, and always have been.*

But must it not have been the case that that in the opinion of these crofters the land was valueless? *No, I think they wished to get one particular spot and won't take anything else.*

Don't you think these people are intelligent people, and that they ought to know what would be for their benefit? *I think they are very intelligent people, and I think they are very nice people and very hard-working people.*

And perfectly capable of forming an opinion as to the value of the land offered them? *But I think that when other land is offered to them it is rather hard that they won't take it, but wish to spoil another place which would become utterly valueless.*

The following statement was then read on behalf of the witness:

'*The very name of this island, Jura, from Dhiura or Dera, is, in itself, significant that deer have always been abundant; indeed they are prehistoric, for a fossil stag's antler was dug out of Jura gravel not very long ago. In olden times they were able to roam wherever they liked, no part of the island being fenced off from them.*'

In 1875, the late proprietor, Mr Richard D. Campbell of Jura, let some 27,000 acres as a deer forest. To do this no crofters or cottars were turned out of the island, or even removed, and it was Mr Campbell's own stock that had to be taken off the ground.

The stock (sheep and cattle) kept by Mr Campbell on what is now called deer forest was never large; part of it was only summered there; the ground being chiefly high bleak land, is poor and only suited for deer, and if the small particles of better ground were taken from the deer forest and converted into a few indifferent crofts, the rest of this large tract of poor land would become utterly valueless even for deer, for unless hinds get a little better feeding in winter they cannot rear their calves, and in a short time the stock would be nil.

Doing away with the existing deer forest would injure the Jura crofters instead of benefitting them, as the few facts hereafter stated will go to prove:

1st. The yearly rates paid by Mr Evans, lessee of the deer forest, in a great measure reduce what must otherwise fall on the crofters.

2nd. A large portion of from £5000 to £6000 spent annually by Mr Evans in Scotland is circulated in this island. The sum of £1300 is paid in wages alone to outdoor servants, all Highlanders. [Many of these statements are questionable, but only a few can be proved one way or the other. The census shows the birthplaces of the people that Evans employs, and they are *not* Highlanders.]

3rd. Mr Evans distributes venison freely among the Jura people. He has fenced, gratis, a good many small crofts, and put wooden lofts and partitions into houses, besides helping the people in many other ways too numerous to mention. In 1892, Mr Evans spent £105 in providing cement, which, with some additional help from Mr Campbell, laid floors in every house from Lagg to Small Isles. If these few facts are taken into consideration, it will, I think, prove that the deer forest is a decided gain to each and all of us in Jura.

[It is curious that Miss Campbell is so eager to describe the largesse and good works of Mr Evans, when one would have thought that all these matters were properly the responsiblility of the laird.]

The farm of Tarbert, some 24,000 acres in extent, which is under sheep and deer, used to be farmed by the proprietor, but is now let. The present tenant, Mr Dugald Fletcher, a well known farmer, will, I think, be present himself to state how impossible it would be to settle crofters on any part of Tarbert excepting the few fields close to his own house, without which the farm could not be worked. This farm when first let returned a rental of £800 a year, but owing to the poor prices for sheep and wool the rent had to be reduced to £500 a year.

Keanuachdrach farm, about 3500 acres in extent, under sheep and deer, situated at the north of Jura, is let to Mr Archibald MacCormick at a rent of £135. This farm in better times returned a yearly rent of £200. The present tenant maintains that he cannot make the farm pay, even at the present reduced rent, unless Mr Campbell gives him the shooting and fishing along with it at the nominal rent of £15 a year. This shooting includes three deer as well as other game.

The farms of Ardfin, Strone and Sanaig, in all about 900 acres in extent are farmed by Mr Campbell of Jura himself. Sheep, cattle and deer graze all over them together as in olden times.

[The portions of Jura now let by Campbell amount to 54,500 acres. Approximately 20,500 acres remain, most of which is owned by McFarlane of Ardlussa. Only a small proportion of the island now remains either as crofted townships or as Campbell's own farm land.]

Mr Campbell, shortly after succeeding his late brother in the management of these estates, with a view to lighten the burdens on the people in such depressed and altered circumstances of the times, voluntarily dispensed with the duty work which every tenant was bound to render him, valued at £2 a year as estimated by themselves.

Mr Campbell, a few years ago, was reluctantly compelled to part with his fine well-known herd of Highland cattle, the expense of labour to provide wintering being so high that it far exceeded the prices they realised. Even with his three farms Mr Campbell has to winter from 300 to 400 of his hoggs away from Jura; and, those wintered at home having to be artificially fed, the expense is great. Besides this the heavy death-rate makes the keeping up of stock extremely difficult, and to obtain anything of a price for sheep or wool, fresh blood must be continually brought in. This the crofters do not seem to realise, which perhaps accounts for the fact that sheep sold by crofters invariably fetch the very lowest price in the market. Farms of even small size can only be worked by men possessed of a certain amount of capital. Crofters do not (at least in Jura) care for working a farm together; each and all of them prefer a croft entirely to themselves.

If the better spots of land were taken from Mr Campbell, Mr Evans, and Mr Fletcher, thus rendering the rest of the ground valueless for any purpose, some thirty to forty families, almost entirely Jura people, at present employed as servants by these three gentlemen, would be thrown out of work, and the local rates, which are high enough already, would be very greatly increased.

The distribution of compulsory rates was for the year to Whitsunday 1894 as follows:

Mr Campbell of Jura's proportion	£402
Mr Evan's (Jura Forest)	20
Mr Fletcher, farmer, Tarbert	44
Mr Archibald Maccormick, Kenuachdrach	13
Crofters	20

Mr Campbell will be glad to show the return of his farm for 1893, and although worked as economically as possible his loss is very considerable.

Mr Campbell for the benefit of his people keeps up three ferries, and a meal mill at a great loss to himself; and if the large tracts of bare bleak land are left valueless on his hands through picking out a few spots where imported crofters might manage to exist, it would be impossible for him to continue to do so.

[Why should the ferries and the mill run 'at a great loss'?]

No crofters have ever been sent out of the island by Mr Campbell or his predecessors.

Mr Campbell advanced considerable sums of money to several tenants and crofters. In every case the money advanced is still owing. One of these parties, just declared a bankrupt, has run his debt into hundreds of pounds. Out of fourteen crofters, who, in 1890, had their rents fixed by the Crofters Commission, several are very considerably over a year in arrears of rent; this will prove that even with ready made crofts, money lent and every advantage for procuring seaware, etc., the crofters rarely succeed in eking out a bare subsistence. How would it, therefore, be possible for them to do so where everything had to be made, no seaware convenient and no roads to their crofts? Then who is to take over the existing sheep stock which could not be kept on by Mr Campbell or Mr Fletcher without the better grounds for wintering? And what is to become of the large number of Jura people who would be thrown out of work by Mr Campbell, Mr Evans and Mr Fletcher?

Except for the distillery, which does not afford work to many, people have no means of earning money in Jura; and I have no hesitation in saying that the young people, male and female, as a rule, all wish to get away to the low country. Regular wages paid by Mr Campbell, Mr Evans and Mr Fletcher to Jura people amount to about £1200 per annum, and extra labour to about £200.

Mr Campbell can show the Commissioners a field on his own home farm about fifteen acres in extent, reclaimed by his late brother some fifty years ago; and though labour was to be had at that time for very little, it cost £1100 to reclaim the same and build a dyke round it.

The rainfall in Jura is very heavy, the yearly average being 65 inches (one year was as high as 94 inches) which is greatly against stock of all kinds. The distance from markets and the scarcity of transit reduces the value of all products very considerably. Steamer freights are high, which also adds greatly to the expense of goods coming to or going from the island. Stock has often to be kept in towns for several days, having arrived either too late or too soon for the markets.

(Signed) I.H.Campbell

[There is no doubt that the climate and the geographic remoteness of Jura make life expensive and difficult in modern times, and the problem Miss Campbell outlines are familiar to employers and to all residents to the present day.]

After considerable questioning about comparative values of the land, and possible income from it:

And is it not rather the process that has been going on already, confining them to a few green spots, and taking the pasture from them? *I don't think they can complain of that in Jura.*

There has been a statement made to us today that they have been deprived of their pasture? *You will see for yourselves whether they were deprived of it.*

And you yourself object to them being confined to narrow bounds? *I don't think the crofters in Jura are confined to narrow bounds, and I think, as I have said, that where they pastured out they pastured simply as a privilege on the ground where the laird had his own stock; as Neil Clark himself told you, he gathered the laird's sheep off that ground.*

[Miss Campbell's use of the word 'privilege' is interesting. Although the custom was enshrined in ancient tradition, the crofters were not protected by law and had no redress when they were put off this 'common' land.]

Of course we know this, that cattle were allowed to cross boundaries; there were not fences, and they have stated that although these boundaries were set out and declared still they were not rigidly kept; the laird's cattle wandered upon their ground, they don't deny that? *Yes, but we do not admit that they had these boundaries; we say their stock just grazed on the laird's ground where he had his own stock.*

You say it was yours and they say it was theirs? *They say it was theirs.*

But still the stock of both were there, and they are not there now; they have been confined now to a small spot, which was not the old condition of affairs? *Yes, but there are very few now in comparison with what there used to be in the island; and that was not through any fault of ours, but owing to the failure of the kelp industry.*

[There follows the exchange about kelp recorded in Chapter 32, after which the sitting is adjourned]

SUMMARY

A change in tenure had actually come in 1886 with the Crofters Act. The 1884 Report which led to it, limiting to crofters those with rents of under £30, listed the banes of the peasantry: minute, scattered holdings; insecurity of tenure; lack of compensation on departure, for improvements; high rents; withdrawal of land to sport; poor communications; defective education; justice; and emigration facilities. The Act itself provided for tenure security, improvement compensation, and, by application to the Crofters Commission, enlargement of holdings.

However, 'enlargement of holdings' proved but a mirage on the crofters' limited boundaries. In Argyll as a whole, hundreds of applications were received, but as the 'Crofters Commission' report of 1895 shows, nothing was ever done.

'Fair rents' applications were more successful. As soon as it became obvious that his tenants would apply en masse, Campbell made 10 per cent reductions and cancelled the duty work and peat cutting, considered worth twenty days in all.

The Commission still made sweeping cuts, however. Four Keils holdings, each with 10 acres arable and a sixth share in 460 acres of pasture were dropped from £11 to £8. Six Knockrome crofters, with 13 acres arable and a fourteenth share of 1650 acres pasture, fell from £15 to £12. Four at Ardmenish with 12 acres and a quarter share of 892, from £23 to £18. Rent arrears ranged from £18 to £90. The Commission cancelled some three-fifths, the balance to be paid in instalments. Despite these reductions many crofters on Jura continued in arrears, including those still working in the 1930s, at the end of available records.

Soumings. The Commission considered the general regulation of the townships, until now entirely under the owners' control. The main aspect was the 'souming' or number of animals each tenant could have on the land. In the last few years of the century this clause was the centre of a protracted struggle between Campbell and six Keils tenants. They doubtless had exceeded their soumings, a perennial state in many of the island's tiny crofts, since they lost both the case, with heavy costs, and the subsequent appeal.

As an example of the Commission's ruling, in 1900 the larger Ardmenish and Knockrome crofters were permitted fourteen cows, six heifers, six stirks, fourteen calves, two horses, four pigs and twenty-four sheep. The smaller ones had half as many and the Keils defendants had lesser soumings still. There were many still smaller soumings, for the very poor, the old, and the craftsmen, down to the Knockrome teacher's one cow.

It should be noted that the other great Commission, the Red Deer Commission, as a result of its 1895 report, mapped the existing and reclaimable crofting land on Jura. Oddly, they ignored the northern half, so that the evolution of land tenure there remains obscure. The mapping produced no benefits, however.

The *Oban Times* of 1895 records:

The Royal Commission on Deer Forests
Sitting in Jura: A Lady's Evidence.

The Royal Commission have now completed their work on the islands of Islay, Jura and Colonsay. On Friday they held a sitting in Jura, where delegates from the townships of Knockrome and Keils spoke of the necessity of getting additional pasture, such as had formerly been in the occupation of crofters in the island. The grazing farms of Sanaig, Strone and Cnockbreac were suitable for cutting up into small-holdings for the excess population.

Miss Isabella Campbell, of Jura, who appeared on behalf of her father, the proprietor, said that the island had been the abode of deer from prehistoric times, but it was not until 1875 that part of it, extending to about 2700 acres, was let as a deer forest. No evictions had ever taken place on the island at the instance of Mr Campbell or his predecessors. The decrease in the population of Jura was due to the fact that on the failure of the kelp industry hundreds of people left the island because there was no occupation for them. One of the lots in Knockrome was at present vacant, and the proprietor wished to divide it among the other crofters, but they could not agree among themselves about it. The tenants had never asked for an extension of their boundaries. and they had been offered additional grazing and refused it, apparently because they considered it of little value. It was good enough however, for the laird to graze his stock on. Miss Campbell argued the abolition of the deer forest would entail a large increase on the rates, and deprive thirty or forty families of their means of subsistence. A few years ago the laird was obliged to sell off his fine herd of well-known Highland cattle on account of the cost of providing wintering for them. The low price realised by crofters for their stock was perhaps due to the want of fresh blood to keep up the stock.

It will be seen that Miss Campbell's evidence to the Red Deer Commission is almost word for word identical to what she said to the Crofters' Commission.

In the last years of the nineteenth century, Miss Campbell seems to have enjoyed a high profile on the island and in the local press. Opinions are evidently divided as to her influence on the community. In 1897 the Election of the School Board provoked some interest:

Eight candidates for the five seats on the Board. Mr Colin Campbell of Jura, for many years a member, has withdrawn in favour of his sister, Miss Isabella Campbell. It is commonly believed that the action of the present Board in taking the commendable step of advancing the cause of education in accordance with modern requirements has brought Miss Campbell to the fore. This lady is a 'ratepayers' candidate. Her father is the largest ratepayer in the parish. This is the first contested election in Jura and more interest is being taken in it than in any previous one.

Sir, Permit me to correct some errors in the above. Miss Campbell does not come forward as a 'ratepayers' candidate', but because she has been requested to do so by many who believe her to be particularly competent. Her consent to do so was largely determined by her honest conviction that the action of the Board in recent years, so far from being 'commendable' left considerable room for improvement. If the writer of the above, criticising her motions were to sign his name, I feel sure his connections with recent School Boards, would explain, though not excuse, his criticism. I am, etc. A Native of Jura.

13 April 1897. The result of the School Board election is as follows:

Miss Campbell, Jura House (87); Rev. Angus MacCuaig (50); Angus Mac-Kechnie, crofter (18); Alexander Keith, crofter (16); John Shaw, crofter (15); John MacKechnie (15); James MacLean,crofter (15); Donald Darroch, crofter (9). The first five now form the new Board.

This was a sweeping victory, and in line with the various notes of appreciation in the press, e.g. 1899: 'Small Isles; A most successful concert was held here on Thursday evening last, in aid of the District Jubilee Nurses' Scheme for the County of Argyll.'

The dignitaries who attended are listed, ex-Provost Ferguson of Govan in the chair. The entertainers are listed and thanked.

This concert, together with the one held on 8th August for the same purpose, realised in all £8 15s These entertainments, which we understand are to be held annually, have been promoted by Miss Isabella H. Campbell, of Jura House, whose active interest in all matters pertaining to the good of the island is well known, and much appreciated, especially by the sick poor.

Not everybody is happy, though.

Jura, 1897: Jura, which is now the proud and happy possessor of telegraph wires is all the same in a less prosperous condition than it was earlier in the decade. It is not so long since there was a bustling village, with many children about the doors, where there are only one or two small households left. The young people have all emigrated, for Jura has not many attractions to offer to their ambitions. Apart from that, the conditions of life have changed under the virtual rule of Miss Campbell, who, though not the actual 'laird', is in residence, and represents him on the island. It is said that the telegraph arrangements were for a long time delayed because the Government would not put up as many danger flags for the birds as was deemed desirable in the interests of game.

Jura: Local Notes: The extension of the telegraph to Jura has been completed for some time back, but the estate authorities will not allow the wire to enter the Post Office until they are satisfied that a sufficient number of 'guards' are placed on the wire to keep the game from hurting themselves against it. Originally they wanted a few thousands of these guards to be put up beyond the number that is usual elsewhere. In the meantime we have only to submit patiently to this arbitrary conduct.

Considerable comment is caused by the treatment that Hugh McDougall and his sister are receiving at present from the estate officials. Their forefathers have been in the service of the Jura family for about 130 years. A year ago, because McDougall could not agree to the monetary terms which the Campbells wished to make with him, he could not get a house on the property to dwell in, nor was he allowed to erect even a removable house of corrugated iron. Last week he had to remove from the lodgings that he occupied at Small Isles, as his landlord was warned that he must not give him lodgings. It may be added that McDougall is engaged for a part of four days a week as postman in the district, and that there is nothing to be said against his character.

'Petticoat Goverment' may be a very good thing in theory, but is not always successful in practice.

No doubt Miss Campbell produced very strong feelings on Jura. When the author arrived there he found a number of elderly residents who still had vivid memories of her. They seemed to look back on her with a mixture of admiration and considerable alarm.

The present study of the Crofters' Commission's visit to Jura, and Miss Campbell, concludes with a general summary of the question of the clearances.

THE CLEARANCES
We studied the population of Jura during the second half of the nineteenth century through the records provided by the national censuses and watched it drop from

1158 to 614 during the fifty years from 1841 to 1891. During this time 47 per cent of the number of inhabitants present at the first census were absent by the last. We know that many families left the island, both to emigrate and to settle on the mainland. Much of the period during which this exodus took place is given the term 'the clearances', in the Highlands and Islands at large. We must now see whether this description applies to Jura. Was Jura 'cleared' of people to make way for sheep and deer, and to allow the landowners to gain bigger incomes than those supplied by the rents of the settled tenants? Miss Campbell insisted to the Commission that nothing of the kind ever took place on the island. 'Not one single family was ever evicted from their dwelling,' she said, 'and those who left did so voluntarily, because they preferred to go.'

There is no doubt that the word 'clearance', has been applied to the crofting township of Cnocbreac, which appears in Jura's early history and still features in the 1841 census. John Mercer had no doubt about Cnocbreac and says: 'In Jura there is the clearly recorded Cnocbreac eviction of the 1840s.' As we have seen through the censuses it is not quite as simple as that. In 1841 there were five families there, all of them young, although supporting several elderly relatives. One emigrant family with descendants in North Carolina traces its ancestry to Cnocbreac. However, by the 1851 census four of the five households have been resettled elsewhere in Jura. John and Mary Buie have gone to be the first tenants at Inver, newly built. Alexander Clark and his brother Neil have gone to Dunans. Their mother-in-law of seventy probably died, and Mary, their twelve-year-old sister disappeared. The McCartan family with their three children and two servants went to New Brosdale, and the other John and Mary Buie with two small children, two elderly parents, a forty-year-old sister and a servant all moved along the coast to Dainsgeir. The Buies of Inver were there until the sixties, and the Buies of Dainsgeir were there until the end of the century. The McArtans also remained on Jura until the 1890s, staying all this time in their new house in New Brosdale. Neil Clark's mother went to Dunans, and he stayed with her for a time before moving on, as did his brother Alexander who was a lodger in Dunans for several years. We have Miss Campbell's testimony that Neil Clark lived there with his mother, and that the crofters were all 'river watchers' and 'sheep minders', and that all but one family was resettled elsewhere.

If this story amounts to 'clearance', then it is a very strange example. Four of the five tenant households were found other accommodation in the laird's possession. Two of these homes are brand new and all are probably a great improvement on the old cottages of Cnocbreac. It may well be that Campbell had his eye on the western terraces below the Paps for a big flock of sheep, and John Buie of Inver, who was a herd, may have continued to be responsible for these animals. However, in all fairness, it is not reasonable to apply the word eviction to this process. Indeed it seems unlikely that the three young Shaws, John, Neil and Duncan, who are occupying the fifth Cnocbreac house alone at the ages of fifteen, twelve and ten, were not offered similar alternative accommodation before choosing to make their way off the island. We cannot easily force Cnocbreac into the pattern of a 'cleared township'.

Lergybreck is also on Mercer's list. This is an altogether different situation.

In 1841 Lergybreck was a considerable township. There were nine inhabited dwellings and fifty-six souls. Between 1841 and 1851 three quite substantial families leave the township and the island, presumably to emigrate. They take eighteen children and young people with them. In another house, Marion McNiven, a forty-year-old pauper is left on her own as various other family members move away. The Blacks of Keils move into one of the vacant houses, leaving seven dwellings occupied in the 1851 census. By the census of 1861 the situation is transformed. Only Marion McNiven, now aged sixty-one, has survived and still occupies her family home. The Gillies family, composed of brother and sisters have left the island, as have the Blacks who had settled from Keils in 1851. The other four families have gone to other crofting townships. One just across the Corran to Corran House, two to Knockrome and one to Ardfernal. Two widows in their fifties are occupying two of the vacant houses. Only three are now inhabited, all by single women over fifty.

By the census of 1871 they have all gone, and only one cottage survives, occupied by Neil Clark (36), from Cnocbreac (see above), who will continue as the caretaker for the new Jura Forest Lodge until the next century. His cottage still survives to this day.

Local tradition on Jura ascribes the destruction of this community, not to Campbell of Jura, but to Neil McLeod the Farmer at Feolin, who seems to have been farmer, factor and old-style tacksman all rolled into one. Oral tradition recalls that he had the right from Campbell to renew or not to renew leases as he saw fit, and chose not to renew them. More than that, he suffered the old buildings to be demolished as they fell vacant, and indeed it is very hard to find any trace of them where the old charts show that they once stood.

Neil McLeod's father Archibald McLeod was farming Feolin before the 1841 census, and subsequently handed it on to his son. He was ninety years old in 1851, and his wife Janet was still alive at eighty-five. The farm itself is mentioned throughout the eighteenth century, and may well have had a special status associated with a tacksman. Certainly, when Campbell came to lease the land for Jura Forest, Feolin Farm went with it, now unencumbered by unprofitable tenants on Lergybreck. It seems very likely that the motive for getting rid of this particular township was deer and not sheep. The Jura Forest ground must have been profitable to the Campbells long before Henry Evans time, and the stalking would have gone much better without the crofters livestock sharing the same ground.

Miss Campbell puts the responsibility squarely on Colin Campbell, her grand-father and says: 'he removed the crofters from Learganbreac, distributing them on other parts of the estate where there were vacant crofts; and put his factor to Learganbreac; giving him a sheep stock, and grazing his own cattle there.'

It is interesting that the local people were content to leave the responsibility at McLeod's door, rather than let it rest with the Laird. Neil McLeod did not emulate his father, and died in 1874 at the age of sixty-nine. His widow and the younger members of his family left the island.

Although Lergybreck bears out Mercer's contention that it was cleared much better than Cnocbreac, it looks as though in Jura it was not necessary to resort to outright eviction. Tenancies were short and leases expired quickly. When people had already proposed to leave the island there was no need for more unpleasantness, and the same applied when they decided to move to Knockrome. All that was necessary was to wait, and move firmly when the opportunity presented itself. It didn't really take very long. However, in this case we do have the single simple word, 'removed', and I suppose some would call that 'clearance' no matter where the people were 'removed to'.

We have already commented on the curious case of An Carn in the far north. Mercer refers to the oral tradition of its clearance by 1868, but we have noted that there is no evidence of this community in any of the island's records, and unless it was extremely short-lived, it really must have been occupied and deserted well before the 1841 census.

Mercer's view of all of this was that the above examples were simply the big, indignation-provoking cases, but that here and there, one by one, farmer's tenancies were quietly not renewed, and the ground turned over to the owner's sheep and deer. Our population charts bear out this assessment, for many communities with a number of dwellings in 1841 are reduced by 1891 to a single house.

The problem about finding out what was really happening is, as always, the absence of contemporary evidence. In this difficulty we are not alone, for the Crofters' Commission were faced with finding out exactly the same things which interest us.

38

The Northern Isles

There has been comment on the islands to the north of the main island of Jura during the greater part of this book.

These islands were always somewhat inaccessible and had a feeling of remoteness. It seems likely that in historical times the folk on the nearby mainland were not interested in them, and no doubt the troubled waters of the Sound of Luing presented a formidable barrier to traffic with the mainland.

The human population seems to have been small since medieval times, perhaps for similar reasons to those which restricted the number of people on Jura. Scarba certainly is rocky and difficult to cultivate except on the eastern shore. The other islands, though lower than Scarba still tend to be harsh moorland, and present a hostile environment for everything except sheep. The Garvellachs, with a different underlying geology, produce some lush pasture land, but they are the most distant from centres of population, and this may have worked against continuing settlement. Belnahua, alone, with its historic slate deposits seems to have supported a substantial human population in the past.

A late sixteenth-century report on Scarba regarding potential recruitment says: 'it is all woodis and craigis, except two tounis, and would raise seventeen fighting men.'

We have the famous perambulation of Presbytery in 1724, which gives the number of 'catechisable persons' – that is adult males and females including children down to the age of twelve.

This document lists sixty persons on Scarba: thirty on Lunga; sixteen on Belnahua; eighteen on the largest of the Garvellachs; and an unstated, but doubtless much smaller number on Eilean Naomh.

These catechisable people would consist of married couples and their older children together with elderly adults, so we might be looking at about ten dwelling houses on Scarba, four on Lunga, four on Belnahua, where there would be only working families, and a similar number in the Garvellachs.

Despite their remoteness and the small population, these islands had an appeal for business-minded landowners, possibly attracted to the profits from sheep farming, or sensing the potential for quarrying. In 1788 the map-maker Langlands produced a 'schemed rent' for a lease of the Garvellachs. This has survived and gives the acreages of 'Garvillich, Dunchonnel, Culbrandan, and Elachnive' and assesses them as worthy of £74 4/8 in rent.

By 1814 we know the various proprietors: Charles Campbell of Combey for the Garvellachs; Mr Dennistoun of Scarba (Mulbuie & Kilmory); Mr Stevenson of Belnahua and Mr McDougall of Lunga and Pendules.

In 1794 Francis Stewart is writing his *Statistical Account* and seems quite definite about the population. Scarba he says has fifty souls in fourteen families, including three widows. The forty-seven family members will consist of about twenty-eight parents and nineteen children. He tells us that these fourteen families live in two townships, presumably the settlements of Kilmory and Mulbuie which show on the early maps. Langlands' map of 1787 only shows six houses, but Francis Stewart knows of more than twice that number,

Stewart puts the rest of the population in Lunga and Belnahua, without mention of Lunga's northern islands, or of the Garvellachs. He collects everyone into a single township in Lunga, which he credits with six families and twenty-nine souls: twelve adults and seventeen children. He lists no widows.

We noted elsewhere that Francis Stewart had only been a short time in the ministry of Jura when he was required to turn out the *Statistical Account*, so he himself may have been lacking the necessary information for this remote part of his parish.

He is, however, undoubtedly right when he notes that the slate island of Belnahua is supporting a population of 132 souls, in twenty-eight families, for by 1794 the quarry is booming.

Stewart's physical description of these islands is limited to a few lines, and he makes no mention of the Garvellachs at all. His comment on Belnahua is, however, interesting:

> Balnahuaigh is about a mile in circumference, and is all a slate quarry. This quarry has been worked for many years back, and found to yield very good slate. There are generally about thirty men employed in it, who work by the piece, or at so much the thousand of slate.

We know that, in 1843, Alexander Kennedy compiled the *Second Statistical Account*. His population figures for the northern isles are less detailed than Stewart's:

	males	females	total
Scarba	25	23	48
Lunga	10	14	24
Belnahua	77	74	151
Garvelloch or Holy Island			7

These figures suggest that the Scarba population has hardly changed since Stewart's time, but Lunga has dropped a little and industrial colony on the slate island is on the increase. The Garvellachs get a mention, but only produce one or two families.

By the time of Kennedy's account, however, we have available the returns from the first national census of 1841. This reveals a completely different position in these islands from that in the minister's report. Far from having forty-eight residents, the census shows Scarba as having only twenty-three. They are in four households, so here we have firm records which show that Alexander Kennedy's figures in the *Statistical Account* are a complete fiction. It looks as if he simply went back to Francis Stewart's, and made a wild guess. If he did not know why there were only four families in Scarba, instead of the fourteen his return suggests, it may be relevant to ask ourselves why he didn't.

The same story emerges in the case of Lunga. The true account from the census gives one family on the main island of Lunga, and another on the island the census calls 'Fiulla Island'. This is Fiola Meadhonach, adjacent to Lunga to the north, which has the ruins of a house and a grain drying kiln. The real situation here is of two families instead of Kennedy's five or six.

By the 1841 census, Belnahua has twenty-eight families at work on the twenty-seven acre islet. Water had to be brought from the mainland in barrels, and laundry taken out. This large community evidently desired the benefits of the Church and its sacraments for there are many records of infant baptisms in Kennedy's time. Perhaps this is why he seems more in touch with the population there than with that of Scarba and Lunga.

Nearby Fladda, an eight-acre rock with a notable lighthouse on it, was said by Munro in 1549 to be inhabited. It later had a small slate quarry which was worked until the 1860s. After that its two resident families were there to man the light.

The human population of all these islands declined during the nineteenth century. The census returns show Scarba down to two families from 1861, and from 1921 there was only a single family in residence. Lunga was also down to a single family by the turn of the century, with no entry in the census after the Second Word War. The Garvellachs were deserted from 1881, although on the date of the 1911 census there were two shepherds on the island.

Fladda Lighthouse had to be manned and lighthouse keepers continued until 1951.

The owner of Scarba in due course built Kilmory Lodge as a holiday retreat, and the farmhouses on Lunga and Garbh Eileach continued in occasional use and in reasonable repair until recent times. In modern times there is an Outward Bound Centre on Rubha Fiola and the Fladda Lighthouse is a holiday home.

BELNAHUA AND THE SLATE QUARRY

Since this small island supported a considerable number of people for so many years it seems appropriate to produce a general note on the quarry.

Belnahua and Fladda were already being quarried on a small scale as early as the sixteenth century, but it was from about 1750 that these islands and the rest of the Easdale Dalradian slate zone began to be commercially exploited. At this time it was discovered that Jura also had workable slate, at Tarbert and Inverlussa.

The Belnahua slate was 'medium fine' or quite high grade, blue-grey to black, small grained except for protruding crystals of pyrites, which both caused working difficulties and stopped the slates lying flat on the roof. The Inverlussa slate also suffered from quartzite bands mixed into the slate.

Belnahua was owned by various entrepreneurs, of whom the best known was Robert Stevenson. He had a descendant whom Betsy McKechnie of Craighouse was proud to claim as an ancestor and as her namesake. She always referred to this woman as Betsy Stinson, and the Jura censuses show her living on Jura during the nineteenth century.

In 1795 the slate workers got 12s a thousand. This produced 25s for the owners and reached the Glasgow builder at £2 5s to £3. Up to 1834 there was a slate tax of 7s 6d per every thousand slates carried in a boat, which favoured the mainland quarries.

The Jura owners ran the Isle of Jura quarries. In 1834, one sold 'sizeable slates' at £2 a thousand and, in 1879, at £4 15s About this time competition struck at them all. The low-grade Jura quarries closed, although an Edinburgh letter contains a sketch, probably done about 1897, for their re-opening down to 450ft. It was about the time of the First World War that Belnahua was finally abandoned. It was by then a slate shell hollowed out to 90ft, far below sea-level.

The quarriers had an intimate knowledge of the rock; its folding, cleavage and jointing.

The Belnahua beds dipped regularly and were worked towards the rise of the cleavage, so as to leave terraces 12–20ft deep parallel to the strike. The six-man crews took an agreed area for a period. Ten yards for six weeks was standard. The two face workers loosened the rock with explosives, then used heavy chisels to divide the blocks along the cleavage into slabs. These then went to two pairs of dressers, working in a shed away from the face. The splitters and dressers produced full-size slates which averaged 14in by 9in, the minimum allowed being 12in by 7in About 90 per cent of the slate quarried was lost in the process. The finished slates were loaded into the ships in thousands of 1200, as well as forty more for breakages, after which the crew was paid an agreed rate.

The population of Belnahua grew steadily until in 1871 it was at its height, with 146 inhabitants. The quarry began to decline in the 1870s, under the influence of competition, and the next four censuses show 108, 68, 39 and 32 inhabitants. The thirty-two in 1911 are the last to be recorded, for the 1921 census shows no one on the island. The slate had run out and the sea flooded the old workings. Today the many ruined houses stand around a sullen lagoon and create a ghostly atmosphere as the evening comes on.

It should be noted that during the time of the slate quarries, marble was being seriously quarried in the Garvellachs. In 1800 the output was of flags up to 4ft by 3ft, of fine grain and giving a good polish.

Between 1792 and 1836, white quartz sand was being taken from the shore of the Garvellachs, and of Jura, for the glassworks at Dumbarton. The few records show 200 tons a year, brought to an end probably by the location of less remote deposits. In 1801, Campbell of Jura was demanding payment from the sand boats,

In 1882 there was another outrage and a telegram intended to produce an arrest read: 'Janet of Belfast, John Boyle Master and Owner, left here last night for Liverpool loaded with Stones taken from the shores of Loch Tarbert.' However, the police could never be persuaded to act, and there are still Irish streets paved with Jura cobbles.

Presumably because of the small and remote populations on these islands very few human stories have survived. About 1602, according to Loder, a pirate band from Mull was conducting raids on the surrounding islands. It was routine in those days to maroon helpless victims on small islets, and the Rock of Thumbs, a third of a mile north of the north end of Quern Strait in the Lunga Isles is believed to have got its name from the time that the Mull band left nine Lunga men there without their thumbs. The name 'Quern Strait' may possibly preserve the distant memory of a quern factory in Lunga.

In 1687 a Lunga man was found to have stolen two horses:

> Twa mares; viz ane belled browne mare fore or fyve yeirs old worth twentie merks and ane young gray mare worth ten pund. He sold them in ane public mercat for ane horse and fourtie shilling; the justice having received information of the honnestie and peaceable behaviour of the said accused; in mitigation ... ordained that the said accused be scourged throw the towne of Inverary, and his whole goods and gear to be confiscate; and the bond of caution given for his good behaviour in tyme coming to continue.

Since another man who had lately stolen a cow was hanged a few years earlier, the Lunga man seems to have got off lightly.

In 1749, the grandfather of a petitioner to the Campbell chief had 'forcibly obtained possession of the Garvellachs', after the resident MacLeans had refused to pay tribute to the the Campbells:

> Although the MacLeans did for a time smother their resentment, yet at length a band of them came fully armed under cloud of night ... and most riotously plundered the whole effects and bestial, to the value of 3000 marks, and after destroying the houses and byres, stript the possessors of the living, and left their wives and children stript naked to the inclemency of the weather. There were however no killings.

Much more recently, perhaps sometime in the nineteenth century, there was the well-known story of an old couple who lived in the farmhouse in Lunga. The old man died and, because of the wild winter weather, his wife was unable to attract the attention of anyone on the mainland and, in due course, she hanged herself outside the house. By the time people arrived and discovered what had happened, the two were long dead, and there were also the usual concerns about the burial of a suicide. The old man was buried in the cemetery in Scarba, but his suicide wife was buried on a little island called Eilean a' Bhealaich (Isle in the Gap), which lies in the midst of the Channel of the Grey Dog.

It seems sad that more stories of these former communities should not apparently have survived. In modern times all the islands of the group are used to graze livestock, although the shepherds and cattlemen do not remain with their animals.

During the summer months these islands are visited by all kinds of people using every kind of vessel, from large yachts to ocean-going canoes. For the rest of the year most of them are little visited. The natural history of the group had a brief mention in the appropriate chapter, but there seems little else to record here about the Northern Isles of the parish of Jura.

X

Tales of Jura

39

Legends, Stories,
Superstitions and Sayings

The stories in this book come from three different collectors: the Rev. Charles Robertson, in Jura in 1913, the Rev. Donald Budge, in Jura in the 1950s; and the Rev. Peter Youngson, in Jura from 1975.

CHARLES ROBERTSON

Born in 1864 at Aberfeldy, Charles Robertson trained for the ministry at New College. He worked in various parishes in the Highlands and Islands as a missionary for the United Free Church of Scotland. He was a notable Gaelic scholar, with a passion for local dialects, and regional variations, and for tales and stories, which he collected everywhere he went. Charles Robertson came to the United Free Kirk in Jura about 1908 and remained until 1914, when he became minister of the United Free Church in the parish of Kilchoman and Portnahaven in Islay. Charles Robertson was on Jura for part of the long ministry of the Rev. Donald John Robertson. The Church of Scotland minister was short and stocky, while the U F missionary was very tall indeed. The two men were familiarly known on the island of Jura as 'Robertson beag' and 'Robertson fada' ('little Robertson' and 'long Robertson'). Robertson fada's exercise books in the National Library of Scotland contain ninety-five pages of handwritten material, mostly consisting of stories and lore collected from natives of Jura. The bulk of this seems to have been assembled in an intense period of work in January 1913.

Robertson fada died on 11 June 1927 at the age of sixty-three years.

Stories for which Charles Robertson is the principal source have the initials RF after their titles.

DONALD BUDGE

Donald Budge's book on Jura contains a numbers of stories collected from various sources. Most had never been in print before. Some were taken down about 100 years ago in Jura, and in Gaelic, from the lips of Jura men, by John Dewar who was one of those who collected tales for J. F. Campbell of Islay, when he was compiling his popular *Tales of the West Highlands*. They were never published and came into Donald Budge's hands through the kindness of the Rev. Angus P. Fletcher, minister of Skipness, Argyll; who was of the former Jura family of Fletchers. Jura men who recited the tales to John Dewar were: Malcolm Macdonald, Lagg; John Campbell, Tarbert; and Malcolm Darroch, Lussagiven.

Stories for which Donald Budge is the principal source have the initials DB after their titles.

PETER YOUNGSON

The author spent time with some remarkable men and women of his own day. His main intention was to establish how many of the earlier stories that Donald Budge knew were still current on the island and, later, to try to do the same with the Robertson fada material. In the process, a great deal of additional information came to light and this is published here.

His principal informants were: Archie Black, Dougie Buie, Sandy Buie, Donald Darroch, Katie Darroch, Alick Keith, Dan Macdougall, Effie Macdougall, Alec McIsaac, Janet McKechnie, Betsy McKechnie, Katie McLean, Neil McMillan and John Shaw. There were many others. Stories for which these and other informants were the sources have the initials PY after their titles. Such Gaelic passages as seem important for the original flavour of the story follow the English in italics. The stories are numbered for ease of reference.

1. The Witch of the Paps of Jura (DB)

Cailleach a' Bheinn Mhoir, the Witch of Jura, lived at Largiebreac. She had a ball of thread by which she could draw towards her any person or any thing if she could throw the ball beyond them. She got Macphie of Colonsay into her coils and would not allow him to depart. Every time he attempted to leave her she used to intercept him, and even after he had got into his birlinn and got off from the shore, she would get him ashore again by throwing the ball into his boat. At last he pretended that he was perfectly content in his bondage, and managed to get the secret from her that she had a hatchet that would cut the thread. He watched his opportunity and stole the hatchet, having previously ordered his boat to be waiting at Knockbreac at the foot of Beinn a'Chaolais. He set out at dawn of day and was seated in his boat before the Cailleach got to the top of the hill, which she climbed with speed as soon as she missed him. When she saw him in the boat, she called out piteously to him:

> Oh, Macphie, my heart's treasure.
> Hast thou left me on the shore?
>
> *A Mhic-a-Phì, a ghaoil mo chridhe,*
> *An d'fhàg thu air a' chladach mi?*

This she oft repeated, throwing at the same time the magic ball (*Ceirsle draoid-heachd*) into the boat and drawing it into the shore. But when she saw the thread cut and saw the boat sailing beyond her reach, she tried desperately to follow it and slid down from the top of the Ben leaving a mark from the top to the shore. This is called to this day the 'Old Woman's Furrow or Slide' (*Sgrìob na Caillich*).

As she descended she was crying out:

> Oh, Macphie, rough-skinned and ugly
> Hast thou left me on the shore?
>
> *A Mhic-a-Phì, charraich ghrànnda.*
> *An d'fhàg thu air a' chladach mi?*

2. Buie of the Deer (RF)

Mac Ille-bhuidhe who lived at Cnocbreac asked his sons one day in his old age to help him to reach the high face of Beinn an Oir. When seated there he said:

> I am Buie of the deer,
> I'm sitting on the side of Beinn an Oir,
> And though I am aged and grey,
> God has the power to make me young.

> *Is mise Mac' Ill' Bhuidh' nam fiadh,*
> *'S mi 'm shuidh' air sliabh Bheinn an Oir,*
> *'S ged a tha mi aosmor liath,*
> *Is comasach le Dia mo dhèanamh òg.*

And he walked home as active and supple as any of his sons.

The Buies were long connected with the deer. For example, it was said: 'To dream of deer was to dream of the Buies.'

3. Field of the Quarrel (DB)

Not far from the farm of Strone in south Jura there can be seen the remains of an enclosure which is to this day called 'field of the quarrel' (*Acha na h'urraghail*). On a hillside nearby there was a small community of cottars. There was given to them, a piece of land in common which they proceeded to prepare and cultivate and sow with corn. The work was all done by communal effort, each family giving a certain amount of labour, the arrangement being that when the crop grew and was secured it should be shared equally by all. The corn grew well. It ripened and was now ready to be harvested and so, before proceeding to cut the field, the people met together to decide as to how the crop was to be divided. Certain people had contributed more labour than others. There was discussion and then argument, and as tempers rose there was quarrelling, and the strife was so bitter that bloodshed was feared. Finally darkness fell and the parley ceased, but they went on their way full of muttering and resentment and discontent.

There was one wise old woman who looked on and listened and saw how things had resulted. She knew that unless something were done, blood would be shed on the morrow and lives lost.

After bedtime a bright glow was seen in the direction of the disputed corn-field, and by the time the people had hastened to the scene, a great fire had swept the length and breadth of the golden yellow cornfield and nothing now remained but blackened turf. It was not until long afterwards that they discovered that the fire was no mere accident, but that the old woman had decided in her wisdom that human lives were of more value than golden corn.

4. Jura Burials (DB)

At one time Jura was not considered to be consecrated ground, sacred for burials. The people who lived in south Jura buried their dead in Kilchoman, Islay, and the people of north Jura buried their dead in Colonsay. It happened that 'the man of Achacobhais' (*Fear Acha Cobhais*) died and his remains were being carried for burial to Daiseadail. (Achacobhais seems to have been a place on the hill behind the kirk, not far from Keils.) The burial party with the body arrived at the shore and the bier was rested on a rock called Leac Earnadail.

A great storm arose and it was found to be impossible to cross to Islay. The mourners all departed until only the two sons of the dead man were left. When they found that nothing else could be done they carried the body back to their own farmland and here they made a burial at Achachobais. From Kenuachdrach, north Jura, the remains of the dead used to be conveyed to consecrated ground in Colonsay. The biers were carried to Corpach, at the boundary between the lands of the Campbells of Jura, and the lands of the McNeills in Jura, near to Rudha an t-sailean and there put on board a vessel for Colonsay.

On the occasion of the last burial in this way, a storm arose and so great was the danger that the coffin and bier had to be thrown overboard into the sea. The boat and crew succeeded in reaching the Jura shore, and on arriving there found that the coffin and bier had already been thrown ashore by the waves. The burial finally took place in Ardlussa, and that was the beginning of burials in Ardlussa graveyard.

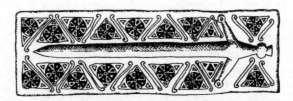

5. Traditions of Kilearnadale Cemetery (RF)

There is an area of elevated ground immediately inside the gate of Kilearnadale graveyard which is called 'the big ruin' (*An larach mhor*). This was the site of St Columba's Chapel, and is the burying place of the old native inhabitants.

Strangers found a burial place to the north of this but were prohibited from entering by the gate from the south, and were obliged to go round by the outside so as not to trample on the graves of the natives. When a stranger was to be buried, some of the older men with sticks in their hands took their station at the gate of the churchyard and made the bearers of the remains go round and enter at the other gate. Men who were alive within living memory are said to have taken part in preventing the funerals of strangers from entering by the gate. One of the last cases, if not the last, was the funeral of a sailor who was a stranger, in which instance there was a scuffle, and an oak stick was broken on the head of one of the participants.

The old parish church stood in the northern part of the ground. The last minister to preach in the old church was the Rev. Neil McLeod, who was the author, according to tradition, of the song, 'My swarthy maid, beautiful and black-haired' (*Mo nighean dubh ga boidheach dubh*), and is buried in that part of the churchyard with an inscribed stone to mark his grave. A son of Mr McLeod, named Archibald, and nick-named 'Baldy', lived at Aoireann, now called Feolin Farm, and is remembered by Dugald Buie, who gave these particulars.

Note: Neil McLeod was minister from 1759 to 1766. He was married to Elizabeth Campbell. His son Archibald died between 1851 and 1855, at over 90 years of age. The said Dugald Buie was eight years old in 1855, and so could indeed have remembered him.

A ford on the stream below the churchyard is named 'ford of the old woman' (*ath na caillich*), and nearby is 'the Clerk's Field' (*achadh a' chleirich*). Local informants said 'before the whins grew everywhere you could see all the houses. There must have been a lot of folk there at one time.' Dwelly gives a possible meaning for the Clerk as the 'beadle', and local folk gave evidence in 1766 that a piece of ground nearby was called 'beadle's glebe'. The Ordnance Survey map of 1890 gives '*Acair a' chleirich*'.

Up above on the hillside are 'the crofts' (*na Croitean*), and you can see lazy-beds all over it.

A small knoll on the south or west side of the road, about twenty or thirty yards from the gate of Kilearnadale was a burying place for unbaptised infants.

The old road to the burying place came down the brae from Keils, and at the top of the brae on either side of the road are two little mounds of unequal height at which Mrs Campbell of Jura used to mount and dismount from the pony which she rode to church. The sloping path down from this spot is still called 'Lady Walk'.

The remains of three or four dwelling houses can still be traced beside the churchyard of Kilearnadale, and its entrance on the west. The last inhabitants of these houses died of a plague. When they were ill no one would go near them for fear of the plague. Milk and other necessities were left at the brink of the hollow and fetched by two men, one blind and the other lame. The blind man carried the lame man on his back to direct the way. By and by no one was able to come for the food and it became clear at last that all were dead. They were never buried, but were left lying in their places and the houses were allowed to fall down round about.

The name given to this plague was *an carrasan*. It also carried off the inhabitants of a small hamlet to the west of Campbell's house at Knockrome. Another version of this story is still current in Jura. In it the blind and lame individuals are sisters, who were the last survivors in the plague village, and came to a meeting place for food. This was brought by a hunchback youth from Keils who could do no useful work. The arrangement ended when the sisters died.

The story lingered on until modern times, for, when the local authority arrived to create a new car park, they found local stalwarts forbidding the breaking of the ground just to the left of the entrance to the graveyard. 'This is where the plague victims are buried! You'll not touch this ground.' They prevailed, and the car park remained an odd L-shape. There are the ruins of a small building on the spot in question.

The site first chosen for the new church was the spot on which the big cairns rests on top of the bank behind the United Free Church manse. It was abandoned for the final site after building operations had begun, in consequence of the fact that what the masons built one day was found taken down the next day, presumably by the fairies, although the truth is that the undoing of the work was by the hands of some of the inhabitants who objected to the site.

The name of the cairn is 'cairn of the preaching' (*carn na searmoin*. The great-grandfather of John and Donald Keith wrought at the building of the present parish church for a wage of 7d per day, and was one of the most highly paid men employed at the work.

6. Raid on Colonsay; Darroch and Buie (RF)

There are several stories about an ancestral Darroch and his struggles with an ancestral Buie. In these tales Darroch is given his old Gaelic name of *Mac Ille riabhach*, which means 'son of the grey lad or grizzled lad', although here he will be called Darroch.

Buie is called *Mac Ille bhuidhe*, which means 'son of the yellow-haired lad'. Here he will be called Buie.

Darroch was employed by the land-grabbers of his day to secure possession of new lands. Though few men could stand up to him, he met his match in Buie, who owned a great part of Jura, and had his home in Lergybreck. Darroch was engaged by Argyll to take possession of Colonsay and exterminate the MacPhee family who held the island at that time.

As Darroch was getting his followers together, Buie came up to him and asked him for a passage to Port Askaig in his war galley. He did not tell Darroch that he knew they were going to Colonsay. When the boat arrived at Port Askaig, Darroch announced that he was going on to Colonsay.

'If that's where you're off to,' said Buie, 'I wouldn't mind if I ended up on Colonsay myself.'

When they reached Colonsay, Darroch and his men set off for MacPhee's house to carry out their mission. Buie followed at a safe distance. He saw a young woman running into an outhouse with something concealed in her arms, and quickly followed her. 'What have you got there, lass?'

'It's nothing of any value,' she replied.

'Don't be afraid," said Buie. 'Although I'm here along with these men, I don't belong to their company, and I mean you no harm.'

The girl showed him a baby boy, and said, 'That is the only one now alive of the family of MacPhee.'

Buie took the infant and concealed him against his own breast underneath his plaid. When Darroch's company had finished their work he joined them on the return journey. Buie wanted Darroch to make straight for Jura, and set him off at the nearest point, but Darroch chose to make for the Sound of Islay, the way he had come. Buie was doing his share of the rowing, and, trying hard to keep the head of the boat towards Jura, he broke his oar. His hands flew back and struck his chest, or rather struck the baby on his breast. The child gave a cry.

Darroch exclaimed, 'There's a stowaway in the boat.' (*Seo! Tha arrabhalach sa bhàta.*)

'It's only the creaking of the oar,' said Buie. (*Chan eil ach diosgan nan ràimh.*)

They gave him another oar, but he broke it as well. 'You'll have to give me a stronger oar,' said Buie. (The words he used were '*am buirbid mor*'.) This was the great heavy oar the galley carried to use for steering, so they gave him that. So well did he wield his oar that he brought the boat to land in Jura, just north of the opening of the Sound of Islay. When they were near enough, Buie used his oar as a vaulting pole, and before the others were aware of what was happening, he was ashore and facing them with his drawn sword in his hand.

'You'll need all your sprightliness now, Buie.' (*Cha b'fhuilear dhut, Mhic 'Ille Bhuidh', bhith cho ealamh.*)

'Land if you like,' said Buie, 'for I'm ready for you.' (*Thigeadh sibhse air tir a-nis.*)

'I don't think so,' replied Darroch, declining the invitation. (*Chan e sin bhios ann.*)

Buie held the baby aloft in his arms and called out, 'This is the heir of the MacPhees, and there are as many arrows in the quiver as you have men, and not one of you will pass.' (*Seo oighre Mhic-a-Phi Cholasa, agus co-lion saighead anns an lùireach, agus tha daoine agad, agus cha tèid aon dhiùbh seachad.*)

Buie was afraid to take the child to his own house, lest his enemies might come while he was away from home, so he took the boy to a remote cave on the side of Beinn an Oir, the highest of the Paps of Jura, and hid him there. He went regularly with food to the child, and would leave a piece of meat, tied to the child's toe with a piece of cord of such a length that if the meat were to go into the child's throat so that he was on the point of choking, the sudden straightening of his body would automatically pull the meat out of his throat.

In due course the boy grew up, and with Buie's help he was able to win back his inheritance in Colonsay, although it is said that he lost it again later. As long as he held it, however, if Buie was in need of any help against an enemy, he had only to light a signal fire in sight of Colonsay, and MacPhee and all the men he could muster would be over in hot haste to help him.

It is said that the MacPhees, the sugar refiners of Greenock, are descended from that child.

7. Yellow-Haired John of the Deer (DB)

Macphie of Colonsay left a son who was a child at the time when his father perished. It was known that Colkitto was anxious to get hold of the child to destroy him, lest he should later revenge the death of his father whom Colkitto had killed. In Jura there was a forester of the Macdonalds, who had a great regard for the MacPhies or MacDuffies of Colonsay, and so it was planned to send the child to Jura to be cared for by the forester who was called Yellow-Haired John of the Deer. The child was hidden first in Colonsay by a man named Currie, who then brought the child to Jura. The forester agreed to take charge of him and brought him to a cave in Beinn an Oir, where he put up a bed and slept at nights with the child held to his breast. He was afterwards removed to Kintyre, where he was brought up.

8. MacIain Riabhach (DB)

On one occasion, MacIain Riabhach (brindled or grizzled MacIain, a notorious outlaw), being away from home, the men of Rathlin raided his country. They sacked the country, they assaulted the women folk and departed. MacIain vowed vengeance upon the men of Rathlin. He led a counter-attack upon Rathlin with his warriors, upon which the Rathlin men fled and landed upon Jura. MacIain and his band followed them and engaged them in combat. Making them prisoners they were tied in couples, chest to chest, and shot through with arrows, after which their bodies were thrown over the rocks at the Red Cave ('*uamh dearg*), in Glen na Baitraich.

Landing upon Jura on one occasion MacIain Riabhach burned every home between the west of Jura and the township of Lagg. There is a gulley between the rocks at Rudha na Traighe (headland by the strand), and a flat rock bridging the gulley or cleft. It was in this place that MacIain used to hang his prisoners.

MacIain Riabhach was at one time pursuing some of his enemies who were Jura men, along the shoreside of West Loch Tarbert, Jura. One of the Jura men swam out to sea toward Sgeir a Bhuderich. This was noticed by MacIain and one of his young men. Said he to his follower, 'Swim after him, my lad, and kill him.' The young man did so, swimming after the Jura man, holding his sword between his teeth. On reaching the rock the Jura man said, 'Be courageous my man, and I will come to your aid.' He swam back to meet him, and grasping the sword from between the young man's teeth, swung it and severed his head from his body. When the companions of the dead man saw what had happened, no other of them dared to pursue the fugitives.

9. An Gillie Riabaich (RF)

Old Darroch was known as An Gille Riabhach, duine gaisgeil, a tha cho dorch' 's a bha a thuineadh (son of the grizzled man, a hero who is as black as was his dwelling house, dark indeed in those days). According to one tradition he came originally from the north of Ireland, an adherent of John Garve Maclean of Coll.

Darroch used to imprison men, women and children in a cave on the west coast of Jura called 'cave of the two doors' (uamh an dà dhorais'). This cave was a tunnel, open at both ends. Darroch would have heather and other combustibles heaped up at the mouths of the cave and, setting fire to them, would suffocate the prisoners.

He also had some favourite rocks in Loch Tarbert called 'drowned sunken rocks' (*na bogacha bàithte*), and he would tie women prisoners by their hair to the seaweed on these rocks and leave them to drown when the tide came in.

Darroch can be dated by the tradition that he was continually at war with the great warrior called Alasdair MacColla, or Alasdair Colkitto, who was the son of the famous Colkitto, whose full name was Coll MacGillespie. Alasdair Colkitto was lieutenant to Montrose in his brilliant but unsuccessful attempt to win the throne for the House of Stewart in 1646.

Darroch's equipment lasted a long time. A Keith from Crackaig told Robertson, 'I remember seeing the halter on Darroch's gallows in my own lifetime.' He used the old word 'withe'. But the halter has long since disappeared, and the cross-stone has itself fallen owing to the decay in the rock.

The old villain was apparently reluctant to leave the scene. An informant recalled, 'When Darroch was on his death bed he lingered so long that it seemed as if he would never die, and to hasten his departure a plough coulter was heated red hot and thrust down his throat.' A violent end for a violent man.

10. Darroch and Red Cave (RF)

Darroch was a contemporary of Duncan Campbell of Sannaig, the first Baillie of Jura, who died in 1695 at the age of ninety-nine.

One encounter between these two worthies has been remembered.

Darroch and the 'great baillie' were once passing the night together with some followers in a cave near Glen Batrick which is called Red Cave (*an uamh dhearg*). Now there is a continual dripping from the roof of this cave, and the droplets are red in colour, which gives the cave its name. Darroch made several attempts to find a place to sit where the red drip would not fall directly down on him, but always in vain.

The baillie said, 'It is no wonder that the Red Drop (*am boinne dearg*) will always find you.' He was referring to Darroch's reputation for being a man of blood.

Darroch replied, 'If it were a matter of a blood feud, I'd not be slow in setting the blade to the neck.' (*Nam b'fhalachd a bha ann, chuirinn an t-snàthad air a' choltair air a' mhuineil.*)

His actual words in the Gaelic refer to using the coulter or blade of the plough, which cuts open the turf, to rip open his enemy.

Darroch sounded so grim, that the baillie became very nervous, and made an excuse to go outside the cave. Once he was safely out, he took to his heels and did not stop until he was back on his own side of the island, and far away from that terrible old man.

11. Gillour MacCraine (RF)

We have encountered the reputation of Gillour MacCraine as famously long lived, but several stories of his exploits have survived.

Gillour is reputed to have been very adept at the use of the bow and arrow. One one occasion there was a raid by cattle lifters upon the south of Jura, and Gillour's cow was amongst the animals seized. Gillour came upon the scene, when the thief holding his cow with the one hand, laid hold of the boat with his other hand, preparatory to inducing the cow to board. Drawing his bow, and letting fly with an arrow, Gillour pinned the hand that was on the boat to the wood.

He then warned the depredator that it was not by any mistake in aiming, the arrow was in his hand and not in his heart.

The culprit was obliged to let the cow go, and got himself quietly away to a safe distance with what speed he could, without offering further provocation to such a dangerous archer.

Budge's version is substantially the same, but has some nice details missing from the above. For example it mentions that Gillour overlooked the scene from the crag above the bay.

Gillour's son when about a hundred years of age, though some say eighty, asked his father for a pair of boots, as he meant to get married. He had never had a pair of boots up to that time. Gillour, when the proposal was mooted to him, said, '*Is òg d'iomairt.*' This proves to be hard to translate, but probably means, 'You're a bit young for that kind of frolic!'

There is also a proverb current in Jura that was first said by Gillour to his son one day when they were both out on the hill. The young man, who according to the age of his father was already an old man, complained of fatigue.

'*Is olc an là a thug thu!*' said Gillour. Again this is difficult, but possibly ironic. (Poor soul, you've had a hard time of it.' or 'You've chosen a bad day.')

Gillour was once forced by Mac-an-riabhaich to shoot at an apple set upon his boy's head. Instead of drawing one arrow from his quiver when about to aim, he drew two, and put the extra arrow in readiness for an extra shot. He hit the apple and left the son unscathed. Mac-an-riabhaich asked him why he had drawn the second arrow.

'It was for you if ought had happened to my son.'

Robertson commented on the format of the above story, which parallels the William Tell story. He was evidently aware of another Scottish version which he believed predated the Swiss legend.

Gillour MacCraine was once asked how he was able to retain the freshness of his complexion despite his great age. He replied, 'I have never at any time partaken of food of greater heat than the warm milk of the cattle-fold, and I have never at any time warmed myself at a fire.' (DB)

The Earl of Argyll enquired of Gillour what was his attitude was toward whisky. Said Gillour, 'I have never at any time turned aside from my path to partake of it, nor have I ever avoided it when it met me in the way.' (DB)

When Gillour's son was 120, his strength began to fail. During one night some deer entered their land and were destroying the standing corn. Gillour called to his son to arise and chase the deer away.

'I am not able to do it,' said his son.

'When I was your age,' said Gillour, 'I should soon have put them to flight.'

He then got up, stretched his hand for his bow and arrows, went outside and slew four of the intruding deer and, having bled them, returned to his son, saying, 'We shall be safe from these for some time, they will not trouble us.' Meaning that deer shun any place where they can smell the blood of their own kind. Gillour died about the year 1671. (DB)

12. Witchcraft and the Corp Creadha (RF) (PY)

The most famous witchcraft story of Jura, and one the author has also been told by a number of people, is about the practice of the clay doll (*corp creadha*). There are several versions. Robertson's is probably the best.

The Campbells of Jura were Campbells of Craignish, and before becoming proprietors of Jura were baillies of the island. One of them, the 'great baillie' (*am baillidh mòr*), on one of his visits to the island, was met after he landed at Kinuachdrach by a wise woman (*ban-fhiosaiche*) and urged by her to make for Knockrome at his utmost speed, that his life was being practised against there by means of a 'corp creadha', and his only hope of life was to be there in time to destroy the image before the death wound should be given to it. She directed him when Knockrome was reached to make for the first light seen there.

The baillie and his man started off in all haste. As they neared Knockrome, the baillie's legs began to fail him, and at last he became so weak that his man got him on his back and carried him. Still the baillie's weakness increased, so much that the man saw, though they were now very near Knockrome houses, he would have to leave his master and get forward quickly.

So saying, 'This will do no good.' (*Cha dèan seo feum*) and setting him down on a great flat topped boulder behind the Knockrome houses, he got permission to leave him there and go on by himself. Making for the first light he saw, and peeping in, he saw the pins being stuck into the clay doll, and let out a shout.

At the heart of the story there are various versions of what the man shouted; at least three were known to Robertson. The author's favourite is: 'The bitch's house is on fire' (*Taigh na galla, taigh ri theine.*). Until recently local people were still able to identify the house in Knockrome which used to be called 'the bitch's house'.

The women within rushed out at this alarm being given to see where the fire was, and the man slipped into the house and trampled the 'corp creadha' into powder. When he returned to the big stone the baillie had recovered his strength and was as well as ever.

The baillie's man who did him this service was great-grandfather of John Shaw of Caigenhouse, and the Campbells of Jura to this day show favour to the descendants of the man who thus saved their ancestor's life. The name of the women practising with the corp creadha was MacGille- riabhaich or, as that sept now call themselves, Darroch.

Here are the other versions that Robertson recorded of what was shouted to distract the women:

'A house on fire, a house on fire, belonging to the old woman of Cnoc Crom.'
'*Taigh ri theine, taigh ri theine air a' chaillich an Cnoc Crom.*'

In the Gaelic, '*taigh na galla*' can be a curse, roughly equivalent to 'to blazes with'.

So, 'To blazes with the old woman, there is a house on fire in Cnoc Crom.'
'*Taigh na galla do'n chaillich taigh ri theine an Cnoc Crom.*'

In another version of the story it is a rascally and unpopular factor who is the victim.

13. Una's Elopement (DB)

It was in Kenuachdrach in the north end of Jura that peace was made between the eloping daughter of Donald of Islay and her pursuing and irate parent. Dugald of Craignish, son of Gillespic of Craignish, was sent by his father to be nursed and educated in the home of the Tossach Bane Maceachairn of Nether Craignish. The Maceachairns were at this time a numerous and strong clan about the western coast of Argyll, and had their prestige augmented by this new relationship of co-altship, or fostership, with the knights of the Lochawe family. On coming of age, Dugald of Craignish married Una, daughter of Donald of Islay, from whom the Macdonalds of Islay and Kintyre were afterwards descended. The marriage was brought about chiefly by the good offices and skill of the Tossach Bane.

The Tossach had, by his own personal merits, got himself much in favour with Donald, who was chieftain of Islay, and on account of frequent visits was considered no stranger to the family. In consequence of this he found opportunity of speaking to Una on behalf of his 'dalt' or 'foster-son', whom she had frequently seen and admired. Dugald, however, being a younger son, was not likely to be considered a suitable match by the young lady's father, so the Tossach Bane planned a clever strategy in order to win for Dugald the lady Una as his bride.

Having obtained the young lady's consent to his plan, and also the agreement of her stepmother, he sailed to Dunnyveg with his own galley and, having secured his prize, set out in the beginning of a long winter night for Craignish. The sympathetic stepmother delayed the supper as long as possible and until she was satisfied that the galley was well on its way. Supper was finally got ready and when the family sat down the young lady was immediately missed, as was also the Tossach Bane and, on enquiry being made, the flight was discovered. Orders were immediately issued that a strong band of men be ready next morning to follow in pursuit, rescue his daughter and revenge the affront.

Wild weather prevented a sea voyage, so Donald led his men by land through Jura, accompanied by his wife. On the evening of the second day they pitched camp at Kenuachdrach opposite the Craignish shore.

Tossach Maceachairn and his party, who happened to be encamped on the Craignish shore opposite Kenuachdrach, saw the camp fires of the Islay party and, in order to give the impression of having a great retinue of followers, caused to be set going as many fires as they could find fuel for, and kept the fires going all night, it being usual in these days to assess the number of an enemy by the number of his camp fires after dark.

Donald of Islay's lady by this time had won to her side some of the chiefs and leaders of the party and, with a woman's wit, rushed in and alarmed her lord telling him of the mighty number of the host on the other side. She advised him that it would be unwise to attack so large a body, saying that whosoever could command to his side so great a body must be a person worthy of any great man's daughter. She also advised the sending across of an ambassador with a view to making terms. The leaders seconded her proposal, to which Macdonald agreed, and messengers were dispatched across the water.

These were immediately received with welcome and friendship by Dugald and Maceachairn, and no less so by the lady Una herself. On delivering their message they were informed that the man who sought Una of Islay as his bride was Dugald, brother to the Knight of Lochawe, and, if their master was willing to come to an amicable agreement, and have the marriage solemnised in a peaceable way, that the two parties should meet midway on the island of Reis-an-t'sruth. This was agreed to and all the differences adjusted, the Tossach Bane Maceachairn obliging himself that, failing children of his own he would bequeath the estate to his foster-son after his death. (From *The Manuscript History of Craignish.*)

14. The Terrible Woman of Dainskeir (DB)

In the valley of the Dainskeir Burn is to be seen the grave of the woman who bore the name 'the big old woman of Dainskeir' (*Cailleach mhòr Dhainnsgeir*). She is reputed to have been named Maclean and to have hailed from Mull. She was a terror to all who passed by and, when it was discovered that she had killed her own child, there was only one thing to be done in those days and that was to put her to death. At last a man named Buie undertook to face up to her, but she, knowing that he was determind to kill her, promised him, for she had the gift of prophecy as well as more evil gifts, that there would be a Buie as forrester on Beinn an Oir for all time if he would save her life. Buie, however, determined to rid the land of her terror and he put her to death.

Another version is in Campbell's *Popular Tales of the West Highlands*, as follows. The Cailleach would not let the Islay post pass through Jura and always killed the man as he crossed the ferry. At last a man called Buie, who lived at Largiebreac, the residence of the Cailleach, was promised the neighbouring farm if he would kill her. Buie hesitated, but his eldest son went forth to tackle her. They wrestled and the Cailleach brought the youth to his knees.

'Thou art in extremity, a'Mhic Mheadh Bhuie,' she said, 'and a pity it is so'.

'My grandmother, who is on the hinder side of Alba, is here,' he replied, putting his hand on his dirk, 'and will come to help me if I be.'

They grappled once more, and again she brought him down uttering the same words. Young Buie managed to draw his dirk and stabbed her to the heart. The promised farm was duly handed over and is said to have been held by the family for centuries.

15. Murder at Strone (DB)

In the time of the second Baillie Campbell of Jura there lived near Strone a man of the name of Olafson (MacOlonfhaidh), who was a thief. The man who farmed Strone at the time was named MacKellar (MacEalair) and he was in the habit of grazing his cattle on the hill-ground near Strone. On one misty day, MacOlonfhaidh drove a farrow cow belonging to MacKellar into a deep ravine and there he killed the cow. The farmer's daughter had been sent to bring home the cattle and, missing the farrow cow, continued to search for her. She happened to pass the ravine into which the thief had driven the cow and, looking down, saw what had taken place. MacOlonfhaidh had just killed the cow and opened her, and having done so he exclaimed aloud, 'May God bless this cow, inside and out.' The girl, overhearing him, called out, 'God will not bless you, you wicked thief!' and so saying fled. MacOlonfhaidh, knowing that the girl would give him away, pursued her and, overtaking her, killed her and, dragging her body through the bushes, concealed, the body by burying it in a cairn of stones. Her mother, having heard the girl's despairing cries and realising that her daugher must be in great danger, sent a search party out to find her dead or alive. MacOlonfhaidh joined himself to those who searched and, after some time, the searchers found some strands of a woman's fair hair on the bushes and feared the worst. The body was then found, hidden in a cairn. It was MacOlonfhaidh himself who found the body.

The girl's body was then carried to where Baillie Campbell was, and a council held on the matter. It was believed at that time that, if a guilty party were to lay his hand upon the body of his victim, blood would flow forth from him. Suspicion was thrown first upon a member of a family of Paterson (MacPhaidir), who lived nearby, but all present were convinced that he was not the person who committed the crime. Moreover, the man's family declared that no member of the family would be permitted to suffer death without the death of the whole. Also each one of them submitted to the test but no one gushed blood. MacOlonfhaid was then made to come nigh to the corpse and made to lay his hand upon it. A feeling of great guilt overcame him, and his face grew red as blood. 'The guilt of blood is upon his face,' declared Baillie Campbell. 'Confess thy crime,' said he, addressing the man, 'and if there be any clemency it can only be through thine own confession.' MacOlonfhaidh then admitted his guilt and confessed to the crime. He was sentenced to death and hanged. This was the last time that a person was put to death by hanging in Jura.

16. Press Gang (PY)

We pored over the old map together, looking at the names around Knocknafeolaman. Dan stabbed out with a finger: 'the shoulder' (*an slinnean*), that's where the press gang took John Campbell of Keils. Aye, they manacled his wrists and his ankles, and they took him off down to the ferry in a horse and cart. And he didn't come back to Jura for twenty-two years, and when he came home his beard was down around his waist and his own mother didn't know him. And he went and took a drink out of the Keils burn with the stoup, and it was when he was doing that that she knew her son. And he was supposed to have been at the Battle of the Nile with Nelson. At any rate it was twenty-one years they served at that time.

17. Tragedy at the Corran River (PY)

A young man living in Corran House was courting a lass from Knockrome, and one night they went off to a dance down at Craighouse. When their daughter didn't come home, and it was very late on a rainy night, her family roused Knockrome and after a search, they went down to Corran House. They hammered on the door, but the folk were not for opening up until they threatened to break the door down. The boy was in bed, and had to be knocked up to come and give an explanation.

Confronted with the family he said that he had brought the girl back from the dance behind him on his pony. As they were crossing the ford, they found the river in spate from all the rain, and the girl got swept off the pony into the water, and was lost to sight. The boy claimed to have panicked, and gone home, tied up his horse and gone to bed without a word to anyone.

They searched down the banks of the Corran and they found the girl's body on the sand at the mouth of the river. She had not been dead long, for her body was still warm.

There was some confusion then about the matter, for folk at the dance claimed to have been witnesses to a quarrel between the young couple. Although it was finally decided in the community that the girl's death had been an accident, the feeling against the people in Corran House was so strong that they were forced to leave the island. They were called McPhee, although the name of the girl's family seems to have been forgotten.

Several Knockrome folk were reluctant to tell this story. There seems to have been some sense of guilt that the reaction which drove the Corran House folk off the island had been less than completely just.

The best account came from a Keils informant who remembered a night when his father was angered by the idea of his sisters going off to a dance in wild weather, and had warned them that they would end up like the poor girl drowned in the Corran River.

18. The Rev. McCuaig (RF) (PY)

There were frequently things needing to be done to repair the manse and this was the responsibility of the Campbells of Jura. Now on this occasion Mrs McCuaig undertook to write the letter requesting that some work be done to improve the house. It was Miss Belle Campbell herself who arrived at the manse to discuss the matter with the minister's wife. Before she left she had been so persuasive that she talked Mrs McCuaig round and they agreed that the work wouldn't be done at that time.

Now Mrs McCuaig had been a Macdonald before her marriage and, when Mr McCuaig came home and heard of the discussion, he laughed, and said to his wife, 'Well, I never knew the Macdonalds and the Campbells could be so friendly till today!'

So Mrs McCuaig sat down right away and wrote Miss Campbell a strong letter, insisting that the work be carried out at once.

Mr McCuaig always had the old practice of reading the Banns on three successive Sundays. Now there was a man and woman in the place, and we had better not name them even yet – and they had been courting for years and years. Well, they finally decided that they had better get married, and Mr McCuaig had been reading the Banns for two weeks. On the last occasion he made it very clear in his reading that this was the very last opportunity anyone had to object. Now Sandy Lindsay of Caigenhouse was in the congregation, and he got to his feet and said: 'Devil an objection, Minister, they should have been married long ago!'

Mr McCuaig used to rent the flat island, Pladda, from the Laird, for a bit of extra grazing, and he would put his milk cows on it for the summer. Well, this day, one of his elders, a Darroch it was, was ferrying the minister to and fro from Pladda with his bull. The minister's job was to sit in the stern of the boat and hold the head rope on the bull and keep the beast's head above the water while it made the crossing. Well, on the way back, a discussion arose on a point of theology and, between the rowing and the pipe smoking and the argument, the minister forgot all about the bull and, when they arrived at the manse bay, the poor beast had drowned.

The cook in the manse in these days was Kate Clark (Katie Chleirach) from Feolin Farm. (Plate 20) There had been a wet spell, and then came a fine day, and the minister called all hands to get out and bring in the hay.

'I cannot come,' said Kate, 'I have the bannocks to make!'

And Mr McCuaig raised his eyes and said, 'The heavens may fall, and the end of the world may come, but Kate Chleirach will still be making her bannocks in Jura Manse.'

The said Kate Chleirach was short and stout and homely of appearance, and Angus Buie had been away from the island for some time and, on his return, met Kate on the road.

'My,' he said, 'You must be the woman they're telling me is the bonniest woman on the whole of Jura.'

'Yes,' she said, 'and you'll be the man they're telling me is the biggest liar.'

When Mr McCuaig arrived to be the minister it was an elder called Keith who introduced the other two members of the Kirk Session and himself. His introduction was a thumbnail sketch of each in the Gaelic. His actual words seem to have been: *Tha Buie, duine gun math, gun chron.* And *'Tha Galbhraith, duine le teanga leam leat.'*

The phrases he used still produce smiles today, for they were fairly unkind. The first meant: 'This is Buie, a man without good, without harm.' The second translates as: 'He'll never do you a bad turn, but he won't go out of his way to do you a good one.' To Jura people in the past, this seemed to ring true about some Buies.

The second man was an incomer, Galbraith, who was a lighthousekeeper on Skervuile Rock and an elder of the kirk.

He was introduced: 'This is Galbraith, a man whose tongue agrees with me and with you at the same time.'

Keith finished the introductions with his own character: *''S mise MacCithich, duine a bheir a bheachd ge b'e chòrdas e riut no nach còrd.'* ('I myself am a Keith and I will give you my opinion whether you like it or not.') Indeed, Keiths of later generations were still proud of their reputation for straight speaking.

19. The White Horse of Jura (DB)

One of the most fascinating of the Jura stories is the one which concerns the Campbells of Jura and the White Horse. A certain Campbell many many years ago found occasion to evict an old woman who lived on a part of his estate which he wished to use for some other purpose, probably to stock it with either cattle or deer. The old woman's family had lived on that spot for numberless generations before ever there was a Campbell in Jura and she naturally fiercely resented being evicted from the land.

The day will come,' she said, 'and it is not far distant, when there will not be a proud Campbell left in Jura. When that day comes, the last of the Campbells will be one-eyed, and despite all that the Campbells now possess, he will leave the island, and all that he will take away with him when he departs will be carried to the ship in a cart drawn by a white horse.

The old woman's prophecy was widely known among the people of Jura. In the course of the years the Campbells disposed of parts of their estate. First they sold Kenuachdrach, then Tarbert and later they sold Lergie Forest and Inver with Knockbreac. But they still retained Jura House and the estate of Ardfin; they were still the Campbells of Jura and the old prophecy was half forgotten. Some years ago, however, new horses were required at Ardfin Farm and a horse dealer on the mainland was asked to supply them. They duly arrived and were found to be greys and on another pretext they were returned with a request that another two be sent. The second pair arrived and as fortune would have it they also were grey in colour, but this time, despite the ancient prophecy and the fact that they were of that colour they were retained.

It also happened that the Lady of Jura had an English maid who at times visited some of the Jura homes and who, on hearing of the prophecy, related it to her mistress who laughed and considered it very amusing. She later told her husband what her maid had heard. He, however, did not think it at all amusing. He was the last of the Campbells of Jura, and was without the sight of one eye which he lost before the First World War. It is possible, too, that he had estate matters on his mind, for he was yearly losing much money on the estate.

In 1938, and shortly after the above incident, a remarkable thing happened, namely, that he sold the estate to Mr W. Riley-Smith, of Tadcaster, Yorkshire, who took over not only the estate and Jura House, but also much of its valuable and historic furnishings. The family belongings, which Mr Campbell removed on his departure from Jura, were conveyed to Craighouse Pier in a cart which was drawn by a grey horse, now turning white. The white horse was still alive in Jura while this narrative was being written.

20. A Helpful Spirit (RF)

There was a man at Airidh an t-Sratha who had a haystack to make. Airidh an t-Sratha was a summer shieling on the west coast between Loch Tarbert and Inver.

Waking early in the morning, he saw that the day was going to be a good one, so he said to his wife, 'Rise up and help me, and we will make the stack.'

He put on his clothes and went out. She made her appearance bye and bye, and they worked together until the haystack was finished. The man sent his wife back into the house, saying: 'I will be putting the finishing touches to the haystack, as befits the man of the house.'

When he was satisfied he went inside to see if there was some food ready and, to his great astonishment, he found his wife in bed, apparently waking up out of a deep sleep.

'What possessed you to go back to bed so quickly?' he said.

'I have not yet been out of bed,' she replied.

'Were you not out with me building the stack?' he asked.

'How could I be making the stack when I've been sound asleep.'

'Then who has been helping me all morning whom I took to be yourself?'

To which question of course there was no good answer.

21. Hugh of the Little Head (RF)

A headless apparition, known by the name of 'Hugh of the Little Head' (*Eòghan a' chinn Bhig'*), haunts one of the two septs of Macleans in Jura. The appearance of the spectre betokens that some evil is about to befall some member of that sept. Hardly any, if any, of that sept, whether man or woman, will go out of doors alone after nightfall.

It is understood that he has a 'little head' because half of it was hacked away in a battle.

22. The Rider at the Door (RF)

Small Isles Bay used to be much frequented by the smacks and schooners which carried the traffic of the West Highlands before the steamboats came, and Craighouse Inn did a thriving trade. The household used to be kept up late working on Saturday nights, so that they were guilty of the sin of encroaching upon the Sabbath Day. One Saturday night something happened which made them give up this evil practice, and a man who was staying overnight in the inn witnessed the whole event and gave a detailed account. This man, who was in a room upstairs, observed a man on horseback riding backwards and forwards from the bridge on one side of the inn to the bridge on the other side. Each time he passed the back door, which faced towards the bay, the horse struck the door with its heels. A great stone, hollowed out as a mortar for husking barley, was kept behind the door at night to keep it closed. This was the 'knotting stone' (*a' chnotag eòrna.*) (literally 'the barley husking mortar').

So violent were the blows given to the door by the horse that the stone was forced away from the door. The rider did not disappear until the household stopped work, and the strange visitation caused them to be careful never again to work so late on the Saturday night as to encroach upon the Sunday morning.

23. The Evil Eye (PY)

Superstitions relating to the Evil Eye seem to have been widespread in Jura in the past, and have survived to recent times. The Evil Eye is concerned with the welfare of livestock, and a beast afflicted with it is likely to sicken or die.

The author enountered these beliefs in a most striking manner when minister of Jura in the early 1970s, and tells his experiences in the first person.

A crofter of my acquaintance contacted me to ask if I had heard that his neighbour had a Highland cow which had just given birth to twin calves. This being quite an unusual event in the community, he was just wondering if I would be interested in seeing the beasts.

I expressed enthusiasm and presented myself at the township later that morning. My informant conducted me into the nearby byre where the mother cow and the calves were, and there also was the proud crofter himself.

New-born Highland calves are most attractive creatures, and the fact that there were the two of them increased my excitement. I said how fine they appeared to be, probably not once, but a number of times, and also gave it as my opinion that the mother cow was as fine an animal as I had seen.

I heard a slight clearing of the throat, and looked up to see the friend who had introduced me, standing looking at me with a face like thunder. He made a slight gesture of his head, which indicated that we should at once go outside, and when we were in the open air together he turned on me.

'Minister! Minister! What on earth do you think you are doing, man?'

I protested, 'I'm sorry. What have I done? I haven't done anything!'

'We never praise a man's beasts like you were doing in there, did you not see you were making him most anxious. We never praise a man's stock like that, it's a sure way for them to get the Evil Eye.'

'But what should I have said?' I asked in considerable confusion.

'Och! "They're fine enough beasts." would have been more than sufficient.'

On long reflection after the event I found myself thinking that there was a parallel with folk who become anxious if we seem to be 'tempting providence' in our speech. The person who, on hearing someone say they've been driving for many years without an accident, feels obliged to say, 'Touch wood, touch wood!'

There was a sequel. A few days later I was visiting a remote croft house, inhabited by an elderly bachelor and his unmarried sister. I put the question to him: 'Now you're a man of the Kirk. Would you be worried if I went into your byre and saw one of your beasts and began to heap praise on it, that it would get the Evil Eye.'

'Oh, Minister, you're speaking to the wrong one of us. I'll get the expert through.' So saying, he called his sister from the kitchen. 'Tell her what you've been telling me, and ask her your question.'

I said exactly the same thing to the lady, ending with; 'Would you be worried it would get the Evil Eye.'

She looked hard straight at me and said, 'Not a bit, Minister, you don't have it!' and went back to the kitchen.

The second half of the story left me as confused as the incident itself, but I began to ask around and collect some other strands to the story. Although in these enlightened days very few people would admit to actually believing in the matter, they were very willing to speak about how important it was in the past.

Although all animals could be affected, cattle seem most commonly to have been the victims. Milk cows were particularly susceptible, and could become sterile, or lose their calves, or lose their milk, or have it altered so that it was no use for butter or cheese.

It seems to have been the belief that the person with the Evil Eye had no control over it and had no intention to do any harm to the beast or its owner. It could be well known that someone had it.

For example, there was a seaman who often went to visit an old couple on the west coast. Someone took the old man aside and said, 'I wouldn't show any beast of mine to that man!'

'Oh, why is that?'

'Oh! He is well known for possessing the Evil Eye.'

Anyway the next day the old man went into the byre and the cow was lying there dead.

It was also believed that a man could harm his own livestock.

'There was a man in Jura. He was manager on a home farm for one of the lairds, and then he had farm of his own. They said he could not praise one of his own beasts or the animal would be dead the next day.'

Another informant recalled, 'There were a couple of two-year-olds we had ourselves. Well, a man came by and began to praise them. Well, they didn't die, but they lost their calves from the Evil Eye. The man who came by wasn't even a drover, he was just a visitor who came for a walk this way in spring, and the cows were in just before calving time. He went to the byre and saw them, and he praised them, and praised them. And they lost their calves.'

'One of the drovers was famous for it. If he was keen on an animal, you would do better to just let him have it, for if you didn't it would never do much afterwards.'

Since the problem seems to have been widespread, it seemed important to find out about any possible remedy.

The most reliable cure appears to have been 'water over silver'. The beast afflicted with the Evil Eye was given a pail of water which had a silver coin immersed in it, and began to improve at once.

People who could provide a cure for such curses as the Evil Eye were said to have the 'Knowledge of Rebuking' (*Eòlas a' Chronachaidh'*). Such a person could apply the cure and was often given the silver coin to keep, not as a payment, but to put the seal on the cure.

Another belief which seems to have been widespread was that if any person praised a beast, the owner of the beast should praise it even more, and thus counteract the original praise by surpassing it. One informant said that was very common on Jura.

24. Skulls (RF)

There seem to be many superstitions about skulls and bones in Jura's past. There was a famous skull in Glengarrisdale until the mid-1970s, about which there were many stories. The skull and associated bones were reputed to belong to a man who was killed in a clan battle.

This skull was described in detail by a Mr Tom Speedy, who wrote notes on his visit to the place for the *Oban Times* in May 1907, when his guide was Angus MacKechnie of Glengarrisdale. The author has a photograph of this man actually posing for the camera while holding the skull in his hand. The author himself visited the place in 1971 and saw the skull in its place, but it finally disappeared around 1976, with no explanation.

Robertson fada records these comments:

> The Glengarrisdale skull always lies in the same spot under a shelf of rock, and it is alleged, wherever it may be removed to, it will be found to have been returned by some unknown agency to the accustomed 'resting place' by the following morning.

A farmer by the name of McCormick of Crinan took the skull away, and went with it, or sent it, to Edinburgh, but brought it back, or sent it back subsequently.

John Mackay of Tarbert, who gave these particulars, when staying a night with Angus MacKechnie, hid the skull in order to test the story, and sure enough, found it in its usual place the following morning. He had watched Angus MacKechnie's movements as effectively as he could during the interval and, but for finding the skull back in its own place, would have thought it impossible that he could have moved the skull unknown to him.

There was a married couple at Tarbert whose children were all dying in infancy from the 'sickness of a week' (*Anshocair na seachduin* or '*Tinneas na seachduin*). This was an ailment which infants took when they were about eight days old, and of which they died. An ailment of the same kind was found in St Kilda about twenty-five years ago, and in Arran in the first half of the nineteenth century.

A remedy for this condition was recommended to the family at Tarbert. The skull in Uamh Maol an t-Sornaich was to be fetched after sunset. Gruel was to be made in it and given to the child, and the skull was to be restored to its place in the cave before sunrise. Another said that the skull had to be taken after Rudha Mhail lighthouse was lighted and restored before the light was extinguished the next morning. This was done and the child lived.

25. Stories about Adders (RF)

If a person handles an adder without knowing that it is an adder, it will not hurt him. A visitor to Jura on one occasion found an adder, but thought it was an eel and put it in his pocket and took it home, without its making any attempt to injure him.

A Colonsay man, arriving at the east side of Jura, told that, while crossing the island from the side next to Colonsay, he had seen an adder:

'And it kept hissing.' (*Agus bha i a' srathail, a' srathail.*)

'And did you kill it?' (*An do marbh thu i?*)

'No, but I gave it a good threatening with my stick.' (*Cha do mharbh ach mhaoidh mi am bata oirre gu math.*)

26. 'Who's Killing the Stirk?' (RF)

Malcolm Macdougall, when a young man, worked one winter at sheep drains at Ardmenish, and used to go with some of his fellow workmen to ceilidh at Knockrome. One night they were at a house where the entrance was through the byre. When they rose to leave, his two companions, who were quite familiar with the house, went out quickly and, intentionally no doubt, left him to find his way out as best he could. Flurried by their desertion and his unfamiliarity with his surroundings, he missed the right way through the byre and fell headlong over a stirk.

The stirk began to bellow and the housewife fell a raging and crying out: 'Who's killing the stirk?' (*Cò a tha a' marbhadh a' ghamhainn?*)

Hearing also the rattling of the tongs, he made the utmost haste to get outside, but had not gone two steps when he collided with the belly of a cow and increased the uproar. However, he made his escape at last, somehow, without further misadventure, and without having felt the weight of the tongs.

27. The Knockrome Herd (RF)

The herd at Knockrome fell out with his employers, who were in fact the whole community of Knockrome. And wanting, or at all events, professing to want, to fight them, he invited them to come on.

'Come on a pair of you.' (*Thigeadh caigeann agaibh.*)

Come on two pair.' (*Thigeadh dà chaigeann.*)

'Come on the whole lot of you.' (*Thigibh uile còmhla.*)

28. Welding at the Smithy (PY)

Welding jobs were always tricky, and it was usual for the smith to enlist the help of the customer. It was necessary to use the great big hammer for the back of the weld and the small hammer to beat the weld out at the same time. One day there was a crofter in working with the smith, and he was wielding the big hammer where the smith directed, when his wife looked in through the smiddy door and saw them. Later she could be heard complaining to a friend: 'That smith's no use at all. He's got my poor man struggling away with a great enormous hammer in there, and he's just playing himself with the wee one!'

29. Harvest Traditions (PY)

The harvest season more than any other abounded in traditions and traditional methods, although few are preserved to the present day.

The first tenant to complete the reaping tied the last sheaf to be cut by him with a coloured ribbon and kept it on display in the kitchen corner until the following spring. This sheaf was called 'The Maiden' (*a' mhaighdean*) and was given to the horses on the first day of the spring ploughing. The very last sheaf to be cut in the whole village was called the 'Old Woman' (*a' chailleach*). To own the maiden was looked on as an honour, and to be in possession of the old woman was considered a disgrace.

The first family to complete the harvest joined in with their neighbours, and so on, until everyone was finished. When they finished, each family celebrated 'harvest home' (*deireadh-buana*). This was an informal gathering with dancing, drinking, singing and general chatting about the favourability of the year's harvest. For the celebrations each family invited everyone who had helped them with the harvest.

Two old next-door neighbours from Ardfernal were reputed not to have been on speaking terms except at harvest home. The last one was held about 1920.

When the corn stacks were made, the base of each one was laid out and covered with ragwort (*baltan buidhe*) to protect the corn from rats. The sheaves were then laid down, and as each layer was put in place, rough salt was sprinkled over it before the next layer was laid.

30. The Proper Fare (PY)

From a Port Askaig informant: 'There was a man on Jura called James McKechnie; he was living at Corran House; and this was at the time when the fare to get rowed across the Sound to Port Askaig was one shilling. This man was very loth to part with the fare, and he had the habit of being ready to jump off the boat the minute she touched the land, and he would throw the fare over his shoulder into the bottom of the boat; and it would always be a sixpence, not the proper fare at all; and from this they called him *Sheumais an t'sgillin* (James of the Shilling).

Well, the two ferrymen on the Jura side were Sutherlands and they were mild mannnered men who didn't like any unpleasantness – but the third man from the Islay side was very annoyed about the business.

'When next he wants to cross over,' he said, 'you let me have the ferrying of him.'

So, the next time James was crossing, he had the Islay ferryman and he rowed half-way across. When he was about the middle of the Sound, he shipped one oar and he raised the other one high over his head with both hands. 'Pay now!' he shouted. (*Pàigh a-nis!*)

So on that journey Sheumais an t'sgillin paid in full.

31. The Exciseman at the Bridge (PY)

Sandy Buie was always proud to tell this story of his grandfather.

He was a great hand at the distilling and made fine whisky. The inn was in sore need of a supply so this night my grandfather and his young lad set off for the inn with the pony and two kegs of whisky in the panniers on its back. The exciseman's house was over the bridge, on the way to the inn, and he was waiting for them. He grappled with the old man and they rolled together on the ground. My grandfather shouted to the lad, 'Make for the hill.'

My grandfather got the better of the struggle and made off into the darkness but, in the fight, in the dark, the exciseman had felt grandfather's bald head. He shouted after him, 'I'll know you! I'll know you! I'll know you at the church!'

The next Sunday the exciseman stood at the kirk door and watched every man on the island into his seat. He was not to know that, on a visit to Glasgow, my grandfather had given in to a moment of vanity and had purchased a wig, which he never wore.

He wore it that Sunday though and completely foiled the exciseman.

32. A Straight Answer (PY)

In 1920 the second Lord Astor purchased the Tarbert Estate. Lord Astor was very jealous of his land. He was stalking this day with a keeper called Darroch, who was a man of few words. The Lord and the keeper were high up on the moor when His Lordship looked down and saw a pleasure yacht moored in the sea loch, Loch Tarbert.

His Lordship was annoyed at the boat being there and said to his keeper.'What the devil's that boat doing in my water, Darroch?'

Darroch surveyed the scene, and replied with civility, 'No harm, My Lord.'

For which fine answer it is believed that he lost his post and left the island.

33. Saying in the Cemetery (PY)

Dan Macdougall approached the author in the cemetery after the conclusion of the burial of a very aged member of the community and, with some emotion, uttered a short sentence in Gaelic. The words were not immediately understood but it was clear that the saying had great importance for him. When asked where he had heard it, he said that it had been said to him when he was at a funeral in the same graveyard when he was only a child. On that occasion also the person who had died had been nearly a hundred years old.

At a suitable time a little later still the saying was repeated again. It was:

'*Ged's fada an dàil, thig an cuireadh.*' which means: 'Though long be the wait, still comes the invitation.'

34. Three Gaelic Sayings from Jura (RF)

'Much bellowing, little rutting.' (*Mòran bùiridh's beagan dàmhair.*) As of stags, a lot of noise for nothing.

Said by a man sitting on the raised beach and feeling threatened by some animal: 'Here I am sitting on top of Maol an t'Sornaidh, and I can't even find a pebble.' (*Mi am shuidh' air muin clach Mhaol an t-Sòrnaidh, 's mi gun dòirneag.*)

'Christmas Day, New Year and Easter. If they all came on the same day I would get my fill.' (*Là Nollaig, Collain agus Càisg. Nan robh sin air aon là gheibhinn-sa mo shàth.*)

35. Some of Katie Darroch's Sayings (PY)

Katie Darroch used to repeat many of the local sayings to the author until I could get them clear:

> 'I married a slovenly girl for her property.
> The property's all gone, but she's still here.'

> (*Phòs mi luid airson a cuid,*
> *Dh'fhalb a cuid, ach dh'fhan an luid.*)

This was an important saying about the lucky things to see early in the New Year.

> 'I saw a foal with its backside to me
> And a snail on a bare slab,
> And I heard the cuckoo without having taken a morsel of bread.
> And I knew the year would be sorrowful for me.'

> (*Chunnaic mi searrach 'sa chuile rium,*
> *Is seilcheag air leac lom,*
> *Cuthag gun mirium bhreim,*
> *Dh'aithnith mi nach soirbhicheadh a' bhliadhna rium.*)

And this was a favourite saying:

> 'There are three things that have no flavour,
> Egg without salt,
> Tea without sugar,
> And a kiss without whiskers.'

> ('*Tha trì rudan gun blas,*
> *Ugh gun salann,*
> *Ti gun siùcar,*
> *Agus pòg gun fheusagan.*')

Katie said she had heard an old woman, who had just come back from a wedding in Islay, who said: 'I would rather be at one funeral in Jura than at two weddings in Islay.' (*B'àill leamsa bhith aig aon tòrragh an Diùra na bhith aig dà bhanais an Ile.*)

Katie was proud of her family connection with 'Dunacha Sha', Duncan Shaw of Ardfernal, who corresponded so usefully with his emigrant relatives. She was pleased to be able to give a translation of the message which he sent to his Uncle Neil in North Carolina to explain why he wasn't considering emigrating himself.

'I guess I never will marry,
I will pay no attention to love-making,
I prefer my cat and my dog,
And I am happy as a bachelor.'

('*A chaoidh cha phòs mi, tha mi'n dùil,
Cha tog mi sùil ri leannanachd,
B'annsa leamsa mo chat's mo chù,
'S gur sunndach mi' s mi 'm bhaidsealair.'*)

(Plate 17)

36. Stories of Donald Black (PY)

Donald Black died before I took up my position in Jura, but I seemed for ever to be hearing his name in connection with his witty sayings. He had lived as a crofter in Keils, and was renowned for his quick responses to all kinds of situations. Various people said that his sayings should be written down but, as far as I know, they never have been. There must have been many, and I now remember only a few, and these without the Gaelic, but I feel that a collection of Jura stories would not be complete without at least a few Donald Black stories.

A young tradesman was working for Donald on his house. He came out and said, 'Mr Black, could I borrow your bicycle to go down to the village for some cigarettes?'
'By all means,' replied Donald.
'Where is it, Mr Black?'
'It's over there!'
The man walked over to Donald's bike, which was leaning against the wall. He would not have known that Donald Black's bike was famous all over the island. He pulled it up and looked at it somewhat doubtfully.
'Does this bike go, Mr Black?'
'Aye. If you pedal it!'

One night the shopkeeper Lamont had shut up shop and gone to bed. A hammering on the shop door roused him, and he put on his dressing gown and went down to see who it was. When he unbolted and opened the shop door he found Donald Black.
'What on earth are you wanting here at this hour?' he said.
'Paraffin,' said Donald.

510 Tales of Jura

'But man, it's night time!' shouted the shopkeeper.
'It's at night that you need it.' ('*S ann air an oidhche a tha feum agad àir.*)

The famous tradesman MacSporran had been working on Donald's roof with his apprentice for some days. In due course he finished.
'That's me done, Mr Black,' he said.
'You'll be back with my account?'
'I'll be back next week, Mr Black.'
The following week MacSporran presented his account. Donald Black examined it for so long that Mr MacSporran got anxious.
'Is everything in order, Mr Black? It's all there – my time, the lad's time.'
'Oh, I dare say it is quite in order,' said Donald, 'but I see from this that it would be more profitable for me to be working for you, than to have you working for me.'

A visitor to the island was in the bar and turned to Donald, who was standing there, and asked him what he did for a living.
'I'm a crofter,' said Donald.
'Oh, that's a job anyone could do,' said the visitor.
'Indeed?' said Donald.
'Oh yes, there's not a single job on a croft that I can't do!'
'Indeed?' said Donald, 'Can you lay an egg?'

On one occasion Donald was in Oban for the cattle sales with a number of other men from Jura. They were all together in a local public house and Donald was entertaining those around with a continual stream of stories.
The young men in the bar who didn't know Donald became more and more amazed. Finally one young fellow approached and asked Donald, 'And where do you come from, sir?'
Donald replied, 'Mars.'

37. The McCraine Sisters (PY)
There was a time when there were plenty of McCraines living in Jura, but they have all left or died out.
A well-known family lived in Caigenhouse. The father, Donald, was famous for his feats of strength. He was involved in the building of the present road. The men found a mighty boulder in the path of the road some little way before Crackaig, and no amount of effort would move it. They all went off for some food and, when they came back, they found that Donald Mor had moved it out of the way by himself. It still lies where he put it and can be seen by the roadside.
The last of the family were two unmarried daughters called Marion and Mary. They didn't speak to one another, and Marion lived in the kitchen and Mary in the room. They had their own way of doing things and they used to go gathering hazel nuts in the wood above the village – collecting them in a pillowcase.
Marion was given to nodding off in the midst of a conversation and was nicknamed 'Nodan'. She was a very good washer-woman and extremely neat in

her appearances and habits. Mary had somewhat twisted legs and was nicknamed 'Cham', which means 'bandy-legged' in the Gaelic.

The shop was next door to their house, and the sisters of course were regular customers. The shop assistant was also a McCraine, known as Calum Beag ('Wee Malcolm').

Calum Beag had a problem with Cham. He had noticed that, while she was waiting to be served, she would put her hand into the meal tub and bring out a fistful of meal, which she would drop into the pocket of her apron. Calum did not want to make any public fuss with such a worthy old lady, but was determined to put a stop to the matter. After some thought, he got a wee mouse trap and set it in the meal in the tub. There was no more heard of the affair.

Cham and Nodan lived to a good age. Mary died in 1908, aged eighty-five, and Marion lived until 1916 when she was eighty-four.

38. McLever, the Robber (PY)

McLever was a robber who had a treasure. He buried his treasure at the top of Eagle Hill (Cnoc an Iolaire), which looks down over Lergiebreck. The finding of his treasure is an easy matter. You climb to the top of the hill and then fix your eye on Lowlandman's Bay. Now you move around until you can see just enough of the bay to cover a blue bedspread. You dig at that point and there is your treasure. There are some who say it should be a blue pocket handkerchief, and not a bedspread, but they haven't found the treasure either.

McLever was running from his pursuers, when he took the path which runs out into Lowlandman's Bay from the north. He gained ground by making his famous leap, and then swam across the mouth of the bay to land below Ardfernal Hill. He crossed the neck of land and swam again, this time landing at the rocks by Jura Forest.

He crawled into the cave nearby and, exhausted by his efforts and thinking himself safe, he fell asleep. It was there in the cave that his pursuers finally caught up with him and, finding him asleep, slew him.

39. The Birth at Bog Airidh (PY)

There was a croft house at Bog Airidh in the old days. Bog Airidh means the Wet Shieling and it lies above Ardmenish, just beside the modern road. There is a small bridge at NR 561747, and the ruins can still be seen close to the road on the seaward side.

There was a family of Darrochs lived there, and the young woman was going to have a baby. When her time was near she sent to Feolin for the midwife, Granny Darroch. When she heard of it, she would not attend, for she believed that it was not ethical for her to practise on one of her own kin, and she was related to the girl. She decided that it would be more seemly if the doctor in Islay were to attend, so she put in a call for the man. Doctors in those days were no more willing than they are today to make house calls, and he put the matter off for some time. However, in due course, he made the journey. He crossed in the boat while his horse swam behind. At any rate, he reached Bog Airidh, and asked admittance, and the child that had been born opened the door to him!

40

Poetry and Songs

There must have been ballads, songs and poetry in the Gaelic in Jura from early times but, although many stories have survived, most of the minstrels of the past are lost and largely forgotten. Two important individuals survive in the memories of native Diurachs, and these recollections are supported by historical record.

First there is Neil Shaw, who, according to Donald Budge, always referred to himself as Niall Macillesheathanaich and was for many years secretary to An Comunn Gaidhealach. Neil Shaw was immensely proud of his Jura ancestry and must have been bitterly disappointed when he was old enough to know that he had not in fact been born on the island.

A certain amount of his family background can be found in the census and other records. His grandfather and grandmother were John and Mary Shaw who were in Lussagiven in 1851, 1861 and 1871, and across the road in Mulbuie in 1881. They were not in the 1841 census, although John's parents were Neil Shaw and Margaret Darroch, both well-known Jura names.

The censuses show their children as Mary, Isabella and Duncan. It is Duncan who will become the bard's father, and whose story concerns us. In 1861 he was still living at home, aged twenty-four, and was a boatman like his father. In 1868 he married Mary McLean of Gatehouse. She was a daughter of Malcolm McLean and Marion Shaw, who are mentioned in the McLean family history of the twentieth century.

The 1871 census shows Duncan and Mary settled in Lussagiven, although he was then working on the land. Duncan's parents, John and Mary Shaw, living nearby, still had their daughter Isabella living at home, and also three young grandchildren. In the birth register we find Duncan's family. By the date of the census record of 1881, the family had left Jura and were living at Duntrune Private House, close to the Castle of Duntrune. Here, in the parish of Kilmartin, and just north of Crinan, they were still in sight of the north end of Jura, and here Neil was born. T. M. Murchison's obituary on Neil Shaw in the *Perthshire Advertiser* of 21 June 1961 makes it clear that Neil Shaw was 'born a mainlander, close to the old Castle of Duntroon, in the Parish of Kilmartin, in the ancient Kingdom of Dalriada'. He suggests that 'soon thereafter the family moved to Jura', he might well have said 'moved back to Jura'. The family were certainly back in Jura by 1884, for another child, Dougald was born that year. The census of 1891 shows them back in residence in Mulbuie, on the opposite side of the road from Lussagiven, their former home. Neil Shaw was now back in Jura as a baby, and would grow up there. He later spoke with affection of his schoolmaster, Malcolm McNiven, of Ardlussa Primary School. This teacher also appears in the 1891 census and lives in Lussagiven. Although Neil evidently enjoyed his early schooling and learnt to be fluent in both Gaelic and English, he did not persist with further education and, according to Mr Murchison, he left school at the earliest opportunity and went to sea. At some time in his early years, he took instruction in piping and soon became a competent piper. Neil's seafaring days took him to many parts of the world. In trading to the Mediterranean countries, he found himself off the coasts of modern Greece. Within sight of the famed peak of Helicon, the prime mountain of Greek poetry and lore, he wrote one of his earliest Gaelic poems. This poem won his first prize in the Gaelic Mod.

None of the somewhat sparse references we have to him during these early years give evidence of his considerable gifts in the Gaelic language. However, he obviously continued to build on an early talent and enthusiasm for the Gaelic tongue. As early as 1906, this gift was being recognised, and he was elected Bard of the Rothesay Branch of An Comunn Gaidhealeach. In 1911 he applied for a full-time position on the staff of An Comunn Gaidhealeach, and although initially not appointed, two years later, in 1913, at the age of thirty-two, he was made the Permanent Secretary. Neil Shaw was to hold this influential post for forty years. He had a break from the work during the First World War, when he engaged in military service. At the end of the war he returned to his duties and was then sent out on a series of propaganda tours around Scotland. He formed and founded a large number of local branches. In 1934, the year his mother, Mary, died in Jura, Neil formed, in Barra, the first Branch of the Gaelic League of Youth. He retired as Secretary in 1953, but he became President from 1954 to 1956. Neil Shaw was a Member of the Scottish Arts Council. He was awarded a Civil List Pension and was made an OBE. Fine photographs of Neil Shaw have survived, especially with his mother Mary Shaw, who was known on the island as 'The Queen', either from her resemblance to Victoria or from her imperious manner. (Plate 19) Latterly Neil spent an increasing amount of his time on Jura. He died in 1961 at the age of eighty. Among Neil Shaw's poetic output is the song 'Null thar an Aiseig', which has become the most famous song about Jura, and is sung on every occasion that Jura people gather for a ceilidh. Here, as reproduced in the frontispiece of his book, is Donald Budge's version of the song, accompanied by his own skilful and sensitive translation into English:

'Null thar an Aiseig'		'Crossing to Jura'
Fonn: Theid mi null gu tir mo rùin,	*Chorus:*	I shall sail across the Sound,
Theid mi null thar an aiseig,		I shall sail across the ferry,
Theid mi null gu tir mo rùin,		To my native Isle I'm bound,
S'mor mo shunnd a' tilleadh dhachaidh.		Braving wind and wave and skerry.
Theid mi null ann thar a chaoil,		Soon I'll cross to Jura isle
Far a' bheil mo dhaoin a fanachd,		Where my dearest ones are dwelling,
Gheibh mi fàillt bho'm mhàthair chaoin,		Mother waits to welcome me,
'Nuar bu mhaoth mi 's i rinn m'altrum.		Mine's a joy beyond all telling.
Chi mi 'm bàta fo a siuil		Sailing swiftly toward the lea
A tighinn dlùth do na chala,		Strong brown hand upon the tiller,
Chi mi m'athair aig an stiùir,		Now my father's form I see,
Cha bhi cùram orm bho'n chas-shruth.		Wind and tide can hold no terror.

As a' bheinn gun toir mi fiadh,	Flesh of deer will hill provide,
Gheibh mi iasg as an abhainn,	Fresh-run salmon shall the river,
Le mo ghunna mar is miann	Shy grey-hen and mallard wild
Gheibh mi liath-chearc is lacha.	To my gun will fall as ever.
Bidh mo chridhe leum le mùirn,	Calm delight my heart shall warm
'S mòr mo shunnd is chan airsneul,	Light my step to Lussa-given,
Chan 'eil coimeas tir mo rùin	Gaelic speech my ear shall charm,
Ann an dùthaich eil' air thalamh.	Dearest island under Heaven.
Composed by Neil Shaw	*Translation by Donald Budge*

Our second subject, and the man widely known as the 'Jura Bard,' was called Donald MacKechnie, although in Gaelic he called himself Domhnull MacEacharn. He was born in 1836, the first of the ten children of Malcolm McKechnie and Catherine McKechnie who were living in Glengarrisdale in 1881. Donald himself left Jura and went to Edinburgh where he married Elizabeth Sutherland in 1869. They had seven children. He earned his living as a spirits merchant and died in Edinburgh in 1908.

One of Donald's brothers, Neil McKechnie married in 1889 Isabella Shaw, a descendant of many generations of Jura Shaws. Among their family were Calum McKechnie and Uncle Angus of Inverlussa. The McKechnies of the north end who were important personalities during the post-war years on Jura, and who lived until the 1970s and 1980s, were nephews and nieces of the 'Jura Bard'.

A respected encyclopedia gives an entry under 'Gaelic Literature' as follows: 'Gaelic in the Modern World. A sharp decline in technique and content were evident in the nineteenth century. Some excellent writers of prose however were Dr Norman Macleod and Donald Mackechnie.' The *Encyclopaedia Britannica* gives under 'Celtic literature': 'among original prose writers of the nineteenth century was Donald Mackechnie.'

The *Companion to Gaelic Scotland* states:

Domhnall MacEachern lived latterly in Edinburgh as part of the distinguished circle which included Donald Mackinnon, Alexander Carmichael and Sheriff Nicolson. A frequent prize winner at Mods at the turn of the century, his poetry is light, sometimes sentimental, and only a few pieces are remembered ('An Sruthan', 'Am Bothan Beag', 'Bean a' Chotain Ruaidh') He also translated from the Rubváiyát. His prose has worn better, his essays on various animals in particular illustrating his light, humorous touch, his use of incisive and idiomatic language and his unpretentious style; 'Am Fiadh' (The Deer) is the best known of these.

Donald McKechnie's stories and poems were collected together and published under the title *Fear Ciuil* (*The Minstrel*). The collection's longest poem has this title, and the publication not only has the fine photograph of the 'Jura Bard'(Plate 18), but also contains an English translation of the poem. There are forty-eight four-line stanzas in the poem. It is in some ways not unlike 'The Ancient Mariner'. The traveller on a journey stops at an inn and finds there, by the bar, a tall, thin stranger for whom he feels compelled to buy a drink. The man talks of music and its power to unlock the secrets of the heart, and then he begins to play on his harp. While the traveller smokes his pipe, the harpist's music plays and breaks over him with many different sounds. He seems to experience the sea, and the hillsides and moors of his native land. He is transported to the business and bustle of the city, and to the material competition that has claimed his soul. He glimpses a simpler and purer way that he once knew in his own native country and reacts angrily at what the harper has shown him. The minstrel asks him if the storm comes from outside or from within his own heart. The question has no answer, but the encounter leaves him with new insight and strength.

XI

The Twentieth Century

41

Jura and the Gaelic Language

In common with the whole of the Highlands and Islands of Scotland, the language of the people of Jura throughout most of the period dealt with in this book was Gaelic. Indeed, as recently as the latter part of the nineteenth century many people evidently spoke little English, or were at least very uncomfortable with it.

Most of the natives of the island who gave evidence to the Crofters' Commission in 1894 did so in Gaelic with an interpreter. We have already seen the difficulties that excisemen had in pursuing their business while not properly understanding what was being said to them.

Previous chapters have revealed something of the richness of the native tongue, and of its wit and humour. Two men became famous for using their language to great effect in prose and poetry, and earned the title 'Bard', although in the past every community had its story-tellers and singers of songs.

The Rev. Charles Robertson (Robertson Fada) was a considerable Gaelic scholar and, as well as collecting stories wherever he went, he made a considerable number of notes on individual regional dialects. He filled a notebook with what he considered to be the distinctive elements in Jura's Gaelic. The topic is beyond the wit of the present author, but no doubt some modern scholar will investigate and write up the results at some point. Suffice it to say that Jura's Gaelic is quite distinct from that of the neighbouring island of Islay, and it seems likely that Robertson was aware of a difference even between the Gaelic of the north and of the south of Jura itself.

By the early part of the twentieth century Jura's schoolchildren were being discouraged from speaking Gaelic in the playground, and stories abound of punishments meted out for such offences. No doubt the teachers thought they were serving the long-term needs of their pupils by teaching them 'good English', without which they would have difficulty finding worthwhile employment, but one of the consequences was the development of a sense of inferiority and of insecurity about their own tongue.

The author frequently found that, if he was unable to grasp a Gaelic phrase on first hearing and asked for it to be repeated, the speaker would jump to the conclusion that he or she was in error in what they had first said and would attempt to produce the phrase in a different and more acceptable form.

With such real or imaginary pressures it is not surprising that those willing to converse in their native tongue became less plentiful as the century advanced.

By the mid-1970s, only a small group of people on Jura were prepared to help students learn Gaelic. Dan Macdougall, Archie Black and Katie Darroch were perhaps the most generous of these. In 1975, when the author arrived to live on Jura, the number of residents who spoke Gaelic fluently was probably about thirty. Most of these would have been elderly or even aged, although a number of younger members of some of their families, though shy of conversing in Gaelic in public, were evidently speaking it within the family circle.

The author has visited Jura recently, and it is sad to record that virtually all of the members of the Gaelic-speaking network he knew twenty-five years ago have died. It is perhaps fortunate that the School of Scottish Studies at the University of Edinburgh has a good collection of recordings made in the early 1970s by John McLean and others. It is to be hoped that Jura's dialect will be preserved here for posterity even if there are no contemporary residents still speaking it.

42

Place-names of Ardfernal
and Knockrome

At many places in earlier chapters our debt to Malcolm McArthur, presently of Dunfermline, has been made clear. Born into a Jura family with crofting lands in Ardfernal, Calum had a perfect opportunity to become intimately familiar with the two crofting townships of Ardfernal and Knockrome. In 1986 Calum decided to try to reduce to some order the considerable collection of Gaelic names of which he was aware in the two townships and the surrounding country. I was privileged to be allowed to help in finding some kind of suitable format, and the result was a small booklet of sketches made by a long-term Jura holiday-maker at Ardfernal, called Jim Harrison, whose paintings of the area were always much sought after by the folk of the island.

The booklet contained eight such sketches made from various viewpoints around the area in question. Each contained numbers with lines leading to the named feature. These pages are not the place to reproduce these charming and artistic sketches in full, but Sketch Four has been chosen as an example and appears here with its names and its key.

Calum gave a simple rationale for the book. 'In Gaelic, neighbour used place-names to help neighbour. If you were told your missing cattle beast was at a certain place, time and trouble were saved. If these names continue in use it will only be for this reason.' A phonetic version was included for all the Gaelic names. This has been omitted here. No doubt those people seriously concerned will avail themselves of an original copy of the work.

The book contains a remarkable total of 204 place-names. It is earnestly to be hoped that this work will continue to be reproduced from time to time so that those who live and work in the area, as well as those who visit it, will still have the opportunity to learn and use these names after those in whom the oral tradition long reposed have passed away.

The plan in this chapter is to reproduce the names appropriate to Sketch Four here in full, and follow this by printing a selection from the others, intended to show something of the richness and variety of the name in use.

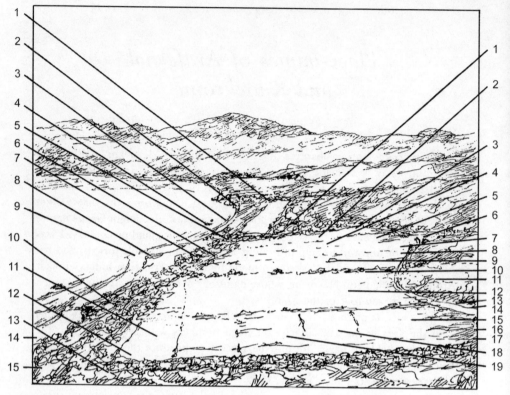

Viewpoint at the South end of Ardfernal Hill looking West

Figure 5. Place-names of Ardfernal and Knockrome – Sketch four.

Left

1 *Corran River* River of the Sickle point
2 *Corran House* Former Change House or Inn
3 *Corran* A Sickle Point
4 *Sgeir mhic ruitean* Rock of the Hunchback's son
5 *Allt ruadh* Red Burn
6 *Cladh Mhic* Iain MacDonald's Burials
7 *Goirtean na mallachd* Field of Damnation
8 *Rubh na tosgaid* Point of the Overflows or Norse Burial place, or possibly 'hogsheads'
9 *Gil na murlach* Dogfish Strand
10 *A'chroit* The Croft
11 *Am mas* The Buttock
12 *Cul a ruighe* Back to the Ridge, i.e. to the west
13 *An ruigh* The Ridge
14 *Port na murlach* Dogfish Port
15 *Rubh Bhride* Bridget's Point, running south of the view

Right

1 *Eadar a Dhiura* Between the Two Juras
2 *Tom an tairbh* Bull Clump
3 *Buail a earraich* Spring Fold
4 *Duble na coille* Woody Double Rig (farmed strip)
5 *Tom* Clump
6 *Geadhail* Infield
7 *Croit mhor* Big Croft
8 *Torran ghlas* Grey Rocks
9 *Tom uinsean* Ash Clump
10 *Garadh criche* Division Wall
11 *Lon dubh* Black Field
12 *Geadhail a'chruithneach* Wheat Field
13 *Parc* Park
14 *Uchd a buie* Yellow Breast
15 *Doit a chiobair* Shepherd's Patch
16 *Bealach* Gateway, to right of view
17 *Ardfernal* Promontory of Alder Trees (or Terns)
18 *Ruigh Iain Campbell* Ian Campbell's Slope
19 *Ruig nan carn* Slope of the Cairns

Here is a collection of various picturesque names from Calum's book:

Cnoc soillear (Shining Hill); Tigh nan cuthaig (Cuckoo House);

Port na meirlich (Thieves Port); Druim linn (Flax Ridge);

Torran h-aon ghraidh (Rocks of the Beloved); Goirtean creadh (Clay Field);

Uaigh mearsanta ruadh (Grave of the Ginger-Haired Pedlar);

Moine beisteagan (Worms' Moor); Moine Martin (Martin's Moor);

Port nan gobhair (Goats' Port); Rubh na h-acarsaid (The Anchorage Point);

    Clach Shamson (Samson's Stone); Fearan muintir Eachan (Hector's Land);

Clach Domhnaidh Shaw (Donnie Shaw's Stone); Cul na sionnaich (Fox's Corner);

Rubh an leanachais (Point of the Sad Accident); Geadhail nam fiadh (Deer Park);

Tobar cnoc an t-seann duine (Well of Old Man's Hill); Iodhlainn Uisdean (Hugh's Yard);

Garadh na beiste duibh (Otter Wall); Buaile lean dris (Bramble Patch Fold);

Suainean beag (The Wee Wreathe); Clach na feannag (Crow Stone);

Cnoc na h-easgaidh phrabain (Hill of the Entangled Bog);

Cul a'bhaile (Back of the Town – the name of the prehistoric house);

Bruach ruadh Joseph (Joseph Brown's Quarry); Doire chlagain (Skull Bushes);

An ath nigheadaireachd (Washing Ford, for Shrouds); Tom Sheonaid (Janet's Bush);

Abhainn a' bhog aire (The Stream of the Soft Sheiling).

Here then is a 'taste of the Gaelic' of Knockrome and Ardfernal from Calum McArthur.

43

The First Three-Quarters
of the Twentieth Century

The sitting of the Crofters' Commission in Jura in 1896 reveals clearly the problems the people faced in trying to win a livelihood on the island. They were losing the right to graze and pasture on their traditional lands. Although they were not being evicted, their conditions were becoming no easier. Although the members of the Commission were clearly in sympathy with the plight of the local crofters, they were completely outmanoeuvred by Miss Campbell, and they simply lacked the 'teeth' to do anything to make more than minor improvements. They made a number of rulings in favour of the crofters. For example, in 1900 the larger Ardmenish and Knockrome crofters were permitted fourteen cows, six heifers, six stirks, fourteen calves, two horses, four pigs and twenty-four sheep. This was too little, too late for the people of Jura. In 1911 the Commission and its functions, together with the Congested Districts Board, formed in 1897 to attack crofting problems, were absorbed by the Scottish Land Court. The crofters once more had lost the means of effective protest the Commission had represented.

The decline in population which was traced through the nineteenth century now continued into the twentieth. The ten-yearly national census returns make sad reading, with figures from 1901 to 1951 as follows:

1901	625
1911	570
1921	461
1931	382
1941	337
1951	220

During this period the landowners were also encountering what they experienced as serious difficulties. James Campbell, ninth of Jura died in 1901 and the estate passed to Colin Campbell, tenth. He served for a time with the 91st Highlanders. Budge considered him to be the best of the old-time lairds, who was 'chieftain and leader to his people in the best sense of the term'. Perhaps if Donald Budge had sought the opinion of the oldest of the Jura crofters he would have found a different assessment, for the author has often been told of Campbell's autocratic and high-handed manner and harsh application of the estate regulations.

A short time before the outbreak of the First World War he had the following letter published in the Scottish press:

In the island of Jura, with a population of 500 souls and only some thirty to thirty-five of these being men of military age, twenty-seven recruits have stepped forward to join the 8th Battalion of the Argyll and Sutherland Highlanders this year. Four generations of the Jura family in direct descent have served their country in this regiment, one of whom is still serving. If this catches the eye of any man connected with Jura, let him enrol himself at once.

In due course the war broke out and two of Colin Campbell's sons died in it – James, of wounds received at Neuve Chapelle in 1915 and Ronald on the Somme in 1917. The 'men of military age' from Jura went off to the Front (Plate 21) and the Memorial Tablet on the wall of the parish church records the names of the fourteen men who did not return.

Tribute is paid here, in turn, and their names are recorded in full:

TO THE GLORY OF GOD AND IN MEMORY OF THOSE
WHO GAVE THEIR LIVES IN THE GREAT WAR 1914–1919

Capt. James Archibald Lochnell Campbell, Yr. of Jura
A. & S. High^{rs} – 19 March 1915
Capt. Ronald Walker Francis Campbell
10th Royal Fusiliers – 11 August 1916
Lieut. Archibald Darroch
H. M. Yacht *Rhuma* – 16 October 1918
Lieut. Dugald Shaw
5th Seaforth High^{rs} – 27 July 1917
Sergt. Archibald A. Shaw, M. M.
11th Royal Scots – 22 October 1916
Pte. Archibald Darroch
1st Cameron High^{rs} – 12 May 1916
Pte. Donald Darroch
7th A. & S. High^{rs} – 25 April 1917
Pte. Donald Darroch
9th Royal Scots – 9 April 1917
Pte. Alexander McDougall
9th H. L. I. – 26 September 1917
Pte. John McDougall
4th A. & S. High^{rs} – 21 July 1916
Pte. Angus McKechnie
17th H. L. I. – 18 November 1916
Pte. John McKechnie
8th A. & S. High^{rs} – 13 November 1916
Pte. Robert McPherson
8th A. & S. High^{rs} – 17 December 1914
Pte. John Shaw
8th A. & S. High^{rs} – 29 January 1920

The Voters' Roll of 1918 gives us a useful picture of the population at the end of the war, although of course only women of thirty years and over had the vote.

Twenty-four men are recorded as absent by reason of being soldiers not yet home. Fourteen men are absent through being at sea. If those termed 'sailors' are naval personnel and those called 'seaman' are merchantmen, there are nine naval men, and five in the merchant service. One absentee is an engineer, and John Campbell of Inverlussa is an ammunition worker. We know of at least one other in an ammunition factory, namely Jean Handley, Mary Keith's mother.

After deducting those absent, the Voters' Roll records 147 adults on Jura in 1918. It is not possible to reconstruct complete families because of the voting system, as mentioned above, however, occupations of the men are recorded, and are of some interest.

We shall shortly be looking at the history of the various estates. The voting record shows gamekeepers, gillies, stalkers, gamewatchers, etc. There are seven men in all employed at Inver, Jura House, Tarbert and Ardlussa. Ardfin employs six men in connection with the estate and the farm. There are three estate gardeners.

The Distillery Contract came to an end in 1918, and only John and James Ferguson, the owners, are still on Jura, along with the sole remaining cooper.

Crofters are found now only in the traditional townships: Keils (five); Knockrome (three); Ardfernal (two); and Ardmenish (two). However, people are still called farmers at Feolin Ferry, Sanaig, Crackaig, Craighouse, Keils, Feolin Farm, Corran House, Knockrome (three), Lagg (two), and Kinuachdrach. In all, thirteen.

Eight men are designated as shepherds or herds throughout the island, while nine are ploughmen. There are two farm workers, a cattleman and a cowherd, together with four ordinary labourers, making an additional twenty-five men who work on the land in various ways. There is one smallholder.

Taking note of all the ways people can work on the land in Jura, there are fifty-six men employed in farming.

There are the expected service folk: one doctor, two ministers, three teachers and an inspector of poor. There is a hotelkeeper, a harbourmaster, a piermaster, a postmaster and two postmen. There is also a blacksmith, a carter and a team of four roadmen. Skervuile Lighthouse has three lightkeepers and a boatman. There is one fisherman and one lobsterman.

An army pensioner and three widows make up the Voters' Roll for Jura for 1918.

During the 1970s and 1980s many of the inhabitants of Jura donated old family photographs to the author. These were re-photographed by Norman Tait, and copies were put on display in the parish church. Most of the black-and-white illustrations used in this book come from this collection. As we consider the first half of the twentieth century on Jura, the opportunity will be taken to show some of the ordinary activities of the people. (Plates 22, 23, 24, 25, 26, 27, 28, 32)

In 1920, Colin Campbell, by now nearly seventy, made over the estate to his son Charles Graham, who continued to manage it for a further eighteen years. (Plate 28)

It will be remembered that the estate now contained the independent enclave of Jura Forest, first leased to Henry Evans. In 1904, Mr Evan's lease expired, and the ground north of the Corran River was re-assigned to the Tarbert division. The lodge and shootings were let to various sportsmen, until in 1925 the Jura

Forest Estate was sold outright to Sir James Lithgow. In due course the estate passed to Mr and Mrs Geoffrey Rickman.

During this period the Campbells also disposed of the west coast estate of Inver, which was purchased by Mr Henry Lithgow, and passed on to his nephew Sir James Lithgow.

In 1920 the Campbells put another huge piece of the island on the market, and the 2nd Lord Astor purchased Tarbert and Corrynahera. As we know, these were formerly large sheep farms, but were now converted to deer forests. The new estate ran down the island as far as the Corran River and Small Isles Bay, and extended to the north as far as Lussagiven, making it the largest single land-holding on the island.

By 1938, Colin Campbell decided that the remaining estate was no longer profitable and put it on the market. What became known as the Jura Estate was bought by Mr W. Riley-Smith of Tadcaster, Yorkshire. The new owner died in 1954, and the estate was inherited by his son, Mr A. F. Riley-Smith.

The Ardlussa Estate is 25,000 acres, and comprises Kenuachdrach, Barnhill, Ardlussa, Inverlussa and Lussagiven, together with the remote bothy of Glengarrisdale. The McNeills of Colonsay had long owned the north of Jura, and Duncan McNeill had rebuilt Ardlussa House before they sold the estate in 1854 to Lord Murray. On his death in 1858 they bought it back again, and held it until 1874 when they sold it again to Walter Macfarlane. In 1902 it was bought by Alexander Crossman, who in the winter of 1919 sold the whole estate to Lord Astor. It was Mr Crossman who, in 1913, bought the farm of Kenuachdrach from Campbell of Jura. The Campbells had long owned this remote northern enclave, but now the whole of the north end of the island was brought under one ownership.

Mr Walter Hargreaves-Brown, having rented the estate for a couple of seasons, purchased it outright from Lord Astor in 1928. He died in 1936, and the estate was managed by trustees. In due course in 1945, his daughter Margaret, who was married to Robert Fletcher, bought the estate from the trustees, and they made Ardlussa their home.

These complicated changes of fortune saw the island of Jura settle down to a completely new pattern of land ownership by the years after the Second World War.

Instead of the situation where the southern part of the island was controlled by the Campbells of Jura and the northern part by the McNeills of Colonsay, Jura was now divided into five estates, as follows:

Inver	Sir William Lithgow
Jura Estate	Anthony Riley-Smith
Jura Forest	The Rickman Family
Tarbert Estate	Lord Astor
Ardlussa	The Fletchers

The Crofters' Commission revealed the first signs of what would happen to the community as the leasing of land for hunting became more general. We recall the presentation of conflicting evidence about the effect of the Jura Forest Estate on the population. A number of crofting families had disappeared but the estate was supporting a number of new ones where the men were engaged as gillies, keepers, gardeners and estate workers and their wives looked after the house and the guests. The new century saw this pattern developing as each individual estate found a balance between its hunting and fishing interests and the needs of the Jura residents.

The *Inver Estate* concentrated largely on its deer, but maintained a fine herd of Highland cattle, in this case the black variety. The land had long been thought unsuitable for crofting, and indeed its crofting community of Cnocbreac had disappeared long before. The population thus resolved itself into a single family consisting of a joint estate manager and farmer.

The *Jura Forest Estate* had been brought into existence for its deer hunting, and this continued, with the south bank of the Corran River giving a fishing interest as well. The land contained the long established farm of Feolin, and the isolated croft house of Corran. The old crofting community of Leargybreck had long disappeared, although the Free Kirk building still stood beside the sole surviving cottage, and the ruins of the township. Several families occupied newly built houses as noted above.

The *Tarbert Estate* existed primarily for shooting and fishing, with the northern bank of the Corran River supplying its sea trout. A house which had been built in connection with slate quarrying was enlarged into the present Tarbert Lodge, which produced a residence of great comfort for the new owners, the Astors, on their visits. They also maintained the lodge of Glenbatrick, on the remote west coast, and in the early part of the last century a wooden lodge at Cruib, which has since been demolished.

The remains of the former sheep farm survived, with some farming at Tarbert and at Lagg. The population thus consisted of keepers and farmers, and traditional crofters largely disappeared. Some dwellings at Tarbert Village and at Lagg became holiday homes. The old croft house at Corrynahera was finally deserted and became a ruin. The community at Lagg declined with the loss of the school and in due course the post office. The old Change House remained as an estate worker's home, and Gatehouse as the dwelling of the estate manager.

However, the Tarbert Estate contained the three crofting townships of Ardmenish, Knockrome and Ardfernal, and crofting legislation protected the rights and lifestyle of the inhabitants of these communities. They simply exchanged a Campbell for Lord Astor and a local factor, and went on about their business as usual. None-the-less it was in these three townships that the fifty years to 1950 saw the most dramatic reduction in the population. By the time the author was on the island in the 1970s, there was only one active croft at Ardmenish, four at Knockrome and none at Ardfernal, although about eight habitable dwellings remained as absentee holiday homes. The lighthouse staff also lived on the Tarbert estate, again with little contact with the landowner.

Ardlussa. Once more this was a story of deer shooting, with fishing on the Lussa, which had been engineered to improve the run of sea trout, and some serious farming centred on the estate centre of Ardlussa House. Again there were stalkers and farmers and a gardener, and again the old crofting townships declined and almost disappeared. Kinuachdrach, once a thriving community, shrank to a single inhabited house. Barnhill house was sold to an English owner, and enjoyed fame for some time while George Orwell lived and wrote there in the 1940s. In recent years it has only been the extreme difficulty of reaching Barnhill which has prevented the place becoming a place of pilgrimage for Orwell enthusiasts the world over. Lealt also became a leased house, and home later of John Mercer, the author. The community of Inverlussa, formerly centred on the slate quarry, became a mixture of residences for ageing inhabitants, and holiday homes run by the estate. The local school there closed. The same story applied to Lussagiven, with holiday homes and retired local folk. The estate by the 1970s contained no crofting and no farming, except that run by the estate.

Jura Estate. When the Campbells sold the last part of their territory, the new owner acquired land totalling 14,000 acres. This differed from the other estates in the island in that the new proprietor found himself the inheritor to some extent of the mantle of the Campbells. The purchase was no doubt made purely in the interests of sport, but the proprietor found life more complicated than the other landlords did. The estate contained the splendid Jura House, with its superb walled garden. The home farm of Ardfin was at the centre of the best farming land on the island, and the farm was maintained in operation. The owner sold land to the Forestry Commission, so some of the oldest inhabited communities such as Sannaig and Dunans became lost, and only individual houses such as Camustac and Strone remained as leased residences, although they were not farmed in any way. The community of New Brosdale declined to a line of ruins, and the school at Cabrach closed. The large crofting township of Crackaig also ran down until, by 1970, it had only a single occupied house, and no crofting was being carried on.

The crofting township of Keils was in this estate, and it continued in its traditional life, much like Knockrome, but once again with a decline in the number of crofters, ultimately to two, surrounded by a small number of surviving dwellings, mostly holiday homes.

Throughout the above description of the development of the modern pattern of the Jura estates, there has been continual mention of the decline of their associated settlements and the ruin of buildings.

The complete picture comes as something of a shock, when it is realised that, of the 159 houses being lived in in 1891, only thirty-seven were still occupied as full-time residences in Jura in the 1970s.

A further forty-three still survived in the form of holiday homes, but seventy-nine were no longer habitable, having either been taken over for farm purposes or become ruins.

This loss of houses took place all over the island. Some small historic settlements disappeared for ever: Dainsgear, Dunans, Sannaig, Corrynahera, Auchintarbert, Mulbuie and Glengarrisdale.

The ferry communities of Lagg and Kinuachdrach, in 1891 still showing eleven houses, by the mid-1970s had only three.

One of the major townships, that at New Brosdale, has gone from having twelve homes in 1891 to the point at which only its former schoolhouse is in use as the dwelling for an estate worker.

The four big crofting townships of Keils, Knockrome, Ardfernal and Ardmenish, which between them had forty-four households in 1891, had been reduced to nine full-time houses, and ten holiday homes.

By the early part of the twentieth century, the island had already seen the population begin to concentrate on the shores of Small Isles Bay. The township of Knocknafeolaman, up on the hill above the inn, had long since disappeared, but Ballard had survived as the home of the blacksmith, and was an active croft, while down on the shore the smithy and the mill were still going concerns well into the century. The distillery was, of course, in operation until just after the First World War, and had become the focus of housing for its workers. The substantial manager's house at Torran Mor remained standing. About this time the island got its first resident GP, and later Dr Stewart Sandeman took up residence in the said Torran Mor. The hotel continued on from the old inn, and in due time became the only licensed premises on the island. The excise house remained in place. There was a small village store.

However, with the coming of the First World War and the closure of the distillery, Jura continued to decline. There was still a steady movement away to the mainland, and even a few late emigrants. Many traditional crofters became aged and were not succeeded by their families. Their neighbours took double holdings. It seems likely that this dreadful decline was slowed by growing prosperity in the 1930s which saw Jura's wealthy owners employing more housekeeping and gamekeeping staffs on their various estates.

At Small Isles Bay the community of Caigenhouse seems to have survived the general decline. It was during the period between the wars that many men of Jura returned to the sea for a livelihood and, as in the previous century, proved themselves to be successful seafarers. As we have seen, Caigenhouse was for a time known as 'Mariners' Row' for it boasted, within living memory, ten master mariners. Communities such as Knockrome and Keils made similar claims.

Other buildings continued to provide a focus along the bay. Small Isles School remained part of the community, as did Holly House, the home of the inspector of poor. The parish church still stood by the shore, and north on the outskirts of the community was Jura manse. A little to the south stood the United Free Church and its fine manse at Carraig.

The desire grew for modernisation and improvement, and, largely as a result of the activites of the builder Robert Shaw, second storeys began to appear on many cottages, and thatched roofs were replaced with corrugated iron or slates. Robert had strong Jura connections, and, having been dispatched to Jura to establish a bridgehead for his firm, remained and became a success. He built in time a fine solid house for himself and his family on the hill about Lagg, where it still looks down over the bay.

The original pier at Craighouse had been erected by the distillers, James Ferguson & Son. It was a wooden structure, and finally became unsafe. Duncan

McKechnie, of Craighouse, who was the local councillor for many years, campaigned for a new pier, and the present concrete and iron pier was opened in 1952, just before Mr McKechnie died. The community also acquired a hall, built by the Territorial Association, and sold after the First World War to the late Miss Lithgow, who presented it to the community.

Over most of this increasingly complicated structure around the bay, the new owner of the Jura Estate presided as landlord – not necessarily a comfortable position.

There has been a great deal of time spent in describing the difficulties of making a living on Jura, but it should not be thought that there was no time for enjoyment in the community. We have already seen that music and storytelling were part of the life of the island as was the strong tradition of piping.

Three other social occasions can be mentioned here. There was certainly a 'Jura Show' during the latter part of the nineteenth century and well into the twentieth. All the ingredients of an Agricultural Show were present, with livestock being walked and shown. (Plate 33)

In 1926 a regatta was established to give residents and visitors the opportunity to show their skills in small boats. Mr William Nicholson, senior, was responsible for organising the regatta for many years, and the event has shown a great ability to persist, going on to the present time.

In recent years the Ardlussa Sports have also been a pleasant feature of summer life on Jura.

Having become the main population centre in the island, the community on Small Isles Bay continued to expand. In due course a new distillery company was formed by two Jura owners, and the re-born distillery was completed in 1963. Now there was a need again for mashmen, stillmen and coopers, a management staff, and a re-born excise service.

In due course the local authority began to provide council houses, and where else but on the shore of Small Isles Bay. The name Craighouse, formerly and properly attached only to the hotel, began to be used for the whole of the increasing ribbon development along the coast.

Four very ordinary-looking houses were put up in 1956 adjacent to the Old Schoolhouse, and called Kilearnan Place. The new forestry plantations needed workers, and four small cottages were built for them just north of the school.

Five pairs of semi-detached houses were built on the hill leading down to the hotel from the south, alongside Craighouse Ravine. These were intended for distillery workers and this developement was called Woodside.

Still further along the coast, fifteen new houses were built, spanning the mouth of the Keils Burn. This development in 1968, contained some homes intended for elderly retired folk, and the strip of new buildings was called Burnside.

There were thus created thirty-three new dwellings, some of which were inhabited by people who had formerly lived in the old townships.

After the Second World War there had been a growing tendency for natives of Jura, who had left the island in their youth and done well, to return in their mature years and spend their retirement on the island. Others, with no blood ties to Jura had forged long connections with the island, and they too came to settle. These folk brought capital to Jura, and often had money to spend on a retirement bungalow. New houses began to spring up where there was a hereditary claim to land, or where building permission could be obtained. For example the MacKechnies of Craighouse built above the hotel in the 'Red Gap', Bealach Dearg. The McIsaacs, formerly of the mill, built the bungalow of Braeside below Ballard. The Patons came to live and built The Shieling. Faskadh was built alongside the post office at Caigenhouse.

In outlying parts of the island, a modern bungalow replaced The Kennels at Ardfin. At Tarbert, a large house was built for the Astors, as Tarbert Lodge.

Even later, and about the time when this study is coming to an end, a new school and schoolmaster's house, and a surgery and doctor's house were built between Burnside and Carraig, and the Astor estate sprouted some timber holiday houses. No doubt this development of modern building will continue.

New roads were built: one in 1951 between Knockrome and Ardfernal, and another in 1953 up to the township of Keils. A modern telephone system was installed in 1950–1.

By this period, as we have seen, the island contained a large number of houses which were not occupied throughout the year, many of which were retained by the families of those who formerly occupied them as crofters and tenants. These families retained a close bond with the island, and folk such as these formed the Glasgow Jura Association, which was often influential in questions of the development of the island.

Jura gradually began to catch up with the standards expected by people living on the mainland. Through the activities of the Argyll County Council, with the co-operation of the various landowners, and as a result of the desires of the people, various services began to be provided. Kitchens and bathrooms began to appear in ordinary houses and bottled gas arrived for lighting and cooking. Some houses generated their own electricity. A water supply was arranged for Craighouse. In due course mains electricity arrived, first generated in Islay, and coming the shortest way across the Sound of Islay, and later coming by the longer under-sea cable from the mainland. Many old-established places and customs disappeared. The smithy and the mill closed down and the excise house became a holiday home. Coal began to be delivered to the island, and largely replaced peat-cutting, which was reduced to a traditional activity pursued only by a few of the older generation crofters. Traditional crofting practices were gradually modified or abandoned, and the tractor became universal, replacing the shire horse.

By this time, and far too late for Jura, the question of the crofters had come once again to Government notice. A new Commission was set up in 1954, specifically to report on ways to regenerate crofting. A croft was now defined as under £50 rent or under fifty acres apart from common grazing. This limit was raised to seventy-five acres in 1961. The new Commission retained most of the nineteenth-century rules, but with additional powers, such as the power to end the holdings of incompetent or absentee crofters. Residence within ten miles became the standard in 1961. A permanent Commission was established in Inverness, with a register of all crofts. Tenure of land as a croft now carries many privileges. Not only is there special agricultural aid, but the crofter has for some years been able to get a grant and loan to build a house on which he has an almost freehold chance of recouping the state's money on leaving. In 1972 it was announced that a crofter could, if he wished, buy his holding, at a price to be decided by the Scottish Land Court, or he might acquire only the house and garden, or just inbye land for non-agricultural development, such as the building of 'cottages' for which aid was being offered. What could the nineteenth-century crofters on Jura not have accomplished with this legal support? Doubtless such changes would have continued to create stress between crofters and landlords, at a time when the Scottish Landowners Federation could give public utterance, 'regretting the consequent drop in the sporting value of estates, and the destruction of the landlord and tenant system'.

44

People of the Twentieth Century

Much of this book has been concerned with people who have lived on Jura through the centuries. This chapter will mention some residents of the first half of the twentieth century. Far more than those few which have been chosen could find a place here, and it is hoped that descendants of families not pictured will understand the many omissions.

We consider first some families with traditional Jura names:

BLACK

Donald Black and Flora Smith of Keils had four children who lived and died on Jura.

Euphemia died unmarried in Keils in 1913, aged sixty-seven.

Donald died unmarried in Caigenhouse in 1943, aged seventy-five.

Anne died unmarried in Keils in 1945, aged eighty-five.

John, the widower of Isabella, died in Keils in 1947, aged eighty-five.

John and Bella were the parents of the present-day Donald and Archie. Some of Donald's stories are in the collection. It is interesting to see such an important surname in the history of Jura reduced to just a single line in the twentieth century. (Plate 31)

BUIE

By the middle of the twentieth century, two families were still living on Jura which bore the historic surname Buie. Sandy Buie was one of the few full-time crofters in Knockrome, and lived there with his wife Nan and his family. Dougie Buie lived in Carraig with his wife Tottie and their son, Duncan. Dougie was one of those people you find in the Islands who had so many roles in the community that it took some time to list them all. In addition to his joiner-work, and all the other jobs, he was also the Kirk Session Clerk.

(a) Sandy Buie. Sandy Buie's parents were Angus Buie and Marrion Darroch. Angus Buie's sisters, Christina, Lily and Margaret, all died on Jura: in 1908 aged thirty-eight; in 1916 aged forty-two; and in 1924 aged sixty-seven. Lily was single, but Christina was the wife of John Kelly and died at Ardfernal, while Margaret was the wife of James McKechnie and died at Tarbert.

(b) Dougie Buie. Dougie Buie always insisted that, as far as he could tell, he and Sandy Buie were not related, although his wife's mother and Sandy's wife's mother were sisters.

Dougie's parents were Duncan Buie and Marion McKenzie. Duncan died in Craighouse in 1946, aged seventy-two. His sisters Mary and Margaret lived to be seventy-seven and eighty, and died in 1953 and 1964, but not on Jura.

(c) Donald Buie and Christina Shaw had two daughters who lived into the century.

Ann Buie, the widow of John McArthur, died in Knockrome in 1900, aged eighty-seven, and Flora Buie, the widow of Duncan Darroch, died in Knockrome in 1905, aged eighty-one. Flora Buie was the mother of a big family which included one of the many Donald Darrochs, whose sons crofted at Knockrome until recent times.

Ann Buie was the mother of Malcolm McArthur, who in turn was the father of Calum, who, with his wife Mary, was the father of four daughters who remain important members of the community to the present day. Here the Buie line is still strong, but in the absence of sons, the family name has become obscured.

(d) Donald Buie and Ann Black had three children who lived into the twentieth century.

Ann died in Knockrome in 1900, aged fifty-one. She was the widow of John Campbell.

Malcolm, married to Annie Darroch, died at Knockrome in 1916, aged sixty. They had a son called Donald Buie, who lived in Knockrome.

Catharine died in Knockrome in 1917, aged eighty. She was the widow of John McGregor. This was Kate Buie, who survives in at least two fine photographs. She was the mother of Flora McGregor, who married Neil Darroch. They became the parents of Katie and Donald and Ian and Mary and other notable members of the modern community. Again the Buie name became submerged in this line.

Two other Buie families were still on the island in the early twentieth century. None of them left descendants on the island.

Many Buies could be portrayed here, and indeed we have already seen a picture of Duncan Buie, father of Dougie. There were two well known Buie sisters called Peggy and Catherine. Peggy worked as a servant at Feolin Farm. The family came from Dainskeir, and in due course the sisters retired to Caigenhouse. Kate Buie was always known as 'Stramash', since she caused some disturbance wherever she went. (Plate 29)

CAMPBELL

By the twentieth century there are a number of families of Campbells on Jura, and some have a continuing presence:

(a) John Campbell, a seaman, and his wife Catherine McLellan have two sons, William and Alexander, both of whom marry and live on the island, dying in 1903 and 1908. William and his wife Ann Clark have Dugald and Mary, who live and die in Keils. Dugald married, and died in 1929, aged sixty-three, and Mary, unmarried, died in 1945, aged eighty-five. Mary was the famous character in Keils told about in the stories, and Dugald's widow Bella was the woman who was tragically drowned in the Keils burn.

(b) Campbells also lived at the north end. Duncan Campbell, a postman, and his wife Mary McDougall were at Inverlussa where he died in 1903, aged sevety-seven. A daughter, Marrion, married James Darroch and died at Inverlussa

in 1912, aged forty-two, and a son, Neil, who was married to Mary McLean, lived until 1943, when he died at Inverlussa, aged eighty-eight. Neil Campbell and Mary McLean had a son Dugald, who married Catherine McKechnie, a member of the important family of McKechnies of Inverlussa. They were the parents of Peter Campbell, for many years estate manager at Ardlussa.

CLARK

The Clarks were an early and significant family in Jura. Once more by the twentieth century there are only a few family lines.

An important family was Alexander Clark and Mary McConnel who lived in Keils during the nineteenth century and died in 1875 and 1885. A number of their large family died before the turn of the century, but six lived on into the next.

One, Alexander, was married to Catherine McArthur, and died in Keils in 1923, aged eighty-four. Through their daughter, Mary, this couple were Alick Keith's grandparents. One of their sons, Alexander, was a seaman and died unmarried at Keils in 1953, aged sixty-six.

We hear of Catherine Clark of Feolin in her stories of service in the Manse. She appears in the death register as an illegitimate child who died in 1917 at the age of sixty-nine.

DARROCH

Once more we are dealing with an important ancestral name, and the Darrochs remain numerically dominant into the twentieth century, outnumbering the historically plentiful Shaws, Buies and Macdougalls. There are fifty-two individual deaths of people with the name Darroch recorded in the Register from 1900. We will look first at some Darrochs of the twentieth century whose modern descendants played a part in the island's recent history.

(a) The Darroch ancestors of the Darrochs and Buies of Knockrome.
Sandy Buie and Sandy Darroch shared common great-grandparents.

Archibald Darroch and Marrion Buie were born at the end of the eighteenth century. Amongst their children were Donald and Mary who both lived into the twentieth. Donald died in 1900, aged sixty-seven at Knockrome. He and his wife Ann McLean were the parents of a big family, of whom two died on Jura. John Darroch, a bachelor died in Knockrome in 1935, aged eighty. Marrion married Angus Buie and died in Knockrome in 1937, aged sixty-six. They were Sandy Buie's parents.

Archibald Darroch and Marrion Buie also had a daughter called Mary who lived until 1902 and died in Knockrome, aged seventy-eight. She was married to yet another Donald Darroch, a son of Alexander Darroch and Mary Campbell. Donald was ninety when he died in Knockrome in 1900.

Two of their children died on the island. Donald, died in Knockrome in 1947, a bachelor, aged ninety-one. Alexander married Janet McGregor and died in Knockrome in 1929, aged seventy-nine. They were the parents of the most recent family of Darrochs in Knockrome: Sandy, Janet McKechnie, Peter, Annie and Katie.

(b) The Darroch ancestors of Donald Darroch of Inver, and of his brother and sisters (Ian, Katie, Annie, Neilina, Janet, Flora and Mary).

There was a Donald Darroch in Knockome, in the 1900s whose second wife was Ann Shaw. Amongst their large family, two died on Jura in the twentieth century. Neill married Flora McGregor and died in Ardfernal in 1922, aged sixty-two. Neil was born in Knockrome into the family of his step-brothers. He inherited the croft from his father. He was the Neil after whom Katie Darroch was familiarly called 'Katie Neil', and they were the parents of her family. His sister Janet married Malcolm McArthur and died in Ardfernal in 1915, aged fifty-four. They were the parents of the McArthur family of Ardfernal, whose son Calum married Katie and Donald's sister, Mary. (Plate 33)

(c) Charlotte Darroch, late of Knockrome, and Rob Darroch of Jura.
Duncan Darroch and Flora Buie lived in Corran House in the nineteenth century. Some of their large family lived into the twentieth century and died on Jura.

Malcolm and Donald stayed in Knockrome and worked the croft known later as the White House. Malcolm did not marry and died in 1953, aged sixty-nine. Donald married Charlotte McIntyre, who had come to Jura to be housemaid to Dr Sandeman and his family. Donald died in 1951, aged sixty-two. Charlotte survived him in her house in Woodside for many years. Many photographs survive of life in Knockrome in this family.

Duncan Darroch and Flora Buie had a daughter, Ann, in 1838. She married John Darroch and they lived in Corrynahera. They had a large family, two of whom died on Jura. Their son Duncan died at Corrynahera in 1882, aged eleven, and they had a daughter Margaret who died in infancy in Corrynahera in 1884. It seems that the family then left the island. One of their sons, Archibald, became the father of Duncan Darroch, who became a minister of the Church of Scotland, and, until his death, kept close ties with the island. His son Rob became a resident of Jura in recent years.

(d) Margaret Darroch of Tarbert. Roderick Darroch and Flora Peddie had a son Neil Darroch who was born in Colonsay in 1823. He married Christina McLellan and they lived in Lagg and Auchintarbert. Both lived into the twentieth century. Neil died at Tarbert in 1901, aged seventy-three, and Christina also died there in 1918, aged seventy-nine. Two of their family also died on Jura. Flora, the wife of James McLullich died at Tarbert in 1948, aged seventy-eight. Neil died there, unmarried, in 1949, aged seventy-three. With their brother, Richard, this was the family of their descendant Margaret Darroch of Tarbert who has kept a lifelong connection with Tarbert and Jura.

(e) The Holly House connection. John Darroch and Marrion Darroch lived at Knockrome in the nineteenth century. Among their children was Neil who died at Ardmenish in 1901, aged eighty-five. He was married to Mary McColl, who died in 1926, aged ninety-eight. This lady was the famous 'Granny Darroch' of Feolin Ferry, who was the local midwife for many years, and of whom fine photographs survive. This couple had a large family, five of whom lived and

died on Jura. One, Angus, married Margaret McIsaac and left the island. He was the father of Alec Darroch of Holly House. (Plate 34)

(f) The McSweins of Caigenhouse. Neil Darroch and his wife Janet had among their family a daughter, Jean, who married Robert McSwein. She died on Jura in 1946, aged seventy-nine. Their descendants retain the family house in Caigenhouse and remain in contact with Jura.

KEITH

Another important family in the island's history were the Keiths, represented in the middle of the twentieth century by Alick Keith, crofter at Keils and the island's postman. Alick was a Kirk Elder, as were his father and grandfather before him. His family tree shows relatives alive in the twentieth century.

Duncan Keith and Flora McDougall were Alick's great-grandparents on his father's side. Their son, John Keith, was Alick's grandfather. He married Mary Buie, and died at Keils in 1914, aged eighty-eight. Two of their children lived until the 1940s. Isabella married John Black and died at Feolin Farm in 1946, aged seventy. Alick's father John married Mary Clark. He died in Keils in 1940, aged sixty-six. His wife Mary lived until 1964 and died in Caigenhouse, aged eighty-four. They had a son, John, who died in Keils in 1916 only a year old, and a daughter, Mary, who died at only twenty-three years in 1927, in Keils. Their brother, Alick, and his sisters, Isa, Katie and Morag, all survived to be senior citizens.

LINDSAY

It was Donald Budge's belief that the Lindsays first came to Jura to work on the Ferry at Lagg, and certainly the connection with Lagg remains dominant well into the twentieth century.

John Lindsay, the post-runner of Lagg, and his wife Elizabeth McColl are the ancestors of most of the twentieth-century Lindsays. Three of their seven children lived into the century, and one at least of those had significant offspring.

John Lindsay's son, Archibald, the postman at Lagg, was married to Euphemia McGilp, who came from Knapdale. Archibald died before 1900, but Effie, his wife, lived until 1902 and died in Lagg, aged eighty-eight. She had a brother, Neil McGilp, whose daughter, Euphemia, would marry her son, Alexander, thus creating confusion with identical names in the next generation. Archibald Lindsay and his wife had nine children. Four lived into the twentieth century and two are noted here.

Alexander Lindsay married his cousin Euphemia McGilp. He was also a postman and died in Lagg in 1912, aged fifty-four. Their daughter Flora married the builder, Robert Shaw.

Neil Lindsay married Mary McIndeor, of Kilchoman in Islay. This was the famous Lindsay who went to San Francisco and returned after the earthquake in which he lost his business. Neil died in Caigenhouse in 1945, aged eighty. His daughter Effie, married Dan McDougall and remained a notable modern resident in Jura.

MCCRAINE

It seems unreasonable to omit a famous family name like McCraine from this study, and yet it must be accepted that the deaths register contains only five references to a McCraine dying on the island in the twentieth century. Indeed there are only a handful of references in the second half of the nineteenth century, although the church officer role of Archibald McCraine was well known, and the tendency of McCraines to marry members of the miller's family, the McIsaacs, is also noticeable.

Donald McCraine and Mary McIsaac both died in the nineteenth century, but lived in Caigenhouse in its earliest days. They had two daughters, both unmarried, who lived into the twentieth century and died in Caigenhouse. Mary McCraine (Cham), died in 1908, unmarried. She was eighty-five. Marion (Nodan), her sister, died in 1916. She was also a spinster and was eighty-five. These sisters feature in stories of Caigenhouse.

MCDOUGALL

At one time there were more people called McDougall on Jura than any other name. During the nineteenth century the death register is full of entries. However, by the middle of the twentieth century, only the family of the blacksmith of Craighouse remained. The smiths had lived in Ballard. Their family line ran back from Coll and Dan McDougall and their sister, Katie McLean. Their father and mother were Donald McDougall and Mary McIsaac. The smith and the miller lived near one another, and the families were closely connected. Donald died in 1918, aged sixty-four, but Dan's mother lived until 1947 and died at the age of eighty-three. Behind them were their parents Coll McDougall and Flora Shaw, and before that Alexander McDougall and Ann McDougall. The contemporary family contained a sister Flora who died in 1899 aged fourteen; a brother Alexander who was killed at Passchendale in 1917, and sisters Ann and Jane who lived until after the Second World War. Coll and Dan's sister Katie married Donald McLean, who died in 1960, aged sixty-three. Coll McDougall died in 1972, but Dan and Effie continued to contribute to Jura life for many years.

The Death Register for the twentieth century still contains many entries under the name McDougall, but none seem to have left much trace of their presence on the island to the present time.

MCISAAC

As we have seen, the millers were called McIsaac. There were McIsaacs still living on Jura in the mid-part of the twentieth century. These were people like Jeannie McIsaac of the Pier Cottage, Alec McIsaac of Braeside, the bungalow nearest to the old Miltown, and Mary McIsaac, the wife of Dr John Renwick of Yorkshire. These belong to the same generation as Dan McDougall and are first cousins of his, through his mother.

Their great-great grandparents were John McIsaac and Catherine Shaw, and their great-grandparents were Duncan McIsaac and Ann Darroch. This generation had children who lived into the twentieth century. In Duncan and Ann McIsaac's family was also their son, Alexander, who was Alec McIsaac's grandfather.

MCKECHNIE

The McKechnies are another significant family in the history of Jura and, in this case, there are at least three separate families whose descendants are still connected with the island. We will look at the families of Betsy McKechnie of Bealach Dearg, of Sandy Buie's wife, Nan, and of Lily McInnes, and her family at Inverlussa.

(a) Betsy McKechnie. Betsy was one of a family of nine. Her grandparents were Angus McKechnie and Janet Darroch. Angus was a joiner at Ardfin who died in the 1880s. His mother was Betsy Stevenson. She was a daughter of Robert Stevenson, the owner of Belnahua. Her parents were John McKechnie and Mary McLean. John died in 1907 in Craighouse, aged sixty-eight, and his wife died in 1939, aged eighty. Having been off the island for a time, John came back and founded the village shop called Jura Stores and, later, he managed the Craighouse Hotel and ran its farm. After John McKechnie died, his sons Archie, Duncan and Angus, took on the farm and the shop. Archie died in 1962. Duncan married Janet Darroch of Knockrome and died quite recently. Angus married Lizzie Beveridge and died in Dundee in 1968. Other members of the family lived to the present day. Jane was unmarried and died in 1950, aged sixty-nine. John James became a postmaster and died in 1965, aged seventy-seven. Catherine became Catherine Horne and died in 1969. Her daughter Carol married Gordon Wright and settled lately on Jura.

Betsy herself, having been a student teacher at Knockrome School, went away to pursue her career and, having been a headmistress near Stirling, she retired to Jura, living in the modern bungalow above the hotel and dying in 1982, at the age of ninety-three.

Betsy's grandfather, Angus McKechnie, lost his wife Janet in 1855 and married again, one Ann McDougall, who lived until 1914, and died at the age of eighty-eight. Amongst their family were two children who notably lived into the twentieth century.

Angus McKechnie married Mary Keith. He was the merchant who ran the shop in Caigenhouse, mentioned elsewhere. He died in Caigenhouse in 1915, aged fifty-three, his wife Mary living until 1937, and dying at the age seventy-eight. They lost a son, Angus, in the First World War and had a daughter, Mary, who lived until 1974, and died aged seventy-seven.

Angus McKechnie and Ann McDougall had a son, Duncan, who married Christina McNeill. He died in 1952, agèd eighty-eight in Craighouse. He became a local councillor and a JP.

(b) Nan Buie of Knockrome. Sandy Buie's wife, Nan, and her sister, Mrs Leonard, were the grand-daughters of Dugald McKechnie and Mary McDougall. Two of their children lived on Jura in the twentieth century. Isabella died unmarried in Ardfernal in 1911, aged sixty-nine, and her brother Angus was Nan Buie's father.

(c) The family of Calum McKechnie of Inverlussa.

The grandparents of Calum McKechnie and his family were Malcolm McEachern and Catharine McEachern. Malcolm died in the nineteenth century, but his wife, Catherine, the daughter of Malcolm McKechnie and Catharine Shaw, lived until 1906 and died at Glengarrisdale, aged eighty-seven. Their son Neil, McKechnie, married Isabella Shaw, and they became the parents of Calum. Neil lived until 1925, and died at Inverlussa, aged seventy-two. His wife's death is not on record. Neil had a brother called Angus, who lived in Inverlussa until his death, unmarried, in 1928, aged seventy-one. (Plate 30)

Neil McKechnie and Bella Shaw had a large family. Their son, Duncan, died unmarried, in Inverlussa in 1916, aged twenty-five. Another son, Neil, also died unmarried, in Inverlussa in 1932, aged thirty-five. Elizabeth married Dugald Campbell and became Peter Campbell's mother. Angus remained unmarried and lived to a great age in Inverlussa, known to all as 'Uncle Angus'. Calum McKechnie married Margaret MacKellar and they became the parents of a large family, living to recent times in the island. Their daughter, Lily, married Neil McInnes of Gatehouse. Other family members lived beyond Jura. Another well known contemporary resident, Annie Welsh of Inverlussa, was sister to Margaret McKellar and so sister-in-law to all the McKechnies. She became Annette Campbell's grandmother.

McLean

A number of families called McLean remained significant into the twentieth century. Some, of course, connect with people we have already studied.

(a) Malcolm McLean and Marion Shaw. This couple lived at Gatehouse in the nineteenth century, where Malcolm was a gamekeeper. He died in 1898, while his wife lived to 1903 and died aged eighty-four. Four of their children lived on Jura in the twentieth century.

Dugald died, unmarried, in Gatehouse in 1923, aged sixty-four. Donald married Marion Kennedy. They lived at Ardfernal where he died in 1931, aged seventy-nine. His wife was known as 'Mor Ceinidheach' and died in 1941, aged eighty-three. It was their son, Donald, who married Dan McDougall's sister, Katie. Mary married Duncan Shaw. She died at Inverlussa in 1934, aged eighty-nine. Her husband had died in 1908, at Buaile a Bhuidhe, aged seventy-two. He was the son of John Shaw and Mary Shaw. They were the parents of the famous Neil Shaw, the Bard of Jura. Isabella married Donald Darroch, one of the Darrochs of Knockrome.

(b) Duncan McLean married Mary Shaw and lived at Lagg. He died in 1928, aged seventy-five. She lived until 1945 and died, aged eighty-three. Her parents were John Shaw, a shepherd, and Ann McIsaac. Their eighteen-year-old daughter Ann, died in 1902 in Gatehouse. Their daughter, Marion, died at Lagg, in 1932, aged thirty-two. She had married the builder, Robert Shaw, who thus tragically lost his first wife. Their daughter, Peggy, became Peggy McLeod, Nancy McLean's mother.

(c) James McLean and Marrion Keith had a son, Lachlan, who died unmarried at Craighouse in 1900, aged twenty-seven. Curiously, Kilearnadil graveyard contains a stone commemorating another of their children, Catherine McLean who died in Glasgow in 1892, aged twenty-one. The stone records 'through the

result of an accident by falling over a window three storeys high'. It is interesting to speculate that Catherine may not have seen a three storey house before and was not aware of the danger of cleaning its upper windows.

SHAW

These families of Shaws had a significant presence on the island in recent years:

(a) The Shaws of Ardmenish. Behind this family lie Donald Shaw and Mary McLean who lived in Ardmenish and died near the end of the nineteenth century. They had at least nine children and were great-grandparents of Dougie Buie. Five of their children left the island. Ann Shaw, their daughter, married Angus McKechnie and died at Knockrome in 1943, aged eighty-three. As we have already seen she was Nan Buie's mother. Of the others of the large family, Gilbert, Jessie, Morag, John and Neil all lived in Ardmenish in recent times.

(b) More Shaws of Ardmenish. John Shaw and Margaret Buie lived in Ardmenish and died near the end of the nineteenth century. Of their children, one, John Shaw, married Agnes Lindsay, as we saw under Lindsays. John died in Ardmenish in 1951, aged ninety-three. Their children were important members of the twentieth-century community. Archie died in 1918 in the First World War. John died at Ardmenish in 1920, aged twenty-seven. Mary died in 1964, aged seventy-three. Effie married Archie Kerr who died, leaving his widow on Jura until recent times. Sandy married Mary Campbell. He died in 1955 and his widow lived on in Jura.

(c) The Shaws of Inverlussa. Duncan Shaw and Margaret McDougall of Lussagiven had four children living on Jura in the twentieth century. All were significant, but Bella and Donald perhaps specially so. Bella Shaw married Neil McKechnie and became the mother of the Inverlussa McKechnies.

Donald Shaw married Margaret Speirs and died at Inverlussa in 1952, aged seventy-seven. This couple were the parents of Mary Shaw, of Inverlussa post office, and of Alistair Shaw, Alistair Ruadh, lately gardener at Ardlussa House.

(d) Robert Shaw of Lagg. Robert Shaw lived for much of his life on Jura. We have sketched his role as a builder. He was also an elder of the Kirk and a finalist in the Mod. However, he was not born on Jura. We take this opportunity to use his family tree as an example of what was happening in the early part of the twentieth century.

We start with John Shaw and Mary Darroch. He was a boatbuilder and lived at Lagg and Lussagiven. His wife died at Ruantallain. They were the parents of Catherine Shaw, the wife of Niven Darroch. They had six children, among whom was a son, John.

John Shaw married Ann McIsaac (see under McIsaacs). John Shaw was born at Lussagive and died at New Brosdale in 1902, aged eighty-four. His wife died at Gatehouse in 1905.

We are fortunate to have a detailed family tree of this family and, since we are using it as an example, the members are listed here in full:

1   Calum; b. 1857; married Margaret McPhail. Three children but no offspring.

2   John; b. 1858; went to Australia. Married. Descendants survive.

3   Neil; b. 1860; went to Philadelphia. Married. Descendants survive.

4   Mary; b. 1863; married Duncan McLean. Lived at Gatehouse. See under McLeans.

5   Duncan; b. 1865; became a seaman and Chief Officer. Went to Glasgow and married. Was Robert Shaw's grandfather, see below.

6   Dugald; b. 1868; accidental death.

7   Alexander; b. 1871; became the Rev. Sandy Shaw. Married Catherine Kirk.

8   Donald; b. 1873; died in infancy.

9   Anne; b. 1875; married Alfred Turner and went to Australia.

10   Archibald; b. 1878; became the Rev. Archie Shaw. Married Anne Ross.

11   Donald; b. 1880; married Margaret Murchison and went to Australia.

Duncan Shaw was married in Glasgow and among his children was his son, Robert, born in 1901.

Robert became a builder and returned to Jura to live and work. He married, first; Marion McLean, who as we have seen, died young, and second, Flora Lindsay in 1936. He and his wife were highly respected on the island and his daughter Effie, who was brought up on Jura, retains the strong family connection.

(e) Dunacha Sha. Of historical interest are the relatives of Torquil Shaw and Anne Shaw who emigrated from Cnocbreac in 1830. Anne's brother, John Shaw, married Catherine Darroch. Their daughter, Mary, married Donald McCraine and has been noted in the McCraines. They also had a son, Duncan Shaw, who lived at Ardfernal and died, unmarried, in 1901, aged seventy-one. Duncan was known locally as 'Dunacha Sha', and was the one-legged man remember by Katie Darroch, whose letters to his American cousins provided a valuable link in tracing their history.

MCARTHUR

As far as the twentieth century is concerned, the McArthur dynasty starts with John McArthur and Ann Buie. Four of their children feature in the Death Register, and three had families.

Donald McArthur was unmarried and died in Ardfernal in 1906, aged sixty-five.

Catharine McArthur married Alexander Clark. She died in Keils in 1934, aged eighty-eight. As we have seen in the Clark section, they were Alick Keith's grandparents.

Mary McArthur married John McNeill. She died at Inverlussa in 1944, aged ninety-two. Malcolm McArthur married Janet Darroch. He died at Knockrome in 1912, aged sixty-four. His wife died in Ardfernal in 1915, aged fifty-four. Among their family was Calum McArthur, who married Mary Darroch ('Mary Neil', Katie and Donald Darroch's sister). From this family came Nina Cameron, Kathy Hunter, Flora McDonald and Mary McDonald, and their families, and their sister Janet. Calum McArthur's brother John was the father of the present-day Calum McArthur of Dunfermline and the family croft at Ardfernal.

Incoming families have always been important in the life of the island and no less in the twentieth century, as, for example, the following show.

THE MCDONALDS OF ARDFIN

Angus McDonald and his wife Isabella came from Skye to manage the home farm at Ardfin. Their three sons continued to be important members of the local community. Norman and his wife Agnes, and Angus and his wife Nancy, continued to farm at Ardfin, while their brother, Allan, married Flora, one of the McArthur girls.

THE MCINNES FAMILY

Ewen McInnes of Glencoe and his wife, Mary Ann McKinnon of Tiree, came to Gatehouse to work on the Astor Estate. Their son, Neil, married Lily McKechnie and continued at Gatehouse. Their daughter, Nancy, married Angus McDonald of Ardfin and their daughter, Isa, married Donald Darroch of Inver.

THE CAMERONS

Willie Cameron and his wife, Bella, came to work on Jura. They lived at Strone and Willie worked as the gardener at Ardfin. Their son, Ian, married Nina McArthur, and they and their family remained on the island.

Plate 36 captures something of the character of the many individuals who came to the end of their lives in Jura in the twentieth century.

45

In Conclusion

The author lived and worked on Jura from 1975 to 1987 and has maintained a regular, though infrequent, contact with the island since then. This book is being written in the year 2000.

It was never the intention that the book should be 'contemporary' or 'up to date', for the author deemed it advisable to leave a 'ventilated space' beween the end of this study and the present day. The rapidly accelerating rate of change in society at large makes this decision seem ever more sensible. It is difficult for anyone to predict where our communities, our country or our world are going as we enter a new Millennium. It is certainly quite impossible to see into the future of a Hebridean Island like Jura.

Since the 1950s some dramatic changes have taken place and, yet, many things have stayed the same. A number of sporting landowners have changed and two of the estates have been further subdivided, but the principal motives of the various estate owners seem to remain unchanged, and deer are still being shot and, at the moment at least, fish are still being caught. The new Distillery seems well established, with Jura Malt Whisky as a prestigious commodity the world over. Various offshore creatures have been fished, and dived for and sold to new markets. These have included scallops, crawfish, velvet swimming crabs and various other more exotic animals. Modern electronic technology seems to imply that it may be possible to conduct a successful business from any remote location, in which case Jura qualifies more easily than most.

Many people who do not live on the island still have an ongoing 'love affair' with Jura and, while, that continues, they are always going to want to be able to visit it at will and, if necessary, retire and die and be buried there.

It is against the background of this contemporary scene that this book has been conceived and produced. The author believes that the better the past history of the Island is researched, documented and made available, the more likely it is that Jura will continue to be populated, and to survive and prosper in the future. This is the author's dearest wish and the sole end to which this book is dedicated.

Bibliography

Scottish National Archives:
  Statutory Registers of Births, Marriages and Deaths
  Old Parish Registers
  National Censuses of 1841; 1851; 1861; 1871; 1881; 1891
  Campbell of Jura Papers
  Minutes of the Commissioners of Supply (1744–1774)
The National Library; Maps and Charts
Ordnance Survey; 1 inch, 6 inch and other maps.
Origines Parochiales Scoticae. Edited C. Innes, Edinburgh, 1845
Archives at Lochgilphead:
  'Records of the Parochial Poor Board of Jura' (1845–1890)
  Records of the Commisioners of Supply. Voters' Rolls and Valuations
Presbytery Minutes of Kintyre
Royal Commisions; Report on Crofters (1884) Red Deer (1895)
Crofters' Commission; Sitting on Jura (1894)
Royal Commission on Ancient Monuments; 'The Argyll Inventory, Vol. 5; Islay and Jura.'
Statistical Accounts of Scotland: First (1792); Second (1845); Third (1961)

Historic Accounts:
Adomnán, *Life of St Columba* Edmonston & Douglas (1874)
Daniell, W. A. A., *Voyage around Great Britain* (1818)
Jameson, Robert, *Mineralogy of the Scottish Isles* (1800)
Lightfoot, Rev. John, *Flora Scotica* (1772)
MacCulloch, John, *A Description of the Western Isles of Scotland* (1819)
Macdonald, James, *A General View of the Agriculture of the Hebrides* (1811)
Martin Martin, *A Description of the Western Islands of Scotland London* (1703), ed. Dr D. J. MacLeod (1934)
Munro, *Description of the Western Isles of Scotland* (1594), ed. Dr D. J. Macleod (1934)
Pennant, Thomas, *A Voyage to the Hebrides* (1772)
Teignmouth, Lord, *Sketches of the Coasts and Islands of Scotland, Vol. 2* (1836)
Walker, John, *An Economic History of the Hebrides and Highlands of Scotland* (1808)

General
Baird, Bob, *Shipwrecks of the West of Scotland* (1995)
Budge, Donald, *Jura, an Island of Argyll* (1960)
Cowan, I.B. & Easson, D.E., *Mediaeval Religious Houses of Scotland* (1976)
Darling, F. Fraser, *West Highland Survey; An Essay in Human Ecology* (1955)
Evans, Henry, *The Red Deer of Jura* (1890)
Fenton, Alex, *Scottish Country Life* (2000)
Fordun, John of, *Chronia Gentis Scotorum* (1447)
Franklin, T. Bedford, *A History of Scottish Farming* (1998)
Gordon, Seton, *Hebridean Memories*

Haldane, A. R. B., *The Drove Roads of Scotland* (1997)
Hopkins, Paul, *Glencoe and the End of the Highland War*
McArthur, Calum, *Place Name of Jura; a Guide* (1986)
MacEachern, Donald, *The Lands of the Lordship* (1976)
Mackay, James A., *Islands Postal History Series: No. 10: Islay and Jura* (1979)
Mercer, John, *Hebridean Islands; Colonsay, Gigha, Jura* (1974)
Muir, T. S. , *Characteristics of Old Church Architecture* (1861)
Murray, W. H., *The Islands of Western Scotland* (1973)
Rickman, John, *The Laird of the Lighthouses* (1994)
Roman Catholic Archives, *Irish Franciscan Mission to Scotland* (1619–1646), ed.
   Cathaldus Giblin, OFM, (1964)
Scott, Hew, *Fasti Ecclesiae Scoticanae* (1923)
Sheets, John Wilson, *Articles on Population Structure relating to Colonsay and Jura*
S.P.C.K., *Records of the Society for the Propagation of Christian Knowledge* (various
   dates)
Thom, A, *Megalithic Sites in Britain* (1967)
Tucker, D. G., *History of the Scottish Slate Industry* (1977)
Watson, W. J., *Celtic Place-names of Scotland* (1926)
Weyndling, Walter, *Ferry Tales of Argyll and the Isles* (1996)
Whyte, Ian, *Agriculture & Society in Seventeenth-Century Scotland* (1979)
Wright, Gordon, *Jura's Heritage; a Brief History of the Island* (1991)
——, *Jura; A Guide for Walkers* (1983)
——, *Jura Parish Church; a Brief History* (1997)
Wright, Gordon and Tait, Norman, *The Isle of Jura; Images from the Past* (1994)
——, *The Isle of Jura; Memories of the Past* (1998)

Science and Natural History:
Anderton, R., *Guide to the Dalradian Rocks of Jura* (1977)
Ashmore, P. J., *Neolithic and Bronze Age Scotland* (1996)
Booth, C. Gordon, *Birds in Jura* (1976)
Countryside Commission for Scotland, *Beaches of Islay, Jura and Colonsay* (1973)
Dawson, A. G., *Late Glacial Shorelines, etc.* Quaternary Research Association Field
   Guide (1983)
——, *A Fossil Lobate Rock Glacier in Jura* (1977)
Horne, David J., *The Geology of Jura* (1985)
Mercer, John; Proceedings: Society of Antiquaries of Scotland:
      'Stone Tools from a Washing Limit Deposit of the Highest Post-Glacial
      Transgression'
      'Lealt Bay, Isle of Jura' Vol. 100 (1967–8)
      'A Regression-time Stone-Workers' Camp, Lussa River, Isle of Jura'
      Vol. 103 (1970–1)
      'Flint Tools from the Present Tidal Zone, Lussa Bay, Isle of Jura'
      Vol. 102 (1969–70)
      'Lussa Wood 1: the Late-Glacial and Early Post-Glacial Occupation of Jura'
      Vol. 110 (1978–80)
      'Glenbatrick Waterhole, a microlithic site on the Isle of Jura' Vol. 105 (1972–4)
      'Microlithic and Bronze Age Camps, N. Carn, Isle of Jura' Vol. 104 (1971–2)
      'The Neolithic Level at Lussa Wood 1, N. Jura' Glasgow Arch, J, 3 (1974)
Morton, J. K., *The Flora of Islay and Jura*, (1959)
Rideout, Eric Hardwicke, *Standing Stones & Other Antiquities in Jura* (1932)

Royal Society of Edinburgh and the Nature Conservancy Council: 'The Natural Environment of the Inner Hebrides' (1983)

Sissions, J. B., *Quarternary Geomorphology of the Inner Hebrides: a Review*

Smith, Shelagh M., *The Shores of Jura and Islay: Marine Flora and Fauna* (1982)

United States References

Buie, T. R. and Buie, Scott, *The Family Buie: Scotland to North America* (1983)

Clark, Lt-Col. Victor, *The Argyle Colony* (1970)

Darroch, Frank, *A Darroch Family in Scotland and in Canada* (1974)

Dobson, David, *Directory of Scots in the Carolinas* (1986)

Fowler, Malcolm, *They Passed This Way* (1976)

Kelly, Douglas, F., *Carolina Scots* (1998)

MacKenzie, Rev. James Donald, *Colorful Heritage* (1969)

Meyer, Duane, *The Highland Scots of North Carolina*

Patten, Jennie, 'The Argyle Patent' in *History of Somonauk Church* (1979)

Ross, Malcolm, *The Cape Fear* (1965)

Thomas, Maud, *Away Down Home: a History of Robeson County, North Carolina* (1982)

Index

the raiders, 492; Gillour; other tales, 493; Harvest traditions, 506; heir of the McPhees, 489; Helpful spirit, 500; Hugh of the little head, 501; Jura burials, 486; Kate Clark at the manse, 499; Katie Darroch' sayings, 508; Kilearnadale cemetery; traditions, 486; Knockrome herd, 505; MacIain Riabhach, 490; McCraine sisters, 510; McCuaig, the Rev.; stories of, 498; McLever the robber, 511; meat on a string, 489; Murder at Strone, 496; Old Darroch; An Gillie Riabaich, 490; Plague at Kilearnadale, 487 Press gang, 497; Proper fare; The, 506; Raid on Colonsay, 488; Rider at the door, 501; Skulls, 503; stowaway in the boat, 488; Straight answer, 507; Terrible woman of Dainskeir, 495; Tragedy at Corran river, 497; Una's elopement, 494; Welding at the smithy, 505; White horse of Jura, 499; Who's killing the stirk?, 505; Witch of the Paps, 485; Witchcraft at Knockrome, 493; Yellow-haired John of the deer, 490
swarm of inhabitants, 376

Tait, Norman and Pearl, 30; 34
Tarbert, 75; 112; 528
Taylor, Angus, land surveyor, 212
Teignmouth, Lord; on the life of the people, 379; agriculture neglected, 379; funeral; comments on Teignmouth's account, 381; funeral; account of, 380; list of amenities, 379; Loch Tarbert; herring fishermen, 379; mill; corn ground at, 379; 'Sketches of the Coast and Islands of Scotland', 379; small isles; good anchorage, 379
teinds, 257
Telford's road, 443
Tenants and rents, 415; Keils and Ballard note (1836), 415; McGilvray, Neil; action for damages (1831). 415
Terrible woman of Dainskeir, 495
Tertiary dykes, 21; 23
thatching, 398
theft, 369
Thomson, John; Atlas of Scotland (1832), 171
ticks, 36

titles to Jura; 86
Tragedy at Corran river, 497
Tramaig bay, 10
tree planting, 29
Triantorran, 107
Troach, 113
tunicates, 33
Turner, Sir James; account of Jura, 95
Twentieth Century; first three-quarters, 524; Ardlussa sports, 531 Council housing, 531; County Council provisions, 531; Crofters rights, 532; Distillery, 531; holiday homes, 531; Jura Show, 531; landowners difficulties, 524; loss of dwelling houses, 529; new roads, 532; new private housing, 532; Occupations, 526; photograph collection, 526; population decline, 524; Regatta, 531; Small Isles bay; concentration of population, 530; social life on Jura, 531; War Memorial, 525; World War One, 525
Twentieth Century; people of, 534; Black, 534; Buie, 534; Cameron, 544; Campbell, 535; Clark, 536; Darroch, 536; Elderly quartet, 544; Keith, 538; Lindsay, 538; McArthur, 543; McCraine, 539; McDonald, 544; McDougall, 539; McInnes, 544; McIsaac, 539; McKechnie, 540; McLean, 541; Shaw, 542

Una's elopement, 494
Upper Lussagiven, 112

Valuation of lands (1770), 252; new names in valuation doc., 252; Agey, Robert, 252; Campbell, Donald, 252; McArthur, Duncan, 252; McDugald, John, 252; McIlerioch, John, 252; McIleroy, Duncan, 252; Shaw, Neil, 252
Valuation of Shire of Argyll; comment, 256
view from the Paps, 164
Vikings, 79; Alexander of Scotland, 81; Angus Mor, 81; vikings; early contacts, 59; Annals of Ulster, 79; Ceile De; Culdees, 79; Cripplehand, Bjorn, 79; Crovan, Godred, 79; David, King, 80; division of his lands, 80; Donald I, 81; Edgar, King of Scots, 79; Gaelic